MAX ELLERY'S VEHICLE REPAIR MANUALS

An All Australian Production

PROUDLY PRINTED IN AUSTRALIA

EP.TLP

LANDCRUISER
PETROL / GASOLINE 4&6 Cyl
1969 - 1990
FJ   RJ

40's   55's   60's   70's   Bundera

Automobile Repair Manual

D1737588

* Tune-up
* Repairs
* Mechanical
* Body Work
* Electrical Diagrams
* Restoration Reference
* Factory Specifications

This repair and maintenance manual has been published to provide Toyota Landcruiser (Petrol / Gasoline engine) owners and enthusiasts with an invaluable, comprehensive and thorough guide in all aspects of restoration, maintenance and mechanical repair work.

ACKNOWLEDGEMENTS.

I would like to thank AMI Toyota Ltd and associated Companies for assisting with information in the production of this Manual.

DISCLAIMER

Every endeavour has been made to ensure all information in this manual is accurate. Mistakes and omissions can always occur, and the publisher does not assume any duty or care, or legal responsibility in relation to the contents of this book.

Published by:
M.R. Ellery Publishing Co.,
R.S.D. Axedale, Victoria, 3551 Australia.
Phone (054) 395000.

Printed by McPhersons Printing Group
Maryborough, Vic.

National Library of Australia Card number and ISBN
  ISBN   0 646 12409 9

TOYOTA LANDCRUISER
PETROL / GASOLINE ENGINES
1969 -1990

CONTENTS   PAGE

VEHICLE IDENTIFICATION

VIN / FRAME NUMBER

In order to identify vehicles, two different coding systems are used depending on the destination of the vehicles. On vehicles for Europe and Australia the VIN (Vehicle Identification Number) system is used. For other areas the conventional Frame Numbering system is used. For each reference, the VIN or Frame Number is stamped on the "manufacturer's plate" installed in the engine compartment for bonnet type vehicle.

1. VIN on vehicles for Europe
On the manufacturer's plate, the VIN is stamped on one line in three sections being defined as WMI, VDS and VIS.

2. VIN on Vehicles for Australia
On the plate, the VIN is stamped on the "Frame No." line, in three sections being defined as WMI, VDS and VIS.

3. Frame Number on vehicles for other areas
On the plate, the Frame Number is stamped on the "Frame No." line, divided into two sections, corresponding to VSD and VIS respectively.

VIN SYSTEM IDENTIFICATION

ENGINE IDENTIFICATION INFORMATION

EUROPE   J T 4 W O Y R 2 1 0 1 2 3 4 5 6 7

Engine Serial Number

The engine serial number is stamped on the side of the engine block.

JT4 WMI (World Manufacturer Identifier)
WOYR21 VDS (Vehicle Description Section)
01234567 VIS (Vehicle Indicator Section)

JT4 Geographical Area, Country & Manufacturer
JT4 Asia, Japan, Toyota
W Body Style - i.e., W .. Wagon, P .. Pickup
O Not used (for Engine No. with 3 figures)
Y Engine Type - i.e., Y .. 2Y, R .. 22R
R Car Line - i.e, R..Model-F, J..Land Cruiser
21 Model No.
0 Dummy
1234567 Plant Sequential Number

EUROPE AND AUSTRALIA since 1988

J T 7 3 1 Y N 8 5 0 1 2 3 4 5 6 7

JT7 WMI (World Manufacturer Identifier)
31YN85 VDS (Vehicle Description Section)
01234567 VIS (Vehicle Indicator Section)

JT7 Geographical Area, Country & Manufacturer
JT7 Asia, Japan, Toyota
31 Body Style - i.e., 31.. Standard Cab Truck
Y Engine Type - i.e., Y..2Y, L..2L
N Car Line - i.e., N..Hilux, J..Land Cruiser
8 Model Number - i.e., 8..8, B..11
5 Engine Type and Drive Type,i.e.,4..22R, 2L/4- WD
0 Dummy Number
1234567 Plant Sequential Number

MAINTENANCE AND TUNE UP PETROL ENGINES

MAINTENANCE AND TUNE UP

PETROL ENGINES - 6 CYLINDER (2F & 3F)

Description   **Page**

Engine Coolant

1.Check Engine Coolant Level at Reserve Tank.

The coolant level should be between the "LOW" and "FULL" lines. If low, check for leaks and add coolant up to the "FULL" line.

2.Check Engine Coolant Quality.

There should not be excessive deposits of rust or scales around the radiator cap or radiator filler hole, and the coolant should be free from oil.

If excessively dirty, replace the coolant.

Engine Oil

Check the engine oil level. The oil level should be between the "L" and "F" marks on the level gauge. If low, check for leakage and add oil up to the "F" mark.

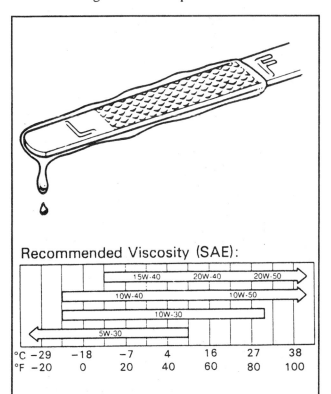

Recommended Viscosity (SAE):

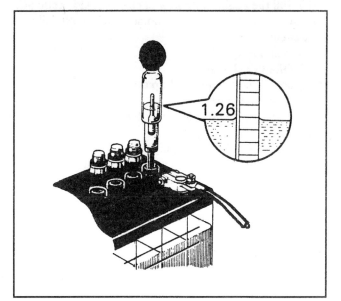

Oil Filter

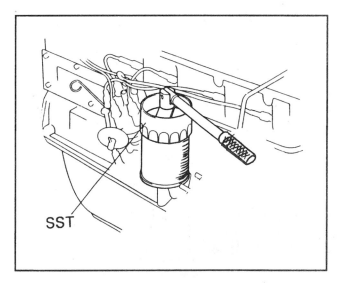

Battery

1.Check Battery Specific Gravity.

(a) Check the specific gravity of each cell.

Standard specific gravity:

1.25 - 1.27 when full charged at 20 degrees centigrade (68 degrees fahrenheit)

(b) Check the electrolyte quantity of each cell.

If insufficient, refill with distilled (or purified) water.

2.Check Battery Terminals, Fusible Links and Fuses.

(a) Check that the battery terminals are not loose or corroded.

(b) Check the fusible link and fuses for continuity.

1.Drain Engine Oil.

(a) Remove the oil filler cap.

(b) Remove the oil drain plug and drain the engine oil into a container.

2.Replace Oil Filter.

(a) Remove the oil filter.

(b) Check and clean the oil filter installation surface.

(c) Apply clean engine oil to the gasket of a new oil filter.

(d) Lightly screw in the oil filter by hand until you feel some resistance.

(e) Tighten the oil filter an extra 3/4 turn.

3.Fill with Engine Oil.

(a) Clean and install the oil drain plug with a new gasket. Torque the drain plug.

Torque: 400 kg-cm (29 ft-lb, 39 N.m)

(b) Fill the engine with new engine oil, API grade SC, SD, SE, SF, or better and recommended viscosity oil.

Capacity:

Drain and refill:

w/o Oil filter change

7.0 litres (7.4 US qts, 6.2 Imp.qts)

w/ Oil filter change

7.8 litres (8.2 US qts, 6.9 Imp.qts)

Dry fill:

8.0 litres (8.5 US qts, 7.0 Imp.qts)

(c) Install the oil filler cap with the gasket.

4.Start Engine and Check for Leaks.

5.Recheck Engine Oil Level.

Air Filter

Paper Filter Type:

Clean Air Filter.

Clean the element with compressed air, first blowing from the inside thoroughly and then the outside.

Oil Bath Type:

Clean Air Filter.

(a) Wash the oil case and air filter in kerosine by agitating and rubbing.

(b) Wipe the oil case and air filter with a clean rag.

(c) Place the oil case on a level work stand.

(d) Pour in clean engine oil until it reaches the 'OIL LEVEL' mark.

(e) Place the air filter on a tray.

(f) Saturate the air filter with clean engine oil.

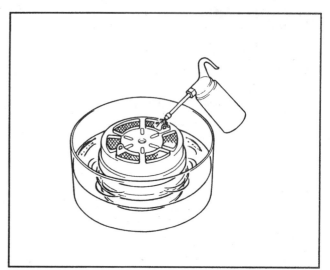

SPARK PLUGS

1.Remove Spark Plugs.

2.Clean Spark Plugs.

Using a spark plug cleaner or wire brush, clean the spark plug.

3.Visually Inspect Spark Plugs.

Check the spark plug for electrode wear, thread damage and insulator damage. If abnormal, replace the plugs.

Recommenced spark plugs: ND W14EX-U

NGK BP4EY

4.Adjust Electrode Cap.

Carefully bend the outer electrode to obtain the correct electrode gap.

Spark plug gap: 0.8 mm (0.031 in.)

5.Install Spark Plugs.

Torque: 180 kg-cm (13 ft-lb, 18 N.m)

Alternator Drive Belt

1.Inspect Drive Belt.

(a) Visually check the drive belt for cracks, oiliness or wear. Check that the belt does not touch the bottom of the pulley groove.

If necessary, replace the drive belt.

(b) Check the drive belt deflection by pressing on the belt at the points indicated in the figure with 10 kg (22.0 lb, 98 N) of pressure.

Drive belt deflection:

New belt: 7.0 - 9.0 mm (0.278 - 0.354 in.)

Used belt: 9.0 - 12.0 mm (0.354 - 0.472 in.)

If the belt deflection is not within specification, adjust it.

* "New belt" refers to a new belt which has never been used.

* "Used belt" refers to a belt which has been used on a running engine for 5 minutes or more.

Adjust of Valve Clearances

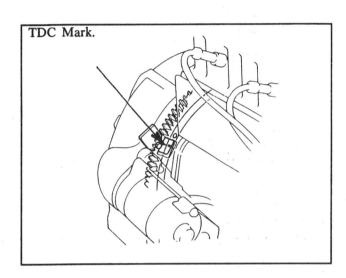

TDC Mark.

* Inspect and adjust the valve clearance after engine has reached normal operating temperature.

1. Remove Cylinder Head Cover.

2. Set No. 1 Cylinder to TDC/Compression.

(a) Set the No. 1 cylinder to TDC/compression. Align the TDC mark of the flywheel with the timing pointer by turning the crankshaft clockwise with a wrench.

(b) Check that the rocker arms on the No. 1 cylinder are loose and rocker arms on the No. 6 cylinder are tight.

If not, turn the crankshaft one revolution (360 degrees) and align the mark as above.

3. Inspect and Adjust Valve Clearances.

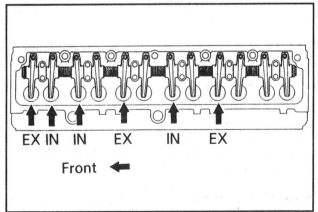

(a) Measure only those valves indicated by arrows.
Valve clearance (Hot):
Intake -   0.20 mm (0.008 in.)
Exhaust - 0.35 mm (0.014 in.)

* Using a feeler gauge, measure the valve clearance between the valve stem and rocker arm. Loosen the lock nut and turn the adjusting screw to set the proper clearance. Hold the adjusting screw in position and tighten the lock nut.

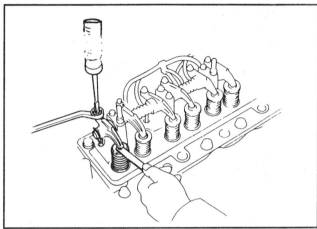

* Recheck the valve clearance. The feeler gauge should slide with a very slight drag.

(b) Turn the crankshaft one revolution (360 degrees) and align the mark as above. Adjust only the valves indicated by arrows.

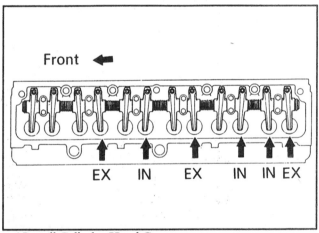

4. Install Cylinder Head Cover.

Inspect and Adjust Ignition Timing

1. Connect Tachometer and Timing Light to Engine.

Connect the test probe of a tachometer to the ignition coil negative (-) terminal.

* NEVER allow the ignition coil terminals to touch the ground as it could result in damage to the ignition coil.

TACHOMETER   IGNITION COIL

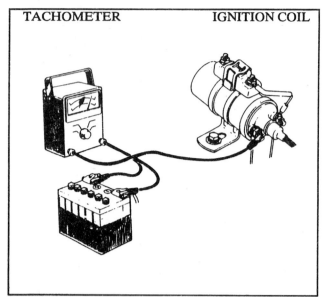

* It is recommended that you consult with the manufacturer before using a tachometer as some are not compatible with this system.

2.Inspect Dwell Angle.

Check the dwell angle at the engine idling.

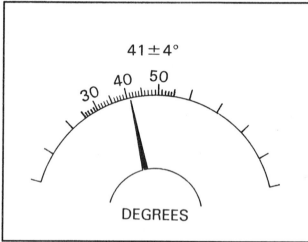

41 ± 4°

DEGREES

Dwell angle: 41 +/- 4 degrees

If the dwell angle is not as specified, adjust the rubbing block gap.

3.Inspect and Adjust Ignition Timing.

(a) Check the ignition timing.

Ignition timing:

7 degrees BTDC @ Max. 900 rpm

(b) Loosen the bolt and nut holding the distributor to the clamp.

(c) Adjust by turning the distributor.

(d) Tighten the bolt and nut, and recheck the ignition timing.

7 Degrees BTDC MARK.

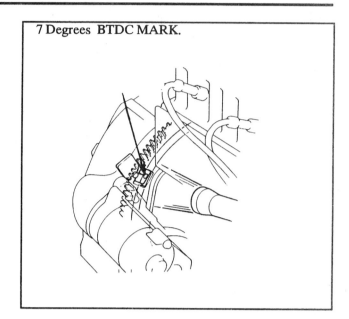

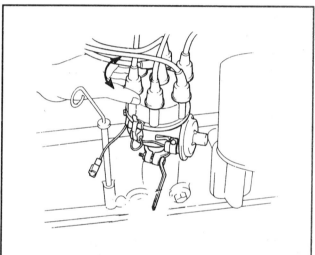

Inspect and Adjust Idle Speed

1.Warm Up Engine.

2.Connect Tachometer.

3.Inspect Idle Speed.

Idle speed: M/T 650 rpm

             A/T 750 rpm

If not as specified, adjust according to the following procedure:

* Always use a CO meter when adjusting the idle mixture. It is not necessary to adjust with the idle mixture adjusting screw in most vehicles if they are in good condition.

* If a CO meter is not available and it is absolutely necessary to adjust with the idle mixture adjusting screw, use the alternative method listed below.

A. Method with CO Meter

1.Visually Inspect Carburettor.

(a) Check for loose screws or a loose mounting to the manifold.

(b) Check for wear in the linkage, missing snap rings or excessive looseness in the throttle shaft. Correct any problems found.

2.Initial Conditions:

(a) Air cleaner installed.

(b) Normal operating coolant temperature.

(c) Choke fully open.

(d) All accessories switched off.

(e) All vacuum lines connected.

(f) Ignition timing set correctly.

(g) Transmission in the "N" range.

(h) Fuel level should be about even with the correct level in the sight glass.

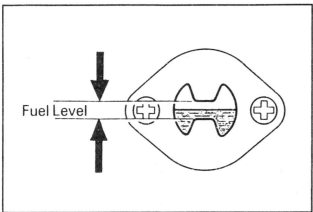

(i) CO meter operates normally.

(j) If there is an idle limiter cap on the idle mixture adjusting screw, remove it.

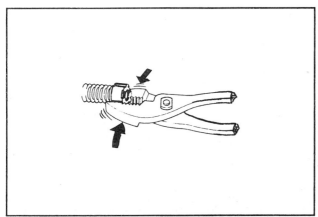

3.Adjust Idle Speed and Idle Mixture.

(a) Start the engine.

(b) Using a CO meter to measure the CO concentration in the exhaust, turn the idle speed and idle mixture adjusting screws to obtain the specified concentration value at idle speed.

Idle speed: M/T - 650 rpm; A/T - 750 rpm

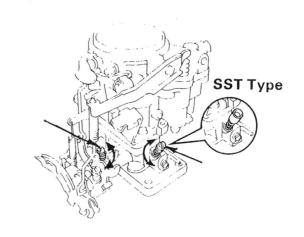

SST Type

Idle Speed Adjusting Screw.   Idle Mixture Adjusting Screw.

4.Inspect CO Concentration.

(a) Check that the CO meter is properly calibrated.

(b) Race the engine 30-60 seconds at about 2,000 rpm before measuring concentration.

(c) Wait 1-3 minutes after racing the engine to allow the concentration to stabilize.

(d) Insert a testing probe at least 40 cm (1.3 ft) into the tailpipe, and measure the concentration within a short time.

Idle CO concentration: 1.5 +/- 1.0 %

* If the CO concentration is within specification this adjustment is complete.

* If the CO concentration is not within specification, turn the idle mixture adjusting screw to obtain the specified concentration value.

* If the CO concentration cannot be corrected by adjusting the idle mixture, see table below for other possible causes.

Problem Solving:

1) Rough Idle - CO Normal:
   Causes:
   * Faulty ignition:
     - Incorrect timing
     - Fouled, shorted or improperly gapped plugs
     - Open or crossed ignition wires
     - Cracked distributor cap
   * Leaky exhaust valves
   * Leaky cylinder

2) Rough Idle (fluctuating HC reading) - CO Low:
   Causes:
   * Vacuum leak:
     - Vacuum hose
     - Intake manifold
     - PCV line
     - Carburettor base

3) Rough Idle (black smoke from exhaust) - CO High:

Causes:

* Restricted air filter
* Plugged PCV valve
* Faulty carburettor:
  - Faulty choke action
  - Incorrect float setting
  - Leaking needle or seat
  - Leaking power valve

5.[w/ Idle Limiter Cap] Install New Idle Limiter Cap.

After this adjustment is completed, install a new idle limiter cap on the mixture adjusting screw.

* After completing adjustment, perform a road test to make certain engine performance has not changed.

B. Alternative Method

* To be used only if CO meter is not available.

1.Visually Inspect Carburettor.

(a) Check for loose screws or loose mountings to the manifold.

(b) Check for wear in the linkage, missing snap rings or excessive looseness in the throttle shaft. Correct any problems found.

2.Initial Conditions.

(a) Air cleaner installed.

(b) Normal operating coolant temperature.

(c) Choke fully open.

(d) All accessories switched off.

(e) All vacuum lines connected.

(f) Ignition timing set correctly.

(g) Transmission in the "N" range.

(h) Fuel level should be about even with the correct level in the sight glass.

(i) If there is an idle limiter cap on the idle mixture adjusting screw, remove it.

3.Adjust Idle Speed and Idle Mixture.

(a) Start the engine.

(b) Set to the maximum speed by turning the IDLE MIXTURE ADJUSTING SCREW.

(c) Set to the idle mixture speed by turning the IDLE SPEED ADJUSTING SCREW.

Idle mixture speed: M/T - 690 rpm; A/T - 790 rpm.

(d) Before moving to the next step, continue adjustments (b) and (c) until the maximum speed will not rise any further, no much the IDLE MIXTURE ADJUSTING SCREW is adjusted.

(e) Set to the idle speed by screwing in the IDLE MIXTURE ADJUSTING SCREW.

Idle speed: M/T - 650 rpm; A/T - 750 rpm.

This is a lean Drop Method for setting idle speed and mixture.

4.[w/ Idle Limiter Cap] Install New Idle Limiter Cap.

After this adjustment is completed, install a new idle limiter cap on the idle mixture adjusting screw.

* After completing adjustment, perform a road test to make certain engine performance has not changed.

Inspect and Adjust Fast Idle Speed

1. Warm Up and Stop Engine.

2.Remove Air Cleaner Assembly or Air Intake Connector from Carburettor.

3.Connect Tachometer.

4.Inspect and Adjust Fast Idle Speed.

(a) Start the engine.

(b) Fully turn the choke lever counterclockwise, and fully open the choke valve.

(c) Check the fast idle speed.

Fast idle speed: 1,800 rpm

(d) Adjust the fast idle speed by turning the FAST IDLE ADJUSTING SCREW.

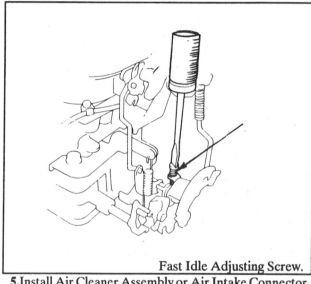

Fast Idle Adjusting Screw.

5.Install Air Cleaner Assembly or Air Intake Connector.

Inspect and Adjust Throttle Positioner Setting Speed (S.Arabia M/T only)

1.Warm Up and Stop Engine.

2.Connect Tachometer.

3.Start Engine.

4.Inspect and Adjust Throttle Positioner (TP) Setting Speed.

(a) Disconnect the vacuum hoses from the TP and plug the hose end.

(b) Rev the engine to 2,000 rpm for a few seconds, release the throttle and check the TP setting speed.

TP setting speed: 1,000 rpm

(c) Adjust the TP setting speed by turning the TP AD-JUSTING SCREW.

(d) Rev the engine to 2,000 rpm for a few seconds, release the throttle and recheck the TP setting speed.

(e) Reconnect the vacuum hoses to the TP.

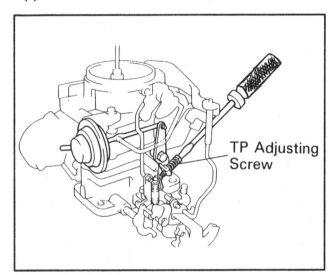

TP Adjusting
Screw

through the spark plug hole and repeat steps (a) through (c) on the cylinder with low compression.

* If adding oil helps the compression, the piston rings and/or cylinder bore may be worn or damaged.

* If pressure stays low, a valve may be sticking or seating improperly, or there may be leakage past the gasket.

5. Connect Distributor Connector.

6. Install Spark Plugs.

Torque: 180 kg-cm (13 ft-lb, 18 N.m).

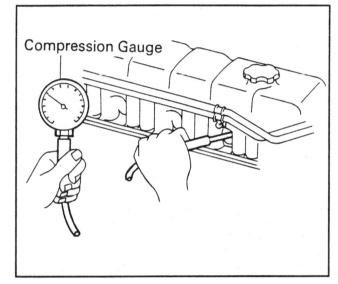

Compression Gauge

Compression Check

* If there is lack of power, excessive oil consumption or poor fuel mileage, measure the cylinder compression pressure.

1. War Up and Stop Engine.

2. Remove Spark Plugs.

3. Disconnect Distributor Connector.

4. Check Cylinder Compression Pressure.

(a) Insert a compression gauge into the spark plug hole.

(b) Fully open the throttle valve.

(c) While cranking the engine with the starter, measure the compression pressure.

* Always use a fully charged battery to obtain engine revolutions of more than 200 rpm.

(d) Repeat steps (a) through (c) for each cylinder.

Compression pressure:

10.5 kg/cm2 (149 psi, 1,030 kPa) or more

Minimum pressure:

8.0 kg/cm2 (114 psi, 785 kPa)

Difference between each cylinder:

1.0 kg/cm2 (14 psi, 98 kPa) or less

(e) If the cylinder compression in one or more cylinders is low, pour a small amount of engine oil into the cylinder

ENGINE TUNE-UP & MAINTENANCE - 21R, 21R-C & 22R PETROL ENGINES

Drive Belt.

Look for:

(a) Cracks, deterioration, stretching or wear, and look for oil or grease.

(b) Improper belt-to-pulley contact.

Check & Adjust Belt Tension.

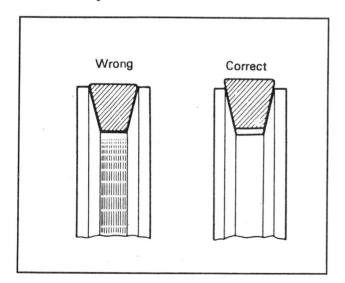

Battery.

Look for:

(a) Rusted battery support.

(b) Loose terminal connections.

(c) Corroded or deteriorated terminals.

(d) Damaged or leaking battery.

Measure Specific Gravity.

1. Check the specific gravity of the electrolyte with a hydrometer.

Specific gravity: 1.25-1.27

[When fully charged at $20^{\circ}C$ ($68^{\circ}F$)]

2. Check the electrolyte quantity of each cell. If sufficient, refill with distilled water.

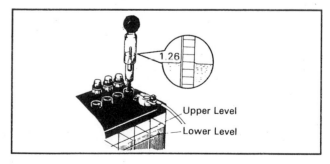

Engine Oil.

Check Oil Level.

The oil level should be between the L and F marks. If low, check for leakage and add oil up to the F mark.

Check Oil Quality.

Look for:

(a) Deterioration.

(b) Water (Milky colour)

(c) Discolouration or thinning

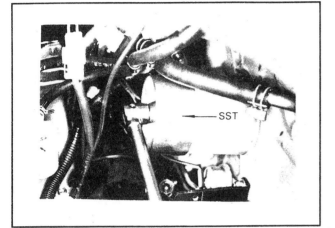

Oil Filter

Replace Oil Filter.

1. Remove the oil filter with filter clamp.

2. Inspect and clean the oil filter installation surface.

3. Apply clean engine oil to the gasket of the new oil filter.

4. (Non-Removal Type gasket)

* Lightly screw in the oil filter to where you feel resistance and tighten an extra 2/3 of a turn.

(Removal Type gasket)

Install new filter and tighten firmly by hand.

* Do not tighten with any tool.

5. Start the engine and check for oil leakage.

Cooling System.

Check Coolant Level. If low fill reservoir to FULL line.

* To maintain freeze protection, use a recommended anti-freeze.

Check Coolant Quality.

Look for:

(a) Coolant cleanliness.

(b) Rust or scale deposits around the radiator cap and filler neck.

(c) Entry of oil.

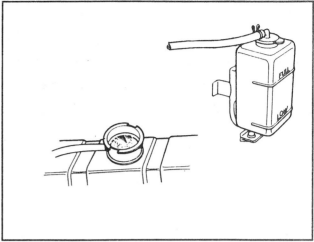

Check Cooling System Parts.

Look for:

(a) Damaged or deteriorated radiator and water hoses.

(b) Loose hose clamps.

(c) Damaged or corroded radiator core.

(d) Leakage from the water pump, radiator core or loose water drain cock.

(e) Faulty operation of radiator cap. Inspect the spring tension and seating condition of the radiator cap vacuum valves. If the valve opens at a pressure below specification or is otherwise defective, replace the radiator cap.

Valve opening pressure:

STD 0.75-1.05 kg/cm^2 (10.7-14.9psi)

Limit 0.6 kg/cm^2 (8.5psi)

Air Cleaner

(Oil Bath Type)

Clean Element.

1. Remove the air cleaner cup and element.

2. Wash the element and case with kerosene and dry them thoroughly.

Install Air Cleaner.

1. Refill the case up to the indicated level with clean engine oil.

2. Cover the element entirely with clean engine oil.

3. Install the cap and element.

4. Tighten the air cleaner on the air cleaner support.

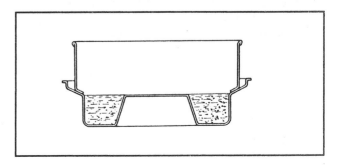

(Paper Element Type)

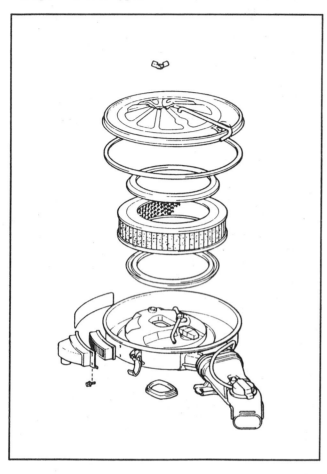

Clean Element.

1. Remove the air cleaner.

* Be careful not to get dirt or other foreign matter into the carburettor.

2. Take the element out and blow compressed air from the inside.

3. If the element is torn or really dirty replace with a new one.

Look for:

(a) Damaged, worn or deteriorated gaskets.

(b) Damaged, or worn seal washer.

Install Air Cleaner.

(a) Install the gaskets

(b) Tighten the front and rear stays with your fingers.

(c) After putting the element back in, tighten the air cleaner caps with clips.

(d) Tighten the wing nut and both stays.

Spark Plugs

Look for:

(a) Cracks or other damage on the threads and insulator.

(b) Electrode wear.

(c) Damaged or deteriorated gaskets.

(d) Burnt electrode or heavy carbon deposits.

Clean Spark Plugs.

Adjust Spark Plug Gap.

Check each plug gap with a spark plug gap gauge. If necessary, adjust by bending the outer electrode.

Spark plug gap: 0.8 mm (0.031 in.)

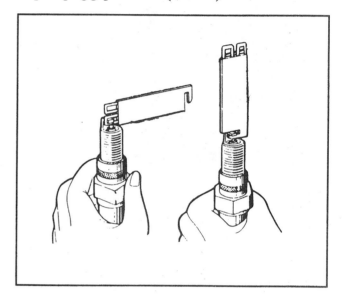

Distributor.

Check Distributor Cap. Clean the distributor cap and check the cap and rotor for:

(a) Corrosion, burning or dirty cord holes, cracks or damage.

(b) Burnt electrode terminal.

(c) Weak centre piece spring action.

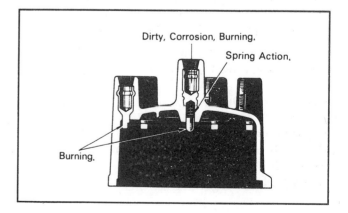

Adjust Gap.
1. Adjust the air gap.(Breaker points less type)
Air gap: 0.2-0.4 mm (0.008-0.016 in.)

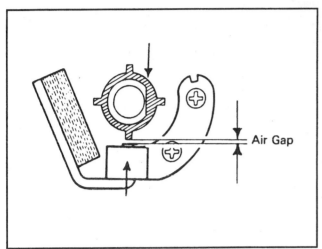

2. Adjust the rubbing block gap and damping spring gap.(Breaker points type)
Rubbing block gap: 0.45 mm (0.0177 in.)
Damping spring gap: 0.1-0.4 mm (0.004-0.016 in.)

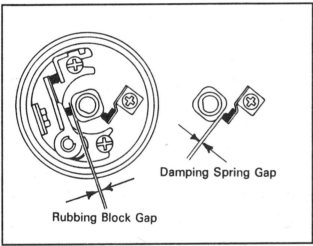

Check Vacuum Advancer Operation. Apply vacuum to the diaphragm and check that the vacuum advancer moves in accordance with the vacuum.

Check Governor Operation.
1. Turn the rotor clockwise and release it.
2. Check for looseness.
3. Start the engine and disconnect the vacuum hoses from the distributor. The timing mark should vary with the engine rpm.

Ignition Timing.

Check Dwell Angle. (Breaker Points Type)
Using a dwell angle tester, check the dwell angle at idle speed before adjusting the ignition timing.
Dwell angle: 52°
If the angle does not meet specification,adjust the rubbing block gap as follows:
More than 53° Decrease the gap.
Less than 51° Increase the gap.

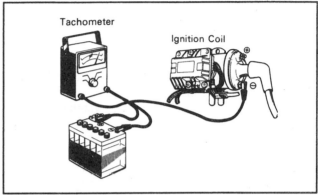

Check Ignition Timing.
1. Connect a tachometer and timing light.
* Australia RJ (Since '85/10)connect the tachometer (+) terminal to the ignition coil (-) terminal.
* **Australia RJ (Since '85/10) remove the rubber cap and connect the tachometer (+) terminal to the service connector from the igniter.**
* Do not keep the ignition switch ON for more than 10 minutes if the engine will not start.
* As some tachometers are not compatible with this ignition system, it is recommended that you consult with the manufacturer.
* NEVER allow the ignition coil terminals to touch ground as it could result in damage to the igniter and/or ignition coil.
* Do not disconnect the battery when the engine is running.
* Make sure that the igniter is properly grounded to the body.
2 Warm up the engine.
3. Disconnect the vacuum hoses from the distributor and plug the ends of them.
4. Check the ignition timing with the engine idling.

Ignition timing:

21R
5° BTDC/Max.750 rpm RA (Since '83/8),RX70
8° BTDC/Max.750 rpm RA (Before '83/8),RX60
(Ex. South Africa)
12° BTDC/Max.750 rpm RX60 (South Africa)

21R-C
*5° BTDC/Max.600 rpm Australia M/T
*5° BTDC/Max.650 rpm Australia A/T
8° BTDC/Max.750 rpm Switzerland,Sweden.
22R
*0° BTDC/Max.850 rpm RB20 (Since '84/8,85 RON version)
*0° BTDC/Max.950 rpm RJ (Australia)
*5° BTDC/Max.850 rpm RB20 (Since '84/8,90 RON version)
RJ (Ex.Australia),RN, RU.
5° BTDC/Max.950 rpm RB20 (Before '84/8,85 RON version)
8° BTDC/Max.950 rpm RB20 (Before '84/8,90 RON version)
* * with vacuum advance cut.

5. If necessary, loosen the distributor set bolt and turn the distributor to line up the timing lights.

6. Recheck the ignition timing after tightening the distributor.

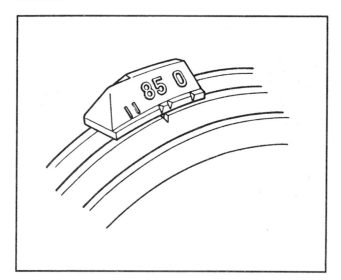

Valve Clearance.

Adjustment.

1. Warm-up the engine, then turn it off.
2. Set No.1 cylinder to TDC/compression.

3. Adjust the valve clearance. The valve clearance is measured between the valve stem and rocker arm adjusting screw. Adjust only the valves as illustrated in the diagram.

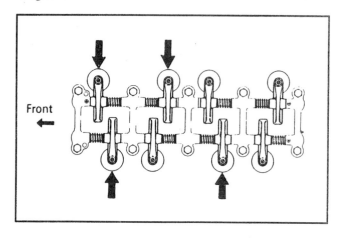

Front

Valve clearance:
Intake: 0.20 mm (0.008 in.)
Exhaust: 0.30 mm (0.012 in.)

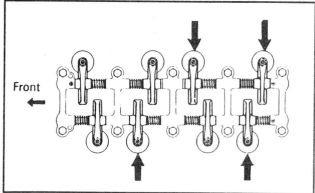

Front

4. Rotate the crankshaft 360° and adjust the remaining valves.

Carburettor.

Automatic Choke.

1. Check the choke valve operation by pushing the valve down with your finger and then letting it go. The valve should return quickly and smoothly.

2. Warm the engine up and check that the choke valve begins to open and the choke housing is heated.

3. (Ex. USA & Canada)

Check the engine starting and running condition. If needed, adjust the automatic choke setting by turning the coil housing.

* If the fuel mixture is too rich....Turn clockwise

 If the fuel mixture is too lean....Turn anti-clockwise.

Choke breaker.

1. While holding the throttle valve slightly open, close the choke valve and hold it closed as you release the throttle valve.

2. Disconnect the vacuum hose between the restrictor and vacuum pipe at the restrictor side.

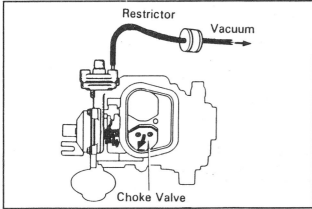

3. Apply vacuum to the restrictor and make sure that the choke valve slightly opens.

Choke Opener.

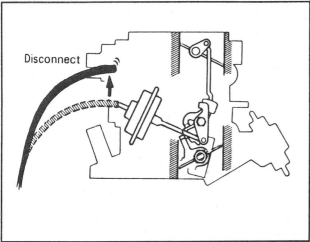

1. With the coolant temperature below 60°C (140°F), disconnect the vacuum hose from the choke opener diaphragm.

2. Press the accelerator pedal down and release it before starting the engine.

3. Connect the vacuum hose and make sure that the choke linkage does not move.

4. Warm the engine up to normal operating temperature and then turn it off.

5. Disconnect the vacuum hose from the choke opener diaphragm.

6. Hold the throttle valve slightly open and at the same time push the choke valve closed and hold it closed as you release the throttle valve.

7. Start the engine , do not touch the accelerator pedal.

8. Connect the vacuum hose, and make sure that the choke linkage moves and that the fast idle cam is released to the fourth step.

Fast Idle Cam Breaker.

1. With the coolant temperature below 30°C (86°F), disconnect the vacuum hose from the FICB diaphragm.

2. Press the accelerator pedal down and release it before starting the engine.

3. Connect the vacuum hose and make sure that the FICB lever does not move.

4. Warm the engine up to normal operating temperature and then turn it off.

5. Disconnect the vacuum hose from the FICB diaphragm.

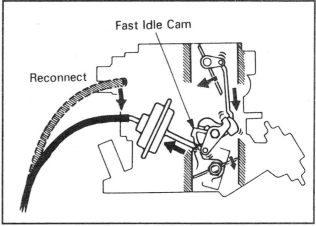

6. Hold the throttle valve slightly open and at the same time push the choke valve closed and hold it closed as you release the throttle valve.

7. Start up the engine , do not touch the accelerator pedal.

8. Connect the vacuum hose, and make sure that the FIBC lever moves and that the fast idle cam is released to the third step or beyond.

Check Float Level.

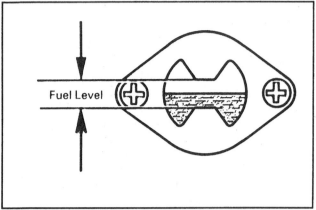

Check the fuel level while the engine is idling.

Check Acceleration Pump.

1. Check the acceleration pump operation. Petrol(Gasoline) should spurt out from the jet when the throttle valve is opened.

2. Check the throttle valve opening. The throttle valve should be completely open when the accelerator pedal is pressed right down.

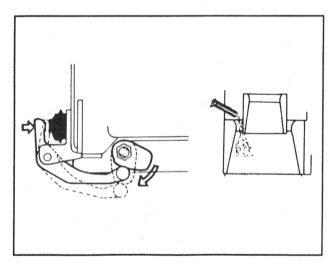

Idle Speed Adjustment

(Ex. RJ, RU, RB, RX, RA60, 61 & RT133)
1. Check the items listed below beforehand.
(a) Air cleaner installed.
(b) Normal operating coolant temperature.
(c) Choke fully open.
(d) All accessories switched off.
(e) All vacuum lines connected.
(f) Ignition timing set correctly.
(g) Transmission in N range

(h) Fuel level should be about even with the correct level in the sight glass.

2. Break the idle limiter cap on the idle speed adjusting screw, if installed.

3. Adjust the idle speed by turning the idle speed adjusting screw.

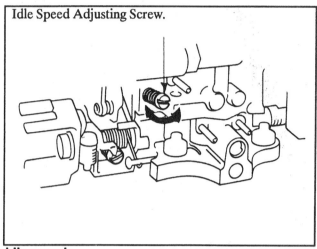

Idle Speed Adjusting Screw.

Idle speed:

M/T	700rpm
A/T	
Fed.RN4-A/T	700rpm
Canada RT,RA-A/T	850rpm
Others A/T	750rpm

4. Install a new limiter cap on the idle speed adjusting screw, if one was installed.

* For the idle mixture adjustment, the idle mixture adjusting screw is adjusted and plugged with a steel plug by the manufacturer. If necessary, remove the plug and follow the procedure described in FUEL SYSTEM section.

Idle Speed & Idle Mixture Adjustment.

(RN (Canada 4x4, Saudi Arabia), RJ, RU, RB, RX, RA60,61.
1. Check the items listed below beforehand.
(a) Air cleaner installed.
(b) Normal operating coolant temperature.
(c) Choke fully open.
(d) All accessories switched off.
(e) All vacuum lines connected.
(f) Ignition timing set correctly.
(g) Transmission in N range.
(h) Fuel level should be about even with the correct level in the sight glass.
(i) If there is an idle limiter cap on the idle adjust screw, remove it.

2. Start the engine.

3. Set to the maximum speed by turning the idle mixture adjusting screw.

Set to maximum speed.

4. Set to the idle mixture speed by turning the idle speed adjusting screw.

Idle mixture speed:

Australia RJ	740rpm
RJ (Ex.Australia)	850rpm

* Before moving to the next step, continue the adjustments (a) and (b) until the maximum speed will not rise any further no matter how much the Idle Mixture Adjusting Screw is adjusted.

5. Set the idle speed by screwing in the idle mixture adjusting screw.

Idle speed:

RJ (Australia)	700rpm
RJ (Ex.Australia)	800rpm

* This is the "Lean Drop Method" for setting idle speed and mixture.

6. Install a new limiter cap on the idle mixture adjusting screw, if one was installed.

Fast Idle Speed Adjustment.

A. 21R, 21R-C Engine

1. Warm up the engine and then turn it off.

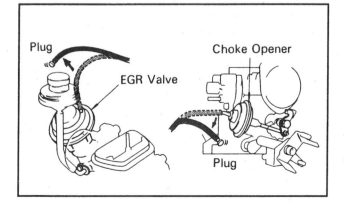

(With choke opener and/or EGR system)

2. Disconnect the vacuum hoses from the choke opener diaphragm and EGR valve, also plug the end of the hoses.

3. Hold the throttle valve slightly open and at the same time push the choke valve closed and hold it closed as you release the throttle valve.

4. Start the engine, do not touch the accelerator pedal.

5. Adjust the fast idle speed by turning the fast idle adjusting screw.

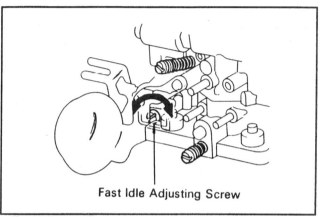

Fast Idle Adjusting Screw

Fast idle speed:

RX60	2,400rpm
RX70	2,600rpm

6. Connect the hose to the FICB diaphragm and make sure that the FICB lever moves and that the fast idle cam is released to third step or beyond.

B. 22R Engine

1. Warm-up the engine and then turn it off.

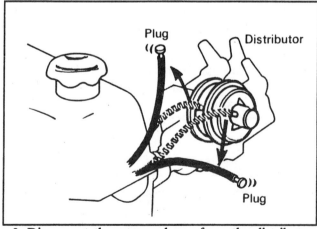

2. Disconnect the vacuum hoses from the distributor vacuum advancer and plug the ends of the hoses.

(With EGR system and/or choke opener system)

3. Disconnect the vacuum hoses from the choke opener diaphragm and EGR valve, and plug the ends of the hoses.

* Choke opener system is equipped on RJ (ECE and Australia).

4. Hold the throttle valve slightly open and at the same time push the choke valve closed and hold it closed as you release the throttle valve.

5. Start the engine and adjust the fast idle speed by turning the fast idle adjusting screw.

Fast Idle Adjusting Screw

Fast idle speed:
RJ   2,600 rpm
* Do not touch the accelerator pedal.

Throttle Positioner.

RJ (Australia)

Check Throttle Positioner.
Operation.
1. Warm the engine up.
2. Make sure that the throttle positioner is released at idle.
3. Connect the throttle positioner diaphragm directly to the intake manifold with a vacuum hose.
4. Check that the throttle positioner is set.

Check Throttle Positioner Setting Speed.
1. After the throttle positioner is set, make sure that the engine speed is correct.
Throttle positioner setting speed
RJ 1,200 rpm

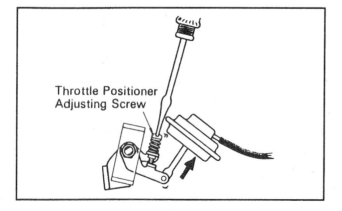

Throttle Positioner Adjusting Screw

2. If needed, adjust with the throttle positioner adjusting screw.

Compression.

Pressure.
1. Warm the engine up.
2. Take all the spark plugs out.
3. Disconnect the high tension cord from the ignition coil to cutoff the secondary circuit.
4. Insert a compression gauge into the spark plug hole and fully open the throttle valve. While cranking the engine, measure the compression pressure.

Compression pressure:
STD
21R More than $11.0kg/cm^2$ (157psi)
21R-C More than $11.5 kg/cm^2$ (164psi)
22R More than $12.0kg/cm^2$ (171psi)
Limit
21R & 21R-C $9.0kg/cm^2$ (128psi)
22R $10.0 kg/cm^2$ (142psi)
Difference between each cylinder:
Less than $1.0 kg/cm^2$ (14psi)
* Always use a fully charged battery to obtain engine revolution of more than 250 rpm.

PETROL ENGINES.

2F & 3F 6 CYLINDER PETROL ENGINES

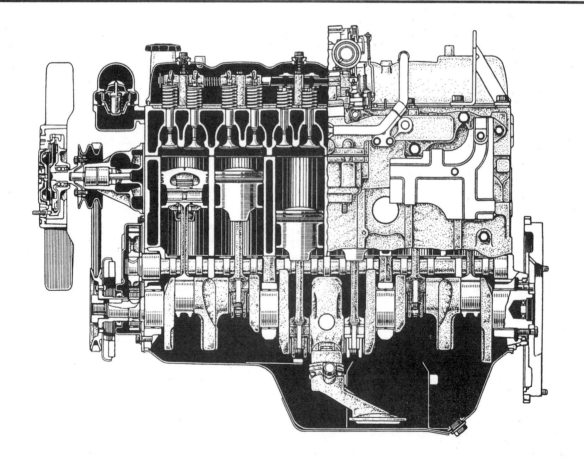

2F & 3F 6 CYLINDER PETROL ENGINES

CYLINDER HEAD   **Components**

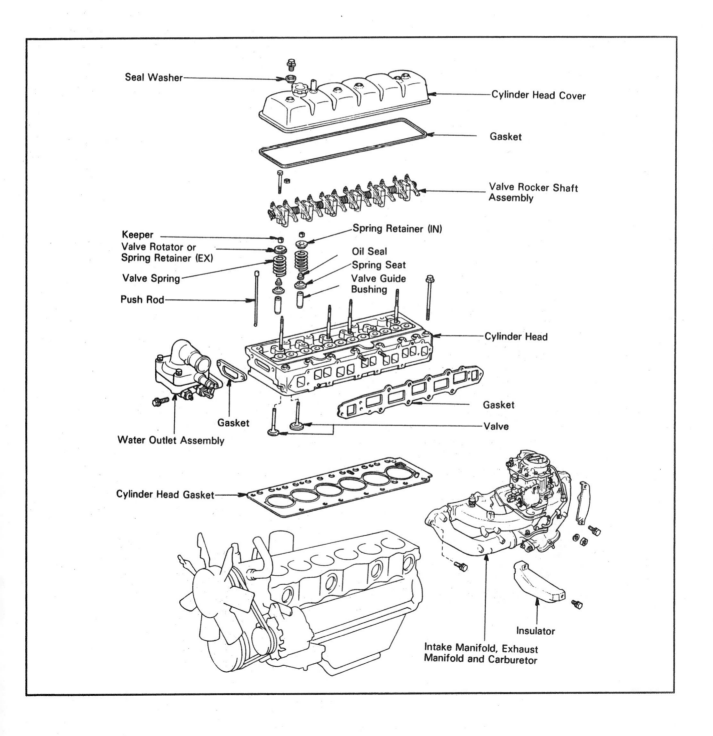

Seal Washer — Cylinder Head Cover

Gasket

Valve Rocker Shaft Assembly

Keeper

Valve Rotator or Spring Retainer (EX)

Spring Retainer (IN)

Oil Seal

Spring Seat

Valve Spring

Valve Guide Bushing

Push Rod

Cylinder Head

Gasket

Water Outlet Assembly

Gasket

Valve

Cylinder Head Gasket

Insulator

Intake Manifold, Exhaust Manifold and Carburetor

Removal

1. Drain Engine Coolant.

2. Remove Heater and Oil Cooler Pipes.

(a) Disconnect the hoses from the water outlet, water pump and oil cooler.

(b) Remove the screws and heater and oil cooler pipes from the cylinder head.

3. Disconnect High-Tension Cords from Spark Plugs.

4. Remove Spark Plugs.

5. Remove Fuel Pipe. Remove the fuel pipe connecting the carburettor to the fuel pump.

6. Remove Cylinder Head Cover. Remove the 4 cap nuts, seals, washers, cylinder head cover and gasket.

7. Remove Water Outlet Assembly.

(a) Disconnect the water by-pass hose from the water outlet.

(b) Remove the 2 bolts holding the water outlet housing to the cylinder head, and remove the water outlet assembly and gasket.

8. Remove Intake, Exhaust Manifolds and Carburettor Assembly.

(a) Remove the 4 bolts and two insulators.

(b) Remove the 12 bolts, 2 nuts and plate washers holding the manifolds to the cylinder head.

(c) Remove the intake, exhaust manifolds and carburettor assembly and gasket.

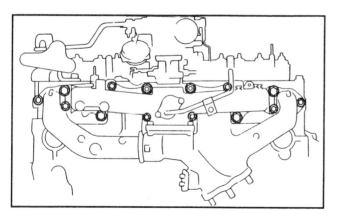

9. Remove Valve Rocker Shaft Assembly.

(a) Uniformly loosen and remove the 8 bolts and four nuts in several passes, in the sequence shown.

(b) Remove the rocker shaft assembly.

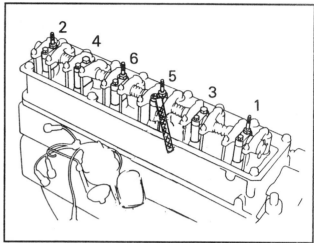

10. Remove Push Rods. Remove the 12 push rods in order, beginning from the No. 1 push rod.

*Arrange the push rods in correct order.

11. Remove Cylinder Head.

(a) Uniformly loosen and remove the 15 head bolts in several passes, in the sequence shown.

*Head warpage or cracking could result from removing out of sequence.

(b) Lift the cylinder head from the dowels on the cylinder block and place the head on wooden blocks on a bench.

*If the cylinder head is difficult to lift off, pry with a screwdriver between the cylinder head and block edges.

*Be careful not to damage the cylinder head or block surface on the cylinder and head gasket sides.

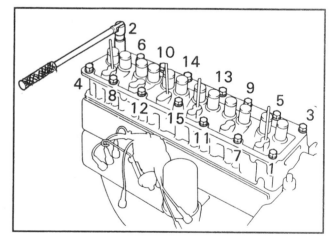

Dismantle

Remove Valves.

(a) Using special tool, press the valve spring and remove the two keepers.

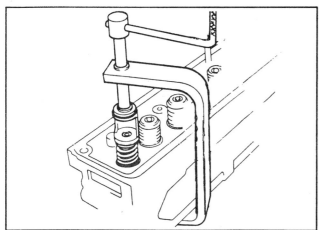

(b) Remove the spring retainer (or valve rotator), valve spring and valve.

(c) Using a screwdriver, pry out the oil seal.

(d) Remove the spring seat.

*Arrange the valves, valve springs and spring retainers (or valve rotators) in the correct order.

Inspection, Cleaning and Repair of Cylinder Head Components

1. Clean Top of Pistons and Top of Block.

(a) Turn the crankshaft and bring each piston to top dead center. Using a gasket scraper, remove all the carbon from the piston top.

(b) Remove all the gasket material from the top of the block.

(c) Blow carbon and oil from the bolt holes.

*Protect your eyes when using high pressure air.

2. Remove Gasket Material. Using a gasket scraper, remove all the gasket material from the manifold and head surface.

*Be careful not to scratch the surfaces.

3. Clean Combustion Chambers. Using a wire brush, remove all the carbon from the combustion chambers.

*Be careful not to scratch the head gasket contact surface.

4. Clean Valve Guide Bushings. Using a valve guide bushing brush and solvent, clean all the guide bushings.

5. Clean Cylinder Head. Using a soft brush and solvent, thoroughly clean the head.

6. Inspect Cylinder Head for Flatness. Using a precision straight edge and feeler gauge, measure the surfaces contacting the cylinder block and manifolds for warpage.

Maximum warpage;

Cylinder block side 0.15 mm (0.0059 in.)

Manifold side   0.10 mm (0.0039 in.)

If warpage exceeds maximum, replace the head.

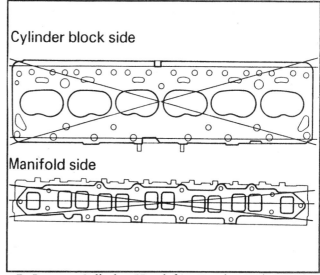

Cylinder block side

Manifold side

7. Inspect Cylinder Head for Cracks. Using a dye penetrant, check the combustion chamber, intake and exhaust ports, head surface and the top of the head for cracks. If cracked, replace the head.

8. Clean Valves.

(a) Use a gasket scraper, chip and carbon from the valve head.

(b) Using a wire brush, thoroughly clean the valve.

9. Inspect Valve Stem and Valve Guide Bushing.

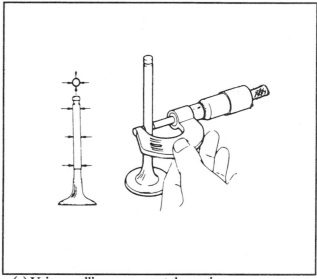

(a) Using a calliper gauge or telescoping gauge, measure the inside diameter of the valve guide bushing.

Bushing inside diameter:

8.010-8.030 mm (0.3154-0.3161 in.)

(b) Using a micrometer, measure the diameter of the valve stem.

Valve stem diameter:

Intake: 7.970-7.985 mm (0.3138-0.3144 in.)

Exhaust: 7.960-7.975 mm (0.3134-0.3140 in.)

(c) Subtract the valve stem diameter measurement from the bushing inside diameter measurement.

Standard stem oil clearance:

Intake: 0.025-0.060 mm (0.0010-0.0024 in.)

Exhaust: 0.035-0.070 mm (0.0014-0.0028 in.)

Maximum stem oil clearance:

Intake: 0.10 mm (0.0039 in.)

Exhaust: 0.12 mm (0.0047 in.)

If the clearance exceeds maximum, replace the valve and valve guide bushing.

10. If Necessary, Replace Valve Guide Bushing.

(a) Using special tool and a hammer, tap out the valve guide bushing.

(b) Using a calliper gauge, measure the bushing bore diameter of the cylinder head.

(c) Select a new valve guide bushing (STD size or O/S 0.05)

If the bushing bore diameter of the cylinder head is more than 14.018 mm (0.5519 in.), machine the bore to the following dimension.

Rebored cylinder head bushing bore dimension:

14.050-14.068 mm (0.5531-0.05539 in.)

If the bushing bore diameter of the cylinder head exceeds 14.068 mm (0.5539 in.), replace the cylinder head.

(d) Using the special tool and a hammer, tap in a new valve guide bushing to where there is

17.3-17.7 mm (0.681-0.697 in.) protruding from the cylinder head.

(e) Using a sharp 8.0 mm reamer, ream the valve guide bushing to obtain the standard specified clearance (as described under Item 9 in this section.) between the valve guide bushing and new valve stem.

11. Inspect and Grind Valves.

(a) Grind the valve only enough to remove pits and carbon.

(b) Check that the valve is ground to the correct valve face angle. **Valve face angle: 44.5°**

(c) Check the valve head margin thickness.

Standard margin thickness

Intake: 1.5-2.1 mm (0.059-0.083 in.)

Exhaust: 1.7-2.3 mm (0.067-0.091 in.)

Minimum margin thickness:

Intake: 1.0 mm (0.039 in.)

Exhaust: 1.2 mm (0.047 in.)

If the valve head margin thickness is less than **minimum**, replace the valve.

(d) Check the valve overall length.

Standard overall length:

Intake 124.8 mm (4.913 in.)

Exhaust

with spring retainer 125.0 mm (4.921 in.)

with valve rotator 128.0 mm (5.039 in.)

Minimum overall length:

Intake 124.3 mm (4.894 in.)

Exhaust

with spring retainer 124.5 mm (4.902 in.)

with valve rotator 127.5 mm (5.020 in.)

(e) If the valve stem tip is worn, resurface the tip with a grinder or replace the valve.

*Do not grind off more than the minimum amount.

12. Inspect and Clean Valve Seats.

(a) Using a 45° carbide cutter, resurface the valve seats. Remove only enough metal to clean the seats.

(b) Check the valve seating position. Apply a thin coat of prussian blue (or white lead) to the valve face. Install the valve. Lightly press the valve against the seat. Do not rotate the valve.

(c) Check the valve face and seat for the following:

* If the blue appears 360° around the face, the valve is concentric. If not, replace the valve.

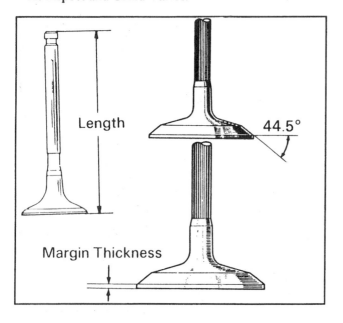

* If the blue appears 360° around the valve seat, the guide and seat are concentric. If not, resurface the seat.

* Check that the seat contact is on the middle of the valve face with the following width:

Intake   1.1-1.7 mm (0.043-0.067 in.)

Exhaust 1.4-2.0 mm (0.055-0.079 in.)

If not, correct the valve seat as follows:

(1) (Intake) If the seating is too low on the valve face, use 70° and 45° cutters to correct the seat.

(2) (Exhaust) If the seating is too low on the valve face, use 65° and 45° cutters to correct the seat.

(d) Hand-lap the valve and valve seat with an abrasive compound.

(e) After hand-lapping, clean the valve and valve seat.

13. Inspect Valve Springs.

(a) Using calliper, measure the free length of the valve spring. **Free length** 51.5 mm (2.028 in.) If the free length is not as specified, replace the valve spring.

(b) Using a spring tester, measure the tension of the valve spring at the specified installed length.

Standard installed tension:

32.5 kg (71.6lb, 319 N) at 43.0 mm (1.693 in.)

Minimum installed tension:

27 kg (59.5lb, 265N) at 43.0 mm (1.693 in.)

If the installed tension is less than minimum, replace the valve spring.

14. Inspect Rocker Arm and Shaft.

(a) Inspect the valve contacting surface of the rocker arm for wear.

(b) Inspect the rocker arm-to-shaft clearance by wobbling each rocker arm. If movement is felt, dismantle and inspect.

(c) Dismantle the valve rocker shaft assembly.

*Arrange the rocker arms and rocker supports in correct order.

If the contacting surface of the rocker arm is worn, resurface it with a valve refacer and oil stone or replace the rocker arm.

(d) Inspect the oil clearance between the rocker arm and shaft.

* Using a calliper gauge, measure the inside diameter of the rocker arm.

Rocker arm inside diameter:

18.494-18.515 mm (0.7281-0.7289 in.)

* Using a micrometer, measure the diameter of the rocker shaft.

Rocker shaft diameter:

18.464-18.485 mm (0.7269-0.7278 in.)

* Subtract the rocker shaft diameter measurement from the inside diameter measurement of the rocker arm.

Standard oil clearance:

0.009-0.051 mm (0.0004-0.0020 in.)

Maximum oil clearance: 0.08 mm (0.0031 in.)

If the clearance exceeds maximum, replace the rocker arm and shaft.

(e) Assemble the valve rocker shaft assembly as shown.

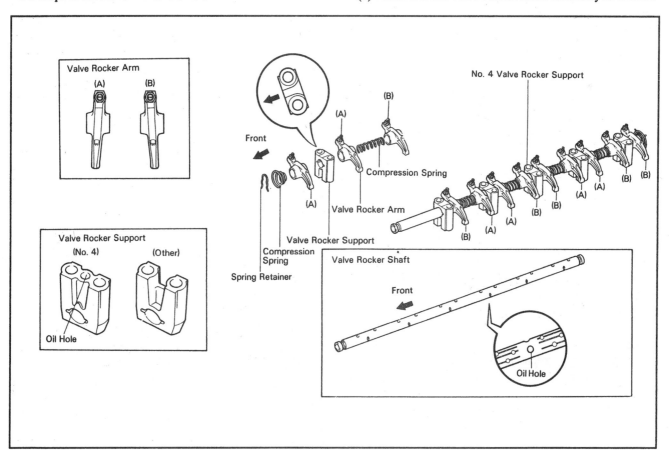

15. Inspect Push Rods.

(a) Place the push rod on V-Blocks.

(b) Using a dial indicator, measure the circle runout at the center of the push rod.

Maximum circle runout: 1.0mm (0.039 in.)

If the circle runout exceeds the maximum, replace the push rod.

16. Inspect Intake and Exhaust Manifolds. Using a precision straight edge and feeler gauge, measure the surface contacting the cylinder head for warpage.

Maximum warpage:

Intake with RH exhaust   0.50 mm (0.0197 in.)

LH exhaust   0.30 mm (0.0118 in.)

If warpage exceeds maximum, separate and inspect the intake and exhaust manifold. If necessary, replace the manifold.

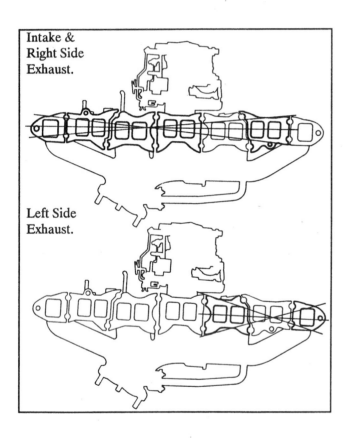

Intake &
Right Side
Exhaust.

Left Side
Exhaust.

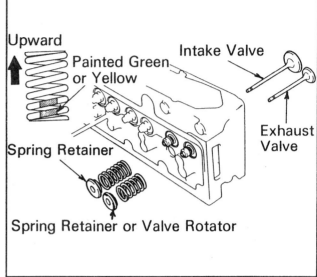

(d) Using special tool, compress the valve spring and place the two keepers around the valve system.

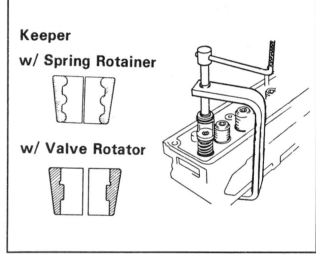

(e) Using a plastic-faced hammer. lightly tap the valve stem to assure proper fit.

Assembly

 * Thoroughly clean all parts to be assembled.

 * Before installing the parts, apply new engine oil to all sliding and rotating surfaces.

 * Replace all gaskets and oil seals with new ones.

Install Valves

(a) Place the spring seat on the cylinder head.

(b) Using special tool and a hammer, tap in a new oil seal.

(c) Install the valve, valve spring and spring retainer (or valve rotator).

Installation

1. Install Cylinder Head.

(a) Place a new cylinder head gasket on the cylinder block.

*Be careful of the installation direction.

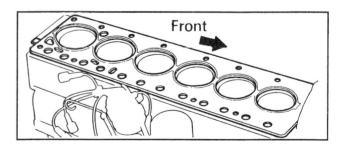

(b) Place the cylinder head on the cylinder head gasket.

(c) Apply a light coat of engine oil on the threads and under the cylinder head bolts.

(d) Install and uniformly tighten the 15 cylinder head bolts in several passes, in the sequence shown.

Torque: 1,250 kg-cm (90ft-lb, 123 N·m)

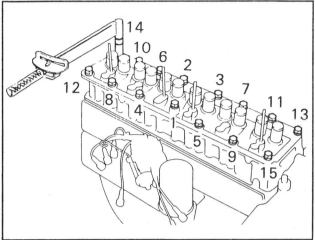

2. Install Push Rods. Install the 12 push rods.

3. Install Valve Rocker Shaft Assembly.

(a) Place the rocker shaft assembly on the cylinder head.

(b) Install and uniformly tighten the 8 bolts and 4 nuts in several passes, in the sequence shown.

Torque:
12 mm bolt head 240 kg-cm (17 ft-lb, 24N·m)
14 mm bolt head and nut 240 kg-cm (25 ft-lb, 33N·m)

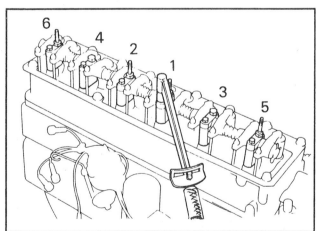

4. Install Intake, Exhaust Manifolds and Carburettor Assembly.

(a) Install a new gasket, the intake, manifolds and carburettor assembly with the 12 bolts, 2 plate washers and nuts. Torque the bolts and nuts.

Torque:
17 mm bolt	700 kg-cm (51 ft-lb, 69 N·m)
14 mm bolt	510 kg-cm (37 ft-lb, 50 N·m)
Nut	570 kg-cm (41 ft-lb, 56 N·m)

(b) Install the 2 insulators with the 4 bolts.

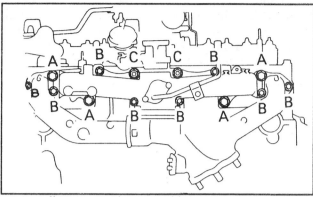

5. Install Water Outlet Assembly.

(a) Install a new gasket and the water outlet assembly with the 2 bolts. Torque the bolts.

Torque: 250 kg-cm (18 ft-lb, 25N·m)

(b) Connect the water by-pass hose.

6. Adjust Valve Clearances.

(a) Set the No.1 cylinder to TDC/compression. Align the TDC mark of the flywheel with the timing pointer by turning the crankshaft clockwise with a wrench.

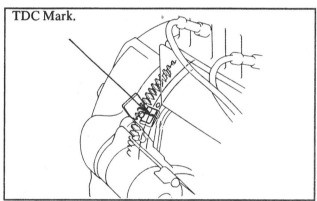

TDC Mark.

(b) Check that the rocker arms on the No.1 cylinder are loose and rocker arms on the No.6 cylinder are tight. If not, turn the crankshaft one revolution (360°) and align the mark as above.

(c) Adjust only those valves indicated by arrows.

Valve clearance (Hot):
Intake 0.20 mm (0.008 in.)
Exhaust 0.35 mm (0.014 in.)

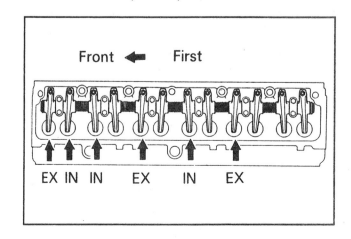

* Using a feeler gauge, measure the valve clearance between the valve stem and rocker arm. Loosen the lock nut and turn the adjusting screw to set the proper clearance. Hold the adjusting screw in position and tighten the lock nut.

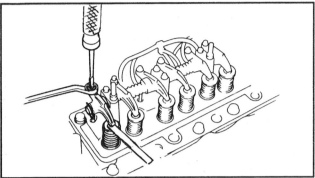

* Recheck the valve clearance. The feeler gauge should slide with a very slight drag.

(d) Turn the crankshaft one revolution (360°) and align the mark as above. Adjust only the valves indicated by arrows.

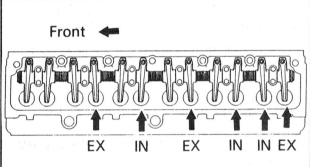

Front ⬅

EX   IN   EX   IN   IN EX

7. Install Cylinder Head Cover.

(a) Install a new gasket to the cylinder head cover.

(b) Install the cylinder head cover with the 4 seal washers and cap nuts.

Torque: 90 kg-cm (78 in.-lb, 8.8 N·m)

8. Install Fuel Pipe.

9. Install Spark Plugs.

10. Connect High-Tension Cords to Spark Plugs.

11. Install Heater and Oil Cooler Pipes.

(a) Install the heater and oil cooler pipes with the screws.

(b) Connect the hoses to the water outlet, water pump and oil cooler.

12. Fill With Engine Coolant.

13. Start the Engine and Check For Leaks.

14. Check Engine Oil Level.

TIMING GEARS AND CAMSHAFT

Components.

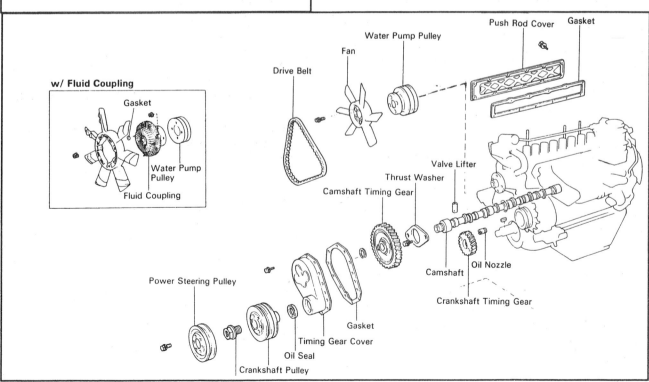

Removal.

1. Remove Distributor.
2. Remove Fuel Pump.
3. Remove Valve Rocker Shaft Assembly.
(As described under cylinder head section.)
4. Remove Push Rod Cover. Remove the 10 bolts, 2 nuts, push rod cover and gasket.
5. Remove Valve Lifters. Using a piece of wire, remove the 12 valve lifters in order, beginning from the No.1 lifter.
*Arrange the valve lifters in correct order.
6. Remove Drive Belts.
7. (With PS) Remove Power Steering (PS) Pulley From Crankshaft Pulley. Remove the 6 bolts and PS pulley.

8. Remove Crankshaft Pulley.
(a) Using special tool and a 46 mm socket wrench, remove the pulley mount bolt.
(b) Using pulley puller to remove the pulley.
9. Remove the Timing Gear Cover. Remove the 12 bolts, gear cover and gasket.
10. Check Timing Gear Backlash. Using a dial indicator, measure the backlash at several places while turning the camshaft clockwise and counterclockwise.
Standard backlash:
0.100-0.183 mm (0.0039-0.0072 in.)
Maximum backlash: 0.25 mm (0.0098 in.)
If the backlash exceeds maximum, replace the camshaft and crankshaft timing gears.
11. Remove Camshaft Timing Gear and Camshaft Assembly.
(a) Remove the 2 bolts mounting the thrust plate to the cylinder block.
(b) Carefully pull out the camshaft and timing gear assembly.
*Be Careful not to damage the camshaft bearings.
12. Remove Crankshaft Timing Gear.
(a) Using a screwdriver and hammer, tap out the crankshaft pulley set key.
(b) Using special tool, remove the timing gear.

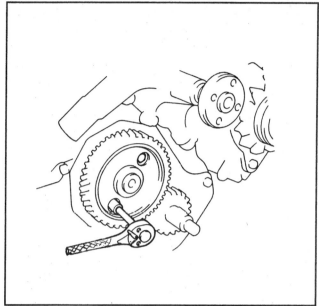

13. If necessary, remove oil nozzle.

Inspection

Inspect Camshaft.
(a) Place the camshaft on V-Blocks and, using a dial indicator, measure the circle runout at the No.2 and No.3 journals.
Maximum circle runout: 0.30 mm (0.0118 in.)
If the circle runout exceeds maximum, replace the camshaft.
(b) Using a micrometer, measure the cam lobe height.
Standard cam lobe height:
Intake 38.36-38.46 mm (1.5102-1.5142 in.)
Exhaust 38.25-38.35 mm (1.5059-1.5098 in.)
Minimum cam lobe height:
Intake 38.0 mm (1.496 in.)
Exhaust 37.9 mm (1.492 in.)
If the lobe height is less than minimum, replace the camshaft.
(c) Using a micrometer, measure the journal diameter.
Journal diameter (from front side):

STD	No.1	47.955-47.975 mm (1.8880-1.8888 in.)
	No.2	46.455-46.475 mm (1.8289-1.8297 in.)
	No.3	44.955-44.975 mm (1.7699-1.7707 in.)
	No.4	43.455-43.475 mm (1.7108-1.7116 in.)
U/S 0.25	No.1	47.715-47.725 mm (1.8785-1.8789 in.)
	No.2	46.215-46.225 mm (1.8195-1.8199 in.)
	No.3	44.715-44.725 mm

(1.7604-1.7608 in.)

No.4   43.215-43.225 mm
(1.7014-1.7018 in.)

U/S 0.50   No.1   47.465-47.475 mm
(1.8687-1.8691 in.)

No.2   45.965-45.975 mm
(1.8096-1.8888 in.)

No.3   44.465-44.475 mm
(1.7506-1.7510 in.)

No.4   42.965-42.975 mm
(1.6915-1.6919 in.)

If the journal diameter is not within specification, check the oil clearance.

(d) Using a feeler gauge, measure the thrust clearance between the thrust plate and camshaft.

Standard thrust clearance:
0.200-0.290 mm (0.0079-0.0114 in.)
Maximum thrust clearance: 0.33mm (0.0130 in.)

If the clearance exceeds maximum, replace the thrust plate. If necessary, replace the camshaft.

Replacement

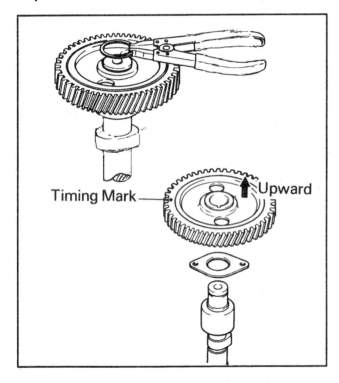

Timing Mark ——   Upward

1. Remove Snap Ring. Using snap ring pliers, remove the snap ring.

2. Remove Camshaft. Using a socket wrench and press, press out the camshaft.

3. Install New Camshaft

(a) Install the timing gear set key to the camshaft.

(b) Assemble the camshaft, thrust plate and timing gear with timing mark facing away from camshaft.

(c) Using special tool and a press, align the timing gear set key with the key groove of the timing gear, and press in the camshaft.

4. Install Snap Ring.

5 Check Camshaft Thrust Clearance.

Thrust clearance:
0.200-0.290mm (0.0079-0.0114 in.)

Inspection of Valve Lifters

Inspect Valve Lifters.

Using a micrometer, measure the valve lifter diameter.

Lifter diameter:
STD   21.387-21.404 mm (0.8420-0.8427 in.)
O/S 0.05   21.437-21.454 MM (0.8440-0.8446 in.)

If the diameter is not within specification, check the oil clearance.

Replacement of Crankshaft Front Oil Seal.

Replace Crankshaft Front Oil Seal.

* There are two methods (A & B) to replace the oil seal as follows:

A. If the timing gear cover is removed from cylinder block:

(a) Using screwdriver and hammer, tap out the oil seal.

(b) Using special tool and a hammer, tap in a new oil seal until its surface is flush with the timing gear cover edge.

(c) Apply Multi purpose grease to the oil seal lip.

B. If timing gear cover is installed to cylinder block:

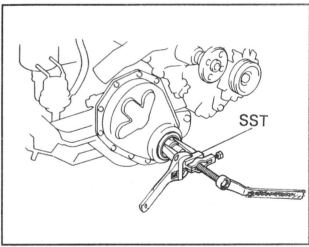

SST

(a) Using special tool, remove the oil seal.

(b) Apply Multi purpose grease to a new oil seal lip.

(c) Using special tool and a hammer, tap in the oil seal until its surface is flush with the timing gear cover edge.

Installation of Timing Gears and Camshaft.

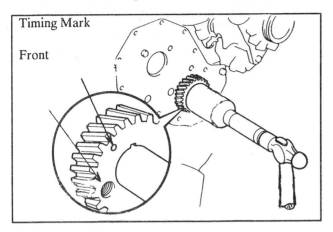

1. Install Crankshaft Timing Gear.

(a) Put the timing gear on the crankshaft with the timing mark facing frontward.

(b) Align the timing gear set key with the key groove of the timing gear.

(c) Using special tool and a hammer, tap in the timing gear.

(d) Using a plastic-faced hammer, tap in the crankshaft pulley set key.

2. Install Camshaft Timing Gear and Camshaft Assembly.

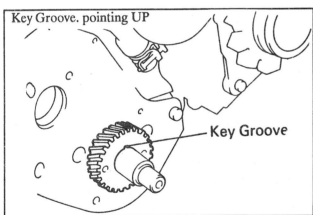

(a) Set the crankshaft timing gear with the key groove facing upward by turning the crankshaft clockwise.

(b) Insert the camshaft into the cylinder block.

* Be careful not to damage the camshaft bearings.

(c) Align the timing marks of the crankshaft and camshaft timing gears and mesh the gears.

* At this time, No.6 cylinder should be at TDC/compression.

(d) Install the 2 bolts mounting the trust washer to the cylinder block. Torque the bolts.

Torque: 120 kg-cm (9 ft-lb, 12 N^{o}m)

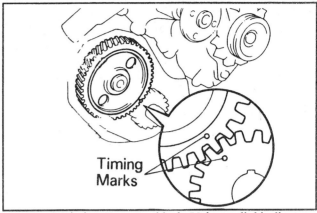

3. Check Timing Gear Backlash. Using a dial indicator, measure the backlash at several places while turning the camshaft clockwise and counter clockwise.

Standard backlash:

0.100-0.183 mm (0.0039-0.0072 in.)

Maximum backlash: 0.20 mm (0.0078 in.)

4. Install Oil Nozzle

(a) Install and set the oil nozzle in position.

(b) Using a Chisel and hammer, stake the threads of the

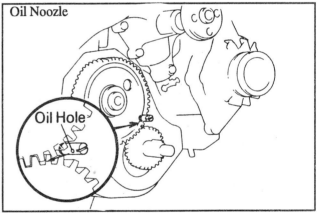

oil nozzle.

5. Install Timing Gear Cover and Crankshaft Pulley.

* There are 3 different size timing gear cover bolts, be ensured to use the correct one.

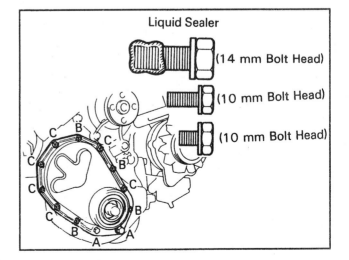

(a) Install a new gasket and the gear cover with the 12 bolts. Finger tighten all bolts.

(b) Align the pulley set key with the key groove of the pulley.

(c) Using special tool and a hammer tap in the pulley.

(d) After installing the pulley, torque the cover bolts.

Torque:

Bolts (14mm) 250 kg-cm (18 ft-lb, 25 N·m)

Bolts (10mm) 50 kg-cm (43 in.lb, 4.9 N·m)

(e) Use a 46 mm socket wrench, install and torque the pulley mount bolt.

Torque: 3,500 kg-cm (253 ft-lb, 343 N·m)

6 (with P/S) Install Power Steering (PS) Pulley to Crankshaft Pulley. Install the PS Pulley with the 6 bolts. Torque the bolts.

Torque: 185 kg-cm (13 ft-lb, 18 N·m)

7. Install and Adjust Drive Belts.

8. Install Valve Lifter. Carefully insert the 12 lifters into the lifter bore.

9. Install Valve Lifter Cover. Install a new gasket and the lifter cover with the 10 bolts and 2 nuts.

Torque: 40 kg-cm (35 in-lb, 39 N·m)

10 Install Valve Rocker Shaft Assembly (as previously described.)

11. Install Fuel Pump.

12. Install Distributor (see ignition section.)

13. Start Engine and Check For Leaks.

14. Check Engine Oil.

CYLINDER BLOCK

Components

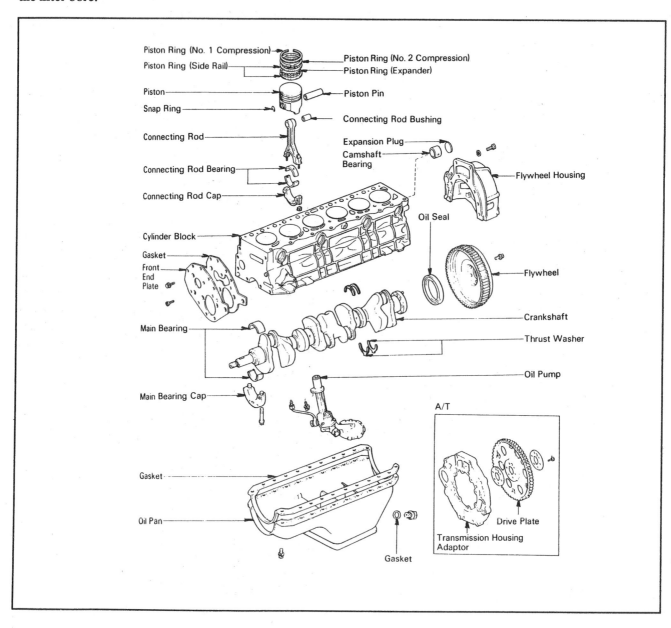

Dismantle

1. (Man.Trans)Remove Clutch Cover and Disc.

2. (Man.Trans)Remove Flywheel.

3. (Auto Trans)Remove Drive Plate.

4. (Man.Trans)Remove Flywheel Housing.

5. (Auto Trans)Remove Transmission Housing Adaptor.

6. Remove Cylinder Head (as previously described).

7. Remove Timing Gears and Camshaft (as previously described).

8. Remove Oil Pan and Oil Pump.

9. Remove Front End Plate.

(a) Using a socket wrench, remove the 3 screws.

(b) Remove the 2 bolts, front end plate and gasket.

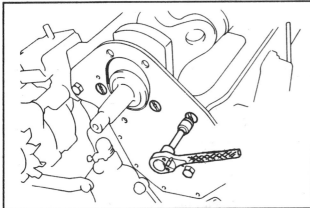

10. Check Connecting Rod Thrust Clearance. Using a dial indicator, measure the thrust clearance while moving the rod back and forth.

Standard thrust clearance:

0.160-0.300 mm (0.0063-0.0118 in.)

Maximum thrust clearance: 0.40 mm (0.0156 in.)

If the clearance exceeds maximum, replace the connecting rod assembly. If necessary, replace the crankshaft.

12. Remove Connecting Rod Caps and Check Oil Clearance.

(a) Using a punch or numbering stamp, place match marks on the connecting rod and cap to ensure correct reassembly.

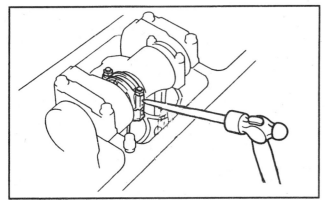

(b) Remove the connecting rod cap nuts.

(c) Using a plastic-faced hammer, lightly tap the connecting rod bolts and lift off the connecting rod cap.

* Keep the lower bearing inserted with the connecting rod cap.

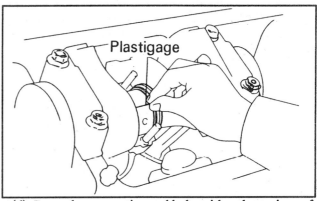

Plastigage

(d) Cover the connecting rod bolts with a short piece of hose to protect the crankshaft from damage.

(e) Clean the crank pin and bearing.

(f) Check the crank pin and bearing for pitting and scratches.

If the crank pin or bearing are damaged, replace the bearings. If necessary, replace the crankshaft.

(g) Lay a strip of Plastigage across the crank pin.

(h) Install the connecting rod cap.

Torque: 600 kg-cm (43 ft-lb, 59 N·m)

* Do not turn the crankshaft.

(i) Remove the connecting rod cap.

(j) Measure the Plastigage at its widest point.

Standard oil clearance:

STD

0.020-0.050 MM (0.0008-0.0020in.)

U/S 0.25 and 0.50

0.019-0.063 mm (0.0007 - 0.0025 in.)

Maximum oil clearance: 0.10 mm (0.0039 in.)

If the clearance exceeds maximum, replace the bearing. If necessary, replace the crankshaft.

* If using a standard bearing, replace with one having the same number marked on the connecting rod cap. There are 3 sizes of standard bearings marked A, B and C.

(Reference)

Standard bearing thickness (at centre wall):

Mark A 1.484-1.488 mm (0.0584-0.0586 in.)

Mark B 1.488-1.492 mm (0.0586-0.0587 in.)

Mark C 1.492-1.496 mm (0.0587-0.0589 in.)

(k) Completely remove the Plastigage.

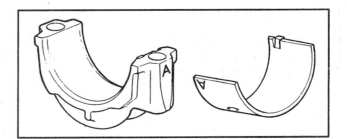

12. Remove Piston and Connecting Rod Assemblies.

(a) Remove all the carbon from the piston ring ridge.

(b) Cover the connecting rod bolts.

(c) Push the piston, connecting rod assembly and upper bearing out through the top of the cylinder.

* Keep the bearings, connecting rod and cap together.

* Arrange the piston and connecting rod assembly in correct order.

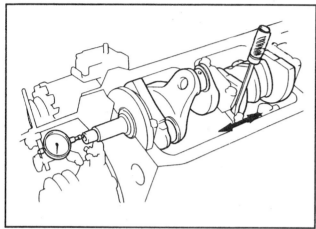

13. Check Crankshaft Thrust Clearance. Using a dial indicator, measure the thrust clearance while prying the crankshaft back and forth with a screwdriver.

Standard thrust clearance:

0.015-0.204 mm (0.0006-0.0080 in.)

Maximum thrust clearance: 0.30mm (0.0118 in.)

If the clearance exceeds maximum, replace the thrust washers as a set.

Thrust washer size: STD, O/S 0.125, 0.250

14. Remove Main Bearing Caps and Check Oil Clearance.

(a) Remove the main bearing cap bolts.

(b) Using the removed main bearing cap bolts, pry the cap back and forth, and remove the main bearing caps, lower bearings and lower thrust washers (No.3 main bearing cap only)

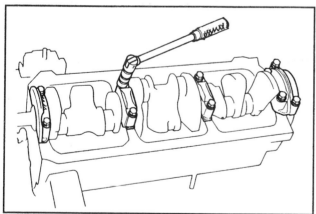

* Keep the lower bearing and main bearing cap together.

* Arrange the main bearing caps and lower thrust washers in correct order.

(c) Lift out the crankshaft.

* Keep the upper bearings and upper thrust washers together with the cylinder block.

(d) Clean each main journal and bearing.

(e) Check each main journal and bearing for pitting and scratches.

If the journal or bearing are damaged, replace the bearing. If necessary, replace the crankshaft

(f) Place the crankshaft on the cylinder block.

(g) Lay a strip of Plastigage across each of the main journals.

(h) Install the main bearing caps .

Torque: 19 mm bolt head

1,375 kg-cm (99 ft-lb, 135 N·m)

17 mm bolt head

1,175 kg-cm (85 ft-lb, 115N·m)

* Do not turn the crankshaft.

(i) Remove the main bearing caps.

(j) Measure the Plastigage at its widest point.

Standard oil clearance:

STD

0.016-0.056 mm (0.0006-0.0022 in.)

U/S 0.25 & 0.50

0.021-0.067 mm (0.0008-0.0026 in.)

Maximum oil clearance: 0.10 mm (0.0039 in.)

* If replacing the cylinder block subassembly the bearing standard clearance will be:

0.004-0.060 mm (0.0002-0.0024 in.)

If the clearance exceeds maximum, replace the main bearing. If necessary, replace the crankshaft.

* If replacing a standard size bearing with a standard oil clearance, replace with one having the same number. If the number of the bearing cannot be determined, select a bearing from the table below according to the numbers imprinted on the cylinder block and crankshaft. There are 5 sizes of standard bearings, marked 1,2,3,4 & 5.

BEARING NUMBER MARK

CRANKSHAFT	3	4	5
CYL..BLOCK	6 7 8	6 7 8	6 7 8
BEARING	3 4 5	2 3 4	1 2 3

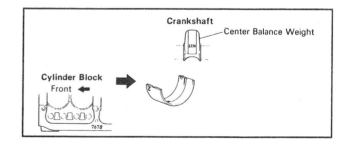

Eg: Crankshaft No.4, Cylinder Block No.6
   = Bearing No. 2

(Reference)
Crankshaft journal diameter:
Mark 3
No.1 66.972-66.980 mm (2.6367-2.6370 in.)
No.2 68.472-68.480 mm (2.6957-2.6961 in.)
No.3 69.972-69.980 mm (2.7548-2.7551 in.)
No.4 71.472-71.480 mm (2.8139-2.8142 in.)
Mark 4
No.1 66.980-66.988 mm (2.6370-2.6373 in.)
No.2 68.480-68.488 mm (2.6961-2.6964 in.)
No.3 69.980-69.988 mm (2.7551-2.7554 in.)
No.4 71.480-71.488 mm (2.8142-2.8145 in.)
Mark 5
No.1 66.988-66.996 mm (2.6373-2.6376 in.)
No.2 68.488-68.496 mm (2.6964-2.6967 in.)
No.3 69.988-69.996 mm (2.7554-2.7557 in.)
No.4 71.488-71.496 mm (2.8145-2.8148 in.)
Cylinder block housing inside diameter:
Mark 6
No.1 72.010-72.018 mm (2.8350-2.8353 in.)
No.2 73.510-73.518 mm (2.8941-2.8944 in.)
No.3 75.010-75.018 mm (2.9531-2.9535 in.)
No.4 76.510-76.518 mm (3.0122-3.0125 in.)
Mark 7
No.1 72.018-72.026 mm (2.8353-2.8357 in.)
No.2 73.518-73.526 mm (2.8944-2.8947 in.)
No.3 75.018-75.026 mm (2.9535-2.9538 in.)
No.4 76.518-76.526 mm (3.0125-3.0128 in.)
Mark 8
No.1 72.026-72.034 mm (2.8357-2.8360 in.)
No.2 73.526-73.534 mm (2.8947-2.8950 in.)
No.3 75.026-75.034 mm (2.9538-2.9541 in.)
No.4 76.526-76.534 mm (3.0128-3.0131 in.)
Standard bearing thickness (at centre wall):
Mark 1
2.493-2.497 mm (0.0981-0.0983 in.)
Mark 2
2.497-2.501 mm (0.0983-0.0985 in.)
Mark 3
2.501-2.505 mm (0.0985-0.0986 in.)
Mark 4
2.505-2.509 mm (0.0986-0.0988 in.)
Mark 5
2.509-2.513 mm (0.0988-0.0989 in.)
(k) Completely remove the Plastigage.
15. Remove Crankshaft.
(a) Lift out the crankshaft.
(b) Remove the upper bearings and upper thrust
washers from the cylinder block.
* Arrange the main bearing caps, bearings and thrust
washers in the correct order.

INSPECTION OF CYLINDER BLOCK

1. Remove Gasket Material. Using a gasket scraper,
remove all the gasket material from the top of the cylinder
block service.
2. Clean Cylinder Block. Using a soft brush and solvent,
clean the block.
3. Inspect Top of Cylinder Block for Flatness. Using a
precision straight edge and feeler gauge, measure the
surfaces contacting the cylinder head gasket for warpage.
Maximum warpage: 0.15 mm (0.0059 in.)
If warpage exceed maximum, replace the cylinder block.

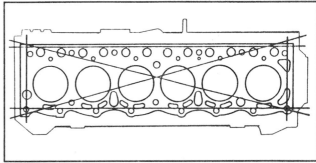

4. Inspect Cylinders For Vertical Scratches. Visually
check the cylinder for vertical scratches. If deep scratches
are present, rebore all 6 cylinders.
5. Inspect Cylinder Bore Diameter. Using a cylinder
gauge, measure the cylinder bore diameter at various
positions in the thrust and axial directions.

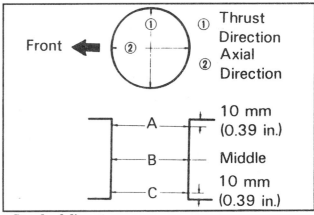

Standard diameter:
STD 94.000-94.030 mm (3.7008-3.7020 in.)
Maximum diameter:
STD   94.23 mm (3.7098 in.)
O/S 0.50   94.73 mm (3.7295 in.)
O/S 1.00   95.23 mm (3.7492 in.)
O/S 1.50   95.73 mm (3.7689 in.)
If the diameter exceeds maximum, rebore all 6 cylinders.
If necessary, replace the cylinder block.
6. Remove Cylinder Ridge. If the wear is less than 0.2
mm (0.008 in.), use a ridge reamer to machine the piston
ring ridge at the top of the cylinder.

Dismantle Piston and Connecting Rod Assemblies.

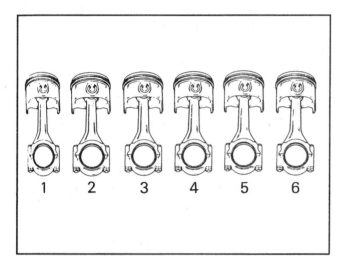

1. Check Fit Between Piston and Pin. Try to move the piston back and forth on the piston pin. If any movement is felt, replace the piston and pin as a set.

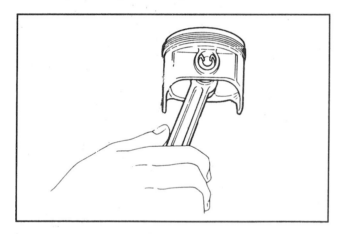

2. Remove Piston Rings.

(a) Using a piston ring expander, remove the compression rings.

(b) Remove the two side rails and oil ring expander by hand.

   * Arrange the rings in correct order.

3. Disconnect Connecting Rod From Piston.

(a) Using needle-nose pliers, remove all the snap rings.

(b) Gradually heat the piston to approx. 80°C (176°F).

(c) Using a plastic-faced hammer and driver, lightly tap out the piston pin and remove the connecting rod.

   * The piston and pin are a matched set.

   * Arrange the pistons, pins, rings, connecting rods and bearings in correct order only.

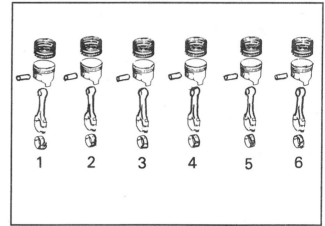

Inspection of Piston and Connecting Rod Assemblies.

1. Clean Piston.

(a) Using a gasket scraper, remove the carbon from the piston top.

(b) Using a groove cleaning tool or broken ring, clean the ring grooves.

(c) Using a solvent and a brush, thoroughly clean the piston.

   * Do not use a wire brush.

2. Inspect Piston Diameter and Oil Clearance.

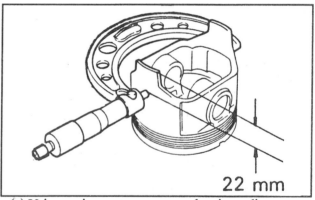

(a) Using a micrometer, measure the piston diameter at a right angle to the piston pin hole centre line, 22 mm (0.87in.) below the skirt bottom edge.

Standard diameter:

STD	93.960-93.990 mm	(3.6992-3.7004 in.)
O/S 0.50	94.460-94.490 mm	(3.7189-3.7201 in.)
O/S 1.00	94.960-94.990 mm	(3.7386-3.7398 in.)
O/S 1.50	95.460-95.490 mm	(3.7583-3.7594 in.)

(b) Measure the cylinder bore diameter in the thrust directions and subtract the piston diameter measurement from the cylinders or replace the cylinder bore diameter.

Oil Clearance:

0.030-0.050 mm (0.0012-0.0020 in.)

If the clearance is not within specification, replace all 6 pistons. If necessary, rebore all 6 cylinders or replace the cylinder block.

3. Inspect Clearance Between Wall of Piston Ring Groove and New Piston Ring. Using a feeler gauge, measure the clearance between new piston ring and the wall of the piston ring groove.

Ring groove clearance:
No.1   0.030-0.070 mm (0.0012-0.0028 in.)
No.2   0.050-0.090 mm (0.0020-0.0035 in.)
[2F] Oil 0.04 -0.19 mm (0.0016-0.0075 in.)

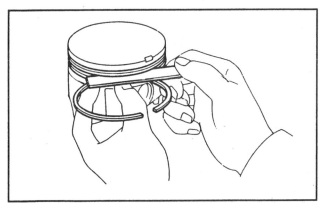

If the clearance is not within specification, replace the piston.

4. Inspect Piston Ring End Cap.

(a) Insert the piston ring into the cylinder bore.

(b) Using a piston, push the piston ring a little beyond the bottom of the ring travel.(70mm or 2.76 in from top surface of cylinder block.)

(c) Using a feeler gauge, measure the end gap.

Standard end gap: No.1 & No.2
0.200-0.520 mm (0.0079-0.0205 in.)

Oil (side rail)
0.200-0.820 mm (0.0079-0.0323 in.)

Maximum end gap:
No.1 & No.2   1.12 mm (0.0441 in.)
Oil (side rail)   1.42 mm (0.0559 in.)

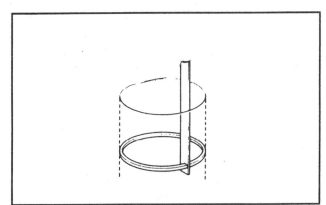

If the gap exceeds maximum, replace the piston ring. If the gap exceeds maximum, even with a new piston ring rebore the cylinder and use and O/S piston ring.

5. Check Piston Pin Fit. At 80°C (176°F) you should be able to push the pin into the piston with your thumb. If the pin can be installed at a lower temperature, replace the piston and pin as a set.

6. Inspect Connecting Rods.

(a) Using a rod aligner, check the connecting rod alignment.

* Check for bend.

Maximum bend:

0.05 mm (0.0020 in.) per 100 mm (3.94 in.) If the bend exceeds maximum, replace the connecting rod assembly.

* Check for twist.

Maximum twist:

0.05 mm (0.0020 in.) per 100 mm (3.94 in.) If the twist exceeds maximum, replace the connecting rod assembly.

(b) Using a calliper gauge, measure the inside diameter of the connecting rod bushing.

Bushing inside diameter:

22.012-22.027 mm (0.8666-0.8672 in.)

(c) Using a micrometer, measure the diameter of the piston pin.

Piston pin diameter:

22.004-22.019 mm (0.8663-0.8669 in.)

(d) Subtract the piston pin diameter measurement from the bushing inside diameter measurement.

Standard oil clearance:

0.005-0.011 mm (0.0002-0.0004 in.)

Maximum oil clearance: 0.03 mm (0.0012 in.)

If the clearance exceeds maximum, replace the connecting rod bushing. If necessary, replace the piston and piston pin assembly.

Replacement of Connecting Rod Bushings

1. Press Out The Connecting Rod Bushing.

2. Install New Connecting Rod Bushing.

(a) Align the oil holes of the bushing and connecting rod.

(b) Using special tool and a press, press in the bushing.

3. Hone Rod Bushing and Check Piston Pin Fit in Connecting Rod.

(a) Using a pin hole grinder, hone the bushing to obtain the standard specified clearance between the bushing and piston pin.

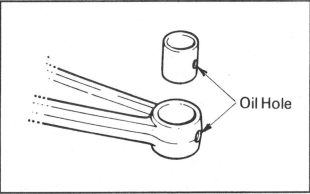

Oil Hole

(b) Check the piston pin fit at normal room temperature. Coat the piston pin with engine oil and push it into the rod with your thumb.

Boring of Cylinders

* Bore all 6 cylinders for the oversized pistons outside diameter.

* Replace the piston rings with ones to match the oversized pistons.

1. Select Oversized Piston

Oversized piston diameter:
O/S 0.50   94.460-94.490 mm (3.7189-3.7201 in.)
O/S 1.00   94.960-94.990 mm (3.7386-3.7398 in.)
O/S 1.50   95.960-95.490 mm (3.7583-3.7594 in.)

2. Calculate Amount to Bore Cylinder.

(a) Using a micrometer, measure the piston diameter at a right angle to the piston pin hole centre line, 22 mm (0.87 in.) below the skirt bottom edge.

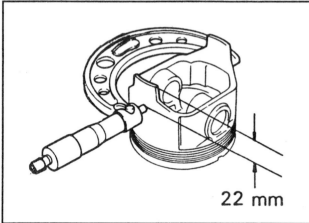

(b) Calculate the amount each cylinder is to be rebored as follows: Size to be rebored = P + C = H

P = Piston diameter C = Piston clearance
0.030-0.050 mm (0.0012-0.0020 in.)
H = Allowance for honing
Less than 0.02 mm (0.0008 in.)

3. Bore and Hone Cylinders to Calculated Dimensions.

Maximum honing: 0.02 mm (0.0008 in.)

* Excess honing will destroy the finished roundness.

Inspection and Repair of Crankshaft:

1. Inspect Crankshaft for Runout.

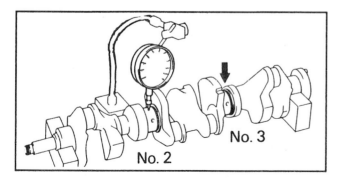

(a) Place the crankshaft on V-Blocks.

(b) Using a dial indicator, measure the circle runout at the No.2 and No.3 journals.

Maximum circle runout: 0.12 mm (0.0048 in.)

If the circle runout exceeds maximum, replace the crankshaft.

2. Inspect Main Journals and Crank Pins.

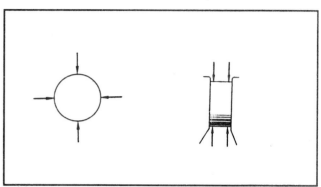

(a) Using a micrometer, measure the diameter of each main journal and crank pin.

Main journal diameter (from front side):
STD
No.1 66.972-66.996 mm (2.6367-2.6376 in.)
No.2 68.472-68.496 mm (2.6957-2.6967 in.)
No.3 69.972-69.996 mm (2.7548-2.7557 in.)
No.4 71.472-71.496 mm (2.8139-2.8148 in.)
U/S 0.25
No.1 66.745-66.755 mm (2.6278-2.6281 in.)
No.2 68.245-68.255 mm (2.6868-2.6872 in.)
No.3 69.745-69.755 mm (2.7459-2.7463 in.)
No.4 71.245-71.255 mm (2.8049-2.8053 in.)
U/S 0.50
No.1 66.495-66.505 mm (2.6179-2.6183 in.)
No.2 67.995-68.005 mm (2.6770-2.6774 in.)
No.3 69.495-69.505 mm (2.7360-2.7364 in.)
No.4 70.995-71.005 mm (2.7951-2.7955 in.)

Crank pin diameter:

STD size	3F	2F
	52.988-53.000 mm	53.98-54.00 mm
	(2.0861-2.0866 in.)	(2.1252-2.1260 in.)

also available as undersized 0.25 mm & 0.50 mm

If the diameter is not within specification, check the oil clearance. If necessary, grind or replace the crankshaft.

(b) Check each main journal and crank pin for taper and out-of-round.

Maximum taper and out-of-round:

0.02 mm (0.0008 in.) If the taper and out-of-round exceeds the maximum, replace the crankshaft.

3. Grind and Hone Main Journals and/or Crank Pins to the undersized finished diameter. Install new main journal and/or undersized crank pin bearings.

Inspection and Repair of Camshaft Bearings

1. Inspect Camshaft Oil Clearance.
 (a) Using a cylinder gauge, measure the inside diameter of the camshaft bearing.

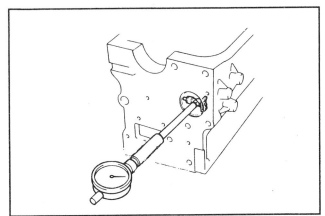

Bearing inside diameter (from front side):
STD
No.1   48.000-48.030 mm (1.8898-1.8909 in.)
No.2   46.500-46.530 mm (1.8307-1.8319 in.)
No.3   45.000-45.030 mm (1.7717-1.7728 in.)
No.4   43.500-43.530 mm (1.7126-1.7138 in.)
Also available as undersized 0.25 mm & 0.50 mm.
 (b) Subtract the journal diameter measurement from the bearing inside diameter measurement.
 Standard clearance:
STD　　　　　　0.025-0.075mm (0.0010-0.0030 in.)
U/S 0.25 and 0.50
No.1 & No.2　　0.025-0.110mm (0.0010-0.0043 in.)
No.3 & No.4　　0.025-0.105mm (0.0010-0.0041 in.)
 Maximum clearance:
STD　　　　　　0.10mm (0.0039 in.)
U/S 0.25 & 0.50　0.15mm (0.0059 in.)
If the clearance exceeds maximum, replace the camshaft bearings. If necessary, grind or replace the camshaft.
 2. If Necessary, Replace Camshaft Bearings.
 * The outside diameter varies with each bearing.

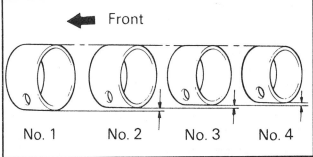

 A. Remove expansion plug using a special tool and a hammer, tap out the expansion plug.
 B. Remove camshaft bearings using special tool.
 C. Install new camshaft bearings with special tool.
 * Align the oil holes of the bearing and cylinder block.

D. Ream camshaft bearings to the finished diameter.
 E. Install expansion plug.
 (a) Apply liquid sealer to the expansion plug surface of the cylinder block.
 (b) Using a hammer, tap in a new expansion plug until its surface is flush with the cylinder block edge.
 3. If Necessary, Grind and Hone Camshaft Journals to the undersized finished diameter.

Inspection of Valve Lifter Bores.

Inspect Valve Lifter Oil Clearance.
 (a) Using a calliper gauge, measure the valve lifter bore diameter.
 Bore diameter:
21.417-21.443 mm (0.8432-0.8442 in.)
 (b) Subtract the valve lifter diameter measurement from the valve lifter bore diameter measurement.
 Standard oil clearance:
0.013-0.056 mm (0.0005-0.0022 in.)
 Maximum oil clearance: 0.10 mm (0.0039 in.)
 If the clearance exceeds maximum, replace the valve lifters.
 Valve lifter size: STD, O/S 0.05

Replacement of Crankshaft Real Oil Seal.

 (a) Using a knife, cut off the oil seal lip.
 (b) Using a screwdriver, pry out the oil seal.
 * Tape the screwdriver tip to prevent damaging the crankshaft.
 (c) Apply Multi purpose grease to a new oil seal lip.
 (d) Using a special tool and a hammer, tap the oil seal in until its surface is level with the cylinder block and main bearing cap edges.

Assembly of Piston and Connecting Rod Assemblies.

 1. Assemble Piston and Connecting Rod.
 (a) Install a new snap ring on one side of the piston pin hole.

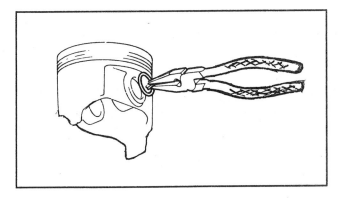

(b) Gradually heat the piston to approximately 80°C (176°F).

(c) Line up the notch of the piston with the protrusion of the connecting rod and push the piston pin in using your thumb.

(d) Install a new snap ring on the other side of the piston pin hole.

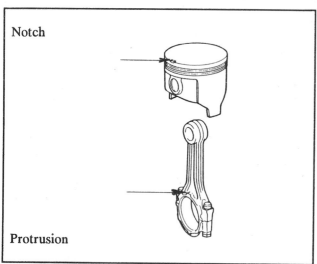

2. Install Piston Rings.

(a) Install the oil ring expander and two side rails by hand.

(b) Using a piston ring expander, install the 2 compression rings with the code mark facing upward.

(c) Position the piston rings so that the ring end gaps so they do not align with each other.(at right angles).

* Do not line up the end gaps.

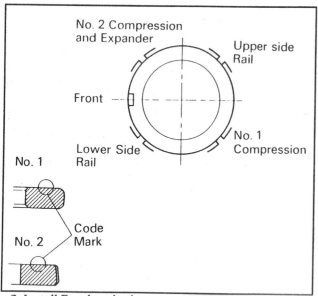

3. Install Bearings in the connecting rod and rod cap.

* Install the bearing with the oil hole in the connecting rod.

Assembly of Cylinder Block

* Before installing all parts make sure they are thoroughly clean.

* Apply new engine oil to all sliding and rotating surfaces before installing the parts.

* Ensure all gaskets and oil seals are replaced with new parts.

1. Install Main Bearings.

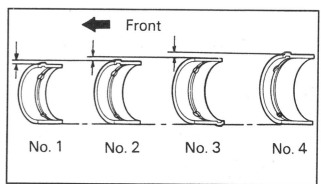

* The outside diameter varies with each bearing.
Install the bearing in the cylinder block and bearing caps.

* Install the bearing with the oil hole in the block.

2. Install Upper Thrust Washers under the No.3 main bearing cap position of the block with the oil grooves facing outward.

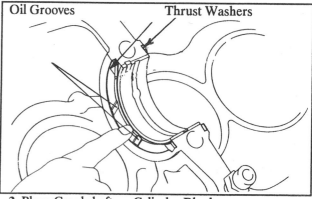

3. Place Crankshaft on Cylinder Block.

4. Install New Crankshaft Real Oil Seal.

(a) Apply Multi purpose grease to the oil seal lip.

(b) Push the oil seal in until its surface is level with the cylinder block edges.

* Be careful not to install the oil seal on an angle.

5. Install Main Bearing Caps and Lower Thrust Washers.

(a) Apply liquid sealer to the main bearing surface of the cylinder block.

* Be carefull not to get liquid sealer on the main bearing.

(b) Install the lower thrust washers in the No.3 main bearing cap with the oil grooves facing outward.

(c) Install the main bearing caps in their proper locations.

(d) Apply a light coat of engine oil to the threads and under the bolt heads of the main bearing caps.

(e) Install and uniformly tighten the 10 bolts of the main bearing caps in several passes.

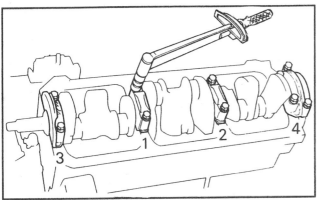

Torque:

19mm bolt head	1,375 kg-cm (99ft-lb, 135 N·m)
17mm bolt head	1,175 kg-cm (85ft-lb, 115 N·m)

(f) Check that the crankshaft turns smoothly.

(g) Check the crankshaft thrust clearance.

6. Install Piston and Connecting Rod Assemblies.

(a) Cover the connecting rod bolts with a short piece of hose to protect the crankshaft and cylinder bore from damage.

(b) Using a piston ring compressor, push the correctly numbered piston and connecting rod assembly into the cylinder with the notch of the piston facing forward.

7. Install Connecting Rod Caps.

(a) Match the numbered cap with the numbered connecting rod.

(b) Install connecting rod cap with the protrusion facing foward.

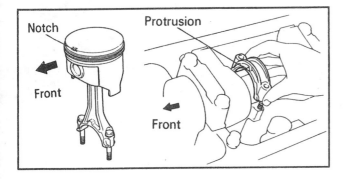

(c) Apply a light coat of engine oil to the threads and under the nuts of the connecting rod cap.

(d) Install and alternatively tighten the nuts of the connecting rod cap in several passes.

Torque: 600 kg-cm (43 ft-lb, 59N·m)

(e) Make sure that the crankshaft turns smoothly.

(f) Check the connecting rod thrust clearance as previously described (dismantle item 11.)

8. Install Front End Plate using the 2 bolts. Using a socket wrench, torque the screws.

Torque: 250 kg-cm (18 ft-lb, 25 N·m)

(c) Torque bolts.

Torque: 310 kg-cm (22 ft-lb, 30 N·m)

(d) Stake the screws using a chisel and hammer.

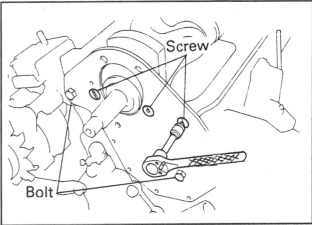

9. Install Timing Gears and Camshaft as previously described.

10. Install Cylinder Head Assembly.

11. Install Oil Pump and Oil Pan.

12. (Man.Trans)Install Flywheel Housing.

13. (Auto Trans)Install Transmission Housing Adaptor.

14. (Auto Trans)Install Flywheel.

(a) Clean and set bolt threads and crankshaft bolt holes of any residual sealer, oil or foreign particles. Remove any oil with kerosine or gasoline.

(b) Apply anaerobic adhesive and sealant [THREE BOND 1324 (Part No. 08833-00070)or equivalent] to 2 or 3 threads of the bolt end.

* This adhesive will not harden while exposed to air. It will act as a sealer or binding agent only when applied to threads, etc, and the air is cut off.

(c) Install the flywheel on the crankshaft.

(d) Install and uniformly tighten the bolts in several passes.

Torque: 890 kg-cm (64 ft-lb, 87 N·m)

15. (Auto Trans)Install Drive Plate.

16. (Man.Trans)Install Clutch Disc & Cover.

NOTES

21R, 21R-C & 22R 4 CYLINDER ENGINES

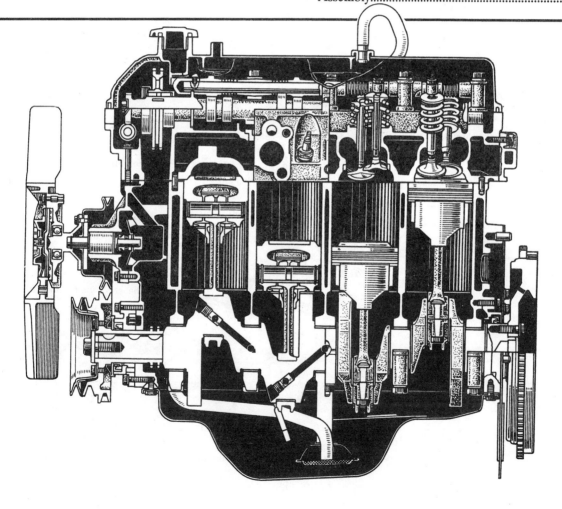

21R, 21R-C & 22R 4 CYLINDER ENGINES

CYLINDER HEAD

Components

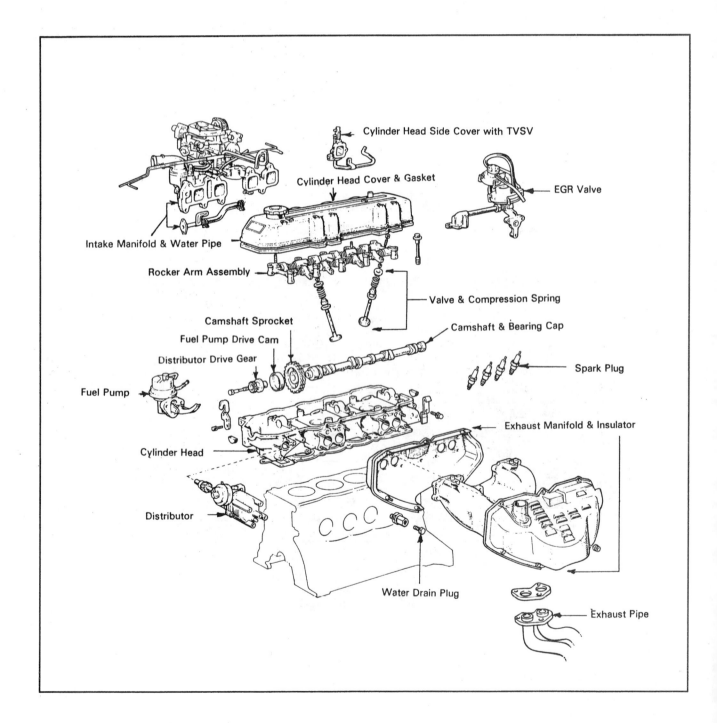

- Cylinder Head Side Cover with TVSV
- EGR Valve
- Cylinder Head Cover & Gasket
- Intake Manifold & Water Pipe
- Rocker Arm Assembly
- Valve & Compression Spring
- Camshaft Sprocket
- Fuel Pump Drive Cam
- Camshaft & Bearing Cap
- Distributor Drive Gear
- Spark Plug
- Fuel Pump
- Exhaust Manifold & Insulator
- Cylinder Head
- Distributor
- Water Drain Plug
- Exhaust Pipe

Dismantle

Dismantle the parts in the order listed:

1. Water Drain Plug.
2. Exhaust Pipe.
3. Fuel Pump.
4. EGR Valve.
5. Intake Manifold & Water Pipe.
6. Cylinder Head Side Cover with TVSV.
7. Exhaust Manifold & Insulator.
8. Spark Plug.
9. Distributor.
10. Cylinder Head Cover & Gasket.
11. Distributor Drive Gear.
(a) Set No.1 cylinder to TDC/Compression.

Position No1 Cylinder at TDC Compression.

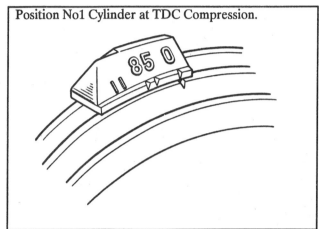

(b) Place matchmarks on the camshaft sprocket and timing chain.

Place Matchmarks.

Matchmarks

(c) Remove the camshaft sprocket set bolt.
(d) Remove the distributor drive gear and fuel pump drive cam from the sprocket. Allow the camshaft sprocket and chain to remain.
12. Fuel Pump Drive Cam.
13. Camshaft Sprocket.
14. Rocker Arm Assembly.
15. Cylinder Head.
(a) Remove the chain cover bolt.

(b) Loosen and remove each cylinder head bolt in the order shown.

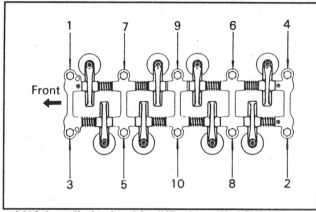

Front

(c) If the cylinder head is difficult to lift off, pry with a screwdriver between the head and block.
16. Camshaft & Bearing Cap.
(a) Measure the camshaft thrust clearance.
Thrust clearance:
Limit: 0.25mm (0.0098 in.)
17. Valve & Compression Spring.
(a) Remove the valves and springs with special tool.
(b) Arrange the valves and springs in order.

Inspection

Cylinder Head

1. Clean the combustion chamber and remove any gasket material from the manifold and head surface. Check the cylinder head for cracks or excessively burnt valve seat surfaces.
2. Check the cylinder head underside surface and manifold mounting surface for warpage with a precision straight edge and thickness gauge.
3. If warpage exceeds the limit, correct it by machining, or replace the head.
Cylinder head surface warpage:
Limit: 0.15 mm (0.0059 in.)
Manifold mounting surface warpage:
Limit: 0.20 mm (0.0079 in.)
Maximum reface:
Limit: 0.20 mm (0.0079 in.)
4. Clean the cylinder block upperside surface. Check the cylinder block as described later.

Valve & Guide

1. Clean and check valves for bending, wear or scores.

2. Check the valve stem to valve guide clearance of each valve by inserting the valve stem into the guide and moving it backwards & forwards.

3. Measure the valve stem oil clearance.

(a) Measure the inside diameter of the valve guide at several places with an inside dial gauge.

(b) Measure the valve stem diameter.

(c) Calculate the clearance between the valve stem and valve guide by subtracting the difference where the clearance is the largest.

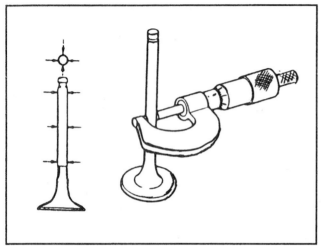

Stem oil clearance:

Limit: IN   0.08 mm (0.0031 in.)

       EX   0.10 mm (0.0039 in.)

If the clearance exceeds the limit, replace both valve and guide.

4. Replace the valve guide bushing.

(a) Break off the bushing and remove the snap ring.

(b) From the top, drive out the guide toward the combustion chamber with special tool.

(c) Using special tool, drive in the guide until the snap ring makes contact with the cylinder head.

* Make sure that the hole is clean.

(d) Ream the guide to the specified clearance with an 8 mm (0.31 in.) reamer.

Stem oil clearance:

STD IN   0.02-0.06 mm (0.0008-0.0024 in.)

      EX   0.03-0.07 mm (0.0012-0.0028 in.)

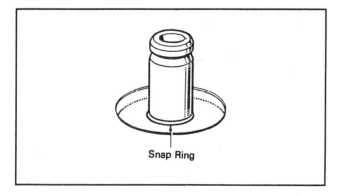

Snap Ring

5. Grind the Valve Seat Surface.

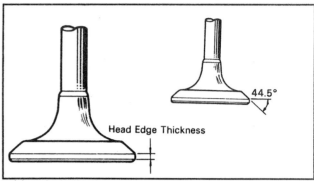

Head Edge Thickness   44.5°

(a) Grind all valves to remove the pits and carbon.

Valve face angle: 44.5°

(b) Check the valve head margin and replace if less than the limit.

Head edge thickness:

Limit: 0.6 mm (0.024 in.)

(c) Check the valve stem tip.

(d) If the valve stem tip is worn, resurface with a valve grinder, but do not grind off more than 0.5 mm (0.020 in.)

Overall length:

STD

21R

IN113.8 mm (4.480 in.)

RA (Since '84/8)

RX70 (Before '85/9)

114.0 mm (4.488 in.)

RX70 (Since '85/9)

115.5 mm (4.547 in.)

RA (Before '84/8)

RX60

EX113.9 mm (4.484 in.)

RA (Before '84/8)

112.9 mm (4.445 in.)

Others

22R-C

IN115.5 mm (4.547 in.)

RX60

113.5 mm (4.468 in.)

Others

EX112.9 mm (4.445 in.)

22R

IN113.5 mm (4.468 in.)

RJ (Australia)

113.8 mm (4.480 in.)

Others (Before '85/9)

114.0 mm (4.488 in.)

Others (Since '84/9)

EX112.4 mm (4.425 in.)

RJ (Australia)

112.9 mm (4.445 in.)

Others

Stem end refacing:

Limit: 0.5 mm (0.020 in.)

Valve Seat.

1. Check the width and position of the valve contact with the seat. Coat the valve face with prussian blue or red lead. Locate the contact point on the valve by rotating the valve against the seat.

Contact width:
IN & EX   1.2-1.6 mm (0.047-0.063 in.)
Contact position: Middle of valve face.

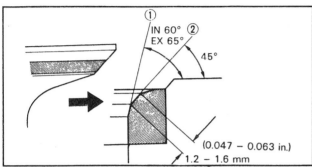

2. Resurface the valve seat with a 45° cutter to clean the seat.

3. Correct the seat position.

(a) If the seat position is too high, use 60° & 45° cutters (for intake), 65° and 45° cutters (for exhaust) in the order indicated.

(b) If the seat position is too low, use 30° and 45° cutters in the order shown.

4. After correction, the valve and valve seat should be lapped lightly with a lapping compound.

Valve Spring

1. Check the squareness of the valve springs with a steel square and surface plate. Turn the spring around slowly and take note of the space between the top of the spring and the square. Replace the spring if it is out of square more than the specified limit.

Squareness; Limit 1.6 mm (0.063 in.)

2. Measure the spring free length. Replace the springs that do not meet specification.

Free length:
(Before '84/8) 45.8 mm (1.803 in.)
(Since '84/8)   48.5 mm (1.909 in.)

3. Using a spring tester, measure the tension of each spring at the specified installed length. Replace any spring that does not meet specification.

Installed length: 40.5 mm (1.594 in.)
Installed load:
STD   25.0 kg (55lb) (Before '84/8)
           30.0 kg (66lb) (Since '84/8)
Limit   22.5 kg (50lb) (Before '84/8)
           28.5 kg (63lb) (Since '84/8)

Rocker Arm & Shaft.

1. Check the rocker arm to shaft clearance if worn excessively, disassemble and check.

2. Measure the clearance with a dial indicator and outside micrometer. If clearance exceeds the limit, replace the rocker arm and/or shaft.

Oil clearance:
STD   0.01-0.05 mm (0.0004-0.0020 in.)
Limit: 0.08 mm (0.0031 in.)

3. Check the contact surface for wear or damage.

4. If only a light ridged wear, correct the cam containing surface of the rocker arm with a valve refacer and oil stone.

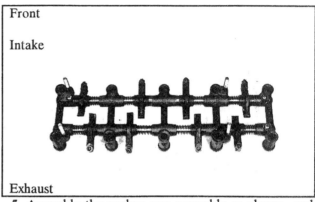

5. Assemble the rocker arm assembly as shown, and install three screws.

* All rocker arms are the same, but all rockers arm support are different and must be assembled in the correct order.

Camshaft & Camshaft Bearing Cap.

1 Inspect the cam and journal for damage or wear. If damaged replace the camshaft.

2. Measure the camshaft for runout. Replace the camshaft if it exceeds the limit.

Circle runout:
Limit: 0.2 mm (0.008 in.)

3. Measure the cam lobe height. If wear exceeds limit, replace the camshaft.

Cam height:
STD   IN 42.63-42.72 mm (1.6783-1.6819 in.)
       EX 42.69-42.78 mm (1.6807-1.6842 in.)
Limit: IN 42.43 mm (1.6705 in.)
        EX 42.49 mm (1.6728 in.)

4. Measure the journal diameter. If it is less than specified, replace the camshaft.

Journal diameter:
STD 32.98-33.00 mm (1.2984-1.2992 in.)

5. Inspect the bearing caps and cylinder head for flaking or scoring. If bearing caps and cylinder head are damaged, replace the caps and cylinder head.

6. Measure the camshaft oil clearance.

(a) Clean the cylinder head, bearing caps and camshaft.

(b) Place a piece of plastiguage across the full width of the journal surface.

(c) When installing the bearing caps, insure that the front marks and engraved numbers match.

(d) Install the bearing cap, and tighten the bolts to specified torque.

Tightening torque: 1.7-2.3 kg-m (13-16ft-lb)

* Do not turn the camshaft while the plastigauge is in place.

(e) Remove the bearing caps.

(f) With the plastigauge scale, measure the width of the plastigauge at tis widest point. If the clearance exceeds the specification limit, replace the caps and cylinder head.

Oil clearance:

STD   0.01-0.05 mm (0.0004-0.0020 in.)

Limit: 0.1 mm (0.004 in.

7. Measure the camshaft thrust clearance.

(a) Install the bearing cap, and tighten the bolts to specified torque.

Tightening torque:

1.7-2.3 kg-m (13-16 ft-lb)

(b) Measure the thrust clearance.

Thrust clearance:

STD   0.08-0.18 mm (0.0031-0.0071 in.)

Limit: 0.25 mm (0.0098 in.)

8. Inspect the distributor drive gear and fuel pump drive cam for wear or damage.

Manifold.

1. Check the cylinder head contacting surfaces for warpage with a precision straight edge and thickness gauge.

2. If warpage exceeds the limit, correct it by machining, or replace the manifold.

Contacting surface warpage:

Limit: IN 0.20 mm (0.0079 in.)

       EX 0.70 mm (0.0276 in.)

Maximum reface:

Limit: 0.20 mm (0.0079 in.)

Assembly

Assemble the parts in the order listed below but take note of extra instructions.

1. Valve & Compression Spring.

(a) Cost the valve stem with engine oil. Insert the spring seat and new oil seal.

(b) Assemble the valve spring and install the retainer locks with special tool.

(c) Tap the valve stems lightly with a plastic hammer or such to assure proper fit.

2. Camshaft & Bearing Cap.

(a) Install the bearing caps in numerical order beginning from the front with arrows pointing toward the front.

Tightening Torque: 1.7-2.3 kg-m (13-16 ft-lb)

3. Cylinder head.

(a) Clean the bolt holes.

(b) Apply liquid sealer to the cylinder head were the timing case cover meets the cylinder block.

4. Rocker Arm Assembly

(a) Tighten each cylinder head bolt a little at a time in the sequence shown in the diagram.

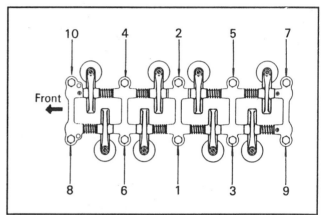

(b) Tighten the cylinder head bolts to specified torque.

Tightening toque: 7.2-8.8 kg-m (53-63 ft-lb)

(c) Tighten the chain cover bolt to the specified torque.

Tightening torque: 1.6-2.4 kg-m (12-17 ft-lb)

5. Camshaft Sprocket

(a) Set the No.1 cylinder to TDC/compression. Install the cam sprocket and chain to the camshaft while aligning the matchmarks put on during removal.

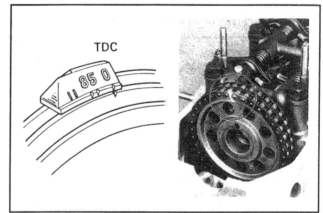

(b) Align the camshaft timing hole with the front mark of rocker support.

* If the chain does not seem long enough, turn the camshaft backwards and forward while pulling up on the chain and sprocket.

6. Fuel Pump Drive Cam.

7. Distributor Drive Gear.

(a) Install the fuel pump cam and distributor drive gear.

Tightening torque: 7.0-9.0 kg-m (51-65 ft-lb)

8. Distributor.

(a) Install the distributor as described in distributor section.

(b) Adjust the valve clearance. Confirm that the No. 1 cylinder is at TDC/compression.

(c) First, adjust the valve clearance of only the valves indicated by arrows in the diagram.

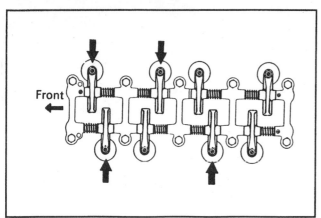

Valve clearance (Hot):
IN   0.20 mm (0.008 in.)
EX   0.30 mm (0.012 in.)

(d) Turn the crankshaft 360° and line up the TDC mark.

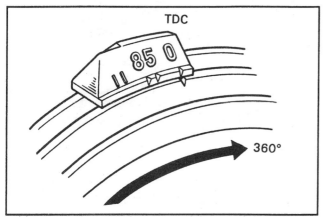

(e) Next, adjust the clearance of the remaining valves.

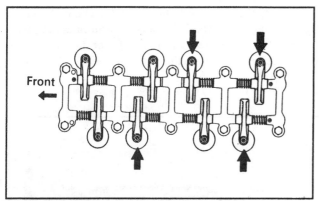

9. Cylinder Head Cover & Gasket.
(a) Apply liquid sealer at the semi-circular plug.
10. Spark Plug.
11. Exhaust Manifold & Insulator.
(a) Tighten each exhaust manifold bolt and nut a little at a time to the specified torque.

Tightening torque: 4.0-5.0 kg-m (29-36 ft-lb)
12. Cylinder Head Side Cover with TVSV

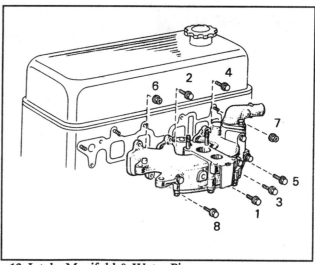

13. Intake Manifold & Water Pipe
(a) Tighten each intake manifold bolt and nut a little at a time to the specified torque.

Tightening torque: 1.6-2.4 kg-m (12-17 ft-lb)
14. EGR Valve.
15. Fuel Pump.
16. Exhaust Pipe.
17. Water Drain Plug.

TIMING CHAIN

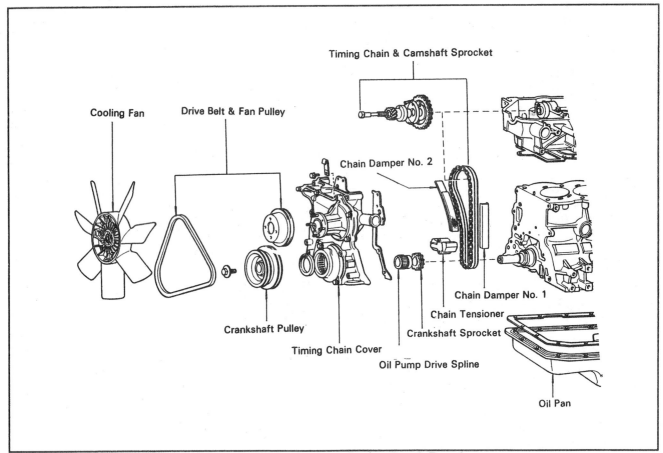

Dismantle

Dismantle the parts in the order listed.
1. Cooling Fan.
2. Drive Belt & Fan Pulley.
3. Oil Sump.
(a) When removing the oil sump, be careful not to damage the oil sump flange.
4. Crankshaft Pulley.
(a) Remove the crankshaft pulley with a pulley puller.
5. Timing Chain Cover.
(a) Remove the timing chain cover.
6. Timing Chain & Camshaft Sprocket.
7. Chain Damper No.1..
8. Chain Damper No.2.
9. Chain Tensioner.
10. Oil Pump Drive Spline.
(a) Remove the oil pump drive spline and crankshaft sprocket with special tool.
11. Crankshaft Sprocket.

Inspection & Repair

Timing Chain.

Measure the length of 17 links with the chain stretched tight by one hand. Make the same measurement at three other locations selected at random. If over the limit at any one place, replace the chain.

Timing Chain elongation:

Limit at 17 links 147.0 mm (5.787 in.)

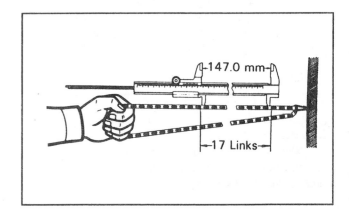

Chain Tensioner.

1. Inspect the tension plunger to see that it slides smoothly in the body cylinder.

2. Measure the tensioner head thickness. If the thickness is less than the limit, replace the cylinder and plunger as a set.

Thickness: Limit 11.0 mm (0.433 in.)

Chain Damper.

Measure the wall thickness of the vibration dampers.

Wall thickness (Double chain type):
Vibration damper No.1 Limit 5.0 mm (0.197 in.)
Vibration damper No.2 Limit 4.5 mm (0.177 in.)
Wear (Single chain type):
Limit 0.5 mm (0.020 in.)

Assembly.

Assemble the parts in the order listed.

1. Crankshaft Sprocket.

(a) Position the crankshaft keyway upward.

(b) Install the crankshaft sprocket and oil pump drive spline with special tool.

2. Oil Pump Drive Spline.

3. Chain Tensioner.

(a) Install the chain tensioner.

Tightening torque:
1.5-2.1 kg-m (11-15 ft-lb) (Double Chain Type)
1.6-2.4 kg-m (12-17 ft-lb) (Single Chain Type)

4. Chain Damper No.2.

(a) Install the chain dampers.

Tightening torque:
1.0-1.6 kg-m (8-11 ft lb) (Double Chain Type)
1.8-2.6 kg-m (13-19 ft-lb) (Single Chain Type)

5. Chain Damper No.1.

6. Timing Chain & Camshaft Sprocket.

(a)Align the chain and sprocket matchmarks and install.Use the proper bolt when installing the chain cover.

7. Timing Chain Cover.

8. Crankshaft Pulley

9. Oil Sump

(FIPG Type) Remove any old packing material and be careful not to drop any oil on the contacting surfaces of the oil sump and cylinder block.

* Using a razor blade and gasket scraper, remove all the packing (FIPG) material from the gasket surfaces.

* Thoroughly clean all components to remove all the loose material.

* Clean both sealing surfaces with a non-residue solvent.

* Do not use a solvent which will affect the painted surfaces.(FIPG type) Apply seal packing to the joint part of the cylinder block and chain cover, cylinder block and chain cover,cylinder block and rear oil seal retainer and oil sump.

Seal Packing: Part No. 08826-00080 or equivalent.

* Install a nozzle that has been cut to a 5-mm (0.20 in.) opening.

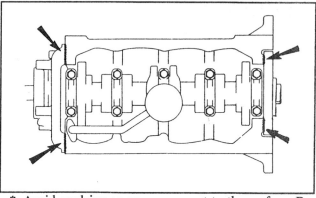

* Avoid applying an excess amount to the surface. Be especially careful near oil passages.

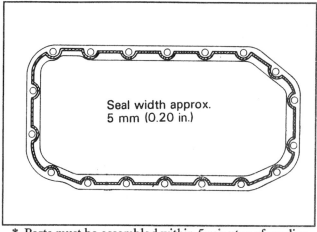

Seal width approx. 5 mm (0.20 in.)

* Parts must be assembled within 5 minutes of application. Otherwise, the material must be removed and re-applied.

* Immediately remove nozzle from tube and reinstall cap.

Install the oil sump over the studs on the block with 16 bolts and two nuts. Torque the bolts and nuts.

Tighten the oil sump bolts.

Tightening torque:
0.3-0.9 kg-m (26-78 in-lb) (Preformed gasket type)
1.0-1.6 kg-m (7-12 in-lb) (FIPG Type)

10. Drive Belt & Fan Pulley

(a) Tighten the crankshaft pulley bolt.

Tightening torque:
14.0-18.0 kg-m (102-130 ft-lb)

11. Cooling Fan.

CYLINDER BLOCK

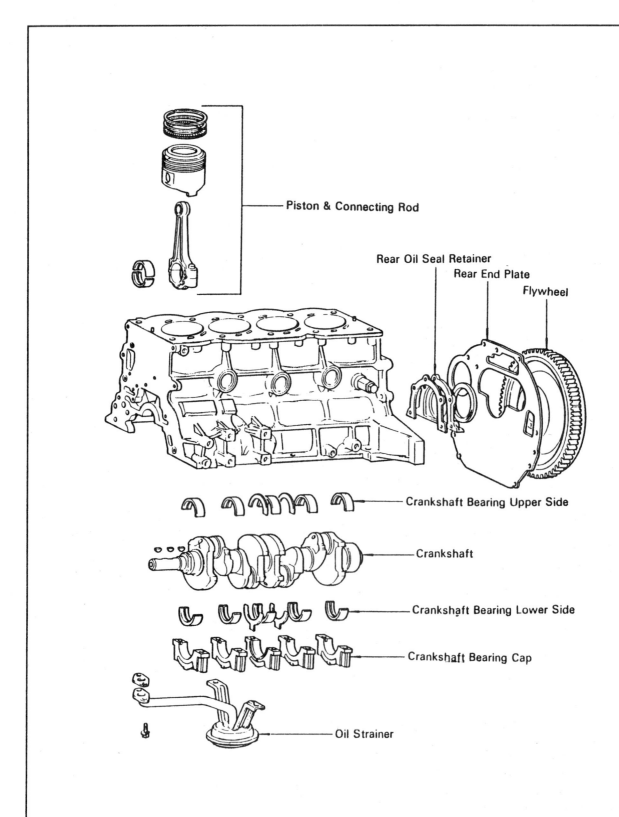

Piston & Connecting Rod

Rear Oil Seal Retainer

Rear End Plate

Flywheel

Crankshaft Bearing Upper Side

Crankshaft

Crankshaft Bearing Lower Side

Crankshaft Bearing Cap

Oil Strainer

Dismantle

Dismantle the parts in the order listed.
1. Flywheel.
2. Rear End Plate.
3. Rear Oil Seal Retainer.
4. Oil Strainer.
5. Piston with Connecting Rod.

(a) Measure the connecting rod thrust clearance. If it exceeds the limit, replace the connecting rod.

Thrust clearance: Limit 0.3 mm (0.012 in.)

(b) Place the matchmarks on the cap and connecting rod.

(c) Cover the rod bolts with short pieces of hose.

* To prevent the crankshaft pin and cylinder bore from damage, this step must be performed before removing the pistons.

(d) Arrange the piston and connecting rod caps in order.

6. Crankshaft Bearing Cap.

(a) Measure the crankshaft thrust clearance. If it exceeds the limit, replace the thrust washer as a set.

Thrust clearance: Limit 0.3 mm (0.012 in.)

(b) Remove each crankshaft bearing cap as shown in the diagram.

(c) If the crankshaft bearing cap will not come off, remove by raising the bolts and prying backwards and forwards.

(d) Arrange the crankshaft bearings and caps in order.
7. Crankshaft Bearing Lower Side.
8. Crankshaft.
9. Crankshaft Bearing Upper Side.

Inspection.

Cylinder Block.

1. Clean and check the cylinder block for cracks or scoring.

2. Check the block gasket surface for warpage. If warpage exceeds the specified limit, replace the block.

Warpage: Limit 0.05 mm (0.0020 in.)

3. Check for warpage on several angles across the top of the cylinder block.

4. Visually check the cylinder for vertical scratches. If deep scratches are present, the cylinder must be rebored.

5. Measure the cylinder bore at various positions in the thrust and axial directions.

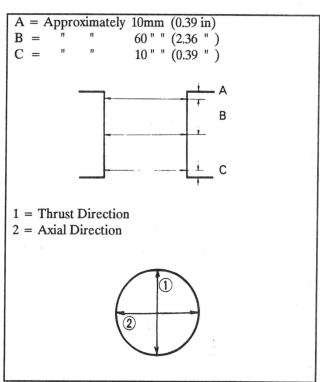

1 = Thrust Direction
2 = Axial Direction

6. If the bore exceeds specification, it must be rebored.

Cylinder bore:
STD 21R, 21R-C
84.00-84.03 mm (3.3071-3.3083 in.)
22R
92.00-92.03 mm (3.6220-3.6232 in.)

Wear: Limit 0.2 mm (0.008 in.)

7. If wear is less than 0.2 mm (0.008 in.), use a ridge reamer to machine the piston ring ridge at the top of the cylinder.

Piston & Connecting Rod.

1. Try to move the piston backwards and forwards on the piston pin. If any movement is felt, replace the piston and pin.

2. Remove the piston ring with a piston ring expander.

3. Remove the snap rings in the hole.

* Use new snap rings for assembly.

4. Heat the piston to about 80°C (176°F) with piston heater or such.

5. Push the piston pin out.

6. After dismantling, place the parts in order.

7. Check the piston pin fitness. Heat the piston up to about 80°C (176°F), and coat the pin with engine oil. It should then be possible to push the pin into the piston hole with thumb pressure.

8. Measure the oil clearance between the connecting rod bushings and piston pin.

Oil clearance:
STD   0.005-0.011 mm (0.0002-0.0004 in.)
Limit   0.015 mm (0.0006 in.)

9. If the bushing is worn or damaged, replace it with special tool.

* Line up the bushing oil hole with the connecting rod oil hole.

10. The fitting between bushing and pin should be such that the pin, when coated with engine oil, can be pushed in with thumb pressure at normal temperature.

Piston Clearance.

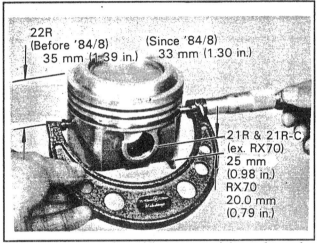

1. Measure the piston diameter at right angle to the piston pin centre line. Measurement must be made at room temperature (20°C or 68°F).

Piston diameter:
STD 21R, 21R-C
83.96-83.99 mm (3.3055-3.3067 in.)
22R
91.938-91.968 mm (3.6196-3.6208 in)
(Before '84/8)
91.96-91.99 mm (3.6205-3.6216 in.)
(Since '84/8)

2. Measure the cylinder bore and subtract the piston measurement. If clearance exceeds specification, replace the piston.

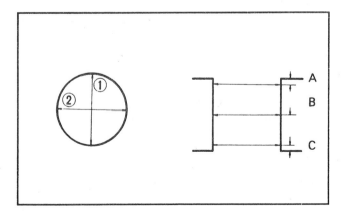

Piston oil clearance:
21R, 21R-C   0.03-0.05 mm (0.0012-0.0020 in.)
22R   0.052-0.072 mm (0.0020-0.0028 in.)

* Use the measurement where the wear is at maximum.

Piston Ring.

1. Measure the ring end gap.

(a) Insert the ring into the cylinder using a piston. Position the ring at the lower part of the cylinder bore.

(b) Measure the end gap. If it exceeds specification, the ring must be replaced.

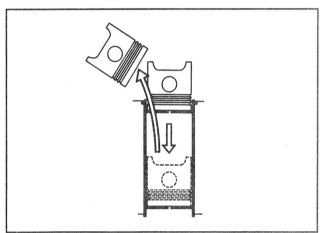

End gap:
21R & 21R-C
No.1 ring   0.25-0.47 mm (0.0098-0.0185 in.)
No.2 ring   0.15-0.42 mm (0.0059-0.0165 in.)
Oil ring   0.20-0.82 mm (0.0079-0.0323 in.)
22R
No.1 ring   0.24-0.39 mm (0.0094-0.0154 in.)
No.2 ring   0.18-0.42 mm (0.0071-0.0165 in.)
(Before '84/8)
0.60-0.70 mm (0.0236-0.0276 in.)
(Since '84/8 Ex.Australia RJ)
Oil ring   0.20-0.82 mm (0.0079-0.0323 in.)
Limit:
21R & 21R-C
No.1 ring   1.07 mm (0.0421 in.)
No.2 ring   1.02 mm (0.0402 in.)
Oil ring   1.42 mm (0.0559 in.)
22R
No.1 ring   0.99 mm (0.0390 in.)
No.2 ring   1.02 mm (0.0402 in.)(Before '84/8)
1.30 mm (0.0512 in.)
(Since '84/8 Ex.Australia RJ)
Oil ring   1.42 mm (0.0559 in.)

2. Measure the ring groove clearance. If it exceeds specification, replace the ring and/or piston.

Ring groove clearance;
Compression No.1 & No.2
Limit 0.2 mm (0.008 in.)

Crankshaft Pin & Bearing.

1. Check the bearings for flaking or scoring. If bearings are damaged, replace them.

2. Measure the crank pin oil clearance.

(a) Clean the crankshaft pin, rod, cap and bearing.

(b) Lay a strip of plastigauge across the pin.

(c) Tighten the cap nuts to specified torque.

Tightening torque: 5.7-6.9 kg-m (39-50 ft-lb)

(d) Loosen the cap nuts.

* Do not turn the connecting rod.

(e) Measure the plastigauge at its widest point. If clearance is not within specification, replace the bearings.

Bearing oil clearance:

STD   0.025-0.055 mm (0.0010-0.0022 in.)

Limit   0.08 mm (0.0031 in.)

U/S Bearing size: U/S 0.25

Assemble The Piston & Connecting Rod.

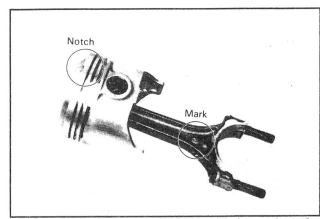

1. Line up the notch on the piston with the mark on the connecting rod.

2. Install a new snap ring in the hole on one side.

* Always replace the snap ring with a new one when assembling.

3. Heat the pistons to about 80°C (176°F).

4. Push the piston pin in.

5. Install a new snap ring on the other side.

* Always replace the snap ring with new one when assembling.

6. Rock the piston and check that movement is smooth.

7. Install the piston rings with a piston ring expander. Install 2 compression rings with the code marks facing upwards.

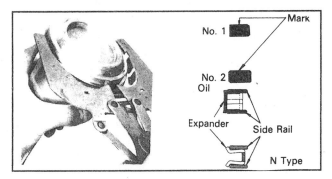

Crankshaft & Bearing.

1. Measure the crankshaft oil clearance.

(a) Clean the journal, cap and bearing.

(b) Lay strip of plastigauge across the journal.

(c) Tighten the cap bolts to specified torque.

Tightening torque:

9.5-11.5 kg-m (69-83 ft-lb)

(d) Loosen the cap bolts.

* Do not turn the crankshaft.

(e) Measure the plastigauge at its widest point. If clearance is not within specification, replace the bearing.

Journal oil clearance:

STD   0.025-0.055 mm (0.0010-0.0022 in.)

Limit   0.08 mm (0.0031 in.)

U/S bearing size: U/S 0.25

Rear Oil Seal.

1. Check the oil seal lip for wear or deformation.

2. Replace the rear oil seal.

(a) Remove the oil seal with a screwdriver.

(b) Drive in a new oil seal with special tool.

* Drive in the oil seal until it is about even with the rear oil seal retainer.

* Be careful not to drive it in on an angle.

(c) After fitting the seal, coat the seal lip lightly with Multi purpose grease.

Bearing (for Input Shaft Front)

1. Inspect for wear or damage and replace if necessary.

2. Replace the bearing.

(a) Remove the bearing with special tool.

(b) Install a new bearing with special tool.

Flywheel.

1. Check the surface contacting the clutch disc.

2. Measure the runout of the surface contacting the clutch disc.

Runout: Limit 0.2 mm (0.008 in.)

3. Check the ring gear.

Assembly.

Assemble the parts in the order listed.

1. Crankshaft Bearing Upper Side.

(a) Do not allow oil to get on the back side of the bearing.

2. Crankshaft.

3. Crankshaft Bearing Cap & Bearing Lower Side.

(a) Face the oil groove of the thrust washer toward the outside.

(b) Face the arrows toward the front.

(c) Tighten each bearing cap a little at a time as shown in the diagram.

(d) Tighten the bearing caps to specified torque.

Tightening torque: 9.5-11.5 kg-m (69-83 ft-lb)

(e) After tightening each bolt, check the rotation.

(f) Measure the crankshaft thrust clearance. If it exceeds the limit, replace the thrust washer as a set.

Thrust clearance:

STD 0.02-0.22 mm (0.0008-0.0087 in.)

Limit 0.3 mm (0.012 in.)

Thrust washer thickness:

STD 2.69-2.74 mm (0.1059-0.1079 in.)

RX70, RN (Saudi Arabia), RU RB20 (Since '84/8),RJ:
 1.94-1.99 mm (0.0764-0.0783 in.)

O/S washer size 0.125, 0.25

Cover the rod bolts with a hose to protect the crank pin and cylinder bore from damage.

4. Piston with Connecting Rod.

(a) Position the ring gap at 90° from each other as illustrated in the diagram.

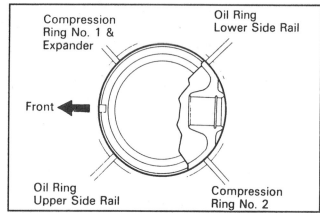

(b) Push in each correctly numbered piston/rod assembly with the notch facing forward. The mark on the connecting rod should face toward the front.

(c) Insert the pistons into the cylinder while compressing the ring with a piston compressor.

(d) Line up the rod and cap marks, and fit on the cap.

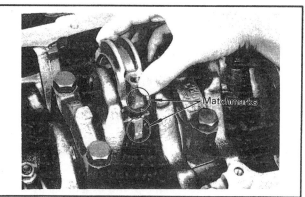

(e) Tighten the rod cap to specified torque.

Tightening torque: 5.4-6.6 kg-m (40-47 ft-lb)

* Check for smooth rotation after tightening each cap.

(f) Make sure that the crankshaft rotates smoothly.

(g) Check the connecting rod thrust clearance.

Thrust clearance:

STD 0.16-0.26 mm (0.0063-0.0102 in.)

Limit 0.3 mm (0.012 in.)

5. Oil Strainer.

6. Rear Oil Seal Retainer.

7. Rear End Plate.

8. Flywheel.

(a) Tighten the flywheel to specified torque.

Tightening torque: 10.0-12.0 kg-m (73-86 ft-lb)

FUEL SYSTEM

FUEL SYSTEM 2F & 3F 6 CYLINDER ENGINES.

FUEL SYSTEM 2F & 3F 6 CYLINDER ENGINES.

IN VEHICLE INSPECTION

1. Remove Air Cleaner or Air Intake Connector From Carburettor.

2. Inspect Carburettor and Linkage.

(a) Be sure that the various set screws, plugs and union bolts are tight and installed correctly.

(b) Examine the linkage for excessive wear and missing snap rings.

(c) Make sure that the throttle valves open fully when the accelerator pedal is fully pressed down.

3. Inspect Float Level. Ensure that the float level is about even with the correct level in the sight glass. If not, check the carburettor needle valve and float level and adjust or repair as necessary.

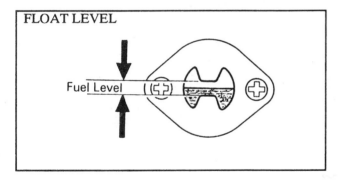

FLOAT LEVEL

Fuel Level

Cold Engine
4 .(with choke breaker)

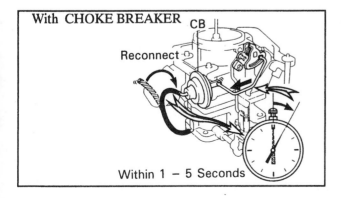

With CHOKE BREAKER   CB

Reconnect

Within 1 – 5 Seconds

Inspect Choke Breaker (CB) System.

(a) Start the engine.

(b) Disconnect the vacuum hose from the CB and ensure that the choke linkage moves.

(c) Connect the vacuum hose to the CB and check that the choke linkage moves within the stated time after connecting the hose.

Time: 1-5 seconds.

Hot Engine.
5. Inspect Acceleration Pump. Open the throttle valve, and ensure that petrol (gasoline) spurts out from the acceleration nozzle.

6. Fit Air Cleaner or Air Intake Connector to Carburettor.

7. Inspect and Adjust Idle Speed Speed and Mixture as in Tune-Up and Maintenance Section.

8. Inspect and Adjust Fast Idle Speed as in Tune-Up and Maintenance Section.

9. Inspect and Adjust Throttle Positioner Setting Speed as in Tune-Up and Maintenance Section.

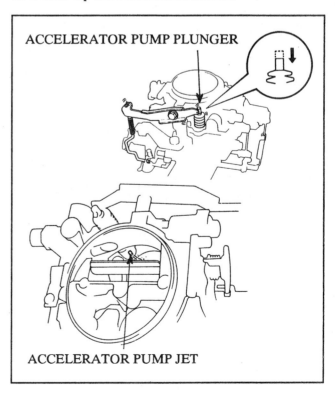

ACCELERATOR PUMP PLUNGER

ACCELERATOR PUMP JET

CARBURETTOR F3 (F2-USA)

Carburettor Circuit.
1. Acceleration Pump Plunger.
2. Secondary Slow Jet.
3. Secondary Main Nozzle.
4. Choke Valve.
5. Acceleration Nozzle.
6. Primary Main Nozzle.
7. Choke Breaker.
8. Fuel Cut Solenoid Valve.
9. Power Piston.
10. Needle Valve.

11. Secondary Main Jet.
12. Secondary Throttle Valve Diaphragm.
13. Secondary Throttle Valve.
14. Primary Throttle Valve.
15. Idle Mixture Adjusting Screw.
16. Primary Slow Jet.
17. Primary Main Jet.
18. Power Valve.

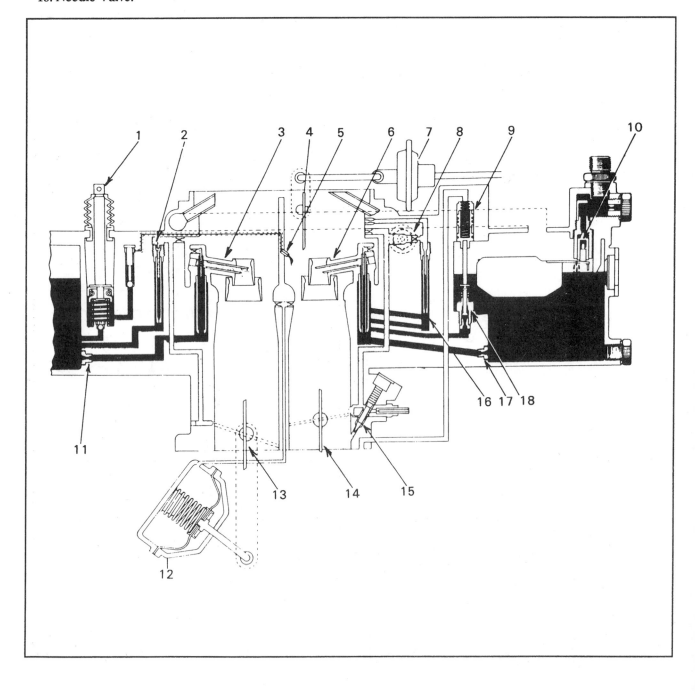

Components

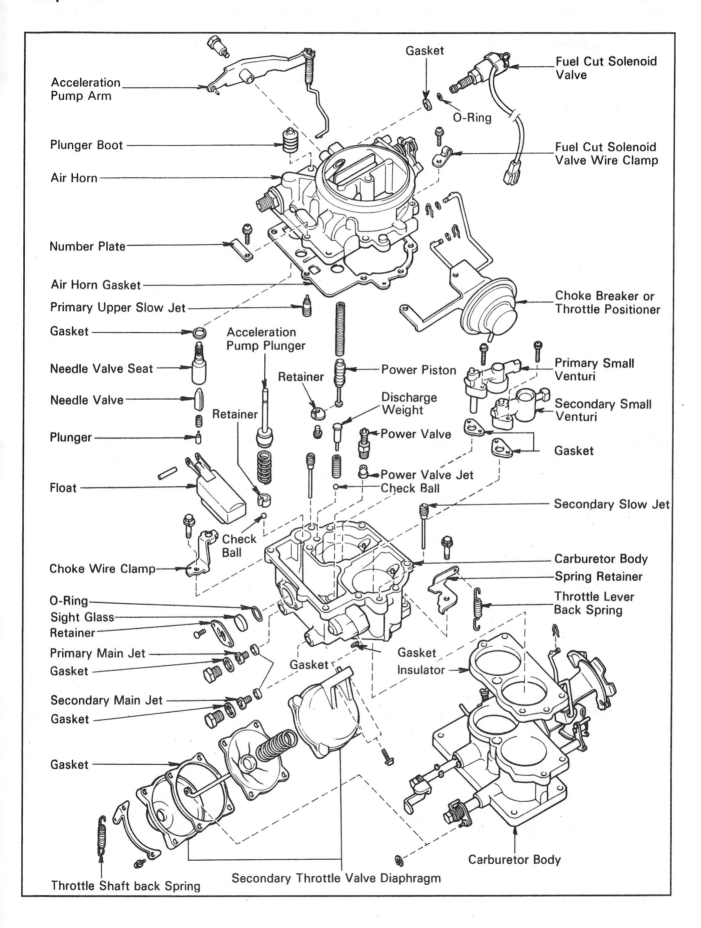

Acceleration Pump Arm

Plunger Boot

Air Horn

Number Plate

Air Horn Gasket

Primary Upper Slow Jet

Gasket

Needle Valve Seat

Needle Valve

Plunger

Float

Choke Wire Clamp

O-Ring
Sight Glass
Retainer

Primary Main Jet
Gasket

Secondary Main Jet
Gasket

Gasket

Throttle Shaft back Spring

Gasket

Acceleration Pump Plunger

Retainer

Retainer

Check Ball

Fuel Cut Solenoid Valve

O-Ring

Fuel Cut Solenoid Valve Wire Clamp

Choke Breaker or Throttle Positioner

Power Piston

Discharge Weight

Power Valve

Power Valve Jet
Check Ball

Primary Small Venturi

Secondary Small Venturi

Gasket

Secondary Slow Jet

Carburetor Body
Spring Retainer
Throttle Lever Back Spring

Gasket
Insulator

Carburetor Body

Secondary Throttle Valve Diaphragm

Removal.

1. Remove Air Cleaner Assembly or Air Intake Connector.

2. Disconnect Connector of Fuel Cut Solenoid.

3. Disconnect Linkages.

(a) Accelerator throttle cable.

(b) Choke cable.

(c) Automatic Transmission throttle cable.

4. Disconnect Fuel Inlet Pipe.

5. Disconnect Hoses.

(a) Emission control hoses.

* Before disconnecting the emission control hoses, use tag to identify how they should be reconnected.

(b) (with Outer Vent Control Valve) Outer vent control hose.

6. Remove Carburettor.

(a) Unscrew the four mount nuts and take them out.

(b) Remove the carburettor

(c) Using a cloth, cover the inlet hole of the intake manifold.

Dismantle

The following instructions are organised so that you work on only one component group at a time. This will help avoid confusion with parts that look similar from different sub-assemblies being on your bench at the same time.

(a) Arrange parts in order to assist when assembling.

(b) Ensure not to get clips and springs mixed up or lost.

Dismantle of Air Horn.

1. Remove Acceleration Pump Arm.

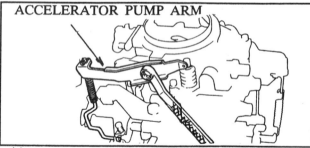

ACCELERATOR PUMP ARM

(a) Remove the pivot bolt.

(b) Disconnect the pump arm from the pump plunger.

(c) Disconnect the pump connecting link from the throttle lever and take out the pump arm and pump connecting link.

2. Disconnect Vacuum Hoses from Flange Ports.

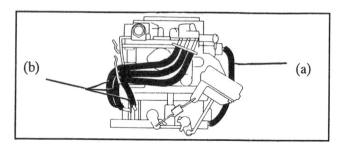

(b)   (a)

(a) (with CB only) Choke Breaker (CB) vacuum hose

(b) (S.Arabia and Australia) Other 3 vacuum hoses.

3. Disconnect Links from Levers

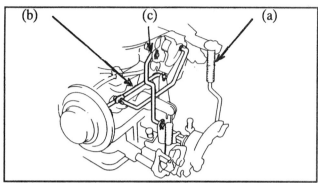

(b)   (c)   (a)

(a) (with CB) Choke breaker (CB) link

(b) (with TP) Throttle positioner (TP) link

(c) Fast Idle Link.

4. Remove Air Horn Assembly.

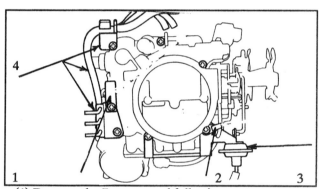

(1) Remove the 7 screws and following parts:

(a) (General countries M/T) Number Plate

(b) Wire clamp of fuel cut solenoid valve.

(c) (with CB or TP) Choke breaker (CB) with hose or Throttle Positioner (TP).

(d) (S.Arabia & Australia) Vacuum pipe supports with 3 hoses.

(2) Lift off the air horn assembly and the air horn gasket.

5. Remove the pivot pin and float.

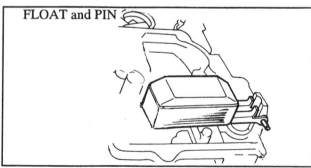

FLOAT and PIN

6. Remove the plunger, spring and needle valve.

7. Remove Acceleration Pump Plunger and Boot.

8. Remove Air Horn Gasket.

9. Remove Needle Valve Seat & Gasket.

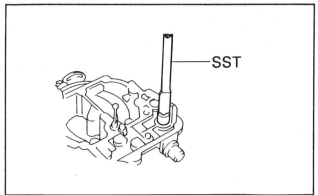

10.Remove the screw, retainer, power piston and spring.

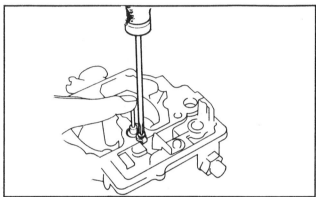

11.Remove Primary Upper Slow Jet.

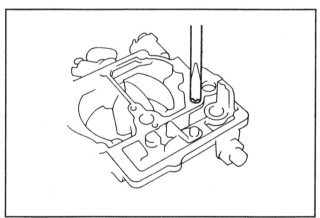

12.Remove the Solenoid valve and gasket.

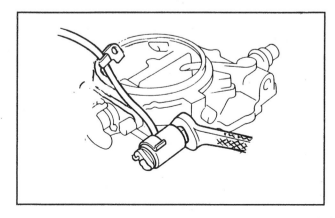

Dismantle Carburettor Body
1. Remove Check Balls for Acceleration.

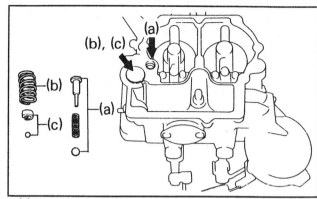

(a) Remove the pump discharge weight, spring and large ball.

(b) Remove the plunger spring.

(c) Using tweezers, remove the plunger retainer and small ball.

2. Remove Primary Slow Jet & Secondary Slow Jet.

Remove Primary Slow Jet & Secondary Slow Jet.

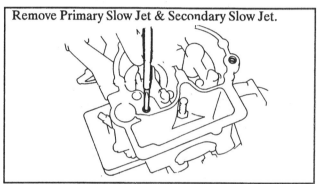

3. Remove Power Valve and Jet Assembly.

Power Valve and Jet

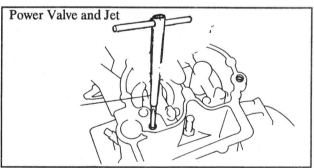

(a) Dismantle the power valve and jet.

4. Remove Main Jets.

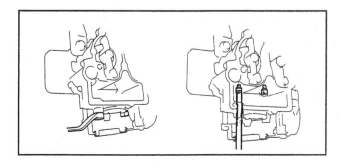

(a) Remove the primary main passage plug & gasket, and the primary main jet and gasket.

(b) Take out the secondary main passage plug and gasket, and the secondary main jet and gasket.

5. Remove Small Venturies.

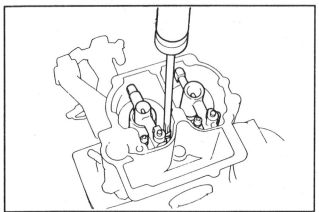

(a) Take out the 2 screws, primary small venturi and gasket.

(b) Take out the 2 screws, secondary small venturi and gasket.

6. Remove Secondary Throttle Valve Diaphragm.

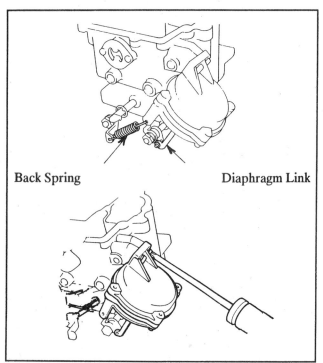

Back Spring   Diaphragm Link

(a) Take out the throttle shaft back spring.

(b) Remove the E-Clip and disconnect the diaphragm link.

(c) Unscrew the 2 screws, and take out the throttle valve diaphragm assembly & gasket.

(d) If necessary, unscrew the 4 screws, take out the spring retainer and dismantle the throttle valve diaphragm.

7. If Necessary, Remove Sight Glass. Unscrew the 2 screws and also take out the retainer and O-Ring.

8. Separate Carburettor Body and Flange.

(a) Take the throttle lever back spring out.

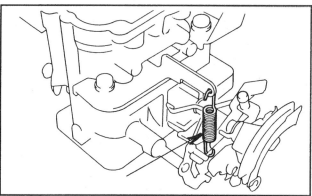

(b) Remove the passage screw and spring washer.

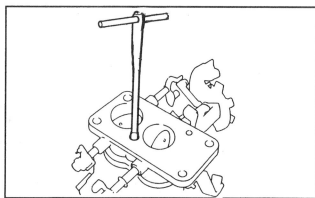

(c) Take out the bolt, spring washer and choke wire clamp.

(d) Remove the bolt, spring washer and spring retainer.

(e) Separate the body and flange.

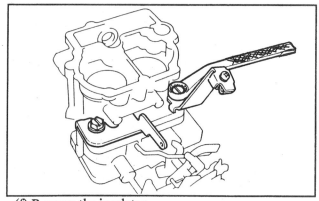

(f) Remove the insulator.

Inspection of Carburettor.

1. Clean Dismantled Parts Before Inspection.

(a) Wash and clean the cast parts with a soft brush and carburettor cleaner.

(b) Clean off all the carbon from around the throttle valve.

(c) Using carburettor cleaner also wash the other parts thoroughly.

(d) Blow all dirt and other foreign matter from the jets, fuel passages and restrictions in the body.

2. Inspect Float and Needle Valve.

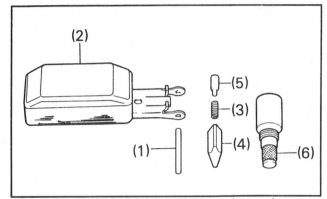

(a) Check pivot pin (1) for scratches and excessive wear.

(b) Check the float (2) for broken lips and wear in the pivot pin holes.

(c) Check spring (3) for breaks and deformation.

(d) Check the needle valve (4) and plunger (5) for wear or damage.

(e) Check the strainer (6) for rust and breaks.

3. Inspect Power Piston and ensure that it moves smoothly.

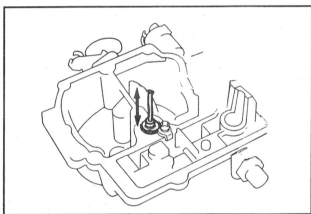

4. Inspect Power Valve for faulty opening and/or closing action. Air should pass through when open.

5. Inspect Fuel Cut Solenoid Valve.

(a) Connect the valve body and terminal to the battery terminals.

(b) Check to feel a click from the solenoid valve when the battery power is connected and disconnected. If the solenoid valve does not operate properly, replace it.

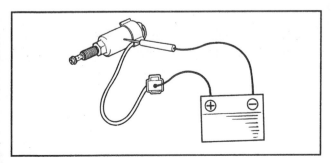

Assembly of Carburettor Body.

* Use new gaskets and O-Ring throughout.

1. Assemble Carburettor Body & Flange together with a new insulator.

(a) Connect the spring retainer with the bolt

(b) Connect the choke wire clamp with the bolt.

(c) Install the passage screw together with the spring washer.

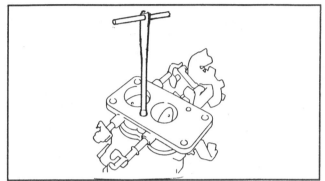

(d) Connect the throttle lever back spring.

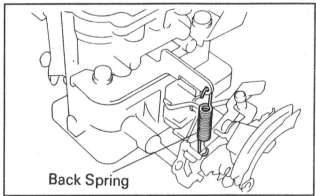

Back Spring

2. Install Sight Glass with the 2 screws, a new O-Ring and a retainer.

3. Fit Secondary Throttle Valve Diaphragm.

(a) Assemble the housing (1), a new gasket (2), the diaphragm (3), spring (4), and cover (5).

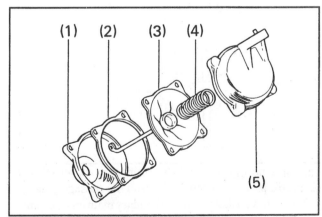

(b) Using 4 screws fit the spring retainer.

(c) With 2 screws fit the throttle valve diaphragm using a new gasket.

(d) Connect the diaphragm link with the E-Clip.

(e) Fit the throttle shaft back spring.

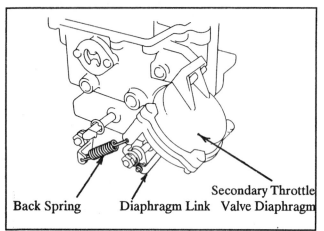

Back Spring   Diaphragm Link   Valve Diaphragm

Secondary Throttle

4. Install Small Venturies.

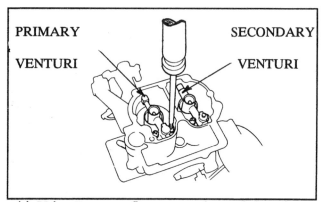

PRIMARY   SECONDARY

VENTURI   VENTURI

(a) Using 2 screws, fit a new gasket and the primary venturi.

(b) Fit a new gasket and the secondary venturi using 2 screws.

5. Fit Main Jets.

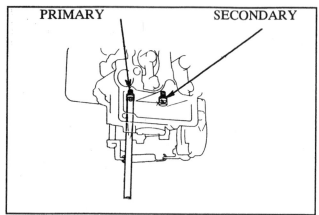

PRIMARY   SECONDARY

(a) Fit a new gasket and the primary main jet (Brass coloured), and also a new gasket and the passage plug.

(b) Fit a new gasket and the secondary main jet (Chrome coloured) and also a new gasket and the passage plug.

6. Assemble the power valve and jet, then install.

7. Install Primary Slow Jet & Secondary Jet.

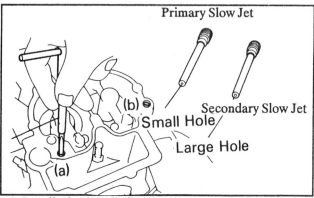

Primary Slow Jet

Secondary Slow Jet

Small Hole

Large Hole

8. Install Check Balls for Acceleration.

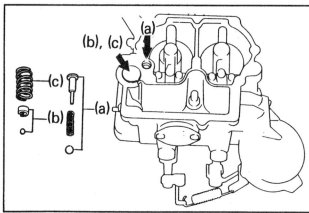

(a) Fit the pump discharge large ball, spring & weight.

(b) Install the plunger small ball and retainer using tweezers.

(c) Fit the plunger spring.

Assembly of Air Horn

1. Install Fuel Cut Solenoid Valve

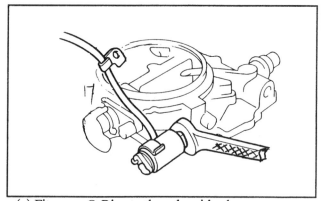

(a) Fit a new O-Ring to the solenoid valve.

(b) With a new gasket fit the solenoid valve.

2. Install Primary Upper Slow Jet.

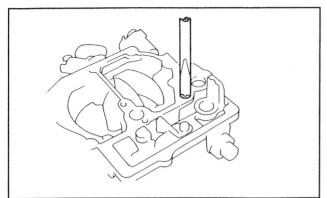

3. With retainer and screw, fit the spring and power piston.

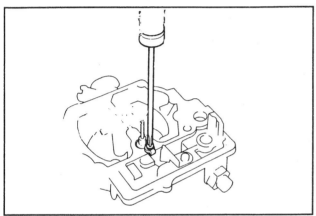

4. Using a new gasket fit the needle valve seat.

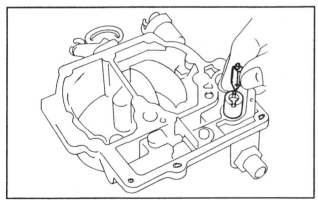

5. Insert the needle valve, spring and plunger into the needle valve seat.

6. Adjust Float Level.

(a) Using pivot pin install the float.

(b) Allow the float to hang down by its own weight. Using special tool, measure the distance between the float tip and air horn.

Float level (raised position): 6.0mm (0.236 in.)

* This measurement should be made without a gasket on the air horn.

(c) Adjust by bending the portion of the float lip as shown

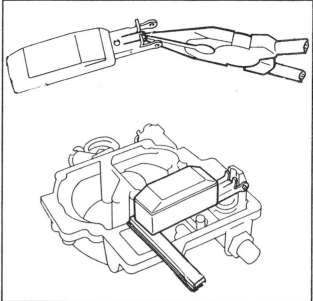

(d) Lift up the float. Using special tool measure the difference between the needle valve plunger and float lip.

Float level: (lowered position): 1.1 mm (0.043 in.)

(e) Adjust by bending the position of the float lip as shown.

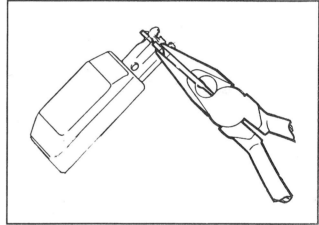

7. Fit New Air Horn Gasket in the Air Horn.

8. Install a new boot and accelerator pump plunger.

9. Using the pivot pin, fit the float.

10. Install Air Horn Assembly.

(a) Place the air horn in the carburettor body.

(b) Using 7 screws, fit the following parts:

(1) (S.Arabia & Australia) Vacuum pipe supports with 3 hoses.

(2) (General Countries M/T) Number Plate.

(3) (with CB or TP) Choke Breaker (CB with hose or throttle positioner (TP).

(4) Wire clamp of fuel cut solenoid valve.

11. Connect Links.

(a) (with CB) Choke Breaker (CB) Link.

(b) (with TP) Throttle positioner (TP) Link.

(c) Fast Idle Link.

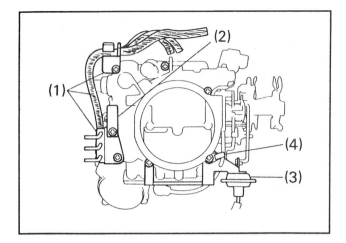

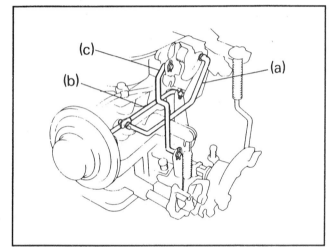

12. Connect Vacuum Hoses.

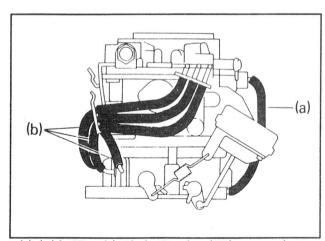

(a) (with CB only) Choke Breaker (CB) vacuum hose.

(b) (S.Arabia & Australia)Other 3 vacuum hoses.

13. Fit Acceleration Pump Arm.

(a) Connect the pump connecting link to the throttle lever.

(b) Fit the pump arm to the pump plunger.

(c) Install the pump arm with the pivot bolt.

14. Check Operation of All Parts.

Adjustment.

1. Check & Adjust Throttle Valve Opening.

(a) Check the full opening angle of the primary throttle valve.

Standard angle: $90°$ from horizontal.

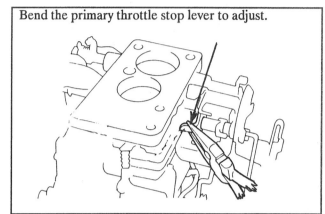

Bend the primary throttle stop lever to adjust.

(b) Bend the primary throttle stop lever to adjust.

(c) Check the full opening angle of the secondary throttle valve.

Standard angle; $90°$ from horizontal.

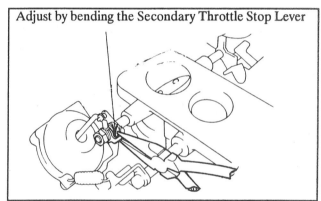

Adjust by bending the Secondary Throttle Stop Lever

(d) Bend the secondary throttle stop lever to adjust

2. Check and Adjust Kick-Up Setting.

(a) Check the opening angle of the secondary throttle valve, ensure that the primary throttle valve is fully opened to do this.

Standard angle: $25°$ from horizontal.

(b) Bend the secondary throttle kick-up lever to adjust.

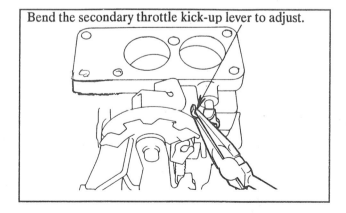

Bend the secondary throttle kick-up lever to adjust.

3. Check and Adjust Secondary Touch Angle.

(a) Check the primary throttle valve opening angle at the same time the primary kick lever just touches the secondary kick lever.

Standard angle: 67° from horizontal.

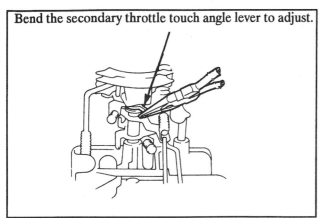

Bend the secondary throttle touch angle lever to adjust.

(b) Bend the secondary throttle touch angle lever to adjust.

4. Check and Adjust Fast Idle Setting.

(a) Check the primary throttle valve angle, with the choke valve fully closed..

Standard angle: 23° from horizontal.

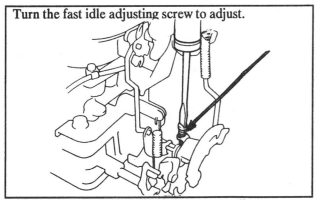

Turn the fast idle adjusting screw to adjust.

(b) Turn the fast idle adjusting screw to adjust.

5. Check & Adjust Choke Breaker (CB)

(a) With the choke valve fully closed, apply vacuum to the CB.

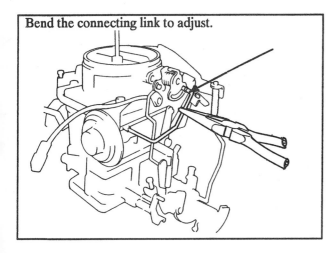

Bend the connecting link to adjust.

(b) Check the choke valve angle.

Standard angle: 38° from horizontal.

(c) Bend the connecting link to adjust.

6. Preset Idle Speed Adjusting Screw.

(a) Check the primary throttle valve angle.

Standard angle: 14° from horizontal

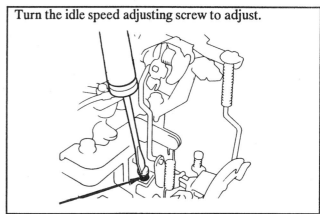

Turn the idle speed adjusting screw to adjust.

(b) Turn the idle speed adjusting screws to adjust.

7. Preset Idle Mixture Adjusting Screw. If the idle mixture adjusting screw has been removed, screw it right in and then unscrew it the following amount:

Standard:

S.Arabia M/T Return 3 3/4 turns from fully closed.

S.Arabia A/T Return 4 1/2 turns from fully closed.

Other   Return 2 turns from fully closed.

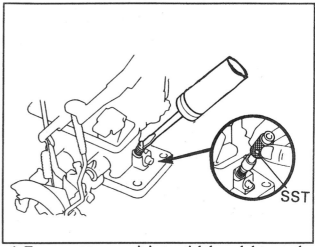

SST

* Ensure not to screw it in too tightly and damage the screw tip.

* If there is an idle limiter cap on the idle mixture adjusting screw, remove it.

8. Check and Adjust Acceleration Pump Stroke.

(a) Rotate the throttle shaft and check the length of the stroke.

Standard stroke: 9.5 mm (0.374 in.)

(b) Adjust the pump stroke by bending the connecting link.

9. Ensure Smooth Operation of Each Part.

Installation

1. Install Carburettor
(a) Place the insulator on the intake manifold.
(b) Using the 4 nuts, fit the carburettor.
2. Connect Hoses.
(a) Emission control hoses
(b) (with Outer Vent Control Valve) Outer vent control hose.
3. Connect Fuel Inlet Pipe.
Torque: 150 kg-cm (11 ft-lb, 15N'm)
4. Connect Cables.
(a) Accelerator throttle cable.
(b) Choke Cable.
(c) Throttle cable for automatic transmission.
5. Connect Connector of Fuel Cut Solenoid Valve.
6. Fit Air Cleaner or Air Intake Connector.
7. Check and Adjust Idle Speed and Idle Mixture as described in Tune-Up & Maintenance Section.
8. Check and Adjust Fast Idle Speed as described in Tune-Up and Maintenance Section.
9. Check & Adjust Throttle Positioner Setting Speed as described in Tune-Up & Maintenance Section.

CARBURETOR 2F ENGINE

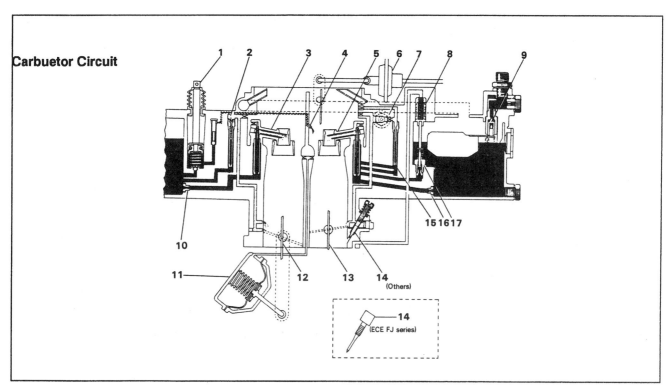

Carbuetor Circuit

1. **Pump Plunger.**
2. 2nd Slow Jet.
3. 2nd Main Nozzle.
4. Pump Jet.
5. 1st Main Nozzle.
6. Choke Breaker (Throttle Positioner Diaphragm) (Australia & Environment Control Equipment 40 FJ Series).
7. Solenoid Valve.
8. Power Piston.
9. Needle Valve.
10. 2nd Main Jet.
11. Diaphragm.
12. 2nd Throttle Valve.
13. 1st Throttle Valve.
14. Idle Mixture Adjusting Screw.
15. 1st Slow Jet.
16. 1st Main Jet.
17. Power Valve.

Components.

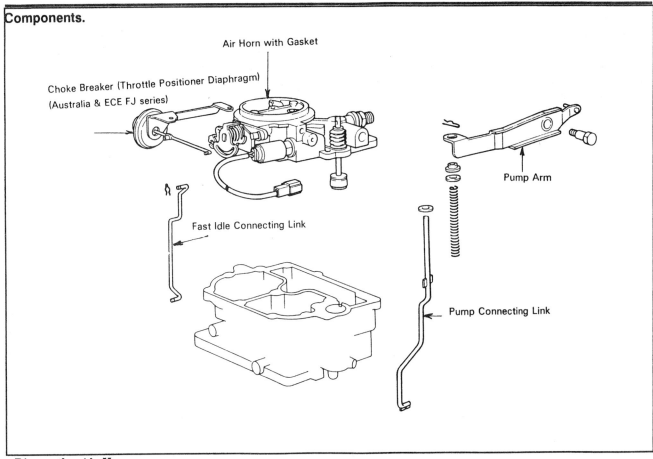

Air Horn with Gasket

Choke Breaker (Throttle Positioner Diaphragm)
(Australia & ECE FJ series)

Pump Arm

Fast Idle Connecting Link

Pump Connecting Link

Dismantle - Air Horn

Dismantle the parts in the order listed:

1. Pump Connecting Link.
2. Pump Arm.
3. Fast Idle Connecting Link.
4. Choke Breaker (Throttle Positioner Diaphragm) (Australia & ECE FJ Series).
5. Air Horn with Gasket.

Dismantle - Float

Dismantle the parts in the order listed:

1. Solenoid Valve.
2. Pump Plunger.
3. Boot.
4. Float Lever Pin.
5. Float.
6. Air Horn Gasket.
7. Needle valve, Spring and Pin.
8. Needle Valve Seat.
9. Power Piston Retainer.
10. Power Piston and Spring.

Dismantle - Choke System

FLOAT

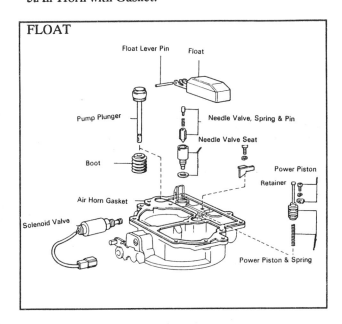

Float Lever Pin   Float

Pump Plunger

Needle Valve, Spring & Pin

Needle Valve Seat

Boot

Power Piston

Retainer

Air Horn Gasket

Solenoid Valve

Power Piston & Spring

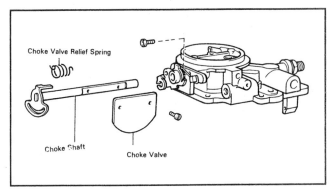

Choke Valve Relief Spring

Choke Shaft

Choke Valve

Dismantle the parts in the order listed:

1.Choke Valve. To remove the choke valve, file off the ends of the set screws.

* Do this only if it is necessary to replace the choke shaft.

2.Choke Valve Relief Spring. Unhook the choke valve relief spring and pull out ...

3.Choke Shaft.

Carburetor Body

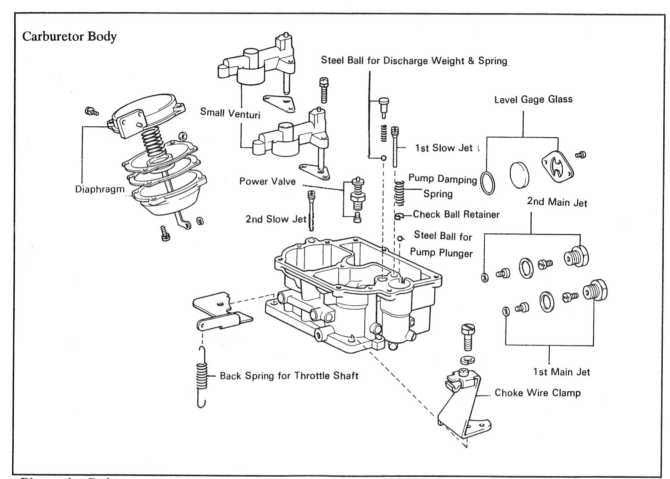

Dismantle - Body

Dismantle the parts in the order listed:

1.Steel Ball for Discharge Weight and Spring. Drop out the steel ball for the discharge weight and springs.

* Be careful not to lose the steel ball.

2.Pump Damping Spring. Drop out the steel ball for the discharge weight and springs.

* Be careful not to lose the steel ball.

3.Check Ball Retainer. Remove the check ball retainer with a pair of tweezers and then remove the steel ball for the pump plunger.

* Be careful not to lose the steel ball.

4.Steel Ball for Pump Plunger.

5.1st Slow Jet.

6.2nd Slow Jet.

7.Power Valve.

8.1st Main Jet.

9.2nd Main Jet.

10. Small Venturi.

11. Level Gauge Glass.

12. Diaphragm.

13. Choke Wire Clamp.

14. Back Spring for Throttle Shaft.

Carburetor Flang

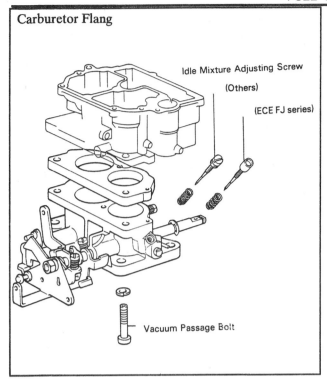

Idle Mixture Adjusting Screw

(Others)

(ECE FJ series)

Vacuum Passage Bolt

Dismantle - Flange

Dismantle the parts in the order listed:

1. Vacuum Passage Bolt.
2. Idle Mixture Adjusting Screw. Remove the idle mixture adjusting screw with (E.C.E.) or screwdriver for other models.

Inspection

* Before inspection, wash all parts thoroughly with gasoline or kerosine.
* Using compressed air, blow all dirt and other foreign matter from the jets and similar parts, and from the fuel passages and apertures in the body.
* Never clean the jets or orifices with wire or a drill. This could enlarge the openings and result in excessive fuel consumption.

Inspect the following parts and replace any part damaged:

1. Air Horn Parts

(a) Air Horn - Inspect for cracks, damaged threads and wear on choke shaft bores.
(b) (i) Power Piston - Inspect for damage.
 (ii) Spring - Inspect for deformation or rust.
 (iii) Power piston bore: Inspect for wear or damage.

(c) Make sure that the power piston moves smoothly in the air horn bore.
(d) Float and float lever pin: Inspect for wear or breaks.
(e) Strainer: Inspect for rust or breaks.
(f) Needle valve surface.
(g) Needle valve seat.
(h) (i) Choke valve - Inspect for deformation.
 (ii) Choke shaft: Inspect for wear, bending or improper fit in housing.
(i) Solenoid valve: Connect the wiring to the battery positive terminal and ground the body. Make sure that the needle valve is pulled in.
(j) Choke breaker (throttle positioner diaphragm) (Australia & ECE FJ Series): Apply vacuum to the diaphragm. Then check that the vacuum does not drop immediately and the link moves when vacuum is applied.

* The throttle positioner diaphragm is used in common with the choke breaker system.

(k) (i) Pump plunger: Inspect for wear on sliding surface and for damaged or deformed leather.
 (ii) Boot: Inspect for damage.

2. Body Parts

(a) Body: Inspect for cracks, scored mounting surfaces and damaged threads.
(b) Small venturis: Inspect for damage of clogging.
(c) Jets: Inspect for damage or clogging and for damaged contact surface, threads and screwdriver slots.
(d) Power valve: Check for faulty opening and closing action and for damaged contact surfaces and threads.
(e) Remove the jet with special tool.
(f) (i) Pump damping spring: Inspect for deformation or rust.
 (ii) Steel ball: Inspect for damage or rust.
(g) Diaphragm: Inspect the diaphragm, housing and spring for wear or damage.
(h) Assemble the diaphragm as illustrated.

3. Flange Parts

(a) Flange: Inspect for cracks, damaged mounting surfaces, threads and for wear on throttle shaft bearings.

ECE FJ Series

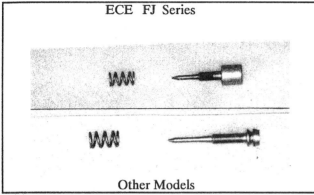

Other Models

(b) Throttle valves: Inspect for worn or deformed valve and for wear, bending, twisting or faulty movement inside the housing shaft.

(c) Idle mixture adjusting screw: Inspect for damaged tapered tip or threads.

Assembly - Flange

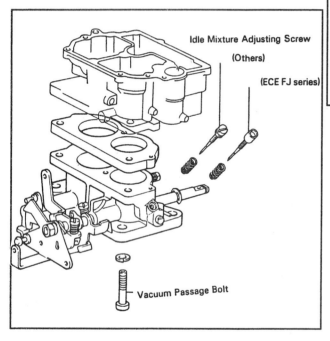

Assemble the parts in the order listed:

1. Idle Mixture adjusting Screw. Install the idle mixture adjusting screw temporarily with special tool ECE (or a screwdriver for others).

2. Vacuum Passage Bolt. Tighten the vacuum passage bolt with special tool.

* Use a new gasket.

Assembly - Body

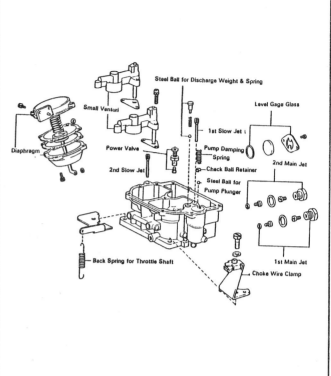

Assemble the parts in the order listed:

1. 1st Slow Jet.
2. 2nd Slow Jet.
3. Power Valve.
4. 1st Main Jet using special tool.
* The 1st main jet is brass coloured.
5. 2nd Main Jet using special tool.
* The 2nd main jet is chrome coloured.
6. Venturi:
1st small venturi - chrome coloured.
2nd small venturi - brass coloured.
7. Level Gauge Glass.
8. Diaphragm.
9. Back Spring for Throttle Shaft.
10. Choke Wire Clamp.
11. Steel Ball for Pump Plunger. Install the steel balls, being careful not to mix up the two sizes of balls:
Smaller ball - for pump plunger.
Larger ball - for discharge weight.
12. Check Ball Retainer.
13. Pump Damping Spring.
14. Steel Ball for Discharge Weight and Spring.

Assembly - Choke System

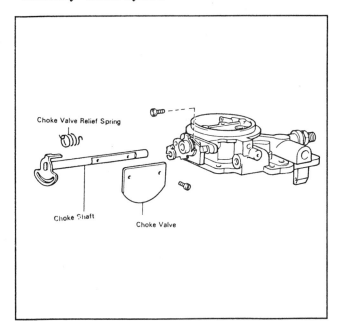

Assemble the parts in the order listed:

1.Choke Shaft.
2.Choke Valve Relief Spring.
3.Choke Valve and check the choke valve action.
* Stake the choke shaft screws after assembling.

Assembly - Float

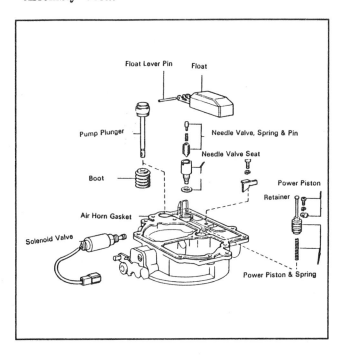

Assemble the parts in the order listed:

1.Power Piston and Spring.

2.Power Piston Retainer. Make sure that the power piston moves smoothly.
3.Needle Valve Seat.
4.Needle Valve, Spring and Pin.
5.Air Horn Gasket.
6.Float.
7.Float Lever Pin.
(a) Adjust the Float Level. Allow the float to hang down by its own weight. Then check the clearance between the float tip and air horn with special tool. Adjust by bending Part A of the float lip.

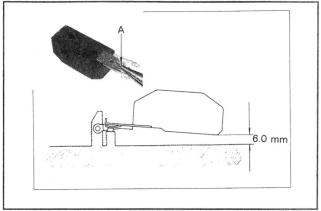

Float upper level: 6.0 mm (0.236 in)
* This measurement should be made without a gasket on the air horn.
(b) Adjust the Lowered Position. List up the float and check the clearance between the needle valve plunger and float lip using special tool. Adjust by bending Part B of the float lip.

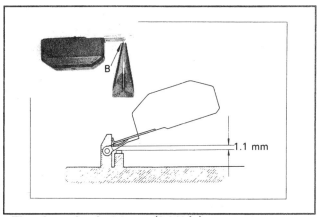

Float lower level: 1.1 mm (0.043 in)
8.Boot.
9.Pump Plunger. Ensure that the pump plunger moves smoothly.
10. Solenoid Valve.

Assembly - Air Horn

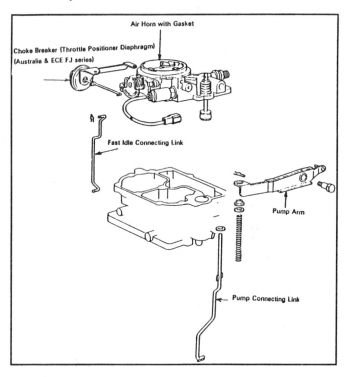

Assemble the parts in the order listed:

1.Air Horn with Gasket. Before installing the air horn, make sure that the pump discharge weight is properly assembled.

2.Choke Breaker (Throttle Positioner Diaphragm) (Australia & ECE FJ Series).

3.Fast Idle Connecting Link.

4.Pump Arm.

5.Pump Connecting Link. After assembly, make sure that each link moves smoothly.

Adjustments

1.Primary Throttle Valve Opening.

(a) Fully open the primary throttle valve and check the opening angle.

Opening angle from horizontal plane: 90°

(b) Adjust by bending the throttle lever stopper as illustrated.

2.Secondary Throttle Valve Opening.

(a) Fully open the secondary throttle valve and check the opening angle.

Opening angle from horizontal plane: 90°

(b) Adjust by bending the throttle lever stopper as illustrated.

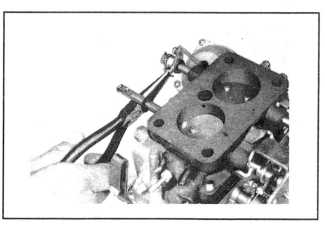

3.Kick-Up.

(a) Fully open the primary throttle valve, then check the secondary throttle valve opening angle with special tool.

Kick-up angle: 25°

(b) Adjust by bending the secondary throttle lever indicated in the figure.

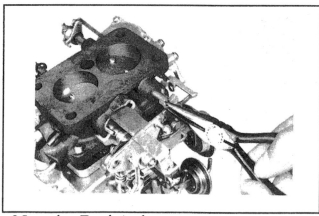

3.Secondary Touch Angle.

(a) Check the primary throttle valve opening with special tool. At the same time, the secondary throttle valve begins to open.

Secondary touch angle from horizontal plane: 67°

(b) Adjust by bending the touch lever indicated in the figure.

4.Fast Idle Clearance.

(a) Fully close the choke valve by turning the choke shaft lever.

(b) Check the clearance between the primary throttle valve and carburetor flange using special tool.

Fast idle clearance: 1.3 mm (0.051 in)

(c) Adjust by turning the fast idle adjusting screw indicated in the figure.

5.Check Breaker (U.S.A., Australia and E.C.E. FJ Series).

(a) Apply vacuum to the choke breaker diaphragm.

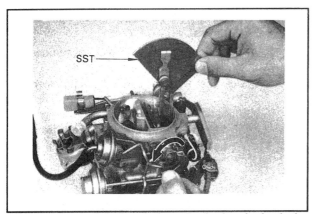

(b) While closing the choke valve by hand, check the choke valve angle with special tool.

Choke valve opening angle from horizontal plane:
U.S.A. 45°
Others 38°

(c) Adjust by bending the choke breaker link indicated in the figure.

6.Choke Opener (U.S.A., FJ 4..ˢ and 60 Series).

(a) Fully close the choke valve by turning the choke shaft lever.

(b) Apply vacuum to the diaphragm and then check the choke valve angle with special tool.

Choke valve opening angle from horizontal plane: 75°

(c) Adjust by bending the choke shaft stopper indicated in the figure.

7.Throttle Positioner (Australia and ECE FJ Series).

(a) Apply vacuum to the throttle positioner diaphragm.

(b) Check the throttle valve opening with special tool.

Throttle valve opening angle from horizontal plane:
N.S.W. 11°
Others 10°

(c) Adjust by turning the throttle positioner adjusting screw indicated in the figure.

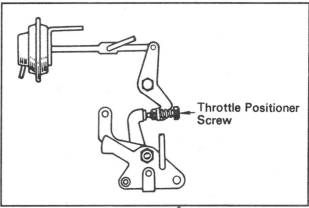

8.Slow Cut Valve (U.S.A., FJ 4..ˢ and 60 Series).

(a) Set the primary throttle valve opening to the secondary touch angle (67°).

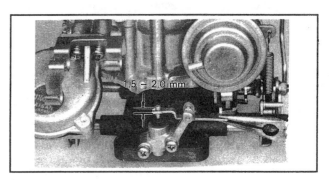

(b) Inspect the slow cut valve stroke and adjust by bending the lever indicated in the figure.

Slow cut valve stroke: 1.5 - 2.0 mm (0.059 - 0.079 in)

9. Acceleration Pump.

(a) While rotating the throttle shaft, check that the pump connecting link moves smoothly.

(b) Check the acceleration pump stroke and adjust by bending the pump connecting link.

Acceleration pump stroke: 9.5 mm (0.374 in)

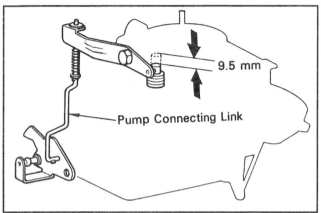

9.5 mm

Pump Connecting Link

10. (i) [Except U.S.A.] Idle Mixture Adjusting Screw. Tighten the idle mixture adjusting screw fully and then unscrew as follows: (using special tool for ECE or screwdriver (others))

Return from fully closed:

ECE & N.S.W.   2-1/2 turns

Others   2 turns

(ii) [U.S.A., FJ 4..ˢ & 60 Series] If necessary, remove the steel plug and idle mixture adjusting screw referring to the following procedure:

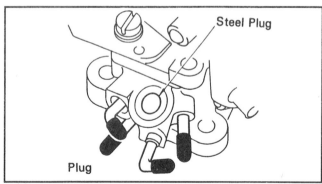

Steel Plug

Plug

(a) Mark the centre of the plug with a punch.

* Plug each carburetor vacuum port to prevent entry of steel particles when drilling.

(b) Drill a 8.5 mm (0.335 in) hole in the centre of the plug.

* As there is only 1 mm (0.04 in) clearance between the plug and screw, drill carefully and slowly to avoid drilling onto the screw.

(c) Through the hole in the plug, fully screw in the mixture adjusting screw with a screwdriver.

* Be careful not to damage the screw tip by tightening the screw too tight.

(d) Use a 9.5 mm (0.374 in) drill to force the plug off.

(e) Blow off any steel particles with compressed air and remove the screw.

* If the drill has gnawed into the screw tip or if the tapered position is damaged, replace the screw.

(f) Fully screw in the idle mixture adjusting screw and then unscrew it about 2 turns.

* Be careful not to damage the screw tip by tightening the screw too tight.

* Do not install the steel plug until the idle mixture adjustment is finished.

11. Idle Mixture Adjustment (U.S.A., FJ 4..ˢ and 60 Series). In the case of the steel plug being removed, check the idle mixture speed, referring to the following method:

(a) Inspect the following items before adjustment:

1) Air cleaner installed,

2) Normal operating coolant temperature,

3) Choke fully open,

4) All accessories switched off,

5) All vacuum lines connected,

6) Ignition timing set correctly,

7) Transmission in neutral,

8) Fuel level should be about even with the correct level in the sight glass.

(b) Break the idle limiter cap on the idle speed adjusting screw if installed.

(c) Start the engine and set to the maximum speed by turning the idle mixture adjusting screw.

(d) Set to the idle mixture speed by turning the idle speed adjusting screw.

Idle mixture speed: 690 rpm

* Before moving to the next step, continue adjustments 3 and 4 until the maximum speed will not rise any further no matter how much the IDLE MIXTURE ADJUSTING SCREW IS ADJUSTED.

(e) Set to the idle speed by screwing in the idle mixture adjusting screw.

Idle speed: 650 rpm

* This is the LEAN DROP METHOD for setting the idle speed and mixture.

(f) Install a new limiter cap on the idle speed adjusting screw (if one was installed).

(g) Tap in a new plug until it is even with the carburetor flange surface.

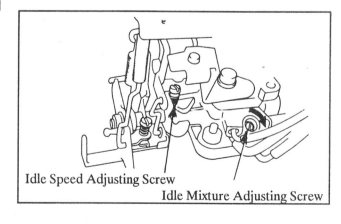

Idle Speed Adjusting Screw

Idle Mixture Adjusting Screw

FUEL PUMP

Inspection of Fuel Pump.(Airtight Test)

CUTAWAY VIEW

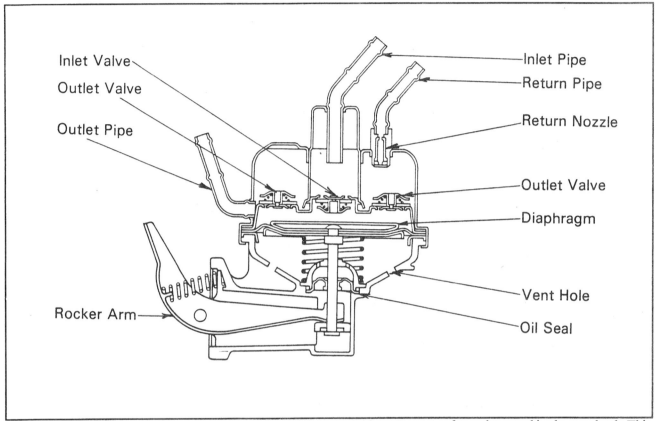

Inlet Valve
Outlet Valve
Outlet Pipe
Rocker Arm

Inlet Pipe
Return Pipe
Return Nozzle
Outlet Valve
Diaphragm
Vent Hole
Oil Seal

Prechecks.

Before carrying out any of the following checks on the fuel pump:

(a) Run some fuel through the pump to ensure that the check valves seal tightly (a dry check valve may not seal properly)

(b) Without blocking off any pipes, operate the rocker arm and check the amount of force needed for operation and the amount of arm play. This same amount of force should be used in the checks.

1. Check Inlet Valve. Block off the outlet and return pipes with your finger and make sure that there is an increase in rocker arm play and that the rocker arm moves easily (no reaction force).

2. Check Outlet Valve. Block off the inlet pipe with your finger and ensure that the rocker arm locks (does not operate with the same amount of force used in the precheck above.)

* Never use more force than used in the precheck. This applies to checks 3 and 4 also.

3. Check Diaphragm. Block off the inlet, outlet and return pipes and ensure that the rocker arm locks.

* If all 3 of these checks are not as described, the sealing of the body and upper casing is defective.

4. Check Oil Seal. Block off the vent hole with your finger and ensure that the rocker arm locks.

5. If fuel pump does not perform correctly, replace with a new pump.

Installation of Fuel Pump

1. Install Fuel Pump with new gaskets, using the 2 bolts and insulator.

Torque: 185 kg-cm (13 ft-lb, 18N·m)

2. Connect Fuel Hoses to Fuel Pump.

3. Start Engine and check for leaks.

PROBLEM DIAGNOSIS

Problem: Engine will not start or hard to start but cranks OK.

Possible Causes & Remedies:

* Choke Operation. Remedy-Check choke system.

* Needle Valve sticking or clogged/Vacuum hose disconnected or damaged. Remedy-Check float and needle valve.

* Fuel cut solenoid valve not open. Remedy-Check fuel cut solenoid valve.

Problem: Rough Idle or stalls.

Possible Causes & Remedies:

* Idle speed incorrect/Slow jet clogged. Remedy-Adjust idle speed.

* Idle mixture incorrect. Remedy-Adjust idle mixture.

* Fuel cut solenoid valve not open. Remedy-Check fuel cut solenoid valve.

* Fast idle speed setting incorrect (cold engine). Remedy-Adjust fast idle speed.

* Choke valve open (cold engine). Remedy-Check choke system.

Problem: Engine hesitates/poor acceleration.

Possible Causes & Remedies:

* Float level too low/Accelerator pump faulty. Remedy-Adjust float level.

* Power valve faulty. Remedy-Check power piston & valve.

* Choke valve closed (hot engine). Remedy-Check choke system.

* Choke valve stuck open (cold engine). Remedy-Check choke system.

* Fuel line clogged. Remedy-Check fuel line.

Problem: Engine Pre-Igniting (runs after ignition has been turned off).

Possible Causes & Remedies:

* Linkage sticking/Idle speed or fast idle speed out of adjustment. Remedy-Adjust idle speed or fast idle speed.

* Fuel cut solenoid faulty. Remedy-Check fuel cut solenoid valve.

Problem: Poor Petrol (gasoline) milage.

Possible Causes & Remedies:

* Choke faulty. Remedy-Check choke system.

* Idle speed too high. Remedy-Adjust idle speed.

* Deceleration fuel cut system faulty/Power valve always open. Remedy- Check deceleration system.

* Fuel leak. Remedy-Repair as necessary.

Problem: Insufficient fuel supply to carburettor.

Possible Causes & Remedies:

* Fuel filter clogged. Remedy-Replace fuel filter.

* Fuel pump faulty. Remedy-Replace fuel pump.

* Fuel line clogged. Remedy-Check fuel line.

* Fuel line bent or kinked. Remedy-Replace fuel line.

FUEL SYSTEM 21R, 21R-C & 22R
4 CYLINDER ENGINES

FUEL SYSTEM 21R, 21R-C & 22R 4 CYLINDER ENGINES

Fuel Pump

Cutaway view.

Inspection. Operate the lever and ensure that fuel is being pumped out. If not replace with a new fuel pump.

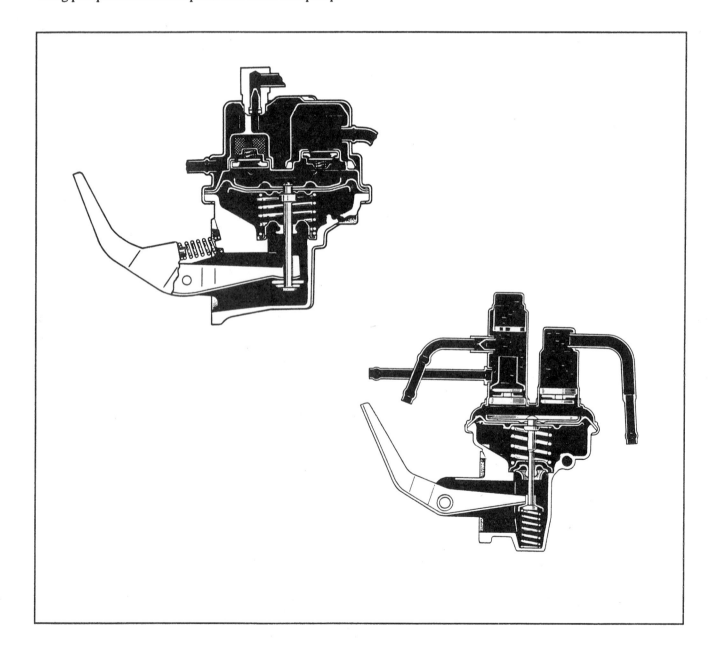

Carburettor (USA & Canada)

1. Pivot Pin.
2. Float.
3. Needle Valve.
4. Needle Valve Seat.
5. Power Piston Retainer.
6. Power Piston (Check for free movement).
7. Spring.

DISMANTLE.

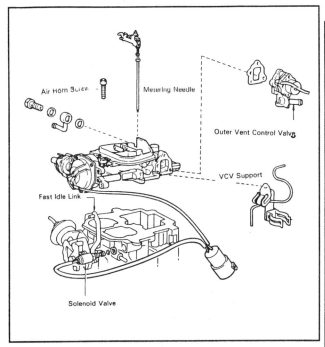

Body.

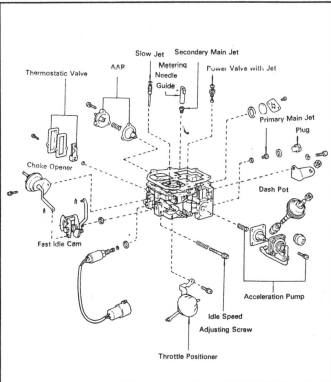

Air Horn.

Dismantle the parts in the order listed.
1. Metering Needle.
2. Fast Idle Link.
3. Air Horn Screw.
4. VCV Support (Ex.Canada RN 4x4).
5. Outer Vent Control Valve (Ex.Canada RN 4x4).
6. Solenoid Valve.

Float.

Dismantle the parts in the order listed.

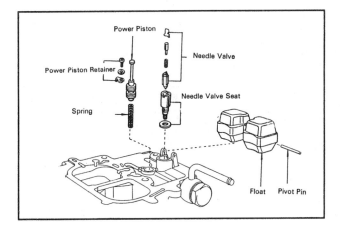

Dismantle the parts in the order listed.
1. Slow Jet.
2. Power Valve with Jet.
3. Metering Needle Guide.
4. Secondary Main Jet.
5. Plug.
6. Primary Main Jet.
7. Acceleration Pump.
8. AAP.
9. Thermostatic Valve.
10. Throttle Positioner.
11. Fast Idle Cam.
12. Choke Opener.
13. Idle Speed Adjusting Screw.
14. Dash Pot.

INSPECTION.

1. Before inspection, clean all parts thoroughly with petrol (gasoline).

2. Using compressed air, blow all dirt and other foreign matter from the jets and similar parts, and from fuel passages and apertures in the body.

3. Never clean the jets or orifices with wire or a drill. This could make the opening bigger and result in using excess fuel.

Inspect the following parts and replace any parts damaged.

Air Horn Parts.

1. Air horn: Examine for cracks, damages and excessive deformation of the air valve and choke valve.

2. Ensure that the power piston moves smoothly in the air horn bore.

3. Power Piston: Examine for damage. Spring: Inspect for deformation or rust. Power Piston Bore: Examine for wear or damage.

4. Float & Pivot Pin: Inspect for wear or breaks.

5. Strainer: Check for rust or breaks.

6. Needle valve surface.

7. Needle valve seat.

8. Metering needle: examine for bending or damage at the tapered tip.

9. Outer vent control valve (except Canada RN 4x4): examine the valve and valve seats for damage and ensure that the valve rod moves smoothly. Using a ohmmeter, measure the resistance between the terminal and solenoid body.

Resistance: 63-73 ohms at 20oC (68oF)

10. Choke oil: Using ohmmeter, measure the resistane between the terminal and coil housing.

Resistance: 16-20 ohms at 20°C (68°F)

Body Parts.

1. Body: Examine for cracks, scored mounting surface and damaged threads.

2. Jets: Inspect for damage or clogging. Examine for damaged contact surface, threads and screwdriver slots.

3. Power valve: Examine for faulty opening and closing action. Check for damaged contact surface and threads

4. Remove the jet.

5. Acceleration pump: Inspect the diaphragm, housing and spring for wear or damage.

6. AAP: Check the diaphragm, housing and spring for wear or damage.

7. Solenoid valve:

8. Choke opener: Apply vacuum to the diaphragm. Check that vacuum does not drop immediately and the link moves when with vacuum is applied.

9. Throttle positioner (Calif. RN 4x4 and RN C&C): Apply vacuum to the diaphragm. Ensure that vacuum does not drop immediately and the link moves when vacuum is applied.

10. Thermostatic valve: Examine for damage.

11. Dash pot (USA RT A/T and USA RA A/T): Inspect the body and boot for cracks for damage.

Flange Parts.

1. Flange: Examine for cracks, damaged mounting surfaces, threads and for wear on throttle shaft bearings.

2. Throttle valves: Inspect for worn or deformed valves and for wear, bending, twisting of shafts or faulty movement inside the housing shaft.

3. Idle mixture adjusting screw (Canada RN 4x4): Examine for damaged tapered tip or threads.

* For other vehicles, the idle mixture adjusting screw is adjusted and plugged with a steel plug by the manufacturer.

ASSEMBLY.

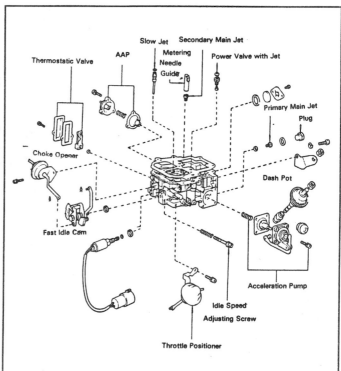

1. Primary Main Jet & Plug.
2. Secondary Main Jet.
3. Metering Needle Guide.
4. Power Valve with Jet.
5. Slow Jet.
6. Thermostatic Valve.
7. AAP.
8. Acceleration Pump.
9. Choke Opener.
10. Fast Idle Cam.
11. Idle Speed Adjusting Screw.
12. Throttle Positioner (Calif.RN 4x4 and RN C&C).
13. Dash Pot (USA RT A/T and USA RA A/T).

Float.

Assembly.
1. Power Piston & Spring.
2. Power Piston Retainer.

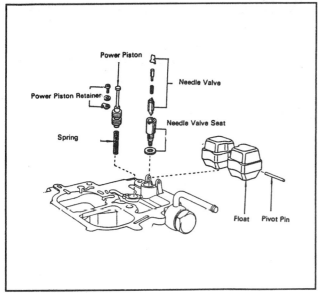

3. Needle Valve Seat.

4. Needle Valve.

5. Float.

6. Pivot Pin.

(a) Insert the lip of the float under the wire of the needle valve.

(b) Alter the float level. Allow the float to hang down by its own weight. Measure the difference between the float top and air horn with special tool.

Float level: 10.5 mm (0.413 in.)

* Measure the difference without a gasket on the air horn.

(c) Bend the arm of the float to adjust.

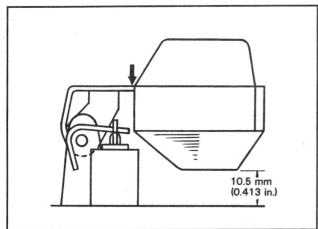

(d) Lift the float up and examine the clearance between the needle valve plunger and the float lip with special tool.

Float level (lowered position):

0.9-1.1 mm (0.035-0.043 in.)

(e) Bend the float tip that comes into contact with the needle valve plunger to adjust.

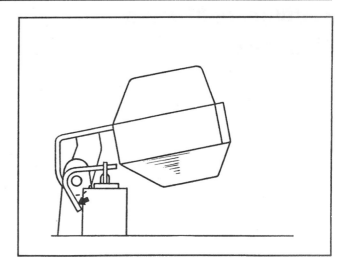

Air Horn.

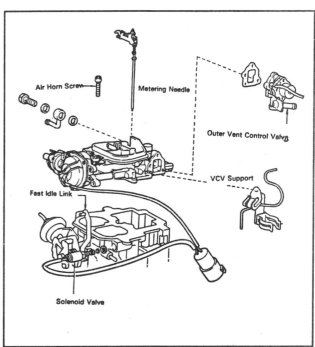

Assemble.

1. Solenoid Valve.

2. Outer Vent Control Valve (Ex. Canada RN 4x4).

3. VCV Support (Ex. Canada RN 4x4).

4. Air Horn Screw.

5. Fast Idle Link.

6. Metering Needle.

After assembly, ensure all lines move smoothly.

Carburettor (General Countries)

2. Float.
3. Needle Valve.
4. Needle Valve Seat.
5. Power Piston Retainer.
6. Power Piston, ensure it moves freely.
7. Spring.

DISMANTLE.

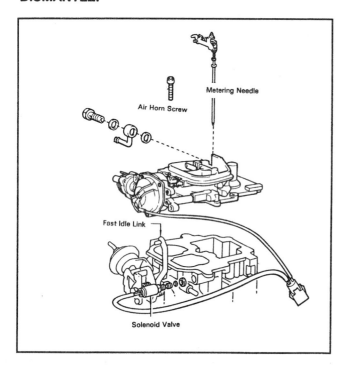

Dismantle the Choke System.

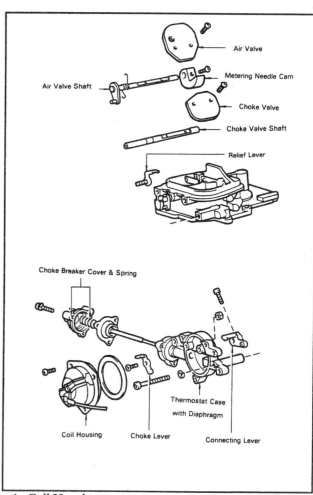

Dismantle Air Horn.
1. Metering Needle.
2. Fast Idle Link.
3. Air Horn Screw.
4. Solenoid Valve.

(a)Loosen the solenoid valve and remove it from the body by rotating the body anti-clockwise.

  * Be careful not to bend or distort the lead wires.

Dismantle the Float.
1. Pivot Pin.

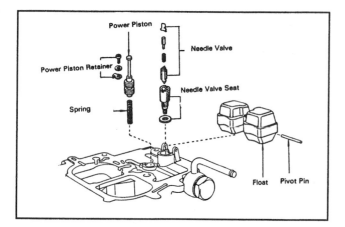

1. Coil Housing.
2. Choke Lever.
3. Choke Breaker Cover & Spring.
4. Thermostat Case with Diaphragm.
5. Connecting Lever.
6. Relief Lever.
7. Air Valve.
8. Choke Valve.
9. Metering Needle Cam.
10. Air Valve Shaft.
11. Choke Valve Shaft.

Dismantle Body.

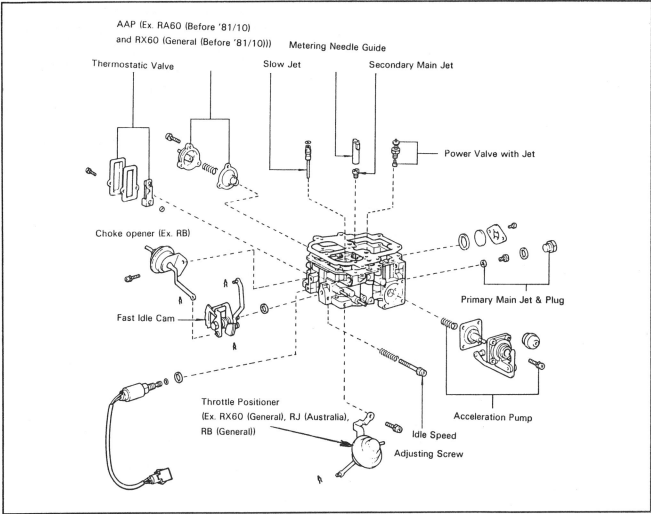

1. Slow Jet.
2. Power Valve with Jet.
3. Metering Needle Guide.
4. Secondary Main Jet.
5. Plug.
6. Primary Main Jet.
7. Acceleration Pump.
8. AAP [Ex.RA60 (Before '81/10) and RX60 (General (Before '81/10)].
9. Thermostatic Valve.
10. Throttle Positioner.
11. Fast Idle Cam.
12. Choke Opener (Ex.RB).
13. Idle Speed Adjusting Screw.

Dismantle Flange.

1. Idle Mixture Adjusting Screw.
2. Carburettor Flange.

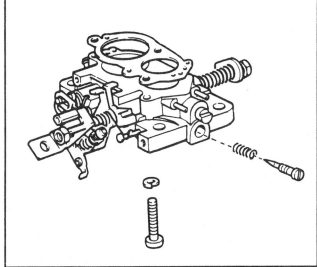

INSPECTION.

1. Before Inspection, clean all parts thoroughly with petrol (gasoline).

2. Using compressed air, blow all dirt and other foreign matters from the jets and similar parts, and from the fuel passages and apertures in the body.

3. Never clean the jets or orifices with wire or a drill. This could make the opening bigger and result in using excess fuel.

Inspect the following parts and replace any part damaged.

Air Horn Parts:

1. Air Horn: Examine for cracks, damaged threads and excessive wear on the choke and air valve shaft holes.

2. Ensure that the power piston moves smoothly in the air horn bore.

3. Power Piston: Inspect for damage. Spring: Examine for deformation or rust. Power piston bore: Check for wear or damage.

4. Float & Pivot Pin: Examine for wear or breaks.

5. Strainer: Check for rust or breaks.

6. Needle valve surface.

7. Needle valve seat.

8. Air and choke valve: Examine for deformation. Air and choke valve shaft: Inspect for wear, bending or improper fit in the housing.

9. Metering needle: Examine for bending or damage at the tapered tip.

10. Coil Housing: Check for cracks, and deformation of thermostatic bi-metal coil.

11. Choke coil: Using a ohmmeter, measure the resistance between the terminal and coil housing.

Resistance: 16-20 ohms at 20°C (68°F).

Body Parts.

1. Body: Check for cracks, scored mounting surfaces and damaged threads.

2. Jets: Inspect for damage or clogging and /or damaged contact surface, threads and screwdriver slots.

3. Power valve: Examine for faulty opening and closing action. Check for damaged contact surface and threads.

4. Remove the jet.

5. Acceleration pump: Examine the diaphragm, housing and spring for wear or damage.

6. AAP [Ex. RA60 (Before '81/10) & RX60 (General (Before '81/10))]: Check the diaphragm, housing and spring for wear or damage.

7. Solenoid valve: To test, connect a battery to the positive and negative terminals of solenoid. If you feel or hear a click from the solenoid valve when the power is connected , the solenoid valve is functioning correctly.

8. Choke Opener (Ex.RB): Apply the vacuum to the diaphragm. Check that vacuum does not drop immediately and the link moves when vacuum is applied.

9. Throttle positioner [Ex. RX60 (General), RJ (Australia)]: Apply vacuum to the diaphragm. Ensure that

vacuum does not drop immediately and that the link moved when vacuum is applied.

10. Thermostatic valve: Inspect for damage.

Flange Parts.

1. Flange: Check for cracks, damaged mounting surfaces, threads and for wear on throttle shaft bearings.

2. Throttle valves: Examine for worn or deformed valves and for wear, bending, twisting of shafts or faulty movement inside the housing.

3. Idle mixture adjusting screw: Inspect for damaged tapered tip or threads.

ASSEMBLY.

Assembly of Flange.

1. Carburettor Flange.
2. Idle Mixture Adjusting Screw.
3. Flange Screw.

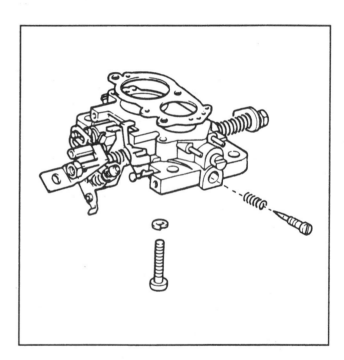

Assembly of Body.

1. Primary Main Jet & Plug.
2. Secondary Main Jet.
3. Metering Needle Guide.

4. Power Valve with Jet.   9. Choke Breaker Cover & Spring.

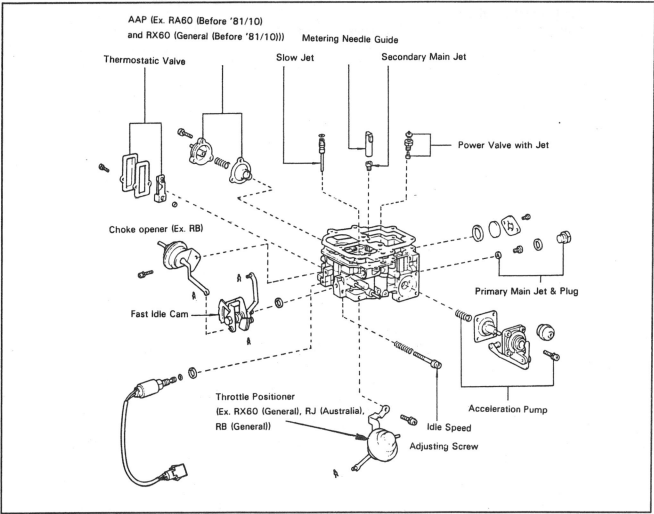

5. Slow Jet.

6. Thermostatic Valve.

7. AAP [Ex. RA60 (Before '81/10) and RX60 (General (Before '81/10))].

8. Acceleration Pump.

9. Choke Opener (Ex.RB).

10. Fast Idle Cam.

11. Idle Speed Adjusting Screw.

12. Throttle Positioner [Ex. RX60 (General), RJ (Australia), RB (General))]

Assembly of Choke System.

1. Choke Valve Shaft.

2. Air Valve Shaft.

3. Metering Needle Cam.

4. Choke Valve.

5. Air Valve.

6. Relief Lever.

7. Connecting Lever.

8. Thermostat Case with Diaphragm..

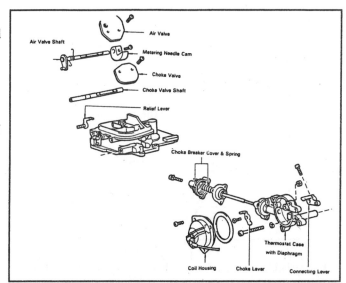

10. Choke Lever

(a) Hook the choke lever to the bi-metal spring.

11. Coil Housing

(a) Align the case scale standard line with the housing scale line.

(b) Check the choke valve action.

* Stake the choke valve shaft and air valve shaft screws after assembling.

Assembly of Float.

1. Power Piston & Spring.
2. Power Piston Retainer.
3. Needle Valve Seat.

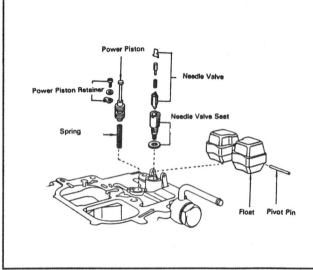

4. Needle Valve.
5. Float.
6. Pivot Pin.

(a) Insert the lip of the float under the wire of the needle valve.

(b) Alter the float level. Allow the float to hang down by its own weight. Check the difference between the float top and air horn with special tool.

Float level: 9.8 mm (0.386 in.)

* Measure the difference without a gasket on the air horn.

(c) Bend the arm of the float to adjust.

(d) Lift the float up and examine the clearance between the needle valve plunger and the float lip with special tool.

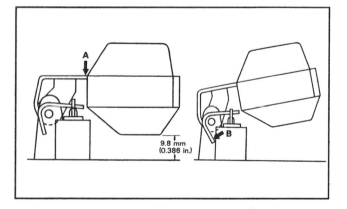

(e) Bend the float tip that comes into contact with the needle valve plunger to adjust.

Assembly of Air Horn.

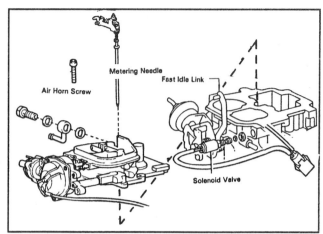

1. Solenoid Valve

(a) Install the solenoid valve into the carburettor body by rotating the carburettor body clockwise.

* Be careful not to bend or distort the lead wires.

2. Air Horn Screw
3. Fast Idle Link
4. Metering Needle

(a) Hook the metering needle spring end into the hole as shown in the diagram. Then install the metering needle and 2 washers.

(b) After assembly, make sure that each link moves smoothly.

Carburettor Adjustment.

Primary Throttle Valve Opening.

1. Fully open the primary throttle valve and check the opening angle.

Opening angle from the horizontal place: 90°

2. Bend the throttle arm lever to adjust.

Secondary Throttle Valve Opening

1. Fully open the secondary throttle valve and check the opening angle.

Opening angle from horizontal place: 90°

2. Bend the throttle arm lever to adjust.

Fast Idle Setting.

1. Set the throttle shaft lever to the first step of the fast idle cam.

2. With the choke valve fully closed, check the primary

throttle valve angle with special tool.

Fast idle angle from horizontal plane:

RA, RT, RX   22°
RN, RU, RB, RJ   23°
Others   24°

3. Turn the fast idle adjusting screw to adjust.

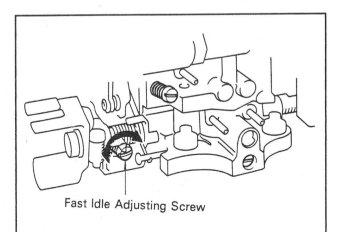

Fast Idle Adjusting Screw

Unloader.

1. With the primary throttle valve fully opened, check the choke valve angle with special tool.

Choke valve angle from horizontal plane:

RA (Since '84/8), RX (Since '84/8), RN, RJ   45°
Others   ,,,,,,,,,,,,   50°

2. Bend the first throttle arm to adjust.

Choke Opener.

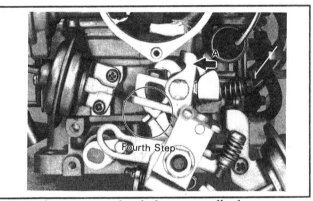

1. Apply vacuum to the choke opener diaphragm.

2. Ensure that the fast idle cam is released to the fourth step.If necessary,adjust by bending the choke opener lever A.

3. Close the choke valve and set the fast idle lever to the first step.

4. Ensure that there is clearance between the choke opener lever and fast idle cam.

Throttle Positioner [Calif. RN 4x4, RN C&C, Ex.RX60(General),RJ(Australia)].

1. Apply vacuum to the diaphragm.

2. Examine the throttle valve opening angle with special tool.

Throttle valve opening angle from horizontal plane:

RT, RA, RX   17°
RN, RJ, (Before '84/8)   17.5°

3. Turn the adjusting screw to adjust.

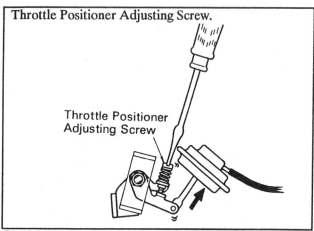

Throttle Positioner Adjusting Screw.

Throttle Positioner
Adjusting Screw

Choke Breaker.

1. Apply vacuum to the choke breaker diaphragm.

2. While closing the choke valve by hand, check the choke valve opening angle with special tool.

Choke valve opening angle from horizontal plane:

RJ (Europe, Australia)	52°
RX (21R-C (from '80/9 to '81/8)	55°
Others	38°

Acceleration Pump.

While rotating the throttle shaft, check that the pump lever and diaphragm rod move smoothly.

Dash Pot [USA RT A/T and USA RA A/T]

1. Fully open the choke valve and release the fast idle cam to the fourth step.

2. Fully open and return the throttle valve. Check the time required for the throttle valve to return to the idle position.

Time required: 3 seconds.

3. Turn the dash pot adjusting nut to adjust.

Idle Mixture Adjusting Screw (RN(Canada 4x4, Saudi Arabia), RA60, 61 RT133, RX, RU, RB, RJ)

Tighten the idle mixture adjusting screw fully and then unscrew it the following amount:

Return: 3 turns from fully closed.

Use special tool if necessary.

* Use care not to screw in too tightly and damage the screw tip.

Dash Pot [Ex.RN (Canada 4x4, Saudi Arabia), RA60, 61, RT133, RX, RU, RB, RJ]

If necessary, remove the steel plug and idle mixture adjusting screw referring to the following procedures:

1. Mark the centre of the plug with a punch.

* Plug each carburettor vacuum port to prevent entry of steel particles when drilling.

2. Drill a 6.5mm (0.256 in.) hole in the centre of the plug.

* As there is only 1mm (0.04 in.) clearance between the plug and screw, drill carefully and slowly to avoid drilling onto the screw.

3. Through the hole in the plug, fully screw in the mixture adjusting screw with a screwdriver.

* Be careful not to damage the screw tip by tightening the screw too lightly.

4. Use a 7.5 mm (0.295 in.) drill to force the plug off.

5. Blow off any steel particles with compressed air and remove the screw.

* If the drill has gnawed into the screw top or if the tapered position is damaged, replace the screw.

6. Fully screw in the idle mixture adjusting screw and then unscrew it about 2-1/2 turns.

* Be careful not to damage the screw tip by tightening the screw too tightly.

* Do not install the steel plug until the idle mixture adjustment is finished.

Idle Mixture Speed Adjustment.

In the case of the steel plug being removed, check the idle mixture speed referring to the following procedures.

1. Check the following items before adjustment:

(a) Air cleaner installe.d

(b) Normal operating coolant temperature.

(c) Choke fully open.

(d) All accessories switched off.

(e) All vacuum lines connected.

(f) Ignition timing set correctly.

(g) Transmission in N range.

(h) Fuel level should be about even with the correct level in the sight glass.

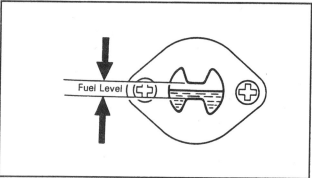

Fuel Level

2. Break the idle limiter cap on the idle speed adjusting screw if installed.

3. Start the engine and set to the maximum speed by turning the idle mixture adjusting screw.

4. Set to the idle mixture speed by turning the idle speed adjusting screw.

Idle mixture speed:

All M/T	740 rpm
USA RA, RT, RN with A/T	
(Ex. Fed. RN with 4-speed A/T)	790 rpm
Fed. RN with 4-speed A/T	740 rpm
Canada RA, RT with A/T	890 rpm
Canada RN with A/T	790 rpm

* Before moving to the next step, continue the adjustments 3 and 4 until the next maximum speed will not rise

any further no matter how much the idle mixture adjusting screw is adjusted.

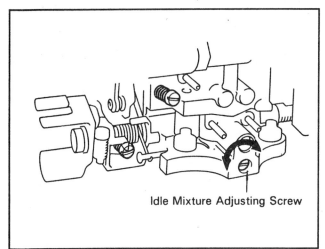

Idle Mixture Adjusting Screw

5. Set the idle speed by screwing in the idle mixture adjusting screw.

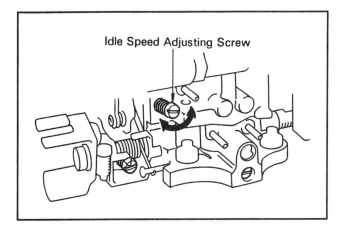

Idle Speed Adjusting Screw

Idle speed:

All M/T	700 rpm
USA RA, RT, RN, with A/T	
(Ex.Fed. RN with 4 speed A/T)	750 rpm
Fed.RN with 4 speed A/T	700 rpm
Canada RA, RT with A/T	850 rpm
Canada RN with A/T	750 rpm

* This is the "Lean Drop Method" for setting idle speed and mixture.

6. Install a new limiter cap on the idle speed adjusting screw of one was installed.

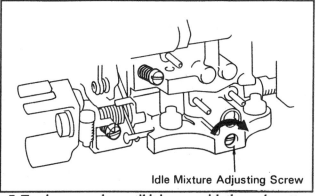

Idle Mixture Adjusting Screw

7. Tap in a new plug until it is even with the carburettor flange surface.

NOTES

LUBRICATION SYSTEMS

LUBRICATION SYSTEM.

Oil Pressure Check.

1. Check Engine Oil Quality. Check the oil for deterioration, entry of water, discolouring or thinning. If the quality is poor, replace the oil. Use API grade SC, SD, SE, SF or better and recommended viscosity oil.

2, Check Engine Oil Level. The oil level should be between the "L" & "F" marks on the level gauge. If low,

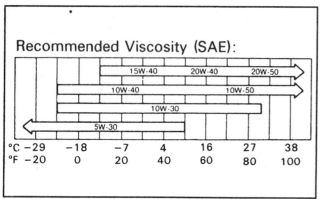

check for leakage and add oil up to the "F" mark.

3. Remove Oil Pressure Switch or Sender Gauge.

4. Install Oil Pressure Gauge.

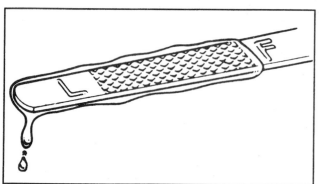

5. Start Engine and Warm Up to normal operating temperature.

6. Check Oil Pressure.

2F & 3F Oil pressure:

At idle $\quad$ 0.3kg/cm^2 (4.3 psi, 29 kPa) or more

At 4,000 rpm $\quad$ 2.5-5.0 kg/cm^2 (36-71 psi, 245-490 kPa)

* Check for oil leakage after reinstalling the oil pressure switch or sender gauge.

21R, 22R

At 4,000 rpm $\quad$ 4.5kg/cm^2 (64psi).

Oil Filter & Engine Oil

1. Drain Engine Oil.

(a) Remove the oil filler cap

(b) Remove the oil drain plug and drain the engine oil into a container.

2. Replace Oil Filter.

(a) Remove the oil filter.

(b) Check & clean the oil filter installation surface.

(c) Apply clean engine oil to the gasket of a new oil filter.

(d) Lightly screw the oil filter in by hand until you feel resistance.

(e) Tighten the oil filter an extra 3/4 turn.

3. Fill with Engine Oil.

(a) Clean and install the oil drain plug, with a new gasket. Torque the drain plug.

Torque: 400 kg-cm (29 ft-lb, 39 N·m)

(b) Fill the engine with new engine oil, API grade SC, SD SE, SF or better and recommended viscosity oil.

Capacity:

2F & 3F Drain and refill-

without oil filter change

$\qquad$ 7.0 ltrs (7.4 US qts, 6.2 Imp.qts)

with oil filter change

$\qquad$ 7.8 ltrs (8.2 US qts, 6.9 Imp.qts)

Dry fill- $\quad$ 8.0 ltrs (8.5 US qts, 7.0 Imp.qts)

21R & 21R-C Drain and refill-

with oil filter change

$\qquad$ 4.3 ltrs (4.5 US qts, 3.8 Imp.qts)

without oil filter change

$\qquad$ 3.6 ltrs (3.8 US qts, 3.2 Imp.qts)

Dry fill- $\quad$ 4.8 ltrs (5.1 US qts, 4.2 Imp qts)

22R Drain and refill-

with oil filter change

$\qquad$ 4.6 ltrs (4.9 US qts, 4.0 Imp.qts)

without oil filter change

$\qquad$ 3.8 ltrs (4.0 US qts, 3.3 Imp.qts)

Dry fill- $\quad$ 4.8 ltrs (5.1 US qts, 4.2 Imp.qts)

(c) Install the oil filler cap with the gasket.

4. Start engine and check for leaks.

5. Recheck Engine oil level.

Oil Pump 2F & 3F

Components.

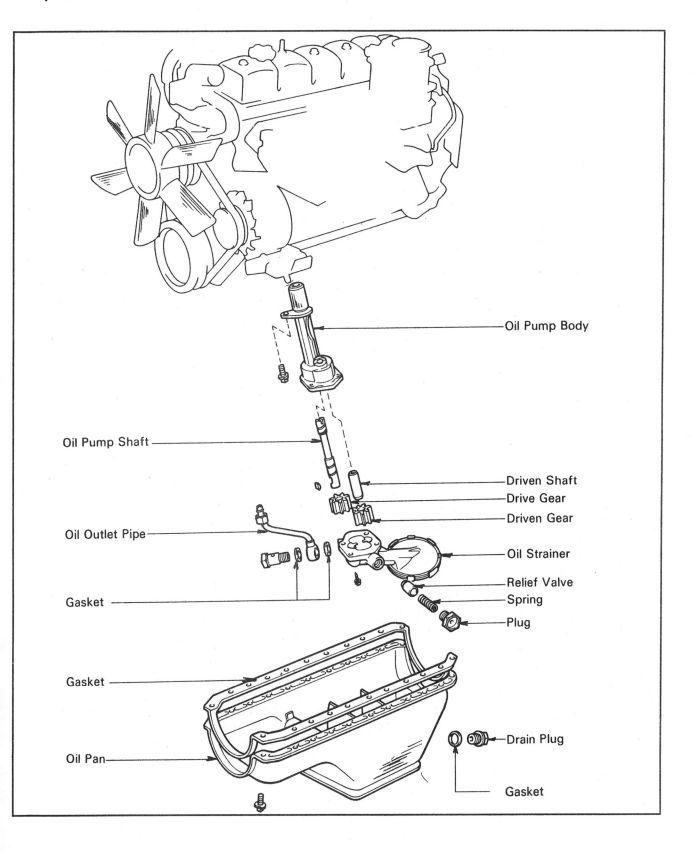

Oil Pump Body

Oil Pump Shaft

Driven Shaft
Drive Gear
Driven Gear

Oil Outlet Pipe

Oil Strainer

Relief Valve
Spring

Gasket

Plug

Gasket

Drain Plug

Oil Pan

Gasket

Removal.

* When repairing the oil pump, the oil sump and strainer should be removed and cleaned.

1. Raise Vehicle.
2. Drain Engine Oil.
3. Remove Oil Sump and gasket by taking the 22 bolts out.
4. Remove Oil Outlet Pipe, firstly take the union nut, bolt, and two gaskets out.

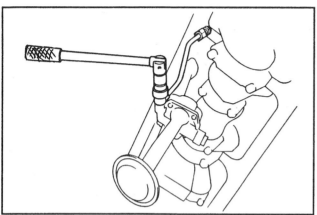

5. Remove Oil Pump by taking out the bolt.

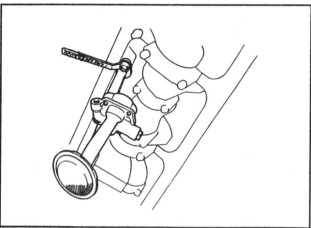

Dismantle.

1. Check Oil Pump Operation.

(a) Using a screwdriver, submerge the oil strainer in oil and rotate the oil pump shaft clockwise. Oil should come out of the oil outlet hole.

(b) Close the oil outlet hole with your thumb and turn the oil pump shaft as previously done. The shaft should be hard to turn.

2. Mount Oil Pump In Vice.
3. Remove the Plug, Spring and Relief Valve.

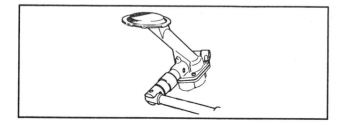

4. Remove Oil Pump Strainer by taking out the 4 screws.
5. Remove Driven Gear.
6. Remove Drive Gear and Oil Pump Shaft Assembly.

Inspection.

1. Inspect Relief Valve. Cover the valve with engine oil and make sure that it fits neatly into the valve hole.

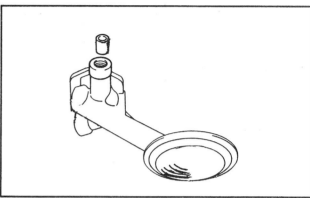

If not, replace the relief valve. If needed, replace the oil strainer.

2. Inspect Gear Body Clearance. Measure the clearance between the gear and body.

Standard body clearance:
0.095-0.175 mm (0.0037-0.0069 in.)
Maximum body clearance: 0.20 mm (0.0079 in.)

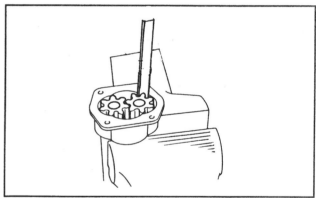

If the clearance is more than maximum, replace the shaft. If needed, replace the gears or oil pump assembly.

3. Inspect Gear Side Clearance. Measure the clearance between the gear and precision straight edge.

Standard side clearance:
0.030-0.090mm (0.0012-0.0035 in.)
Maximum side clearance: 0.15 mm (0.0059 in.)

If the clearance exceeds maximum, replace the gears. If necessary, replace the oil pump assembly.

4. Inspect Gear Backlash. Using a dial indicator, measure the backlash while turning the driven gear clockwise and anticlockwise in several places.

Standard backlash: 0.500-0.600 mm (0.0197-0.0236 in.)

Maximum backlash: 0.95 mm (0.0374 in.)

If the backlash, exceeds maximum, replace the gears. If needed, replace the shaft.

Replacement and Pump Shaft.

1. Replace Drive Gear (or oil pump shaft)

(a) Using an extension bar and press, press out the oil pump shaft from the drive gear.

(b) Line the drive gear set key up with the key groove of a new drive gear.

(c) Using a press, press in the oil pump shaft until it is 0.5 mm (0.020 in.) from the drive gear edge.

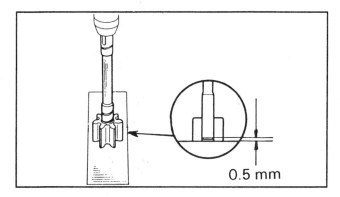

0.5 mm

2. Replace Driven Shaft.

(a) Press out the driven shaft from the oil pump body.

(b) Using a press, press in a new driven shaft until it is 0.5 mm (0.020 in.) from the oil pump body edge.

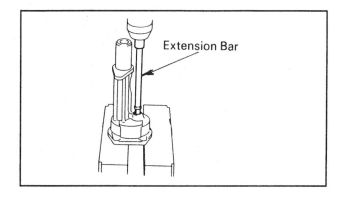

Extension Bar

Assembly.

1. Mount Oil Pump Body In Vice.

2. Install Drive Gear and Oil Pump Shaft Assembly.

3. Install Drive Gear

4. Install Oil Strainer using the 4 screws. Torque the screws.

Torque: 100 kg-cm (7ft-lb, 10 N·m)

5. Install Relief Valve and spring with the plug. Torque the plug.

Torque: 375 kg-cm (27 ft-lb, 37N·m)

6. Check Oil Pump Operation as previously described.

Installation.

1. Install Oil Pump.

(a) Line the oil pump shaft slot of the oil pump up with the governor shaft potrusion of the distributor.

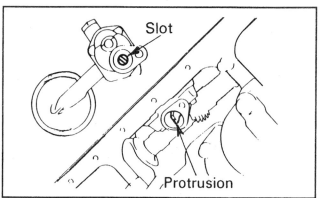

Slot

Protrusion

(b) Install the oil pump with the bolt. Torque the bolt.

Torque: 180 kg-cm (13 ft-lb, 18 N·m)

2. Install Oil Outlet Pipe.

(a) Place the outlet pipe in position.

(b) Install and torque the union bolt with the 2 gaskets.

Torque: 450kg-cm (33 ft-lb, 44 N·m)

(c) Install and torque the union nut.

Torque: 450kg-cm (33 ft-lb, 44 N·m)

3. Install Oil Sump.

(a) Apply liquid sealer to the cylinder block, the No.1 and No.4 main bearing caps as shown.

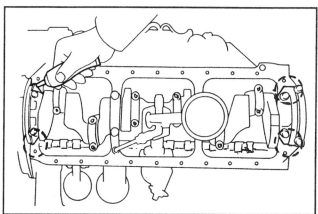

(b) Install a new gasket and the oil sump with the 22 bolts. Torque the bolts.

Torque: 80 kg-cm (69 in-lb, 7.8 N·m)

4. Fill with Engine Oil.

Oil Pump 21R, 21R-C & 22R

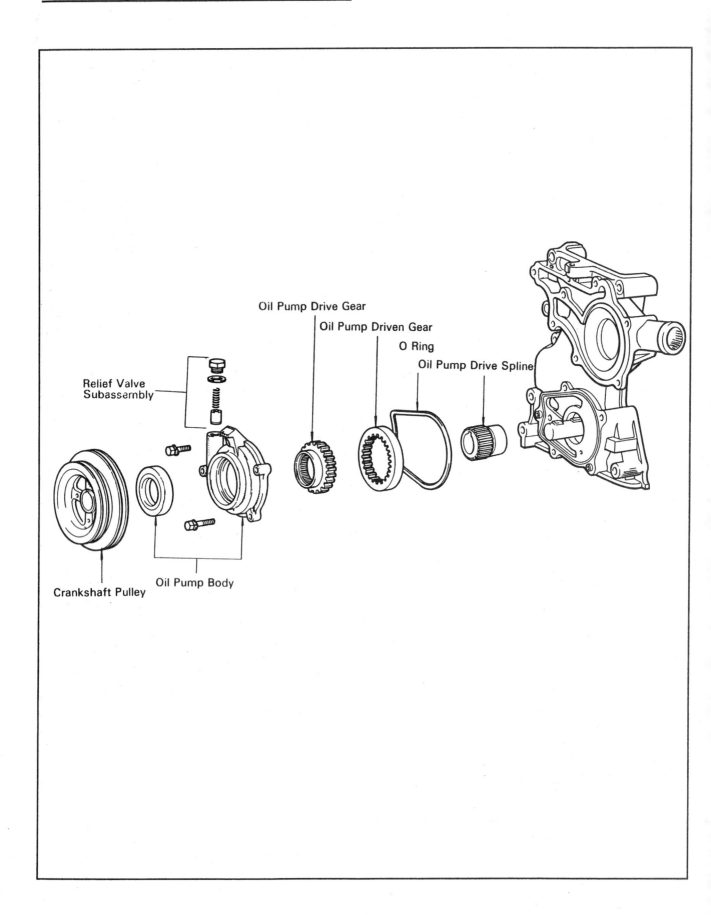

Oil Pump Drive Gear

Oil Pump Driven Gear

O Ring

Oil Pump Drive Spline

Relief Valve
Subassembly

Crankshaft Pulley

Oil Pump Body

Dismantle.

Dismantle parts in the order listed below.
1. Crankshaft Pulley.
(a) Remove the crankshaft pulley with pulley puller.
2. Oil Pump Body.
3. Oil Pump Drive Gear.
4. Oil Pump Driven Gear.
5. O Ring.
6. Oil Pump Drive Spline.
7. Relief Valve Subassembly.

Inspection & Repair.

1. Examine the dismantled parts for wear or damage.
2. Inspect the contact surfaces of the timing chain cover for wear or damage.
3. Measure the body clearance. If it exceeds the limit, replace the gear and/or body.

Body clearance:
STD 0.09-0.15 mm (0.0035-0.0059 in.)
Limit 0.20 mm (0.0079 in.)

4. Measure the tip clearance. If it exceeds the limit, replace the gears and/or body.

Tip clearance:
STD Drive 0.22-0.25 mm (0.0087-0.0098 in.)
     Driven 0.15-0.21 mm (0.0059-0.0083 in.)
Limit   0.33 mm (0.012 in.)

5. Check the relief valve for wear or scoring and see if it slides smoothly.

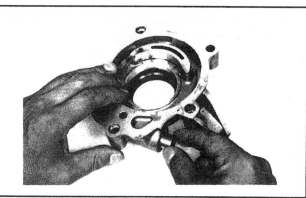

6. Replace the crankshaft front oil seal
(a) Remove the oil seal with a screwdriver.
(b) Install a new oil seal with special tool.
* Drive in the oil seal until it is about even with the oil pump body.
* Be careful not to drive it in on an angle.
* After driving in the seal, cover the seal lip lightly with Multi Purpose grease.

Assembly.

Assemble the parts in the order listed.
1. Relief Valve Subassembly.
2. Oil Pump Drive Spline.
3. O Ring.
4. Oil Pump Driven Gear.
5. Oil Pump Drive Gear.
6. Oil Pump Body.
7. Crankshaft Pulley.

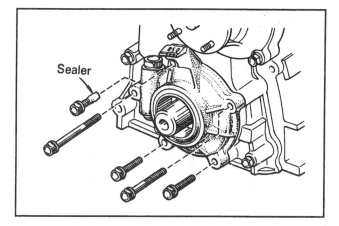

Sealer

Oil Cooler and Relief Valve.

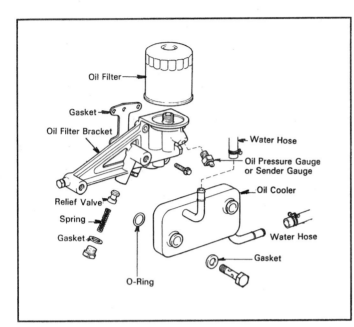

Components.

Removal of Oil Cooler and Relief Valve.
1. Drain Engine Coolant.
2. Remove Oil Filter.
3. Remove Oil Pressure Gauge or Sender Gauge.
4. Disconnect Oil Cooler Hoses.
5. Remove Oil Cooler by taking out the union bolts, gaskets and O-Rings.
6. Remove the Plug, gasket, spring and relief valve.
7. Remove the 4 bolts, oil filter bracket and gasket.

Inspection.

1. Inspect Oil Cooler for damage and sludge.
2. Inspect Relief Valve. Cover the valve with engine oil and check that it fits neatly into the valve hole. If not, replace the relief valve. If needed, replace the oil filter bracket.

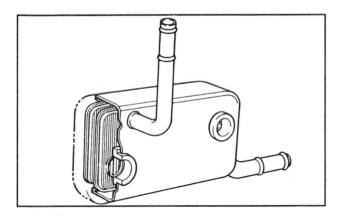

Installation.

1. Install the Oil Filter Bracket. Install a new gasket and oil filter bracket with the 4 bolts.
Torque: 185 kg-cm (13 ft-lb, 18 N·m)
2. Install the relief valve, spring, a new gasket and the plug.
3. Install Oil Cooler.
(a) Place 2 new O-Rings in position on the oil cooler.
(b) Install the oil cooler, two new gaskets and the union bolts. Torque the bolts.
Torque: 650 kg-cm (47 ft-lb, 64 N·m)
4. Connect Oil Cooler Hoses.
5. Install Oil Pressure Gauge or Sender Gauge.
6. Install Oil Filter.
7. Fill with Engine Coolant.
8. Start Engine and Check for leaks.
9. Check Engine Oil Level.

Problem Diagnosis.

Problem: Oil Leakage!
Possible Cause & Remedies:
* Cylinder head, cylinder block or oil pump body damaged or cracked. Remedy- Repair as necessary.
* Oil seal faulty. Remedy- Replace oil seal.
* Gasket faulty. Remedy- Replace gasket.

Problem: Low Oil Pressure!
Possible Cause or Remedy:
* Oil Leakage. Remedy- Repair as necessary.
* Relief valve faulty. Remedy- Repair relief valve.
* Oil Pump Faulty. Remedy-Repair oil pump.
* Engine oil poor quality. Remedy-Replace engine oil.
* Crankshaft bearing faulty. Remedy-Replace bearing.
* Connecting rod bearing faulty. Remedy-Replace bearing.
* Oil Filter clogged. Remedy-Replace oil filter.

Problem: High Oil Pressure!
Possible Cause or Remedy:
* Relief valve faulty. Remedy-Repair relief valve.

IGNITION SYSTEMS

IGNITION SYSTEM 2F & 3F ENGINES

IGNITION SYSTEMS 2F & 3F ENGINE

Precautions.

1. Do not keep the ignition switch on for more than 10 minutes if the engine does not start.

2. When a tachometer is used, connect the test probe of the tachometer to the ignition coil negative (-) terminal.

3. It is recommended that you consult with the manufacturer before using a tachometer as some are not compatible with this system.

4. NEVER allow the ignition coil terminals to touch ground as it could result in damage to the ignition coil.

5. Do not disconnect the battery while the engine is running. Make sure that the igniter is properly grounded to the body.

In Vehicle Inspection.

Spark Test.

* Perform this test to check that there is voltage from the distributor to each spark plug.

Crank Engine and Check that Light Flashes. Connect a timing light to the spark plug. If the timing light does not flash, check the wiring connections, ignition coil and distributor.

High Tension Leads.

1. Carefully Remove High-Tension Leads by Rubber Boot from Spark Plugs.

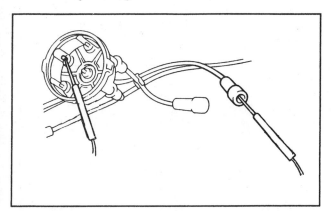

* Pulling on or bending the cords may damage the conductor inside.

2. Inspect High-Tension Leads Resistance. Using a ohmmeter, measure the resistance without disconnecting the cap.

Maximum resistance: 25 k ohms per cord.

If resistance, exceeds maximum, examine the terminals. If needed, replace the high-tension cord and/or distibutor cap.

Spark Plugs.

1. Clean Spark Plugs.

2. Visually Examine Spark Plugs. Check the spark plug for electrode wear, thread damage and insulator damage. If abnormal replace the plugs.

Recommended spark plugs:
ND   W14EX-U
NGK   BP4EY

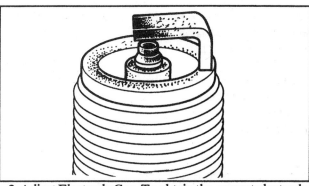

3. Adjust Electrode Cap. To obtain the correct electrode gap carefully bend the outer electrode.

Correct electrode gap: 0.8 mm (0.031 in.)

4. Install Spark Plugs.

Torque: 180 kg-cm (13 ft-lb, 18N`m)

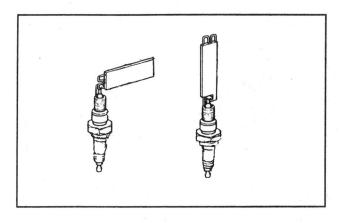

Ignition Coil [with Internal Resistor].

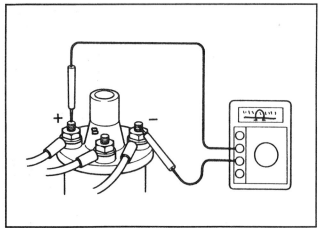

1. Check Primary Coil Resistance. Using an ohmmeter, measure the resistance between the + and - terminals.

Primary coil resistance (cold): 1.5-1.9 ohms.

2. Check Secondary Coil Resistance. Using an ohmmeter, measure the resistance between the B terminal and the high-tension terminal.

Secondary coil resistance (cold): 13.7-18.5 k ohms.

3. Inspect Resistor Resistance. Using a ohmmeter, measure the resistance between the B and + terminals.

Resistor resistance (cold): 0.9-1.2 ohms.

4. Inspect Power Source Line.

(a) With the ignition switch at ON and using a voltmeter, connect the positive (+) probe to the B terminal and the negative (-) probe to body ground.

Voltage: Approx. 12V

(b) With the ignition switch at "Start" and using a voltmeter, connect the positive (+) probe to the + terminal and the negative (-) probe to body ground.

Voltage: Approx. 12V

If abnormal, check the ignition switch and wire harness.

Ignition Coil [With External Resistor].

1. Disconnect High-Tension Leads.

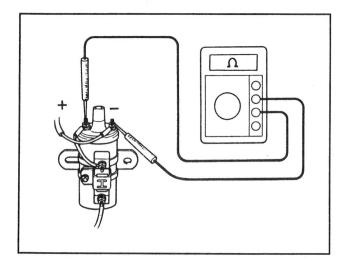

2. Inspect Primary Coil Resistance. Using an ohmmeter, measure the resistance between the + and - terminals.

Primary coil resistance (cold): 1.3-1.6 ohms.

3. Inspect Secondary Coil Resistance. Using an ohmmeter, measure the resistance between the + terminal and high tension terminal.

Secondary coil resistance (cold): 10.7-14.5 k ohms.

4. Examine Resistor Resistance. Using an ohmmeter, measure the resistance between resistor terminals.

Resistor resistance (cold): 1.3-1.5 ohms

5. Inspect Power Source Line.

(a) With the ignition switch at "on" and using a voltmeter, connect the positive (+) probe to the + terminal of the resistor and the negative (-) probe to body ground.

Voltage: Approx. 12V

(b) With the ignition switch at Start and using a voltmeter, connect the positive (+) probe to the + terminal of ignition coil and the negative (-) probe to body ground.

Voltage: Approx. 12V

If abnormal, check the ignition switch and wire harness.

Distributor.

1. Examine Breaker Point. Using a feeler gauge, measure the gap between the cam and rubbing block.

Rubbing block gap: 0.3 mm (0.012 in.)

If the gap is not within specification, adjust the gap as described under Assembly of Distributor.

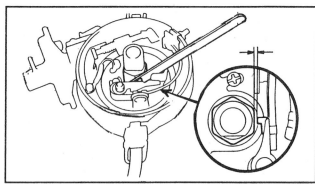

2. Inspect Vacuum Advance.

(a) Disconnect the vacuum hose and connect a vacuum pump to the vacuum advancer.

(b) Apply vacuum and check that the vacuum advancer moves.

If the vacuum advancer does not work, repair or replace as needed.

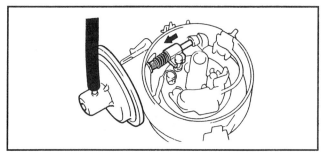

3. Examine Governor Advance.

(a) Turn the rotor clockwise, release it and check that the rotor returns quickly anticlockwise.

(b) Check that the rotor is not excessively loose.

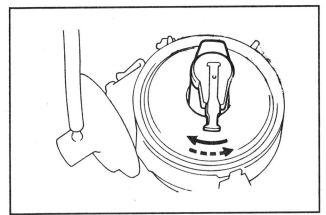

4. (with antioverrun) Inspect Rotor.

Check that the rotor weigh moves smoothly. If abnormal, replace the rotor.

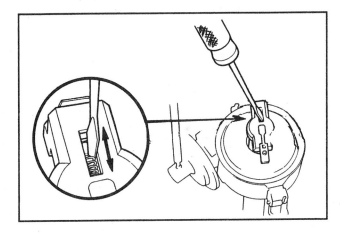

Distributor [with Octane Selector 6 Cylinder]

Dismantle

1. Remove Distributor Cap Without Disconnecting High-Tension Cords.

2. Remove Rotor & Dust Cover.

3. Remove Distributor Wire. Remove the nut, spring washer, distributor wire, plate washer and No.2 insulator.

Components.

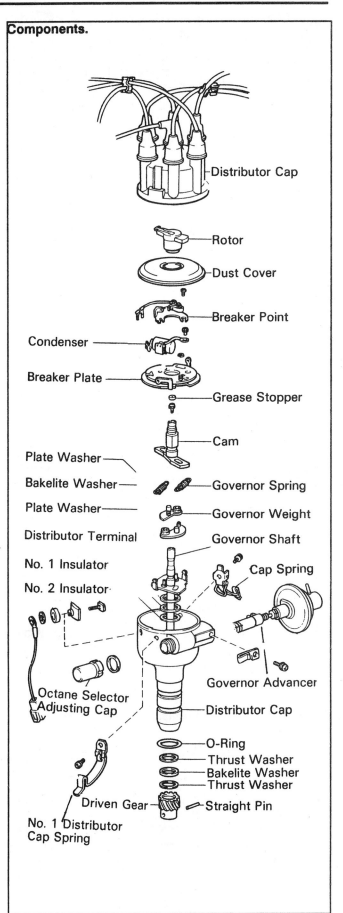

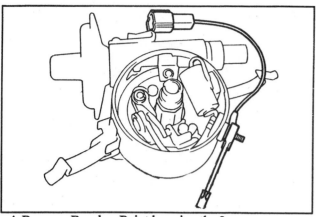

4. Remove Breaker Point by using the 2 screws.

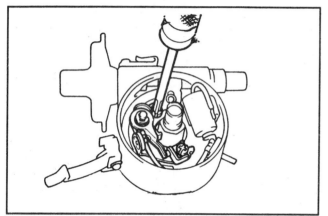

5. Remove Condenser (1 screw with distributor cap inside & 1 screw inside distributor).

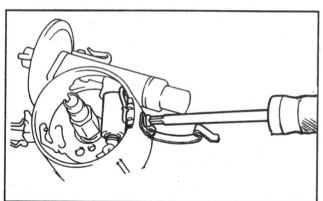

6. Remove Distributor Terminal and No.1 Insulator.

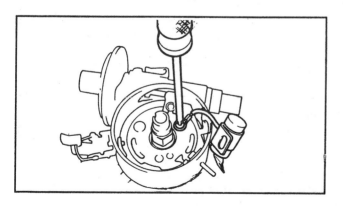

7. Remove Vacuum Advancer.
(a) Remove the screw and clamp.
(b) Pull out the vacuum advancer.

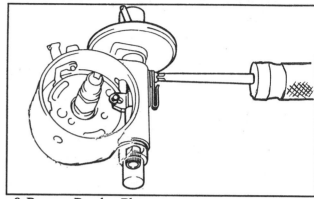

8. Remove Breaker Plate.
(a) Remove the screw and No.2 distributor cap spring.
(b) Pull out the breaker plate.

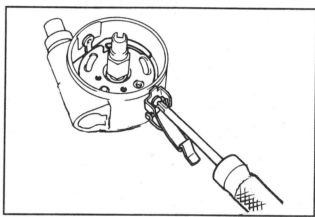

9. Remove Cam.
(a) Remove the grease stopper.
(b) Take the screw out at the end of the governor shaft.
(c) Pull the cam out.

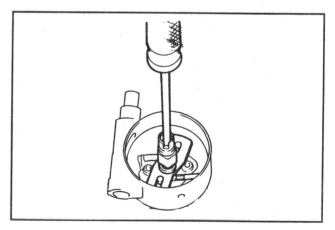

10.Remove Governor Springs.

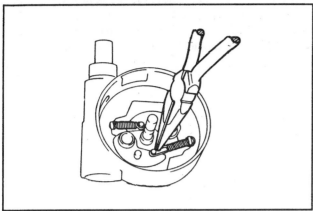

11.Remove Governor Weights.

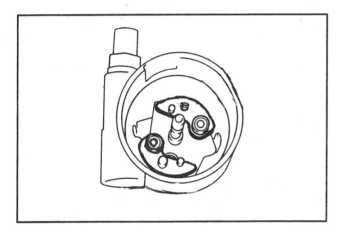

Inspection of Distributor.

1. Inspect Breaker Plate. Turn the breaker plate and check that it has a slight drag. If it sticks or strongly resists, replace the breaker plate.

2. Inspect Governor Shaft.

(a) Turn the governor shaft and check that it is not rough or worn. If it feels rough or worn , replace it.

(b) Using a feeler gauge, measure the governor shaft thrust clearance.

Thrust clearance: 0.15-0.50 mm(0.0059-0.0197 in.)

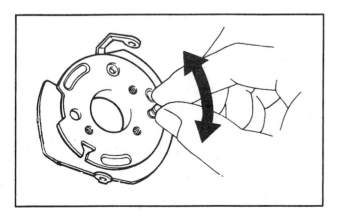

If the thrust clearance is not within specification, increasing or decreasing the number of the thrust washers to adjust.

3. Inspect Cam. Install the cam to the governor shaft and ensure that they fit correctly. If they dont fit, replace the cam and/or governor shaft.

Replacement of Governor Shaft & Drive Gear.

1. Remove Drive Gear.

(a) Using a grinder, grind the drive gear and straight pin.

* Be careful not to damage the governor shaft.

(b) Mount the drive gear in a vice.

(c) Using a pin punch and hammer, tap out the straight pin.

(d) Remove the drive gear, thrust washers and bakelite washer.

2. Remove Governor Shaft. Remove the governor shaft, plate washers and bakelite washer.

3. Install New Governor Shaft.

(a) Lightly coat the governor shaft with high temperature grease.

(b) Slide the upper plate washer, bakelite washer and lower plate washer onto the governor shaft.

(c) Push the governor shaft into the housing.

4. Install New Drive Gear.

(a) Slide the thrust washer, bakelite washer, thrust washer and driven gear onto the governor shaft.

(b) Install a new straight pin.

(c) Examine the governor shaft thrust clearance.(Item 2)

Thrust clearance: 0.15-0.50mm(0.0059-0.0197 in.)

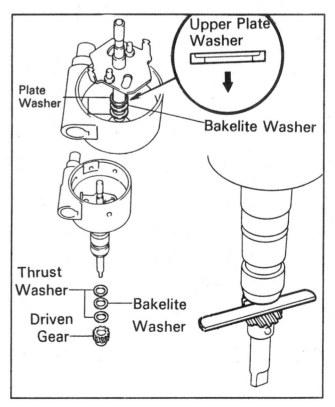

Assembly.

1. Install Governor Weights
(a) Lightly coat the pivot pin of governor shaft with high-temperature grease.
(b) Install the 2 governor weights.
2. Install Governor Springs.
3. Install Cam.
(a) Coat the governor shaft lightly with high-temperature grease.
(b) Install the cam on the governor shaft as shown.

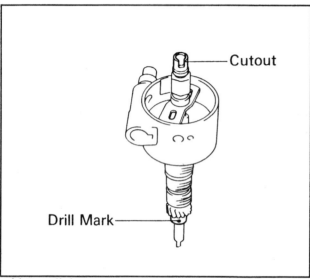

(c) Install the screws.
(d) Pack high-temperature grease into the shaft.
(e) Push the grease stopper on.
4. Install Breaker Plate & No.2 distributor cap spring with the screw.
5. Install Vacuum Advancer.
(a) Install the E-Clip to the pivot pin of the breaker plate.
(b) Put the vacuum advancer into the housing, connecting the pivot pin to pivot.
(c) Using a screw, install the clamp.

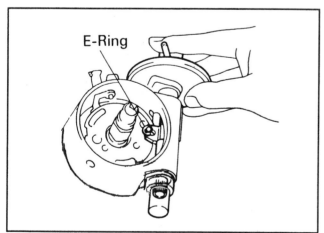

6. Install No.1 Insulator and Distributor Terminal.
7. Install Condenser.

8. Install and Adjust Breaker Point.
(a) Clean the contact surfaces of the points with a piece of cloth covered in solvent.
(b) Apply high-temperature grease to the rubbing block.
(c) Using the 2 screws loosely install the breaker point.
(d) Using a feeler gauge, adjust the gap between the cam and rubbing block.
Rubbing block gap: 0.3 mm (0.012 in.)

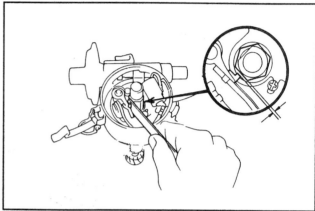

9. Install Distributor Wire.
(a) Install the No.2 insulator and plate washer.
(b) Connect the lead wires of the breaker point and distributor.
10. Install New O-Ring.
(a) Lightly coat the O-Ring with engine oil.
(b) Install the O-Ring onto the housing.

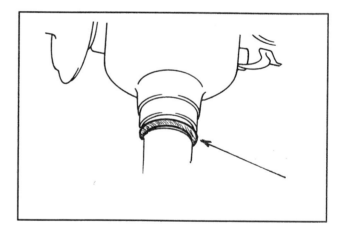

Installation.

1. Set No.1 Cylinder to TDC/Compression.
Set to TDC/Compression in the following way:
(a) Remove the No.1 spark plug.
(b) Place your finger over the hole of the No.1 spark plug and rotate the crankshaft clockwise to TDC. if pressure is felt on your finger, this is TDC/compression of the No.1 cylinder. If not, repeat the process.
(c) Install the No.1 spark plug.

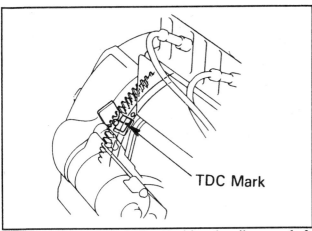

TDC Mark

2. Set Oil Pump Shaft Slot. Position the oil pump shaft slot in the direction shown.

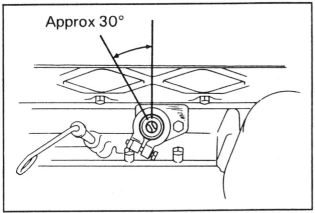

Approx 30°

3. Set Octane Selector.
(a) Remove the adjusting cap.
(b) Set the octane selector at the standard line.
(c) Install the adjusting cap.

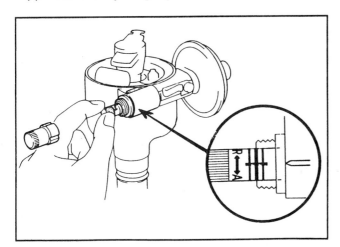

4. Install Distributor.
(a) Start installation of the distributor with the rotor pointing as displayed in the diagram.

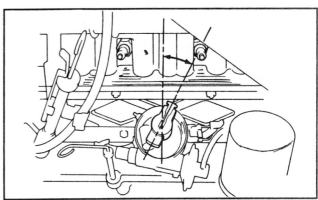

(b) When fully fitted, the distributor should point as displayed in the diagram.

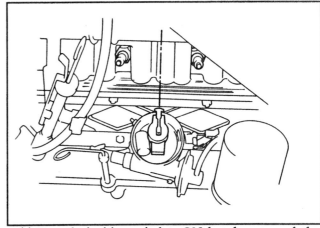

(c) Turn the ignition switch to ON, but do not crank the starter motor.
(d) Turn the distributor body anti-clockwise until a spark jumps between the points and tighten the clamp bolt in that position.

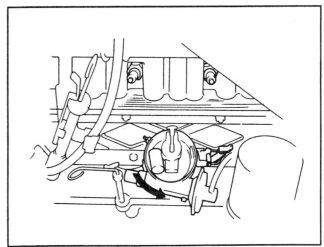

5. Install Dust Cover, Rotor and Distributor Cap with High-Tension Leads.
6. Connect High Tension Leads.
7. Connect Distributor Connector and Vacuum Hose.
8. Adjust Ignition Timing.

Distributor [without Octane Selector 6 Cylinder]

Components

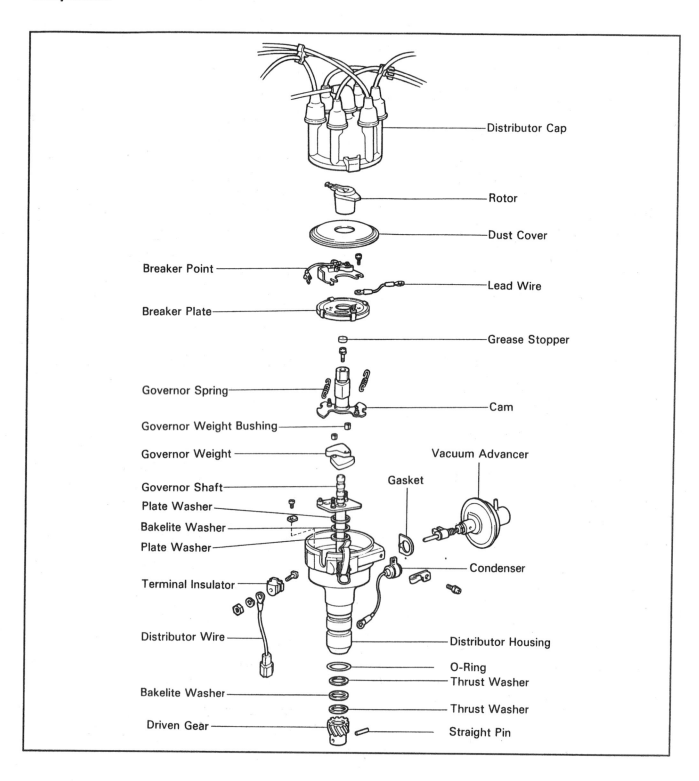

Distributor Cap

Rotor

Dust Cover

Breaker Point

Lead Wire

Breaker Plate

Grease Stopper

Governor Spring

Cam

Governor Weight Bushing

Governor Weight

Vacuum Advancer

Governor Shaft

Gasket

Plate Washer

Bakelite Washer

Plate Washer

Condenser

Terminal Insulator

Distributor Wire

Distributor Housing

O-Ring

Thrust Washer

Bakelite Washer

Thrust Washer

Driven Gear

Straight Pin

Dismantle

1. Remove Distributor Cap without Disconnecting High-Tension Leads.

2. Remove Rotor and Dust Cover.

3. Remove Distributor Terminal.

(a) Remove the nut, spring washer and distributor wire.

(b) Disconnect the lead wires of the condenser and breaker point.

(c) Remove the terminal and insulator.

4. Remove Breaker Point by unscrewing the 2 screws.

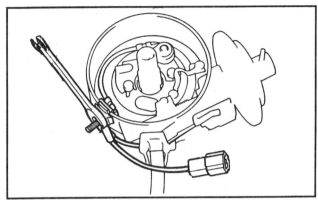

5. Remove Vacuum Advancer.

(a) Remove the screw, clamp and condenser.

(b) Pull the vacuum advancer out.

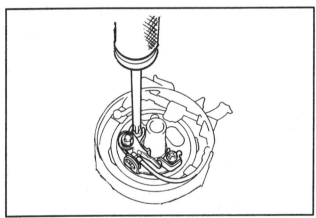

6. Remove Breaker Plate.

(a) Remove the screw and disconnect the lead wire from the breaker plate.

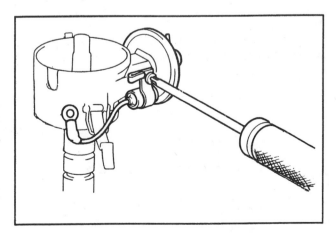

(b) Remove the 2 screws, plate washers and lead wire.

(c) Pull out the breaker plate.

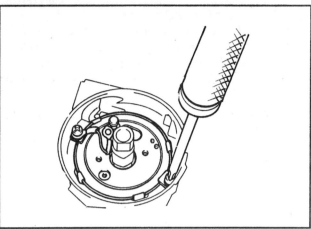

7. Remove Governor Spring. Remove the 2 springs using needle-nose pliers.

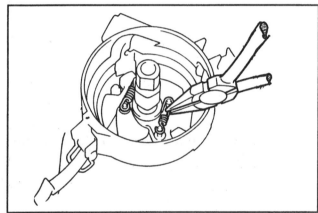

8. Remove Cam.

(a) Remove the grease stopper.

(b) Remove the screw at the end of the governor shaft.

(c) Pull the cam out.

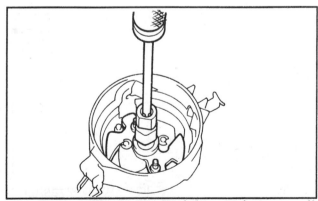

9. Remove Governor Weights. Using a small screwdriver, remove the E-Clips and pull out the weight and bushing. Remove the 2 weights.

Inspection.

1. Inspect Breaker Plate. Rotate the breaker plate and ensure that it has a slight drag. If it sticks or strongly resists, replace the breaker plate.

2. Inspect the Governor Shaft.

(a) Turn the governor shaft and check that it is not rough or worn. If necessary, replace the governor shaft.

(b) Using, a feeler gauge, measure the governor shaft thrust clearance.

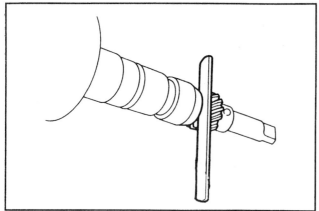

Thrust clearance: 0.15-0.50 mm (0.0059-0.0197 in.)

If the thrust clearance is not within specification, adjust by increasing or decreasing the number of the thrust washers.

3. Inspect Cam. Install the cam to the governor shaft and ensure that they fit correctly. If they dont fit, replace the cam and/or governor shaft.

Replacement of Governor Shaft and Drive Gear.

1. Remove Drive Gear.

(a) Using a grinder, grind the drive gear and straight pin.

* Be careful not to damage the governor shaft.

(b) Mount the drive gear in a vice.

(c) Using a pin punch and hammer, tap out the straight pin.

(d) Remove the drive gear, plate washers and bakelite washer.

2. Remove Governor Shaft, thrust washers and bakelite washer.

3. Install New Governor Shaft.

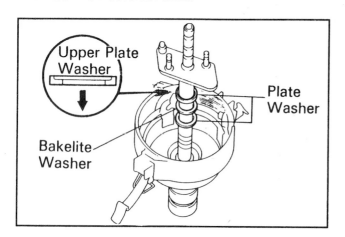

(a) Lightly coat the governor shaft with high temperature grease.

(b) Slide the upper plate washer, bakelite washer and lower plate washer onto the governor shaft.

(c) Push the governor shaft into the housing.

4. Install New Driven Gear.

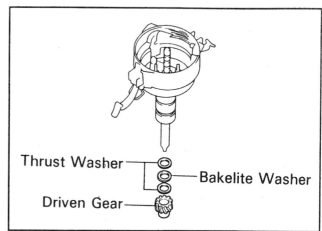

(a) Slide the thrust washer, bakelite washer, thrust washer and driven gear onto the governor shaft.

(b) Position the drill mark on the driven gear and stopper pin as shown.

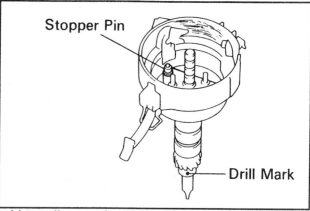

(c) Install a new pin.

(d) Check the governor shaft thrust clearance (Item 2)

Thrust clearance: 0.15-0.50mm(0.0059-0.0197 in.)

Assembly.

1. Install Governor Weights. Install the bushing and weight with the E-Clip using needle-nose pliers. Install the two weights.

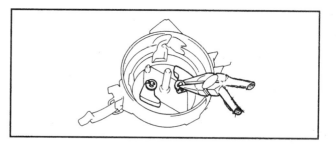

2. Install Cam.

(a) Lightly coat the governor shaft with high-temperature grease.

(b) Install the cam on the governor shaft. as in diagram.

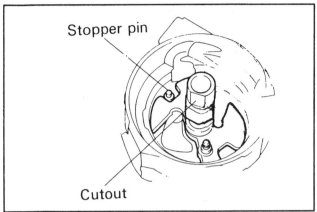

(c) Install the screw.

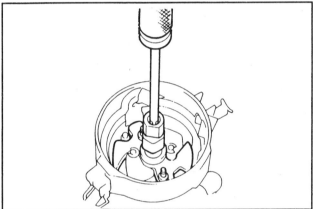

(d) Pack high-temperature grease into the cam.

(e) Push on the grease stopper.

3. Install Governor Springs.

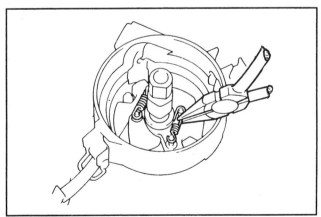

4. Install Breaker Plate.

(a) Line up the 4 clips on the breaker plate with the cutout parts of the housing and insert the breaker plate.

(b) Install the 2 plate washers, lead wire and 2 screws as shown in diagram.

(c) Connect the lead wire with the screw.

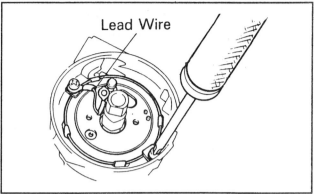

5. Install Vacuum Advance Unit.

(a) Install a new gasket to the advancer.

(b) Insert the vacuum advancer into the housing connecting the pivot pin to the pivot.

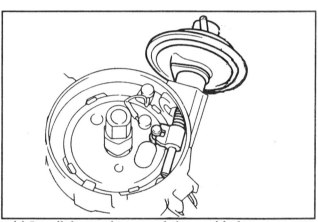

(c) Install the condenser and clamp with the screw.

6. Install and Adjust Breaker Point.

(a) Clean the contact surfaces of the points with a piece of cloth soaked in solvent.

(b) Apply high-temperature grease to the rubbing block.

(c) Install the breaker point loosely with the 2 screws.

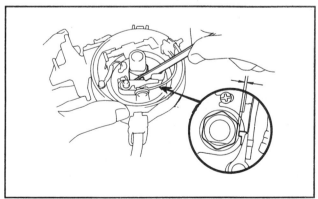

(d) Using a feeler gauge, adjust the gap between the cam and rubbing block.

Rubbing block gap: 0.3 mm (0.012 in.)

7. Install Distributor Terminal.

(a) Install the insulator and terminal to the housing.

(b) Connect the lead wires of the breaker point A, condenser B and distributor C to the terminal.

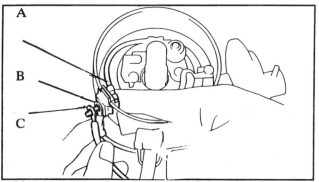

(c) Install the spring washer and nut.

8. Install New O-Ring to Distributor Shaft.

Installation.

1. Set No.1 Cylinder to TDC/Compression.

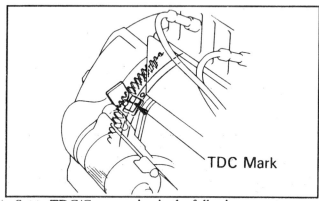

TDC Mark

Set to TDC/Compression in the following way:

(a) Remove the No.1 spark plug.

(b) Place your finger over the hole of the No.1 spark plug and turn the crankshaft clockwise to TDC. If pressure is felt on your finger, this is TDC/Compression of the No.1 cylinder. If not, repeat the process.

(c) Install the No.1 spark plug.

2. Set Oil Pump Shaft Slot. Place the oil pump shaft slot in the direction shown in the diagram.

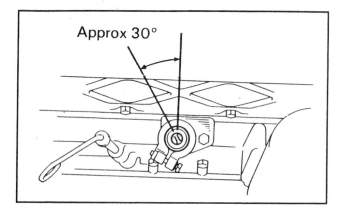

Approx 30°

3. Install Distributor.

(a) Begin installation of the distributor with the rotor pointing as shown in the diagram.

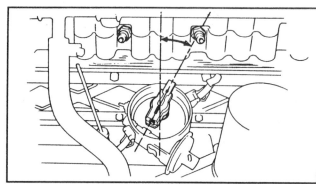

(b) When fully installed, the distributor should point as shown in the diagram.

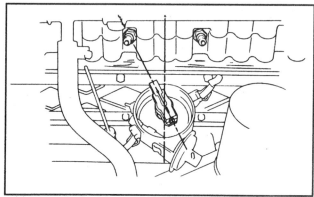

(c) Turn the ignition switch to "on", but do not crank the starter motor.

(d) Rotate the distributor body anticlockwise until a spark jumps between the points and tighten the clamp bolt in that position.

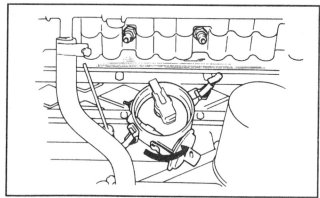

4. Install Dust Cover, Rotor and Distributor Cap with High Tension Leads.

5. Connect the High Tension Leads.

6. Connect Distributor Connector & Vacuum Hose.

7. Adjust Ignition Timing.

IGNITION SYSTEM 21R, 21R-C & 22R ENGINE

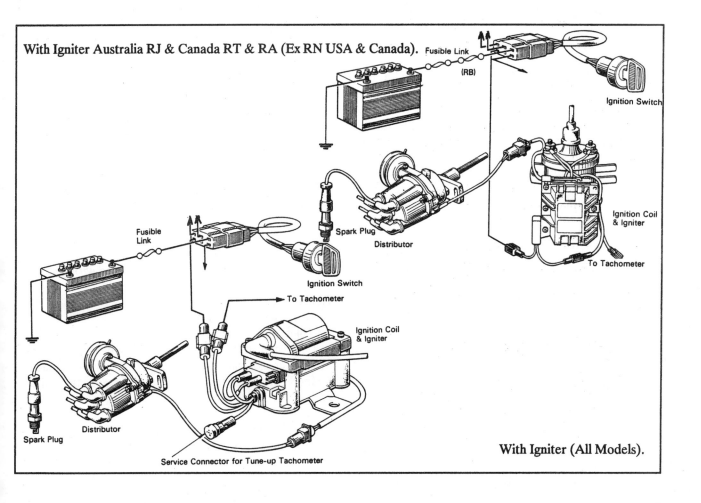

With Igniter Australia RJ & Canada RT & RA (Ex RN USA & Canada).

With Igniter (All Models).

Without Igniter.

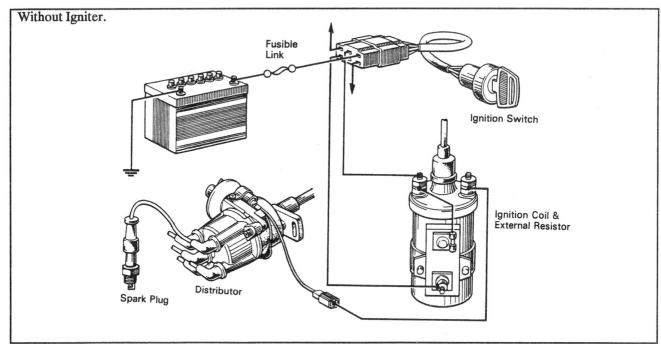

In Vehicle Inspection.

Precautions.

1. For the vehicles equipped with an igniter, take note of the following items:

(a) Do not keep the ignition switch "on" for more than 10 minutes if the engine will not start.

(b) As some tachometers are not compatible with this ignition system, it is recommended that you consult with the manufacturer.

(c) NEVER allow the ignition coil terminals to touch ground as it could result in damage to the igniter and/or ignition coil.

(d) Do not disconnect the battery when the engine is running.

(e) Make sure that the igniter is properly grounded to the body.

(f) When a tachometer is connected to the system:

For Ex.RN (USA & Canada), Canada (RT,RA) & Australia RJ (Since '85/10), connect the tachometer (+) terminal to the ignition coil (-) terminal.

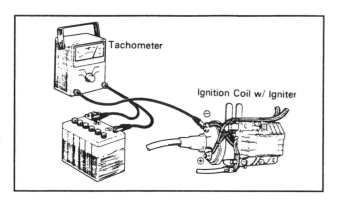

For RN (USA & Canada), Canada (RT,RA) & Australia RJ (Since '85/10), the service wiring connector covered with a rubber cap should be used only for the engine tune-up tachometer.

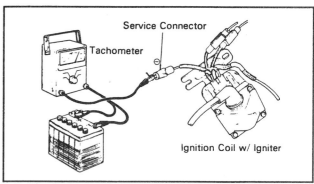

2. Check the spark. Pull the distributor resistive cord, connected to the ignition coil, from the distributor and hold its end close to a ground. Then start the engine and check for spark.

* The check must be made within as short a time as possible.

3. Connector. Examine the connector and wiring.

Resistor.

1. Turn the ignition switch to"on".

2. Check the power source line voltage.

(a) Disconnect the wiring connector brown & yellow.

(b) Connect a voltmeter (+) lead to the brown connecter for the wire harness side, and the (-) lead to the igniter body.

Voltage: Approx. , ^ eY,

3. Check the power transistor "off" condition.

(a) Connect the wiring connector for brown.

(b) Connect a voltmeter (+) lead to the yellow connector for igniter side, and the (-) lead to the igniter body.
Voltage: Approx. 12V

4. Check the power transistor "on" condition.

(a) Disconnect the wiring connector from the distributor.

(b) Using a dry cell battery (1.5V), connect the positive pole to the pink wire terminal and the negative pole to the white wire terminal.

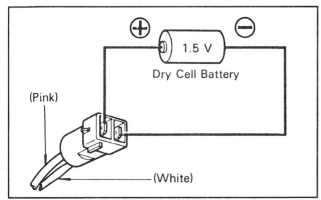

Dry Cell Battery

(Pink)

(White)

* The check must be made within 5 seconds.

(c) Connect a voltmeter (+) lead to the yellow connector for igniter side, and the (-) lead to the igniter body.
Voltage: 5V-less than battery voltage.

Ingition Coil [with Igniter] Australia RJ & Canada RT & RA (Ex RN USA & Canada).

Check the ignition coil resistance with an ohmmeter.

1. Primary coil resistance between the positive and negative terminals.

      Resistance: .8 - 1.1 ohm

2. Secondary coil resistance between the Positive terminal and high tension terminal.

      Resistanxe   10.7 - 14.5 k ohm

Ignition Coil. [With Igniter] All Models.

Check the ignition coil resistance with an ohmmeter.

1. Primary coil resistance: between the (+)(Brown side)and(-)

(Black side) terminal.

Resistance: 0.4-0.5 ohms

2. Secondary coil resistance: between the (+) terminal(Brown side) and high tension terminal.

Resistance: 8.5-11.5 k ohms.

Ignition Coil without Igniter.

Check the ignition coil resistance with an ohmmeter.

1. Primary coil resistance: between the (+) and (-) terminals.

Resistance: 1.2-1.5 ohms

2. Secondary coil resistance: between the (+) terminal and high tension terminal.

Resistance: 8.5-11.5 k ohms.

Resistor (without Igniter)

Check the resistor resistance with an ohmmeter.
Resistance: 1.3-1.5 ohms.

Distributor.

1. Check the governor. Turn the rotor clockwise and release it. The rotor should return smoothly to its original position.

2. Check the vacuum advancer operation. Disconnect the vacuum hose and connect a vacuum pump to the diaphragm. Apply vacuum and ensure that the advance moves.

3. Inspect the air gap.(Breaker points less type.) Examine the air gap between the signal rotor and signal generator projection with a thickness gauge.

  Air gap: 0.2-0.4 mm (0.008-0.016 in.)

4. Check the rubbing block gap and damping spring gap. (Breaker points type.)

  Rubbing block gap: 0.45 mm (0.0177 in.)

  Damping spring gap: 0.1-0.4 mm (0.004-0.016 in.)

5. Check the signal generator.(22R) Check the resis-

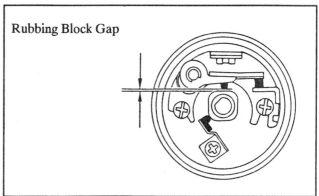

Rubbing Block Gap

tance of the signal generator with an ohmmeter.
  Resistance: 130-190 ohms.

Spark Plug Gap.

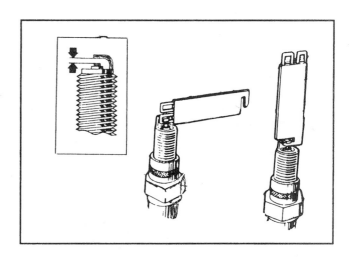

Distributor.

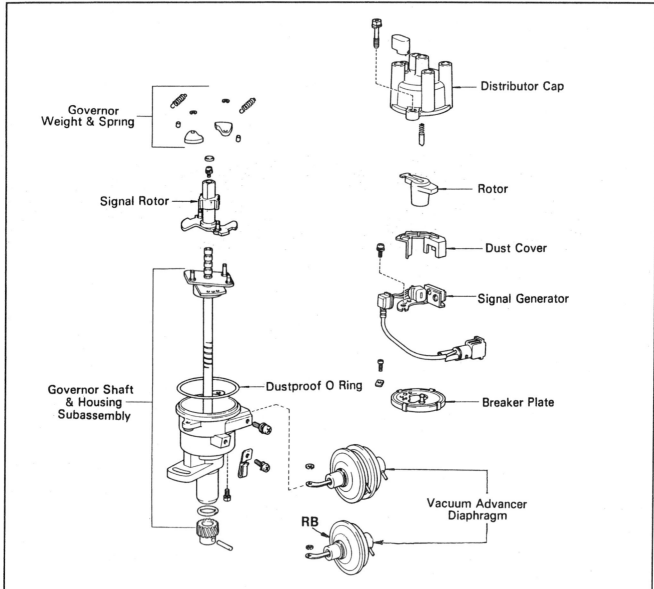

- Distributor Cap
- Rotor
- Dust Cover
- Signal Generator
- Breaker Plate
- Vacuum Advancer Diaphragm
- Governor Weight & Spring
- Signal Rotor
- Governor Shaft & Housing Subassembly
- Dustproof O Ring
- RB

DISMANTLE.

1. Dismantle the parts in the order listed.
1. Distributor Cap.
2. Rotor.
3. Dustproof Cover.
4. Gasket.
5. Terminal.
6. Breaker Point.
7. Damping Spring.
8. Vacuum Advancer & Condenser.
9. Breaker Plate.
10. Governor Weight & Spring.
11. Cam.
12. Governor Shaft & Housing Subassembly.

2. Dismantle the parts in the order listed.
1. Distributor Cap.
2. Rotor.
3. Dustproof O Ring.
4. Dust Cover.
5. Signal Generator.
6. Vacuum Advancer Diaphragm.
7. Breaker Plate.
8. Governor Weight & Spring.
9. Signal Rotor.
10. Governor Shaft & Housing Subassembly.

INSPECTION & REPAIR.

Cap.

Check for cracks, carbon tracks, burnt or corroded terminals and check the centre contact for wear.

Rotor.

Inspect for cracks, carbon tracks, burnt or corroded terminals.

Breaker Plate.

Check for smooth turning.

Cam & Shaft.

(a) Check the cam for wear or damage.
(b) Examine the fit between the cam & shaft.

Governor Weight & Pin.

(a) Turn the governor weight to check for binding.
(b) Inspect the governor weights and bearings for wear or damage.

Governor Shaft & Housing.

1. Make sure that the governor shaft turns smoothly. If needed, disassemble.
2. Disassemble the governor shaft.
(a) Scrape the peened end of the pin with a grinder and drive out the pin.

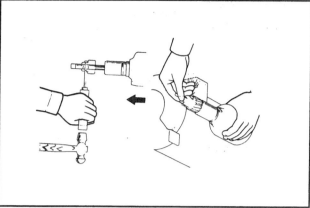

(b) Remove the 2 screw and drive out the governor shaft.
(c) Check the governor shaft for wear or damage.

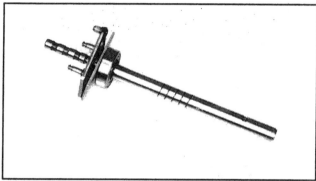

(d) Inspect the bearing for wear, sticking or damage.
(e) Examine the needle roller bearing, washers and spring for sticking, scoring or damage (21R, 21R-C).
(f) Check the housing, bushing and O ring for wear, deformation or damage.
(g) Arrange the spring, bearing and washers as displayed in the diagram.

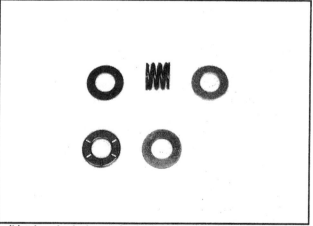

(h) Line the holes up in the bearing retainer and housing and install the 2 screws.
(i) Peen both ends with a vice.

ASSEMBLY.

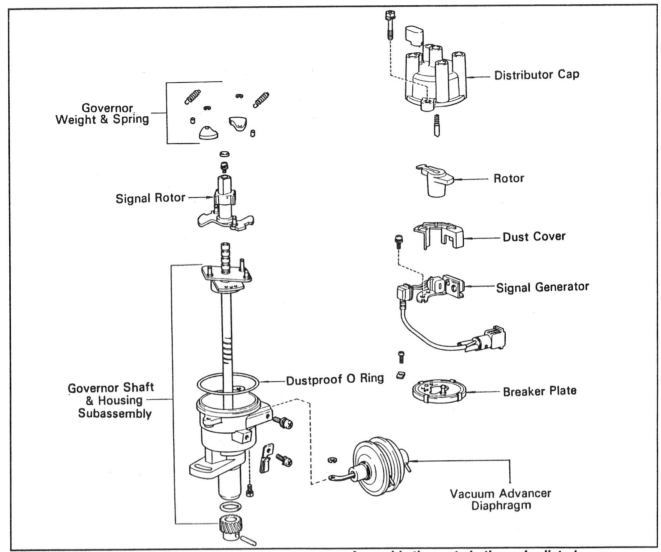

Assemble the parts in the order listed.

1. Governor Shaft & Housing Subassembly.
2. Cam.
3. Governor Weight & Spring.
4. Breaker Plate.
5. Vacuum Advancer & Condenser.
6. Damping Spring.
7. Breaker Point.
8. Terminal.
9. Gasket.
10. Dustproof Cover.
11. Rotor.
12. Distributor Cap.

Assemble the parts in the order listed.

1. Governor Shaft & Housing Subassembly.
2. Signal Rotor.
(a) Match the mark (12 for 22R/14.5 for 21R and 21R-C) with the stopper and fit on the cam.
3. Governor Weight & Spring.
(a) Install the bearing into the pin hole.
(b) Be sure the E-Clip is installed in the groove correctly.
(c) Ensure the governor spring is installed correctly,
4. Breaker Plate.
5. Vacuum Advancer Diaphragm.
(a) Be sure the E-Clip is installed in the breaker plate correctly.
6. Signal Generator.
7. Dust Cover.
8. Dustproof O Ring.
9. Rotor.
10. Distributor.

ADJUSTMENTS.

* Adjust the air gap. (Breaker points less type)
Air gap: 0.2-0.4 mm (0.008-0.016 in.)

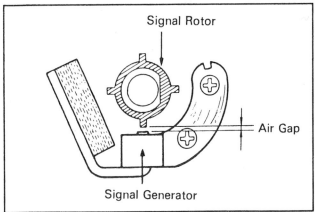

* Adjust the rubbing block gap and damping spring gap (Breaker points type)

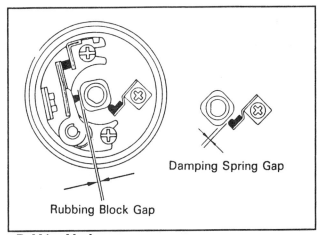

Rubbing block gap:
0.45 mm (0.018 in.)
Damping Spring gap:
0.1-0.4 mm (0.004-0.016 in.)

INSTALLATION.

1. Set the No.1 cylinder to the ignition timing position.

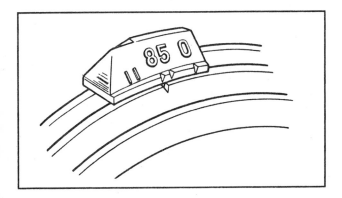

2. Begin insertion of the distributor with the rotor pointing to the vacuum advancer setting screw and the distributor mounting hole approximately at centre position of the bolt hole.

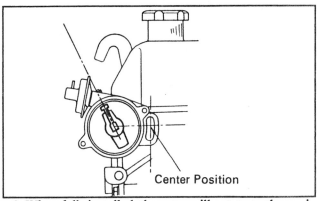

3. When fully installed, the rotor will rotate to the position shown in the diagram.

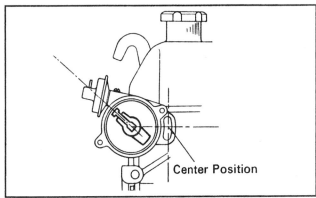

4. Align the rotor tooth with the signal generator, and tighten the clamp bolt in that position.

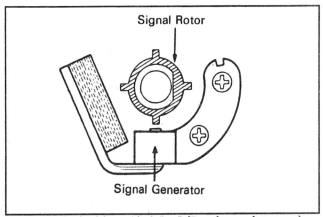

5. Turn the ignition switch "on" (Breaker points type)
* Do not turn the starter motor.
6. Turn the distributor body anticlockwise until a spark jumps between the points, and tighten the clamp bolt in that position.

7. Check that ignition timing at idle speed.

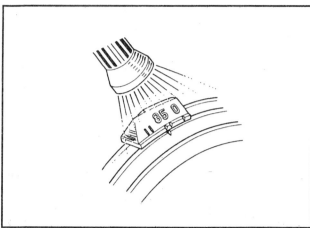

21R

5°   BTDC/Max. 750rpm, RA (Since '83/8), RX70,
8°   BTDC/Max. 750rpm, RA (Before '83/8)
     RX60 (Ex. South Africa)
12°   BTDC/Max.750rpm, RX60 (South Africa)

21R-C

*5°   BTDC/Max.600rpm Australia M/T
*5°   BTDC/Max.650rpm Australia A/T
8°   DTDC/Max.750rpm Switzerland,Sweden.

22R

*0°   BTDC/Max.850rpm. RB20 (Since '84/8,85 RON
version)
*0°   BTDC/Max.950rpm. RJ Australia
*5°   BTDC/Max.850rpm. RB20 (Since '84/8,90 RON
version)
     RJ (Ex.Australia)
5°   BTDC/Max.950rpm. RB20 (Before '84/8,85 RON
version)
8°   BTDC/Max.950rpm. RB20 (Before '84/8,90 RON
version)

*   * without vacuum advance cut.

8. If needed, align the timing marks by turning the distributor body.

Problem Diagnosis.

Problem: Engine will not start/hard to start but cranks OK!
  Possible Causes & Remedies:
   * Incorrect ignition timing. Remedy-Reset timing.
   * Ignition coil faulty. Remedy- Examine coil.
   * Distributor faulty. Remedy-Examine distributor.
   * High tension cord faulty. Remedy- Inspect high tension cords.
   * Spark Plug faulty. Remedy-Examine plugs.
   * Ignition wiring disconnected or broken. Remedy-Inspect wiring.

Problem: Rough Idle or Stalls!
  Possible Causes & Remedies:
   * Spark plug faulty. Remedy-Check plugs.
   * Ignition wiring faulty. Remedy-Check wiring.
   * Incorrect Ignition Timing. Remedy-Reset timing.
   * Ignition coil faulty. Remedy-Inspect coil.
   * Distributor faulty. Remedy-Inspect distributor.
   * High-tension cord faulty. Remedy-Inspect high-tension leads.

Problem: Engine hesitates/poor acceleration!
  Possible Causes & Remedies:
   * Spark plug faulty. Remedy-Check plugs.
   * Ignition wiring faulty. Remedy-Examine wiring.
   * Incorrect ignition timing. Remedy-Reset timing.

Problem: Engine pre-igniting (runs after ignition switch is turned off)!
  Possible Causes & Remedies:
   * Incorrect ignition timing. Remedy-Reset timing.

Problem: Muffler explosion (after-fire) all the time!
  Possible Causes & Remedies:
   * Incorrect Ignition Timing. Remedy-Reset timing.

Problem: Engine backfires!
  Possible Causes & Remedies:
   * Incorrect Ignition Timing. Remedy-Reset timing.

Problem: Poor petrol (gasoline) mileage!
  Possible Causes & Remedies:
   * Spark plug faulty. Remedy-Inspect plugs.
   * Incorrect ignition timing. Remedy-Reset timing.

Problem: Engine overheats!
  Possible Causes & Remedies:
   * Incorrect ignition timing. Remedy-Reset timing.

COOLING SYSTEM

COOLING SYSTEM

ENGINE COOLANT

1.Check Engine Coolant Level at Reserve Tank. The coolant level should be between the "LOW" and "FULL" lines. If low, check for leaks and add coolant up to the "FULL" line.

2.Check Engine Coolant Quality. There should not be any excessive deposits of rust or scales around the radiator cap (water outlet cap) or radiator filler hole (water filler hole), and the coolant should be free from oil. If excessively dirty, replace the coolant.

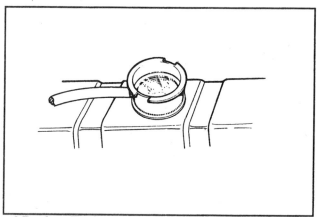

3.Replace Engine Coolant.

(a) Remove the radiator cap and drain the coolant from radiator and engine drain cocks. (Engine drain cock is at left front of engine block.)

(b) Close the drain cocks and fill the system with coolant. Use a good brand of ethylene-glycol base coolant, mixed according to the manufacturer's directions.

Capacity (w/ Heater):
BJ4..'s
         13.3 lts (14.1 US qts, 11.7 Imp.qts)
BJ6..'s
         13.3 lts (14.1 US qts, 11.7 Imp.qts)

FJ70, 73, 75 series
with heater
         15.0 ltrs (15.9 US qts, 13.2 Imp qts)
with Front heaters
         17.0 lts (18.0 S qts,15.0 Imp qts)
with front & rear heaters
         19.0 lts (20.1 US qts, 16.7 Imp qts)

FJ62 Series
without Heater
         15.5 lts (16.4 US qts, 13.6 Imp qts)
with Front Heater
         17.5 lts (18.5 Us qts, 15.4 Imp qts)
with Front and rear heaters
         19.5 lts (20.6 US qts, 17.2 Imp qts)

RJ7..'s series
with heater
         10.3 lts (10.9 US qts, 9.1 Imp qts)
without heater
         8.1 lts (8.6 US qts 7.1 Imp qts)
(c) Recheck the coolant level and refill as necessary.

WATER PUMP - 21R, 21R-C & 22R ENGINES

COMPONENTS.

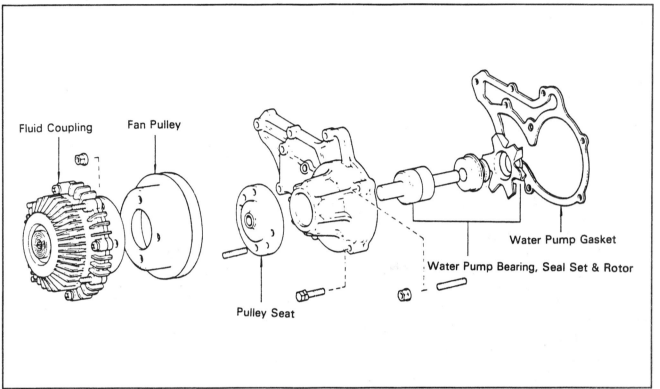

DISMANTLE.

Dismantle the parts in the order listed.
1. Fluid Coupling.
2. Fan Pulley.
3. Water Pump Gasket.
4. Pulley Seat.
5. Water Pump Bearing, Seal Set & Rotor.
(a) While holding the pulley seat, press the shaft with special tool.
(b) Heat the water pump body to about 85°C (185°F).
(c) [30 mm (1.18 in.) diameter bearing] Press out the outer race of the bearing and remove the bearing and the rotor with the special tool.
(d) [30 mm (1.18 in.) diameter bearing] Press out the pump bearing from the rotor with special tool.
(e) [35 mm (1.38 in.) diameter bearing] Press out the shaft of the bearing and remove the rotor and bearing with special tool.

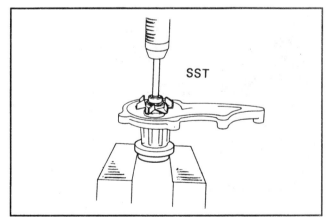

INSPECTION.

1. Examine the operating condition of the bearing. If damaged it produces noise or does not turn properly, replace.
2. Examine the fluid coupling for damage and silicone oil leak. If necessary, replace the coupling assembly.
* Do Not press on the bi-metal.

ASSEMBLY.

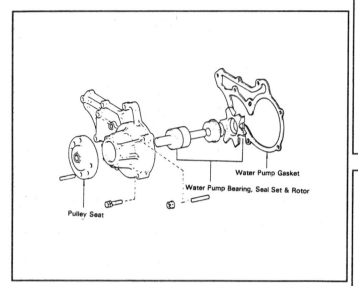

Assemble the parts in the order listed.

1. Water Pump Bearing

(a) Heat the water pump body to about 85°C (185°F)

(b) Press in the bearing with special tool.

* The bearing end face should be level with the body top surface.

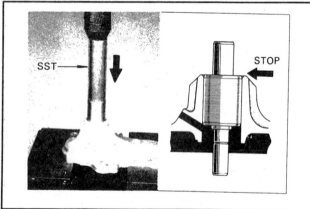

2. Seal Set

(a) Apply a little liquid sealer to the seal set.

* Always replace the seal set with a new one when reassembling.

(b) Press the seal set into the pump body with special tool.

3. Rotor

(a) Install the packing and seat into the rotor.

(b) Press in the rotor.

* Use a new rotor for assembly.

* The distance from the rotor edge to the pump body should be 6.1 mm (0.240 in.)

4. Pulley Seat

(a) Press in the pulley seat with special tool.

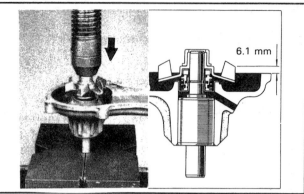

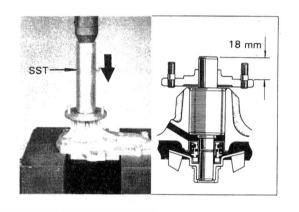

* The distance from the bearing shaft end to the pulley seat should be 18 mm (0.71 in.)

(b) After assembly, make sure that the rotor rotates smoothly.

5. Fan Pulley

6. Fluid Coupling

WATER PUMP - 2F & 3F ENGINES

REMOVAL.

1. Drain Engine Coolant.

2. Remove Drive Belt.

3. Remove Fan and Water Pump Pulley.

(i) **[w/o Fluid Coupling]** Remove the 4 bolts holding the fan to the pulley seat, and remove the fan, fan spacer and pump pulley.

(ii) **[w/ Fluid Coupling]** Remove the 4 nuts holding the fluid coupling to the pulley seat, and remove the fan and fluid coupling assembly and the pump pulley.

4.Remove Water Pump. Remove the inlet hose, water bi-pass hose, heater hose, and oil cooler water hose.

INSPECTION.

1.Inspect Water Pump. Turn the pulley seat and check that the water pump bearing moves smoothly and quietly. If necessary, replace the water pump bearing.

2.Inspect Fluid Coupling. Check that the fluid coupling for damage and silicon oil leakage. If necessary, replace the fluid coupling.

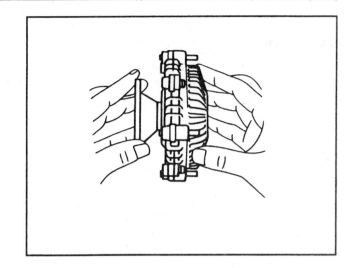

COMPONENTS.

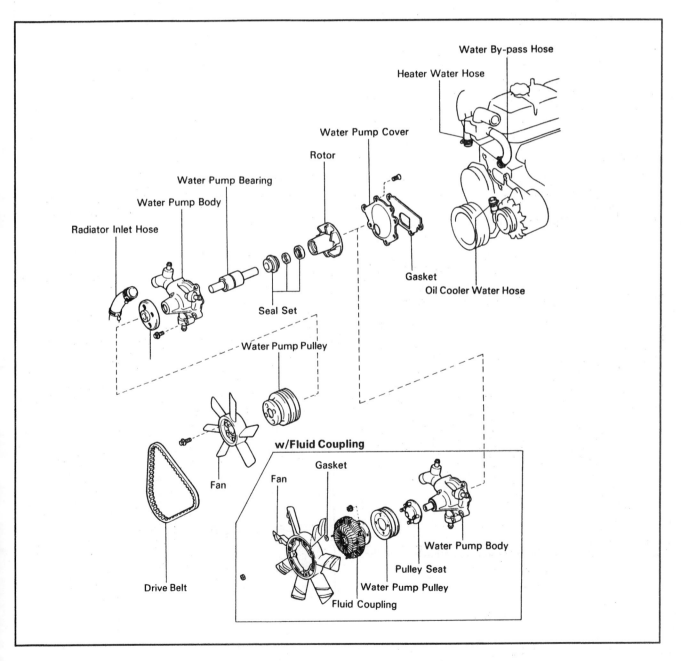

DISMANTLE.

Aluminium Body

1. Remove Water Pump Plate & gasket by unscrewing the 3 screws.

2. Remove Pulley Seat by pressing the shaft of the bearing.

Cast Iron Body.

1. Remove Water Pump Plate & gasket by unscrewing the 3 screws.

2. Remove Pulley Seat by pressing the shaft of the bearing.

3. Remove the Water Pump Bearing.

(a) Gradually heat the water pump body to approx. 85°C (185°F).

(b) Using special tool and a press, press the outer race of the bearing and remove the bearing together with the rotor.

4. Remove Rotor by pressing the shaft of the bearing.

5. Remove Seal, Seat & Packing.

ASSEMBLY.

Aluminium Body.

1. Install Water Pump Seat. Press the shaft of the bearing and install the pulley seat to a distance specified below from the water pump body edge.

Distance:

with Fluid Coupling.	117.3 mm (4.618 in.)
without Fluid Coupling.	152.3 mm (5.996 in.)

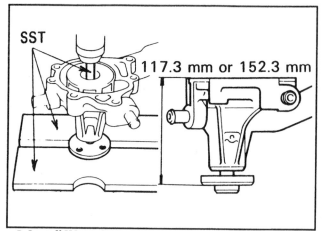

2. Install Water Pump Plate. Install a new gasket and the water pump plate with the 3 screws.

Cast Iron Body.

* Always assemble the water pump with a new seal set.

1. Install Water Pump Bearing.

(a) Gradually heat the water pump body to approx. 85°C (185°F).

(b) Press the outer race of the bearing until its surface is level with the water pump body edge.

2. Press In a New Seal.

3. Install Rotor.

(a) Place a new packing and seat into the rotor.

(b) Press in the rotor to a clearance of 0.7 mm (0.028 in.) from the water pump body.

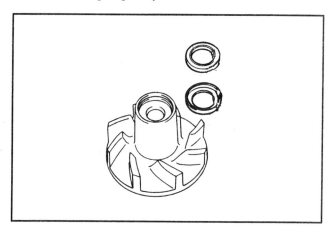

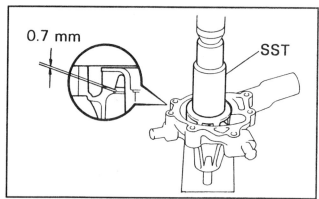

4. Install Pulley Seat. Press the shaft of the bearing and install the pulley seat to a distance specified below from the water pump body edge.

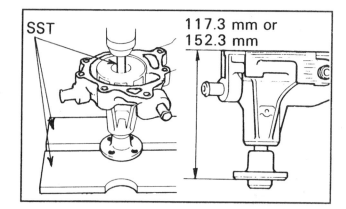

Distance:

with Fluid Coupling.   117.3 mm (4.618 in.)
without Fluid Coupling.   152.3 mm (5.996 in.)

5. Ensure that Water Pump Bearing Rotates Smoothly.
6. Install Water Pump Plate & new gasket using the 3 screws.

INSTALLATION.

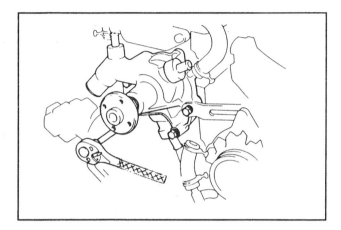

Reverse the REMOVAL procedures.

THERMOSTAT

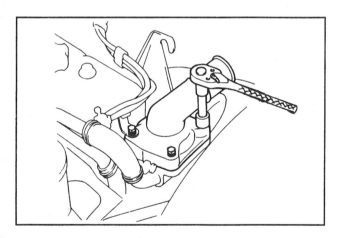

INSPECTION.

* The thermostat is numbered with the valve opening temperature.
1. Immerse the thermostat in water and gradually heat the water.
2. Check the valve opening temperature.

Valve opening temperature:
High temperature type 86 - 90°C (187 - 194°F)

Low temperature type   80 - 84°C (176 - 183°F)
If the valve opening temperature is not within specification, replace the thermostat.
3. Check the valve lift.
10 mm (0.39 in) or more at 100°C (212°F)
If the valve lift is less than specification, replace the thermostat.

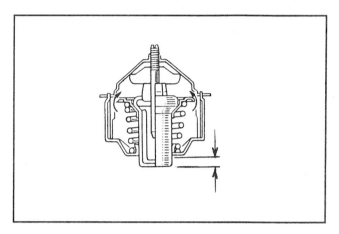

INSTALLATION.

1. Place Thermostat in Water Inlet.
2. Install Water Outlet. Install a new gasket and the water outlet with the 3 bolts. Torque the bolts.
   Torque: 185 kg-cm (13 ft-lb, 18'm)
3. [Water Outlet Cap Type] Connect Coolant Reservoir Hose and Water By-Pass Hose(s).
4. Connect Radiator Inlet Hose.
5. Fill Engine with Coolant.
6. Start Engine and Check for Leaks.

RADIATOR

CLEANING.

Using water or a steam cleaner, remove any mud and dirt from the radiator core.
* If using a high pressure type cleaner, be careful not to deform the fins of the radiator core. If the cleaner nozzle pressure is 30-35 kg/cm^2 (427-498 psi, 2,942-3,432 kPa), keep a distance of at least 40-50 cm (15.75-19.69 in.) between the radiator core and cleaner nozzle.

INSPECTION.

1. Inspect Radiator Cap. Using a radiator cap tester, pump the tester and measure the relief valve opening pressure.
   Standard opening pressure:
   0.75-1.05 kg/cm^2 (10.7-14.9 psi, 74 - 103 kPa)

Minimum opening pressure:
0.6kg/cm° (8.5 psi, 59 kPa)
If the opening pressure is less that minimum, replace the radiator cap.

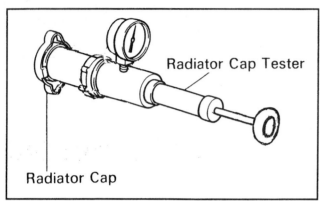

Radiator Cap Tester

Radiator Cap

2. Inspect Cooling System for Leaks.

(a) Fill the radiator with coolant and attach a pressure tester.

(b) Warm the engine up.

(c) Pump it to 1.2 kg/cm° (17 psi, 118 kPa), check that pressure does not drop.

If the pressure drops, check for leaks from the hoses, radiator or water pump. If no external leaks are found, check the heater core, block and head.

PROBLEM DIAGNOSIS

* If the engine tends to overheat, removal of the thermostat will adversely effect cooling efficiency.

Problem: Engine Overheats!
Possible Causes and Remedies:

* Fan belt loose or missing. Remedy - adjust or replace belt.

* Dirt, leaves or insects in radiator or condenser. Remedy - Clean radiator or condenser.

* Hoses, water pump, thermostat housing, radiator, heater, core plugs or head gasket leakage. Remedy - repair as necessary.

* Thermostat faulty. Remedy - check thermostat.

* Injection timing retarded. Remedy - adjust timing.

* Fluid coupling faulty. Remedy - replace fluid coupling.

* Radiator hose plugged or rotted. Remedy - replace hose.

* Water pump faulty. Remedy - replace water pump.

* Radiator plugged or cap faulty. Remedy - check radiator.

* Cylinder head or block cracked or plugged. Remedy - repair as necessary.

STARTING SYSTEM

STARTING SYSTEM 2F & 3F 6 CYLINDER ENGINES.

STARTER

Components

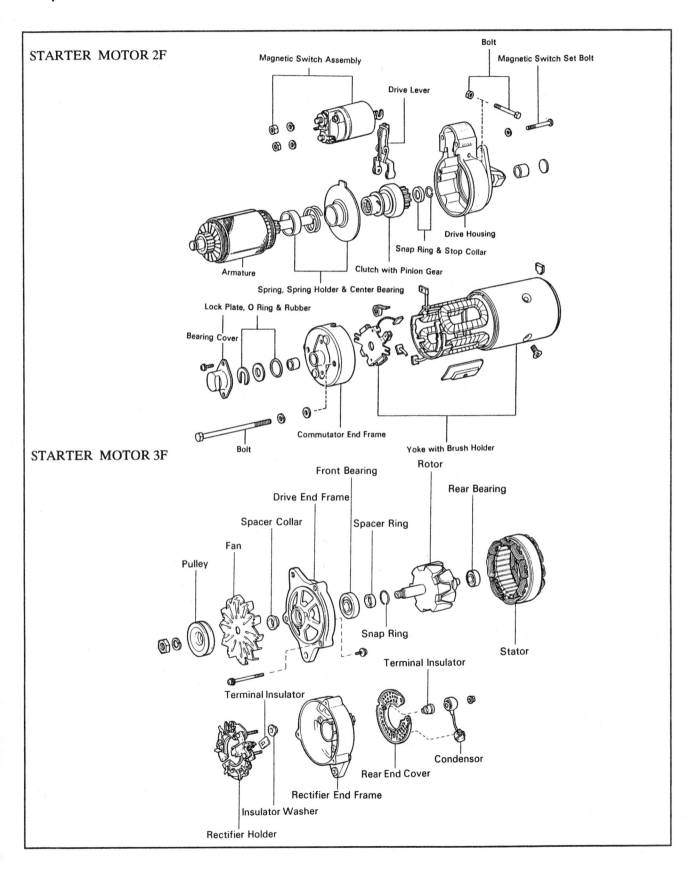

STARTER MOTOR 2F

Magnetic Switch Assembly

Bolt

Magnetic Switch Set Bolt

Drive Lever

Drive Housing

Snap Ring & Stop Collar

Clutch with Pinion Gear

Armature

Spring, Spring Holder & Center Bearing

Lock Plate, O Ring & Rubber

Bearing Cover

Bolt

Commutator End Frame

Yoke with Brush Holder

STARTER MOTOR 3F

Rotor

Front Bearing

Rear Bearing

Drive End Frame

Spacer Ring

Spacer Collar

Fan

Pulley

Snap Ring

Stator

Terminal Insulator

Terminal Insulator

Condensor

Rear End Cover

Rectifier End Frame

Insulator Washer

Rectifier Holder

Dismantle

1.Remove Field Frame and Armature Assembly.

(a) Remove the nut and disconnect the lead wire from the magnetic switch terminal.

(b) Remove the 2 through bolts.

(c) Pull out the field frame together with the armature.

(d) Remove the felt seal and lock plate.

2.Remove Starter Housing, Clutch Assembly and Gear.

(a) Remove the 2 screws.

(b) Remove the following parts from the magnetic switch: 1) starter housing, 2) clutch assembly, 3) return spring, 4) idle gear, 5) bearing.

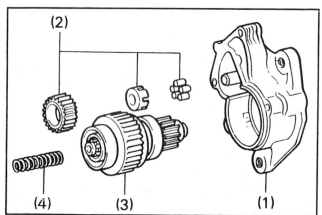

3.Remove Steel Ball. Using a magnetic finger, remove the steel ball from the clutch shaft hole.

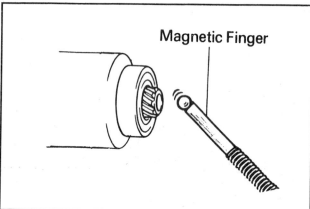

Magnetic Finger

4.Remove Brush Holder.

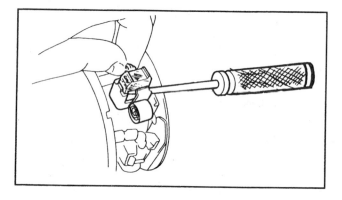

(a) Remove the 2 screws and end cover from the field frame.

(b) Using a screwdriver, hold the spring back and disconnect the brush from the brush holder. Disconnect the 4 brushes and remove the brush holder.

5.Remove Armature from Field Frame.

Inspection

1. Armature Coil.

(a) Inspect commutator for open circuit. Using a ohmmeter, check that there is continuity between the segments of the commutator. If there is no continuity, replace the armature.

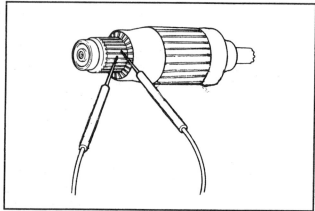

(b) Inspect commutator for ground. Using an ohmmeter, check that there is no continuity between the commutator and armature coil core. If there is continuity, replace the armature.

2.Commutator.

(a) Inspect commutator for dirty and burnt surface. If the surface is dirty or burnt, correct with sandpaper (no. 400) or on a lathe.

(b) Inspect diameter of commutator.

Standard diameter: 30 mm (1.18 in.)

Minimum diameter: 29 mm (1.14 in.)

If the diameter is less than minimum, replace the armature.

(c) Check that the undercut depth is clean and free of foreign particles. Smooth out the edge.

Standard undercut depth: 0.6mm (0.024 in.)

Minimum undercut depth: 0.2mm (0.008 in.)

If the undercut depth is less than minimum, correct it with a hacksaw blade.

3.Field Coil (Field Frame)

(a) Inspect field coil for open circuit. Using an ohmmeter, check that there is continuity between the lead wire and field coil brush lead. If there is no continuity, replace the field frame.

(b) Inspect field coil for ground. Using an ohmmeter, check that there is no continuity between the field coil end and field frame.

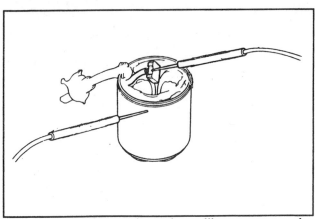

4.Inspect Brush Length. Using callipers, measure the brush length.

Standard length: 13.5 mm (0.531 in.)

Minimum length: 8.5 mm (0.3535 in.)

If the length is less than minimum, replace the brush holder and field frame.

5.Inspect Brush Spring Load. Take the pull scale reading the instant the brush spring separates from the brush.

Standard load: 1.79-2.41 kg (3.9-5.3 lb, 18-24 N)

Minimum load: 1.20 kg (2.6lb, 12 N)

If the reading is not within specification, replace the brush springs.

6.Inspect Insulation of Brush Holder. Using an ohmmeter, check that there is no continuity between the positive (+) and negative (-) brush holders. If there is continuity, repair or replace the brush holder.

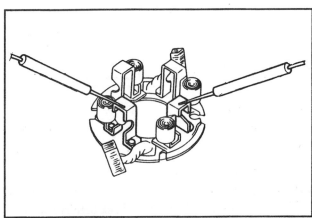

7.Clutch and Gears.

(a) Check the gear teeth on the pinion gear, idler gear and clutch assembly for wear or damage. Replace if damaged. If damaged, also check the flywheel ring gear fro wear or damage.

(b) Inspect Clutch Pinion Gear. Rotate the pinion gear clockwise and check that it turns freely. Try to rotate the pinion gear counterclockwise and check that it locks. If necessary, replace the clutch assembly.

8.Bearings.

(a) Inspect bearings. Turn each bearing by hand while applying inward force. If resistance is felt or if the bearing sticks, replace the bearing.

(b) If necessary, replace bearings.

9.Magnetic Switch.

(a) Perform Pull-in Coil Open Circuit Test. Using an ohmmeter, check that there is continuity between the two terminals. If there is no continuity, replace the magnetic switch.

(b) Perform Hold-in Coil Open Circuit Test. Using an ohmmeter, check that there is continuity between terminal and switch body. If there is no continuity, replace the magnetic switch.

Assembly

* Use high-temperature grease to lubricate the bearings and gears when assembling the starter.

1.Place Armature into field Frame. Apply grease to the armature bearings and insert the armature into the field frame.

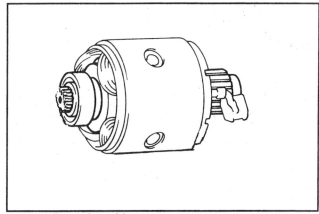

2.Install Brush Holder.

(a) Place the brush holder on the armature.

(b) Using a screwdriver, hold the brush spring back, and connect the brush into the brush holder. Connect the 4 brushes.

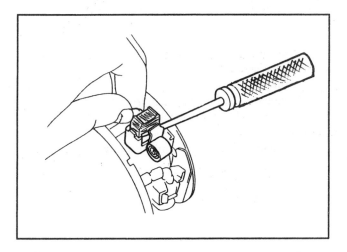

* Check that the positive (+) lead wires are not grounded.

(c) Install the end cover with the 2 screws.

3.Insert Steel Ball Into Clutch Shaft Hole.

(a) Apply grease to the steel ball.

(b) Insert the steel ball into the clutch shaft hole.

4. Install Clutch Assembly and Idle Gear.

(a) Apply grease to the return spring, the clutch assembly, idle gear and bearing.

(b) Insert the return spring into the magnetic switch hole.

(c) Place the following parts in position on the starter housing:

(1) Clutch Assembly, (2) Idler gear and bearing.

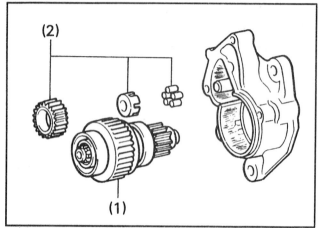

(d) Assemble the starter housing and magnetic switch with the 2 screws.

5.Install field Frame and Armature Assembly.

(a) Place the felt seal in position on the armature shaft.

(b) Align the lock plate with the notch on the field frame.

(c) Install the field frame and armature assembly with the 2 through bolts.

(d) Connect the lead wire to the magnetic switch terminal, and install the nut.

TEST

* These tests must be performed within 3 to 5 seconds to avoid burning out the coil.

1.Perform Pull-In Test.

(a) Disconnect the field coil lead from terminal.

(b) Connect the battery to the magnetic switch as shown. Check that the pinion gear moves outward. If the pinion gear does not move, replace the magnetic switch assembly.

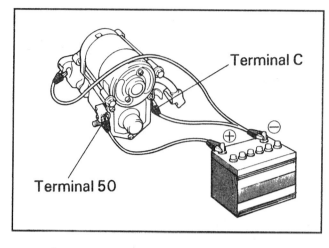

Terminal C

Terminal 50

2.Perform Hold-In Test. While connected as above with the pinion gear out, disconnect the negative (-) lead from the terminal. Check that the pinion gear remains out. If the pinion gear returns inward, replace the magnetic switch assembly.

3.Inspect Plunger Return. Disconnect the negative (-) lead from the switch body. Check that the pinion gear returns inward. If the pinion gear does not return, replace the magnetic switch assembly.

4.Perform No-Load Performance Test.

(a) Connect the battery and ammeter to the starter as shown.

(b) Check that the starter rotates smoothly and steadily with the pinion gear moving out. Check that the ammeter reads the specified current.

Specified current: 90 A or less at 11.5V

PROBLEM DIAGNOSIS

Problem: Engine will not crank!

Possible Causes and Remedies:

* Battery charge low. Remedy - check battery specific gravity; or (ii) charge or replace battery.

* Battery cables loose, corroded or worn. Remedy - repair or replace cables.

* Neutral start switch faulty (A/T only). Remedy - replace switch.

* Fusible link blown. Remedy - replace fusible link.

* Starter faulty. Remedy - repair starter.

* Ignition switch faulty. Remedy - replace ignition switch.

Problem: Engine cranks slowly!
Possible Causes and Remedies:

* Battery charge low. Remedy - (i) check battery specific gravity; or (ii) charge or replace battery.

* Battery cables loose, corroded or worn. Remedy - repair or replace cables.

* Starter faulty. Remedy - repair starter.

Problem: Starter keeps running!
Possible Causes and Remedies:

* Starter faulty. Remedy - repair starter.

* Ignition switch faulty. Remedy - replace ignition switch.

* Short in wiring. Remedy - repair wiring.

Problem: Starter spins but engine will not crank!
Possible Causes and Remedies:

* Pinion gear teeth broken or faulty starter. Remedy - repair starter.

* Flywheel teeth broken. Remedy - replace flywheel.

STARTING SYSTEM.21R, 21R-C & 22R PETROL ENGINES.

STARTING SYSTEM.21R, 21R-C & 22R PETROL ENGINE.

Conventional Starting System Circuit.

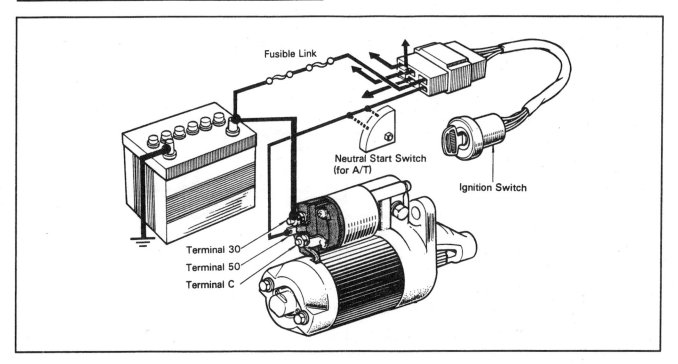

Performance Test.

No-Load Performance Test.

1. Secure the starter in a vice to prevent an accident.
2. Connect the starter to a battery as illustrated in the diagram.

Positive side:

Battery (+) ------------------------ Ammeter (+)

Ammeter (-) ------------------------ Terminal 30

Negative side:

Battery (-) -------------------------- Starter Body

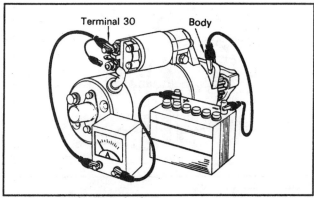

3. Connect the Terminal 50.

If the starter shows smooth and steady rotation with the pinion jumping out and drawing less than specified current, it is satisfactory.

Specified Current: Less than 50A (at 11V)

Magnetic Switch Test.

* Each test must be performed within a short time (3-5 seconds) to prevent the coil from burning out.

1. Disconnect the terminal C lead wires.

2. Pull-in test.

Connect the magnetic switch to a battery as illustrated in the diagram.

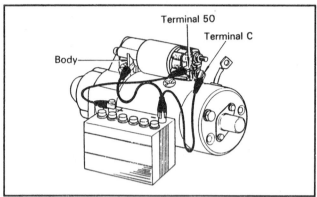

Negative side:

Battery (-) ------------------ Starter body and terminal C

Positive side:

Battery (+) ----------------- Terminal 50

If the pinion has definitely jumped out, the pull-in coil is satisfactory.

3, Hold-in Test.

Disconnect terminal C. The pinion should remain projected.

4. Check the plunger return. When disconnecting the switch body, the pinion should return quickly.

5. Inspect pinion clearance.

(a) Connect the field coil lead to terminal C.

(b) Connect the magnetic switch to a battery as illustrated in the diagram.

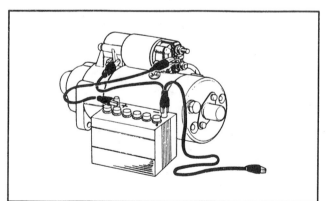

Positive side:

Battery (+) ------------------- Terminal 50

Battery (-) --------------------- Starter Body

(c) Move the pinion to the armature side to eliminate slack, and inspect the clearance between the pinion end stop collar.

Clearance: 0.1-4.0mm (0.004-0.157 in.)

(d) For 1.0 kw

Loosen the lock nut and adjust if needed.

Clearance	Stud
Too large ------------------	screw in
Too small -----------------	screw out

Conventional Starter.

CUTAWAY VIEW.

1.0 kw MODEL.

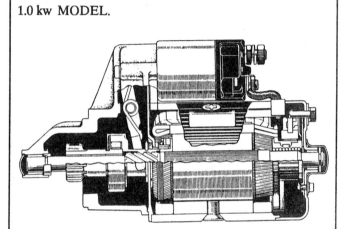

0.8 kw MODEL.

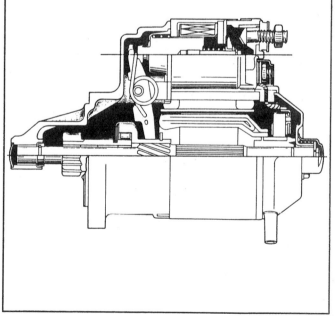

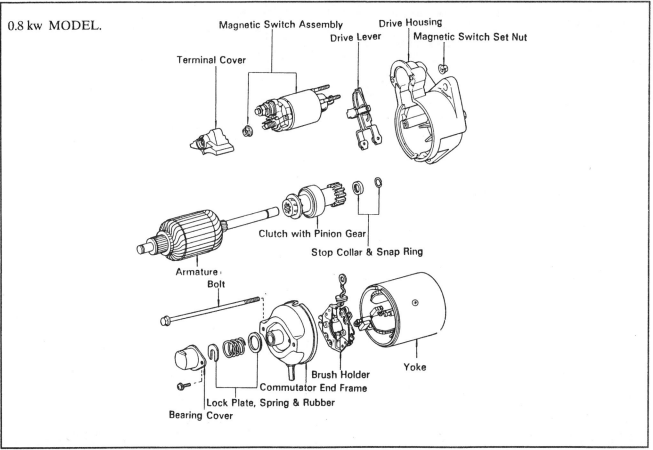

0.8 kw MODEL.

DISMANTLE - 0.8 kw Model.

1. Terminal Cover.
2. Magnetic Switch Set Nut.
3. Magnetic Switch Assembly.

(a)Disconnect the terminal C lead wire from the magnetic switch.

(b)Remove the magnetic switch as illustrated in the diagram.

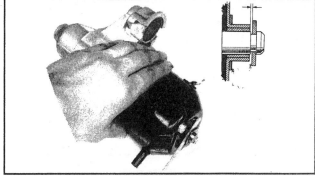

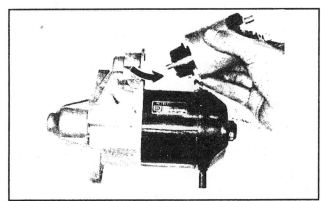

4. Bearing Cover
5. Lock Plate, Spring & Rubber

(a)Measure the armature shaft thrust clearance.

Thrust clearance:
STD   0.05-1.00 mm (0.0020-0.0394 in.)
Limit 1.00 mm (0.0394 in.)

6. Bolt.
7. Commutator End Frame.
8. Brush Holder.

(a)Remove the Brushes from the brush holder.

9. Yoke.
10.Drive Lever.
11.Armature.
12.Drive Housing.
13.Snap ring & Stop collar.

(a) Using a screwdriver, tap in the stop collar.

(b) Using a screwdriver, pry off the snap rings and remove the stop collar.

* Smooth the shaft with an oil stone, if the pinion was difficult to pull out.

14.Clutch with Pinion gear.

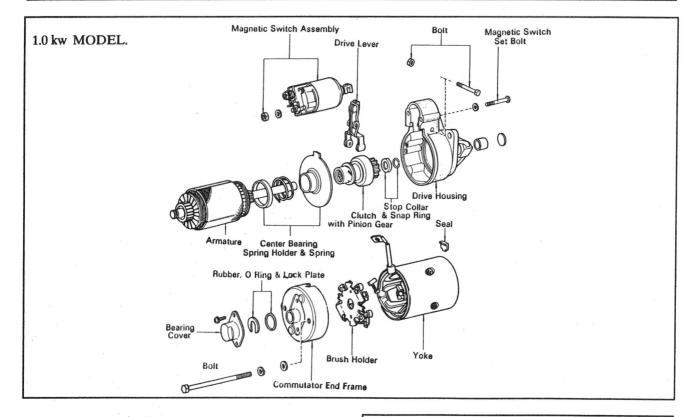

1.0 kw MODEL.

DISMANTLE - 1.0 kw Model.

1. Magnetic Switch Bolt.
2. Magnetic Switch Assembly.

(a)Disconnect the terminal C lead wire from the magnetic switch.

(b)Remove the magnetic switch as illustrated in the diagram.

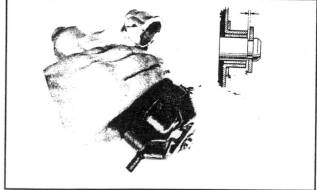

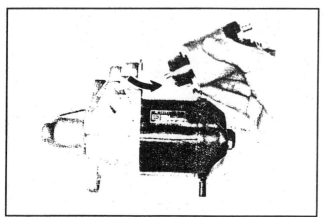

3. Bearing Cover.
4. Lock Plate, O Ring & Rubber.

(a)Measure the armature shaft thrust clearance.

Thrust clearance:

STD   0.05-1.00 mm (0.0020-0.0394 in.)
Limit 1.00 mm (0.0394 in.)

5. Bolt.
6. Commutator End Frame.
7. Brush Holder.

(a)Remove the Brushes from the brush holder.

8. Yoke.
9. Seal.
10.Bolt.
11.Drive Housing.
12.Drive Lever.
13.Armature.
14.Snap ring & Stop Collar.

(a) Using a screwdriver, tap in the stop collar.

(b) Using a screwdriver, pry off the snap rings and remove the stop collar.

* Smooth the shaft with an oil stone, if the pinion was difficult to pull out.

15.Clutch with Pinion Gear.
16. Spring, Spring Holder and Centre bearing.

INSPECTION & REPAIR.

Commutator

Inspect for the following, repair or replace as needed.

1. Dirty or burnt surface. Correct using sandpaper if needed.

2. Depth of segment mica.

Mica depth:
STD   0.4-0.8 mm (0.016-0.031 in.)
Limit 0.2 mm (0.008 in.)

3. Repair the segment mica..

(a) Of the mica depth is below the limit, correct it using a hacksaw blade.

(b) Smooth out the edges using a hacksaw blade.

(c) Use #400 sandpaper to smooth the commutator surface.

4. Runout. Correct on a lathe if it exceeds the limit.

Runout:
STD   Less than 0.1 mm (0.004 in.)
Limit 0.3 mm (0.012 in.)

5. Surface Wear.

Replace the armature if below the limit.

Commutator outer diameter:
0.8 kw STD   28.0 mm (1.102 in.)
       Limit 27 mm (1.06 in.)
1.0 kw STD   32.7 mm (1.287 in.)
       Limit 31 mm (1.22 in.)

Armature Coil.

1. Ground Test.

Inspect the commutator and armature coil core. If there is continuity, the armature is grounded and must be replaced.

2. Short Circuit Test.

Place the armature on an armature tester and hold a hacksaw blade against the armature core while turning the armature. If the hacksaw blade is attracted or vibrates, the armature is shorted and must be replaced.

3. Solder condition.

Inspect for continuity between the commutator and armature coil.

Field Coil.

1. Open circuit test.

Examine for continuity between the field coil brushes. If there is no continuity, there is an open circuit in the field coil and it should be replaced.

2. Ground Test.

Inspect for continuity between the field coil end and field frame.

If there is continuity, repair or replace the field coil. (for 1.0 kw)

Brush.

Measure the brush length and replace if below the limit.

Brush length:
0.8 kw STD   16 mm (0.63 in.)
        Limit 10 mm (0.39 in.)
1.0 kw STD   19 mm (0.75 in.)
        Limit 10 mm (0.39 in.)

Brush Spring.

Measure the brush spring load with a pull scale. If the reading is below the specified value, replace the spring.

Tension: 1.02-1.38 kg (2.2-3.0 lb.)

* Take the pull scale reading at the immediately as the brush spring separates from the brush.

Brush Holder.

Inspect the insulation between the (-) brush holder and (+) brush holder. Repair or replace, if continuity is indicated.

Drive Lever.

Check the drive lever and spring for wear. Replace, if needed.

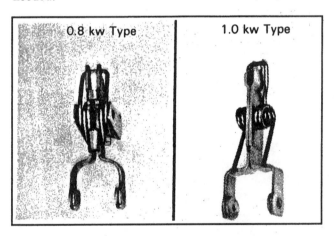

| 0.8 kw Type | 1.0 kw Type |

Starter Clutch & Pinion Gear.

1. Inspect the spline teeth for wear or damage. Replace, if needed.

2. Check the pinion for smooth movement.

3. Examine the pinion gear teeth and the chamfer for wear or damage.

4. Rotate the pinion. It should rotate freely in clockwise direction but lock when turned anticlockwise.

Magnetic Switch.

1. Push in the plunger and release it, it should quickly return to its original position.

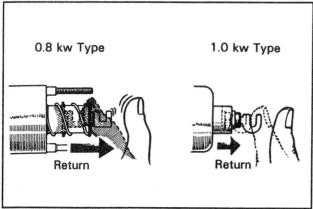

2. Pull-in coil open circuit test.

Check for continuity between the terminal 50 and terminal C.

3. Hold-in coil open circuit test.

Check for continuity between the terminal 50 and switch body.

4. For 1.0 kw

Measure and adjust the distance from the switch mounting surface to the stud end.

Moving stud length:

STD 34 mm (1.34 in.) (Reference only)

Armature Shaft, Bushing & Centre Bearing.

1. Examine the armature shaft, drive housing bushing and end frame bushing for wear or damage.

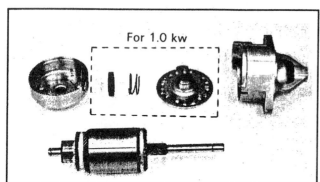

2. Replace the drive housing bushing and end frame bushing if any contact is suspected.

(a) Pry out the bushing cover and press out the bushing.

(b) Line up the bushing hole with the housing groove and press in a new bushing.

(c) Ream the bushing to obtain the specified clearance.

Bushing to shaft clearance:

STD 0.035-0.077 mm (0.0014-0.0030 in.)

Limit 0.2 mm (0.008 in.)

(d) Assemble the parts temporarily.

(e) Ensure that the armature shaft turns smoothly.

(f) Clean the bore, install a new bushing cover and stake the housing at 4 positions.

3. 1.0 kw type.

Examine the spring holder, spring and centre bearing for cracks, wear or damage. Replace if needed.

ASSEMBLY.

0.8 kw Model.

Assemble the parts in the order illustrated.

1. Armature.
2. Clutch with Pinion Gear.
3. Stop Collar & Snap Ring.
4. Drive Housing.
5. Drive Lever.

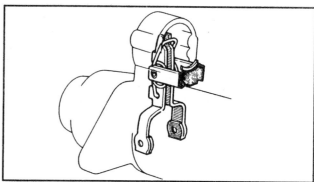

6. Yoke.
7. Brush Holder.
8. Commutator End Fram.
9. Bolt.
10. Lock Plate, Spring and Rubber.
11. Bearing cover.
12. Magnetic Switch Cover.
13. Magnetic Switch Set Nut.
14. Terminal Cover.

1.0 kw Model.

Assemble the parts in the order illustrated.

1. Armature.
2. Centre bearing, Spring Holder and Spring.
3. Clutch with pinion gear.
4. Stop Collar & Snap ring.
5. Drive Lever.

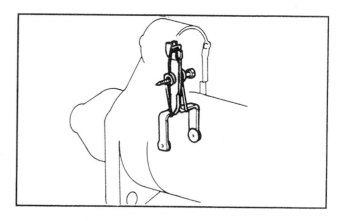

6. Drive Housing.
7. Bolt.
8. Seal.
9. Yoke.
10. Brush Holder.
11. Commutator End Frame.
12. Bolt.
13. Rubber, O Ring & Lock Plate.
14. Bearing Cover.
15. Magnetic Switch Assembly.
16. Magnetic Switch Set bolt.

Reduction Starting System Circuit.

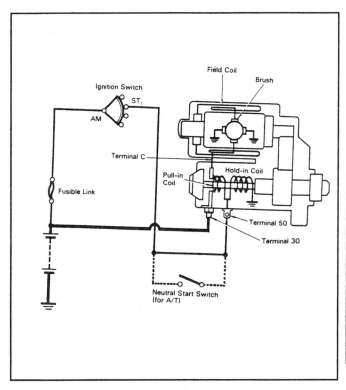

Performance Test.

No-Load Performance Test.

1. Secure the starter in a vice to prevent an accident.
2. Connect the starter to a battery as illustrated in the diagram.
Positive side:
Battery (+) -------------------- Ammeter (+)
Ammeter (-) -------------------- Terminal 30

Negative side:
Battery (-) ------------------- Starter housing.

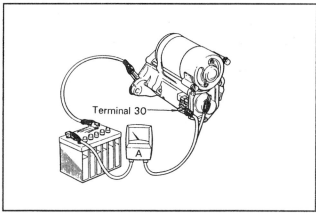

3. Connect the terminal 50.
If the starter shows smooth and steady rotation with the pinion jumping out and drawing less than specified current, it is satisfactory.
Specified current: Less than 90A (11.5 V)

Magnetic Switch Test.

* Each test must be performed within a short time (3-5 seconds) to prevent the coil from burning out.
1. Disconnect the terminal C lead wire.
2. Pull-in test.
Connect the magnetic switch to a battery as illustrated in the diagram.

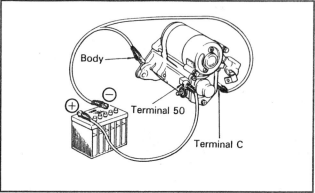

Negative side:
Battery (-) -------------------- Starter body and terminal C
Positive side:
Battery (+) ----------------- Terminal 50
If the pinion has definitely jumped out, the pull-in coil is satisfactory.
3. Hold-in Test.
Disconnect the terminal C. The pinion should remain project.
4. Check Pinion return.
When disconnecting the cable from the starter housing, the jumped-out pinion should quickly return.

Reduction Starter.

CUTAWAY VIEW.

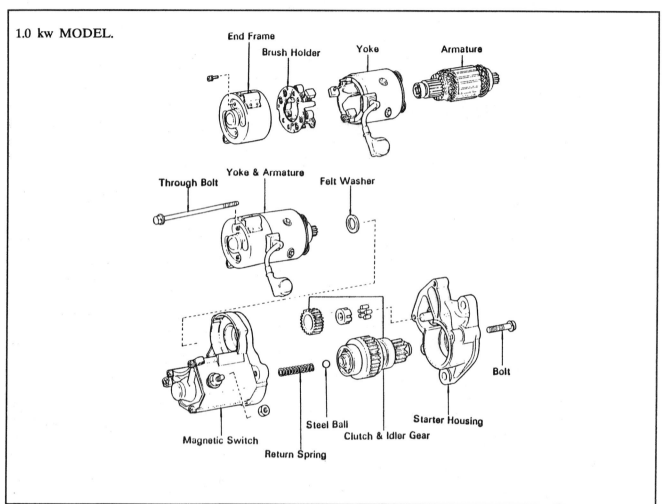

1.0 kw MODEL.

End Frame — Brush Holder — Yoke — Armature

Through Bolt — Yoke & Armature — Felt Washer

Bolt

Magnetic Switch — Return Spring — Steel Ball — Clutch & Idler Gear — Starter Housing

DISMANTLE - 1.0 kw Model.

1. Through Bolt.
2. Yoke & Armature.
(a) Disconnect the terminal C lead wire from the magnetic switch.
3. Felt Washer.
4. Bolt.
5. Starter Housing.
(a) 1.0 kw type. Remove the starter housing together with the idler gear and clutch.
6. Clutch & Idler Gear.
7. Steel Ball.
8. Return Spring.
(a) Remove the steel ball from the clutch shaft hole using a magnet.

9. Magnetic Switch.
10. End Frame.
11. Brush Holder.
(a) Remove the brushes from the brush holder.
* Be careful not to damage the brush and commutator. Also avoid getting oil or grease on them.
12. Yoke.
13. Armature.

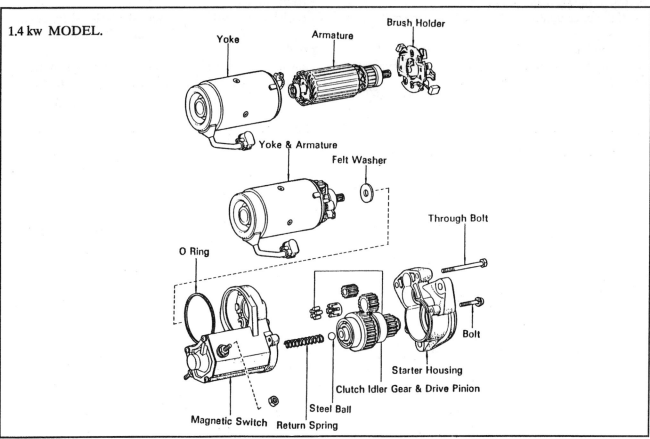

1.4 kw MODEL.

DISMANTLE - 1.4 kw Model.

1. Through Bolt.
2. Yoke & Armature.
(a) Disconnect the terminal C lead wire from the magnetic switch.
3. Felt Washer.
4. O-Ring.
5. Bolt.
6. Starter Housing.
7. Clutch Idler Gear & Drive Pinion.
(a) 1.4 kw type. Remove the starter housing together with the drive pinion, idler gear and clutch.
8. Steel Ball.
(a) Remove the steel ball from the clutch shaft hole using a magnet.
9. Return Spring.
10. Magnetic Switch.
11. Brush Holder.
(a) Remove the brushes from the brush holder.
* Be careful not to damage the brush and commutator. Also avoid getting oil or grease on them.
12. Armature.
13. Yoke.

Inspection & Repair.

Commutator.

Inspect for the following and repair or replace as needed.

1. Dirty or burnt surface, correct with sandpaper if necessary.

2. Depth of segment mica.

Mica depth:
STD   0.45-0.75 mm (0.0177-0.295 in.)
Limit 0.2 mm (0.008 in.)

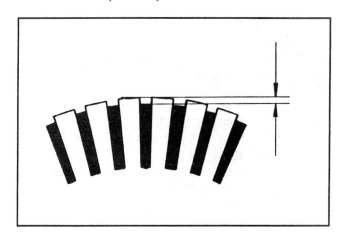

3. Repair the segment mica.

(a) If the mica depth is below the limit, correct it with a hacksaw blade.

(b) Smooth out the edge with a hacksaw blade.

(c) Use #400 sandpaper to smooth the commutator surface,

4. Runout. Correct on a lathe if it exceeds the limit.

Runout:

STD   Less than 0.02 mm (0.0008 in.)

Limit 0.2 (0.008 in.)

5. Surface wear. Replace the armature if below the limit.

Commutator outer diameter:

STD   30 mm (1.18 in.)

Limit 29 mm (1.14 in.)

Armature Coil.

1. Ground test. Inspect the commutator and armature coil core. If there is continuity, the armature is grounded and must be replaced.

2. Short Circuit Test. Place the armature on the armature tester and hold a hacksaw blade against the armature core while turning the armature. If the hacksaw blade is attracted or vibrates, the armature is shorted and must be replaced.

3. Solder Condition. Inspect for continuity between the commutator and armature coil.

Field Coil.

1. Open Circuit Test. Check for continuity between the lead wire and soldered connection of the field coil brush. If there is no continuity, there is an open circuit in the field coil and it should be replaced.

2. Ground test. Check for continuity between the field coil end and field frame. If there is continuity, repair or replace the field coil.

Brush.

Measure the brush length and replace if below the limit.

Brush length:

1.0 kw   STD   13.5 mm (0.531 in.)

         Limit 10 mm (0.39 in.)

1.4 kw   STD   14.5 mm (0.571 in.)

         Limit 10 mm (0.39 in.)

Brush Spring.

1. Measure the brush spring load with a pull scale. If the reading is below the specified value, replace the spring.

Tension:

1.0 kw   STD   1445-1955 g (3.2-4.3 lb)

         Limit 1200 g (22.6 lb.)

1.4 kw   STD   1785-2415 g (3.9-5.3 lb)

         Limit 1200 g (2.6 lb)

* Take the pull scale reading immediately as the brush spring separates from the brush.

Brush Holder.

1. Check the insulation between the (-) brush holder and (+) brush holder. Repair or replace, If continuity is indicated.

2. Clean and fit the brushes using #400 sandpaper, so as they make proper contact with the commutator.

* Secure the armature gear in a vice or such.

Gear.

1. Inspect the gears for damage or wear.

2. Examine the gear teeth for damage or wear. Also, inspect the flywheel ring gear for same.

Clutch.

Rotate the pinion. It should rotate freely in clockwise direction but lock when rotated anticlockwise.

Magnetic Switch.

1. Pull-in coil open circuit test. Check for continuity between the terminal 50 and terminal C.

2. Hold-in coil open circuit test. Inspect for continuity between terminal 50 and the magnetic switch body.

3. Examine for damage or wear.

Bearing.

1. Inspect the bearing for damage or wear.

2. Replace armature bearing, if defective.

(a) Replace the front bearing, and drive in the rear bearing.

Starter Housing.

Examine for damage or wear.

Assembly.

ASSEMBLY - 1.0 kw Model.

* Use high temperature grease to lubricate bearings and gears in the places indicated by arrows in the diagram.

1. Starter Housing.

2. Clutch & Idler Gear.

3. Steel Ball.

4. Return Spring.

5. Magnetic Switch.

6. Bolt.

7. Armature.

8. Yoke.

9. Brush Holder.

10. End Frame.

11. Felt Washer.

12. Yoke & Armature.

13. Through Bolt.

Performance Test Load.

ASSEMBLY - 1.4 kw Model.
* Use high temperature grease to lubricate bearings and gears in the places indicated by arrows in the diagram.
1. Starter Housing.
2. Clutch, Idler Gear & Drive Pinion.

Connect the starter to a battery. The starter should show uniform and steady rotation with the pinion jumping out and drawing less than the specified current.

Specified Current: Less than 90 Amp at 11.5 Volts.

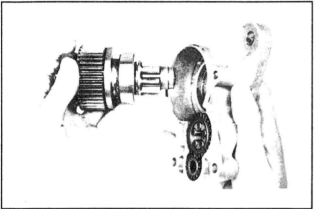

3. Steel Ball.
4. Return Spring.
5. Magnetic Switch.
6. Bolt.
7. Yoke.
8. Armature.
9. Brush Holder.
10.O Ring.
11.Felt Washer.
12.Yoke & Armature.
13.Through Bolt.

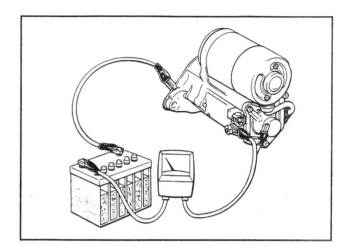

NOTES

ALTERNATOR SYSTEMS

ALTERNATOR SYSTEMS 2F & 3F 6 CYLINDER ENGINES

ALTERNATOR SYSTEMS 2F & 3F 6 CYLINDER ENGINES

In Vehicle Inspection.

1. Check Battery Specific Gravity.

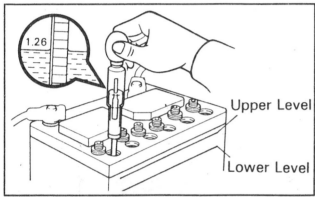

(a) Check the specific gravity of each cell.
Standard specific gravity:
1.25-1.27 when fully charged at 20°C (68°F).
(b) Check the electrolyte quantity of each cell. If insufficient, refill with distilled (or purified) water.
2. Check Battery Terminals, Fusible Links and Fuses.
(a) Check that the battery terminals are not loose or corroded.
(b) Check the fusible link and fuses for continuity.
3. Inspect Drive Belt.

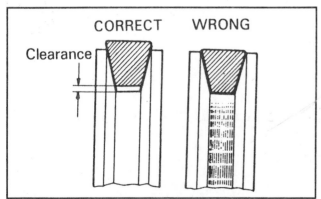

(a) Examine the drive belt for cracks, oiliness or wear. Ensure that the belt does not touch the bottom of the pulley groove. If necessary, replace the drive belt.

(b) Inspect the drive belt deflection by pressing on the belt at the points indicated in the figure with 10 kg (22.0 lb, 98N) of pressure.
Drive belt deflection:
New Belt 7.0-9.0 mm (0.278-0.354 in.)
Used Belt 9.0-12.0 mm (0.354-0.472 in.)
If the belt deflection is not within specification, adjust it.
* "New belt" refers to a new belt which has never been used.
* "Used belt" refers to a belt which has been used on a running engine for 5 minutes or more.
4. Visually Check Alternator Wiring and Listen for Irregular Noises.
(a) Ensure that the wiring is in good condition.
(b) Check that there are no irregular noises from the alternator while the engine is running.

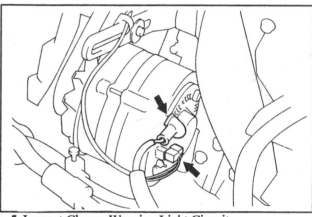

5. Inspect Charge Warning Light Circuit.
(a) Warm up the engine and then turn it off.
(b) Turn off all accessories.
(c) Turn the starter switch to "on". Make sure that the charge warning light is lit.
(d) Start the engine. Ensure that the light goes out.
If the light does not operate as indicated check diagnosis.

6. Check Charging Circuit Without Load.
* If a battery/alternator tester is available, connect the tester to the charging circuit as per the manufacturers instructions.
(a) If a tester is not available, connect a voltmeter and ammeter to the charging circuit as follows:
*Disconnect the wire from terminal B of the alternator and connect it to the negative (-) probe of the ammeter.

*Connect the test probe from the positive (+) terminal of the ammeter to terminal B of the alternator.

*Connect the positive (+) probe of the voltmeter to terminal B of the alternator.

*Ground the negative (-) probe of the voltmeter.

(b) Check the charging circuit as follows:

With the engine running from idle to 2,000 rpm, check the reading on the ammeter and voltmeter.

Standard amperage: Less than 10A

Standard voltage: 13.8-14.8 V at 25°C (77°F)

If the reading is not within standard voltage, adjust the regulator or replace it.

7. Check Charging Circuit with Load.

(a) With the engine running at 2,000 rpm, turn on the high beam headlights and place the heater fan control switch on "hi".

(b) Check the reading on the ammeter.

Standard amperage: More than 30A

If the ammeter reading is less than 30A, repair the alternator.

* If the battery is fully charged, the indication will sometimes be less than 30A.

Alternator.

Dismantle.

1. Remove Drive End Frame and Rotor Assembly from Stator.

(a) Remove the 3 through screws.

(b) Using a screwdriver, pry the end frame and remove it together with the rotor.

* Do not pry on the coil wires.

2. Remove Pulley & Fan

(a) Mount the rotor in a soft jaw vice.

(b) Remove the nut and spring washer.

(c) Remove the pulley, fan and spacer collar.

3. Remove Rotor

(a) Using a press, press out the rotor.

(b) (40A and 45A types) Remove the spacer ring and snap ring.

(c) (50A and 55A types) Remove the spacer ring.

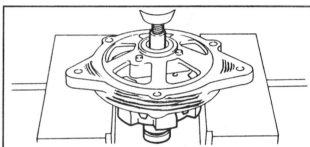

Components.

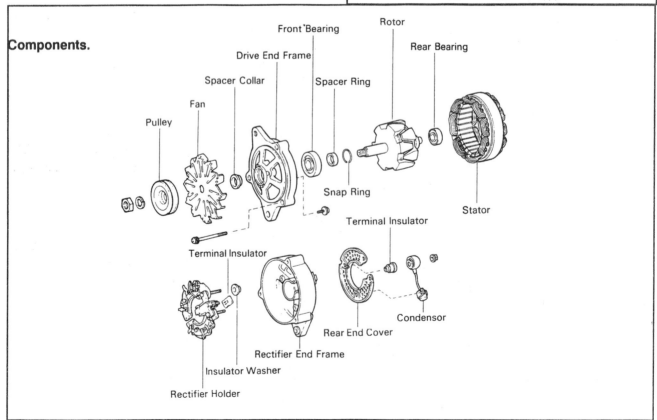

4. Remove Rectifier End Frame.

(a) Remove the 4 nuts, condenser (50A type only) and 2 terminal insulators.

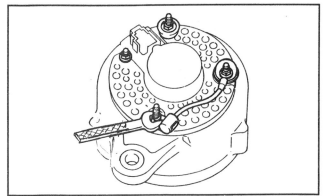

(b) Remove the rear end cover and rectifier end frame.

(c) Remove the 2 insulator washers from the rectifier holder studs.

(d) Remove the insulator washer from the brush holder.

5. Remove Rectifier Holder. Hold the rectifier terminal with needle-nose pliers and unsolder the leads.

  * Protect the rectifiers from heat.

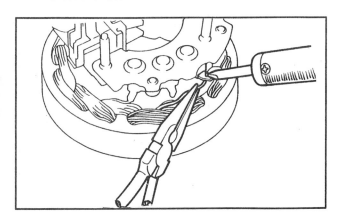

INSPECTION.

Rotor.

1. Inspect the Rotor for Open Circuit. Using an ohmmeter, check that there is continuity between the slip rings.

Standard resistance:
Tirrill regulator type:

3.9-4.1 ohms.

IC regulator type:

2.8-3.0 ohms

If there is no continuity, replace the rotor.

2. Inspect Rotor For Ground. Using an ohmmeter, check that there is no continuity between the slip ring and the rotor. If there is continuity, replace the rotor.

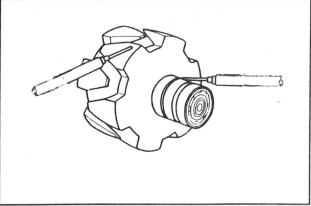

3. Inspect Slip Rings.

(a) Check that the slip rings are not rough or scored. If rough or scored, replace the rotor.

(b) Using callipers, measure the slip ring diameter.

Standard diameter: 32.3-32.5 mm (1.272-1.280 in.)

Minimum diameter: 32.1 mm (1.264 in.)

If the diameter is less than minimum, replace the rotor.

Stator.

1. Inspect Stator for Open Circuit. Using an ohmmeter, check that there is continuity between the coil leads.

  * At this time, the meeting wires should be soldered. If there is no continuity, replace the stator.

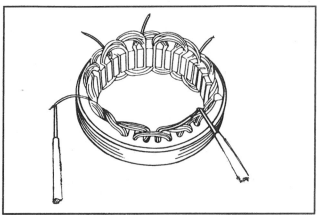

2. Inspect Stator for Ground. Using an ohmmeter, check that there is no continuity between the coil leads and stator core. If there is continuity, replace the stator.

Brushes.

1. Inspect Exposed Brush Length. Using a scale, measure the exposed brush length.

Standard exposed length: 12.5 mm (0.492 in.)

Minimum exposed length: 5.5 mm (0.217 in.)

If the length is less than minimum, replace the brushes.

2. If necessary, replace the brushes.

(a) Unsolder and remove the brush and spring.

(b) Insert the brush wire through the spring.

(c) Install the brush in the holder.

(d) Solder the wire to the holder at specified exposed length.

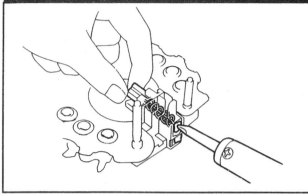

Exposed length: 12.5 mm (0.492 in.)

(e) Ensure that the brush moves smoothly in the holder.

(f) Cut off any extra wire.

Bearings.

1. Inspect Front Bearings. Inspect that the bearing is not rough or worn.

2. If Necessary, Replace the Front Bearing by removing the 3 screws.

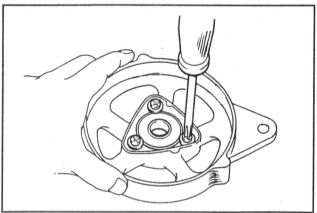

3. Inspect Rear Bearing to ensure that it is not rough or worn.

4. If Necessary, Replace Rear Bearing.

(a) Remove bearing.

(b) Press in a new bearing.

Assembly of Alternator.

1. Hold the rectifier terminal with needle-nose pliers while soldering the leads.

* Protect the rectifiers from heat.

2. Install Rectifier End Frame to Rectifier Holder.

(a) Place the terminal insulator on the brush holder terminal.

(b) Put the 2 insulator washers on the positive studs of the rectifier holder.

(c) Place the rectifier end frame on the rectifier holder.

(d) Place the rear end cover on the rectifier end frame.

(e) Put the 2 terminal insulators on the positive studs of the rectifier holder.

(f) (55A type) Place the condenser in position.

(g) Screw the 4 nuts in.

(h) Make sure that the wires are not touching the rectifier end frame.

3. Install Rotor.

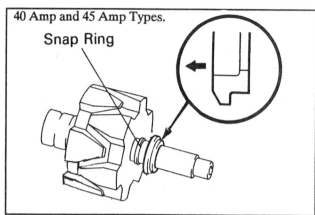

(a) (40A & 45A types) Slide the snap ring and spacer ring onto the rotor shaft.

(b) (50A & 55A types) Slide the spacer ring onto the rotor shaft.

(c) Press in the rotor, using a press.

4. Install Fan & Pulley.

(a) Mount the rotor in soft jaw vice.

(b) Slide the spacer collar onto the rotor shaft.

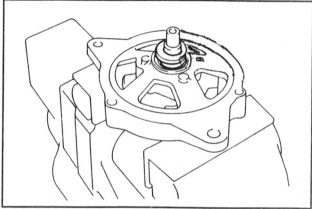

(c) Slide the fan, pulley and spring washer onto the rotor shaft.

(d) Install and torque the nut.

Torque: 625 kg-cm (45 ft-lb, 61 N·m)

5. Assemble Drive End Frame and Rectifier End Frame.

(a) Bend the rectifier lead wires back to clear the rotor.

(b) Using a curved tool, push the brushes in as far as they will go and hold them in position by inserting a stiff wire through the access hole in the rectifier end frame.

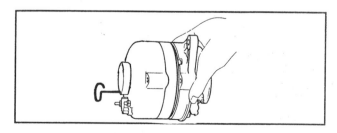

(c) Assemble the drive end frame and the rectifier end frame by inserting the rear bearing on the rotor shaft into the rectifier end frame.

(d) Install the 3 through screws.

(e) Take the stiff wire out of the access hole.

(f) Check that the rotor turns smoothly.

(g) Seal the access hole.

Alternator Regulator.

Inspection.

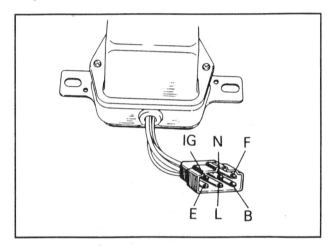

Location: On the left fender apron in the engine compartment.

1. Inspect Point Surfaces For Seizure and Damage. If defective, replace the regulator.

2. Inspect Resistance Between Terminals.

(a) Using ohmmeter, measure the resistance between terminals IG & F.

Resistance (voltage regulator):

At rest   0 ohms

Pulled in Approx 11 ohms

(b) Measure the resistance between terminals E & L.

Resistance (voltage relay):

At rest   0 ohms

Pulled in Approx 100 ohms

(c) Measure the resistance between terminals B & E.

Resistance (Voltage relay):

At rest   Infinity

Pulled in Approx 100 ohms

(d) Measure the resistance between terminals B & L.

Resistance (voltage relay):

At rest   Infinity

Pulled in 0 ohms

(e) Measure the resistance between terminals N & E.

Resistance: Approx 23 ohms

If any of the above checks are not positive, replace the alternator regulator.

Adjustment.

1. Adjust Voltage Regulator by bending regulator adjusting arm.

Regulating voltage: 13.8-14.8 V

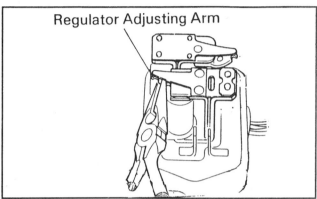

2. Adjust Voltage Relay by bending relay adjusting arm.

Relay actuating voltage: 4.0-5.8 V

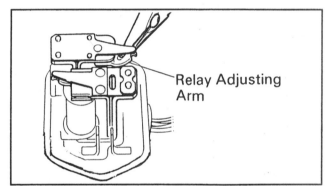

Ignition Main Relay. [FJ 62].

Inspection.

1. Inspect Relay Continuity. Ensure that there is continuity between terminals 1 & 3 and that there is no continuity between terminals 2 & 4.

If continuity is not as stated, replace the relay.

2. Inspect Relay Operation.

(a) Apply battery voltage across terminals 1 & 3.

(b) Make sure there is continuity between terminals 2 & 4 If operation is not as stated above, replace the relay.

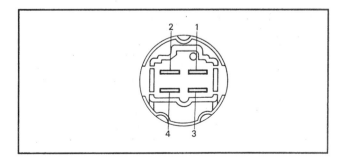

ALTERNATOR SYSTEM.21R, 21R-C & 22R 4 CYLINDER ENGINES.

Tirrill Regulator Type

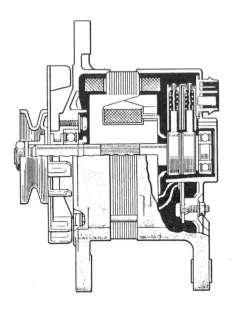

Built-in IC Regulator Type

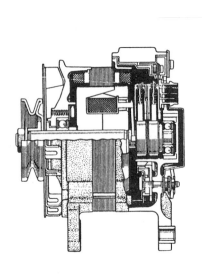

Separate IC Regulator Type

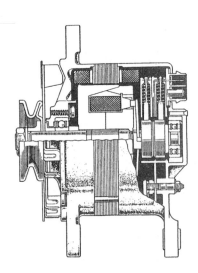

Charging System Circuits.

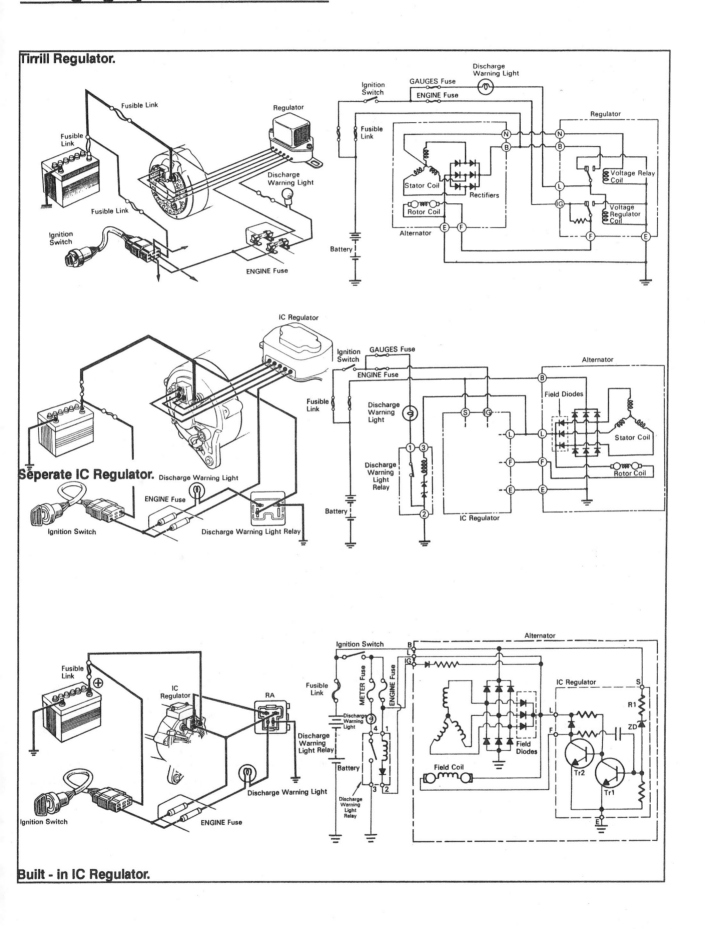

Tirrill Regulator.

Seperate IC Regulator.

Built - in IC Regulator.

In Car Inspection

(Tirrill Regulator Type).

Inspect Following Items.

1. Drive Belt tension. (General Countries.)

Drive Belt Tension at 10 kg (22 lb.)

New Belt 5-7 mm (0.20-0.28 in.)

Used Belt 7-10 mm (0.28-0.39 in.)

2. Fuses.

3. Installed condition of wiring for alternator and regulator.

4. Battery Terminal and fusible link.

5. Alternator in-car condition.

6. Specific gravity.

Specific gravity: 1.25-1.27 at 20°C (68°F)

Performance Test with Voltmeter & Ammeter.

Connect the voltmeter and ammeter as follows:

Ammeter (+) ------------ Alternator B terminal.

Ammeter (-) ------------ Wire B terminal

Voltmeter (+) ---------- Alternator B terminal.

Voltmeter (-) ---------- Ground

* Ensure not to cause a short.

No-load Performance Test.

Check the reading on the ammeter and voltmeter.

Current: Less than 10A

Voltage: 13.8-14.8 V

Engine speed: Idling to 2,000 rpm.

Load Performance Test.

1. Run engine at 2,000 rpm.

2. Turn on the headlights and all accessories.

Then check the reading on the ammeter and voltmeter.

Current: More than 30A

Voltage: 13.8-14.8V

Alternator Inspection.

1. Negative side rectifier short test. Connect an ohmmeter (-) lead to terminal N and (+) lead to terminal E. Meter should indicate infinity.

2. Positive side rectifier short test. Connect an ohmmeter (-) lead to terminal B and (+) lead to terminal N. Meter should indicate infinity.

3. Examine the rotor coil resistance.

Resistance: 3.9 - 4.1 ohms

4. Turn the starter switch to ON position, and inspect to see if there is battery voltage at terminal F. If not, inspect the Engine fuse.

(IC Regulator Type)

Inspect following items:

1. Drive belt tension.

2. Installed condition of wiring for alternator and regulator.

3. Specific gravity.

4. Alternator in-car inspection.

5. Fuses.

6. Battery terminal and fusible link.

Performance Test. Connect the voltmeter and ammeter as follows:

Ammeter (+) ------------- Alternator B terminal

Ammeter (-) -------------- Wire B terminal

Voltmeter (+) ------------ Alternator B terminal

Voltmeter (-) ------------- Ground

* Ensure not to cause a short.

No-load Performance Test. (Separate IC Regulator Type)

Check the reading on the ammeter and voltmeter.

Current: Less than 10A

Voltage: 13.8-14.4 V (25°C or 77°F)

Engine Speed: 2,000 rpm

* If the voltage reading is greater tha 15.0 V replace the IC regulator.

If the voltage reading is less than 13.5 V, check the alternator and IC regulator as follows:

1. Turn off the engine and disconnect the connector from the IC regulator.

2. Turn the starter switch to ON position.

3. Check the voltage reading at the alternator terminal IG. Inspect the engine fuse and/or starter switch, if no voltage.

4. Connect the connector to the IC regulator and then check the voltage reading at the alternator terminal L. If the reading is 1-2 V, inspect the alternator.

No-load Performance Test. (Built-in IC Regulator Type) Inspect the reading on the ammeter and voltmeter.

Current: Less than 10A

Voltage 60A: 14.0-14.7V (25°C, 77°F)

Others: 13.8-14.4V (25°C, 77°F)

If the voltage reading is less than 13.5V, examine the alternator and IC regulator as follows:

1. Turn the starter switch to ON position and check the voltage reading at the alternator IG terminal. If no voltage, inspect the engine fuse and/or starter switch.

2. Remove the end cover from the IC regulator and check the voltage reading at the regulator terminal L. If the voltage reading is zero to 2 volts, check the alternator.

If the voltage reading is same as battery voltage, turn the starter switch to OFF and check that there is continuity between the regulator terminals L & F.

No continuity ------------------ Check the alternator.

Continuity ------------------ Replace the IC regulator.

Load Performance Test.

1. Run engine at 2,000 rpm.

2. Turn on the headlights and all accessories. Then check the reading on the ammeter and voltmeter.

Current: More than 30A
Voltage 60A: 14.0-14.7V
Others: 13.8-14.4V

Alternator.

Dismantle.

Dismantle the parts in the following order:

Tirrill Regulator Type.

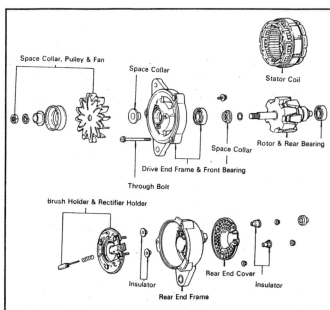

1. Through bolt.

(a) Pry off the drive end frame from the stator.

* Ensure not to damage the coil wires.

2. Space Collar, Pulley & Fan.

(a) Clamp the rotor in a soft jaw vice and loosen the pulley nut.

3. Space Collar.

4. Drive End Frame & Front Bearing.

5. Space Collar.

6. Rotor & Rear Bearing.

7. Insulator.

8. Rear End Cover.

9. Rear End Frame.

(a) Remove the rear end frame from the stator and rectifier holder.

* As for the built-in IC regulator type, remove the IC regulator before separating the rear end frame.

10. Insulator.

11. Brush Holder & Rectifier Holder.

12. Stator Coil.

(a) Disconnect the stator coil from the rectifier holder by melting the solder.

* When unsoldering the leads, hold the rectifier lead with long nose pliers to protect the rectifier from heat.

Separate IC Regulator Type.

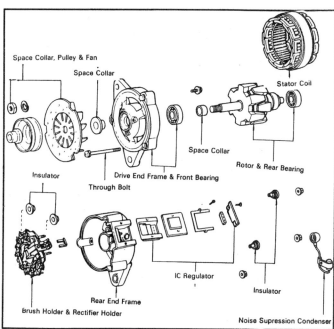

1. Through bolt.

(a) Pry off the drive end frame from the stator.

* Ensure not to damage the coil wires.

2. Space Collar, Pulley & Fan.

(a) Clamp the rotor in a soft jaw vice and loosen the pulley nut.

3. Space Collar.

4. Drive End Frame & Front Bearing.

5. Space Collar.

6. Rotor & Rear Bearing.

7. Noise Suppression Condenser.

8. Insulator.

9. Rear End Frame.

(a) Remove the rear end frame from the stator and rectifier holder.

* As for the built-in IC regulator type, remove the IC regulator before separating the rear end frame.

10. Insulator.

11. Brush Holder & Rectifier Holder.

12. Stator Coil.

(a) Disconnect the stator coil from the rectifier holder by melting the solder.

* When unsoldering the leads, hold the rectifier lead with long nose pliers to protect the rectifier from heat.

Built-in Regulator Type.

1. Through Bolt.

(a) Pry off the drive end frame from the stator.

* Ensure not to damage the coil wires.

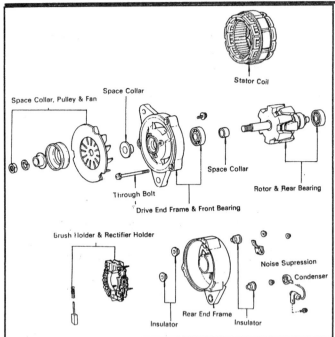

2. Space Collar, Pulley & Fan.

(a) Clamp the rotor in a soft jaw vice and loosen the pulley nut.

3. Space Collar.

4. Drive End Frame & Front Bearing.

5. Space Collar.

6. Rotor & Rear Bearing.

7. Noise Suppression Condenser.

8. Insulator.

9. IC Regulator.

10.Rear End Frame.

(a) Remove the rear end frame from the stator and rectifier holder.

* As for the built-in IC regulator type, remove the IC regulator before separating the rear end frame.

11.Insulator

12.Brush Holder & Rectifier Holder.

13.Stator Coil.

(a) Disconnect the stator coil from the rectifier holder by melting the solder.

* When unsoldering the leads, hold the rectifier lead with long nose pliers to protect the rectifier from heat.

INSPECTION.

Rotor.

1. Check the slip rings for dirt or burns.

2. Open circuit test. Check for continuity between both slip rings. Replace the rotor if there is no continuity.

Resistance:

Tirrill regulator type: 3.9-4.1 ohms.

IC regulator type: 2.8-3.0 ohms.

3. Ground Test.

Ensure that there is no continuity between the slip ring and rotor. If there is continuity, replace the rotor.

Stator (Tirrill Regulator Type)

1. Open circuit test. Ensure that there is continuity between the 2 leads near each other. Replace the stator if there is no continuity.

2. Ground Test. Check that there is no continuity between the coil leads and stator core. If there is, replace the stator.

Stator. (IC Regulator Type)

1. Open Circuit Test. Check that there is continuity between the three-wire meeting point and the other leads. Replace the stator if there is no continuity.

* Inspect for continuity when the meeting wires are connected with solder.

2. Ground Test. Check that there is no continuity between the coil leads and stator core. Replace the stator if there is continuity.

Bearing.

1. Examine the front & rear bearings for roughness or wear and replace using a new ones if needed.

* Ensure not to press bearing in on an angle.

Brush & Brush Holder.

1. Measure the exposed brush length.

Exposed length:

Minimum 5.5 mm (0.217 in.)

If the brush length is less than minimum, replace the brush.

2. When replacing the brush, assemble them as illustrated in the diagram.

Exposed length: 12.5 mm (0.492 in.)

Rectifier (Tirrill Regulator Type - 40, 45A)

1. Rectifier holder positive side:

Connect an ohmmeter (+) lead to the rectifier holder, and the (-) lead of the meter to each rectifier terminal. If there is no continuity, rectifier assembly must be replaced.

2. Reverse polarity of test leads and examine again. If there is continuity, rectifier assembly must be replaced.

3. Rectifier holder negative side:

Connect an ohmmeter (+) lead to each rectifier terminal, and the (-) lead of the meter to the rectifier holder. If there is no continuity, rectifier assembly must be replaced.

4. Reverse polarity of test leads and inspect again. If there is continuity, rectifier assembly must be replaced.

Rectifier (Tirrill Regulator Type - 50, 55A)

1. Rectifier holder positive side:

Connect an ohmmeter (+) lead to the rectifier holder and the (-) lead of the meter to the rectifier terminal. If there is no continuity, the rectifier assembly must be replaced.

2. Reverse polarity of the test leads and check again. If there is continuity, the rectifier assembly must be replaced.

3. Rectifier holder negative side: Connect an ohmmeter (+) lead to the rectifier terminal, and the (-) lead of the meter to the rectifier holder. If there is no continuity, the rectifier assembly must be replaced.

4. Reverse polarity of the test leads and check again. If there is continuity, the rectifier assembly must be replaced.

Rectifier (IC Regulator Type)

1. Rectifier holder positive side: Connect an ohmmeter (+) lead to the rectifier holder, and the (-) lead of the meter to the rectifier terminal. If there is no continuity, rectifier assembly must be replaced.

2. Reverse polarity of test leads and check again. If there is continuity, rectifier assembly must be replaced.

3. Rectifier holder negative side: Connect an ohmmeter (+) lead to the rectifier terminal, and the (-) lead of the meter to the rectifier holder. If there is no continuity, rectifier assembly must be replaced.

4. Reverse polarity of test leads and check again. If there is continuity, rectifier assembly must be replaced.

Field Diodes (IC Regulator Type)

1. Connect an ohmmeter (+) lead to the rectifier holder, and the (-) lead of the meter to the field diode terminal. If there is no continuity, rectifier assembly must be replaced.

2. Reverse polarity of test leads and check again. If there is continuity, rectifier assembly must be replaced.

Diode (IC Regulator Type)

1. Connect an ohmmeter (+) lead to the resistor side, and the (-) lead of the meter to the diode other side. If there is no continuity, rectifier assembly must be replaced.

2. Reverse polarity of test leads and check again. If there is continuity, rectifier assembly must be replaced.

Resistor (IC Regulator Type)

Measure the resistance of the resistor with an ohmmeter.

Resistance: 19 ohms.

ASSEMBLY.

Assemble parts in the following order:

Tirrill Regulator Type.

1. Brush Holder & Rectifier Holder.
2. Stator Coil.
(a) Solder each lead wire onto the rectifier or terminal as illustrated in the diagram.
3. Insulator.
(a) Assemble the rectifier holder with the insulators.
4. Rear End Frame.
5. Rear End Cover.

6. Insulator.
(a) Assemble the rear end cover with the insulators.
7. Rotor & Rear Bearing.
8. Space Collar.
9. Drive End Frame & Front Bearing.
(a) Push in the brushes and temporarily lock them in place with wire inserted through the access hole in the rear end frame.
(b) Assemble the drive end frame and the rectifier end frame by inserting the rear bearing into the rear end frame. Then, remove the wire from the access hole.
10. Space Collar.
11. Space Collar, Pulley & Fan.
(a) Clamp the rotor with a soft jaw vice and tighten the pulley nut.
Tightening torque: 5.0-6.5 kg-m (37-47 ft-lb).
12. Through bolt.
(a) Check the rotor for smooth rotation after assembly is completed.

Separate IC Regulator Type.

1. Brush Holder & Rectifier Holder.
2. Stator Coil.
(a) Solder each lead wire onto the rectifier or terminal as illustrated in the diagram.
3. Insulator.
(a) Assemble the rectifier holder with the insulators.
4. Rear End Frame.
5. Insulator.
(a) Assemble the rear end cover with the insulators.
6. Noise Suppression Condenser.
7. Rotor & Rear Bearing.
8. Space Collar.
9. Drive End Frame & Front Bearing.
(a) Push in the brushes and temporarily lock them in place with wire inserted through the access hole in the rear end frame.
(b) Assemble the drive end frame and the rectifier end frame by inserting the rear bearing into the rear end frame. Then, remove the wire from the access hole.
10. Space Collar.
11. Space Collar, Pulley & Fan.
(a) Clamp the rotor with a soft jaw vice and tighten the pulley nut.
Tightening torque: 5.0-6.5 kg-m (37-47 ft-lb).
12. Through Bolt.
(a) Check the rotor for smooth rotation after assembly is completed.

Built-in IC Regulator Type.

1. Brush Holder & Rectifier Holder.
2. Stator Coil.
(a) Solder each lead wire onto the rectifier or terminal as illustrated in the diagram.
3. Insulator.
(a) Assemble the rectifier holder with the insulators.

4. Rear End Frame.

5. IC Regulator.

6. Insulator.

(a) Assemble the rear end cover with the insulators.

7. Noise Suppression Condenser.

8. Rotor & Rear Bearing.

9. Space Collar

10.Drive End Frame & Front Bearing.

(a) Push in the brushes and temporarily lock them in place with wire inserted through the access hole in the rear end frame.

(b) Assemble the drive end frame and the rectifier end frame by inserting the rear bearing into the rear end frame. Then, remove the wire from the access hole.

11.Space Collar.

12.Space Collar, Pulley & Fan.

(a) Clamp the rotor with a soft jaw vice and tighten the pulley nut.

Tightening torque: 5.0-6.5 kg-m (37-47 ft-lb).

13.Through bolt.

(a) Check the rotor for smooth rotation after assembly is completed.

Alternator Regulator.

Inspection & Adjustment.

Check the connector fitting condition before inspecting the regulator.

* Always ensure that the regulator connector is pulled out when examining and adjusting.

Inspect each point surface for burn or excessive damage. Replace if defective.

Voltage adjustment.

1. To adjust voltage regulator, bend the regulator adjusting arm.

Regulated voltage: 13.8-14.8 V

2. To adjust the voltage relay, bend the relay adjusting arm.

Relay actuating voltage: 4.0-5.8 V

Discharge Warning Light Relay.

Inspect Relay for Continuity.

1. RN (EX.Saudi Arabia), RA(From Aug.'81 to Aug.'83) Ensure that there is continuity between terminals 1 and 2.

If there is no continuity, replace the relay.

2. Connect (+) lead from the battery to terminal 3 of the relay and (-) lead to terminal 2. Ensure that there is no continuity between terminals 1 and 2. If there is continuity replace the relay.

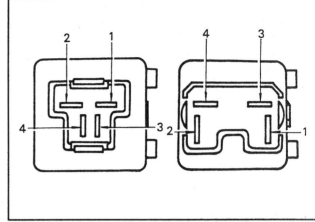

1. (RT,RA(From Aug.'83 to Aug.'84), RB) Ensure that there is no continuity between terminals 3 and 4. If there is continuity, replace the relay.

2. Connect (+) lead from the battery to terminal 1 of the relay and (-) lead to terminal 2. Ensure that there is continuity between terminals 3 & 4. If there is no continuity, replace the relay.

Problem Diagnosis.

Problem: Charge light does not light with ignition "ON" and engine off!

Possible Causes & Remedies:

* Fuse blown. Remedy - inspect IGN, CHARGE and ENGINE fuses.

* Light burnt out. Remedy - replace light.

* Wiring connection loose. Remedy - tighten loose connections

* Alternator regulator faulty. Remedy - inspect regulator.

Problem: Charge light does not go out with engine running (battery requires frequent recharging).

Possible Cuases & Renedies:

* Drive belt loose or worn. Remedy - adjust or replace drive belt.

* Battery cables loose, corroded or worn. Remedy - repair or replace cables.

* Fuse blown. Remedy - inspect ENGINE fuse.

* Ignition main relay faulty. Remedy - inspect relay.

* Fusible link blown. Remedy - replace fusible link.

* Alternator regulator or alternator faulty. Remedy - inspect charging system.

* Wiring faulty. Remedy - repair wiring.

CLUTCH

CLUTCH SYSTEM

Check and Adjust Clutch Pedal & Release Cylinder

1. Check that Pedal Height is Correct.

Pedal Height:

Series	mm	in
FJ, HJ, BJ 4..'s	215	8.46
FJ 55	185	7.28
FJ, BJ, HJ 6..'s	181	7.13
FJ, HJ 7..'s	186	7.32
BJ 70	190	7.48
LJ 70	186	7.32
RJ 70	186	7.32

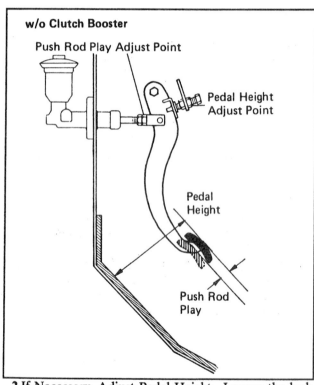

w/o Clutch Booster

Push Rod Play Adjust Point

Pedal Height Adjust Point

Pedal Height

Push Rod Play

2. If Necessary, Adjust Pedal Height. Loosen the lock nut and turn the stopper bolt or clutch switch until the height is correct. Tighten the lock nut.

* After adjusting the pedal height, check and adjust the pedal free play and push rod play or booster air valve stroke.

3. [w/o Clutch Booster] Check that Pedal Freeplay and Push Rod Play are Correct.

(Pedal Freeplay) Push in on the pedal until the clutch begins to resist.

Pedal freeplay: 13 - 23 mm (0.51 - 0.91 in)

(Push Rod Play) Push in on the pedal with a finger softly until the resistance begins to increase a little.

Push rod play at pedal top: 1 - 5 mm (0.04 - 0.20 in)

[w/ Clutch Booster] Check Pedal Freeplay and Booster Air Valve Stroke.

(Pedal Freeplay) Push in on the pedal until the clutch begins to resist.

Pedal freeplay: 15 - 30 mm (0.59 - 1.18 in)

(Booster Air Valve Stroke)

(a) Stop the engine and depress the clutch pedal several times until there is no vacuum left in the clutch booster.

(b) Push in on the pedal with a finger softly until the resistance begins to increase a little.

Booster air valve stroke at pedal top:
5 - 9 mm (0.20 - 0.35 in)

* The booster air valve stroke is the amount of the stroke until the booster piston is moved by the booster air valve.

4. If Necessary, adjust Pedal Freeplay and Push Rod Play or Booster Air Valve Stroke.

(a) Loosen the lock nut and turn the push rod until the freeplay and push rod play or booster air valve stroke are correct.

(b) Tighten the lock nut.

(c) After adjusting the pedal freeplay, check the pedal height.

5. Release Cylinder.

(a) Adjust the play at release fork tip by loosening the lock nut and turn the push rod No. 1 with a spanner while holding the push rod No. 2 with a suitable tool.

Release fork end play:
FJ series 4.0 - 5.0 mm (0.157 - 0.197 in)
BJ series 3.0 - 4.0 mm (0.118 - 0.157 in)
HJ series 4.0 - 5.0 mm (0.157 - 0.197 in)

(b) Check the pedal freeplay at the pedal top.

Pedal freeplay: 30 - 50 mm (1.18 - 1.97 in)

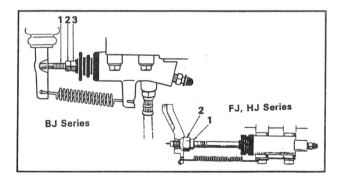

BJ Series

FJ, HJ Series

Test Clutch Booster.

* If there is leakage or lack of vacuum, repair before testing.

1.Operating Check. With the engine stopped, depress the clutch pedal several times. Then, with the pedal at the mid point, start the engine and confirm that the pedal sinks down slightly.

2.Air-tightness Check.

(a) Depress the clutch pedal several times with the engine stopped. Then start the engine and depress the clutch pedal and check that there is a slight difference in pedal effort.

(b) After the engine has been running, push the clutch pedal and ensure that the effort required for at least one pressing of the clutch is equal to the same as when the engine is running.

* If (a) and (b) are not as stipulated, inspect the vacuum check valve and also, if necessary, the clutch booster.

Bleed Clutch System

* If any work is done on the clutch system, or if air is suspected in the clutch lines, bleed the system of air.

* Do not let brake fluid remain on a painted surface. Wash it off immediately.

1.Fill Clutch Reservoirs with Brake Fluid. Check the reservoir after bleeding. Add fluid if necessary.

2.Connect Vinyl Tube to Release Cylinder Bleeder Plug. Insert the other end of the tube in a half-filled container of brake fluid.

3.Bleed Clutch Line.

(a) Slowly pump the clutch pedal several times.

(b) While having an assistant press on the pedal, loosen the bleeder plug until fluid starts to runout. Then close the bleeder plug.

(c) Repeat this procedure until there are no more air bubbles in the fluid.

(d) Torque the bleeder plug.

Torque: 110 kg-cm (8 ft-lb, 11 N·m)

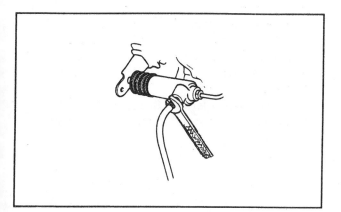

CLUTCH MASTER CYLINDER [W/O Clutch Booster]

Components

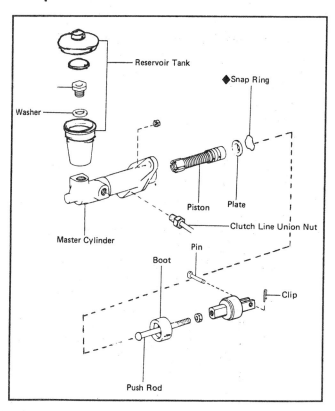

Removal

1.Draw Out Fluid with Syringe or something similar.

2.Disconnect Clutch Line Union.

3.Disconnect Clevis from Clutch Pedal. Remove the clip and clevis pin, disconnect the clevis from the clutch pedal.

4.Remove Master Cylinder. Remove the two mounting nuts, and pull off the master cylinder.

Dismantle

1.Remove Push Rod and Snap Ring.

(a) Pull back the boot and remove the snap ring with a screwdriver.

(b) Pull off the push rod and washer.

2.Remove Reservoir Tank.

3.Remove Piston. Using compressed air, remove the piston from the cylinder.

Inspection

Inspect Master Cylinder. Inspect the dismantled parts for wear, rust or damage.

Assembly

1. Coat Parts with Lithium Soap Base Glycol Grease.
2. Install Piston into Cylinder.
3. Install Push Rod Assembly with Snap Ring.
4. Install Reservoir Tank.
   Torque: **250 kg-cm (18 ft-lb, 25 N·m)**

Installation

1. Install Master Cylinder.
2. Connect Clevis and Clutch Pedal. Connect the clevis and clutch pedal with clevis pin and clip.
3. Connect Clutch Line Union.
4. Adjust Clutch Pedal and Bleed System.

CLUTCH MASTER CYLINDER [w/ Clutch Booster]

Components

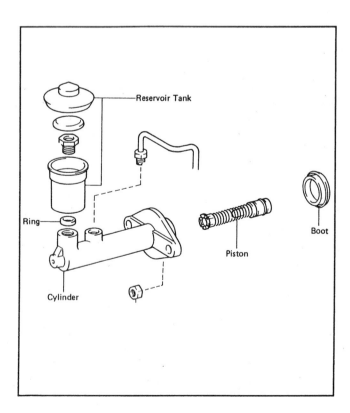

Reservoir Tank

Ring

Cylinder

Piston

Boot

Removal

1. Draw Out Fluid with Syringe or something similar.
2. Disconnect Clutch Line Union.
3. Remove Master Cylinder. Remove the 2 mounting nuts and pull off the master cylinder.

Dismantle

1. Remove Piston. Using compressed air, remove the piston from the cylinder.
2. Remove Reservoir Tank.

Inspection

Inspect Master Cylinder. Inspect the disassembled parts for wear, rust or damage.

Assembly

1. Coat Parts with Lithium Soap Base Glycol Grease.
2. Install Piston into Cylinder.
3. Install Reservoir Tank.
   Torque: 250 kg-cm (18 ft-lb, 25 N·m)

Installation

1. Adjust Length of Clutch Booster Push Rod. See INSTALLATION OF CLUTCH BOOSTER Section.
2. Install Master Cylinder with Mounting Nuts.
3. Connect Clutch Line Union.
4. Adjust Clutch Pedal and Bleed System.

CLUTCH BOOSTER

Removal

1. Remove Master Cylinder.
2. Disconnect Vacuum Hose from Clutch booster.
3. Remove Clutch Pipe and Vacuum Pipe Clamp Bolts.
4. Disconnect Clevis from Clutch Pedal. Remove the clip and clevis pin.
5. Remove Clutch Booster with Booster Cylinder Bracket. Remove the 3 bolts and pull off the clutch booster with bracket.

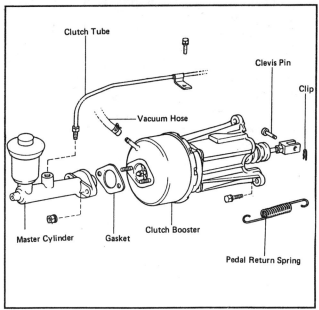

Components

(a) Put matchmarks on the No. 1 and No. 2 booster bodies.

(b) Set the booster in special tool.

* Be careful not to tighten the two nuts of the special tool too tightly.

(c) Turn the No. 1 booster body clockwise, until the No. 1 and No. 2 booster bodies separate.

5. Remove Booster Piston Assembly From No. 2 Booster Body.

6. Remove Booster Diaphragm from Booster Piston. Pull off the diaphragm.

7. Remove booster Air Valve Assembly from Booster Piston.

(a) Push down the booster air valve in the booster piston and remove the stopper key.

(b) Pull off the booster air valve assembly.

8. Remove Reaction Disc from booster Piston.

9. Remove Body Seal from No. 1 Booster Body. Using a screwdriver, pry out the circular ring and remove the body seal.

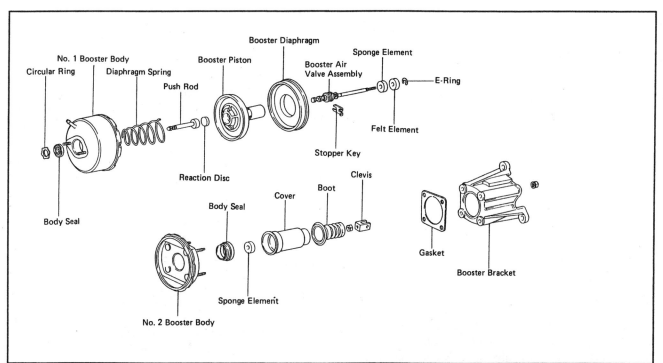

Dismantle

1. Remove Clevis.

2. Remove Piston Cover and Boot.

(a) Remove the booster bracket.

(b) Remove the piston cover and boot.

(c) Remove the sponge element from the boot.

3. Remove Sponge and Felt Element. Using a screwdriver, remove the E-clip and sponge and felt element.

4. Separate No. 1 and No. 2 Booster Bodies.

Remove body Seal with the help of a scew driver.

Inspection

1.Inspect Check Valve Operation.

(a) Check that air flows from the vacuum tank side to the vacuum hose side.

(b) Check that air does not flow from the vacuum hose side to the vacuum tank side.

2.If Necessary, Replace Body Seal fro No. 2 Booster Body.

(a) Using special tool, remove the body sealer.

* Support the No. 2 booster body cylinder base only, using special tool.

(b) Using special tool, drive in the body sealer.

* Support the No. 2 booster body cylinder base only,using special tool.

Assembly

1.Apply Silicone Grease to Parts Shown Below.

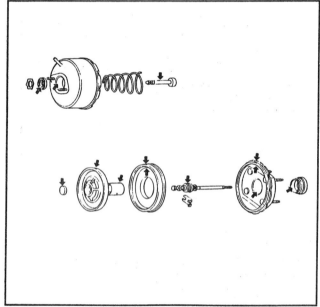

2.Install Body Seal to No. 1 Booster Body.

(a) Place the body seal in position.

(b) Secure the body seal with the circular ring.

3.Install Booster Air Valve Assembly to Booster Piston.

(a) Insert the booster air valve in the booster piston.

(b) Push the booster air valve in the booster piston and install the stopper key.

4.Install Diaphragm to booster Piston. Push in the head of the diaphragm.

5.Install Booster Piston Assembly to No. 2 booster Body.

6.Install Reaction Disc to Booster Piston.

7.Assembly No. 1 and No. 2 Booster Bodies.

(a) Place the No. 1 booster body on special tool.

(b) Place the push rod, diaphragm spring and No. 2 booster body in the No. 1 booster body.

(c) Compress the diaphragm spring between the No. 1 and No. 2 booster bodies.

* Be careful not to tighten the 2 nuts of the special tool too tightly.

(d) Turn the no. 1 booster body counterclockwise, until the matchmarks match.

* If the No. 1 booster body is too tight to be turned, apply more silicone grease on the diaphragm edge that contacts the No. 1 and No. 2 booster bodies.

8.Install Sponge and Felt Element.

(a) Install the sponge and felt elements into the booster.

(b) Install E-clip onto the booster air valve assembly.

9.Install Piston Cover with Boot.

(a) Install the sponge element into the boot.

(b) Install the boot to the piston cover.

(c) Install a new gasket onto the booster and the piston cover with the boot.

10.Install Booster to Booster Bracket with Four Nuts.

11.Install Clevis.

Installation

1.Adjust Length of Booster Push Rod.

(a) Set special tool on the master cylinder, and lower the pin until its tip slightly touches the piston.

* Always adjust the piston after pressing it with a screwdriver and allowing it to return slowly.

(b) Turn special tool upside down, and set it on the booster.

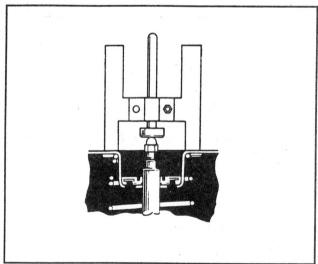

(c) Adjust the booster push rod length until the push rod lightly touches the pin head.

2.Install Clutch Booster with Master Cylinder Bracket to Body.

3.Connect Clevis to Clutch Pedal. Connect the clevis to the clutch pedal with the clevis pin and clip.

4.Install Master Cylinder to Clutch Booster.

5.Connect Clutch Line Union.

6.Connect Vacuum Hose to Clutch Booster.

7.Adjust Clutch Pedal and Bleed System. See ADJUST-MENT Section.

CLUTCH RELEASE CYLINDER

Assembly

1.Coat Piston with Lithium Soap Base Glycol Grease, as per sketch.
2.Install Piston.
3.Install Boot and Insert Push Rod.

Components

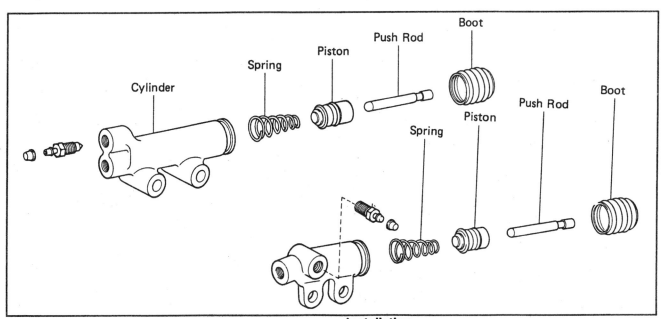

Removal

1.Remove Flexible Hose.
(a) Using special tool, disconnect the union.
(b) Remove the clip from flexible hose.
(c) Loosen and remove the flexible hose from the release cylinder.
2.Remove Release Cylinder.

Dismantle

1.Pull Off Push Rod.
2.Remove boot.
3.Remove Piston. Using compressed air, remove the piston from the cylinder.

Inspection

Inspect Release Cylinder. Inspect the disassembled parts for wear, rust or damage.

Installation

1.Install Release Cylinder with 2 bolts.
Torque: 120 kg-cm(9 ft-lb, 12 N·m)
2.Install Flexible Hose.
(a) Install the flexible hose to the release cylinder.
Torque: 155 kg-cm (11 ft-lb, 15 N·m)
(b) Connect the union.
(c) Install the clip.
3.Bleed Clutch System as described.

Adjustment of Release Cylinder

See ITEM 5, under CHECK & ADJUSTMENT OF CLUTCH PEDAL & RELEASE CYLINDER.

CLUTCH UNIT

(b) Loosen the set bolts one turn at a time until the spring tension is released.

(c) Remove the set bolts and pull off the clutch cover and disc.

3.Remove Bearing, Hub and Fork from Transmission.

(a) Remove the retaining clip and pull off the bearing with hub.

Components

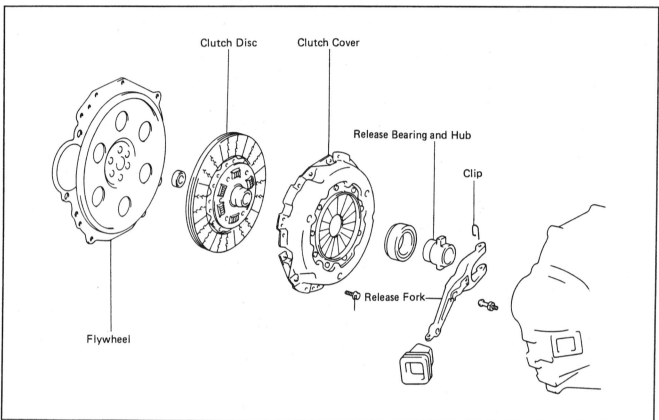

Clutch Disc   Clutch Cover

Release Bearing and Hub

Clip

Release Fork

Flywheel

Removal

(b) Remove the fork and boot.

1.Remove Transmission. See TRANSMISSION Section.

* Do not drain the transmission oil.

2.Remove Clutch Cover and Disc.

(a) Place paint or punch matchmarks on the clutch cover and flywheel to help in installation.

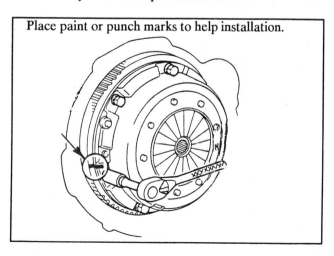

Place paint or punch marks to help installation.

Inspection

1.Inspect Clutch Disc for Wear or Damage. Using callipers, measure the rivet head depth.

Minimum rivet depth: 0.3 mm (0.012 in)

If a problem is found, replace the clutch disc.

2.Inspect Clutch Disc Runout. Using a dial indicator, check the disc runout.

Maximum runout: 0.8 mm (0.031 in)

If runout is excessive, replace the disc.

3.Inspect Pilot Bearing. Turn the bearing by hand while applying force in the axial direction. If the bearing sticks or has resistance, replace the pilot bearing.

* The bearing is permanently lubricated and requires no cleaning or lubrication.

4.If Necessary, Replace Pilot Bearing.

(a) Using special tool, remove the pilot bearing.

(b) Using special tool, install the pilot bearing.

5.Inspect Diaphragm Spring for Wear. Using callipers, measure the diaphragm spring for depth and width of wear.

Limit: Depth 0.6 mm (0.024 in)

Width 5.0 mm (0.197 in)

6.If Necessary, Replace Pressure Plate.

(a) Drill out the rivet heads.

(b) Disconnect the retracting springs from the pressure plate.

(c) Using a punch, drive out the rivets.

(d) Apply molybdenum disulphide lithium base grease (NLGI No. 2) to the contract surface of the pressure plate and cover.

(e) Connect a new pressure plate and the retracting springs with the special pressure plate bolts and nuts. Torque the nuts.

Torque: 195 kg-cm (14 ft-lb, 19 N·m)

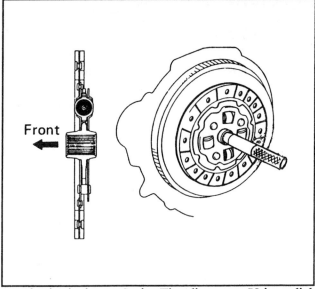

3.Check Diaphragm Spring Tip Alignment. Using a dial indicator and measuring point, check the diaphragm spring tip alignment.

Maximum non-alignment: 1.0 mm (0.039 in)

If alignment is excessive, adjust as follows.

4.If Necessary, Adjust Springs. Using special tool, bend the springs until alignment is correct.

5.Apply Molybdenum Disulphide Lithium Base Grease (NLGI No. 2) or MP Grease.

(a) Apply molybdenum disulphide lithium base grease to the following parts:

- release fork and hub contact point,
- release fork and push rod contact point,
- release fork pivot point,
- clutch disc spline,
- release bearing hub inside groove.

(b) Apply molybdenum disulphide lithium base grease to release bearing front.

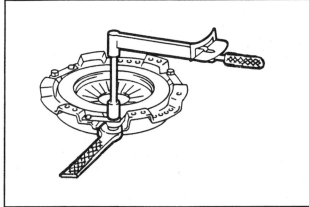

7.Inspect Release Bearing. Turn the bearing by hand while applying force in the axial direction.

* The bearing is permanently lubricated and requires no cleaning or lubrication.

8.If Necessary Replace Release Bearing.

(a) Using a press and special tool, press the release bearing from the hub.

(b) Using a press and special tool, press a new release bearing into the hub.

(c) After installing the bearing, check that there is no drag on the bearing when it is turned under pressure.

Installation

1.Install Disc on Flywheel. Using special tool, install the disc on the flywheel.

2.Install Clutch Cover.

(a) Align the matchmarks on the clutch cover and flywheel.

(b) Tighten the bolts evenly. Make several passes around the cover until it is snug. Torque the bolts.

Torque: 195 kg-cm (14 ft-lb, 19 N·m)

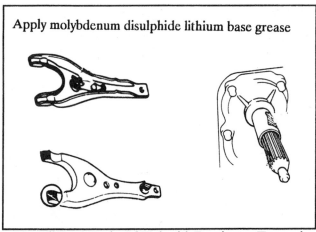

Apply molybdenum disulphide lithium base grease

6.Install Boot, Fork and Hub with Bearing on Transmission.

7.Install Transmission. See TRANSMISSION Section

Problem Diagnosis

Problem: Hard to shift or will not shift!

Possible Causes and Remedies:

*Clutch pedal freeplay excessive. Remedy - adjust pedal freeplay.

* Clutch booster faulty. Remedy - inspect clutch booster.

* Clutch release cylinder faulty. Remedy - repair release cyllinder.

* Clutch master cylinder faulty. Remedy - repair master cylinder.

* Clutch disc out of true, lining greasy or broken Remedy - inspect clutch disc.

* Splines on input shaft or clutch disc dirty or burred. Remedy - repair as necessary.

* Clutch pressure plate faulty. Remedy - replace pressure plate.

Problem: Transmission jumps out of gear!

Possible Cause and Remedy:

* Pilot bearing worn. Remedy - replace pilot bearing.

Problem: Clutch slips!

Possible Causes and Remedies:

* Clutch pedal freeplay insufficient. Remedy - adjust pedal freeplay.

* Clutch booster faulty. Remedy - inspect clutch booster.

* Clutch disc lining oily or worn out. Remedy - inspect clutch disc.

* Pressure plate faulty. Remedy - replace pressure plate.

* Release fork binds. Remedy - inspect release fork.

Problem: Clutch grabs/chatters!

Possible Causes and Remedies:

* Clutch booster faulty. Remedy - inspect clutch booster.

* Clutch disc lining oily or worn out. Remedy - inspect clutch disc.

* Pressure plate faulty. Remedy - repalce pressure plate.

* Clutch diaphragm spring bending. Remedy - align clutch diaphragm.

* Engine mounts loose. Remedy - repair as necessary.

Problem: Clutch pedal spongy!

Possible Causes and Remedies:

* Air in clutch lines. Remedy - bleed clutch system.

* Clutch release cyllinder faulty. Remedy - repair release cyllinder.

* Clutch master cylinder faulty. Remedy - repair master cylinder.

Problem: Clutch noisy!

Possible Causes and Remedies:

* Loose part inside housing. Remedy - repair as necessary.

* Release bearing worn or dirty. Remedy - replace release bearing.

* Pilot bearing worn. Remedy - replace pilot bearing.

* Release fork or linage sticks. Remedy - repair as necessary.

MANUAL TRANSMISSIONS

3 SPEED [J30]

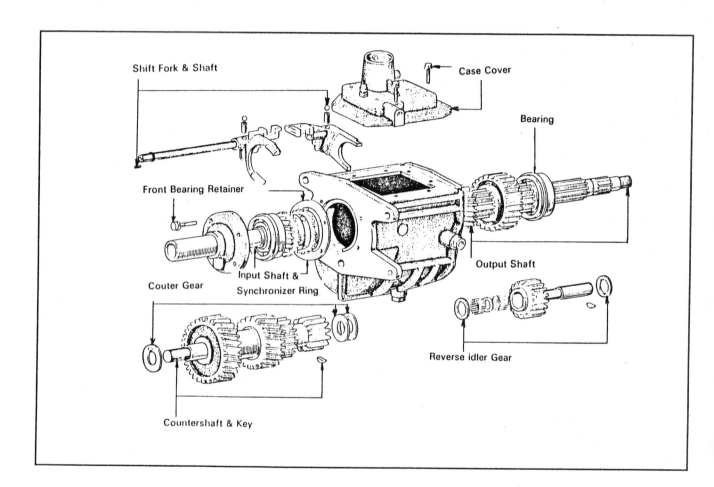

Shift Fork & Shaft

Case Cover

Bearing

Front Bearing Retainer

Output Shaft

Couter Gear

Input Shaft & Synchronizer Ring

Reverse idler Gear

Countershaft & Key

3 SPEED TRANSMISSION [J30]

Removal

Remove the transmission with transfer from the vehicle. Drain the transmission and transfer oil. Remove the transfer to teh transmission in the numerical order shown in the figure.

1. Shift Lever Guide.
2. Lever and Rod.
3. Back-up Light Switch.
4. Power Tawke Off or Cover.
5. No. 2 Case Cover.
6. Spacer, Washer and Nut.
7. Transfer, Gear and Bearing.

Dismantle

Dismantle in the following order:

1. Case Cover.
2. Front Bearing Retainer.
3. Shift Fork and Shaft. Drive out the shaft toward the front.
* Cover the locking ball hole with your finger to prevent the locking ball from jumping out.
4. Countershaft and Key. Drive out the shaft toward the rear with special tool.
5. Input Shaft and Synchronizer Ring.
6. Bearing.
7. Output Shaft.
(a) Using a brass bar, hammer the output shaft until the bearing is separated from the case.
(b) Remove the bearing with special tool.
(c) using a drift pin, drive out the shaft.
8. Reverse Idler Gear.
9. Counter Gear.
10. First and Reverse Gear.
11. Snap Ring.
12. Clutch Hub and Sleeve.

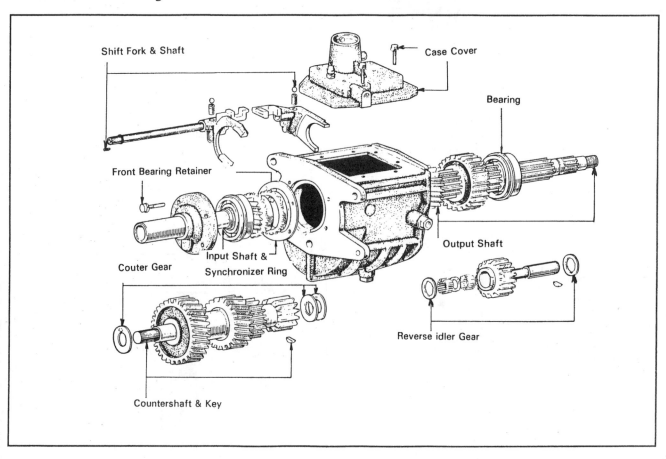

13.Synchronizer Ring.

14.Second Gear.

Inspection

After washing all dismantled parts, inspect them as instructed below. Replace all parts that are found defective.

1.Transmission Case and Front Bearing Retainer. Inspect for wear or damage.

2.Output Shaft. Inspect the shaft for wear or damage at the surfaces where the gears and bearing are installed.

3.1st Gear, 2nd Gear and Bearing.

(a) Inspect the gears for wear or damage at the teeth, thrust faces, inside diameter surfaces, and coned parts.

(b) Inspect the output shaft rear bearing for wear or damage.

(c) Measure the oil clearance.

2nd gear bushing oil clearance (A - B):

Limit 0.09 mm (0.0035 in)

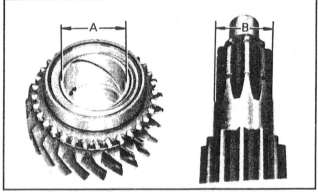

4.Synchronizer Ring.

(a) Fit the synchronizer ring on the gear and measure the clearance.

2nd & 3rd gear synchronizer ring clearance:

Limit 0.8 mm (0.031 in)

5.Clutch Hub Sleeve, Clutch Hub, Shifting Key & Shifting Key Spring.

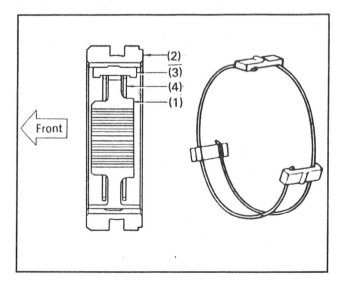

(a) Dismantle the clutch hub and sleeve.

(b) Inspect the splines of hub and hub sleeve for wear or damage.

(c) Inspect the humped part at centre of key for wear or damage.

(d) Inspect the key springs for weakening or damage.

(e) Assemble the hub sleeve (2), three shifting keys (3) and two key springs (4) to the clutch hub (1).

* Hub and hub sleeve are parts having directionality.

* Install the key springs positioned so that their end gaps will not be in line.

* Check the hub and hub sleeve to see that they slide smoothly together.

6.Shift Fork. Check the clearance between the hub sleeve groove and the shift fork.

Clearance: Limit - 0.8 mm (0.031 in)

7.Input Shaft.

(a) Inspect the gear teeth, splines, coned surfaces, and bearings for wear or damage.

(b) Replace the input shaft bearing.

(i) Remove the snap ring with special tool.

(ii) Remove the bearing with a press.

(iii) Using a press and special tool, install the bearing.

(iv) Select a snap ring of the thickness that will allow minimum axial play, and install it on the shaft.

8.Counter Gear and Countershaft.

(a) Inspect the counter gear teeth for wear or damage.

(b) Inspect the bearings and countershaft for wear or damage.

(c) Inspect the thrust washers for wear or damage.

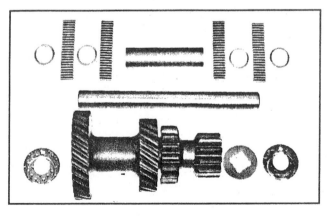

9.Reverse Idler Gear, Bearing and Shaft. Inspect the gear, bearings, and shaft for wear or damage.

Assembly

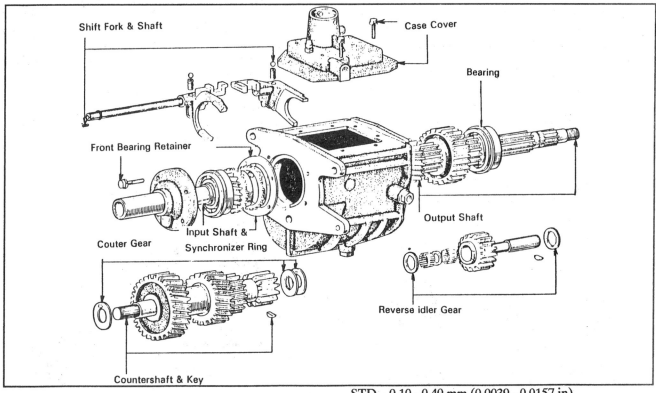

Assemble these in the order shown.

1.2nd Gear. Measure the 2nd gear thrust clearance.

Thrust clearance:
STD   0.10 - 0.40 mm (0.0039 - 0.0157 in)
Limit 0.4 mm (0.016 in)

2.Synchronizer Ring.

3.Clutch Hub and Sleeve.

4.Snap Ring.

5.1st and Reverse Gear. Install as illustrated.

* Coat MP grease on the bearing, washer, and spacer before installing.

6.Reverse Idler Gear.

7.Counter Gear. Assemble the counter gear assembly as illustrated, and install in the case.

* Coat MP grease on the bearing, washer, and spacer before installing.

8.Input Shaft and Synchronizer Ring. Drive in the input shaft with special tool.

9.Countershaft and Key. Measure the counter gear thrust clearance.

Thrust clearance:
STD   0.10 - 0.40 mm (0.0039 - 0.0157 in)
Limit 0.4 mm (0.016 in)

Thrust washer thickness:

Part No.	Thickness mm (in)
33441-61010	1.45 - 1.50 (0.0571 - 0.0591)
33442-61010	1.50 - 1.55 (0.0591 - 0.0610)
33443-61010	1.55 - 1.60 (0.0610 - 0.0630)

10. Output Shaft.

11. Bearing.

12. Shift Fork and Shaft. While holding down the locking ball, drive in the shaft, and then lock the shaft with a straight line.

13. Front Bearing Retainer. Install the retainer with its oil hole positioned downward.

14. Case Cover.

Installation

Install the parts in order.

1.Transfer and Gear.

2.Bearing.

3.Spacer, Washer and Nut.

4.No. 2 Case Cover.

5.Power Take Off or Cover.

6.Shift Lever Guide.

7.Lever and Rod.

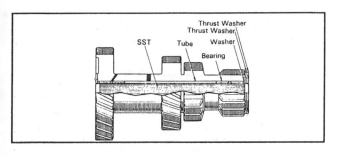

4 & 5 SPEED TRANSMISSIONS [H41, H42 AND H55F]

Removal

1. Disconnect Battery Cable from Negative Terminal.
2. Remove Transmission Shift Lever.
(a) Remove the shift lever boot.
(b) Cover the shift lever cap with a cloth.
(c) Then, pressing down on the shift lever cap, rotate it counterclockwise to remove.
(d) Remove the shift lever.
3. Raise Vehicle and Drain Out Transmission and Transfer.
4. Remove Transmission Undercover.
5. Remove Front and Rear Propeller Shafts.
6. Remove Speedometer Cable.
7. Remvoe Diaphragm Cylinder Vacujm Hose (Electrical Shift Type).
8. Remove 4WD and Back-up Light Switch Connector.
9. Remove L4 Switch Connector (Electrical Shift Type).
10. Remove Transfer Shift Lever From Transfer.
11. Remove Clutch Release Cylinder (BJ, HJ).
12. Remove Starter (BJ, HJ).
13. Remove Exhaust Pipe.
14. Jack Up Transmission Slightly.
15. Remove Engine Rear Support Member.
16. Lower Transmission.
17. Remove Transmission with Transfer.
(a) Remove the transmission mounting bolts from the clutch housing (FJ) or engine (BJ, HJ).
(b) Remove the transmission with the transfer.

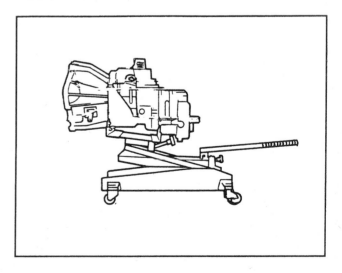

Components

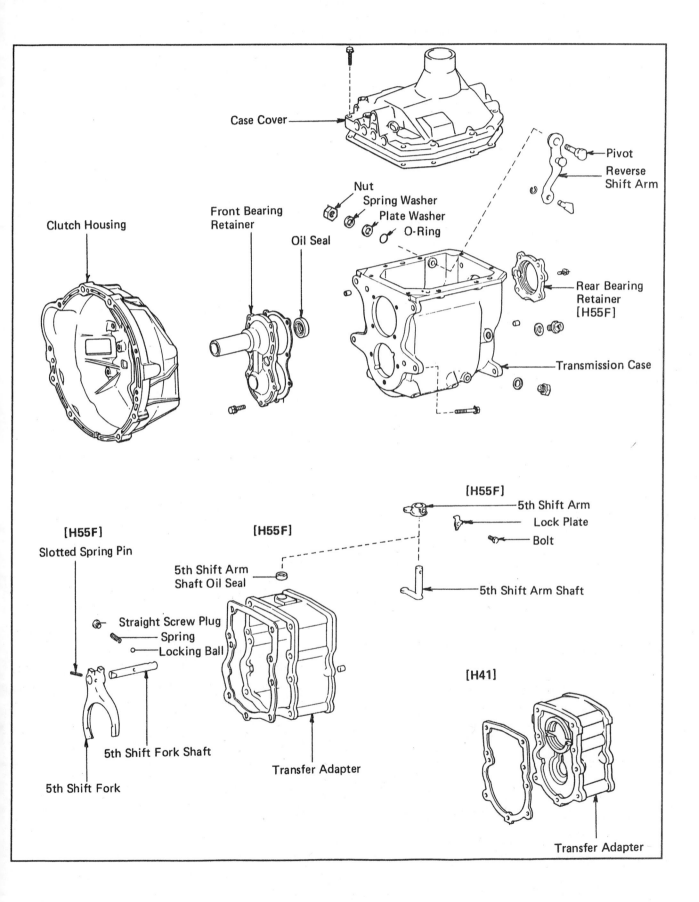

Case Cover

Pivot

Reverse Shift Arm

Nut

Spring Washer

Plate Washer

O-Ring

Clutch Housing

Front Bearing Retainer

Oil Seal

Rear Bearing Retainer [H55F]

Transmission Case

[H55F]

5th Shift Arm

Lock Plate

Bolt

[H55F]

5th Shift Arm Shaft Oil Seal

5th Shift Arm Shaft

[H55F]

Slotted Spring Pin

Straight Screw Plug

Spring

Locking Ball

5th Shift Fork Shaft

Transfer Adapter

[H41]

5th Shift Fork

Transfer Adapter

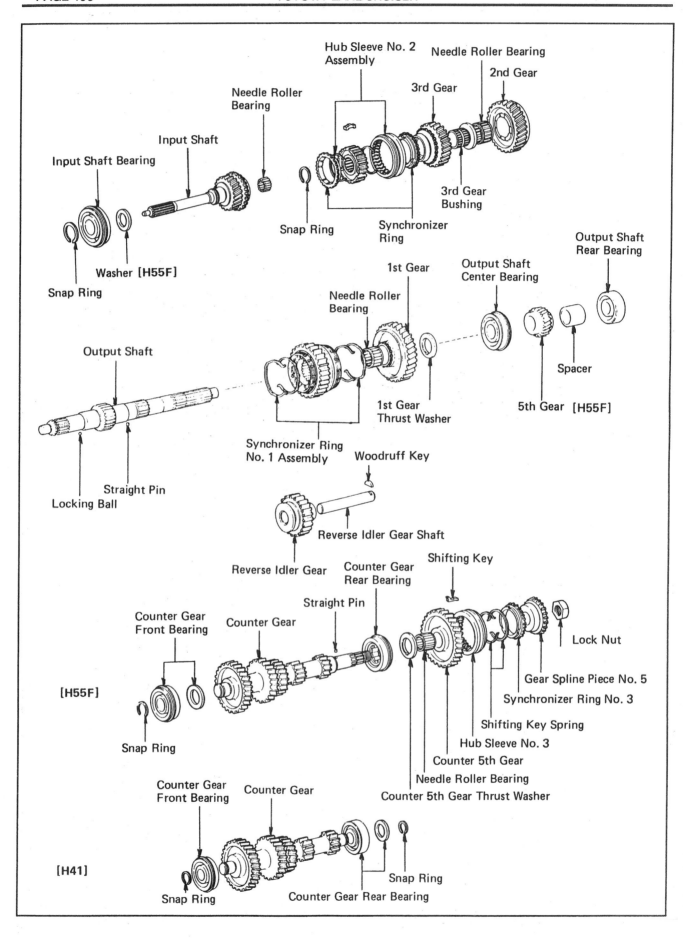

4-Speed " H 41 "

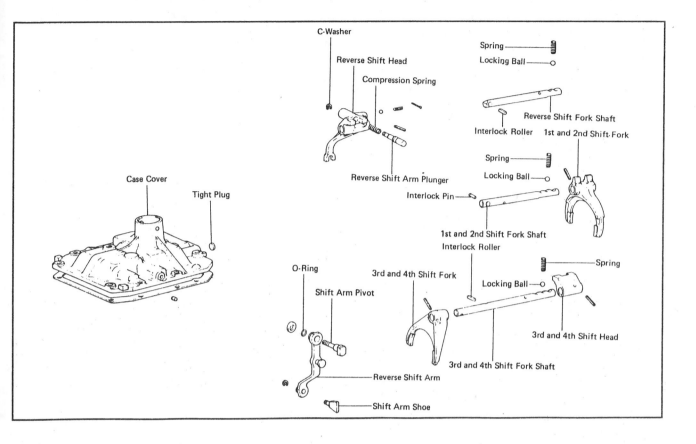

5-Speed " H 55 F "

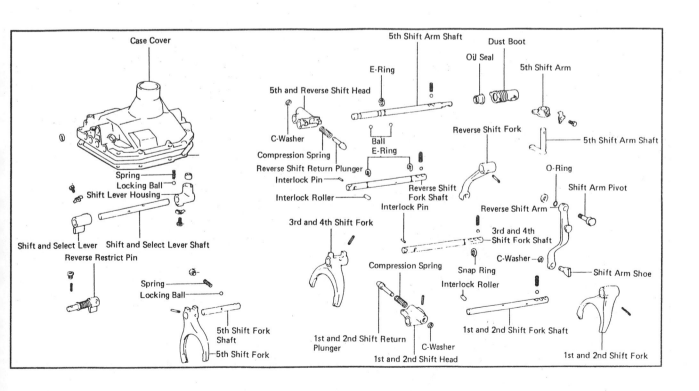

Dismantle Transmission

1.Remove Clutch Housing (HJ, BJ).
2.Remove Transfer. See TRANSFER Section.
3.Remove Back-up Light Switch.

REMOVE REVERSE LIGHT SWITCH.

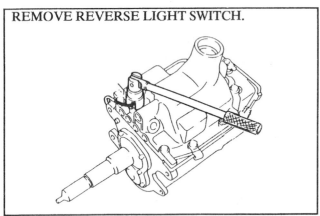

4.Remove Case Cover and Gasket.
(a) **[H55F]** Remove the dust boot.
5.**[H55F]** Remove Fifth Locking Ball and Spring.
(a) Remove the screw plug.
(b) Using a magnetic finger, remove the locking ball and spring.
6.Remove transfer Adapter. Pull up 5th shfit arm and pull the transfer adapter from the transmission case.
7.Measure Each Gear Thrust Clearance. Using a feeler gauge, measure the thrust clearance of each gear.
* For later reference, write down the thrust clearance.
Standard clearance:
1st & 2nd gears
0.175 - 0.325 mm (0.0069 - 0.0128 in)
3rd gear
0.125 - 0.275 mm (0.0049 - 0.0108 in)
Counter 5th gear
0.10 - 0.30 mm (0.0039 - 0.0118 in)
Maximum clearance:
1st & 2nd gears   0.35 mm (0.0138 in)
3rd & Couter 5th gears 0.30 mm (0.0118 in)
8.Remove Output Shaft Rear Bearing. Using special tool, remove the rear bearing.
9.Remove Spacer.

4 Speed Trans	5 Speed Trans

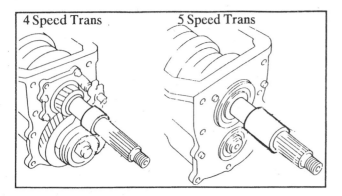

10.**[H55F]** Remove Couter Gear Rear Lock Nut.
(a) Engage the gear double meshing.
(b) Unstake the lock nut.
(c) Using special tool, remove the lock nut.

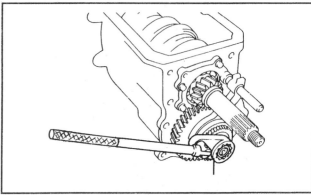

(d) Disengage the gear double meshing.
11.**[H55F]** Remove Gear Spline Piece No. 5, Couter Fifth Gear Assemlby and Fifth Shift Fork. Using special tool, pull the couter 5th gear out of the counter gear rear end with gear spline piece No. 5 and the 5th shift fork.
12.**[H55F]** Remove Straight Pin and Couter Fifth Gear Thrust Washer.
13.**[H55F]** Remove Rear Bearing Retainer.
14. **[H55F]**Remvoe Fifth Gear from Output Shaft. Using special tool and two bolts, remove the 5th gear from the output shaft.
* Use steel plates etc (approx. 2 mm thick) as a backplate to prevent the case from being damaged by the bolts.
* Tighten the two bolts evenly.
* Use bolts with a 12 mm nominal diameter, 1.5 pitch, and approx. 80 mm thread length. (Reference: Par No. 90101-12034).
15.Remove Conter Gear Shaft Rear Bearing.
(a) Using snap ring pliers, remove the snap ring.
(b) Using special tool, remove the counter gear rear bearing.
16.Remove Front Baering Retainer.
* Be careful not to damage the oil seal.
17.Remove Conter Gear Front Bearing.
(a) Using snap ring pliers, remove the snap rings.
(b) Using special tool, remove the couter gear front bearing.
18.**[FJ, HJ series]** Remove Input Shaft and Bearing.

FJ & HJ

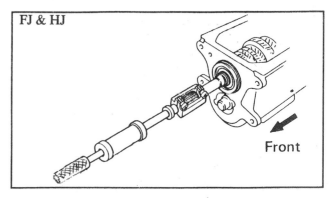

Front

(a) Using special tool, remove the input shaft and bearing.

* Ensure that the input shaft and couter gear do not strike each other.

* Be careful ot to loose the 17 needle roller bearings.

(b) Remove the synchronizer ring.

[BJ series] Remove Input Shaft and Bearing.

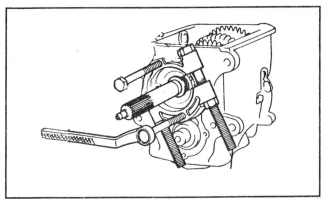

(a) Using snap ring pliers, remove the snap ring of bearing inner.

(b) Set the special tool to the snap ring groove, and using two bolts, remove the input shaft and bearing.

* Use steel plates etc. (approx. 2 mm thick) as a backplate to prevent the case from being damaged by the bolts.

* Tighten the two bolts evenly.

* Use bolts with a 12 mm nominal diameter, 1.5 pitch, and approx. 60 mm thread length. (Reference: Part No. 90101-12034).

19. Remove Output Shaft Centre Bearing.

(a) Using snap ring pliers, remove the snap ring.

(b) using special tool, support the output shaft front end.

(c) Using special tool, remove the centre bearing.

20. Remove Output Shaft and Couter Gear.

(a) Stand the transmission case on its front end.

(b) Remove th eoutput shaft.

(c) Remove the couter gear.

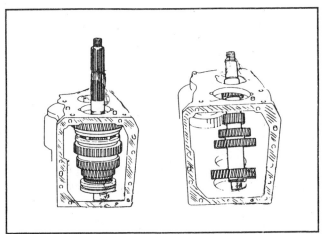

21. Remove Reverse Idler Gear and Shaft.

(a) Tap out the reverse idler gear shaft toward the rear.

(b) Remove the gear and the woodruff key.

22. Remove Reverse Shift Arm From Transmission Case. Remove the nut, washers, O-ring, pivot arm, and reverse shift arm.

23. Remove First Gear Thrust Washer and Straight Pin.

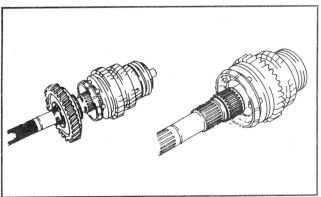

24. Remove First Gear and Needle Roller Bearing.

25. Remove Synchronizer Ring No. 1 Assembly.

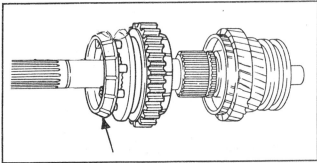

26. Remove Hub Sleeve No. 2 Assembly, Synchronizer Ring, Third Gear, Third Gear Bushing, Needle Roller Bearing and Second Gear from Output Shaft.

(a) Using snap rings pliers, remove the snap ring.

(b) Using a press, remove the hub sleeve No. 2 assembly, synchronizer ring, 3rd gear, 3rd gear bushing, needle roller bearing and 2nd gear.

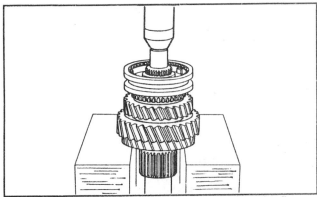

27. Remove Locking Ball. Using a magnetic finger, remove the locking ball.

28. **[H55F]** Remove Fifth Shift Arm and Shaft from Transfer Adapter. Remove the bolt and lock plate, then the 5th arm and shaft.

29.Dismantle Fifth Shift Fork. Using a pin punch and hammer, drive out the slotted pin, then remove the 5th shift fork from the shaft.

[H41] Dismantle Case Cover Assembly

1.Remove 3rd and 4th Shift Head, 3rd and 4th Shift Fork and Shaft.

(a) Using a pin punch and hammer, drive out the slotted spring pins from the shift head and the shift fork.

(b) Using a hammer, drive out the shift fork shaft together with the tight plug.

* Cover the service hole with your hand to prevent the locking ball from flying out.

(c) Remove the fork shaft, shift head, interlock roller, locking ball and spring.

2.Remove Reverse Shift Head.

(a) Using a pin punch and hammer, drive out the slotted spring pin from the reverse shift head, then the shift fork shaft together with the tight plug.

* Cover the service hole with your hand to prevent the locking ball from flying out.

(b) Remove the fork shaft, shift head, interlock roller, locing ball and spring.

3.Remove First and Second Shift Fork and Shaft.

(a) Using a pin punch and hammer, remove the slotted spring pin from the shift fork, then drive out the shift fork shaft together with the tight plug.

* Cover the service hole with your hand to prevent the locking ball from flying out.

(b) Remove the lork shaft, shift fork, interlock pin, locing ball and spring.

4.Dismantle Shift Head.

(a) Compress the spring, and remove the C-clip.

* Be careful as the plunger with spring out.

(b) Remove the plunger and compression spring.

[H55F] Dismantle Case Cover Assembly

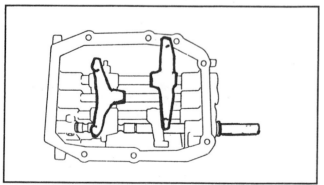

1. Remove 5th Shift Arm Shaft.

(a) Using a screwdriver, pry out the E-clip.

(b) Remove the shaft, two interlock balls, locking ball and spring.

2.Remove 5th and Reverse Shift Head, Reverse Shift Fork and Fork Shaft.

(a) Using a screwdriver, pry out the E-clip.

(b) Using a plastic hammer, tap on the shift fork and remove the tight plug from the case cover.

(c) Using a pin punch, drive out the slotted spring pin from the shift fork.

(d) Remove the fork shaft, shift fork, shift head, interlock roller, interlock pin, locking ball and spring.

3.Remove 1st and 2nd Shift Head, Shift Fork and Fork Shaft.

(a) Using a pin punch and hammer, drive out the slotted spring pin from the shift head.

(b) Using a plastic hammer, tap the shift fork and remove the tight plug from the case cover.

(c) Using a pin punch and hammer, drive out the slotted spring pin from the shift fork.

(d) Remove the fork shaft, shift head, shift fork, locking ball and spring.

4.Remove 3rd and 4th Shift Fork and Fork Shaft.

(a) Using two screwdrivers and a hammer, tap out the snap ring.

(b) Using a plastic hammer, tap the shift fork and remove the tight plug from the case cover.

(c) Using a pin punch, drive out the slotted spring pin from the shift fork.

(d) Remove the fork shaft, shift fork, interlock roller, interlock pin, locking ball and spring.

5.Remove Select Lever, Shaft and Shift Lever Housing.

(a) Unstake the lock plate and remove the lock bolt from the shift lever housing.

(b) Using a plastic hammer, tap the select lever and remove the tight plug from the case cover.

(c) Unstake the lock plate and remove the lock bolt from the lever.

(d) Remove the shaft, select lever and shift lever housing.

6.Remove Reverse Restrict Pin.

'(a) Using a torx wrench, remove the straight screw plug.

(b) Using a pin punch and hammer, drive out the slotted spring pin.

(c) Remove the restrict pin.

7.Dismantle Shift Heads.

(a) Using two screwdrivers and a hammer, remove the C-clip.

* Be careful as the plunger will spring out.

(b) Remove the plunger and compression spring.

* Be careful not to mix up the springs and plungers.

Inspection of Components

1.Inspect Output Shaft and Bushing.

(a) Check the output shaft and bushing fro wear or damage.

(b) Using a micrometer, measure the outer diameter of the output shaft journal and bushing.

Minimum diameter:

1st & 2nd gear journal 43.984 mm (1.7317 in)

Bushing   47.910 mm (1.8862 in)

(c) Using a dial indicator, measure the shaft runout.

Maximum runout: 0.03 mm (0.0012 in)

2.Inspect Counter Gear and Bearings.

(a) Check the gear teeth and bearings.for wear or damage.

(b) **[H55F]** Using a micrometer, measure the outer diameter of the couter gear journal.

Minimum diameter:

Counter 5th gear journal 31.984 mm (1.2592 in)

Rear bearing journal   39.957 mm (1.5731 in)

3. **[H41]** If necessary, Replace Couter Rear Bearing Inner Race.

(a) Using special tool, remove the bearing inner race.

(b) Using special tool and a press, install the bearing inner race.

4.Inspect Oil Clearance of 1st, 2nd and Couter 5th Gears. Using a dial indicator, measure the oil clearance between the gear and shaft with the needle roller bearing installed.

Standard clearance:

1st & 2nd gears

0.020 - 0.073 mm (0.0008 - 0.0029 in)

Counter 5th gear

0.015 - 0.068 mm (0.0006 - 0.0027 in)

5.Inspect Oil Clearance of 3rd Gear. Using a dial indicator, measure the oil clearance between the gear and bushing.

Standard clearance:

0.065 - 0.115 mm (0.0026 - 0.0045 in)

Maximum clearance:

0.12 mm (0.0047 in)

6.Inspect Synchronizer Rings of 1st and 2nd Gears.

(a) Check the inner spline, the raised position of the guide pins, and the thrust pieces and gear moving parts for wear and damage.

(b) Check the guide pin rivet staked parts for play or damage.

(c) Check the synchronizer ring holders for deterioration or wear.

(d) With the synchronizer ring pressed into the gear, measure the distance as shown.

Minimum distance:

1st gear 32.5 mm (1.280 in)

2nd gear 38.0 mm (1.496 in)

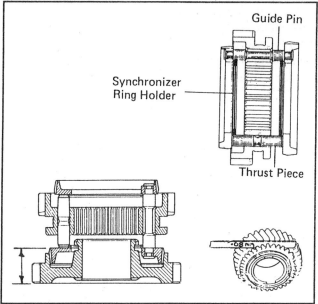

7. **[H55F]**Inspect Synchronizer Rings of 3rd Gear Input Shaft and Gear Spline Piece No. 5.

(a) Check the synchronizer rings for wear and damage.

(b) Turn the ring and push it in to check the braking action.

(c) Measure the clearance between the synchronizer ring back and gear spline end.

Minimum clearance: 0.8 mm (0.031 in)

8.Inspect Shift Forks and Hub Sleeves.

(a) Check the contact surfaces for wear or damage.

(b) Measure the clearance between the hub sleeve and shift fork.

Maximum clearance: 0.8 mm (0.031 in)

9.Inspect Input Shaft and Bearing. Check for wear or damage.

10.If Necessary, Replace Input Shaft Bearing.

(a) Using snap ring pliers, remove the snap ring.

(b) Using special tool and a press, remove the bearing.

(c) Using a press, remove the bearing.

* Do not press in the bearing outer race.

(d) Select a snap ring that will alow minimum axial play and install it on the shaft.

Standard play:

0 - 0.10 mm (0 - 0.0039 in)

Thickness:

3.20 - 3.31 mm (0.1260 - 0.1303 in)

3.31 - 3.42 mm (0.1303 - 0.1346 in)

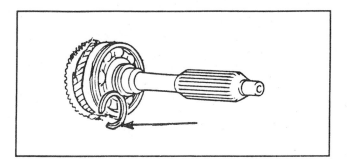

11. Inspect Reverse Shift Arm and Reverse Idler Gear.

(a) Check for wear or damage.

(b) Measure the clearance between the shift arm shoe and idler gear groove.

Maximum clearance: 0.7 mm (0.028 in)

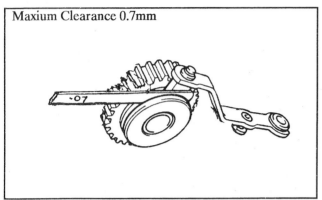

Maxium Clearance 0.7mm

12. Inspect Front bearing Retainer and Check for Wear or Damage. Then check the oil seal for war or damage.

13. If Necessary, Replace Front Bearing Retainer Oil Seal.

(a) Using a screwdriver, pry out the oil seal.

(b) Using special tool, press in a new oil seal.

14. Inspect Transfer Adapter and check for Damage. **[H55F]** Then check the oil seal for wear or damage.

15. [H55F]If Necessary, Replace 5th Shift Arm Oil Seal on Transfer Adapter.

(a) Using a screwdriver, pry out the oil seal.

(b) Using a socket wrench and hammer, drive in a new oil seal.

Drive in depth: 1.0 mm (0.039 in)

16. [H55F]If Necessary, Replace 5th Fork Shaft Oil Seal on Case Cover.

(a) Using a screwdriver, pry out the oil seal.

(b) Using special tool, drive in a new oil seal.

[H41] Assembly of Case Cover Assemlby

1.Assemble Reverse Shift Head.

(a) Install the compression spring and plinger into the shift head.

(b) Press the end of the plunger, and install a new C-clip.

2.Install Reverse Shift Head and Shaft.

(a) Install the spring and locking ball.

(b) Insert the fork shaft through the reverse shift head.

3.Install 1st and 2nd Shift Fork and Shaft.

(a) Install the spring and locking ball.

(b) Coat the interlock roller with MP grease and install it in the case cover.

(c) Coat the interlock pin with MP grease and install it in the shaft.

(d) Insert the fork shaft through the shift fork.

4.Install 3rd and 4th Shift Fork and Shaft.

(a) Install the spirng and locking ball.

(b) Coat the interlock roller with MP grease and install it in the case cover.

(c) Insert the fork shaft through the 3rd and 4th shift fork.

5.Install Slotted Spring Pins.

(a) Align the pin hole of each shaft with the fork, head and the other fork respectively.

(b) Using a pin punch and hammer, drive in the slotted spring pins until they are flush with the fork.

6.Install Tight Plugs. Apply liquid sealer to the tight plugs and drive them in the case cover as shown.

[H55F] Assembly of Case Cover Assembly

1.Assemble Shift Heads.

(a) Install the compression spring and plunger into the shift head.

(b) Press the end of the plunger, and install a new C-spring.

2.Install Reverse Restrict Pin.

(a) Insert the reverse restrict pin into the case cover.

(b) Align the pin holes of the case cover and reverse restrict pin, and drive in the slotted spring pin.

(c) Apply liquid sealer to the plug and torque the plug.

Torque: 190 kg-cm (14 ft-lb, 19 N·m)

3.Install Select Lever, Shaft and Shift Lever Housing.

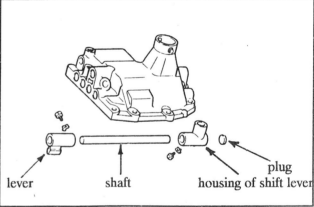

lever   shaft   housing of shift lever   plug

(a) Insert the shaft through the select lever and shift lever housing.

(b) Align the holes of the shaft and select lever, and install the lock bolt with a new lock plate.

Torque: 380 kg-cm (27 ft-lb, 37 N·m)

(c) Align the holes of the shaft and shift lever housing, and install the lock bolt with a new lock plate.

Torque: 380 kb-cm (27 ft-lb, 37 N·m)

(d) Stake the lock plates.

4.Install 1st and 2nd Shift Head, Fork Shaft and Shift Fork.

(a) Install the spring and locking ball.

(b) Insert the fork shaft through the shift fork and shift head.

(c) Install the interlock roller to the case cover.

5. Install 3rd and 4th Shift Fork and Fork Shaft.

(a) Install the spring and locking ball.

(b) Coat the interlock pin with MP grease and install it in the shaft.

(c) Insert the fork shaft through the shift fork.

(d) Install the interlock roller to the case cover.

6. Install Reverse and 5th Shift Head, Reverse Shift Fork and Fork Shaft.

(a) Install the spring and locking ball.

(b) Coat the interlock pin with MP grease and install it in the shaft.

(c) Insert the fork shaft through the shift fork and the shift head.

(d) Install the two interlock balls to the case cover and shift head.

7. Install 5th Shift Arm Shaft.

(a) Install the spring and locking ball.

(b) Insert the shaft through the shift head.

8. Install three E-Clips and Snap Ring.

9. Install Slotted Spring Pins.

(a) Align the pin hole of each shaft with eithe rthe fork, head and other fork or arm respectively.

(b) Using a pin puncgh and hammer, drive in the slotted spring pins until they are flush with the fork.

10. Install Tight Plugs. Apply liquid sealer to the tight plugs and drive them into the case cover as shown.

Assembly of Transmission

1. Install 2nd Gear and Needle Roller Bearing.

(a) Apply gear oil to the output shaft.

(b) Install the needle roller bearing and 2nd gear.

2. Install Locking Ball, Bushing and 3rd Gear.

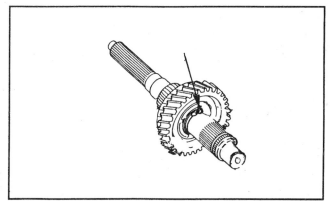

(a) Install the locking ball in the shaft.

(b) Install the bushing on the output shaft and align the bushing notch and locking ball.

(c) Apply gear oil to the bushing.

(d) Install the 3rd gear on the bushing.

3. Insert Clutch Hub No. 2 into Hub Sleeve.

(a) Install the clutch hub and shifting keys to the hub sleeve.

(b) Install the shifting key springs under the shifting keys.

* Install the key springs positioned so that their ends are not in line.

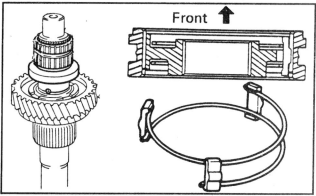

4. Install Hub Sleeve No. 2 Assembly, Using a Press.

* Hold the 3rd gear to prevent the bushing from falling. Be sure that the shifting keys align with the synchronizer ring slots.

5. Install Snap Ring. Select a snap ring that will allow minimum axial play and install it on the shaft.

Mark	Thickness mm (in)
0	2.40 - 2.45 (0.0945 - 0.0965)
1	2.45 - 2.50 (0.0965 - 0.0984)
2	2.50 - 2.55 (0.0984 - 0.1004)
3	2.55 - 2.60 (0.1004 - 0.1024)
4	2.60 - 2.65 (0.1024 - 0.1043)
5	2.65 - 2.70 (0.1043 - 0.1063)

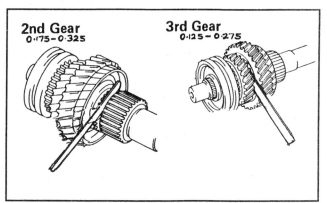

6. Measure Thrust Clearance of 2nd and 3rd Gear. Using a feeler gauge, measure the 2nd and 3rd gear thrust clearances.

Standard clearance:

2nd gear 0.175-0.325 mm (0.0069-0.0128 in)

3rd gear 0.125-0.275 mm (0.0049-0.0108 in)

Maximum clearance:

2nd gear 0.35 mm (0.0138 in)

3rd gear 0.30 mm (0.0118 in)

7. Assemble Synchronizer Ring Holder. Hook the synchronizer ring holder ends to the thrust piece.

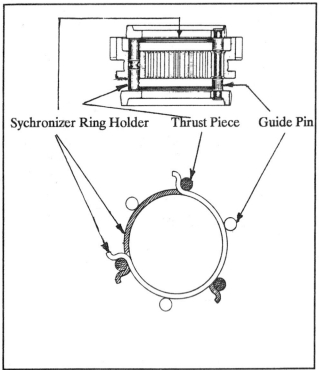

Sychronizer Ring Holder   Thrust Piece   Guide Pin

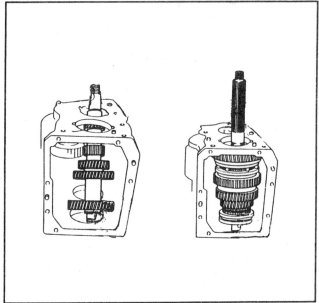

* Align the synchronizer ring holder ends so they are not both facing in the same direction.

* Be sure the synchronizer ring holders are parallel and not intersecting.

8.Install Synchronizer Ring No. 1 and 1st Gear.

(a) Install synchronizer ring No. 1.

(b) Apply gear oil to the needle roller bearing.

(c) Install the needle roller bearing and the 1st gear.

(d) Apply MP grease to the straight pin and 1st gear thrust washer.

(e) Install the 1st gear thrust washer onto the output shaft with the straight pin aligned with the 1st gear thrust washer.

9.Install Reverse Shaft Arm.

(a) Install the reverse shift arm so its pivot is positioned as shown.

(b) Install the O-ring, plate washer, spring washer and nut.

10.Install Reverse Idler Gear and Shaft.

(a) Align the reverse idler gear groove with the reverse shift arm shoe.

(b) Install the reverse idler gear shaft with teh woodruff key through the gear.

11.Put Couter Gear into transmission Case.

(a) Stand the transmission case on its front end.

(b) Put the counter gear into the case.

* Be careful not to damage either end.

12.Put Output Shaft Assemlby into Transmissioin Case.

* Be careful not to damage the front end of the shaft.

13.Install Output Shaft Centre Bearing.

(a) Using snap ring pliers, install the snap ring onto the bearing.

(b) Confirm that the groove of the 1st gear thrust washer and the straight pin are aligned.

(c) Using special tool, install the bearing until it comes into contact with teh 1st gear thrust washer.

14. [H55F] Install 5th Gear to Output Shaft.

(a) Apply MP grease to the inside surface of the 5th gear.

(b) Using special tool, install the 5th gear to the output shaft.

15.Install Input Shaft.

(a) Using snap ring pliers, install the snap ring onto the bearing.

(b) Install the 17 needle roller bearings into the input shaft.

(c) Apply MP grease to the needle roller bearings.

(d) Align the synchronizer ring slots with the shifting keys.

(e) Using a plastic hammer, drive in the input shaft.

* Be sure that the counter gear is low enough so as not to interfere with the input shaft.

16.Install Counter Gear Front Bearing.

(a) Turn the transmission over and align the counter gear centre.

(b) [H55F] Install the thrust collar for the front bearing onto the counter gear.

(c) Using special tool, drive in the bearing.

* When driving in the bearing, support the counter gear in rear with a solid metal or wooden block.

(d) Install the snap ring onto the bearing outer race.

(e) Select a snap ring that will allow minimum axial play and install it on the counter gear front end.

Mark	Thickness mm (in)
1	2.05 - 2.10 (0.0807 - 0.0827)
2	2.15 - 2.20 (0.0846 - 0.0866)
4	2.25 - 2.30 (0.0886 - 0.0906)

17.Install Counter Gear Rear Bearing.

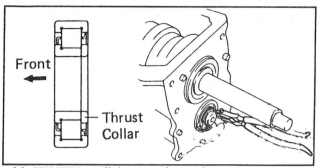

(a) **[H55F]** Install the snap ring to the counter gear rear bearing outer race.

(b) Using special tool, drive in the rear bearing.

* When driving in the bearing, support the counter gear in front with a 3-5 lb hammer or equivalent.

(c) **[H41]** Install the thrust collar fro the rear bearing onto the counter gear rear end.

(d) **[H41]** Using snap ring pliers, install the snap ring onto the counter gear rear end.

18. [H55F] Install Rear Bearing Retainer. Install the rear bearing retainer to the transmission case. Torque the bolts.

Torque: 185 kg-cm (13 ft-lb, 18 N·m)

19. [H55F] Install Straight Pin and Couter 5th Gear Thrust Washer.

(a) Install the straight pin onto the counter shaft.

(b) Align the thrust washer slot with the straight pin and install the thrust washer.

20. [H55F] Assemble Couter 5th Gear.

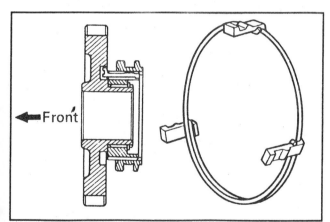

(a) Install the No. 3 hub sleeve and shifting keys to the counter 5th gear.

(b) Install the shifting key springs under the shifting keys so that the spring ends are not in line, as illustrated.

21. [H55F] Install Needle Roller Bearing.

(a) Apply MP grease to the needle roller bearing;

(b) Install the needle roller bearing into the counter 5th gear.

22.[H55F] Assemble 5th Shift Fork.

(a) Install the 5th shift fork to the shaft.

(b) Align the pin holes of the 5th shift fork and shaft.

(c) Using a pin punch and hammer, drive in the slotted spring pin.

23. [H55F] Install Couter 5th Gear Assembly with 5th Shfit Fork.

(a) Install the 5th shift fork and fork shaft onto hub sleeve No. 3.

(b) Install the couter 5th gear assembly with teh 5th shift fork.

24.[H55F] Install Synchronizer Ring and Gear Spline Piece No. 5.

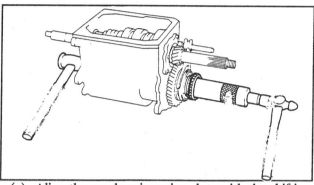

(a) Align the synchronizer ring slots with the shifting keys, and place the synchronizer ring on the rear end of the counter 5th gear.

(b) Using special tool, drive gear spline piece No. 5 into the counter gear to where the lock nut can be installed.

* When driving in gear spline piece No. 5, support the counter gear in front with a 3-5 lb hammer or equivalent.

25.[H55F] Install Lock Nut to Couter Gear Rear End.

(a) Engage the gear double meshing.

(b) Using special tool, install a new lock nut. Torqwue the nut.

Torque: 1,300 kg-cm (94 ft-lb, 127 N·m)

(c) Disengage the gear double meshing.

(d) Using a feeler gauge, measure the counter 5th gear thrust clearance.

Standard clearance:

0.10 - 0.30 mm (0.0039 - 0.0118 in)

Maximum clearance: 0.30 mm (0.0118 in)

(e) Using a punch, stake the lock nut.

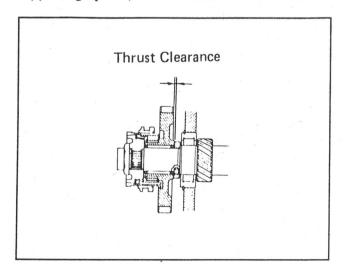

Thrust Clearance

26. Install Front Bearing Retainer with a Gasket.

(a) Install the front bearing retainer with a gasket.

(b) Apply liquid sealer to the bolts.

(c) Install and torque the bolts.

Torque: 170 kg-cm (12 ft-lb, 17 N·m)

27. Install Spacer on the Output Shaft.

28. Install Output Shaft Rear Bearing Using Special Tool.

29. Measure 1st Gear Thrust Clearance Using a Feeler Gauge.

Standard clearance:

0.175 - 0.325 mm (0.0069 - 0.0128 in)

Maximum clearance: 0.35 mm (0.0138 in)

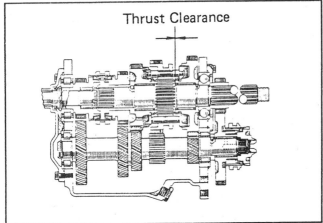

Thrust Clearance

30. [H55F] Install 5th Shift Arm and Shaft.

(a) Install the 5th shift arm shaft through the transfer adapter and install the 5th shift arm.

(b) Install the bolt with a lock washer, and torque the bolt.

Torque: 380 kg-cm (27 ft-lb, 37 N·m)

(c) Stake the lock washer.

31. Install Transfer Adapter with a Gasket.

(a) Place a new gasket in position.

(b) Align the end of the 5th shift arm and 5th shift fork **[H55F]**, and install the transfer adapter.

(c) **[H55F]** Install the locking ball and spring.

(d) **[H55F]** Apply liquid sealer to the plug.

(e) **[H55F]** Using special tool, install and torque the screw plug.

Torque: 250 kg-cm (18 ft-lb, 25 N·m)

32. Install Case Cover.

(a) **[H55F]** Install the dust boot.

(b) Install the case ciover with a gasket. Torque the bolts.

Torque: 400 kg-cm (29 ft-lb, 39 N·m)

33. Install Back-Up Light Switch, Using Special Tool.

34. Install Transfer.

35. [HJ, BJ]Install Clutch Housing. Torque the bolts.

Torque: 650 kg-cm (47 ft-lb, 64 N·m)

36. Adjust Reverse Shift Arm Pivot Position.

(a) Position the adjustment mark on the shift arm pivot end toward the front.

(b) Temporarily install the shift lever, and if the shift lever is catching on something in the selecting direction, adjust by moving the position of the alignment mark by 60°.

(c) Torque the nut.

Torque: 250 kg-cm (18 ft-lb, 25 N·m)

Installation of Transmission with Transfer

1.Install Transmission with Transfer. Align the input shaft spline with the clutch disc, and install the transmission to the clutch housing **[FJ]** or engine **[BJ, HJ]**. Torque the bolts.

Torque:

FJ   650 kg-cm (47 ft-lb, 64 N·m)

BJ   730 kg-cm (53 ft-lb, 72 N·m)

HJ 17 mm 730 kg-cm (53 ft-lb, 72 N·m)

    14 mm 380 kg-cm (27 ft-lb, 37 N·m)

    12 mm 185 kg-cm (13 ft-lb, 18 N·m)

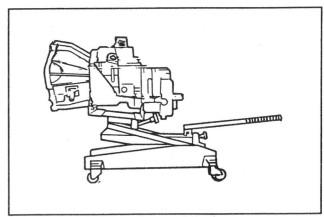

2.Install Engine Rear Support Member.

(a) Install the bolts to both sides of the member.

Torque: 400 kg-cm (29 ft-lb, 39 N·m)

(b) Install the four bolts to the member.

Torque: 600 kg-cm (43 ft-lb, 59 N·m)

3.Install Exhaust Pipe.

Torque: 630 kg-cm (46 ft-lb, 62 N·m)

4.[BJ, HJ] Install Starter.

(a) Install the starter with the two bolts.

Torque: BJ 720 kg-cm (52 ft-lb, 71 N·m)

          HJ 730 kg-cm (53 ft-lb, 72 N·m)

(b) Connect the cable and connector.

5.[BJ, HJ] Install Clutch Release Cylinder.

Torque: 120 kg-cm (9 ft-lb, 12 N·m)

6.Install Transfer Shift Lever to Transfer.

Torque: 250 kg-cm (18 ft-lb, 25 N·m)

7.Install 4WD and Back-Up Light Switch Connector.

8. [Electrical Shift Type]Install L4 Switch Connector.

9.Install Speedometer Cable.

10. [Electrical Shift Type] Install Diaphragm Cylinder Vacuum

Hose.

11.Install Front and Rear Propeller Shafts. See PROPELLER Section.

Torque: 900 kg-cm (65 ft-lb, 88 N·m)

12.Install Transmission Undercover.

13.Install Transmission Shift Lever.

(a) Align the glove of the shift lever cap and the pin part of the case cover.

(b) Cover the shift lever cap with a cloth.

(c) Then, pressing down on the shift lever cap, rotate it clockwise to install.

(d) Install the shift lever boot.

14.Connect Negative Battery Terminal Wire.

15.Fill Transmission and Transfer with Oil.

Oil grade: H41 API GL-4,5 SAE 90

H42 API GL-4,5 SAE 90

H55F API GL-4,5 SEA 90

Capacity:

Transmission

H41   3.5 lts (3.7 US qts, 3.1 Imp.qts)

H42   4.0 lts (4.3 US qts, 3.6 Imp.qts)

H55F 4.9 lts (5.2 US qts, 4.3 Imp.qts)

Transfer

2.2 lts (2.3 US qts, 1.9 Imp.qts)

16.Perform Road Test. Check for abnormal noise and smooth operation.

Problem Diagnosis

Problem:

Hard to shift or will not shift!

Possible causes:

- Splines on input shaft dirty or burred.
- transmission faulty.

Remedy:

- Repair as necessary.
- Dismantle and inspect transmission.

Problem:

Transmission jumps out of gear!

Possible cause:

Transmission faulty.

Remedy:

Dismantle and inspect transmission.

4 AND 5 SPEED TRANSMISSIONS [G40 & G52F] FOR R AND L SERIES LANDCRUISERS

4 AND 5 SPEED TRANSMISSIONS [G40 & G52F] FOR R AND L SERIES LANDCRUISERS

Removal

1.Disconnect Battery Cable From Negative Terminal.

2.[RJ] Drain Out Coolant.

3.[RJ] Disconnect Upper Hose and Engine Rear Heater Hose.

4.Remove Transmission Shift Lever.

(a) Remove the shift lever boot.

(b) Cover the shift lever cap with a cloth.

(c) Then, pressing down on the shift lever cap, rotate it counterclockwise to remove.

(d) Remove the shift lever.

5.Raise Vehicle and Drain Out Transmission and Transfer Gear Oil.

6.Remove Transmission Undercover.

7.Remove Front and Rear Propeller Shafts.

8.Disconnect Bond Cable From Body.

9.Remove Speedometer Cable.

10.[Electrical Shift Type] Remove Diaphragm Cylinder Vacuum Hose.

11.Remove 4WD and Back-Up Light Switch Connector.

12.[Electrical Shift Type]Remove L4 Switch Connector.

13.Remove Transfer Shift Lever.

14.Remove Clutch Release Cylinder.

15.Remove Starter.

(a) Disconnect the cable and connector.

(b) Remove the starter.

16.Remove Exhaust Pipe Clamp and Bracket.

17.Disconnect Engine Rear Support Member From Body.

(a) Support the engine rear support member with the jack.

(b) Remove the bolts from both sides of the support member.

18.Lower Transmission.

19.Remove Transmission with Transfer.

(a) Disconnect the transmission mounting bolts from the engine.

(b) Remove the transmission with the transfer.

20.Remove Engine Rear Support Member. Remove the engine rear support member from the transmission.

Components

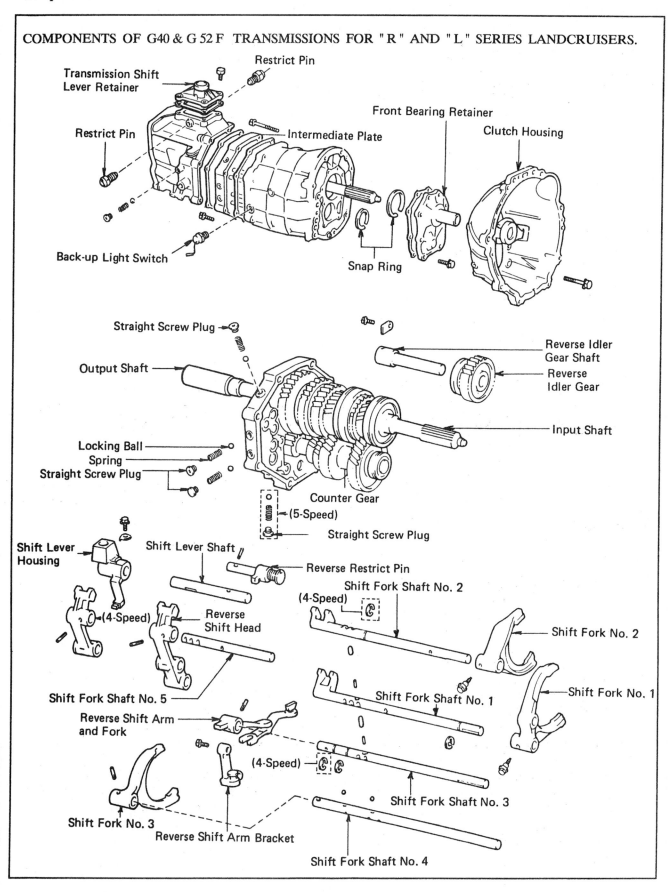

COMPONENTS OF G40 & G 52 F TRANSMISSIONS FOR "R" AND "L" SERIES LANDCRUISERS.

COMPONENTS of G40 & G52F TRANSMISSIONS CONTINUED

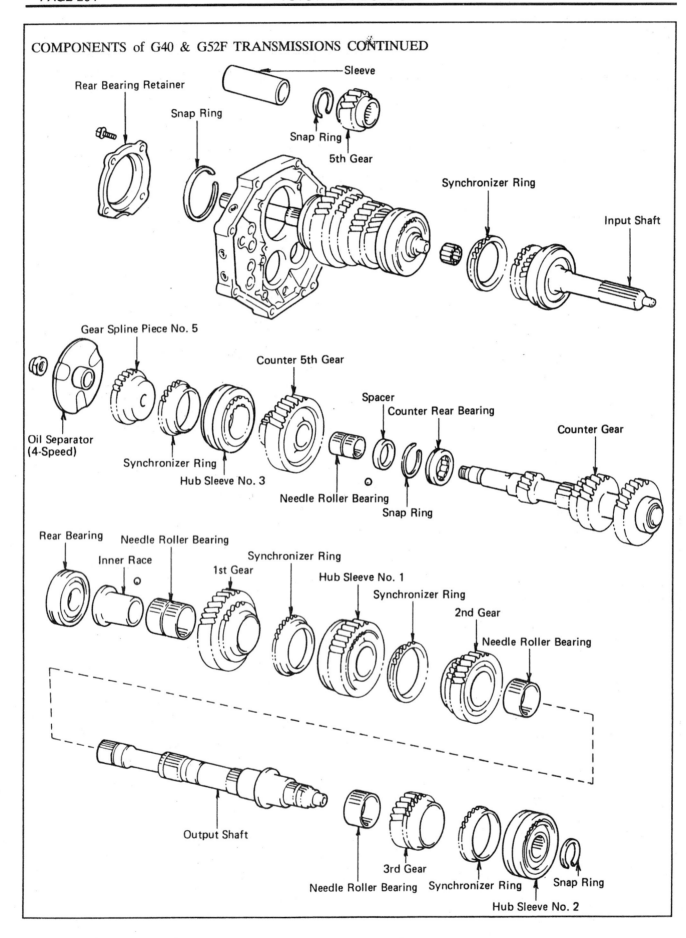

Sleeve

Rear Bearing Retainer

Snap Ring

Snap Ring

5th Gear

Synchronizer Ring

Input Shaft

Gear Spline Piece No. 5

Counter 5th Gear

Spacer

Counter Rear Bearing

Counter Gear

Oil Separator (4-Speed)

Synchronizer Ring

Hub Sleeve No. 3

Needle Roller Bearing

Snap Ring

Rear Bearing

Needle Roller Bearing

Inner Race

1st Gear

Synchronizer Ring

Hub Sleeve No. 1

Synchronizer Ring

2nd Gear

Needle Roller Bearing

Output Shaft

3rd Gear

Needle Roller Bearing

Synchronizer Ring

Snap Ring

Hub Sleeve No. 2

Dismantle

1.Remove Clutch Housing.

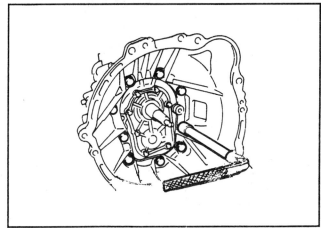

2.Remove Back-Up Light Switch, Shift Lever Retainer and Restrict Pins.

3.Remove Transfer. See TRANSFER Section.

4.Remove Straight Screw Plug, Spring and Ball.

(a) Using a socket wrench, remove the screw plug from the transfer adaptor.

(b) Using a magnetic finger, remove the spring and ball.

5.Remove Transfer Adaptor.

(a) Remove the shift lever housing set bolt and lock washer.

(b) Remove the shift lever shaft and housing.

(c) Remove the eight bolts.

(d) Using a plastic hammer, remove the transfer adaptor.

* Leave the gasket attached to the intermediate plate.

6.Remove Front Bearing Retainer and Two Bearing Snap Rings.

7.Separate Intermediate Plate From Transmission Case.

(a) Using a plastic hammer, carefully tap off the transmission case.

(b) Remove the transmission case from the intermediate plate.

8.Mount Intermediate Plate in Vice.

(a) Use two clutch housing bolts, plate washers and suitable nuts as shown.

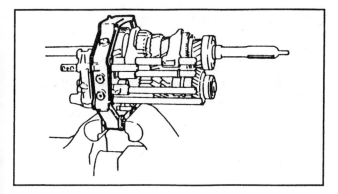

* Install the plate washers in reverse of normal. Increase or decrease plate washers so that the bolt tip and front tip surface of the nut are aligned.

(b) Mount the intermediate plate in a vice.

9.Remove Straight Screw Plugs, Locking Balls and Springs.

(a) Using a socket wrench, remove the plugs.

4-Speed: 3 plugs

5-Speed: 4 plugs

(b) Using a magnetic finger, remove the springs and balls.

10.Remove Bolts and Slotted Spring Pins.

(a) Remove the bolts from the shift fork No. 1 and No. 2.

(b) Using a pin punch and hammer, drive out the pins.

4-Speed: 2 pins

5-Speed: 3 pins

11.Remove E-Clips.

4-Speed: 4 E-clips

5-Speed: 2 E-clips

12. [5 Speed]Remove Shift Fork Shaft No. 4 and Shift Fork No. 3

(a) Pull out the shift fork shaft No. 4 from the intermediate plate.

* The locking balls and interlock pin will fall from the holes so be sure to catch them by hand. If they do not come out, remove them with a magnetic finger.

(b) Remove the shift fork shaft No. 4 and the shift fork No. 3.

13.Remove Reverse Shift Head and Shift Fork Shaft No. 5. Pull out the shift fork shaft No. 5 from the intermediate plate, and remove it with the reverse shift head.

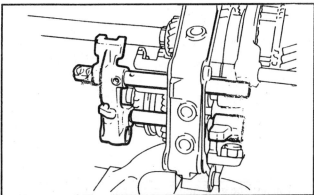

14.Remove Shift Fork Shaft No. 3. Pull out the shift fork shaft No. 3 from the intermediate plate.

* The interlock pins will fall from the hole, so be ready to catch them by hand. If they do not come out, remove them with a magnetic finger.

15.Remove Shift Fork Shaft no. 1. Pull out the shift fork shaft No. 1 from the intermediate plate.

* The interlock pin will fall from the hole so be sure to catch it by hand. If it does not come out, remove it with a magnetic finger.

16. Remove Shift Fork Shaft No. 2, Shift Fork No. 2 and Shift Fork No. 1. Pull out shift fork shaft No. 2 and remove shift fork No. 2 and No. 1.

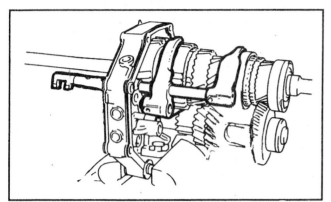

17. Remove Reverse Idler Gear and Shaft.

(a) Remove the reverse idler gear shaft stopper.

(b) Remove the reverse idler gear and shaft.

18. Remove Reverse Shift Arm From Reverse Shift Arm Bracket.

19.[5-Speed] Measure Counter Fifth Gear Thrust Clearance. Using a feeler gauge, measure the counter 5th gear thrust clearance.

Standard clearance:

0.10 - 0.30 mm (0.0039 - 0.0118)

Maximum clearance: 0.30 mm (0.0118 in)

20.[5- Speed] Remove Gear Spline Piece No. 5, Synchroniser Ring, Needle Roller Bearings and Counter Fifth Gear with Hub Sleeve No. 3.

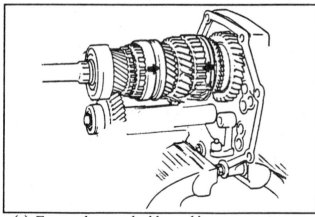

(a) Engage the gear double meshing.

(b) Using a hammer and chisel, loosen the staked part of the nut.

(c) Remove the lock nut.

(d) Disengage the gear double meshing.

(e) Using special tool, remove the gear spline piece No. 5, synchroniser ring, hub sleeve No. 5, needle roller bearing and counter 5th gear.

21.[4-Speed] Remove Oil Separator.

(a) Engage the gear double meshing.

(b) Using a hammer and chisel, loosen the staked part of the nut.

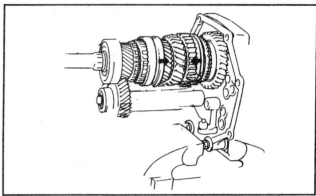

(c) Remove the nut.

(d) Remove the oil separator.

(e) Disengage the gear double meshing.

22.[5-Speed] Remove Spacer and Ball.

23. Remove Reverse Shift Arm Bracket (2 bolts).

24. Remove Rear Bearing Retainer (4 bolts)

25. Remove Bearing Snap Ring.

26. Remove Output Shaft, Counter Gear and Input Shaft as a Unit from Intermediate Plate.

(a) Remove the output shaft, counter gear and input shaft, as a unit, from the intermediate plate by pulling on the counter gear and tapping on the intermediate plate with a plastic hammer.

(b) Remove the input shaft with the 14-needle roller bearings from the output shaft.

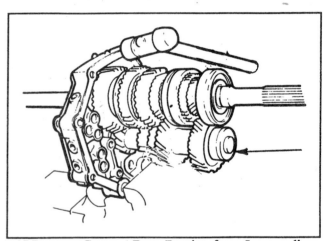

27. Remove Counter Rear Bearing from Intermediate Plate.

28. Remove Sleeve from Output Shaft.

29. Measure Each Gear Thrust Clearance.

Standard clearance:

0.10 - 0.25 mm (0.0039 - 0.0098 in)

Maximum clearance: 0.25 mm (0.0098 in)

30. [5-Speed]Remove 5th Gear, Rear Bearing, 1st Gear, Inner Race and Needle Roller Bearing.

(a) Using two screwdrivers and a hammer, tap out the snap ring.

(b) Using a press, remove the 5th gear, rear bearing, 1st gear and inner race.

(c) Remove the needle roller bearing.

31. [4-Speed]Remove Rear Bearing, 1st Gear, Inner Race and Needle Roller Bearing.

(a) Using two screwdrivers and a hammer, tap out the snap ring.

(b) Using a press, remove the rear bearing, 1st gear and inner race.

(c) Remove the needle roller bearing.

32. Remove Synchroniser Ring.

33. Remove Locking Ball.

34. Remove Hub Sleeve No. 1 Assembly and 2nd Gear Assembly.

(a) Using a press, remove the hub sleeve No. 1, synchroniser ring and 2nd gear.

(b) Remove the needle roller bearing.

35. Remove Hub Sleeve No. 2 Assembly and 3rd Gear Assembly.

(a) Using snap ring pliers, remove the snap ring.

(b) Using a press, remove the hub sleeve No. 2, synchroniser ring and 3rd gear.

(c) Remove the needle roller bearing.

Inspection.

1.Inspect Output Shaft and Inner RAce.

(a) Using callipers, measure the output shaft flange thickness.

Minimum thickness: 4.80 mm (0.1890 in)

(b) Using callipers, measure the inner race flange thickness.

Minimum thickness: 3.99 mm (0.1571 in)

(c) Using a micrometer, measure the outer diameter of the output shaft journal.

Minimum diameter:

2nd Gear 37.984 mm (1.4954 in)

3rd Gear 34.984 mm (1.3773 in)

(d) Using a micrometer, measure the outer diameter of the inner race.

Minimum diameter: 38.985 mm (1.5348 in)

(e) Using a dial indicator, check the shaft runout.

Maximum runout: 0.05 mm (0.0020 in)

2.Check Oil Clearance of 1st Gear. Using a dial indicator, measure the oil clearance between the gear and inner race with the needle roller bearing installed.

Standard clearance:

0.009 - 0.032 mm (0.0004 - 0.0013 in)

Maximum clearance: 0.032 mm (0.0013 in)

3.Check Oil Clearance of 2nd, 3rd and Counter 5th Gears. Using a dial indicator, measure the oil clearance between the gear and shaft with the needle roller bearing installed.

Standard clearance:

2nd & 3rd Gears

0.009 - 0.033 mm (0.0004 - 0.0013 in)

Counter 5th Gear

0.009 - 0.032 mm (0.0004 - 0.0013 in)

Maximum clearance:

2nd & 3rd Gears 0.033 mm (0.0013 in)

Counter 5th Gear 0.032 mm (0.0013 in)

4.Inspect Synchroniser Rings.

(a) Turn the ring and push it in to check the braking action.

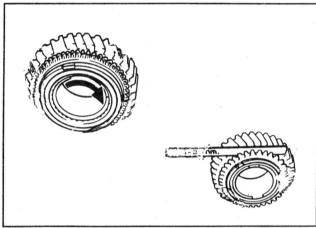

(b) Measure the clearance between the synchroniser ring back and the gear spline end.

Standard clearance:

1.0 - 2.0 mm (0.039 - 0.079 in)

Minimum clearance: 0.8 mm (0.031 in)

5.Measure Clearance of Shift Forks and Hub Sleeves. Using a feeler gauge, measure the clearance between the hub sleeve and shift fork.

Maximum clearance: 1.0 mm (0.039 in)

6.If Necessary, Replace Input Shaft Bearing.

(a) Using snap ring pliers, remove the snap ring.

(b) Using a press, remove the bearing.

(c) Using special tool and a press, install a new bearing.

(d) Select a snap ring that will allow minimum axial play and install it on the shaft (snap rings vary in thickness by .05 mm from 2.05 mm).

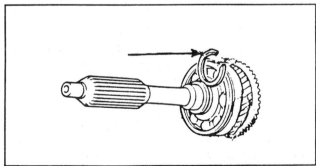

7.If Necessary, Replace Front Bearing Retainer Oil Seal.

Oil seal depth:

12.2 - 13.2 mm (0.480 - 0.520 in) - transmission case installation surface.

8.If Necessary, Replace Counter Gear Front Bearing.

(a) Using snap ring pliers, remove the snap ring.

(b) Press out the bearing.

(c) Replace the side race.

(d) Using a socket wrench, press in the bearing, side race and inner race.

(e) Select a snap ring that will allow minimum axial play and install it on the shaft.

9.If Necessary, Replace Reverse Restrict Pin.

(a) Using a socket wrench, remove the screw pin.

(b) Using a pin punch and hammer, drive out the slotted spring pin.

(c) Pull off the reverse restrict pin.

(d) Install the reverse restrict pin.

(e) Using a pin punch and hammer, drive in the slotted spring pin (snap rings vary in thickness by .05 mm from 2.05 mm).

(f) Using a socket wrench, install and torque the screw plug.

Torque: 190 kg-cm (14 ft-lb, 19 N·m)

Assembly

1.Insert Clutch Hubs No. 1 and No. 2 into Hub Sleeve.

(a) Install the clutch hub and shifting keys to the hub sleeve.

(b) Install the shifting key springs under the shifting keys.

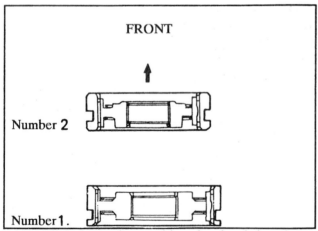

FRONT

Number 2

Number 1.

* Install the key springs positioned so that their end gaps are not in line.

2.Install 3rd Gear and Hub Sleeve No. 2 on Output Shaft.

(a) Apply gear oil to the shaft and needle roller bearing.

(b) Place the synchroniser on the gear and align the ring slots with the shifting keys.

(c) Install the needle roller bearing in the 3rd gear.

(d) Using a press, install the 3rd gear and a hub sleeve NO. 2.

3.Install Snap Ring. Select a snap ring that will allow minimum axial play (snap rings vary in thickness by .05 mm from 1.75 mm).

4.Measure 3rd Gear Thrust Clearance. Using a feeler gauge, measure the 3rd gear thrust clearance.

Standard clearance:

0.10 - 0.25 mm (0.0039 - 0.0098 in)

Maximum clearance: 0.25 mm (0.0098 in)

5.Install 2nd Gear and Hub Sleeve No. 1.

(a) Apply gear oil to the shaft and needle roller bearing.

(b) Place the synchroniser ring on the gear and align the ring slots with the shifting keys.

(c) INstall the needle roller bearing in the 2nd gear.

(d) Using a press, install the 2nd gear and hub sleeve NO. 1.

6.Install Locking Ball and 1st Gear Assembly.

(a) Install the locking ball in the shaft.

(b) Apply gear oil to the needle roller bearing.

(c) Assemble the 1st gear, synchroniser ring, needle roller bearing and bearing inner race.

(d) Install the assembly on the output shaft with the synchroniser ring slots aligned with the shifting keys.

(e) Turn the inner race to align it with the locking ball.

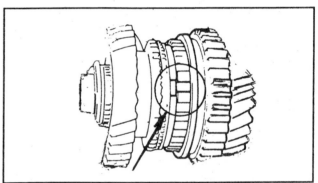

7.Install Output Shaft Rear Bearing. Using special tool and a press, install the bearing on the output shaft with the outer race snap ring groove toward the rear.

* Hold the 1st gear inner race to prevent it from falling.

8.Measure 1st and 2nd Gear Thrust Clearance.

Standard clearance:

0.10 - 0.25 mm (0.0039 - 0.0098 in)

Maximum clearance: 0.25 mm (0.0098 in)

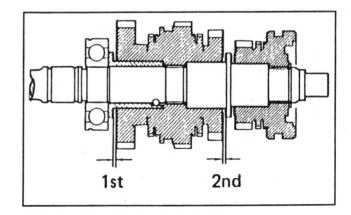

1st   2nd

9. [5-Speed] Install 5th Gear with a Press.

10. Install Snap Ring.

(a) Select a snap ring that will allow minimum axial play.

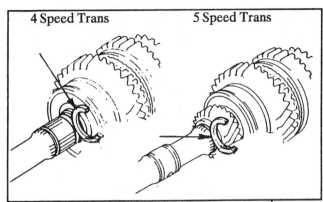

4 Speed Trans   5 Speed Trans

(b) Using a screwdriver and hammer, install the snap ring.

11. Install Sleeve to Output Shaft.

12. Install Output Shaft to Intermediate Plate.

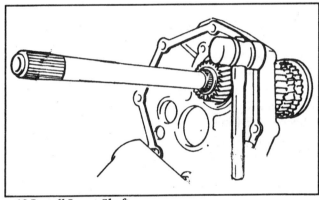

13. Install Input Shaft.

(a) Apply MP grease to the 14-needle roller bearing and install it into the input shaft.

(b) Install the input shaft to the output shaft with the synchroniser ring slots aligned with the shifting keys.

14. Install Counter Gear. Install the counter gear into the intermediate plate while holding the counter gear, and install the counter rear bearing with special tool.

15. Install Bearing Snap Ring.

* Be sure the snap ring is flush with the intermediate plate surface.

16. Install Rear Bearing Retainer.

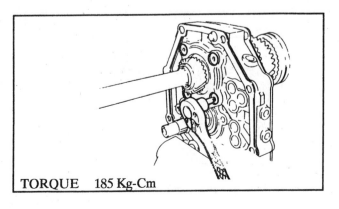

TORQUE   185 Kg-Cm

Torque: 185 kg-cm (13 ft-lb, 18 N·m)

17. Install Reverse Shift Arm Bracket and Torque the Bolts.

Torque: 185 kg-cm (13 ft-lb, 18 N·m)

18. [5-Speed] Install Ball and Spacer.

19. [5-Speed] Insert Counter 5th Gear into Hub Sleeve No. 3.

(a) Install the shifting keys and hub sleeve No. 3 onto the counter 5th gear.

(b) Install the shifting key springs under the shifting keys.

* Install the key springs positioned so that their end gaps are not in line.

20. [5-Speed] Install Counter 5th Gear with Hub Sleeve No. 3 Assembly and Needle Roller Bearings.

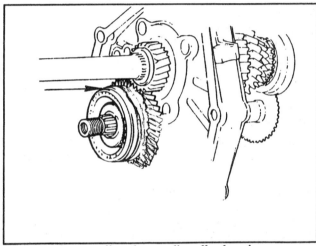

(a) Apply gear oil to the needle roller bearings.

(b) Install the counter 5th gear with hub sleeve No. 3 and needle roller bearings.

21. [5-Speed] Install Synchroniser Ring and Gear Spline Piece No. 5.

(a) Install the synchroniser ring on the gear spline piece No. 5.

(b) Using special tool, drive in the gear spline piece No. 5 with the synchroniser ring slots aligned with the shifting keys.

* When installing the gear spline piece No. 5, support the counter gear in front with a 3-5 lb hammer or equivalent.

22. [4-Speed] Install Oil Separator.

23. Install Lock Nut While Engaging the Gear Double Meshing.

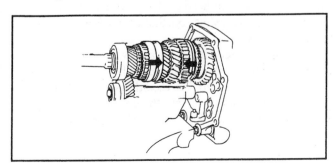

Torque: 1,200 kg-cm (87 ft-lb, 118 N·m)
Stake the lock nut. Disengage the gear double meshing.

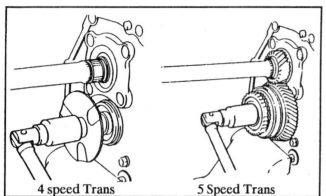

4 speed Trans   5 Speed Trans

24.[5-Speed]Measure Counter 5th Gear Thrust Clearance.

Standard clearance:
0.20 - 0.30 mm (0.0039 - 0.0118 in)
Maximum clearance: 0.30 mm (0.0118 in)

25. Install Reverse Shift Arm to Reverse Shift Arm Bracket.

26. Install Reverse Idler Gear and Shaft.

(a) Install the reverse idler gear on the shaft.

(b) Align the reverse shift arm shoe to the reverse idler gear groove and insert the reverse idler gear shaft to the intermediate plate.

(c) Install the reverse idler gear shaft stopper and torque the bolt.

Torque: 175 kg-cm (13 ft-lb, 17 N·m)

27. Install Shift Fork Shaft No. 2, Shift Fork No. 1 and No. 2. Place shift forks No. 1 and No. 2 into the groove of hub sleeves No. 1 and No. 2 and install fork shaft No. 2 to shift forks No. 1 and No. 2 through the intermediate plate.

28. Install Interlock Pin.

29. Install Shift Fork Shaft No. 1.

(a) Install the interlock pin into the shaft hole.

(b) Install the fork shaft No. 1 to the shift fork No. 1 through the intermediate plate.

30. Install Interlock Pin.

31. Install Shift Fork Shaft No. 3.

(a) Install the interlock pin into the shaft hole.

(b) Install the fork shaft No. 3 to the reverse shift arm through the intermediate plate.

32. Install Shift Fork Shaft No. 5 and Reverse Shift Head.

(a) Install the reverse shift head to the fork shaft No. 5.

(b) Insert fork shaft No. 5 to the intermediate plate and put in the reverse shift head to shift fork shaft No. 3.

33.[5-Speed]Install Shift Fork Shaft No. 4, Shift Fork No. 3 and Two Locking Balls.

(a) Using a magnetic finger and screwdriver, install the locking ball into the reverse shift head hole.

(b) Shift hub sleeve No. 3 to the 5th speed position.

(c) Place shift fork No. 3 into the groove of hub sleeve No. 3 and install fork shaft No. 4 to shift fork No. 3 and reverse shift arm.

(d) Using a magnetic finger and screwdriver, install the locking ball into the intermediate plate and insert fork shaft No. 4 to the intermediate plate.

34. Check Interlock.

(a) Shift the fork shaft No. 1 to the 1st speed position.

(b) Fork shafts No. 2, No. 3, No. 4 and No. 5 should not move.

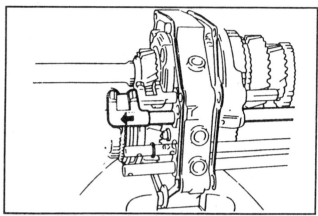

35. Install Slotted Spring Pins.

(a) Install the bolts to the shift fork No. 1 and No. 2.

Torque: 200 kg-cm (14 ft-lb, 20 N·m)

(b) **[5-Speed]** Using a pin punch and hammer, drive in the slotted spring pins into the reverse shift arm, reverse shift head and shift fork No. 3.

36. Install E-Clips.

4-Speed   4 E-Clips
5-Speed   2 E-Clips

37. Install Locking Balls, Springs and Screw Plugs.

(a) Apply liquid sealer to the plugs.

(b) Install the locking balls, springs and screw plugs and torque the screw plugs with a socket wrench.

Torque: 190 kg-cm (14 ft-lb, 19 N·m)

* [5-Speed] Install the short spring into the bottom of the intermediate plate.

38. Dismount Intermediate Plate from Vice.

39. Install Transmission Case with New Gasket to Intermediate Plate. Align each bearing outer race, each fork shaft end and reverse idler gear shaft end with the case installation holes, and install the case. If necessary, tap on the case with a plastic hammer.

40. Install Two Bearing Snap Rings.

41. Install Front Bearing Retainer with New Gasket.

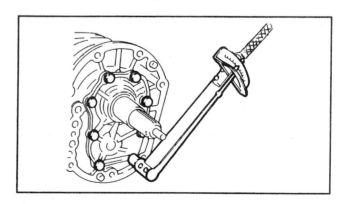

(a) Install the bearing retainer with a new gasket.

(b) Apply liquid sealer to the bolts.

(c) Install and torque the bolts.

Torque: 170 kg-cm (12 ft-lb, 17 N·m)

42. Install Transfer Adaptor, New Gasket, Shift Lever Shaft and Shift Lever Housing.

Torque: 390 kg-cm (28 ft-lb, 38 N·m)

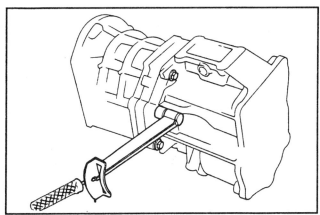

43 Fit locking ball with spring and screw.

44. After Installing Transfer Adaptor Check Following Items.

(a) Check to see that the input and output shafts rotate smoothly.

(b) Check to see that shifting can be made smoothly to all positions.

45. Install Restrict Pins.

(a) Install the black pin on the reverse gear/5th gear side.

(b) Install another pin and torque the pins.

Torque: 280 kg-cm (20 ft-lb, 27 N·m)

46. Install Clutch Housing and Bolts.

Torque: 380 kg-cm (27 ft-lb, 37 N·m)

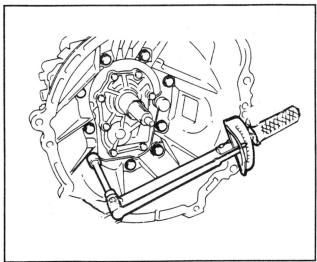

47. Install Shift Lever Retainer With New Gasket. Also install back-up light switch.

48. Install Transfer. See TRANSFER section.

Installation

1. Install Engine Rear Support Member. Install the engine rear support member to the transmission. Torque the bolt.

Torque: 260 kg-cm (19 ft-lb, 25 N·m)

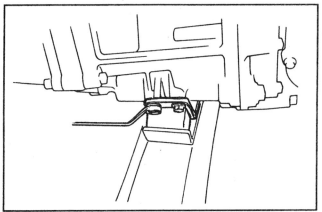

2. Install Transmission with Transfer. Align the input shaft spline with the clutch disc, and install the transmission to the engine.

Torque: 10 mm 380 kg-cm (27 ft-lb, 37 N·m)
   12 mm 730 kg-cm (53 ft-lb, 72 N·m)

3. Connect Engine Rear Support Member to Body. Torque the 8 bolts.

Torque: 400 kg-cm (29 ft-lb, 39 N·m)

4. Install Exhaust Pipe Clamp and Bracket.

5. Install Starter.

(a) Install the starter with the 2 bolts.

Torque: 730 kg-cm (53 ft-lb, 72 N·m)

(b) Connect the cable and connector.

6. Install Clutch Release Cylinder.

Torque: 120 kg-cm (9 ft-lb, 12 N·m)

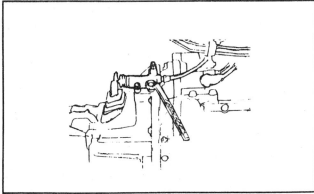

7. Install Transfer Shift Lever to Transfer.

8. Install 4WD and Back-Up Light Switch Connector.

9. **[Electrical Shift Type]** Install L4 Switch Connector.

10. Install Speedometer Cable.

11. Connect Bond Cable to Body.

12.[Electrical Shift Type]Install Diaphragm Cylinder Vacuum Hose.

13. Install Front and Rear Propeller Shafts.

14. Install Transmission Undercover.

15. Install Transmission Shift Lever.

(a) Cover the shift lever cap with a cloth.

(b) Then, install by rotating clockwise while applying downward pressure.

(c) Install the shift lever boot.

16.[RJ] Install Upper Hose and Engine Rear Heater Hose.

17.[RJ]Fill with Coolant.

18. Connect Battery Cable to Negative Terminal.

19. Fill Transmission and Transfer with Oil.

Oil grade: API GL-4, 5 SAE 75W-90

Capacity:

Transmission

G40   2.8 lts (3.0 US qts, 2.5 Imp.qts)

G52F   2.6 lts (2.7 US qts, 2.3 Imp.qts)

Transfer   2.1 lts (2.2 US qts, 1.8 Imp.qts)

20. Perform Road Test. Check for abnormal noise and smooth operation.

AUTOMATIC TRANSMISSION

AUTOMATIC TRANSMISSION

FLUID INSPECTION

1.Check Fluid Level.

* The vehicle must have been driven so that the engine and transmission are at normal operating temperature (fluid temperature: 50 - 80°C or 122 - 176°F).

(a) Park the vehicle on a level surface.

(b) With the engine idling, shift the selector into each gear from the "P" range to the "L" range and return to the "P" range again.

(c) Pull out the transmission dipstick and wipe it clean.

(d) Push it back fully into the filler tube.

(e) Pull it out and check that the fluid level is in the HOT range. If low, add fluid.

Fluid type: ATF DEXRON^R II

* Do not overfill.

2.Check Fluid Condition. If the fluid smells burnt or is black, replace it.

3.Replace Fluid.

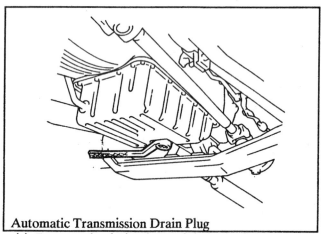

Automatic Transmission Drain Plug

(a) Remove the drain plug and drain the fluid.

(b) Reinstall the drain plug securely.

Torque: 205 kg-cm (15 ft-lb, 20 N·m)

(c) Pour ATF through the filler tube.

Fluid: ATF DEXTRON^R II

(d) With the engine idling, shift the selector into each gear from the "P" range to the "L" range and return to the "P" range again.

(e) With the engine idling, check the fluid level. Add fluid up to the "COOL" level on the dipstick.

(f) Check the fluid level with the normal fluid temperature (50 - 80°C or 122 - 176°F) and add as necessary.

* Do not overfill

Drain and refill capacity:

5.0 lts (5.3 US qts, 4.4 Imp.qts)

Dry fill capacity:

15.0 lts (15.9 US qts, 13.2 Imp.qts)

ADJUSTMENTS

Adjustment of Throttle Cable

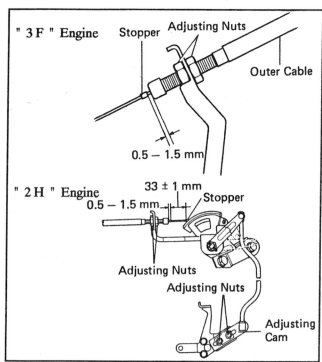

1.Depress Accelerator Pedal and Check that Throttle Valve Opens Fully. If the throttle valve does not open fully, adjust the accelerator link.

2.Check and Adjust Throttle Cable.

(a) Check that the throttle cable is installed correctly and not bending.

(b) When the throttle valve is fully closed, adjust the cable housing so that the distance between the end of the boot and the stopper on the cable is correct.

Distance: 0.5 - 1.5 mm (0.020 - 0.059 in)

(c) **[2H engine only]** - fully depress the accelerator and measure the cable stroke.

Cable stroke: 33 +/- 1 mm (1.30 +/- 0.04 in)

If not within specification, loosen the adjusting nut and adjust by moving the adjusting cam. Then recheck the adjustment.

Adjustment of Shift Linkage

Adjust Floor Shift Linkage.

(a) Loosen the nut on the connecting rod.

(b) Push the manual lever fully toward the front of the vehicle.

(c) Return the manual lever 2 notches to the "N" position.

(d) Set the shift lever at "N".

(e) While holding the lever lightly toward the "R" range side, tighten the connecting rod nut.

Adjustment of Neutral Start Switch

If the engine will start with the shift selector in any range other than "N" or "P", adjustment is required.

1. Loosen Neutral Start Switch Bolts.
2. Set Shift Lever to "N" or "P".
3. Adjust Neutral Start Switch.

(a) Disconnect the neutral start switch connector.

(b) Connect an ohmmeter between the terminals indicated.

(c) Adjust the switch to the point where there is continuity between terminals indicated.

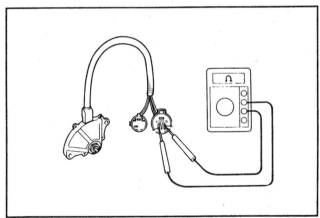

(d) Connect the neutral start switch connector.

4. Tighten Neutral Start Switch Bolts.

Torque: 130 kg-cm (9 ft-lb, 13 N·m)

TESTS

STALL TEST

The object of this test is to check the overall performance of the transmission and engine by measuring the maximum engine speeds in the "D" and "R" ranges.

* Perform the test at normal operational fluid temperature (50 - 80°C or 122 - 176°F).

* Do not continuously run this test longer than 5 seconds.

Measure Stall Speed

1. Check the 4 wheels.
2. Mount an engine tachometer.
3. Fully apply the parking/hand brake.
4. Step down strongly on the brake pedal with your left foot.
5. Start the engine.
6. Shift into the "D" range. Step all the way down on the accelerator pedal with your right foot. Quickly read the highest engine rpm at this time.

Stall speed:
Petrol   1,850 +/- 150 rpm
Diesel   1,900 +/- 150 rpm

7. Perform the same test in the "R" range.

Evaluation

1. If the stall speed is the same for both ranges but lower than the specified value:

* Engine output is insufficient.

* Stator one-way clutch is not operating properly.

* If more than 600 rpm below the specified value, the torque converter could be at fault.

2. If the stall speed in the "D" range is higher than specified:

- line pressure too low,
- front clutch slipping,
- No. 2 one-way clutch not operating properly,
- OD one-way clutch not operating properly.

3. If the stall speed in the "R" range is higher than specified:

- line pressure too low,
- rear clutch slipping,
- No. 3 brake slipping,
- OD one-way clutch not operating properly.

4. If the stall speed in the "R" and "D" ranges is higher than specified:

- line pressure too low,
- improper fluid level,
- OD one-way clutch not operating properly.

TIME LAG TEST

If the lever is shifted while the engine is idling, there will be a certain time lapse or lag before the shock can be felt. This is used for checking the condition of the OD clutch, front clutch, rear clutch and No. 3 brake.

Measure Time Lag

1. Fully apply the parking/hand brake.
2. Start the engine and check the idle speed.
Idle speed: Petrol & Diesel - 750 rpm
3. Shift the shift lever from the "N" to "D" range. Using a stop watch, measure the time it takes from shifting the lever until the shock is felt.
Time lag: Less than 0.7 seconds.
4. In same matter, measure the time lag for "N" - "R".
Time lag: Less than 1.2 seconds.
* Perform the test at normal operational fluid temperature (50 - 80°C or 122 - 176°F).
* Be sure to allow a one minute interval between tests.
* Make 3 measurements and taken the average value.

Evaluation

1. If "N" - "D" time lag is longer than specified:
- line pressure is too low,
- front clutch worn,
- OD one-way clutch not operating properly.
2. If "N" - "R" time lag is longer than specified:
- line pressure is too low,
- rear clutch worn,
- No. 3 brake worn,
- OD one-way clutch not operating properly.

HYDRAULIC TEST

Preparation

1. Warm up the transmission fluid.
2. Shift the transfer shift lever to the "H2" position.
3. Check the front wheels.
4. Jack up rear of the vehicle and support it on stands.
5. Remove the transmission case test plugs and mount hydraulic pressure gauges.
* Perform the test at normal operational fluid temperature (50 - 80°C or 122 - 176°F).

* Measurement can be made with a 1,000 rpm test, but it tests are to be made at 1,800 and 3,500 rpm, it would be safer to do it on road or using a chassis dynamometer because an on-stand test could be hazardous.

Measure Governor Pressure

1. Check that the parking/hand brake is not applied.
2. Start the engine.
3. Shift into the "D" range and measure the governor pressures at the speeds specified in the table.

Evaluation

If the governor pressure is defective:
- line pressure defective,
- fluid leakage in governor pressure circuit,
- governor valve operation defective.

Measure Line Pressure

1. Fully apply the parking/hand brake and check the 4 wheels.
2. Start the engine and check idling rpm.
3. Shift into the "D" range, step down strongly on the brake pedal with your left foot, and while manipulating the accelerator pedal with the right foot, measure the line pressures at the engine speeds specified in table.
* Perform the test at normal operational fluid temperature (50 - 80°C or 122 - 176°F).
* Do not continuously run this test longer than 5 seconds.
4. In the same manner, perform the test in the "R" range.
Line pressure kg/cm^2 [psi] (kPa)
"D" range:
Idling 3.7 - 4.3 [53-61]   (363-422)
Stall 11.1 - 13.6 [158 - 193] (1,089 - 1,334)
"R" range:
Idling 4.5 - 5.5   [64 - 78]   (441 - 539)
Stall   14.0 - 17.0 [199 - 242] (1,373 - 1,667)
5. If the measured pressures are not up to specified values, recheck the throttle cable adjustment and retest.

Evaluation

1. If the measured values at all ranges are higher than specified:
- throttle cable out-of-adjustment;
- throttle valve defective;
- regulator valve defective.
2. If the measured values at all ranges are lower than specified:

- throttle cable out-of-adjustment;
- throttle valve defective;
- regulator valve defective;
- oil pump defective;
- OD clutch defective.

3. If pressure is low in "D" range only:
- "D" range circuit fluid leakage;
- front clutch defective;
- OD clutch defective.

4. If pressure is low in "R" range only:
- "R" range circuit fluid leakage;
- rear clutch defective;
- no. 3 brake defective;
- ID clutch defective.

ROAD TEST

* Perform the test at normal operational fluid temperature (50 - 80°C or 122 - 176°F)

A. "D" RANGE TEST

Shift into the "D" range and, while driving with the accelerator pedal held constant at specified points (throttle valve opening 50% and 100%), check the following points.

1. At each of the above throttle openings, check to see that 1-2, 2-3 and 3-OD up-shift take place and also that the shift points conform to those shown in the automatic shift diagram.

Evaluation
(a) If there is no 1-2 up-shift:
- governor valve is defective
- 1-2 shift valve is stuck
(b) If there is not 2-3 up-shift - 2-3 shift valve is stuck.
(c) If there is no 3-OD up-shift - 3-4 shift valve is stuck.
(d) If the shift point is defective:
- throttle cable is out-of-adjustment
- throttle valve, 1-2 shift valve, 2-3 shift valve, 3-4 shift valve, etc. are defective.

2. In the same manner, check the shock and the slip at 1-2, 2-3 and 3-OD up-shifts.

Evaluation
If the shock is severe:
- line pressure is too high
- accumulator is defective
- check ball is defective.

3. In "D" range OD gear, check for abnormal noise and vibration.

* The check for cause of abnormal noise and vibration must be made with extreme care as they could also be due to an unbalance in the propeller shafts, differential, tire, torque converter, etc. or insufficient bending rigidity, etc. in the power train.

4. While running in the "D" range, 2nd, 3rd gears and OD, check to see that the possible kick-down vehicle speed limits for 2-1, 3-1, 3-2, OD-3 and OD_2 kick-downs conform to those indicated in the automatic shift diagram.

5. Check for abnormal shock and slip at kick-down.

6. While running in the "D" range, OD gear, shift to the "2" and "L" ranges and check the engine braking effect in each of these ranges.

Evaluation
(a) If there is no engine braking effect in the "2" range - brake No. 1 is defective.
(b) If there is no engine braking effect in the "L" range - brake No. 3 is defective.

7. While running at approx. 100 km/h (62 mph) in OD of the "D" range, release your foot from the accelerator. Check that after shifting into the "2" range the OD-3 shift takes place immediately afterward and that the 3-2 shift conforms with the specifications in the automatic shift diagram.

8. While running at approx. 55 km-h (34 mph) in OD of the "D" range, release your foot from the accelerator. Check that after shifting into the "L" range the OD-3-2 shift takes place immediately afterward and that the 2-1 shift conforms with the specifications in the automatic shift diagram.

9. While driving in overdrive at a steady speed (lock-up ON) of about 80 km/h (50 mph), lightly depress the accelerator pedal and check that the engine rpm does not change abruptly.
* If the lock-up is not operating, drive power will not be transmitted via the torque converter fluid. Consequently, the torque converter will slip when the pedal is depressed, causing an abrupt change in engine rpm.

B. "3" RANGE TEST

1. Shift into "3" and run with the throttle valve opening at 50% and 100%, respectively. Then check the 1-2 and 2-3 up-shift points at each of the throttle valve openings to see that it conforms to those indicated in the automatic shift diagram.

2.Check for abnormal noise at acceleration and deceleration, and for shock at u-shift and down-shift.

3.Perform a kick-down from 2nd and 3rd gear of the "3" range, and check the possible 2-1, 3-2, 3-1 kickdowns vehicle speed limit to see if ti conforms to that indicated in the automatic shift diagram.

4.While running in the "3" range, shift into the "2" and "L" range, release the accelerator pedal and check the engine braking effect.

5.While running at approx. 55 km/h (34 mph) in the 3rd gear of the "3" range, release your foot from the accelerator. Check that after shifting into the "L" range the 3-2 shift takes place immediately afterward and that the 2-1 shift conforms to the specifications in the automatic shift diagram.

C."2" RANGE TEST

1.While running in 2nd gear of the "2" range, check to see that there is no -up-shift to 3rd gear.

2.While running in 2nd gear of the "2" range, check to see that there is no down-shift to 1st gear.

3.While running in 2nd gear of the "2" range, release the accelerator pedal and check the engine braking effect.

4.Check for abnormal noise at acceleration and deceleration.

D. "L" RANGE TEST

1.While running in the "L" range, check to see that there is no up-shift to 2nd gear.

2.While running in the "L" range, release the accelerator pedal and check the engine braking effect.

3.Check for abnormal noise at acceleration and deceleration.

E. "R" RANGE TEST

Shift into the "R" range and check for slipping while running at full throttle.

F."P" RANGE TEST

Stop the vehicle on a gradient (more than 9%) and, after shifting into the "P" range, release the parking brake. Then check that the parking lock pawl prevents the vehicle from moving.

AUTOMATIC SHIFT DIAGRAMS

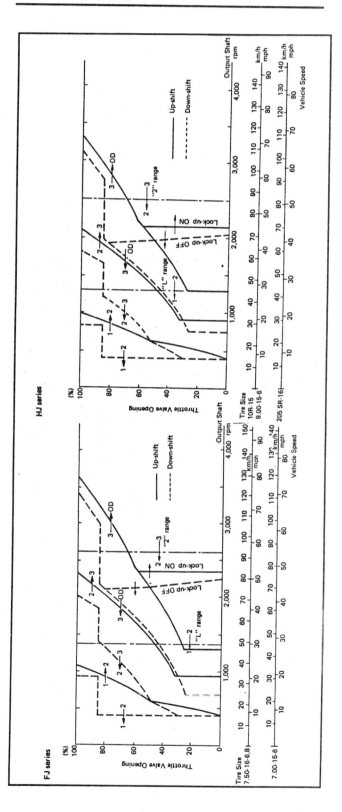

ON-VEHICLE REPAIR

Removal of Valve Body

1.Make Plate to Retain Accumulator Pistons. A retainer is helpful for holding accumulator pistons in the case during removal and installation of the valve body. The plate may be made from aluminium or plastic.

2.Remove Transmission and Transfer Under Covers.

3.Clean Transmission Exterior to Prevent Contamination of Interior of Transmission.

4.Drain Transmission Fluid.

5.Remove Oil Pan and Gasket.

* Some fluid will remain in the oil pan.

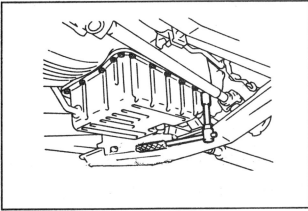

6.Remove Oil Strainer and gasket.

* Be careful as some oil will come out with the filter.

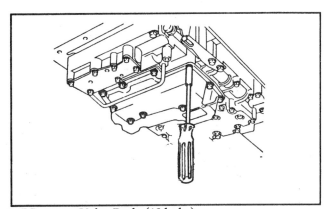

7.Remove Valve Body (18 bolts)

* Support the valve body by hand to prevent it from falling.

(a) Lower valve body slightly, and install the accumulator piston retaining plate. Hold in place with 2 pan bolts, and tighten by hand.

(b) Disconnect the throttle cable from the cam and remove the valve body.

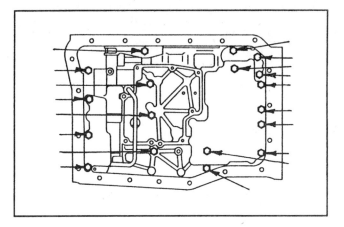

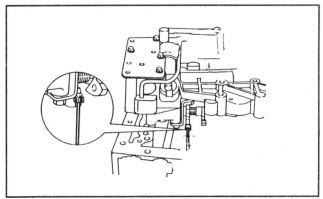

8.Remove 4 Centre Support Gaskets. (O rings)

Installation of Valve Body

1.Install the 4 Centre Support Gaskets, Facing the Pitted Sides Toward the Transmission Case.

2.Push the Cable Fitting into the Cam.

3.Install Valve Body.

(a) Align the manual valve lever with the manual valve.

(b) Remove the 2 pan bolts, and slide out the accumulator retaining plate.

4.Install Valve Body Bolts. Check that the manual valve lever contacts the centre of the roller at the tip of the detent spring.

Torque: 100 kg-cm (7 ft-lb, 10 N·m)

5.Be Sure the Strainer is Clean. Install a new gasket and strainer.

Torque: 5 mm bolt 55 kg-cm (48 in-lb, 5.4 N·m)

6 mm bolt 100 kg-cm (7 ft-lb, 10 N·m)

6.Install Pan with New Gasket. Be sure the pan is clean and the 2 magnets are in place.

* Do not use gasket sealer.

Torque: 70 kg-cm (61 in-lb, 6.9 N·m)

7.Install Drain Plug.

Torque: 280 kg-cm (20 ft-lb, 27 N·m)

8.Install Transmission Undercover and Transfer Undercover.

9.Fill Transmission with ATF. Add 6 lts (6.3 Us qts, 5.3 Imp.qts). Fluid type: ATF DEXRON^R II

* Do not overfill.

10.Check Fluid Level.

Removal of Throttle Cable

1.Disconnect Throttle Cable.

(a) Disconnect the cable housing from the bracket.

(b) Disconnect the cable from the throttle linkage.

2.Remove Valve Body as previously described.

3.Remove 4 Centre Support Gaskets.

4.Disconnect Exhaust Front Pipe from Tail Pipe.

5.Support the frame crossmember with jack, then remove frame crossmember set bolts.

6.Remove Throttle Cable Clamp.

(a) Lower the jack.

(b) Remove the cable clamp from the transmission housing.

7.Push Throttle Cable Out of Transmission Case. Using a 10mm socket, push the throttle cable out.

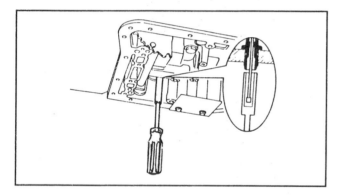

Installation of Throttle Cable

1.Install Cable in Transmission Case.

2.Install Throttle Cable Clamp to Transmission Housing.

3.Install Frame Crossmember Set Bolts.

Torque: 400 kg-cm (29 ft-lb, 39 N·m)

4.Connect Exhaust Front Pipe to Tail Pipe with a new Gasket.

5.Install 4 Centre Support Gaskets.

6.Install Valve Body as previously described.

7.If Throttle Cable is New, Paint Mark on Inner Cable.

* New cables do not have a cable stopper installed. Therefore to make adjustment possible, paint a mark as described below:

(i) Connect the throttle cable to the throttle cam of valve body.

(ii) Pull the inner cable lightly until resistance is felt, and hold it.

(iii) Paint a mark as shown, about 4 mm (0.16 in) in width.

(iv) Pull the inner cable fully, measure the cable stroke.

Cable stroke: 33 +/- 1 mm (1.30 +/- 0.04 in)

8.Connect Throttle Cable.

(a) Connect the cable to the throttle linkage.

(b) Connect the cable housing to the bracket on the valve cover.

(c) Adjust throttle cable.

9.Fill Transmission with ATF. Add 6 lts (6.3 US qts, 5.3 Imp.qts) of ATF. Fluid type: ATF DEXRON^R II

* Do not overfill.

REMOVAL OF TRANSMISSION

1.Disconnect Battery and Upper Radiator Hose.

2.Disconnect Throttle Cable.

(a) Loosen the adjusting nuts, and disconnect the cable housing from the bracket.

(b) Disconnect the cable from the throttle linkage.

3.Disconnect Connectors. Disconnect the connectors located near the starter.

4.Remove transfer Shift Lever Boot.

5.Raise Vehicle and Drain Transmission.

6.Remove Transmission Undercover and transfer Undercover.

7.Drain Transmission Fluid. Remove the drain plug and drain transmission fluid into a suitable container.

8.Remove Transfer Shift Lever.

(a) Remove the slip and pin, disconnect the shift rod from the transfer.

(b) Remove the nut and then remove the washers and the transfer shift lever with control rod.

9.Disconnect Transmission Control Rod. Remove the nut and disconnect the control rod from the control shaft lever.

10.Remove Power Take-Off Shift Lever (w/ Mechanical Winch).

(a) Remove the knob button with an Allen key.

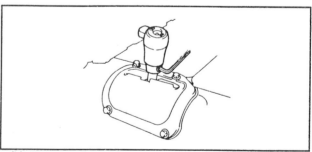

(b) Remove the spring.

(c) Using a hexagon wrench, remove the 2 screws and shift lever knob.

(d) Remove the 4 bolts and shift lever boot.

(e) Remove the nut and disconnect the shift rod from the PTO.

(f) Remove the bolt, and then remove the shift lever with shift rod.

11. Remove Propeller Shaft.

12. Remove Power Take-Off Drive Shaft (w/ Mechanical Winch).

(a) Remove the engine undercover.

(b) Place matchmarks on the yoke and flange.

(c) Remove the bolts and nuts, and disconnect the drive shaft from the PTO.

(d) Remove the front and rear bracket set bolts, and then remove the drive shaft.

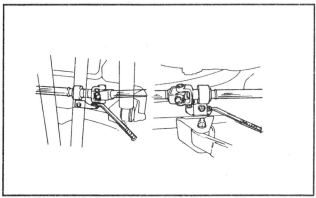

13. Disconnect Speedometer Cable.

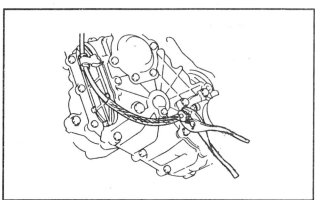

14. Disconnect 2 Vacuum Hoses.

15. Disconnect 2 Oil Cooler Tubes.

16. Remove Starter.

17. Remove Oil Filler Tube.

18. Remove 6 Torque Converter Mounting Bolts after removing the end plate hole plug.

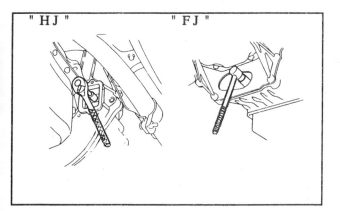

"HJ"   "FJ"

19. Remove Frame Crossmember.

(a) Support the transmission with the transmission jack.

(b) Remove the 8 bolts and 2 nuts, and then remove the frame crossmember.

20. Disconnect Exhaust Front Pipe.

(a) Remove the exhaust pipe clamp.

(b) Remove the 3 bolts, disconnect the front pipe from the tail pipe.

(c) Remove the 3 nuts and front pipe from the exhaust manifold.

(d) Remove the 2 gaskets.

21. Remove Transmission Assembly.

(a) Be sure to put a wooden block between the jack and the engine oil pan to prevent damage. Support the oil pan with a jack.

(b) Lower the rear end of transmission.

(c) Remove the 9 transmission mounting bolts.

(d) Draw out the transmission down and toward the rear.

* Be careful not to snag the throttle cable or neutral start switch cable. Keep the oil pan positioned downward.

22. Place Pan Under Converter Housing, and Remove Converter. Pull the converter straight off, and allow the fluid to drain into the pan.

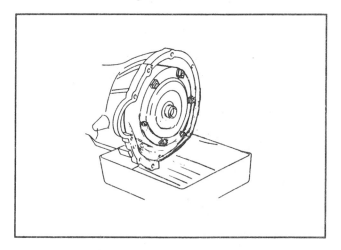

INSTALLATION

1.Measure Drive Plate Runout and Inspect Ring Gear. Set up a dial indicator and measure the drive plate runout. If runout exceeds 0.20 mm (0.0079 in) or if the ring gear is damaged, replace the drive plate. If installing a new drive plate, note the orientation of spacers and tighten the bolts.

Torque: 950 kg-cm (64 ft-lb, 93 N·m)

2.Measure Torque Converter Sleeve Runout.

(a) Temporarily mount the torque converter to the drive plate. Set up a dial indicator. If runout exceeds 0.30 mm (0.0118 in), try to correct by reorienting the installation of the converter. If excessive runout cannot be corrected, replace the torque converter.

* Mark the position of the converter to ensure correct installation.

(b) Remove the torque converter.

3.Apply Grease to Centre Hub of Torque Converter and Pilot Hose in Crankshaft.

4.Install Torque Converter in Transmission. If the torque converter has been drained and washed, refill with fresh transmission fluid.

Refill capacity:

2.0 lts (2.1 US qts, 1.8 Imp.qts)

Dry fill capacity:

5.4 lts (5.7 US qts, 4.8 Imp.qts)

Re-Fill torque converter with Auto Trans Fluid if it has had the drained from it.

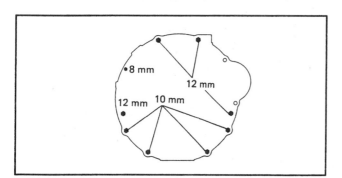

5.Check Torque Converter Installation. Using callipers and a straight edge, measure from the installed surface to the front surface of the transmission housing.

Correct distance:

3F engine 16.5 mm (0.650 in) or more

2H engine 41.2 mm (1.622 in) or more

* Install the converter horizontally to prevent oil seal from damage.

6.Install Transmission Assembly.

(a) Install the guide pin in the torque converter.

(b) Align the guide pin with one of the drive plate holes.

(c) Align two sleeves on the block with the converter housing.

(d) Temporarily install one bolt.

* Be careful not to tilt the transmission forward because the torque converter could slide out.

(e) Install the nine transmission mounting bolts.

Torque: 8 mm bolt 185 kg-cm (13 ft-lb, 18 N·m)

10 mm bolt 380 kg-cm (27 ft-lb, 37 N·m)

12 mm bolt 730 kg-cm (53 ft-lb, 72 N·m)

7.Install Exhaust Front Pipe with New Gasket.

8.Install Frame Crossmember.

(a) Install the frame crossmember, and torque the 8 bolts and 2 nuts.

Torque: Bolt 400 kg-cm (29 ft-lb, 39 N·m)

Nut 600 kg-cm (43 ft-lb, 59 N·m)

(b) Remove the transmission jack.

(c) Remove the jack from the engine oil pan.

9.Install 6 Torque Converter Bolts then Install End Plate Hole Plug.

Torque: 290 kg-cm (21 ft-lb, 28 N·m)

10.Install Oil Filler Tube with New O-Ring.

11.Install Starter.

12.Connect Oil Cooler Tubes.

Torque: 350 kg-cm (25 ft-lb, 34 N·m)

13.Connect 2 Vacuum Hoses.

14.Connect Speedometer Cable.

15.Install Power Take-off Drive Shaft (w/ Mechanical Winch).

(a) Align the matchmarks on the joint flange yoke and drive shaft.

(b) Install the drive shaft.

(c) Install the front and rear bracket.

(d) Align the matchmarks on the drive shaft and PTO.

(e) Torque the nuts.

Torque: 200 kg-cm (14 ft-lb, 20 N·m)

16.Install Engine Undercover.

17.Install Propeller Shafts.

18.Install Power Take-off Shift Lever (w/ Mechanical Winch).

(a) Install the shift lever to the transmission.

(b) Install the shift rod to the PTO

(c) Install the shift lever boot with the 4 bolts.

(d) Install the shift lever knob to the shift lever, and torque the 2 screws with hexagon wrench.

(e) Install the spring and knob button.

19.Connect and Adjust Transmission Control Rod.

20.Install Transfer Shift Lever.

(a) Install the washers and shift lever to the transmission.

(b) Install the shift rod and pin to the transfer.

(c) Install the clip.

(d) Install the shift lever boot with the 4 bolts.

(e) Install the shift lever knob.

21.Install Transmission Undercover and Transfer Undercover.

22.Lower Vehicle and Connect Upper Radiator Hose.

23.Connect Connectors and Battery.

24.Connect Throttle Cable.

25.Adjust Throttle Cable.

26.Fill Transmission with Transmission Fluid and Check Fluid Level.

Total capacity:

15.0 lts (15.9 US qts, 13.2 Imp.qts)

Drain and refill capacity:

5.0 lts (5.3 Us qts, 4.4 Imp.qts)

PROBLEM DIAGNOSIS

General Notes

A. Problems occurring with the automatic transmission can be caused by either the engine or the automatic transmission itself. These two areas should be distinctly isolated before proceeding with diagnosis.

B. Problem diagnosis should begin with the simplest operation, working up in order of difficulty, but initially determine whether the trouble lies within the engine or transmission.

C. Proceed with the inspection in the following order:

1. PRELIMINARY CHECK:
(a) Check the fluid level.
(b) Check the throttle cable mark.
(c) Check the shift linkage.
(d) Check the neutral start switch.
(e) Check the idling speed.
Repair as necessary.
2. STALL TEST. Repair as necessary.
3. TIME LAG TEST. Confirm by road test and repair as necessary.
4. HYDRAULIC TEST. Confirm the shift point and extent of shock by a road test. Repair as necessary.
5. ROAD TEST. Confirm whether the trouble lies within the ATM. If noisy or vibrating, the cause is possibly in the compressor, engine, propeller shaft, tyres, etc.

Problem Diagnosis

Problem: Fluid discoloured or smells burnt!
Possible Causes and Remedies:
* Fluid contaminated. Remedy - replace fluid.
* Torque converter faulty. Remedy - replace torque converter.
* Transmission faulty. Remedy - Dismantle and inspect transmission.

Problem: Vehicle does not move in any drive range!
Possible Causes and Remedies:

* Manual shift linkage out of adjustment. Remedy - adjust shift linkage.
* Valve body or primary regulator faulty. Remedy - inspect valve body.
* Parking brake locked on. Remedy - inspect parking/hand brake.
* Torque converter faulty. Remedy - replace torque converter.
* Drive plate broken. Remedy - replace drive plate.
* Oil pump intake strainer blocked. Remedy - clean strainer.

Problem: Shift lever position incorrect!
Possible Causes and Remedies:
* Manual shift linkage out of adjustment. Remedy - adjust shift linkage.
* Manual valve and lever faulty. Remedy - inspect valve body.
* Transmission faulty. Remedy - dismantle and inspect transmission.

Problem: Harsh engagement into any drive range!
Possible Causes and Remedies:
* Throttle cable out of adjustment. Remedy - adjust throttle cable.
* Valve body or primary regulator faulty. Remedy - inspect valve body.
* Accumulator pistons faulty. Remedy - inspect accumulator pistons.
* Transmission faulty. Remedy - dismantle and inspect transmission.

Problem: Delayed 1-2, 2-3 or 3-OD up-shift, or downshifts from OD-3 or 3-2 then shifts back to OD or 3!
Possible Causes and Remedies:
* Throttle cable out of adjustment. Remedy - adjust throttle cable.
* Throttle cable and cam faulty. Remedy - inspect throttle cable and cam.
* Governor faulty. Remedy - inspect governor.
* Valve body faulty. Remedy - inspect valve body.

Problem: Slips on 1-2, 2-3 or 3-OD up-shift, or slips or shudders on take-off!
Possible Causes and Remedies:
* Manual shift linkage out of adjustment. Remedy - adjust shift linkage.
* Throttle cable out of adjustment. Remedy - adjust throttle cable.
* Valve body faulty. Remedy - inspect valve body.
* Transmission faulty. Remedy - dismantle and inspect transmission.

Problem: Drag, binding or tie-up on 1-2, 2-3 or 3-OD up-shift!
Possible Causes and Remedies:
* Valve body faulty. Remedy - inspect valve body.
* Transmission faulty. Remedy - dismantle and inspect transmission.

Problem: Harsh down-shift!
Possible Causes and Remedies:
* Throttle cable out of adjustment. Remedy - adjust throttle cable.
* Throttle cable and cam faulty. Remedy - inspect throttle cable and cam.
* Accumulator pistons faulty. Remedy - inspect accumulator pistons.
* Valve body faulty. Remedy - inspect valve body.
* Transmission faulty. Remedy - dismantle and inspect transmission.

Problem: No down-shift when coasting!
Possible Causes and Remedies:
* Governor faulty. Remedy - inspect governor.
* Valve body faulty. Remedy - inspect valve body.

Problem: Down-shift occurs too quick or too late while coasting!
Possible Causes and Remedies:
* Throttle cable out of adjustment. Remedy - adjust throttle cable.
* Throttle cable faulty. Remedy - inspect throttle cable.

* Governor faulty. Remedy - inspect governor.
* Valve body faulty. Remedy - inspect valve body.
* Transmission faulty. Remedy - dismantle and inspect transmission.

Problem: No OD-3, 3-2, or 2-1 kick-down!
Possible Causes and Remedies:
* Throttle cable out of adjustment. Remedy - adjust throttle cable.
* Governor faulty. Remedy - inspect governor.
* Valve body faulty. Remedy - inspect valve body.

Problem: No engine braking in "2" range!
Possible Causes and Remedies:
* Valve body faulty. Remedy - inspect valve body.
* Transmission faulty. Remedy - dismantle and inspect transmission.

Problem: Vehicle does not hold in "P"!
Possible Causes and Remedies:
* Manual shift linkage out of adjustment. Remedy - adjust shift linkage.
* Parking/hand brake cam and spring faulty. Remedy - inspect cam and spring.

TRANSFER SYSTEMS

TRANSFER - J30 TRANSMISSION

TRANSFER SYSTEMS for other TRANSMISSIONS

TRANSFER - J30 TRANSMISSION

Components

1. Brake drum, Plate, Shim, Plate and Nut.
2. Backing plat.
3. Driven Gear.
4. Bearing rear retainer and Shim.
5. Drive Gear and Spacer.
6. Companion Flange
7. Extension Housing.
8. Clutch Sleeve.

Removal

Refer to 3-SPEED TRANSMISSION (J30) Section.

9. Case cover and Shifl inner lever.
10. Plug, Spring and ball.
11. Shift fork and Shaft.
12. Clutch sleeve, gear and Output shaft.
13. Low speed gear, Washer and Bearing.
14. High speed gear, Washer and Bearing
15. Idle gear and shaft.

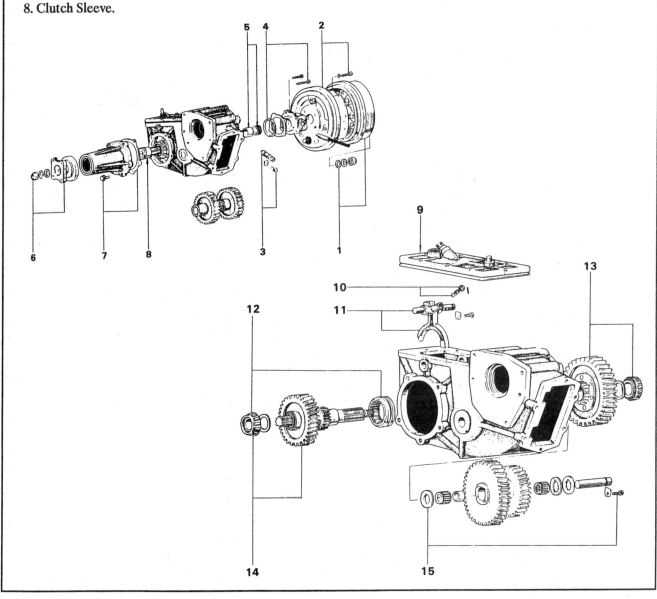

Dismantle

1.Brake Drum, Plate Shim, Plate and Nut.
* Have the system in front drive during the procedure.
2.Backing Plate.
3.Driven Gear.
4.Bearing Rear Retainer and Shim.
5.Drive Gear and Spacer.
6.Companion Flange.
7.Extension Housing.
8.Clutch Sleeve.
9.Case Cover and Shift Inner Lever.
10.Plug, Spring and Ball.
11.Shift Fork and Shaft. Drive out the shaft toward the rear.
12.Clutch Sleeve, Gear and Output Shaft. Set the special tool between the low speed gear and case front side. Force out the output shaft toward the front with a press.
13.Low Speed Gear, Washer and Bearing.
14.High Speed Gear, Washer and Bearing.
15.Idler Gear and Shaft.
(a) Measure the idler gear thrust clearance.
Thrust clearance:
Limit 0.475 mm (0.0187 in)
(b) Remove the shaft with special tool.

Inspection and Repair

* Wash the dismantled parts and inspect them as instructed below. Replace all parts found defective.

1.Transfer Case and Cover. Inspect the casse and cover for cracks or damage. Inspect the oil seals and bushing for wear or damage.
2.Output Shaft. Inspect the parts indicated by arrows for wear or damage.

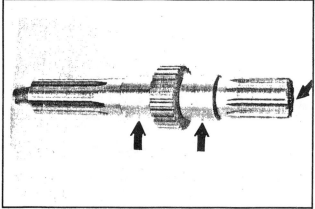

3.Gears.
(a) Inspect the teeth, thrust faces and inside surfaces, for wear or damage.

(b) Measure the oil clearance.
High & low speed output gear:
STD   0.035 - 0.081 mm (0.0014 - 0.0032 in)
Limit 0.081 mm (0.0032 in)

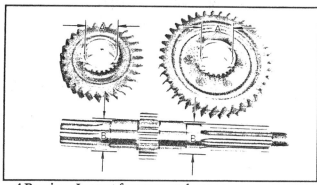

4.Bearing. Inspect for wear or damage.
5.Replace the Bearing Race if Necessary.
6.Sleeve and Fork. Check the clearance between the sleeves and the shift forks.
High & low clearance:
0.05 - 0.35 mm (0.0020 - 0.0138 in)
Front drive clearance:
0.1 - 0.3 mm (0.004 - 0.012 in)

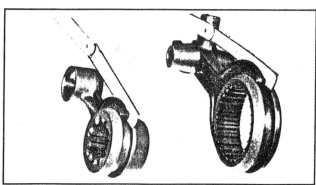

7.Idler Gear. Inspect for wear or damage.
8.Extension Housing.
(a) Inspect the shaft, bearing, and oil seal for wear or damage.
(b) Replace the bearing.
  (i) Remove the oil seal.
  (ii) Remove the snap ring.
  (iii) Remove the bearing together with the shaft using a press.

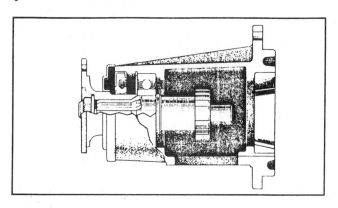

(iv) Replace the bearing.

(v) Using special tool, install the bearing together with the shaft.

(vi) Install the snap ring.

(vii) Install the oil seal with special tool.

Assembly

1.Idler Gear and Shaft. Install the idler gear assembly and shaft as illustrated.

Thrust clearance:

STD   0.125 - 0.475 mm (0.0049 - 0.0187 in)

Limit 0.475 mm (0.0187 in)

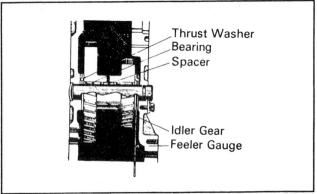

2.High Speed Gear, Washer and Bearing.

* Make sure that the gear is positioned in correct direction.

3.Low Speed Gear, Washer and Bearing.

4.Clutch Sleeve, Gear and Output Shaft. Install the clutch sleeve to the output shaft. Install the output shaft assembly to the case after inserting it through the low speed gear, washer and bearing.

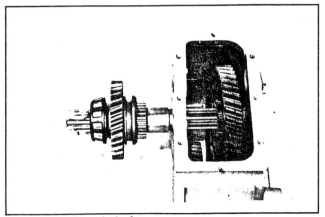

5.Shift Fork and Shaft.

6.Ball, Spring and Plug.

7.Case Cover and Shift Inner Lever. Position the lever tip to align it with the shift fork groove, and install the cover.

8.Clutch Sleeve.

Ensure that the clutch sleeve is installed in the correct direction.

9.Extension Housing.

10.Companion Flange. Using a special tool to keep the companion flange from turning, screw on the nut. Stake the nut after installation.

Tightening torque:

14.0 - 17.0 kg-m (102 - 122 ft-lb)

11.Spacer and Drive Gear.

12.Bearing Retainer and Shim. Install the retainer, using the same thickness of shim as at dismantle.

13.Backing Plate. Install the backing plate assembly.

Tightening torque:

3.0 - 4.5 kg-m (22 - 32 ft-lb)

* Install the short bolt at upper left.

14.Brake Drum, Plate and Nut.

(a) Set the system to front drive. To keep the companion flange from turning, screw on the nut.

Tightening torque:

14.0 - 17.0 kg-m (102 - 122 ft-lb)

(b) Disengage the front drive. Using a spring scale, measure the output shaft bearing preload.

Preload:

New bearing   1.2 - 4.1 kg (2.6 - 9.9 lb)

Reused bearing More than 0.47 kg (1.0 lb)

(c) If the preload is at standard, stake the nut to lock it in plate. If not at standard, adjust by selecting proper thickness shims. Adjust shim thickness range from 0.10 mm (0.0039 in) to 0.25 mm (0.0098 in).

15.Drive Gear.

TRANSFER SYSTEMS for other TRANSMISSIONS .

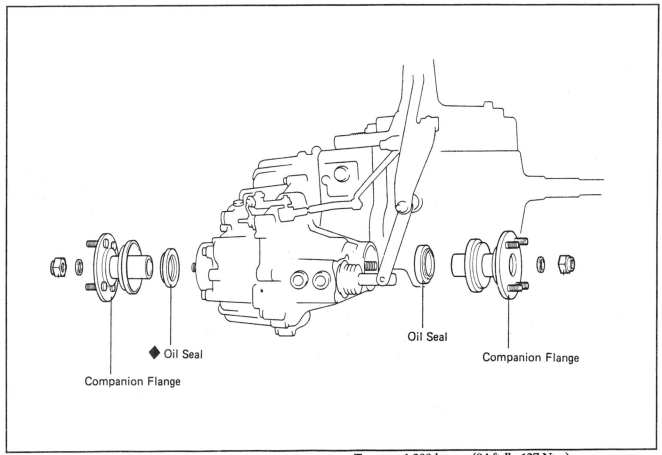

♦ Oil Seal

Companion Flange

Oil Seal

Companion Flange

TRANSFER

Replacement/Front & Rear Output Shaft Oil Seal

1. Drain Gear Oil from Transfer.
2. Remove Transfer Undercover.
3. Remove Front and Rear Propeller Shafts.
4. Remove Companion Flange.
5. Remove the Output Shaft Oil SeaL.
6. Install New Oil Seal.
7. Install Companion Flange and Lock Nut.

Torque: 1,300 kg-cm (94 ft-lb, 127 N·m)
Stake the companion flange lock nut.
8. Install Front and Rear Propeller Shafts.
Torque: 900 kg-cm (65 ft-lb, 88 N·m)
9. Install Transfer Undercover.
10. Fill Transfer With Oil.
Oil Grade: API GL-4,5 SAE 90
Capacity: MTM 2.2 lts (2.3 US qts, 1.9 Imp.qts)
         ATM 2.1 lts (2.2 US qts, 1.8 Imp.qts)

Removal

See REMOVAL OF TRANSMISSION 7 TRANSFER Section [Under 4 & 5 SPEED TRANSMISSION or AUTOMATIC TRANSMISSION].

Components/Diaphragm Cylinder

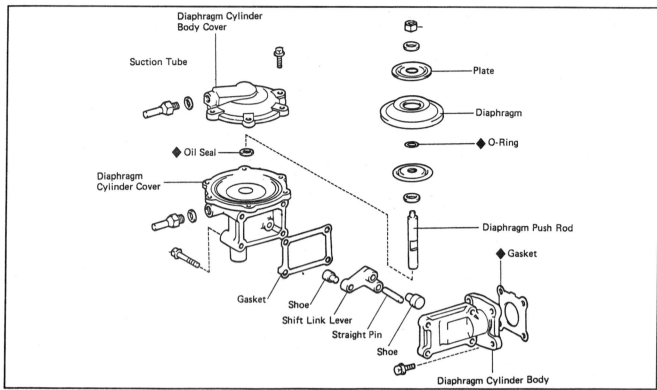

Dismantle/Diaphragm Cylinder

1. Remove Diaphragm Cylinder Assembly and Gasket.
2. Remove Shift Link Lever and Straight Pin.
3. Using a pin punch and hammer, remove the 2 shoes from the shift link lever.
4. Remove Diaphragm Cylinder Body and Gasket Body from the Transfer Case.
5. Inspect Diaphragm Cylinder Assembly.
(a) With at least 400 mmHg (15.75 in.Hg, 53.3 kPa) of vacuum in the diaphragm, confirm that the shaft moves.
Standard stroke: 22 mm (0.87 in)
(b) Confirm again on the diaphragm side.
(c) With at least 400 mmHg (15.75 in.Hg, 53.3 kPa) of vacuum in the diaphragm, confirm the gauge needle is stable.
6. Remove Suction Tube and GAsket.
7. Remove Diaphragm Cylinder Body Cover.
(a) Remove 2 washers, 2 plates, diaphragm and O-ring from diaphragm push rod.

Inspection/Diaphragm Cylinder Components

If Necessary, Replace Oil Seal.
(a) Using a screwdriver, remove the oil seal.
(b) Using a socket wrench, drive in a new oil seal.
(c) Apply MP grease to the oil seal lip.

Assembly/Diaphragm Cylinder

1. Install Following Parts to Diaphragm Push Rod: 1) 2 washers, 2) 2 plates, 3) diaphragm, 4) O-ring.
2. Torque Diaphragm Push Rod Nut.
Torque: 375 kg-cm (27 ft-lb, 37 N·m)
3. Install Diaphragm Push Rod Into Diaphragm Cylinder Cover.
4. Install Diaphragm Cylinder Body Cover. Install the diaphragm cylinder body cover to the diaphragm cylinder cover. Torque the bolts.
Torque: 75 kg-cm (65 in-lb, 7.4 N·m)
6. Install the Diaphragm Cylinder Body with a New Gasket to the Transfer Case. Torque the bolts.
Torque: 185 kg-cm (13 ft-lb, 18 N·m)
7. Using a Press, Install 2 Shoes to Shift Link Lever.
8. Install Shift Link Lever and Straight Pin.
9. Install Diaphragm Cylinder Assembly. Install the diaphragm cylinder assembly with a new gasket to the diaphragm cylinder body. Torque the bolts.
Torque: 185 kg-cm (13 ft-lb, 18 N·m)

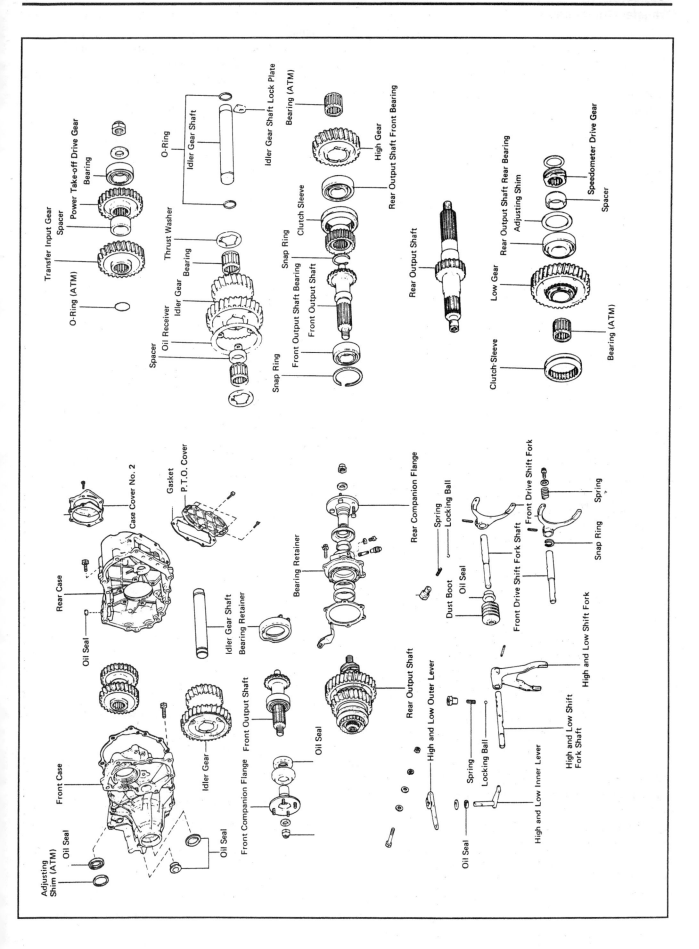

Transfer Components

Dismantle Transfer

1.Remove Diaphragm Cylinder (Electrical Shift Type).

2.Remove Transfer Front Drive Shift Lever (Mechanical Shift Type).

(a) Remove the transfer front drive shift lever.

(b) Remove the dust boot.

3.Remove 4WD Indicator Switch.

4.Remove L4 Position Switch (Electrical Shift Type).

5.Remove Plugs, Springs and Locking Balls.

[Mechanical Shift Type] Remove the plugs and, using a magnetic finger, remove the springs and locking balls.

[Electrical Shift Type] Remove the plug and, using a magnetic finger, remove the spring and locking ball.

6.Remove Speedometer Driven Gear.

7.Remove Transmission Output Shaft Lock Nut.

8.Remove Front and Rear Companion Flange with Nut.

9.Remove the 6 Bolts and Remove the Power Take-off Cover.

10.Measure the Clearance Between the Idler Gear and Thrust Washer Using a Feeler Gauge.

Standard clearance:

0.275 - 0.625 mm (0.0110 - 0.0246 in)

Maximum clearance: 0.625 mm (0.0246 in)

11.Remove Rear Output Shaft Rear Bearing Retainer.

(a) Remove the 6 bolts and remove the rear output shaft rear bearing retainer.

(b) Remove the speedometer drive gear and spacer.

12.Remove Idler Gear Shaft Lock Plate.

13.Remove Transfer Rear Case.

14.Remove Rear Output Shaft Assembly with Shift Fork and Shift Fork Shaft.

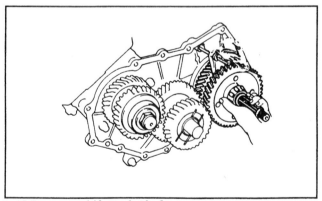

15.Remove Shift Fork Shaft.

(a) Using a pin punch and hammer, drive out the slotted spring pin.

(b) Remove the shift fork shaft from the shift fork.

* Use a set of soft jaws in the vice to protect the shift fork.

16.Remove Transfer Input Gear Bearing, Power Take-Off Drive Gear and Spacer.

(a) Using special tool, remove the transfer input gear bearing.

(b) Remove the power take-off drive gear and spacer.

17.Remove Transfer Input Gear.

18.Remove O-Ring From Transmission Output Shaft (ATM).

19.Remove Idler Gear, Bearings, Spacer Thrust Washers and Idler Gear Shaft.

20.Remove Rear Output Shaft Front Bearing Retainer with a Special Tool.

21.Remove Clutch Sleeve with the Shift Fork and Shift Fork Shaft.

22.Remove Shift Fork Shaft.

[Mechanical Shift Type]

(a) Using a pin punch and hammer, drive out the slotted spring pin.

(b) Remove the shift fork from the shift fork shaft.

[Electrical Shift Type]

(a) Remove the retainer, spring and shift fork from the shift fork shaft.

(b) Using snap ring pliers, remove the snap ring.

23.Remove Transfer Front Case.

(a) Remove the 4 bolts (5-Speed) or 5 bolts (4-Speed).

(b) Using a plastic hammer, remove the transfer front case.

(c) Remove the adjusting shim from the transfer front case (ATM).

24.Remove Front Output Shaft with a Press.

25.Remove Transfer High and Low Shift Outer and Inner Lever.

26.Measure Thrust Clearance of High and Low Gear.

(a) Using a feeler gauge, measure the thrust clearance of the high gear.

Standard clearance:

MTM 0.10 - 0.25 mm (0.0039 - 0.0098 in)

ATM 0.15 - 0.30 mm (0.0059 - 0.0118 in)

Maximum clearance: MTM 0.25 mm (0.0098 in)

ATM 0.30 mm (0.0118 in)

(b) Using a feeler gauge, measure the thrust clearance of the low gear.

Standard clearance:

MTM 0.10 - 0.25 mm (0.0039 - 0.0098 in)

ATM 0.15 - 0.30 mm (0.0059 - 0.0118 in)

Maximum clearance: MTM 0.25 mm (0.0098 in)

ATM 0.30 mm (0.0118 in)

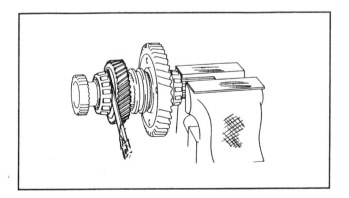

27. Remove High and Low Gear from Rear Output Shaft.

[High Gear]

(a) Using snap ring pliers, remove the snap ring.

(b) Using a press and socket wrench, remove the following parts: 1) clutch hub, 2) output shaft front bearing, 3) high gear, 4) high gear bearing (ATM), 5) clutch sleeve.

[Low Gear] Using a press, remove the following parts: 1) output shaft rear bearing, 2) low gear, 3) low gear bearing (ATM).

Inspection/Transfer Components

1.Inspect Rear Output Shaft.

(a) Check the rear output shaft for wear or damage.

(b) Using a micrometer, measure the outer diameter of the rear output shaft journal surface.

Minimum outer diameter:

Part A 40.009 mm (1.5752 in)

    B 40.009 mm (1.5752 in)

(c) Using a dial indicator, check the shaft runout.

Maximum runout: 0.03 mm (0.0012 in)

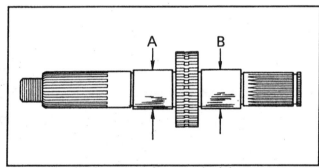

2.Check Oil Clearance of Low and High Gear.

(a) Using a dial indicator, measure oil clearance between the high gear and shaft.

Standard clearance:

MTM 0.035 - 0.081 mm (0.0014 - 0.0032 in)

ATM 0.019 - 0.068 mm (0.0007 -0.0027 in)

Maximum clearance:

MTM 0.081 mm (0.0032 in)

ATM 0.068 mm (0.0027 in)

(b) Using a dial indicator, measure the oil clearance between the low gear and shaft.

Standard clearance:

MTM 0.035 - 0.081 mm (0.0014 - 0.0032 in)

ATM 0.019 - 0.068 mm (0.0007 - 0.0027 in)

Maximum clearance:

MTM 0.081 mm (0.0032 in)

ATM 0.068 mm (0.0027 in)

3.Using a Feeler Gauge, Measure the Clearance Between the Hub Sleeves and Shift Fork.

Maximum clearance: 1.0 mm (0.039 in)

4.If Necessary, Replace Rear Output Shaft Pilot Bearing.

* The bearing will break.

(a) Using special tool, press in a new pilot bearing.

(b) Apply MP grease to the pilot bearing.

5.If Necessary, Replace Rear Output Shaft Front Bearing Outer Race.

(a) Using special tool, remove the rear output shaft front bearing outer race.

(b) Using special tool, press a new front outer race into the front bearing retainer.

6.If Necessary, Replace Rear Output Shaft Rear Bearing Outer Race.

(a) Using special tool, remove the rear output shaft rear bearing outer race and shim.

(b) Install the thinnest shim into the rear bearing retainer.

(c) Using special tool, press in a new rear outer race to the rear bearing retainer.

7.If Necessary, Replace Front OUtput Shaft Oil Seal.

8.If Necessary, Replace Front Drive Shift Fork Shaft Oil Seal.

9.If Necessary, Replace Transmission Rear Oil Seal. Using a screwdriver, remove the transmission rear oil seal. Before inserting new seal, apply some MP grease to the oil seal lip.

10. If Necessary, Replace Rear Output Shaft Oil Seal.

11. If Necessary, Replace High and Low Gear Select Lever Oil Seal.

12. If Necessary, Replace Speedometer Driven Gear Oil Seal. (a) Pull out the oil seal.

(b) Using special tool, drive a new oil seal into the sleeve.

Oil seal depth: 20 mm (0.79 in)

13. If Necessary, Replace Front Output Shaft Bearing.

(a) Remove the oil seal.

(b) Using a screwdriver, remove the snap ring.

(c) Using special tool, press out the bearing.

(d) Using special tool, press in a new bearing.

(e) INstall the snap ring.

(f) Install a new oil seal.

Assembly

1.Install HIgh Gear to Rear Output Shaft. Using special tool, press in the following parts: 1) high gear bearing (ATM), 2) high gear, 3) output shaft front bearing, 4) clutch hub.

2.Install Low Gear to Rear Output Shaft. Using special tool, press in the following parts: 1) clutch sleeve, 2) low gear bearing (ATM), 3) low gear, 4) output shaft rear bearing.

3.Install Snap Ring. Select a snap ring that will allow minimum axial play and install it on the shaft.

Mark	Thickness mm (in)
11	2.30 - 2.35 (0.0906 - 0.0925)
17	2.60 - 2.65 (0.1024 - 0.1043)

4.Install Transfer High and Low Shift Outer and Inner Lever.

5.Install Front Output Shaft. Using special tool, press in the front output shaft to the transfer front case.

6.Install Adjusting Shim to Transfer Front Case (ATM).

(a) Measure the distance between the transfer adaptor and the front case to select a shim to give the standard clearance.

Standard clearance:

0.4 - 0.5 mm (0.016 - 0.020 in)

Adjusting shim thickness:

2.28 - 2.32 mm (0.0898 - 0.0913 in)

2.38 - 2.42 mm (0.0937 - 0.0953 in)

2.48 - 2.52 mm (0.0976 - 0.0992 in)

(b) Install the adjusting shim to the transfer front case.

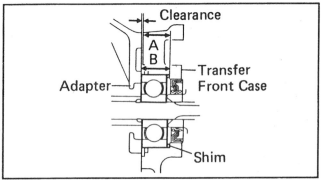

7.Install Transfer Front Case.

(a) Apply MP grease to the oil seal.

(b) Install the front case with a new gasket to the transfer adaptor.

(c) Apply liquid sealer to the bolts, and install and torque as shown: 4-Speed - 4 bolts; 5-Speed - 3 bolts.

Torque: 17 mm 650 kg-cm (47 ft-lb, 64 N·m)

14 mm 400 kg-cm (29 ft-lb, 39 N·m)

(d) Install and torque the other bolts.

Torque: 650 kg-cm (47 ft-lb, 64 N·m)

8.Install Shift Fork Shaft.

[Mechanical Shift Type]

(a) Install the shift fork shaft into shift fork No. 1.

(b) Using a pin punch and a hammer, drive in the slotted spring pin.

* Use a set of soft jaws in the vice to protect the shift fork.

[Electrical Shift Type]

(a) Using snap ring pliers, install the snap ring.

(b) Install the shift fork, spring and retainer to the shift fork shaft.

Torque: 185 kg-cm (14 ft-lb, 18 N·m)

9.Install Clutch Sleeve with the Shift Fork and Shift Fork Shaft.

10. Install Rear Output Shaft Front Bearing Retainer. Using a plastic hammer, install the rear output shaft front bearing retainer.

11. Install Idler Gear.

(a) Install a new O-ring on the idler gear shaft front side groove.

(b) Install the idler gear shaft to the transfer front case.

(c) Install the idler gear thrust washer.

* Be sure that protruding part of washer fits in the case groove.

(d) Apply MP grease to the two bearings.

(e) Install the two bearings and spacer to the idler gear shaft.

(f) Install the idler gear to the idler gear shaft.

12. Install O-Ring to Transmission Output Shaft (ATM).

13. Install Transfer Input Gear. Using special tool, install the transfer input gear.

14. Install Spacer and Power Take-off Drive Gear. Install the spacer and power take-off drive gear to the output shaft.

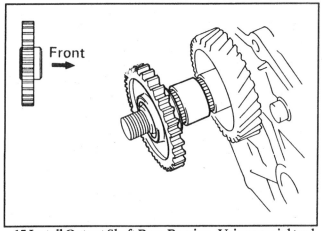

15. Install Output Shaft Rear Bearing. Using special tool and hammer, drive in the output shaft bearing.

16. Install Shift Fork Shaft.

(a) Install the high and low shift fork shafts into the shift fork.

(b) Using a pin punch and a hammer, drive in the slotted spring pin.

* Use a set of soft jaws in the vice to protect the shift fork.

17. Install Rear Output Shaft with Shift Fork and Shaft.

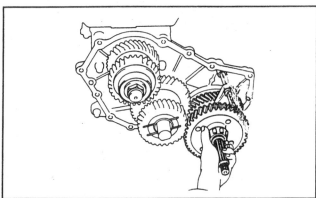

18. Stick on Thrust Washer. Stick the thrust washer to the transfer rear case with MP grease.

* Be sure that protruding part of washer fits in the case groove.

19. Install Transfer Rear Case.

(a) Place a new gasket on the front case.

(b) Install the rear case.

* Align the high and low shift lever tip with the shift fork shaft groove.

(c) Apply liquid sealer to the two bolts, and install and torque as shown.

Torque: 650 kg-cm (47 ft-lb, 64 N·m)

(d) Install and torque the other bolts.

Torque: 17 mm 650 kg-cm (47 ft-lb, 64 N·m)
         14 mm 400 kg-cm (29 ft-lb, 39 N·m)

20. Install O-Ring and Lock Plate.

(a) Align the shaft groove to the bolt hole.

(b) Install an O-ring on the shaft groove.

(c) Using a plastic hammer, drive in the shaft.

(d) Install the lock plate and bolt. Tighten the bolt.

Torque: 130 kg-cm (9 ft-lb, 13 N·m)

21. Install Speedometer Drive Gear and Spacer.

22. Adjust Rear Output Shaft Preload.

(a) Install the rear output shaft rear bearing retainer.

* Align the bearing retainer rib with the case.

(b) Torque the 6 bolts.

Torque: 350 kg-cm (25 ft-lb, 34 N·m)

(c) Shift the transfer lever to the "N" position.

(d) Temporarily install the rear companion flange lock nut.

(e) Using a torque meter, measure the rear output shaft preload (Starting Torque).

Preload:

New bearing

15 - 24.7 kg-cm (13.0 - 21.4 in-lb, 1.5 - 2.4 m·m)

Reused bearing

7 - 12 kg-cm (6.1 - 10.4 in-lb, 0.7 - 1.2 N·m)

If the preload is not within specification, remove the outer race of the rear output shaft rear bearing with special tool. Select an adjusting shim varying in thickness from 0.15 mm (0.0059 in) to 1.5 mm (0.0590 in).

* The preload will change about 10.0 kg-cm (8.7 in-lb, 1.0 N·m) with each shim thickness (vary 0.1 mm).

(f) Remove the rear companion flange lock nut.

23. Remove Rear Output Shaft Rear Bearing Retainer.

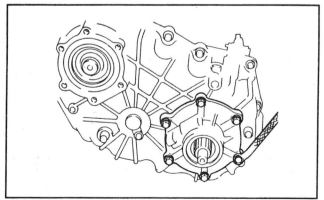

24. Install Rear Output Shaft Rear Bearing Retainer.

(a) Align the bearing retainer rib with the case rib and install the retainer with a new gasket.

(b) Apply liquid sealer to the six bolts.

(c) Install and torque the bolts.

Torque: 350 kg-cm (25 ft-lb, 34 N·m)

25. Install Front and Rear Companion Flange.

(a) Install the companion flange.

(b) Using special tool to hold the companion flange, install the companion flange lock nut.

Torque: 1,300 kg-cm (94 ft-lb, 127 N·m)

(c) Stake the companion flange lock nut.

26. Install Transmission Output Shaft Lock Nut.

(a) Using special tool to hold the rear companion flange, install the transmission output shaft lock nut.

Torque: 1,300 kg-cm (94 ft-lb, 127 N·m)

(b) Stake the transmission output shaft lock nut.

27. Install Power Take-Off Cover.

(a) Install the power take-off cover with a new gasket to the transfer rear case.

(b) Apply liquid sealer to the 2 bolts, and install and torque as shown.

Torque: 170 kg-cm (12 ft-lb, 17 N·m)

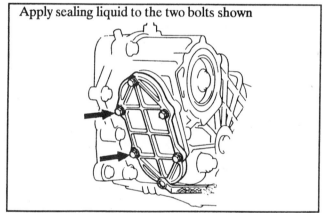

Apply sealing liquid to the two bolts shown

(c) Install and torque the other bolts.

Torque: 195 kg-cm (14 ft-lb, 19 N·m)

28. Install Transfer Case Cover No. 2.

(a) Install the transfer case cover No. 2 with a new gasket to the transfer rear case.

* Face the gasket notch downward.

(b) Apply liquid sealer to the 6 bolts.

(c) Install and torque the bolts.

Torque: 155 kg-cm (11 ft-lb, 15 N·m)

29. Install Speedometer Driven Gear.

Torque: 130 kg-cm (9 ft-lb, 13 N·m)

30. Install Plug, Spring and Locking Ball.

[Mechanical Shift Type] Apply liquid sealer to the plugs and install the locking balls, springs and plugs.

Torque: 450 kg-cm (33 ft-lb, 44 N·m)

[Electrical Shift Type] Apply liquid sealer to the plug and install the locking ball, spring and plug.

Torque: 450 kg-cm (33 ft-lb, 44 N·m)

31. [Electrical Shift Type] Install L4 Position Switch.

Torque: 450 kg-cm (33 ft-lb, 44 N·m)

32. Install the 4WD Indicator Switch.

Torque: 450 kg-cm (33 ft-lb, 44 N·m)

33.Install Dust Boot.

34. **[Mechanical Shift Type]**Install Transfer Front Drive Shift Lever.

35.**[Electrical Shift Type]** Install Diaphragm Cylinder.

Installation

Refer to INSTALLATION OF TRANSMISSION Section.

Problem Diagnosis

Problem: Transfer hard to shift or will not shift!
Possible causes and remedies:
* Splines on input shaft dirty or burred. Remedy - repair as necessary.
* Transfer faulty. Remedy - dismantle and inpsect transfer.

Problem: Transfer jumps out of gear!
Possible cause and remedy:
* Transfer faulty. Remedy - dismantle and inspect transfer.

PROPELLER SHAFTS

PROPELLER SHAFT

Components

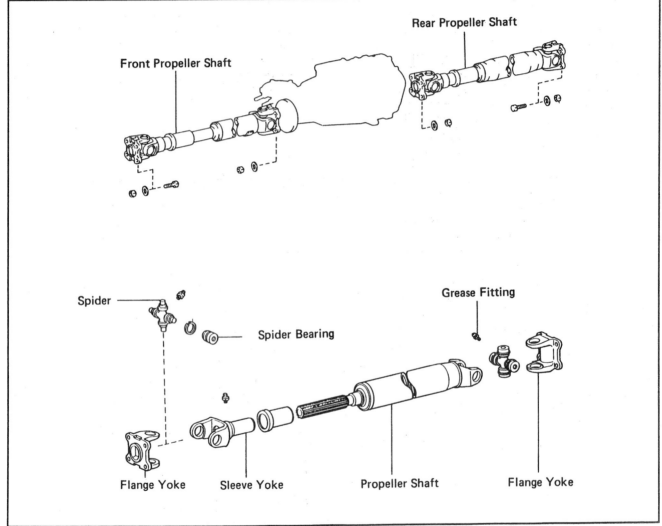

Front Propeller Shaft

Rear Propeller Shaft

Spider

Spider Bearing

Grease Fitting

Flange Yoke   **Sleeve Yoke**   **Propeller Shaft**   **Flange Yoke**

Removal of Front & Rear Propeller Shaft

1. Disconnect Propeller Shaft Flange from Companion Flange on Differential.
   (a) Put matchmarks on the flanges.
   (b) Remove the 4 bolts and nuts.
2. Disconnect Propeller Shaft Flange from Companion Flange on Transfer.
   (a) Put matchmarks on the flanges.
   (b) Remove the 4 nuts.
   (c) Remove the propeller shaft.

Inspection of Components

1. Inspect Front & Rear Propeller Shafts for Damage or Runout. If shaft runout is greater than maximum, replace the shaft.

Maximum runout: 0.8 mm (0.031 in)
2.Inspect Spider Bearings.
(a) Inspect the spider bearings for wear or damage.
(b) Check the spider bearing axial play by turning the yoke while holding the shaft tightly.
Bearing axial play: less than 0.05 mm (0.0020 in)
If necessary, replace the spider bearing.

Dismantle

1.Remove Sleeve Yoke from Propeller Shaft.
(a) Place matchmarks on the sleeve yoke and shaft.
(b) Pull out the sleeve yoke from the shaft.

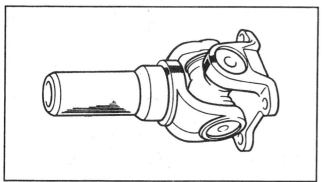

2.Remove Spider Bearing.
(a) Put matchmarks on the sleeve yoke and flange.
(b) Slightly tap in the bearing outer races.
(c) Using 2 screwdrivers, remove the 4 snap rings from the grooves.
(d) Push out the bearing from the flange.
(e) Clamp the bearing outer race in a vice and tap off the flange with a hammer.
* Remove the bearing on the opposite side in the same procedure.
(f) Install the 2 removed bearing outer races to the spider.
(g) Push out the bearing from the yoke.
(h) Clamp the outer bearing race in a vice and tap off the yoke with a hammer.
* Remove the bearing on the opposite side in the same procedure.

Assembly

* When replacing the spider, be sure that the grease fitting assembly hole is facing in the direction illustrated.

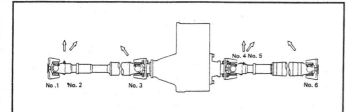

1.Install Spider Bearings.
(a) Apply MP grease to the spider and bearings.
* Be careful not to apply too much grease.
(b) Align the matchmarks on the yoke and flange.
(c) Fit the new spider into the yoke.
(d) Install the new bearings on the spider.
(e) Adjust both bearings so that the snap ring grooves are at maximum and equal widths.
(f) Install 2 snap rings of equal thickness which will allow 0 - 0.05 mm (0 - 0.0020 in) axial play.
* Do not reuse the snap rings.
* Snap rings vary in thickness from 2.00 mm (0.0787 in) to 2.09 mm (0.0823 in).
(g) Using a hammer, tap the yoke until there is no clearance between the bearing outer race and snap ring.
(h) Check that the spider bearing moves smoothly.
(i) Check the spider bearing axial play.
Bearing axial play: Less than 0.05 mm (0.0020 in)
* Install new spider bearings on the flange side in the procedure described above.
2.Insert Sleeve Yoke into Propeller Shaft.
(a) Apply MP grease to the propeller shaft spline and sleeve yoke sliding surface.
(b) Align the matchmarks on the sleeve yoke and propeller shaft.
(c) Install the propeller shaft into the sleeve yoke.

Installation of Front & Rear Propeller Shafts

1.Connect Propeller Shaft Flange to Companion Flange on Transfer.
(a) Align the matchmarks on the flanges and connect the flanges with 4 nuts.
(b) Torque the nuts.
Torque: 900 kg-cm (65 ft-lb, 88 N·m)

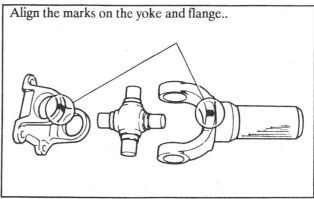

Align the marks on the yoke and flange..

2.Connect Propeller Shaft Flange to Companion Flange on Differential.
(a) Align the matchmarks on the flanges and connect the flanges with 4 bolts and nuts.
(b) Torque the bolts and nuts.
Torque: 900 kg-cm (65 ft-lb, 88 N·m)

3. Apply MP Grease to Grease Fitting. With a grease gun, pump the MP grease into each fitting until it begins to flow from around the oil seal.

* Turn the front propeller shaft until the yoke fitting faces the right side of the vehicle and apply grease to the spider fitting through the side member (MT) or AT oil pan under cover hole.

Problem Diagnosis

Problem: Noise!
Possible Causes and Remedies:
* Sleeve yoke spline worn. Remedy - replace sleeve yoke.
* Spider bearing worn or stuck. Remedy - replace spider bearing.

Problem: Vibration!
Possible Causes and Remedies:
* Propeller shaft runout. Remedy - replace propeller shaft.
* Propeller shaft imbalance. Remedy - balance propeller shaft.
* Sleeve yoke spline stuck. Remedy - replace sleeve yoke.

FRONT AXLE AND SUSPENSION

FRONT AXLE AND SUSPENSION

FRONT WHEEL ALIGNMENT

1.Make Following Check and Correct Any Problems:

(i) Check the tyres for wear and proper inflation. See SPECIFICATIONS Section.

(ii) Check the wheel runout.

Lateral runout: less than 1.2 mm (0.047 in)

(iii) Check the front wheel bearings, front suspension and steering linkage for looseness.

(iv) Use the standard bounce test to check that the front absorbers work properly.

2.Install Wheel Alignment Equipment. Follow the specific instructions of the equipment manufacturer.

3.Check Camber and King Pin Inclination.

Camber: 1° +/- 45'

King pin inclination: $9^o30'$ +/- 45'

If camber or king pin inclination checks are not within specification, recheck the steering knuckle parts and the front wheel for bending or looseness.

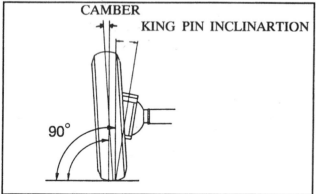

CAMBER

KING PIN INCLINARTION

90°

4.Check Caster.

Caster:

FJ, BJ, HJ 4..^{s} Series	1° +/- 45'
FJ, 55 Series	1° +/- 45'
FJ62, BJ & JH60L (R)G	$0^o50'$ +/- 1°
FJ62, BJ & HJ60L (R)V	$1^o05'$ +/- 1°
FJ & BJ 70 & 73 Series	$1^o05'$ +/- 1°
FJ, BJ & HJ & 75LV & 75RV Series	$0^o45'$ +/- 1°
FJ, BJ & HJ & 75LP & 75RP Series	$0^o55'$ +/- 1°
RJ & LJ 7..^{s} Series	$4^o05'$ +/- 1°

If caster is not as specified, inspect and replace damaged or worn parts.

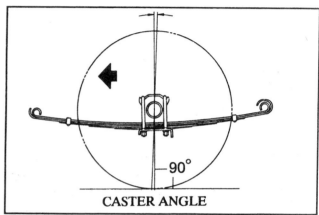

CASTER ANGLE

5.Adjust Toe-In.

(a) Make sure the wheels are positioned straight ahead.

(b) Mark the centre of each rear tread at spindle height and measure the distance between the marks of right and left tyres.

(c) Advance the vehicle until the marks on the rear side of the tyres come to the front.

* The toe-in should be measured at the same point on the tyre and at the same level.

(d) Measure the distance between the marks on the front side of the tyres.

Toe-in:

Bias tyre   4 +/- 2 mm (0.10 +/- 0.08 in)

Radial tyre 1 +/- 2 mm (0.04 +/- 0.08 in)

(e) Make sure the steering gear is centred.

(f) Loosen the nuts holding the clamps to the tie rod.

(g) Adjust toe-in to the correct value by turning the tie rod.

(h) Torque the nuts holding the clamps.

Torque: 375 kg-cm (27 ft-lb, 37 N·m)

* Ensure that the lengths of the tie rod ends are the same.

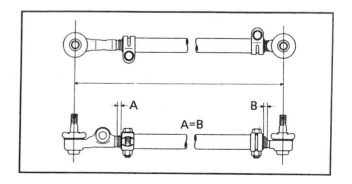

6.Adjust Wheel Angle. Remove the caps of the knuckle stopper bolts and check the steering angles.

Wheel angle:
Maximum - Inside wheel $32^{\circ} + 0^{\circ}$ or -3°)
      - Outside wheel 30°
At 20° (Outside Wheel) - Inside wheel 21°

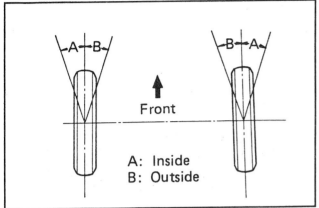

* When the steering wheel is fully turned, make sure that the wheel is not touching the body of brake flexible hose.

If the maximum steering angles differ from the standard value, adjust the wheel angle with the knuckle stopper bolts.

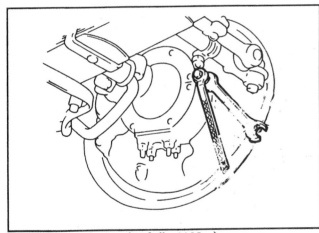

Torque: 450 kg-cm (33 ft-lb, 44 N·m)

If the wheel angle still cannot be adjusted within limits, inspect and replace damaged or worn steering parts.

7.Inspect Side Slip with Side Slip Tester.

Side slip limit:
less than 3.0 mm/m (0.118 in/3.3 ft)

If the side slip exceeds the limit, the toe-in or other front wheel alignment may not be correct.

FREE WHEEL HUB

Components

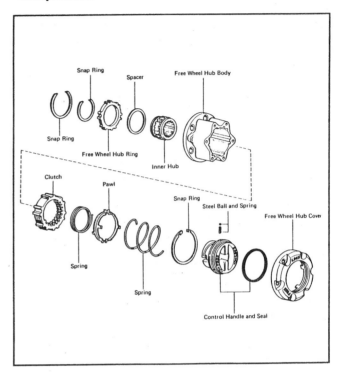

Removal

1.Remove Free Wheel Hub Cover.
(a) Set the control handle to FREE.
(b) Remove the cover mounting bolts and pull off the cover.
2.Remove Snap Ring using snap ring pliers.
3.Remove Free Wheel Hub Body.
(a) Remove the mounting nuts.
(b) Using a brass bar and hammer, tap the bolt heads and remove the cone washers.
(c) Pull off the free wheel hub body.

Dismantle

1.Remove Control Handle from Free Wheel Hub Cover.
(a) using snap ring pliers, remove the snap ring.
(b) Remove the control handle.
(c) Remove the steel ball and spring from the control handle.
2.Remove Inner Hub and Free Wheel Hub Ring from Free Wheel Hub Body.
(a) Using a screwdriver, remove the snap ring.
(b) Remove the inner hub and free wheel hub ring.

3.Remove Free Wheel Hub Ring from Inner Hub.
(a) Using snap ring pliers, remove the snap ring.
(b) Remove the free wheel hub ring and spacer.

Inspection

1.Inspect Cover, Handle and Seal. Temporarily install the handle in the cover and check that the handle moves smoothly and freely.

2.Inspect Body and Clutch. Check that the clutch moves smoothly in the body.

3.Measure Oil Clearance Between Inner Hub and Free Wheel Hub Ring.

Oil clearance (A-B): 0.3 mm (0.012 in)

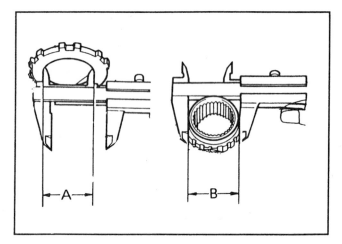

Assembly

1.Apply MP Grease to Sliding Surface of Parts.

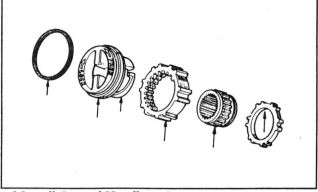

2.Install Control Handle to Cover.
(a) Install the seal, spring and steel ball to the handle.
(b) Insert the handle in the cover and install the snap ring with snap ring pliers.

3.Install Tension Spring in Clutch. Install the tension spring in the clutch with the spring end aligned with the initial groove.

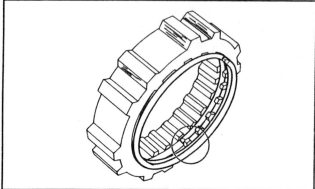

4.Install Follower Pawl to Clutch.
(a) Place the follower pawl on the tension spring with one of the large tabs against the bent spring end.
(b) Place the top ring of the spring on the small tabs.

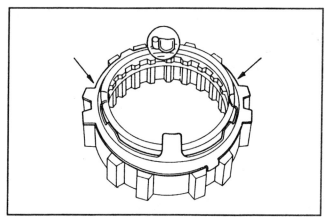

5.Install Clutch and Spring into Cover.
(a) Place the spring between the cover and clutch with the large spring end toward the cover.
(b) Compress the spring and install the clutch with the pawl tab fit to the handle cam.

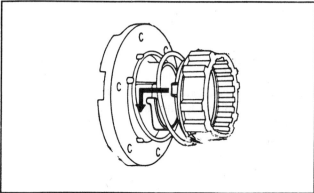

6.Install Spacer and Free Wheel Hub Ring to Inner Hub.
(a) Install the spacer and free wheel hub ring to the inner hub.
(b) Using snap ring pliers, install the snap ring.

7.Install Inner Hub and Free Wheel Hub Ring in Free Wheel Hub Body.

(a) Insert the inner hub and free wheel hub ring in the body.

(b) Using a screwdriver, install the snap ring.

8.Temporarily install Cover to Body and Check Free Wheel Hub.

(a) Set the control handle and clutch to the free position.

(b) Insert the cover in the body and verify that the inner hub turns smoothly.

(c) Remove the cover from the body.

Installation

1.Install Free Wheel Hub Body.

(a) Place the gasket in position on the front axle hub.

(b) Install the free wheel hub body with 6 cone washers and nuts. Tighten the nuts.

Torque: 315 kg-cm (23 ft-lb, 31 N·m)

2.Install Snap Ring.

(a) Install a bolt in the axle shaft and pull it out.

(b) Using snap ring pliers, install the snap ring.

(c) Remove the bolt.

3.Apply MP Grease to Inner Hub Splines.

4.Install Free Wheel Hub Cover with New Gasket.

(a) Set the control handle and clutch to the free position.

(b) Place a new gasket in position on the cover.

(c) Install the cover to the body with the follower pawl tabs aligned with the non-toothed portions of the body.

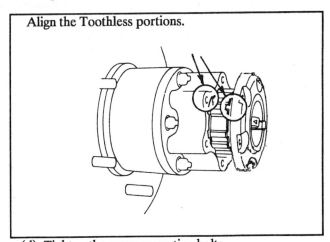

Align the Toothless portions.

(d) Tighten the cover mounting bolts.

Torque: 100 kg-cm (7 ft-lb, 10 N·m)

FRONT AXLE HUB

Components

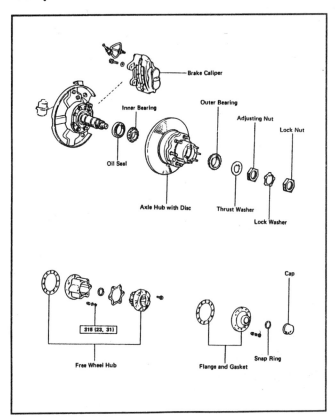

Dismantle

1.Remove Disc Brake Cylinder. Disconnect the brake tube and remove the brake calliper.

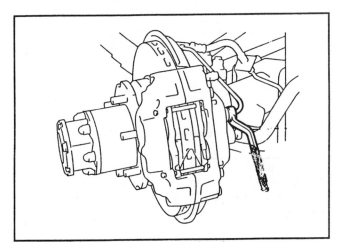

2.Remove Flange or Free Wheel Hub.

* For the free wheel hub.

(a) Remove the cap from the flange.

(b) Using snap ring pliers, remove the snap ring.

(c) Remove the mounting nuts.

(d) Using a brass bar and hammer, tap the bolt heads and remove the cone washers.

(e) Install and tighten the 2 bolts, and remove the flange.

3.Remove Axle Hub with Disc.

(a) Using a screwdriver, release the lock washer.

(b) Using special tool, remove the lock nut.

(c) Remove the lock washer and adjusting nut.

(d) Remove the axle hub with the disc.

4.Remove Inner Bearing and Oil Seal.

(a) Using special tool, remove the oil seal.

(b) Remove the inner bearing from the hub.

Inspection and Repair

1.Inspect Bearing. Clean the bearings and outer races and inspect them for wear or damage.

2.Replace Bearing Outer Race.

(a) Using a brass bar and hammer, drive out the bearing outer race.

(b) Using special tool, carefully drive in the new bearing outer race.

Assembly

1.Pack Bearings with MP Grease.

(a) Place MP grease in the palm of your hand.

(b) Pack grease into the bearing, continuing until the grease oozes out from the other side.

(c) Do the same around the bearing circumference.

2.Coat Inside of Hub and Cap with MP grease.

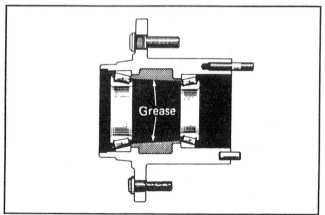

3.Install Inner Bearing and Oil Seal. Place inner bearing into the hub. Using special tool, drive the oil seal into the hub. Coat the oil seal with MP grease.

4.Install Axle Hub on Spindle.

(a) Place the axle hub on the spindle.

(b) Install the outer bearing and thrust washer.

5.Adjust Preload.

(a) Using special tool, torque the bearing adjusting nut.

Torque: 600 kg-cm (43 ft-lb, 59 N·m)

(b) Turn the hub right and left 2 or 3 times.

(c) Using special tool, retighten the bearing adjusting nut.

Torque: 600 kg-cm (43 ft-lb, 59 N·m)

(d) Loosen the nut until it can be turn by hand.

(e) Using a spring tension gauge, measure the frictional force of the oil seal at the hub bolt.

(f) Retighten the adjusting nut.

Torque: 40 - 70 kg-cm (35 - 60 in-lb, 4.0 - 6.8 N·m)

(g) Using a spring tension gauge, measure the preload.

Preload (starting):

Frictional force plus

0.4 - 3.3 kg (0.9 - 7.3 lb, 4 - 32 N)

6.Install Lock Washer and Lock Nut.

(a) Install the lock washer and lock nut.

(b) Using special tool, torque the lock nut.

Torque: 800 kg-cm (58 ft-lb, 78 N·m)

(c) Check that the bearing has no play.

(d) Using a spring tension gauge, check the preload.

Preload (starting):

Frictional force plus

0.4 - 3.3 kg (0.9 - 7.3 lb, 4 - 32 N)

If not within specification, adjust with the adjusting nut.

(e) Secure the lock nut by bending one of the lock washer teeth inward and another lock washer tooth outward.

7.Install Flange or free Wheel Hub.

* In the case of the free wheel hub as described under ASSEMBLY in FREE WHEEL HUB Section.

(a) Place the gasket in position on the axle hub.

(b) Install the flange to the axle hub.

(c) Install 6 cone washers and nuts. Torque the nuts.

Torque: 315 kg-cm (23 ft-lb, 31 N·m)

(d) Install a bolt in the axle shaft and pull it out.

(e) Using snap ring pliers, install the snap ring.

(f) Remove the bolt.

(g) Install the cap to the flange.

8.Install Brake Calliper.

(a) Install the brake calliper to the steering knuckle. Torque the mounting bolts.

Torque: 900 kg-cm (65 ft-lb, 88 N·m)

(b) Using special tool, connect the brake tube.

Torque: 155 kg-cm (11 ft-lb, 15 N·m)

9. Bleed Brake Line.

STEERING KNUCKLE & AXLE SHAFT

Components

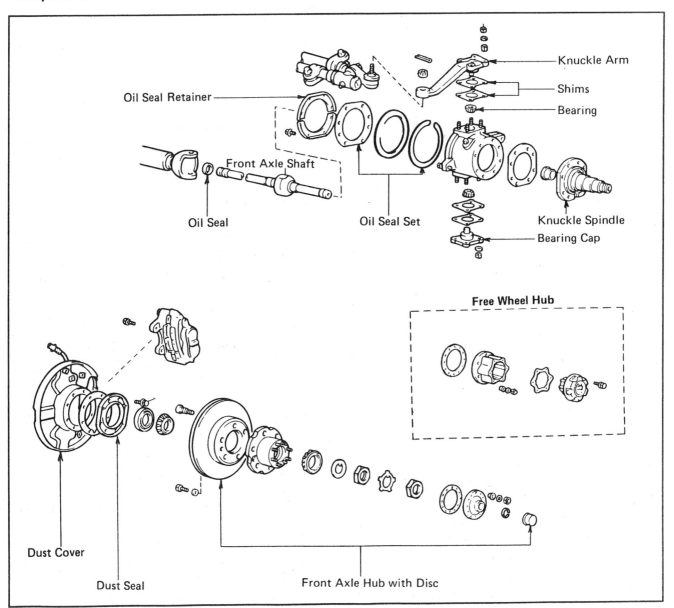

Knuckle Arm

Shims

Bearing

Oil Seal Retainer

Front Axle Shaft

Oil Seal

Oil Seal Set

Knuckle Spindle

Bearing Cap

Free Wheel Hub

Dust Cover

Dust Seal

Front Axle Hub with Disc

Dismantle

1. Remove Front Axle Hub as previously described.
2. Remove Knuckle Spindle Mounting Bolts.
3. Remove Dust Seal and Dust Cover.
4. Drum Brakes. Do not disconnect brake hose. Turn the steering wheel fully to one side, remove the backing

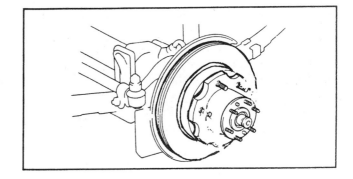

plate assembly out of the way and tie it with wire or light rope.

5.Remove Knuckle Spindle. Using a brass bar, tap the knuckle spindle from the steering knuckle.

6.Remove Axle Shaft. Position one flat part of the outer shaft upward and pull out the axle shaft.

7.Disconnect Tie Rod from Knuckle Arm. Using special tool, disconnect the tie rod from the knuckle arm.

8.Remove Oil Seal Set and Retainer.

9.Remove Knuckle Arm and Bearing Cap.

(a) Remove the knuckle arm and bearing cap mounting nuts.

(b) Using a brass bar, tap the slits of the cone washers and remove them from the knuckle arm.

(c) Using special tool, push out the knuckle arm and shims from the steering knuckle.

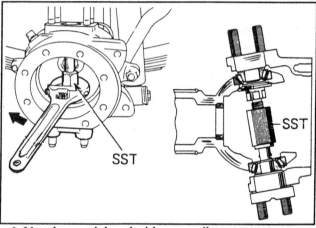

* Use the special tool without a collar.

(d) Using special tool, push out the bearing cap and shims from the steering knuckle.

10. Remove Steering Knuckle and Bearing.

* Mark the removed adjusting shims and bearings to help in the assembly.

Inspection & Repair

1.Inspect Knuckle Spindle. Clean the knuckle spindle and inspect the bushing for wear or damage.

2.Replace Bushing.

(a) Using special tool, remove the bushing.

(b) Using special tool, press a new bushing into the spindle.

3.Inspect Bearing. Clean the bearings and outer races and inspect them for wear or damage.

4.If Necessary, Replace Bearing Outer Race.

(a) Using a brass bar, drive out the bearing outer race.

(b) Using special tool, carefully drive in a new bearing outer race.

5.Inspect Birfield Joint Inner Parts.

(a) Hold the inner shaft in a vice.

(b) Place a brass bar against the joint inner race and drive out the outer shaft.

(c) Tilt the inner race and cage and take out the bearing balls one by one.

(d) Fit the two large openings in the cage against the protruding parts of the outer shaft. Pull out the cage and inner race.

(e) Take out the inner race from the cage through the large opening.

(f) Clean and inspect the joint inner parts for wear or damage.

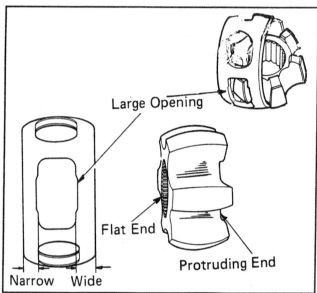

(g) Coat the joint inner parts and inside of the outer shaft with Molybdenum disulphide lithium base grease.

(h) Insert the inner race in the cage through the large opening.

(i) Position the protruding end and the inner race toward the wide side of the cage.

* FJ, BJ, HJ 4..^{s} Series. Make sure you position the protruding end of the race toward the wide side of the cage.

* FJ, BJ HJ, RJ & LJ 6..^{s} & 7..^{s} Series. Ensure to position the protruding end of the race toward the wide chamfering side of cage.

* FJ, BJ, HJ 4..^{s} Series. Make sure you position the cage wide side and race protruding end toward the outside.

* FJ, BJ, HJ, RJ & LJ 6..^{s} & 7..^{s} Series. Ensure to position the cage wide chamfering side end race protruding end toward the outside.

(j) Assemble the cage and inner race to the outer shaft by fitting the 2 large openings in the cage against the protruding parts of the outer shaft.

(k) Make sure to position the wide side of the cage and the inner race protruding end outward.

(l) Fit in the inner race and cage, and install the 6 bearing balls in the outer shaft [see step (c)].

(m) Pack Molybdenum disulphide lithium base grease in the outer shaft.

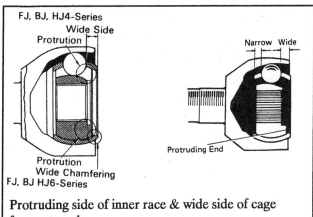

FJ, BJ, HJ4-Series

Protruding side of inner race & wide side of cage face outward.

(n) Install the new snap rings on the inner shaft.

(o) Hold the outer shaft in a vice and, while compressing the snap inner ring, install the inner shaft to the outer shaft.

(p) Verify that the inner shaft cannot be pulled out.

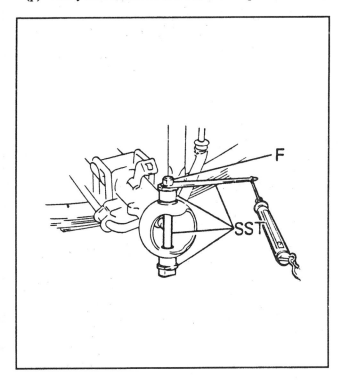

Adjustment of Steering Knuckle Alignment & Bearing Preload

* Whenever the axle housing or the steering knuckle is replaced, the steering knuckle alignment and knuckle bearing preload are to be adjusted.

1. Adjust Bearing Preload.

(a) Using special tool, remove the oil seal.

(b) Coat the knuckle bearings lightly with Molybdenum disulphide lithium base grease.

(c) Mount the special tool on the housing with the bearings.

(d) Add preload to the bearings by tightening nut shown. Using a spring tension gauge, measure the preload.

Preload (starting):

3.0 - 6.0 kg (6.6 - 13.2 lb, 29 - 59 N)

(e) Measure distance A.

(f) Measure distance B. The difference between A and B is the total adjusting shim thickness that is required to maintain the correct bearing preload.

Total shim thickness C: C = A - B

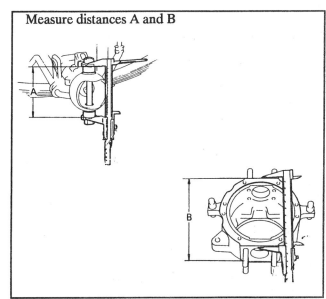

Measure distances A and B

2. Adjust Steering Knuckle Alignment.

(a) Apply a light coat of red lead on the centre part of rod D.

(b) Press adaptors A and B against the housing, press plug C against the rod D and turn lever G so that a line will be described on rod D.

(c) Temporarily install the spindle to the knuckle. Tighten the bolt with 2 washers.

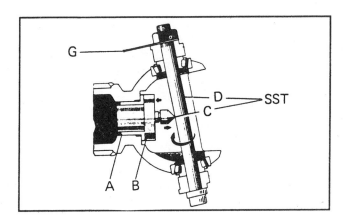

(d) Dismount the special tool from the housing, and mount it on the knuckle.

* Be careful not to erase the line when dismounting and remounting the special tool.

Make sure that rod D is in the same vertical direction that it was when mounted on the housing.

(e) Turn rod D and mark another line on it. Measure distance D between the two lines. The thickness of the steering knuckle lower bearing shim E will be the distance D less 3 mm (0.12 in).

Lower shim thickness E: $E = D - 3$ mm

The thickness of the steering knuckle upper bearing shim F will be the difference between the total adjusting shim thickness C and shim thickness E.

Upper shim thickness F: $F = C - E$

* Compare E and F with the thicknesses of the shims removed when dismantled. If there is considerable difference, remeasure E and F.

(f) Apply Molybdenum disulphide lithium base grease to the front axle shaft bushing.

Assembly

1.Install Oil Seal to Axle Housing. Using special tool, drive the oil seal into the axle housing.

2.Install Oil Seal Set. Install the parts in the following order: 1) felt dust seal, 2) rubber seal, 3) steel ring.

3.Pack Bearings with Molybdenum Disulphide Lithium Base Grease.

(a) Place Molybdenum disulphide lithium base grease in the palm of your hand.

(b) Pack grease into the bearing and continue until the grease oozes out from the other side.

(c) Do the same around the bearing circumference.

4.Install Steering Knuckle and Bearings.

(a) Place the bearings in position on the knuckle and axle housing.

(b) Insert the knuckle on the axle housing.

5.Install Knuckle Arm and Bearing Cap.

(a) Using special tool, support the upper bearing inner race.

* Use special tool with a collar.

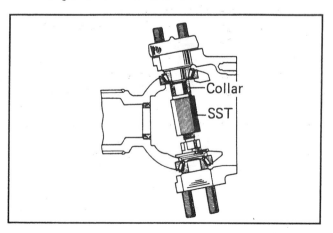

(b) Install the knuckle arm over the shims that were originally used or were selected in the adjustment operations.

(c) Using a hammer, tap the knuckle arm into the bearing inner race.

(d) Using special tool, support the lower bearing inner race.

* Use special tool with a collar.

(e) Install the bearing cap over the shims that were originally used or were selected as described in adjustment operations.

(f) Using a hammer, tap the bearing cap into the bearing inner race.

(g) Remove special tool from the knuckle.

(h) Install the cone washers to the third arm and torque the nuts.

Torque: 975 kg-cm (71 ft-lb, 96 N·m)

(i) Install the cone washers to the knuckle arm and torque the nuts.

Torque: 975 kg-cm (71 ft-lb, 96 N·m)

6.Measure Bearing Preload. Using a spring tension gauge, measure the preload.

Preload (starting):
3.0 - 6.0 kg (6.6 - 13.2 lb, 29 - 59 N)

7.Connect Tie Rod to Knuckle Arm. Torque the castle nut and secure it with a new cotter pin.

Torque: 925 kg-cm (67 ft-lb, 91 N·m)

8.Install Oil Seal Set to Knuckle.

9.Install Axle Shaft. Position one flat part of the outer shaft upward, and install the shaft.

10.Pack Molybdenum Disulphide Lithium Base Grease into the knuckle to about 3/4 of the knuckle.

11.Install Knuckle Spindle, Dust Cover with New Gaskets and Dust Seal.

(a) Place a new gasket in position on the knuckle and install the spindle.

(b) Place the gasket, dust cover and dust seal on the spindle.

(c) Torque the spindle mounting bolts.

Torque: 475 kg-cm (34 ft-lb, 47 N·m)

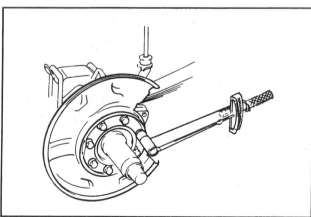

12.Install Axle Hub as previously described.

FRONT DIFFERENTIAL

Components

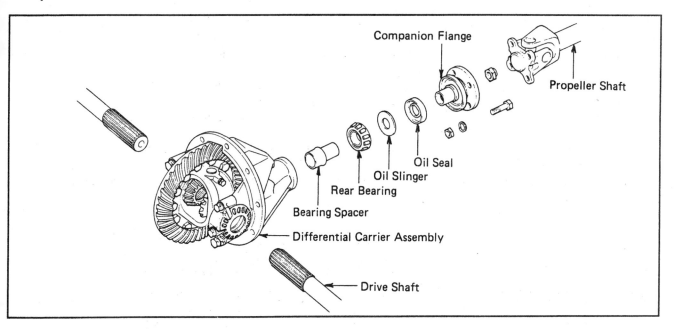

On-Vehicle Replacement of Oil Seal

1. Disconnect Propeller Shaft from Differential.
(a) Place alignment marks on the flanges.
(b) Remove the 4 bolts and nuts.
2.Remove Companion Flange.
3.Remove Oil Seal and Oil Slinger.
(a) Remove the oil seal from the housing.
(b) Remove the oil slinger.
4.Remove Rear Bearing and Bearing Spacer.
5.Install New Bearing Spacer and Front Bearing.
6.Install Oil Slinger and New Oil Seal.
(a) Install the oil slinger facing as shown.
(b) Drive in a new oil seal as shown.
Oil seal drive in depth: 1.0 mm (0.039 in)
(c) Apply MP grease to the oil seal lip.
7.Install Companion Flange.
8.Stake Drive Pinion Nut.
9.Connect Propeller Shaft Flange to Companion Flange.
(a) Align the marks on the flanges and connect the flanges with 4 bolts and nuts.
(b) Torque the 4 bolts and nuts.
Torque: 750 kg-cm (54 ft-lb, 74 N·m)
10.Check Differential Oil Level. Fill with hypoid gear oil if necessary.
Hypoid gear oil: API GL-5
Above - 18°C (0°F) SAE 90
Below - 18°C (0°F) SAE 80W or 80W-90

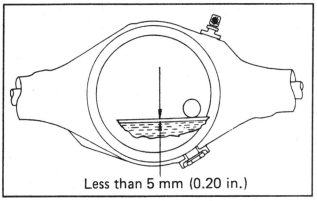

Less than 5 mm (0.20 in.)

Removal

1.Draw Out Fluid with Container.
2.Remove Front Axle Shafts as previously described.
3.Disconnect Propeller Shaft.
4.Remove Front Brake Tube.
(a) Remove the 3 clamp bolts and nut.
(b) Disconnect the brake hose at the frame side and remove the clip.
(c) Remove the three-way with the brake hose and tubes.
5.Remove Differential Carrier Assembly.

Dismantle of Differential

See REAR AXLE Section.

Installation

Reverse Removal Procedures:
* Fit a new gasket.
* Fill differential with oil - API GL-5 HYPOID Gear Oil
SAE 90 above - 18°C (0°F)
SAE 80W or 80W-90 below - 18°C (0°F)
* Bleed brake line.

FRONT SUSPENSION

Components

Shock Absorber and Leaf Spring

Removal

1. Jack Up and Support body.
(a) Jack up and support the body on stands.
(b) Lower the axle housing until the leaf spring tension is free, and keep it at this position.
2. Remove Shock Absorber.
3. Remove U-Bolts.
(a) Remove the U-bolt mounting nuts.
(b) Remove the spring lower seat.
(c) Remove the U-bolts.
4. Remove Leaf Spring.
(a) Remove the hanger pin mounting nut.
(b) Remove the shackle pin mounting nuts.
(c) Remove the hanger pin.
(d) Remove the shackle pin.
(e) Remove the leaf spring.

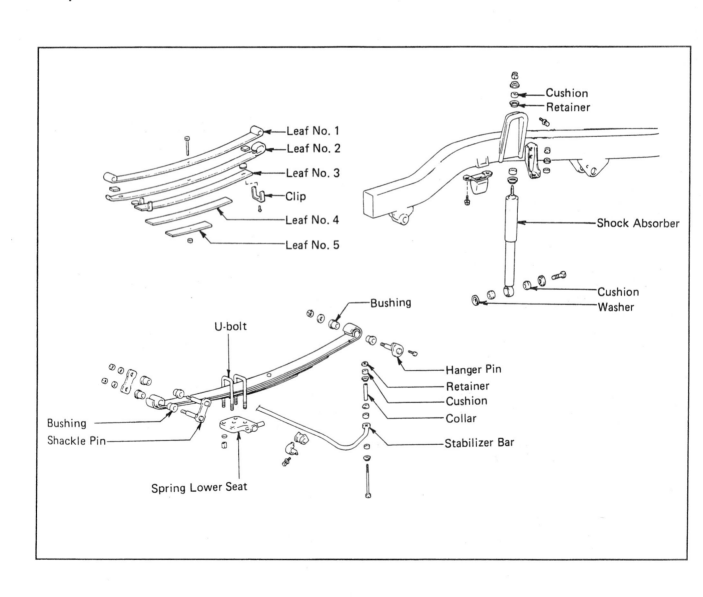

Replacement

1.Bend Open Spring Clip. Using a chisel, pry up the spring clip.

2.Remove Centre Bolt. Hold the spring near the centre bolt in a vice and remove the centre bolt.

3.If Necessary, Replace Spring Clip.

(a) Drill off the head of the rivet, and drive it out.

(b) Install a new rivet into the holes of the leaf spring and clip. Then rivet with a press.

4.Install Spring Centre Bolt.

(a) Attach the spring silencer.

(b) Align the leaf holes and secure the leaves with a vice.

(c) Install and tighten the spring centre bolt.

Torque: 350 - 550 kg-cm (26 - 39 ft-lb, 35 - 53 N·m)

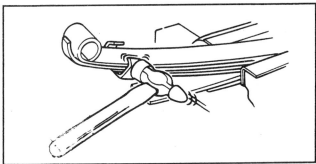

5.Bend Spring Clip. Using a hammer, bend the spring clip into position.

Installation of Spring

1.Install Leaf Spring.

(a) Insert the bushings into the frame and into both ends of the leaf spring.

(b) Place the leaf spring in position.

(c) Install the hanger pin and tighten the nut.

Torque: 130 kg-cm (9 ft-lb, 13 N·m)

(d) Install the shackle pin.

(e) Install the plate an provisionally install the nuts.

2.Install U-bolts.

(a) Insert the head of the leaf spring centre bolt into the hole in the axle housing bracket and install.

(b) Install the spring seat and nuts.

(c) Tighten the U-bolt mounting nuts.

Torque: 1,250 kg-cm (90 ft-lb, 123 N·m)

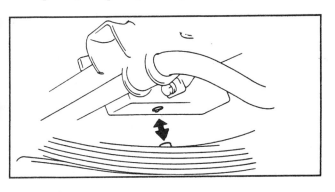

* Tighten the U-bolts so that the length of all the U-bolts under the spring seat are the same.

3.Install Shock Absorber.

(a) Position the shock absorber and install the bushing retainers and nut.

Torque: 260 kg-cm (19 ft-lb, 25 N·m)

(b) Install the lower mounting bolt.

Torque: 970 kg-cm (70 ft-lb, 95 N·m)

4.Stabilise Suspension. Remove the stands and bounce the car to stabilise the suspension.

5.Tighten Hanger Pin and Shackle Pin. Tighten the hanger pin nut.

Torque: 930 kg-cm (67 ft-lb, 91 N·m)

Tighten the shackle pin nut.

Torque: 930 kg-cm (67 ft-lb, 91 N·m)

STABILIZER BAR [IF FITTED]

Removal

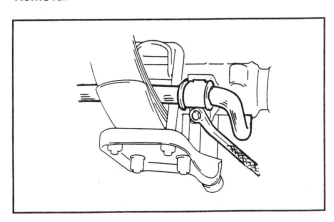

1.Disconnect Stabilizer Bar from Front Axle Housing. Remove both stabilizer bar brackets from the axle housing.

2.Disconnect Stabilizer Bar from Frame. Remove the nuts, cushions and bolts holding both sides of the stabilizer bar to the frame and remove the stabilizer bar.

Installation

　1.Connect Stabilizer Bar to Frame. Connect the stabilizer bar on both sides to the frame with bolts. Use new rubber bushes.
　Torque: 130 kg-cm (9 ft-lb, 13 N·m)
　2.Connect Stabilizer Bar to Axle Housing. Connect the stabilizer bar with the bracket and cushion.
　Torque: 130 kg-cm (9 ft-lb, 13 N·m)

RJ & LJ FRONT SUSPENSION

COMPONENTS

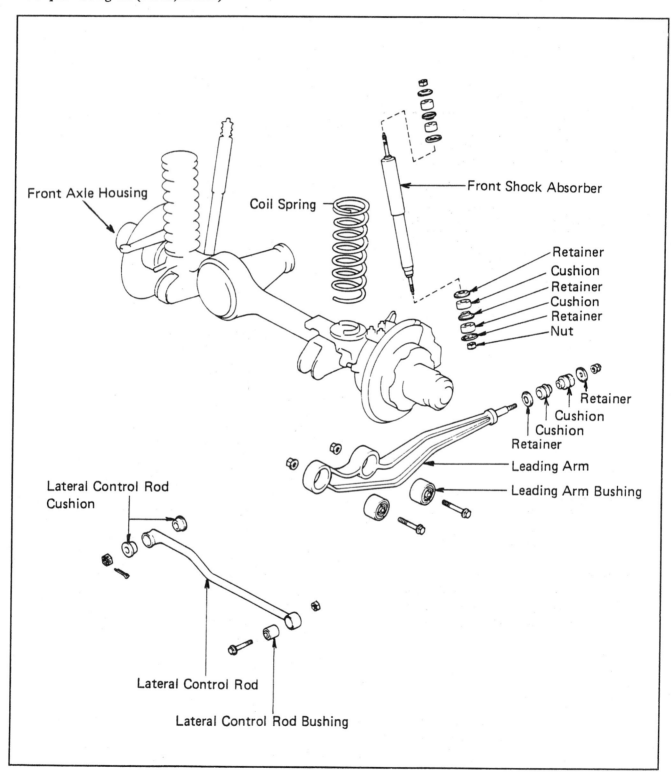

COIL SPRING AND SHOCK ABSORBER

Removal

1. Jack Up and support body.
2. Remove Front Shock Absorber.
(a) Jack up and support the axle housing.
(b) Remove the shock absorber.
3. Lower the jack until the coil spring is free and remove it.
4. Inspect Operation of Front Shock Absorber.

Installation

1. Assemble the spring so its end catches in the hole of the lower seat when installing spring.
2. Raise the jack and install the shock absorber (taking note of the assembly sequence of the retainers and cushions).

LATERAL CONTROL ROD

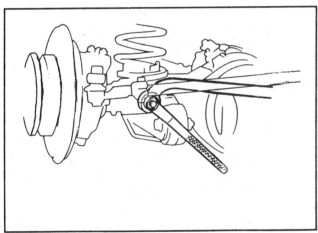

Removal

1. Jack Up and Support Body.
2. Remove the cotter pin and castle nut. Then disconnect the lateral control rod from the front axle housing.
3. Remove the bolt, nut and the lateral control rod.

Replacement of Bushing

1. Press out the bushing from the lateral control rod.
2. Press a new bushing into the lateral control rod.
* Do not use a lubricant when pressing in the bushing.

Installation

1. Install the lateral control rod to the frame with the bolt and nut.
2. Installation to Front Axle Housing.
(a) Install in the following order: 1) washer, 2) cushion, 3) lateral contol rod, 4) cushion, 5)washer, 6) castle nut.

(b) Remove the stands and rock the body up and down to stabilize the suspension.
(c) Jack up the axle housing and torque the nuts.
Torque:
Body side　　　　　1,460 kg-cm (106 ft-lb, 143 N.m)
Axle housing side　1,000 kg-cm (72 ft-lb, 98 N.m)
* When tightening the lateral control rod set nut and bolt, lower the vehicle load until the lateral control rod is horizontal.
(d) Install a new cotter pin into the front axle housing.

LEADING ARM

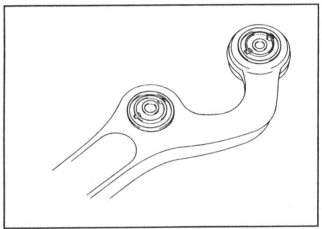

Removal

1. Jack Up Vehicle and Remove Leading Arm.
(a) Remove the nut, retainer and cushion from the leading arm frame side.
(b) Remove the 2 bolts and nuts from the leading arm axle housing side and then the leading arm from body.

Replacement of Leading Arm Bushing

1. Press out the bushings from the leading arm.
2. Press new bushings into the leading arm.
* When assembling the bushing, do so with the holes aligning horizontally.

Installation

1. Install leading arm to frame after installling the cushion, retainer and nut.
2. Install the leading arm to the front axle with the 2 bolts and nuts.
3. Remove the stands and rock the body up and down to stabilize the suspension.
4. Tighten the Nuts.
(a) Jack up the axle housing.
* For safety, place stands under either side of the vheicle's frame. The stands should come up to but not contact the frame.
(b) Torque the nuts.
Torque:
Body side　　　　　1,000 kg-cm (72 ft-lb, 98 N.m)

Axle housing side 2,500 kg-cm (181 ft-lb, 245 N.m)
  * When tightening the nuts, tighten with the vehicle's full weight applied to the axle housing.

PROBLEM DIAGNOSIS

Problem: Oil leak at front axle!
Possible Causes and Remedies:
  * Oil seals damaged or worn. Remedy - replace oil seal.
  * Front axle housing cracked. Remedy - repair as necessary.

Problem: Oil leak at pinion shaft!
Possible Causes and Remedies:
  * Oil level too high or wrong grade. Remedy - drain and replace oil.
  * Oil seal worn or damaged. Remedy - replace oil seal.
  * Companion flange loose or damaged. Remedy - tighten or replace flange.

Problem: Noises in front axle!
Possible Causes and Remedies:
  * Oil level low or wrong grade. Remedy - drain and replace oil.
  * Excessive backlash between pinion and ring or side gear. Remedy - check backlash.
  * Ring, pinion or side gears worn or chipped. Remedy - inspect gears.
  * Pinion shaft bearing worn. Remedy - replace bearing.
  * Wheel bearing worn. Remedy - replace bearing.
  * Differential bearing loose or worn. Remedy - tighten or replace bearings.

Problem: Wanders or pulls!
Possible Causes and Remedies:
  * Tyres worn or improperly inflated. Remedy - replace tyre or inflate tyres to proper pressure.
  * Alignment incorrect. Remedy - check front end alignment.
  * Wheel bearing adjusted too tightly. Remedy - adjust wheel bearing.
  * Front or rear suspension parts loose or broken. Remedy - tighten or replace suspension part.
  * Steering linkage loose or worn. Remedy - tighten or replace steering linkage.
  * Steering gear out of adjustment or broken. Remedy - adjust or repair steering gear.

Problem: Bottoming!
Possible Causes and Remedies:
  * Vehicle overloaded. Remedy - check loading.
  * Shock absorber worn out. Remedy - replace shock absorber.

  * Springs weak. Remedy - replace spring.

Problem: Sways or pitches!
Possible Causes and Remedies:
  * Tyres improperly inflated. Remedy - inflate tyres to proper pressure.
  * Stabilizer bar bent or broken. Remedy - inspect stabilizer bar.
  * Shock absorber worn out. Remedy - replace shock absorber.

Problem: Front wheel shimmy!
Possible Causes and Remedies:
  * Tyres worn or improperly inflated. Remedy - replace tyre or inflate tyres to proper pressure.
  * Wheels out of balance. Remedy - balance wheels.
  * Steering damper worn out. Remedy - replace steering damper.
  * Shock absorber worn out. Remedy - replace shock absorber.
  * Alignment incorrect. Remedy - check front end alignment.
  * Wheel bearings worn or improperly adjusted. Remedy - replace or adjust wheel bearings.
  * Steering knuckle bearing worn. Remedy - replace bearing.
  * Steering linkage loose or worn. Remedy - tighten or replace steering linkage.
  * Steering gear out of adjustment or broken. Remedy - adjust or repair steering gear.

Problem: Tyres improperly inflated!
Possible Causes and Remedies:
  * Tyres improperly inflated. Remedy - inflate tyre to proper pressure.
  * Shock absorbers worn out. Remedy - replace shock absorber.
  * Alignment incorrect. Remedy - check toe-in.

REAR AXLE AND SUSPENSION

REAR AXLE AND SUSPENSION

REAR AXLE
[SEMI-FLOATING TYPE]

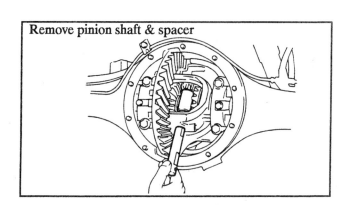
Remove pinion shaft & spacer

Components

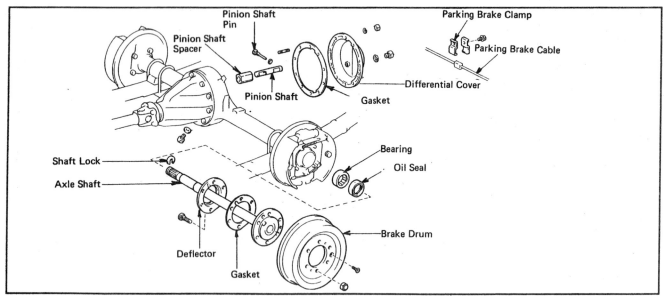

Removal

1. Remove Wheel and Brake Drum.
2. Drain Differential Oil.
3. Remove Parking Brake Cable Clamp.
4. Remove Differential Cover.
5. Remove Pinion Shaft and Pinion Spacer.
(a) Remove the pinion shaft pin from the differential.
(b) Remove the pinion shaft and spacer.
* When the pinion shaft is removed, the pinion gear and thrust washer will come off also.
6. Remove Axle Shaft Lock. Push the axle shaft to the differential side and remove the axle shaft lock.
7. Remove Axle Shaft.

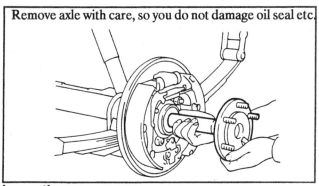
Remove axle with care, so you do not damage oil seal etc.

Inspection

1. Inspect Rear Axle Shaft. Check for wear or damage.
2. Inspect Oil Seal and Bearing for Wear or Damage. If the oil seal and bearing is damaged or worn, replace it.

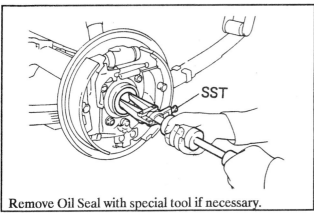

Remove Oil Seal with special tool if necessary.

Installation

1. Install Rear Axle Shaft in Axle Housing. Insert the axle shaft into the housing.

* When inserting the axle shaft, be careful not to damage the oil seal.

2. Install Axle Shaft Lock.

(a) Install the axle shaft lock to the axle shaft.

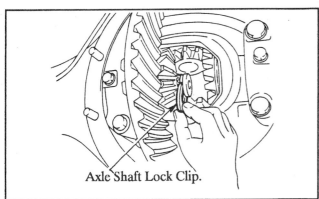

Axle Shaft Lock Clip.

(b) Pull the axle shaft fully toward the outer side of vehicle.

3. Install Pinion Shaft and Pinion Spacer.

(a) Install the spacer and pinion shaft to the differential.

(b) Measure the thrust clearance between the axle shaft and spacer.

Maximum clearance: 0.5 mm (0.020 in)

If necessary, select the spacer.

(c) Install the pinion shaft.

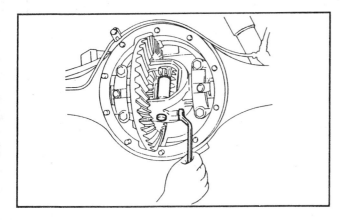

Torque: 275 kg-cm (20 ft-lb, 27 'm)

4. Install Differential Cover.

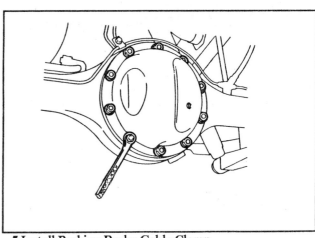

5. Install Parking Brake Cable Clamp.

6. Install Brake Drum and Wheel.

7. Fill Differential With Gear Oil.

Hypoid gear oil: API GL-5

Above - 18°C (0°F) SAE90

Below - 18°C (0°F) SAE 80W or 80W-90

* With LSD fill in hypoid gear oil LSD, SAE 90 API GL-5.

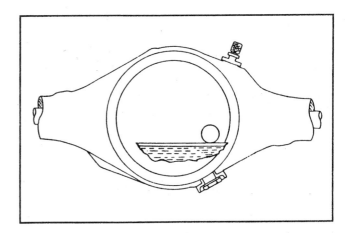

REAR AXLE SHAFT [FULL FLOATING TYPE]

Components

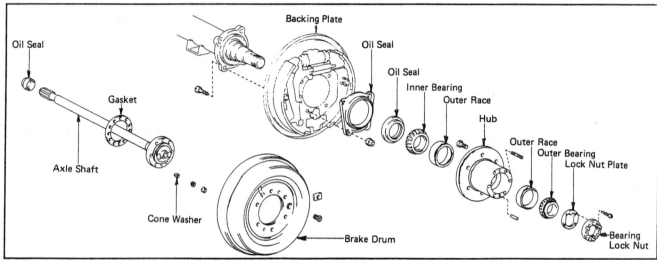

Removal

1.Remove Axle Shaft Set Nut. Remove the 6 set nuts and washers.

2.Remove Cone Washer. Using a hammer and brass-bar, tap on the bolt and remove the 6 cone washers.

3.Remove Rear Axle Shaft.

(a) Install and tighten the 2 service bolts to the service hole.

(b) If the axle shaft separates, remove the 2 service bolts.

(c) Remove the axle shaft with the gasket.

* When pulling out the axle shaft, be careful not to damage the oil seal.

Inspection

1.Inspect Rear Axle Shaft. Check for wear or damage.

2.Inspect Oil Seal for Wear or Damage. If the oil seal is damaged or worn, replace it.

3.If Necessary, Replace Oil Seal.

Installation

1.Apply MP Grease to Oil Seal Lip.

2.Install New Gasket and Insert Axle Shaft.

* When inserting the axle shaft, be careful not to damage the oil seal.

3.Install Cone Washer and Set Nut. Install the cone washers and spring washers with 6 nuts.

Torque: 340 kg-cm (25 ft-lb, 33 N·m)

REAR AXLE SHAFT [LJ AND RJ SERIES]

Components

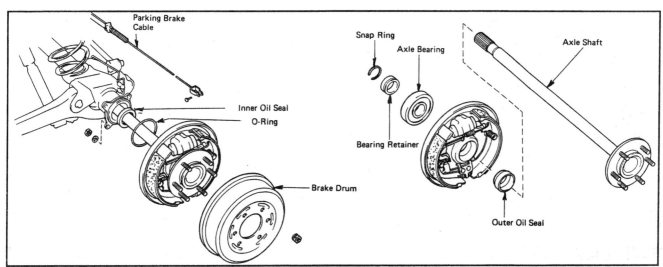

Removal

1. Remove Wheel and Brake Drum.
2. Disconnect Brake Tube and Parking Brake Cable.
3. Remove Rear Axle Shaft Assembly.
(a) Remove the 4 backing plate mounting nuts.
(b) Pull out the rear axle shaft assembly from the rear axle housing.
* When pulling out the rear axle shaft, be careful not to damage the oil seal.
4. Remove O-Ring from Rear Axle Housing.

Dismantle

1. Remove Snap Ring From Rear Axle Shaft.

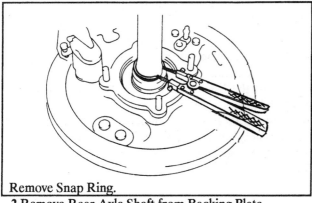

Remove Snap Ring.

2. Remove Rear Axle Shaft from Backing Plate.

(a) Press out the rear axle shaft from the backing plate.
(b) Remove the bearing retainer from the axle shaft.
3. Remove Outer Oil Seal with a Screwdriver.
4. Press Out Rear Axle Bearing.
5. Inspect Rear Axle Shaft and Flange for Wear, Damage or Runout.
Maximum shaft runout: 2.0 mm (0.079 in)
Maximum flange runout: 0.2 mm (0.008 in)
If the rear axle shaft or flange are damaged or worn, or if runout is greater than maximum, replace the rear axle shaft.

Assembly

Reverse DISMANTLING Procedure.

Installation

1. Replace Inner Oil Seal in the Axle Housing. Apply MP grease to seal.
2. Install O-Ring to Rear Axle Housing.
3. Install Rear Axle Shaft Assembly in Axle Housing.
(a) Insert the axle shaft to the housing.
* Be careful not to damage the oil seal.
(b) Torque the 4 backing plate mounting nuts.
Torque: 700 kg-cm (51 ft-lb, 69 N·m)
4. Connect Brake Tube and Parking Brake Cable.
5. Install Brake Drum and Wheel.
6. Bleed Brake System.

REAR AXLE HUB

Removal

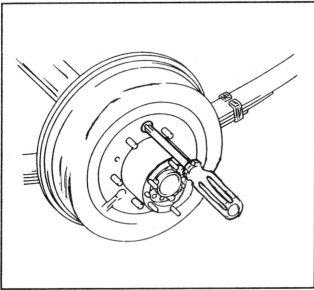

1.Jack Up Vehicle and Remove Wheel.

2.Remove Rear Axle Shaft as previously described under REAR AXLE [FULL FLOATING TYPE] Section.

3.Remove Brake Drum.

(a) Remove the 2 bolts from the brake drum.

(b) Remove the brake drum from the axle hub.

4.Remove Bearing Lock Nut.

(a) Remove the 2 lock nut bolts.

(b) Remove the lock nut.

5.Remove Rear Axle Hub. Remove the axle hub with the lock nut plate and outer bearing.

Inspection

1.Inspect Axle Housing. Using a magnetic flaw detector or flaw detecting penetrant, check for damage or cracks.

2.Remove Oil Seal and Inner Bearing.

(a) Remove the oil seal.

(b) Remove the inner bearing from the axle hub.

3.Remove Bearing Outer Race. Using a hammer and brass bar, drive out the bearing outer race from the axle hub.

4.Install Bearing Outer Race.

5.Pack Bearing with MP Grease.

(a) Place MP grease in the palm of your hand.

(b) Pack grease into the bearing, continuing until the grease oozes out from the other side.

(c) Do the same around the bearing circumference.

(d) Coat inside of hub with grease.

6.Install Inner Bearing and Oil Seal.

(a) Install the inner bearing to the axle hub.

(b) Drive in the oil seal to the axle hub.

(c) Apply MP grease to the oil seal lip.

Installation

1.Install Axle Hub.

(a) Install the axle hub to the axle housing.

* Be careful not to damage the oil seal.

(b) Install the outer bearing.

2.Install Lock Plate and Bearing Lock Nut.

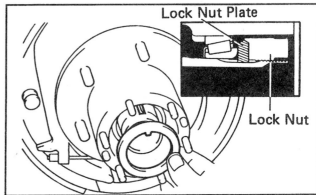

(a) After fully pushing in the outer bearing, position the protrusion of the lock nut plate into the axle housing groove.

(b) Temporarily install the bearing lock nut.

3.Install Brake Drum.

4.Adjust Preload.

(a) Torque the bearing lock nut.

Torque: 600 kg-cm (43 ft-lb, 59 N·m)

(b) Snug down the bearing by turning the hub several times.

(c) Retighten the bearing lock nut to above torque.

(d) Loosen the bearing lock nut until you can rotate it by hand.

(e) Using a spring tension gauge, measure the frictional force of the oil seal.

(f) Retighten the bearing lock nut to above torque.

(g) Using a spring tension gauge, measure the preload at the hub bolt.

Rear wheel bearing preload (at starting):

Frictional force plus 0.4-3.3 kg (0.9-7.3 lb, 4-32 N)

If preload is not within specification, the procedure above must be repeated.

(h) Align the lock nut mark with one of the marks on the axle housing, and place lock bolts in the holes at right angles to the lock nut.

(i) Measure the distance between the top surface of axle housing and the lock nut.

Standard distance: -0.2 - 0.9 mm (-0.008 - 0.035 in)

If not within specification, reinstall the axle hub.

(j) Check the movement of the drum.

5.Install Rear Axle Shaft.

REAR DIFFERENTIAL

6.Install Oil Seal and Oil Slinger.

(a) Install the oil slinger.

(b) Install a new oil seal.

Oil seal drive in depth: 1.00 mm (0.0394 in)

(c) Apply MP grease to the oil seal lip.

7.Install Companion Flange.

Components

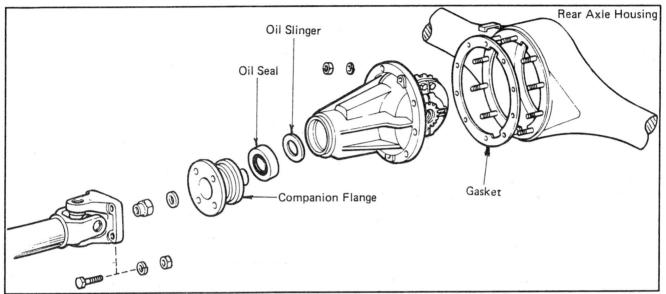

Oil Slinger

Oil Seal

Companion Flange

Gasket

Rear Axle Housing

(a) INstall the companion flange.

(b) Coat the threads of a new nut with gear oil.

(c) Hold the flange and tighten the nut.

Torque:

2,500 - 4,500 kg-cm (181 - 325 ft-lb, 245 - 441 N·m)

* Torque the nut to the values above and the preload indicated below.

Preload (at starting):

9 - 13 kg-cm (7.8 - 11.3 in-lb, 0.9 - 1.3 N·m)

8.Stake Drive Pinion Nut.

9.Connect Propeller Shaft to Companion Flange.

(a) Align the matchmarks on the flanges and connect the flange with 4 bolts and nuts.

(b) Torque the 4 bolts and nuts.

Torque: 900 kg-cm (65 ft-lb, 88 N·m).

10. Check Differential Oil Level. Fill with hypoid gear oil if necessary.

Hypoid gear oil: API GL-5

Above - 18°C (0°F) SAE 90

Below - 18°C (0°F) SAE 80W or 80W-90

Capacity:

BJ, FJ, HJ 2.5 lts (2.6 US qts, 2.2 Imp.qts)

LJ & RJ   2.2 lts (2.3 US qts, 1.9 Imp.qts)

* With LSD fill in hypoid gear oil

LSD, SAE 90 API GL-5

Oil Seal Replacement on The Vehicle

1.Disconnect Propeller Shaft from Differential.

2.Remove Companion Flange.

(a) Using a hammer and chisel, loosen the staked part of the nut.

(b) Remove the nut.

(c) Remove the companion flange.

3.Remove Oil Seal and Oil Slinger.

(a) Remove the oil seal.

(b) Remove the oil slinger.

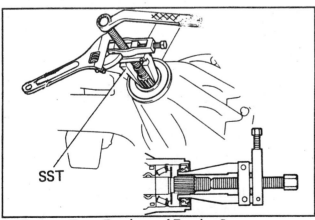

SST

4.Remove Front Bearing and Bearing Spacer.

(a) Remove the front bearing from the drive pinion.

(b) Remove the bearing spacer.

5.Install New Bearing Spacer and Front Bearing.

Removal

1.Drain Differential Oil.

2.Remove Rear Axle Shaft Assembly.

[Semi-floating type: See previous instructions.
* To prevent the pinion and washer from falling, after extracting the axle shaft, install the pinion shaft and shaft pin.]

[Full-floating type: see previous instructions.]

[LJ and RJ Series: see previous instructions.]

3.Disconnect Propeller Shaft from Companion Flange.

(a) Place matchmarks on the flanges.

(b) Remove the 4 bolts and nuts.

4.Remove Differential Carrier Assembly.

Inspection

1.Check Ring Gear Runout. Replace if the runout is greater than the maximum allowable.

Maximum runout: 0.10 mm (0.0039 in)

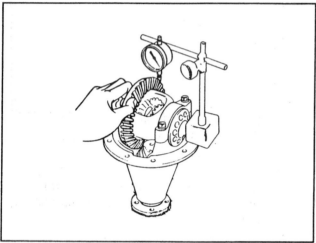

2.Check Ring Gear Backlash. If the backlash is not within specifications, adjust the side bearing preload or repair.

Backlash: 0.15 - 0.20 mm (0.0059 - 0.0079 in)

* Measure the backlash at three or four places and confirm that it is the same value.

3.Adjust Ring Gear Backlash.

(a) Remove the 2 adjusting nut locks.

(b) Loosen the bearing cap bolt until it turns the adjusting nut.

(c) Using special tool, adjust the ring gear backlash until it is within specification.

Backlash: 0.15 - 0.20 mm (0.0059 - 0.0079 in)

* The backlash is adjusted by turning the left and right adjusting nuts equal amounts. For example, loosen the nut on the left side one notch and tighten the nut on the right side one notch.

(d) Torque the bearing cap bolts.

Torque: 800 kg-cm (58 ft-lb, 78 N·m)

(e) Select and install the adjusting nut lock kon the bearing cap.

Torque: 130 kg-cm (9 ft-lb, 13 N·m)

4.Inspect Tooth Contact Between Ring Gear and Drive Pinion.

(a) Coat 3 or 4 teeth at three different positions on the ring gear with red lead.

(b) Hold the companion flange firmly and rotate the ring gear in both directions.

(c) Inspect the tooth pattern.

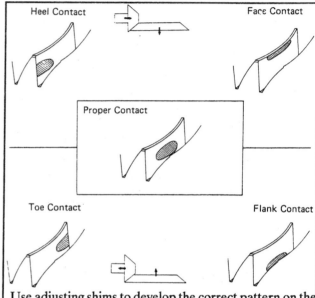

Use adjusting shims to develop the correct pattern on the teeth of the ring gear & pinion.

5.Check Side Gear Backlash (Except Limited Slip Differential). Measure the side gear backlash while holding 1 pinion gear toward the case.

Backlash: 0.02 - 0.24 mm (0.008 - 0.0094 in)

If the backlash is not within specification, install the proper thrust washers.

Installation

1.Install Differential Carrier Assembly with a new gasket, 10 nuts.

Torque: 475 kg-cm (34 ft-lb, 47 N·m)

2. Connect Propeller Shaft to Differential.

3. Install Rear Axle Shaft Assembly.

[Semi-floating type: as previously described.]

[Full-floating type: as previously described.]

[LJ & FJ Series: as previously described.]

4.Fill Differential with Gear Oil.

Hypoid gear oil: API GL-5

Above - 18°C (0°F) SAE 90

Below - 18°C (0°F) SAE 80W or 80W-90

Capacity: 2.5 lts (2.6 US qts, 2.2 Imp.qts)

* With LSD fill in hypoid gear oil

LSD, SAE 90 API GL-5

CONVENTIONAL TYPE DIFFERENTIAL

Components

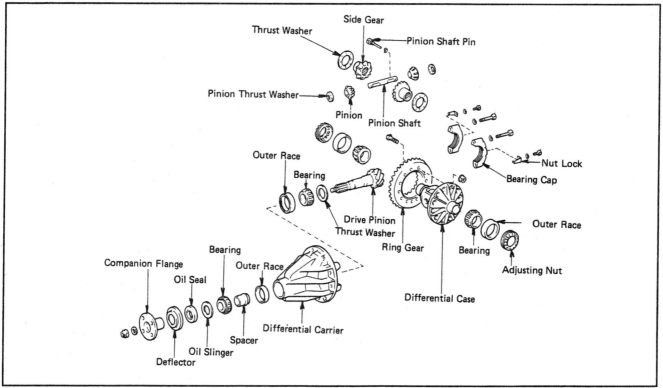

Removal

Dismantle

1.Remove Companion Flange.

(a) Using a hammer and chisel, loosen the staked part of the nut.

(b) Using special tool to hold the flange, remove the nut.

(c) Using special tool, remove the companion flange.

2.Remove Oil Seal and Oil Slinger.

(a) Using special tool, remove the oil seal from the housing.

(b) Remove the oil slinger.

3.Remove Front Bearing and Bearing Spacer.

(a) Using special tool, remove the front bearing from the drive pinion.

(b) Remove the bearing spacer.

* If the front bearing is damaged or worn, replace the bearing.

4.Remove Differential Case and Ring Gear.

(a) Place matchmarks on the bearing cap and differential carrier.

(b) Remove the 2 adjusting nut locks.

(c) Remove the 2 bearing caps and 2 adjusting nuts.

(d) Remove the bearing outer races.

(e) Remove the differential case from the carrier.

* Tag the dismantled parts to show their location for assembly.

5.Remove Drive Pinion From Differential Carrier.

Replace and Inspect Components

1.Replace Drive Pinion Rear Bearing.

(a) Using a press and special tool, pull out the rear bearing from the drive pinion.

(b) Install the washer on the drive pinion with the chamfered end facing the pinion gear.

(c) Using a press and special tool, press the reused washer and new rear bearing on the drive pinion.

2.Replace Drive Pinion Front and Rear Bearing Outer Race.

(a) Using a hammer and brass bar, drive out the outer race.

(b) Using a press and special tool, drive in a new outer race.

3. Remove Side Bearings from Differential Case. Using special tool, pull the side bearing from the differential case.

4. Remove Ring Gear.

(a) Remove the ring gear set bolts and lock plates.

(b) Place matchmarks on the ring gear and differential case.

(c) Using a plastic or copper hammer, tap on the ring gear to separate it from the differential case.

5. Dismantle Differential Case.

(a) Remove the pinion shaft pin.

(b) Remove the following parts: 1) pinion shaft, 2) 2 pinion gears and pinion thrust washers, 3) 2 side gears and side gear thrust washers.

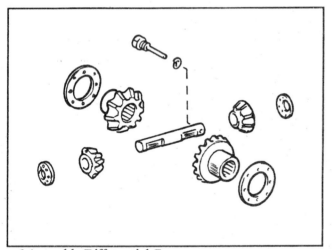

6. Assemble Differential Case.

(a) Install the following parts: 1) 2 side gears with side gear thrust washers, 2) 2 pinion gears with pinion thrust washers, 3) pinion shaft.

(b) Install the pinion shaft pin.

(c) Check the side gear backlash. Measure the side gear backlash while holding 1 pinion gear toward the case.

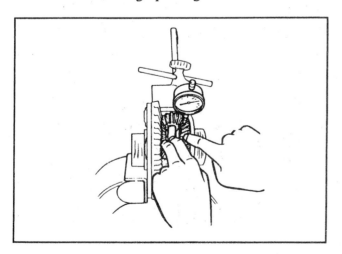

Standard backlash:

0.05 - 0.20 mm (0.0020 - 0.0079 in)

Using the table below, select thrust washers which will ensure that the backlash is within specification. Try to select washers of the same size for both sides.

Thrust washer thickness:

1.55 - 1.65 mm (0.0610 - 0.0650 in)

1.70 - 1.80 mm (0.0669 - 0.0709 in)

1.85 - 1.95 mm (0.0728 - 0.0768 in)

2.00 - 2.10 mm (0.0787 - 0.0827 in)

7. Install Side Bearings. Using a press and special tool, press the side bearings on the differential case.

8. Install Ring Gear on Differential Case.

(a) Clean the contact surface of the differential case.

(b) Heat the ring gear to about 100°C (212°F) in an oil bath.

* Do not heat the ring gear above 110°C (230°F).

(c) Clean the contact surface of the ring gear with cleaning solvent.

(d) Then quickly install the ring gear on the differential case.

(e) Align the marks on the ring gear and differential case.

(f) Coat the ring gear set bolts with gear oil.

(g) Install the new lock plates and set bolts. Tighten the set bolts uniformly and a little at a time. Torque the bolts.

Torque: 1,125 kg-cm (81 ft-lb, 110 N·m)

(h) Using a hammer and drift punch, stake the lock plates.

* Stake one claw flush with the flat surface of the nut. For the claw contacting the protruding portion of the nut, stake only the half on the tightened side.

(i) Check the ring gear runout.

Maximum runout: 0.10 mm (0.0039 in)

Install the differential case onto the carrier and tighten the adjusting nut just to where there is no play in the bearing.

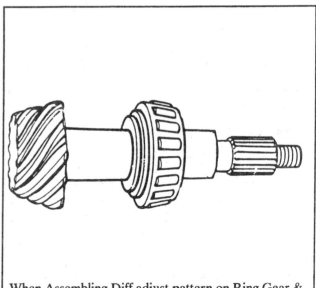

When Assembling Diff adjust pattern on Ring Gear & Pinion as described two pages previously.

LIMITED SLIP DIFFERENTIAL [LSD]

Components

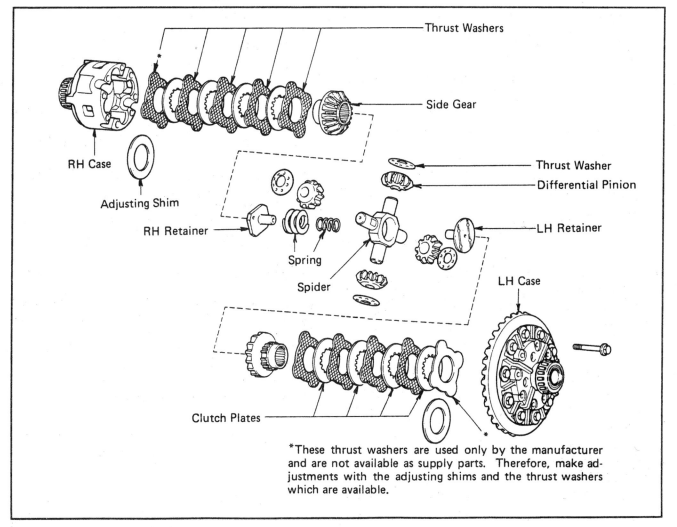

Thrust Washers

Side Gear

RH Case

Adjusting Shim

RH Retainer

Spring

Spider

Thrust Washer

Differential Pinion

LH Retainer

LH Case

Clutch Plates

*These thrust washers are used only by the manufacturer and are not available as supply parts. Therefore, make adjustments with the adjusting shims and the thrust washers which are available.

Removal

As previously described under REAR DIFFEREN-TIAL Section.

Dismantle

1. Put Matchmarks on RH and LH Case.
2. Dismantle Differential Case. Remove the bolts cautiously.

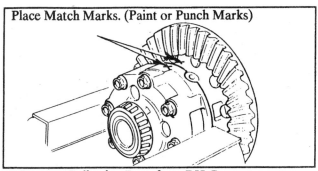

Place Match Marks. (Paint or Punch Marks)

3. Remove Following Parts from RH Case:
(a) side gear,

(b) 1) side gear thrust washer (3 pieces) BJ, FJ and HJ,
    2) side gear thrust washer (5 pieces) LJ and RJ.
(c) 1) clutch plate (3 pieces) BJ, FJ and HJ,
    2) clutch plate (4 pieces) LJ and RJ.
(d) Adjusting washer.

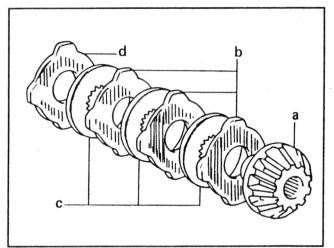

4.Remove Following Parts from LH Case:
(a) Spring RH retainer and spring.
(b) Spider with pinion gear and thrust washer.
(c)Spring LH retainer.
(d) Side gear.
(e) 1) side gear thrust washer (3 pieces) BJ, FJ and HJ.
    2) side gear thrust washer (5 pieces) LJ and RJ.
(f) 1) clutch plate (3 pieces) BJ, FJ and RJ.
    2) clutch plate (4 pieces) LJ and RJ.
(g) Adjusting washer.

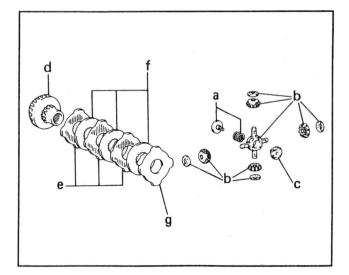

Inspection of Components

1.Replace Parts That are Damaged or Worn.

* If replacing the side gear, also replace the thrust washer making contact with it.

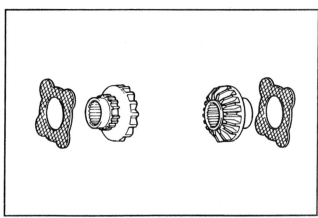

2.Inspect Thrust Washers for Wear or Damage. Check that the contact surface of the thrust washer is even and that no bare metal is showing.

[For reference] Thickness limit: 1.74 mm (0.0685 in)
If necessary, replace the thrust washers.

* If replacing the thrust washer also replace the clutch plate making contact with it.

3.Inspect Clutch Plate for Wear or Damage. Check to see that there is no abnormal wear. If necessary, replace the clutch plate.

4.Inspect Spring Free Length. Measure the free length of the spring.

Limit: 38.6 mm (1.520 in) BJ, FJ and HJ
       31.3 mm (1.232 in) LJ and RJ

Assembly

Reverse Dismantle Proceedure

Installation

See Rear Differential Section

REAR SUSPENSION

Components

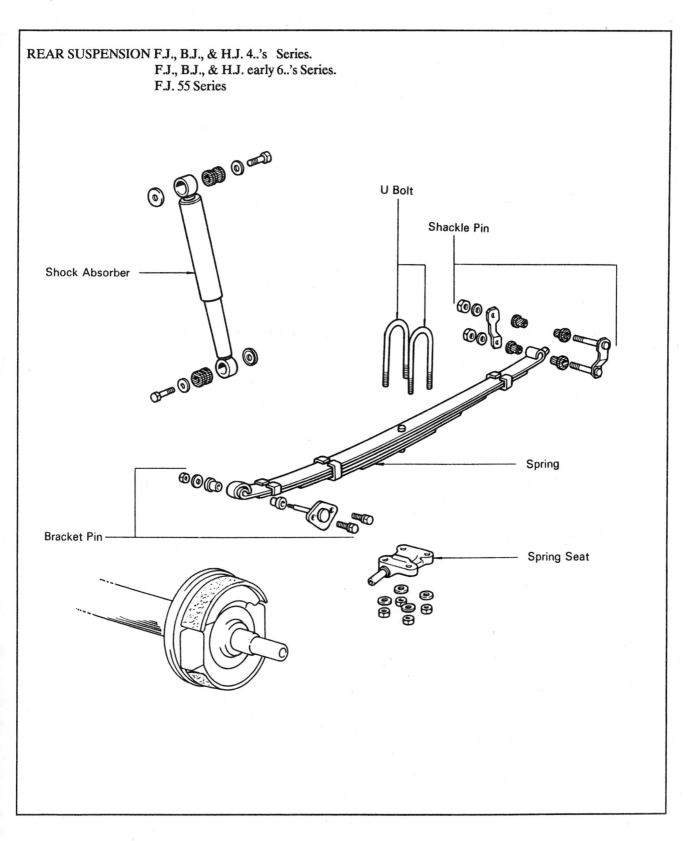

REAR SUSPENSION F.J., B.J., & H.J. 4..'s Series.
F.J., B.J., & H.J. early 6..'s Series.
F.J. 55 Series

U Bolt

Shackle Pin

Shock Absorber

Spring

Bracket Pin

Spring Seat

Rear Suspension F.J. B.J. & H.J. Late 6..'s Series

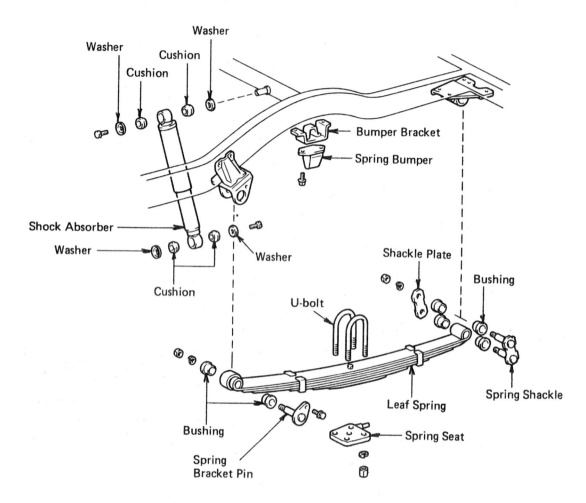

Washer

Washer

Cushion

Cushion

Bumper Bracket

Spring Bumper

Shock Absorber

Washer

Washer

Cushion

Shackle Plate

Bushing

U-bolt

Spring Shackle

Leaf Spring

Bushing

Spring Seat

Spring
Bracket Pin

Leaf Spring Component

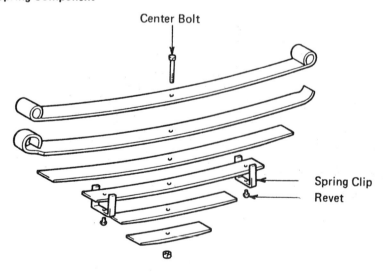

Center Bolt

Spring Clip

Revet

Rear Suspension F.J., B.J. & H.J. 7..'s Series

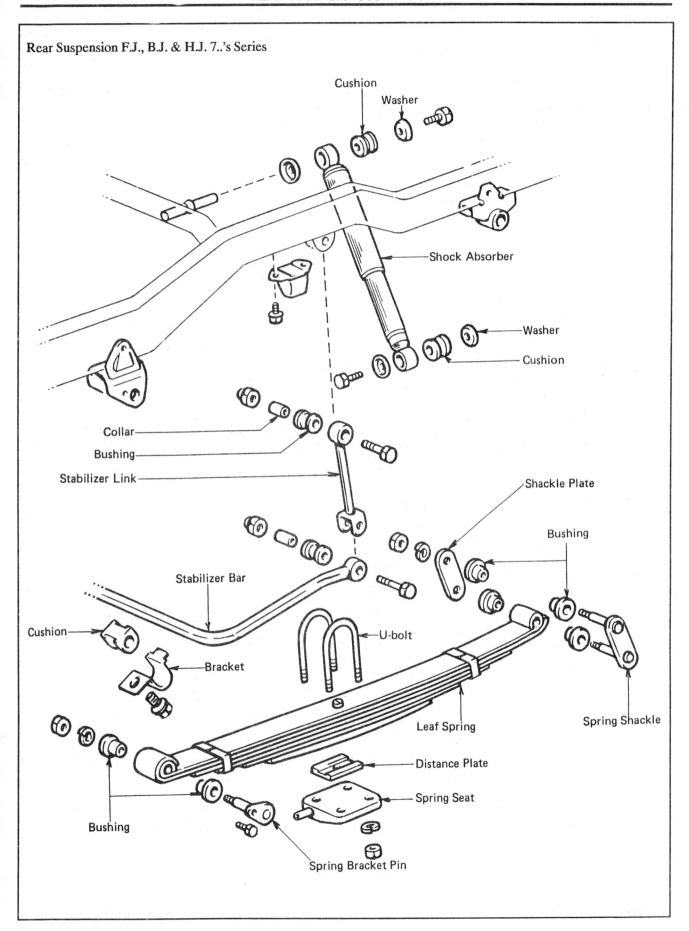

Cushion

Washer

Shock Absorber

Washer

Cushion

Collar

Bushing

Stabilizer Link

Shackle Plate

Bushing

Stabilizer Bar

Cushion

Bracket

U-bolt

Leaf Spring

Spring Shackle

Distance Plate

Spring Seat

Bushing

Spring Bracket Pin

REAR SUSPENSION R.J. & L.J. 7..'s Series.

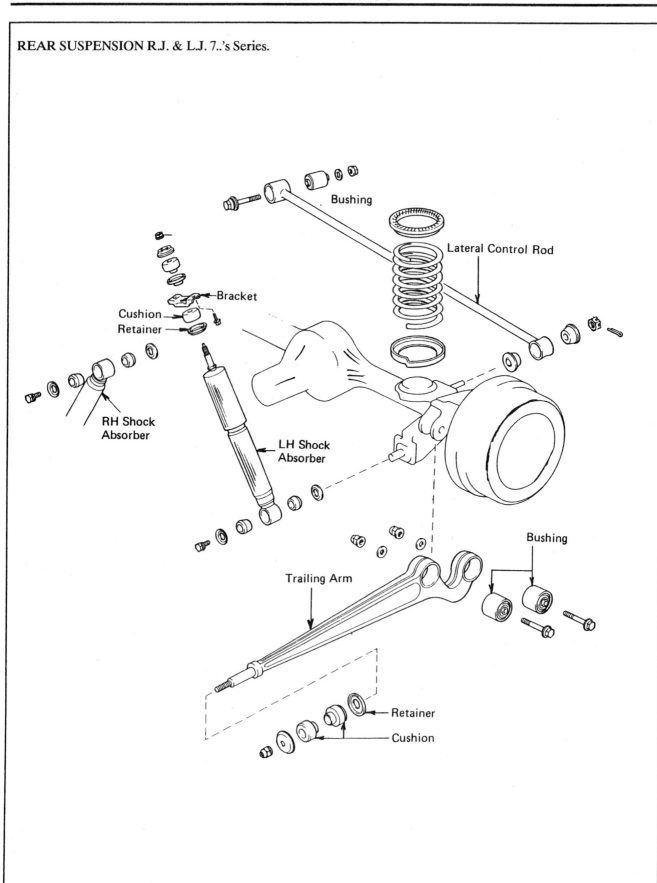

Bushing

Lateral Control Rod

Bracket

Cushion

Retainer

RH Shock Absorber

LH Shock Absorber

Bushing

Trailing Arm

Retainer

Cushion

SHOCK ABSORBER AND SPRING

Removal

1.Jack Up and Support Vehicle.
2.Support Axle Housing. Jack up the axle housing until the leaf spring force is free, and keep it there.
3.Remove Rear Wheel.
4.Remove Shock Absorber.
(a) Disconnect the shock absorber from the frame.
(b) Disconnect the shock absorber from the spring seat.
5.Remove U-Bolts.
(a) Remove the 4 U-bolt mounting nuts with the spring seat and distance plate.
(b) Remove the 2 U-bolts.
6.Remove Spring.
(a) Remove the spring bracket pin nut.
(b) Remove the 2 bolts and spring bracket pin.
(c) Remove the 2 shackle nuts and shackle inner plate.
(d) Remove the spring shackle and spring.

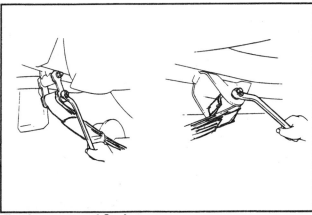

Replacement of Spring

1.Bend Open Spring Clip. Using a chisel, pry up the spring clip.
2.Remove Spring Centre Bolt. Hold the spring near the centre bolt in a vice and remove the centre bolt.
3.Replace Spring Clip.
(a) Drill off the head of the rivet, and drive it out.
(b) Install a new rivet into the holes of the spring leaf and clip. Then rivet with a press.
4.Install Spring Centre Bolt.
(a) Align the leaf holcs and secure the leaves with a vice.
(b) Install and tighten the spring centre bolt.
Torque: 500 kg-cm (36 ft-lb, 49 N·m)
5.Bend Spring Clip. Using a hammer, bend the spring clip into position.

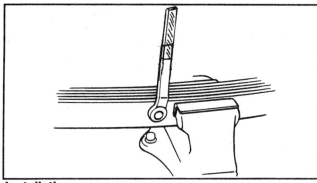

Installation

1.Install Bushing to Leaf Spring.
2.Install Leaf Spring.
(a) Install the spring shackle to the leaf spring.
(b) Place the front end of leaf spring in the front hanger and install the spring bracket pin. Torque the bracket pin bolt.
Torque: 130 kg-cm (9 ft-lb, 13 N·m)
(c) Hand tighten the bracket pin nut.
(d) Place the rear end of leaf spring in the rear bracket, and install the shackle pin.
(e) Install the plate and hand tighten the nuts.
3.Install U-Bolt.
(a) Install the 2 U-bolts onto the leaf spring.
(b) Install the distance plate and spring seat. Torque the 4 U-bolt mounting nuts.
Torque: 1,250 kg-cm (90 ft-lb, 123 N·m)
* Tighten the U-bolts so that the length of all the U-bolts under the spring seat are the same.
4.Install Rear Shock Absorber.
(a) Connect the shock absorber to the frame with the bolt. Tighten the bolt.
Torque: 650 kg-cm (47 ft-lb, 64 N·m)
(b) Connect the shock absorber to the spring seat with the bolt. Tighten the bolt.
Torque: 375 kg-cm (27 ft-lb, 37 N·m)
5.Install Wheel and Lower Vehicle.
6.Stabilise Suspension. Bounce the vehicle to stabilise the suspension.
7.Tighten Spring Bracket Pin and Shackle Pin. Torque the bracket pin nut and the shackle pin nuts.
Torque: 925 kg-cm (67 ft-lb, 91 N·m)

STABILISER BAR

Removal

1.Jack Up and Support Vehicle.

2.Remove Stabiliser Bar.

(a) Remove the stabiliser bar bracket from the axle housing.

(b) Remove the stabiliser bar link with the stabiliser bar from the frame.

(c) Remove stabiliser bar link from stabiliser bar.

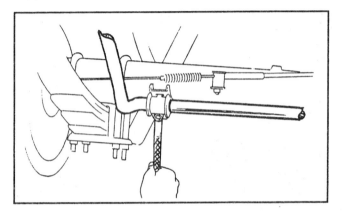

Installation

1.Replace Bushing if Necessary.

2.Install Stabiliser Bar Link to Stabiliser Bar. Install the stabiliser bar link to the stabiliser bar and temporarily install the new nut.

3.Install Stabiliser Bar.

(a) Install the cushion and bracket to the stabiliser bar.

(b) Temporarily install the bracket to the axle housing.

(c) Temporarily install the stabiliser link to the frame with the new nut.

4.Install Wheel and Lower Vehicle.

5.Stabilise Suspension.

6.Tighten Bracket and Link. Torque the bracket bolt and the stabiliser bar link nut.

Torque: 120 kg-cm (9 ft-lb, 12 N·m)

REAR AXLE SHAFT [LJ & RJ SERIES]

Components

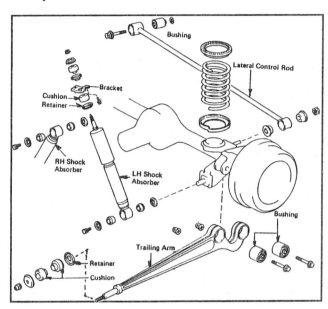

Rear Shock Absorber & Coil Spring

Removal

1.Jack Up Vehicle.

2.Remove Wheel.

3.Remove Rear Shock Absorber.

(a) Using a jack, support the rear axle housing.

(b) Disconnect the shock absorber upper bracket from the body.

(c) Remove the lower bracket bolt and remove the shock absorber.

4.Coil Spring. While lowering the axle housing, remove the coil spring and 2 coil spring insulators.

5.Remove Cushion and Upper Bracket of LH Shock Absorber.

Installation

1.Install Cushion, Retainer and Upper Bracket.

(a) Install the retainer, cushion, bracket, retainer, cushion, retainer and nut.

(b) Torque the nut.

Torque: 320 kg-cm (23 ft-lb, 31 N·m)

2. Install Coil Spring.

(a) Install the coil spring and 2 spring insulators to the axle housing.

(b) Jack up the axle housing and check that the coil spring is installed correctly.

3. Install Shock Absorber to the Rear Axle Housing and Torque the Bolt.

Torque: 650 kg-cm (47 ft-lb, 64 N·m)

4. Connect the shock Absorber to the Body.

Torque:

Left side - 380 kg-cm (27 ft-lb, 37 N·m)

Right side - 650 kg-cm (47 ft-lb, 64 N·m)

5. Remove Jack from Axle Housing.

6. Install Wheel and Lower Vehicle.

Trailing Arm

Removal

1. Support Trailing Arm. Using a jack, support the training arm.

2. Remove Trailing Arm.

(a) Remove the front mounting nut, retainer and cushion.

(b) Remove the 2 rear mounting nuts and bolts from the axle housing.

(c) Lower and remove the trailing arm.

(d) Remove the cushion and retainer from the trailing arm.

Installation

1. Replace Two Trailing Arm Bushings with a Press.

* When assembling the bushing, assemble it so the holes align at a 45° angle.

2. Install Trailing Arm.

(a) Install the rear retainer and cushion to the trailing arm.

(b) Insert the trailing arm to the body.

(c) Install the trailing arm to the axle housing, and torque the 2 nuts and bolts.

Torque: 2,500 kg-cm (181 ft-lb, 245 N·m)

(d) Install the front cushion and retainer to the trailing arm and torque the nuts.

Torque: 1,000 kg-cm (72 ft-lb, 98 N·m)

Lateral Control Rod :R.J. & L.J.

Removal

1. Support Rear Axle Housing. Jack up the rear axle housing and support it with stands.

2. Disconnect Lateral Control Rod from Rear Axle Housing.

(a) Remove the cotter pin.

(b) Remove the nut holding the lateral control rod to the rear axle housing, and disconnect the lateral control rod.

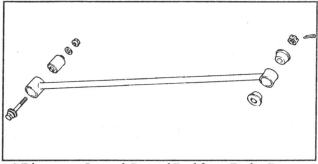

3. Disconnect Lateral Control Rod from Body. Remove the nut and bolt holding the lateral control rod to the body and remove the lateral control rod.

Replacement of Bushing

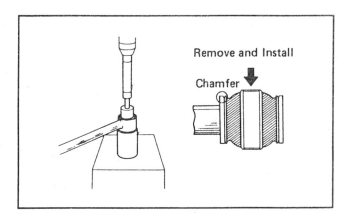

Replace Bushing (if necessary) with a Press.

* When inserting and removing the bushing, press or pull on the metal surface.

* Do not use a lubricant when pressing in the bushing (water acceptable).

Installation

1.Install Lateral Control Rod to Body.

(a) Raise the axle housing until the housing is free from the stands.

(b) Install the lateral control rod to the frame with the nut and bolt.

2.Install Lateral Control Rod to Rear Axle Housing.

(a) Fit in the following order: 1) washer, 2) bushing, spacer, 3) lateral control arm, 4) bushing, 5) washer, and 5) nut.

(b) Remove the stands and bounce the car to stabilise the suspension.

(c) Jack up the axle housing.

(d) Torque the nut and bolt.

Torque:

Body-side   1,460 kg-cm (106 ft-lb, 143 N·m)

Axle housing side   1,000 kg-cm (72 ft-lb, 98 N·m)

* When tightening the lateral control rod set nut and bolt, lower the vehicle load until the lateral control rod is horizontal.

PROBLEM DIAGNOSIS

Problem: Oil leak from rear axle!

Possible Causes and Remedies:

* Oil seals worn or damaged. Remedy - replace oil seal.

* Bearing retainer loose. Remedy - replace retainer.

* Rear axle housing cracked. Remedy - repair as necessary.

Problem: Oil leak from pinion shaft!

Possible Causes and Remedies:

* Oil level too high or wrong grade. Remedy - drain and replace oil.

* Oil seal worn or damaged. Remedy - replace oil seal.

* Companion flange loose or damaged. Remedy - tighten or replace flange.

Problem: Noises in rear axle!

Possible Causes and Remedies:

* Oil level low or wrong grade. Remedy - drain and replace oil.

* Excessive backlash between pinion and ring or side gear. Remedy - check backlash.

* Ring, pinion or side gears worn or chipped. Remedy - inspect gears.

* Pinion shaft bearing worn. Remedy - replace bearing.

* Axle shaft bearing worn. Remedy - replace bearing.

* Differential bearing loose or worn. Remedy - tighten or replace bearings.

Problem: Bottoming!

Possible Causes and Remedies:

* Shock absorber worn out. Remedy - replace shock absorber.

* Springs weak. Remedy - replace spring.

STEERING

STEERING

IN CAR ADJUSTMENTS

Steering Wheel Freeplay

1.Check that Steering Wheel Freeplay is Correct. With the vehicle stopped and tyres pointed straight ahead, rock the steering wheel gently back and forth with light finger pressure. Freeplay should not exceed the maximum limit.
Maximum play: 40 mm (1.57 in)
If incorrect, adjust or repair as required.
2.Point Wheels Straight Ahead.
3.Adjust Steering Gear box.
(a) Loosen the lock nut.
(b) Turn the adjusting screw clockwise to decrease wheel freeplay and counterclockwise to increase it.

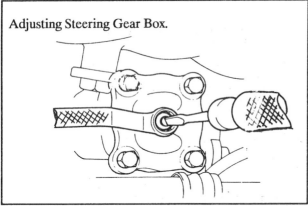

Adjusting Steering Gear Box.

* Turn the adjusting screw in small increments and check the wheel freeplay between each adjustment.
4.Check that Steering Does not Bind. Turn the steering wheel one full turn in both directions. Check that the freeplay is correct and steering is smooth and without rough spots.
5.Hold Adjusting Screw and Tighten Lock Nut.

Oil Level

Check Steering Gear box Oil Level.
Oil Level: 12 - 17 mm (0.47 - 0.67 in) from top

If low, fill with gear oil and check for oil leaks.

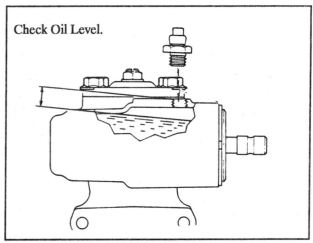

Check Oil Level.

STEERING COLUMN WITH TILT SHAFT

Removal

1.Disconnect Negative Cable from Battery.
2.Disconnect Intermediate Shaft No. 2 from No. 1.
(a) Place matchmarks on the intermediate shaft No. 1 and No. 2 joint yoke.
(b) Remove the set bolt.
(c) Pull out the intermediate shaft No. 1 from No. 2.
3.Remove Steering Wheel.
(a) Remove the steering wheel pad and the set nut.
(b) Place matchmarks on the steering wheel and main shaft.
(c) Remove the steering wheel using special tool.

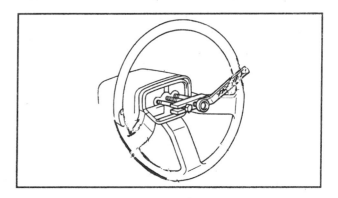

4.Remove Air Duct.

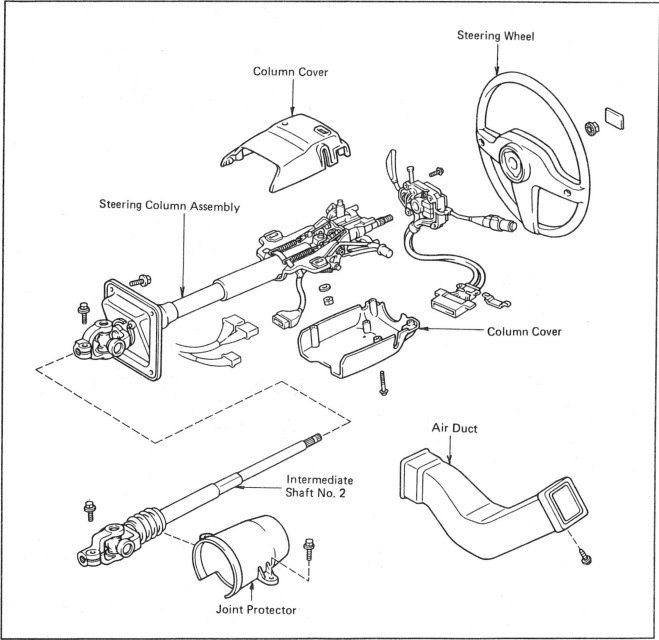

Steering Wheel

Column Cover

Steering Column Assembly

Column Cover

Air Duct

Intermediate
Shaft No. 2

Joint Protector

5.Remove Column Cover.
6.Remove Combination Switch.
7.Remove 4 Bolts from Column Hose Cover.
8.Remove Steering Column Assembly.
(a) Disconnect the ignition switch connector.
(b) Remove the 2 mount nuts.
(c) Pull out the steering column assembly.

1.Remove Tension Springs and Cords.
(a) Fully tilt the main shaft upward.
(b) Release the cord from the hook.
(c) Using a screwdriver, pry out the cord tip and remove the spring and cord.

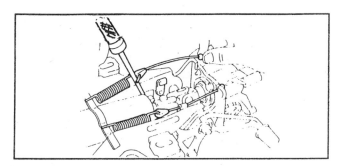

Components

Dismantle

Components of Tilt Steering Column.

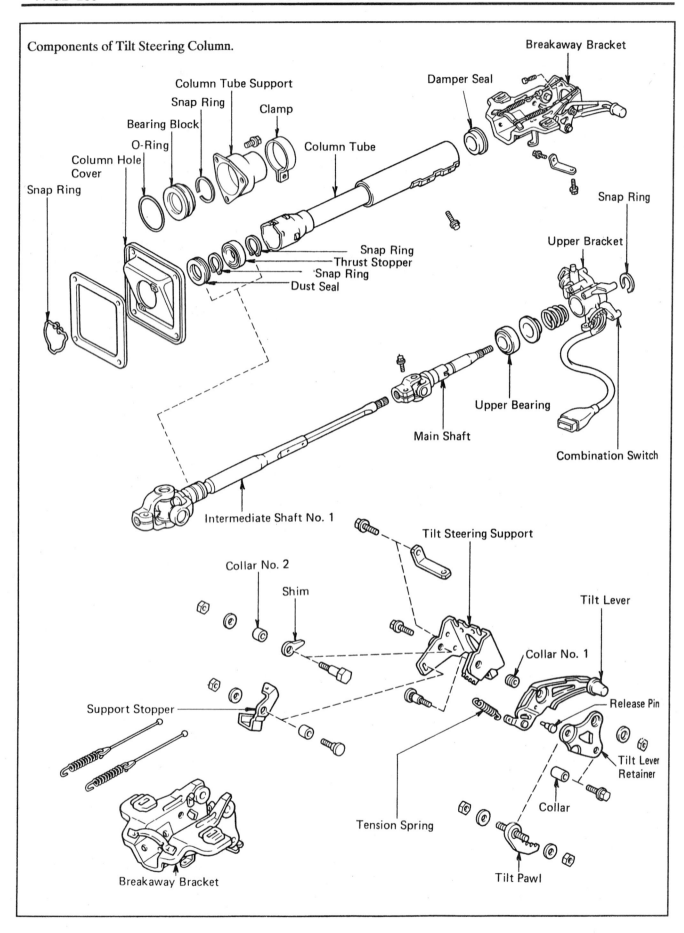

2.Disconnect Intermediate Shaft from Main Shaft.

(a) Place matchmarks on the intermediate shaft and universal joint.

(b) Remove the bolt and the snap ring.

(c) Pull out the intermediate shaft from the main shaft.

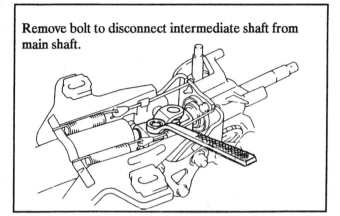

Remove bolt to disconnect intermediate shaft from main shaft.

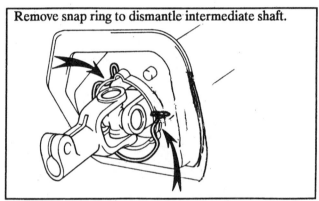

Remove snap ring to dismantle intermediate shaft.

3.Remove Column Tube from Breakaway Bracket. Remove the 4 bolts with a clamp.

4.Remove Ignition Key Cylinder.

(a) Place the ignition key at the "ACC" position.

(b) Push down the stop key with a thin rod, and pull out the key cylinder.

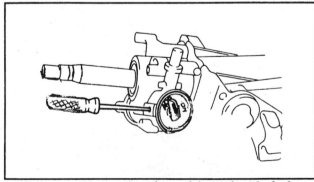

5.Remove Upper Bracket with Main Shaft from Breakaway Bracket.

(a) Remove the support reinforcement with 2 bolts.

(b) Loosen the broken bolt by tapping the chisel.

(c) Remove the 3 bolts.

(d) Disconnect the upper bracket from the breakaway bracket.

6.Remove Ignition Switch.

7.Remove Main Shaft from Upper Bracket.

(a) Compress the main shaft and upper bracket.

(b) Using snap ring pliers, remove the snap ring.

(c) Remove the main shaft, spring and collar from the upper bracket.

8.Dismantle Tilt Steering Support and Breakaway Bracket.

(a) Remove the tension spring, 2 nuts and bolts, the tilt lever retainer and collar, the release pin, the tilt steering pawl, the tilt pawl set bolt, the nut and support stopper bolt with a clamp and the tilt lever set nut.

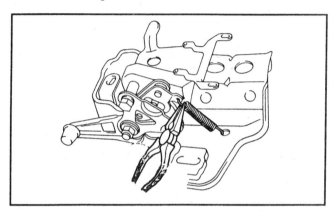

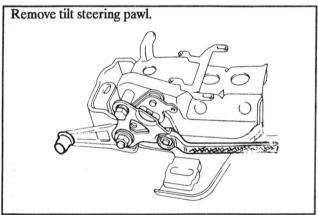

Remove tilt steering pawl.

(b) Temporarily install the nut flat with the end of the bolt and tap it with a hammer.

(c) Remove the nut, the collar and shim, and the other set bolt, nut and collar.

Inspection and Repair

1.[FJ, BJ, HJ 6..ˢ Series] If necessary, Replace Bearing in Upper Bracket.

(a) Remove the bearing.

(b) Pack MP grease into the bearing.

(c) Drive the bearing into the bracket.

2.If Necessary, Replace Lower Bearing.

(a) Remove the lower bearing from the main shaft.

(b) Pack MP grease into the bearing.

(c) Assemble the lower bearing and main shaft.

3.If Necessary, Replace Intermediate Shaft Bearing.

(a) Using snap ring pliers, remove the snap ring.

(b) Pull out the bearing from the intermediate shaft.

(c) Install the bearing.

(d) Using snap ring pliers, install the snap ring.

4.[FJ, BJ, HJ 6..ˢ Series] If Necessary, Replace Spider Bearing.

(a) Using needle-nose pliers, remove the four snap rings.

(b) Using a 12mm and 22mm socket wrench and vice, press out the yoke side outer race.

(c) Clamp the outer race in a vice and tap off the yoke with a hammer.

* Remove the outer bearing races in the same procedure.

(d) Apply molybdenum disulphide lithium base grease to the spider and bearings.

* Be careful not to apply too much grease.

(e) Using a 12mm socket wrench and vice, press the bearing outer race.

(f) Using a 10mm and 12mm socket wrench, adjust both bearings so that the snap ring grooves are at maximum and equal widths.

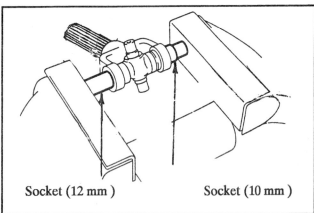

Socket (12 mm)   Socket (10 mm)

(g) Select 2 snap rings of the same thickness, which will allow 0 - 0.05 mm (0 - 0.0020 in) of axial play.

* Do not reuse the snap rings.

Snap ring thickness:

Mark	Thickness mm (in)
None	1.175 - 1.225 (0.0463 - 0.0482)
Brown	1.225 - 1.275 (0.0482 - 0.0502)
Blue	1.275 - 1.325 (0.0502 - 0.0522)

(h) Using needle-nose pliers, install the snap rings.

* Install the bearing outer races in the yoke side using the same procedure.

(i) Using a hammer, tap the shaft and yoke until the clearance between the bearing outer race and snap ring is zero.

(j) Check the spider bearing:

- check that the spider bearing moves smoothly.

- check the spider bearing axial play.

Bearing axial play: 0.05 mm (0.0020 in) or less

Assembly

1.Coat all Rubbing Parts with MP Grease.

2.Assemble Pawl Set Bolt.

Torque: 185 kg-cm (13 ft-lb, 18 N·m)

2.Assemble Tilt Lever to Support.

(a) Select a collar No. 1 which will eliminate play.

(b) Install tilt lever and collar No. 1 to the support.

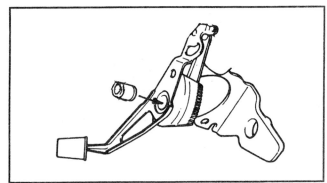

(c) Select a collar No. 2 which will eliminate all play.

(d) Install collar No. 2 to the support.

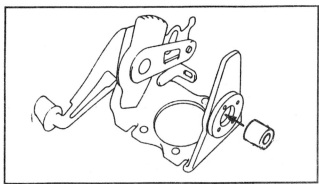

(e) Drive in the serration bolt to the support.

(f) Install the tilt pawl.

(g) Install the tension spring and the release pin.

(h) Assemble the collar and tilt lever retainer.

Torque: 185 kg-cm (13 ft-lb, 18 N·m)

4.Install Shim, Bolt and Nut.

(a) Select a shim which fits snugly when pressed in by hand.

(b) Install the shim, bolt, washer and a lock nut.

Torque: 185 kg-cm (13 ft-lb, 18 N·m)

5.Install Tilt Steering Support Stopper Bolt.

(a) Install the stopper bolt, bracket, washer and nut.

(b) Tighten the nut by holding the bracket as shown.

Torque: 100 kg-cm (7 ft-lb, 10 N·m)

6.Assemble Main Shaft and Upper Bracket.

(a) Assemble the collar, spring and main shaft, and insert them into the bracket.

(b) Install the snap ring by compressing the main shaft and upper bearing.

7.Assemble Upper Bracket and Support.

(a) Apply anaerobic adhesive and sealant to 1 or 2 threads of the bolt end.

* This adhesive will not harden while exposed to air. It will act as a sealer or binding agent only when applied to threads, etc. and the air is cut off.

(b) Install the 2 bolts, 1 with a wiring clamp.

Torque: 75 kg-cm (65 in-lb, 7.4 N·m)

(c) Install the break down bolt and tighten until the bolt head breaks off.

(d) Install the support reinforcement.

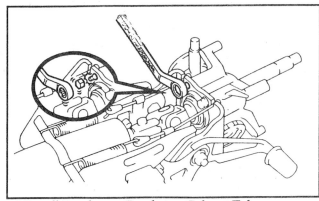

8.Install Breakaway Bracket to Column Tube.

Torque: 185 kg-cm (13 ft-lb, 18 N·m)

9.Install Column Hole Cover to Column Tube.

Torque: 185 kg-cm (13 ft-lb, 18 N·m)

10. Connect Main Shaft and Intermediate Shaft.

(a) Align the marks on the joint yoke and intermediate shaft and tighten the bolt.

Torque: 250 kg-cm (18 ft-lb, 25 N·m)

* Be careful not to push out the damper seal while installing the intermediate shaft.

(b) Install the snap ring.

11. Install 2 Springs and 2 Cords.

(a) Connect the tension spring and cord and hook the spring to the hanger.

(b) Pry the spring end and hook the cord end to the support.

(c) Hook the cord to the cord guides.

12. Check Operation of Tilt Steering Lever and Support.

(a) Check that there is no axial or horizontal play at the end of the main shaft.

(b) Check that the main shaft locks securely in all six positions.

13. Install Ignition Switch.

(a) Turn the ignition key plate to the "ACC" position and install the key cylinder into the upper bracket.

(b) Install the ignition switch.

Installation

1.Install Steering Column Assembly.

(a) Place the steering column assembly in the installed position.

(b) Temporarily install the 2 breakaway bracket mount nuts.

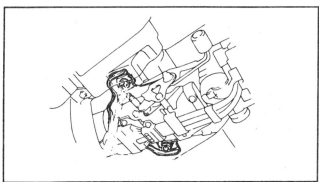

(c) Install and torque the 4 column hole cover bolts.

Torque: 130 kg-cm (9 ft-lb, 13 N·m)

(d) Torque the 2 breakaway bracket mount nuts.

Torque: 250 kg-cm (18 ft-lb, 25 N·m)

2.Install Combination Switch.

3.Install Column Cover and Air Duct.

4.Install Steering Wheel.

(a) Align matchmarks on the steering wheel and main shaft, and install the steering wheel to the main shaft.

(b) Install and torque the set nut.

Torque: 350 kg-cm (25 ft-lb, 34 N·m)

(c) Install the steering wheel pad.

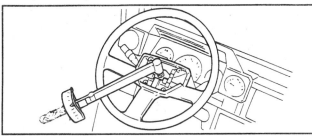

5.Connect Intermediate Shaft No. 1 and No. 2.

(a) Align the matchmarks on the joint yoke of intermediate shaft No. 1 and intermediate shaft No. 2 and connect them.

(b) Install and torque the set bolt.

Torque: 360 kg-cm (26 ft-lb, 35 N·m)

6.Connect Negative Terminal of Battery.

7.Check Steering Wheel Centre Point.

STEERING COLUMN ASSEMBLY

Components

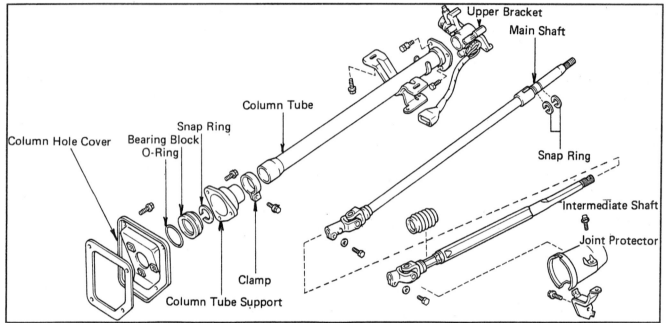

Removal of Steering Column Shaft

1. Turn ignition key to the "ACC" position.
2. Using snap ring pliers, remove the snap ring.
3. Pull out the main shaft.

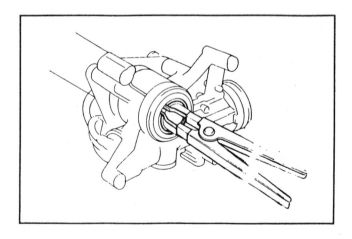

STEERING GEAR - FJ, BJ, HJ4..^{S}, FJ55, FJ, BJ, HJ, 6..^{S} UP TO 1984.

Removal

1. Remove the parts in the following order: 1) main shaft, 2) pitman arm, 3) gear housing.
2. Remove the steering wheel and main shaft.
3. Remove the pitman arm.

F.J., B.J. & H.J. 4..'s Series.

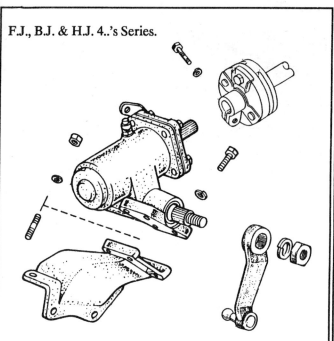

F.J. 55 Series.

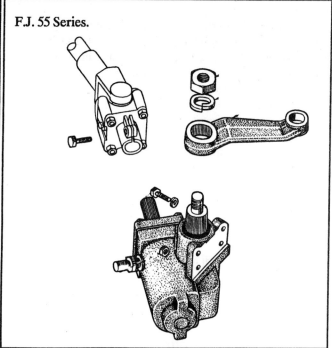

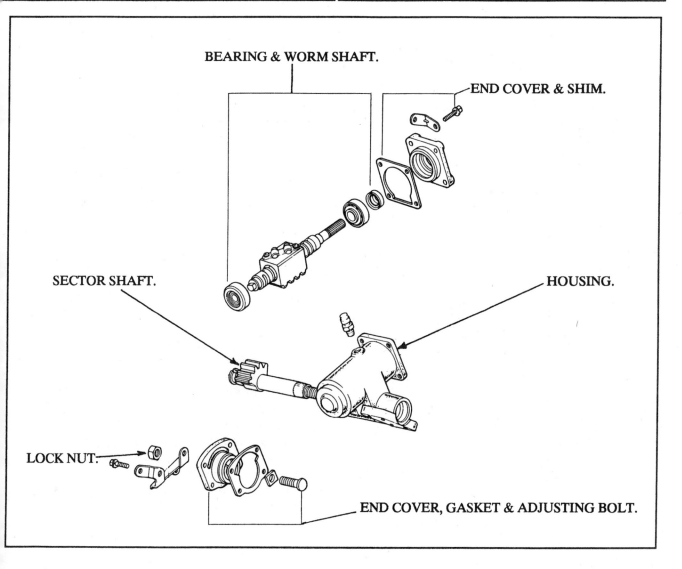

BEARING & WORM SHAFT.

END COVER & SHIM.

SECTOR SHAFT.

HOUSING.

LOCK NUT.

END COVER, GASKET & ADJUSTING BOLT.

Dismantle

1.Dismantle the parts in the following order: 1) lock nut, 2) end cover, gasket and adjusting bolt, 3) sector shaft, 4) end cover and shim, 5) bearing and worm shaft, 6) housing.

2.Screw in the bolt and remove the cover.

* use a receiver to catch the oil from the gear housing.

3.Pull the sector shaft out of the housing.

* Have the sector shaft positioned at its rotational centre.

4.Record the number of shims used.

5.Remove the worm assembly.

* Keep the bearings in proper order so that they can be reassembled to their initial positions.

* Do not attempt to dismantle the steering worm assembly. If any part of it is defective, replace the entire assembly.

* Do not run the ball nut to the worm end.

Inspection

Wash the dismantled parts and inspect them on the following points. Replace any part found defective.

1.Steering Worm and Bearing.

(a) Inspect the bearings, the worm threads and ball nut rack for wear or damage.

(b) Check the turning condition of the ball nut.

2.Replace the Worm Bearing Outer Race.

(a) Remove the outer race at housing end.

(b) Remove the outer race at end cover end.

(c) Install the outer race at housing end.

(d) Install the outer race at end cover end.

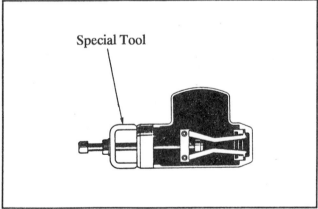

Special Tool

3.Replace the Inner Race.

(a) Force out the inner race with a press.

(b) Press in the inner race.

4.Sector Shaft and Bushing.

(a) Inspect the shaft at bushing contacting surfaces and at gear teeth for wear or damage. Inspect the bushings for wear or damage.

(b) Check the sector shaft oil clearance (A - B).

Oil clearance: Limit - 0.1 mm (0.004 in)

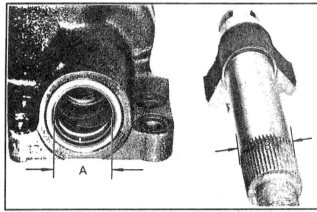

(c) Check the sector shaft oil clearance (A - B).

Oil clearance: Limit - 0.1 mm (0.004 in)

5.Replace the Gear Housing.

(a) Remove the oil seal.

(b) Press out the 2 bushings at the same time in the same direction with special tool.

(c) Press in the bushings from each end of the gear housing with special tool.

(d) Hone the bushings with a pin hole grinder or similar means until standard oil clearance is obtained between the bushings and the sector shaft.

Oil clearance:

STD 0.009 - 0.060 mm (0.0004 - 0.0024 in)

(e) Install the oil seal.

(f) Measure the sector shaft thrust clearance and select a thrust washer that will provide minimum clearance between the sector shaft and the adjusting screw.

Thrust clearance: Limit - 0.05 mm (0.0020 in)

Assembly

1.Assemble the parts in the following order: 1) housing, 2) bearing and worm shaft, 3) end cover and shim, 4) sector shaft, 5) adjusting bolt, 6) end cover, gasket and bolt, 7) lock nut.

2. Install the cover over the same amount of shims removed at DISMANTLE and tighten the cover bolts at specified torque.

Tightening torque: 3.0 - 4.5 kg-m (22 - 32 ft-lb)

* have the worm bearing lubricated with gear oil.

* While tightening the cover bolts, keep checking the worm to see that it will turn properly.

3.Measure the worm bearing preload.

Preload: 3.5 - 6.5 kg-cm (3.0 - 5.6 in-lb)

* Read the scale just when the worm starts to turn. If the preload is not within the specified limits, correct by selecting shim of proper thickness.

4.Position the worm ball nut at the centre and insert the sector shaft.

* Make sure that the worm ball nut and the sector are meshing together at the centre.

5.Loosen the adjusting bolt all the way and install the cover.

6.Tighten the cover bolts at the specified torque.

Tightening torque: 3.0 - 4.5 kg-m (22 - 32 ft-lb)

7.Set the worm shaft preload to the specified value by means of the adjusting bolt.

Preload: 8.0 - 11.0 kg-cm (6.9 - 9.5 in-lb)

* Measurement should be made with the meshing positioned at the centre.

8.Install the pitman arm and check to see that there is no backlash when the worm is rotated with 45° to either side from centre position. Tighten the adjusting screw lock nut.

* After tightening, recheck the preload.

Installation

1.Install the parts in the following order: 1) gear housing, 2) pitman arm, 3) main shaft.

2.Tighten the bolts and nuts at the specified torque.

Tightening torque: 4.0 - 4.5 kg-m (29 - 32 ft-lb)

2.Align the matchmarks on the pitman arm and sector shaft.

3.Tighten at specified torque.

Tightening torque:
16.5 - 19.5 kg-m (120 - 141 ft-lb)

FILL with GEAR OIL.
Capacity 610 cc (37.2 cu.in)
Type :   SAE 90 API GL-4

STEERING GEAR - FJ, BJ, HJ 6..ˢ 1984 ONWARDS, FJ, BJ, HJ 7..ˢ

Removal

1.Disconnect Intermediate Shaft.

(a) Remove joint protector.

(b) Place matchmarks on the worm shaft and intermediate shaft joint yoke.

(c) Remove the 2 set bolts from joint yokes.

(d) Disconnect the intermediate shaft from the worm shaft.

2.Loosen Pitman Arm Set Nut.

3.Disconnect Relay Rod from Pitman Arm.

(a) Remove the cotter pin.

(b) Remove the set nut.

(c) Disconnect the relay rod end from the pitman arm.

4.Remove Gear Housing. Remove the 4 nuts, 4 bolts and gear housing.

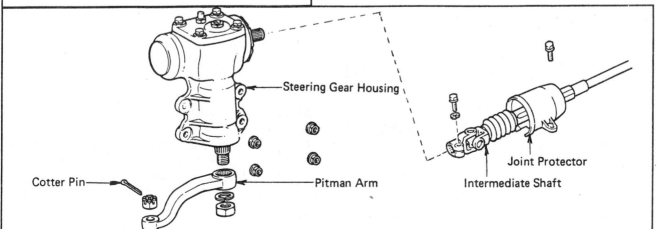

Cotter Pin — Pitman Arm — Steering Gear Housing — Joint Protector — Intermediate Shaft

Components

4.Remove Sector Shaft.

(a) Using a plastic hammer, tap out the sector shaft.

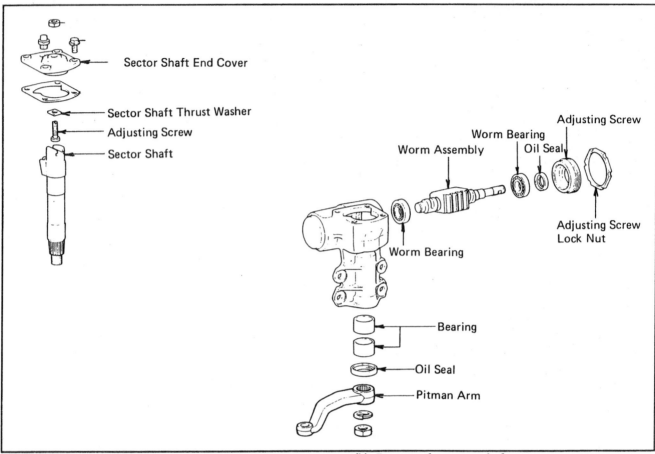

Sector Shaft End Cover

Sector Shaft Thrust Washer

Adjusting Screw

Sector Shaft

Worm Assembly

Worm Bearing

Oil Seal

Adjusting Screw

Worm Bearing

Adjusting Screw Lock Nut

Bearing

Oil Seal

Pitman Arm

Dismantle

1.Remove Breather Plug and Drain Gear Oil.

2.Disconnect Pitman Arm from Gear Housing.

(a) Remove the pitman arm set nut.

(b) Disconnect the pitman arm from the gear housing.

3.Remove End Cover.

(a) Remove the adjusting screw lock nut and 4 nuts.

(b) Remove the end cover by turning the adjusting screw clockwise.

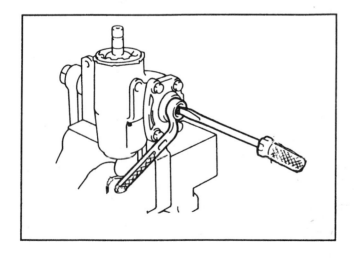

(b) Remove the sector shaft.

5.Remove Worm Bearing Adjusting Screw Lock Nut with Special Tool.

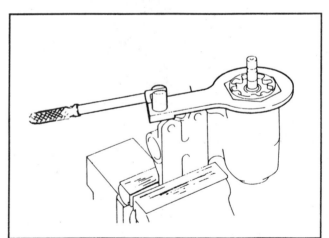

6.Remove Worm Bearing Adjusting Screw with Special Tool.

7.Remove Worm Shaft. Pull the worm shaft out of the gear housing.

* Do not disassemble the ball nut from the steering worm shaft. Do not allow the ball nut to hut the end of the worm shaft.

Inspection

1.Inspect Worm and Ball Nut.

(a) Check the worm and ball nut for wear or damage.

(b) Check that the nut rotates smoothly down the shaft by its own weight.

If a problem is found, repair or replace the worm.

* Do not allow the ball nut to hit the end of the worm shaft.

2.If Necessary, Replace Worm Bearing.

(a) Remove the both side bearings.

(b) Using a press, install both side bearings.

* Be careful not to damage the ball nut while holding it by hand.

(c) Using special tool, remove the outer race from the gear housing.

(d) Using special tool, drive in the other race into the gear housing.

(e) Remove the outer race from the adjusting screw.

(f) Press the outer race into the adjusting screw.

3.If Necessary, Replace Worm Shaft Oil Seal.

(a) Using a socket wrench, drive out the oil seal.

(b) Using a socket wrench, drive in the oil seal.

4.Measure Sector Shaft Thrust Clearance. Using a feeler gauge, measure the shaft thrust clearance.

Maximum clearance: 0.05 mm (0.0020 in) or less

If necessary, install a new thrust washer to provide the minimum clearance between the sector shaft and adjusting screw.

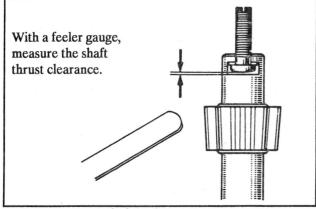

With a feeler gauge, measure the shaft thrust clearance.

5.Inspect Sector Shaft End Cover.

(a) Check for damage.

(b) Check the bushing for wear or damage. If necessary replace the end cover.

* When replacing the end cover, replace with one having the same number.

6.If Necessary, Replace Sector Shaft Oil Seal.

Assembly

1.Apply MP Grease to Bushing, Needle Roller Bearing and Oil Seals.

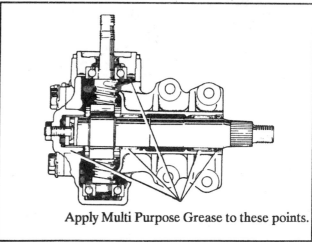

Apply Multi Purpose Grease to these points.

2.Insert Worm Shaft into Gear Housing. Place the worm bearing on the shaft and insert the shaft into the housing.

3.Install and Adjust Bearing Adjusting Screw.

(a) Gradually tighten the adjusting screw until it is snug.

(b) Using a torque meter and special tool, measure the bearing preload in both directions. Turn the adjusting screw until the preload is correct.

Preload (starting):

3.5 - 5 kg-cm (3.0 - 4.3 in-lb, 0.34 - 0.49 N·m)

(c) Hold the adjusting screw in position with special tool and tighten the lock nut with special tool.

Torque: 1,500 kg-cm (108 ft-lb, 147 N·m)

* Check that the bearing preload is still correct.

4.Install Needle Roller Bearing. Apply MP grease to the needle rollers and install them into the housing.

5.Install Sector Shaft.

(a) Install the adjusting screw and thrust washer onto the sector shaft.

(v) Set the ball nut at the centre of the worm shaft. Insert the sector shaft into the gear housing so that the centre teeth mesh together.

6.Install End Cover.

(a) Apply liquid sealer to the gasket and end cover.

(b) Install the end cover over the gasket.

(c) Loosen the adjusting screw as far as possible.

(d) Torque the 3 cover bolts.

Torque: 1,150 kg-cm (83 ft-lb, 113 N·m)

7.Place Worm Shaft in Neutral Position.

(a) Fully turn the worm shaft while counting the rotations.

(b) Then, turn the shaft back half that number. The shaft is now in neutral.

(c) Place the matchmarks on the worm shaft and housing to show neutral position.

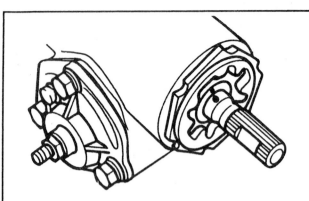

Place matchmarks on worm shaft & housing to show neutral position.

8.Adjust Total Preload. Using a torque meter and special tool, turn the adjusting screw until the preload is correct.

* Be sure that the worm shaft is in neutral.

Preload (starting):

8 - 11 kg-cm (6.9 - 9.5 in-lb, 0.78 - 1.08 N·m)

9.Tighten Adjusting Screw Lock Nut.

(a) Hold the screw with a screwdriver while tightening the lock nut.

(b) Torque the lock nut.

Torque: 450 kg-cm (33 ft-lb, 44 N·m)

* Check that the preload is still correct.

10.Measure Sector Shaft Backlash.

(a) Align the marks on the sector shaft with the pitman arm. Install the pitman arm and tighten the nut finger tight.

(b) Install the backlash gauge. Check that the sector shaft has no backlash within 100° of either side of the neutral position.

11.Replenish Gear Oil.

Oil level: 12 - 17 mm (0.47 - 0.67 in)

Installation

1.Install Gear Housing. Install the gear housing with the 4 bolts and nuts.

Torque: 1,240 kg-cm (90 ft-lb, 122 N·m)

2.Connect Intermediate Shaft.

(a) Align matchmarks on the worm shaft and intermediate shaft joint yoke and connect them.

(b) Install and torque the two bolts.

Torque: 360 kg-cm (26 ft-lb, 35 N·m)

3.Install Joint Protector.

(a) Install the joint protector.

(b) Install and torque the bolt.

Torque: 65 kg-cm (56 in-lb, 6.4 N·m)

4.Connect Relay Rod.

(a) Install the pitman arm to the relay rod.

(b) Install and torque the nut.

Torque: 925 kg-cm (67 ft-lb, 91 N·m)

(c) Install the cotter pin.

5.Torque Pitman Arm Set Nut.

Torque: 1,800 kg-cm (130 ft-lb, 177 N·m)

POWER STEERING

Inspection

1.Check Drive Belt Tension.

2.Check Fluid Level in Reservoir. Check the fluid level and add fluid if necessary.

Fluid: ATF DEXRON^R or DEXRON^R II

* Check that the fluid level is within the HOT LEVEL of the dipstick. If the fluid is cold, check that it is within the COLD level of the dipstick.

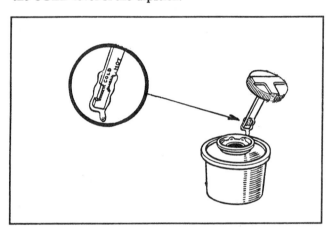

POWER STEERING PUMP

Removal

1.**[2H & 12H-T Engines]** Remove Engine Undercover.

2.Draw Out Fluid From Reservoir Tank.

3.Loosen Drive Pulley Nut. Push on the drive belt to hold the pulley in place and loosen the pulley nut.

4.Remove Drive Belt.

(a) (i) **[3F, 3B & 13B-T Engine]** Loosen the idler pulley nut.

(ii) **[2H & 12H-T Engine]** Loosen the pivot nut.

(b) Loosen the adjusting bolt and remove the drive belt.

5.Remove Drive Pulley and Woodruff Key.

6.Disconnect Pressure Hose.

7.Disconnect Return Hose.

8.Remove Power Steering Pump. Remove PS pump mount bolts and remove the PS pump from the bracket.

Components

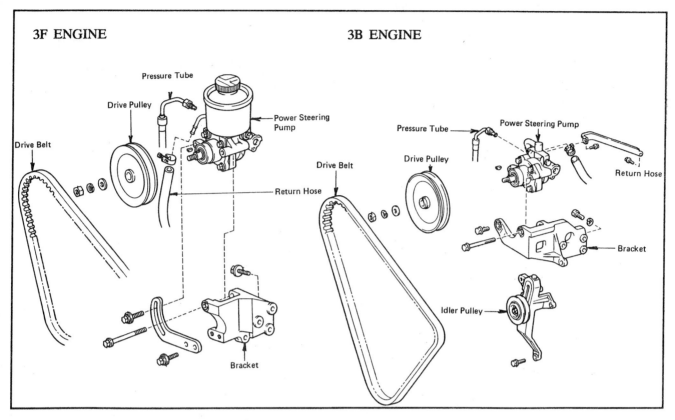

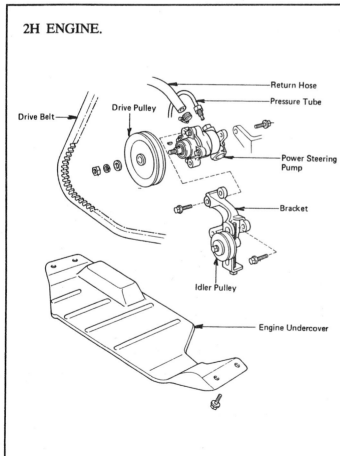

2H ENGINE.

Dismantle

1. Clamp Power Steering Pump in Vice.]
* Do not tighten the vice more than necessary.

2. (a) **[3F & 13B-T Engines]** Remove reservoir tank and O-ring.

(b) **[3B, 13B-T & 2H Engines]** Remove suction port union and O-ring.

3. Remove Front Housing.

(a) Place matchmarks on the front and the rear housing.

(b) Remove the 4 bolts and tap off the front housing with a plastic hammer.

* Be careful that the vane plates, rotor and cam ring do not fall out.

4. Remove Cam Ring, Rotor and Vane Plates.

* Be careful not to scratch the cam ring, rotor or vane plates.

5. Remove Rotor Shaft.

(a) Clamp the front housing in a vice.

* Do not tighten the vice more than necessary.

(b) Using a chisel and hammer, pry off the oil seal.

(c) Using snap ring pliers, remove the snap ring.

(d) Using a press, remove the rotor shaft from the front housing.

6. Remove Rear Plate and Spring.

(a) Using a plastic hammer, tap the bottom end of the rear housing and remove the rear plate and spring.

* Avoid gripping the rear plate with pliers as this could damage it.

(b) Remove the 2 O-rings from the front housing and rear plate.

7. Remove Pressure Port Union.

8. Remove Flow Control Valve and Spring.

* Use care not to drop, scratch or nick this valve.

9. Remove Flow Control Spring Seat.

(a) Using snap ring pliers, remove the snap ring.

(b) Using needle nose pliers, remove the spring seat.

(c) Remove the O-ring from the spring seat.

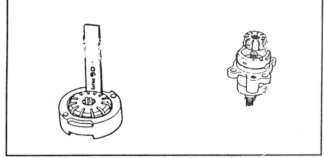

Maximum clearance: 0.06 mm (0.0024 in)

If the difference is excessive, replace the cam ring with

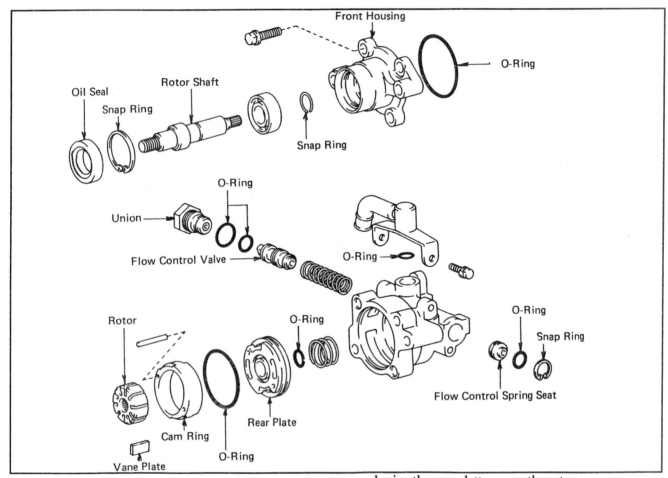

one having the same letter as on the rotor.

4. Inspect and Measure Vane Plates.

(a) Check the vane plates for wear or scratches.

)b) Measure the length, height and width of the vane plates.

Minimum length: 14.97 mm (0.5894 in)

Minimum height: 8.10 mm (0.3189 in)

Minimum width: 1.77 mm (0.0697 in)

(c) Measure the clearance between the vane plate and rotor groove.

Maximum clearance: 0.03 mm (0.0012 in)

* There are 5 vane lengths with the following rotor and cam ring marks:

Inspection

1. Inspect Bushing and Measure Bushing Oil Clearance.

(a) Check bushing for wear or damage. The bushing cannot be replaced separately. If wear or damage is found, replace the entire housing.

(b) Check the oil clearance between the bushing and rotor shaft.

Maximum oil clearance: 0.03 mm (0.0012 in)

2. If Necessary, Replace Rotor Shaft Bearing.

3. Inspect Rotor And Cam Ring. Measure the cam ring clearance.

Rotor & Cam

Ring Mark	Vane Length mm (in)
None	14.996 - 14.998 (0.5904 - 0.5905)
1	14.994 - 14.996 (0.5903 - 0.5904)
2	14.992 - 14.994 (0.5902 - 0.5903)
3	14.990 - 14.992 (0.59016 - 0.59024)
4	14.988 - 14.990 (0.5901 - 0.5902)

Check the Rotor & Cam Ring marks match.

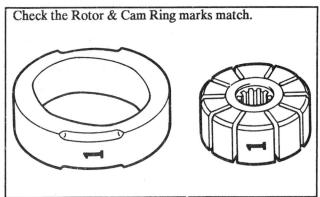

5.Inspect Flow Control Valve and Measure Spring.

(a) Check the flow control valve for wear or damage.

(b) Apply fluid to the valve and check that it falls smoothly into the valve hole by its own weight.

(c) Check the flow control valve for leakage:

- close one of the holes and apply compressed air [4 or 5 kg-cm^2 (57 or 71 psi, 392 - 490 kPa)] into the opposite side.

- confirm that air does not come out from the end hole.

If necessary, replace the valve with one having the same letter as on the rear housing.

6.If Necessary, Replace Union Seat.

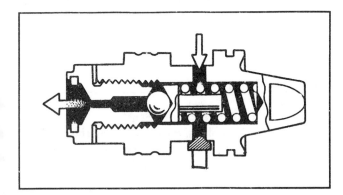

Assembly

1.Install Flow Control Spring Seat.

(a) Install the O-ring to the spring seat.

(b) Push in the spring seat to the front housing.

(c) Using snap ring pliers, install the snap ring.

2.Push in the Spring and Valve to the Front Housing.

3.Install Pressure Port Union.

(a) Install the 2 O-rings to the pressure port union and the front housing.

(b) Install and torque the pressure port union.

Torque: 700 kg-cm (51 ft-lb, 69 N·m)

4.Install Rotor Shaft to Front Housing.

(a) Press in the rotor shaft to the front housing.

(b) Using snap ring pliers, install the snap ring.

5.Install O-Ring and Pin to Front Housing.

6.Install Oil Seal.

7.Align and Install Large Hole of the Cam Ring to the Pin.

* Be sure the letters inscribed on the cam ring face upwards.

8.Install the Rotor with the Letters Inscribed Facing Upward.

9.Install the Vane Plates with the Round End Facing Outward.

Round end facing outwards.

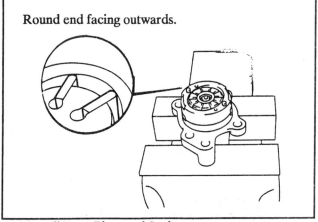

10. Install Rear Plate and Spring.

(a) Install the 2 O-rings to the rear plate.

(b) Place the rear plate on the cam ring with pin holes aligned with the pins.

(c) Place the spring on the rear plate.

11. Install Rear Housing.

(a) Align the matchmarks on the front and rear housing and assemble them.

(b) **[3F Engine]** Install the reservoir tank and O-ring.

(c) Install and temporarily tighten front housing mounting bolts.

(d) Clamp the rear housing in a vice.

* Do not tighten the vice too tightly.

(e) Evenly tighten the 4 housing bolts in several passes.

Torque: 470 kg-cm (34 ft-lb, 46 N·m)

12.[3B, 13B-T and 2H Engines] Install Suction Port Union.

(a) Install the suction port union with an O-ring.

(b) Install and torque the 2 bolts.

Torque: 130 kg-cm (9 ft-lb, 13 N·m)

13. Check Rotor Shaft Rotation Condition.

(a) Check that the rotor shaft rotates smoothly without abnormal noise.

(b) Provisionally install the pulley nut and check the rotating torque.

Rotating torque:

2.8 kg-cm or less (2.4 in-lb, 0.3 N·m)

POWER STEERING PUMP

FJ, BJ, HJ 4..^S; & FJ, BJ, HJ6..^S

UP TO 1984 (and for U.S.A.)

Components

5.Remove Front Housing. Using a plastic hammer, tap off the front housing and remove the O-ring and side plate.

* Do not pull out the rotor or fixed ring.

* Do not allow the slippers or springs to fly out.

6.Remove Rotor Shaft, Spring, Spring Seat and Slipper.

7.Mark Rear Housing and Fixed Ring.

8.Remove Fixed Ring.

(a) Using a plastic hammer, tap off the fired ring.

(b) Remove the O-ring and side plate.

9.Remove Pressure Port Union.

10. Remove Flow Control Valve and Spring.

* Avoid gripping the rear plate with pliers as this could

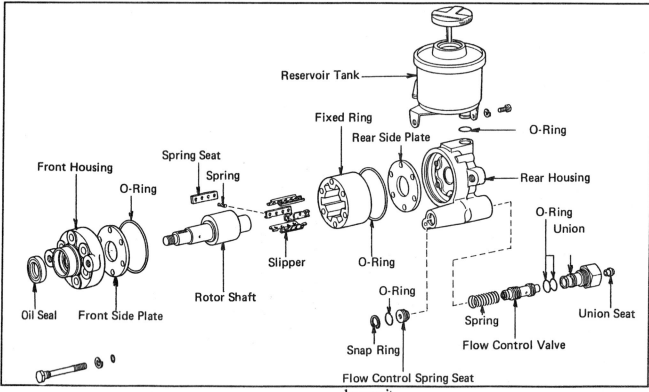

damage it.

11. Remove Flow Control Spring Seat.

(a) Using snap ring pliers, remove the snap ring.

(b) Install a suitable bolt to the spring seat and pull it out.

Dismantle

1.Attach Special Tool to Power Steering Pump and Hold Power Steering Pump.

2.Remove Front Housing Mount Bolts.

3.Remove Reservoir Tank and O-Ring.

4.Mark Front Housing and Fixed Ring.

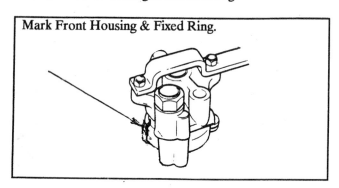

Mark Front Housing & Fixed Ring.

Inspection

1.Inspect Rotor Shaft and Fixed Ring.

(a) Check to oil seal tip contact surface and bushing contact for wear or damage.

(b) Check the circumferential surface of the rotor for abnormal wear (burns and scratches).

(c) Measure the rotor shaft length (side plate contact surface) and the fixed ring length, and check that the difference is within the limit shown below.

Limit: 0.06 mm (0.0024 in)

If not within specification, replace the rotor shaft.

2.Inspect Flow Control Valve and Measure Spring.

(a) Check the flow control valve for wear or damage.

(b) Apply fluid the valve and check that it falls smoothly into the valve hole by its own weight.

(c) Check the flow control valve for leakage:

- Close one of the holes and apply compressed air [4 or 5 kg-cm^2 (57 - 71 psi, 392 - 490 kPa)] into the opposite side.

- Confirm that air does not come out from the end hole.

If necessary, replace the valve with one having the same letter on the rear housing.

Inspect Flow Control Valve

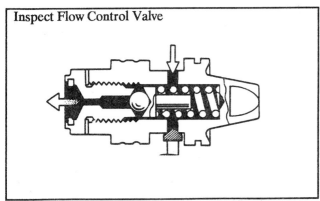

(d) Check that the spring is within specification.

Spring length: 47 - 50 mm (1.85 - 1.97 in)

If the spring is not within specification, replace it.

3.If Necessary, Replace Union Seat.

* Only floating type parts are available.

4.Inspect Slipper and Spring.

(a) Check the slipper for wear or scratches.

(b) Measure the thickness and length of the slipper.

Minimum thickness: 1.40 mm (0.0551 in)

Minimum length: 39.920 mm (1.5717 in)

(c) Check that the spring length is within specification.

Spring length: 13 - 14 mm (0.512 - 0.551 in)

If the spring is not within specification, replace it.

5.Inspect Front and Rear Housing Bushing.

(a) Check the front and rear bushing for wear or cracks.

(b) Measure the clearance between rotor shaft and bushing.

Maximum clearance: 0.03 mm (0.0012 in)

6.If Necessary, Replace Oil Seal.

7.Check the Front and Rear Side Plates on the Rotor Contact Surface. If worn or damaged, replace it.

Assembly

1.Attach Rear Housing to Special Tool and Fix Special Tool to a Vice.

2.Install Spring and Flow Control Valve.

* Be sure the letter inscribed on the flow control valve matches the letter stamped on the rear of the pump body.

Inscribed mark: A, B, C, D, E or F

3.Install Pressure Port Union. Install and torque the union.

Ensure Letter Mark is the same on Flow Control Valve & Pump body.

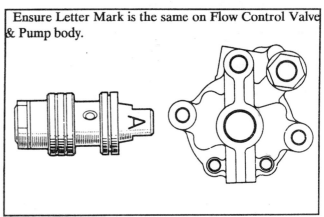

Torque: 700 kg-cm (51 ft-lb, 69 N·m)

4.Install Flow Control Spring Seat.

(a) Temporarily install a suitable bolt to the spring seat.

(b) Push in the bolt and install the snap ring with snap ring pliers.

(c) Remove the bolt.

5.Install Fixed Ring.

(a) Install the side plate to the rear housing.

(b) Install the O-ring to the rear housing.

(c) Align the marks on the fixed ring and rear housing.

(d) Temporarily install the 3 bolts.

(e) Using a plastic hammer, install the fixed ring.

(f) Remove the 3 bolts.

6.Install Rotor Shaft. Select a fixed ring, rotor shaft and slipper with matching code number.

Inscribed mark: 1, 2, 3, 4 or None

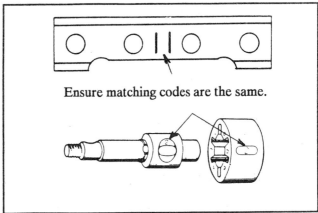

Ensure matching codes are the same.

7.Install Slipper, Spring and Spring Seat. Compress the spring with the slipper and spring seat and install it. Position the slipper notch in the direction illustrated.

8.Install Front Housing.

(a) Install the side plate to the front housing.

(b) Install the O-ring to the front housing.

(c) Align the marks on the fixed ring and front housing.

(d) Temporarily install the 5 bolts.

9.Tighten 5 Housing Bolts. Evenly tighten the 5 housing bolts in several passes.

Torque: 470 kg-cm (34 ft-lb, 46 N·m)

10. Install Reservoir Tank.

(a) Install the O-ring to the reservoir tank.

(b) Install the reservoir tank and torque the 3 bolts.

Torque:

Front Housing Side: 470 kg-cm (34 ft-lb, 46 N·m)

Rear Housing Side: 130 kg-cm (9 ft-lb, 13 N·m)

11. Check Rotor Shaft Rotation Condition.

(a) Check that the rotor shaft rotates smoothly without abnormal noise.

(b) Provisionally install the pulley nut and check the rotating torque.

Rotating torque:

2.5 kg-cm or less (2.2 in-lb, 0.3 ˙m)

Installation

1. Install PS Pump.

(a) **[3F Engine]** Place the PS pump in position and install mount bolts.

˙(b) **[3B, 13B-T, 2H AND 12H-T Engines]** Place the PS pump in position and torque mount bolts.

Torque:

[3B & 13B-T Engines] 375 kg-cm (27 ft-lb, 37 N·m)

[2H & 12B-T Engines] 400 kg-cm (29 ft-lb, 29 N·m)

2.Install Pulley and Drive Belt.

(a) Install the woodruff key, pulley and set nut.

(b) Install the drive belt.

(c) (i) **[3F Engine]** Adjust the drive belt tension and torque mount bolts.

Torque: 400 kg-cm (29 ft-lb, 39 N·m)

Drive belt tension - at 10 kg (22 lb, 98 N):

New belt: 7 - 9.5 mm (0.29 - 0.37 in)

Used belt: 8 - 10 mm (0.31 - 0.39 in)

(ii) **[3B, 13B-T, 2H & 12H-T Engines]** Turn the adjust bolt until the belt tension is the specified value.

Drive belt tension - at 10 kg (22 lb, 98 N):

[3B, 13B-T Engine]

New belt: 13 - 17 mm (0.51 - 0.67 in)

Used belt: 16 - 22 mm (0.63 - 0.87 in)

[2H, 12H-T Engine]

New belt: 6.5 - 8.5 mm (0.26 - 0.33 in)

Used belt: 7.0 - 9.0 mm (0.28 - 0.35 in)

* "New belt" refers to a new belt which has never been used.

* "Used belt" refers to a belt which has been used on a running engine for 5 minutes or more.

(d) **[3B, 13B-T, 2H & 12H-T Engines]** Tighten the idler pulley nut and adjust bolt.

(e) Push down on the drive belt to hold the pulley in place and torque the pulley set nut.

Torque:

[3B & 13B-T Engines]

440 kg-cm (32 ft-lb, 43 N·m)

[3F, 2H & 12H-T Engines]

480 kg-cm (35 ft-lb, 47 N·m)

3.Connect Return Hose to Reservoir Tank.

4.Connect Pressure Tube to Power Steering Pump. Torque the flare nut.

Torque: 450 kg-cm (33 ft-lb, 44 N·m)

5.Fill Reservoir with Fluid.

Fluid: ATF DEXRON^R or DEXRON^R II

6.Bleed Power Steering.

7.Check for Fluid Leaks.

POWER STEERING PUMP - RJ70 & LJ70 SERIES

Components

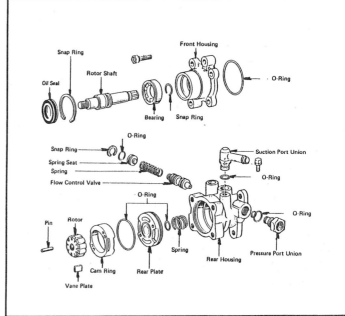

Inspection

1.Inspect Bushing and Measure Bushing Oil Clearance.

(a) Check the bushing for wear or damage. The bushing cannot be replaced separately. If wear or damage is found, replace entire housing.

(b) Check the oil clearance between the bushing and rotor shaft.

Maximum oil clearance: 0.07 mm (0.0028 in)

2.If Necessary, Replace Rotor Shaft Bearing.

3.Inspect Rotor and Cam Ring. Measure the cam ring clearance.

Maximum clearance: 0.06 mm (0.0024 in)

If the difference is excessive, replace the cam ring with one having the same figure as on the rotor.

4.Inspect and Measure Vane Plates.

(a) Check the vane plates for wear or scratches.

(b) Measure the length, height and thickness of the vane plate.

Minimum length: 14.97 mm (0.5894 in)
Minimum height: 7.8 mm (0.307 in)
Minimum thickness: 1.7 mm (0.067 in)

(c) Measure the clearance between the vane plate and rotor groove.

Maximum clearance: 0.06 mm (0.0024 in)

* There are 5 lengths with the following rotor and cam ring numbers:

Rotor & Cam

Ring Number	Vane length mm (in)
None	14.996 - 14.998 (0.5904 - 0.5905)
1	14.994 - 14.996 (0.5903 - 0.5904)
2	14.992 - 14.994 (0.5902 - 0.5903)
3	14.990 - 14.992 (0.59016 - 0.59024)
4	14.998 - 14.990 (0.5901 - 0.5902)

5.Inspect Flow Control Valve.

(a) Check the flow control valve for wear or damage.

(b) Apply fluid to the valve and check that it falls smoothly into the valve hole by its own weight.

(c) Check the flow control valve for leakage:

- Close one of the holes and apply compressed air [4 or 5 kg-cm^2 (57 or 71 psi, 392 or 490 kPa] into the opposite side.

- Confirm that air dies not come out from the end hole.

If necessary, replace the valve with one having the same letter on the rear housing.

6.Inspect Flow Control Valve Spring. Check that the spring is within specification.

Spring length: 47 - 50 mm (1.85 - 1.97 in)

If the spring is not within specification, replace it.

7.If Necessary, Replace Union Seat.

* Only floating type parts are available.

POWER STEERING GEAR

Components (see next page)

Dismantle

1.Remove Pitman Arm.

2.Remove End Cover.

(a) Remove the adjusting screw lock nut.

(b) Remove the 4 bolts.

(c) Screw in the adjusting screw until the cover is removed.

3.Remove Cross Shaft. Using a plastic hammer, tap on the cross shaft end and pull out the shaft.

4.Remove Worm Gear Valve Body Assembly.

(a) Remove the 4 cap screws from the housing.

(b) Hold the power piston nut with your thumb so it cannot move and turn the worm shaft clockwise. Then withdraw the valve body and power piston assembly.

* Ensure that the power piston nut does not come off the worm shaft.

(c) Remove the O-ring.

6.Remove Lock Nut.

(a) Using special tool, hold the adjusting screw and remove the lock nut with special tool.

(b) Using special tool, remove the adjusting screw.

(c) Remove the bearing.

7.Remove O-Ring.

8.Remove Following Parts: 1) worm shaft, 2) thrust bearing, 3) plate washer, 4) teflon ring, 5) O-ring.

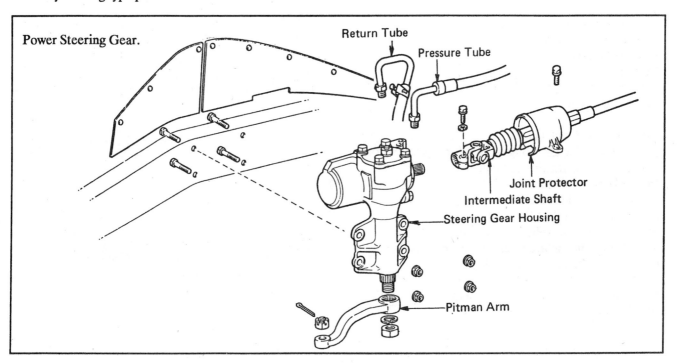

Power Steering Gear.

Return Tube
Pressure Tube
Joint Protector
Intermediate Shaft
Steering Gear Housing
Pitman Arm

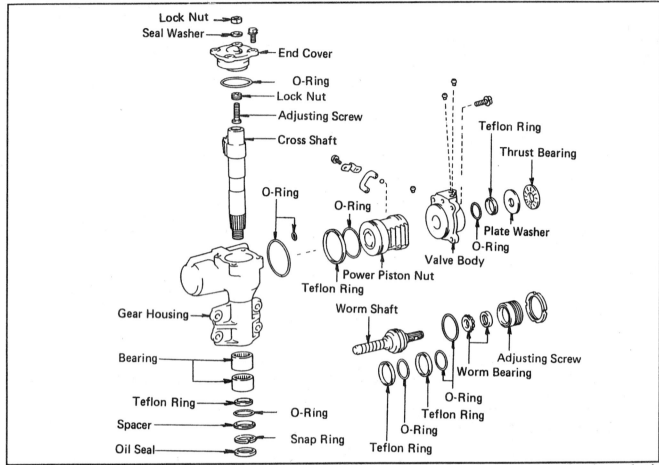

Inspection and Repair

1.Inspect Cross Shaft Adjusting Screw Thrust Clearance.

(a) Clamp the cross shaft in a vice.

(b) Using a dial indicator, measure the thrust clearance.

Thrust clearance:

0.03 - 0.05 mm (0.0012 - 0.0020 in)

If thrust clearance is not correct, adjust the thrust clearance.

2.If Necessary, Adjust Thrust Clearance.

(a) Using a chisel and hammer, remove the lock nut stake.

(b) Loosen the lock nut.

(c) Adjust the adjusting screw for correct thrust clearance and tighten the lock nut.

(d) Stake the lock nut.

3.Replace Needle Roller Bearings.

(a) Remove the oil seal.

(b) Using snap ring pliers, remove the snap ring.

(c) Remove the metal spacer, teflon ring and O-ring.

(d) Press out the bearing.

(e) Press in the upper bearing.

* The bearing top end should be installed so that it aligns with the upper end of the housing hole.

(f) Using special tool, install the lower bearing so that it is positioned 23.1 mm (0.909 in) away from the lower end of the housing hole.

(g) Install the O-ring.

(h) Form the teflon ring into a heart shape and install it with your finger.

(i) Install the metal spacer.

(j) Using snap ring pliers, install the snap ring.

(k) Form the teflon ring.

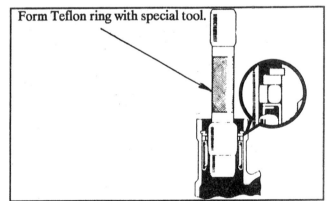

Form Teflon ring with special tool.

(l) Drive in the oil seal.

4.If Necessary, Replace Adjusting Screw Oil Seal.

5.If Necessary, Replace Control Valve Teflon Ring.

* Be careful not to damage the control valve.

Assembly

1. Coat All Parts with Power Steering Fluid.
2. Mount Valve Body in Vice.
3. Install O-Ring and Teflon Ring.
4. Install Worm Shaft with the Thrust Bearing and the Plate Washer to the Valve Body.

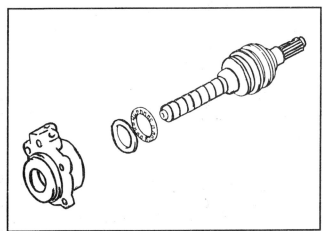

5. Install O-Ring and Bearing to Control Valve.
6. Install Adjusting Screw and Lock Nut. Using special tool, temporarily tighten the adjusting screw and lock nut.
7. Install Power Piston Nut and Balls.

(a) Clean all parts with power steering fluid.

(b) Insert the power piston nut about 15 mm (0.59 in) from the worm shaft end, and align the ball transfer surface with the ball hole.

(c) Insert the balls one at a time into the holes, and turn the worm shaft a little with each insertion. Then securely insert the 33 balls into the piston.

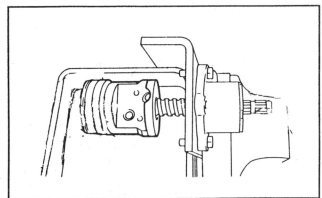

(d) Install 11 new balls to the ball guide and apply MP grease to the ball guide lips so the balls do not fall out.

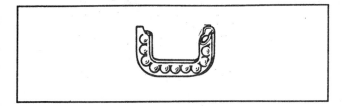

(e) Install the ball guide to the power piston nut.

* Be careful not to damage the ball guide.

(f) Using special tool, install the ball guide clamp.

Torque: 30 kg-cm (26 in-lb, 2.9 N·m)

(g) Check that the power piston nut rotates smoothly.

(h) Turn the power piston nut, and ensure that it is fixed to the tip of the valve body.

* If a ball has fallen out, there will be a gap.

8. Install Worm Gear Valve Body Assembly.

(a) Install the 2 O-rings to the gear housing and valve body.

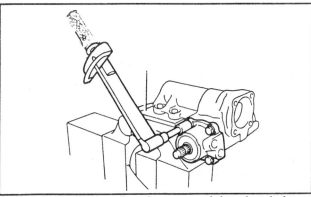

(b) Mount the gear housing on special tool and clamp special tool in vice.

(c) Install and torque the 4 bolts.

Torque: 470 kg-cm (34 ft-lb, 46 N·m)

9. Adjust Worm Bearing Preload.

(a) Remove the lock nut.

(b) Using special tool, tighten the adjusting screw.

(c) Turn the worm shaft to right and left and snug down the bearing.

(d) Slightly loosen the adjusting screw.

(e) Using special tool, slightly tighten the adjusting screw until the preload is correct.

(f) Using special tool and a torque meter, check the preload of the bearing.

Preload:

4.0 - 6.5 kg-cm (3.5 - 5.6 in-lb, 0.4 - 0.6 N·m)

* Hold the power piston nut to prevent it from turning.

(g) Torque the lock nut while holding the adjusting screw with special tool.

Torque: 500 kg-cm (36 ft-lb, 49 N·m)

(h) Recheck the preload.

10. Install Cross Shaft and End Cover.

(a) Install the O-ring on the end cover.

(b) Set the worm gear at the centre of the gear housing.

(c) Insert and push the cross shaft into the gear housing so that the centre teeth mesh.

(d) Fully loosen the adjusting screw and install the end cover with four bolts.

Torque: 470 kg-cm (34 ft-lb, 46 N·m)

11. Adjust Total Preload.

(a) Match the alignment mark on the pitman arm and cross shaft, and install them.

(b) Install and torque the pitman arm set nut.

Torque: 1,800 kg-cm (130 ft-lb, 177 N·m)

(c) Turn the pitman arm until the alignment mark is horizontal.

(d) Tighten the adjusting screw until the backlash is zero.

(e) While measuring the preload, tighten the adjusting screw until the preload is correct.

Total preload:

6.0 - 9.5 kg-cm (5.2 - 8.2 in-lb, 0.6 - 0.9 N·m)

* Be sure that the worm shaft is in the neutral position.

(f) While holding the adjusting screw, install and torque the lock nut.

Torque: 470 kg-cm (34 ft-lb, 46 N·m)

(g) Recheck the total preload.

12. Stake Lock Nut. Using a punch and hammer, stake the lock nut.

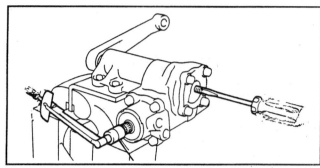

STEERING LINKAGE

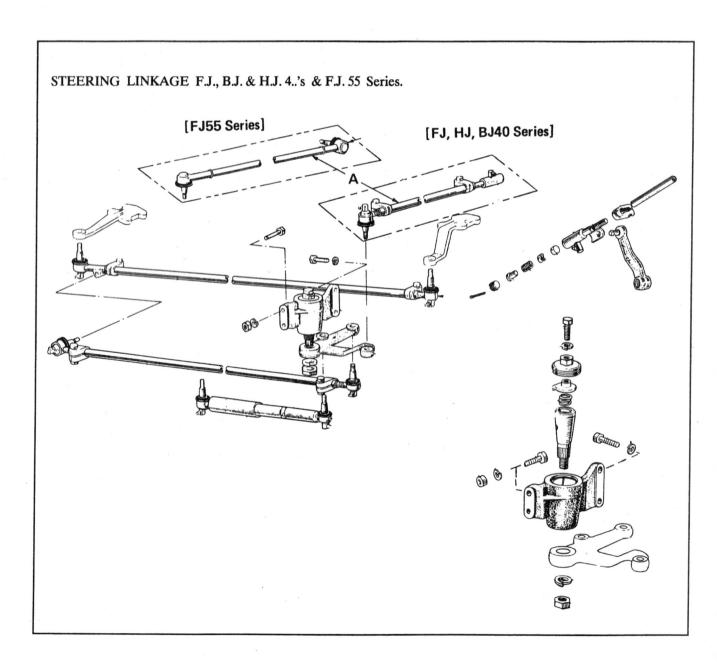

STEERING LINKAGE F.J., B.J. & H.J. 4..'s & F.J. 55 Series.

[FJ55 Series]

[FJ, HJ, BJ40 Series]

A

STEERING LINKAGE F.J., B.J. & H.J. 6..'s & 7..'s Series.

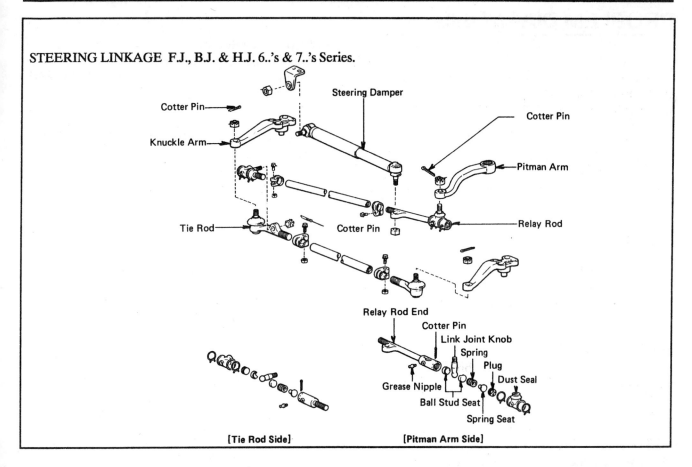

[Tie Rod Side]   [Pitman Arm Side]

STEERING LINKAGE R.J. & L.J. 7..'s Series.

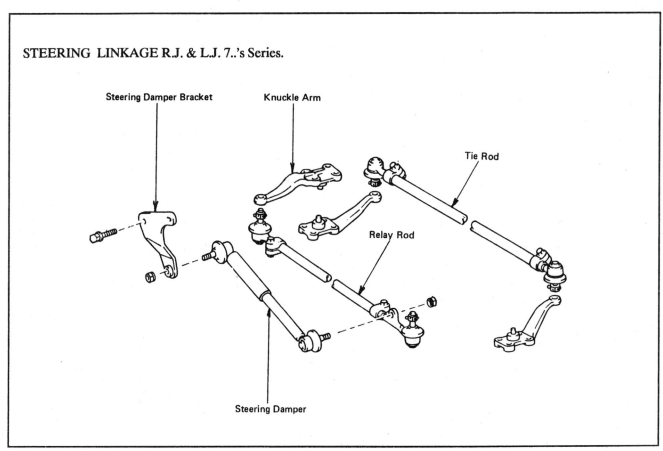

PROBLEM DIAGNOSIS

* Care must be taken to replace parts properly because they could affect the performance of the steering system and result in a driving hazard.

Problem: Hard steering!

Possible Causes and Remedies:

* Tyres improperly inflated. Remedy - inflate tyres to proper pressure.

* Excessive caster. Remedy - check front end alignment.

* Ball joints worn. Remedy - replace ball joints.

* Steering knuckle bearing worn. Remedy - replace knuckle bearing.

* Insufficient lubricant. Remedy - lubricate suspension and steering linkage.

* Steering linkage worn or bent. Remedy - check linkage.

* Steering gear out of adjustment or broken. Remedy - adjust or repair steering gear.

* Power steering belt loose. Remedy - tighten belt.

* Fluid level in reservoir low. Remedy - check reservoir.

* Power steering fluid foaming. Remedy - check power steering fluid.

* Power steering unit faulty. Remedy - check power steering unit.

* Steering column binding. Remedy - check steering column.

Problem: Poor return!

Possible Causes and Remedies:

* Tyre improperly inflated. Remedy - inflate tyres to proper pressure.

* Wheel alignment incorrect. Remedy - check front end alignment.

* Steering column binding. Remedy - check steering column.

* Insufficient lubricant. Remedy - lubricate suspension and steering linkage.

* Steering gear out of adjustment or broken. Remedy - adjust or repair steering gear.

Problem: Excessive play!

Possible Causes and Remedies:

* Steering linkage worn. Remedy - check linkage.

* Steering gear loose. Remedy - tighten gear bolts.

* Steering shaft coupling worn. Remedy - inspect coupling.

* Ball joints worn. Remedy - replace ball joint.

* Steering knuckle bearing worn. Remedy - replace knuckle bearing.

* Steering gear out of adjustment or broken. Remedy - adjust or repair steering gear.

BODY

BODY

FRAMES

FJ 40 , BJ 40 & 42 Series.

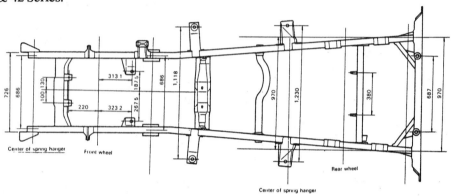

FJ 43, BJ 43 Series.

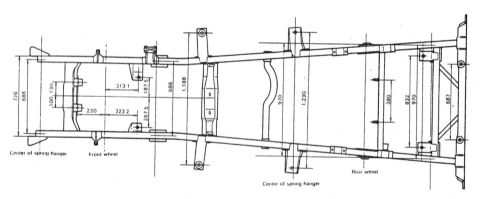

FJ 45, HJ 45, HJ 47 Series.

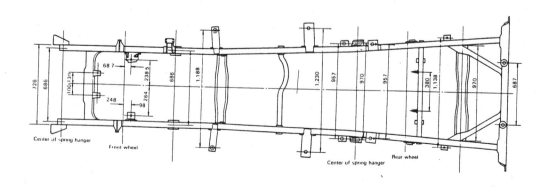

FJ 55.

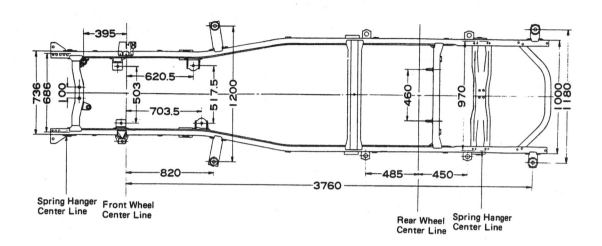

FJ, BJ, HJ 6...'s Series.

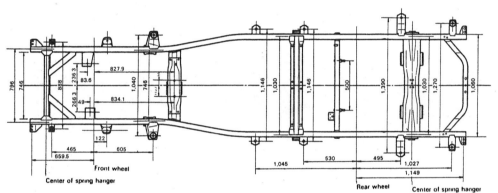

FJ, BJ 70 Series.

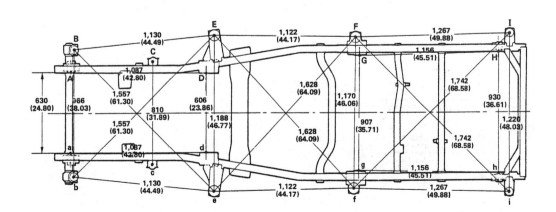

FJ, BJ 73 Series.

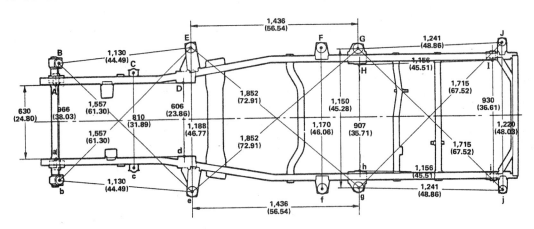

FJ, BJ, HJ 75P Series.

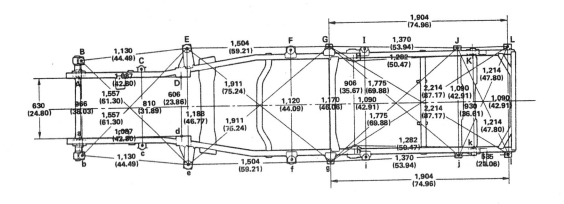

FJ 62 Series.

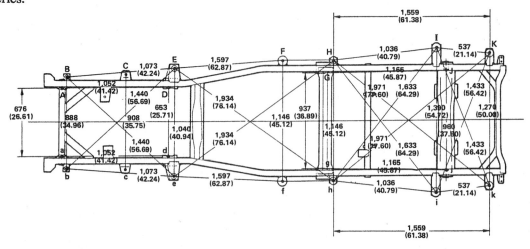

RJ, LJ 70 Series.

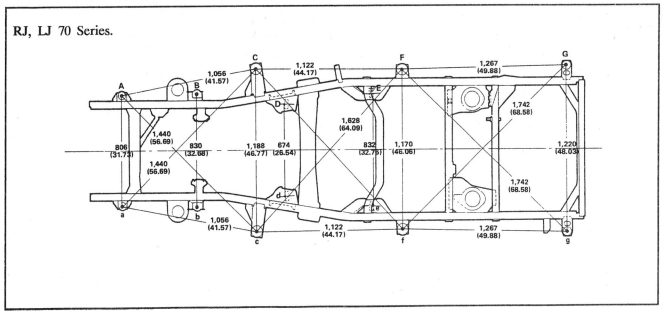

FJ, BJ 4..ˢ SERIES

HOOD

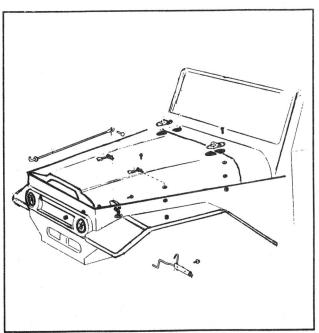

Adjustment

1. Adjust the hood in front-rear direction by loosening the nuts at the hood.

2. Hood Auxiliary Catch Hook. If the catch hook does not latch on properly, correct by bending the stopper.

DOOR

Removal

Door Window Glass Regulator, and Glass Run. Remove in the following order:

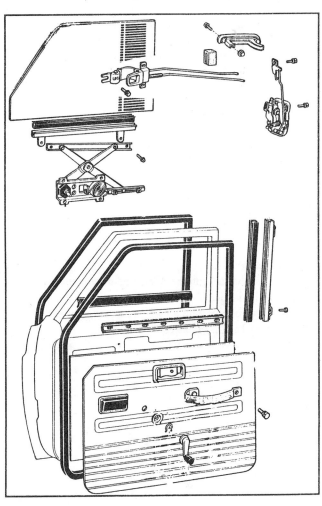

1.Regulator Handle.

2.Pull Handle.

3.Remove the Bezel.

(a) Remove the screws.

(b) Remove in the following order:

 (i) Pull out the rear end.

 (ii) Pull the bezel toward the rear.

 (iii) Remove by pulling out the front end.

4.Trim Board.

5.Service Hole Cover.

6.Remove the Glass Run Rear Channel.

7.Window Glass. Remove the glass:

(a) Remove the bolts.

(b) Remove the glass with the glass holder.

8.Remove the Window Regulator.

(a) Remove the bolts.

(b) Take out the regulator.

9.Remove the Glass Run.

Adjustment

1.Adjust the Door in Front/Rear and Vertical Directions by Loosening the Door Hinges at the Door.

2.Adjust the Gap between the Fender and the Door by loosening the Door Hinges at the Body.

3.Adjust the Door Lock by Aligning the Door Lock Striker.

4.Adjust the Window Glass Tilt as Shown.

5.Adjust Door Outside Handle Play as Shown.

6.Adjust the Door Inside Handle Play as Shown.

7.Adjust the Door Lock as Shown.

REAR DOOR

Removal

1.Tail Gate Lock and Handle.

(a) Remove the tail gate handle by removing the mounting nuts on the inside of the tail gate.

(b) Remove the tail gate lock by removing the screws.

2.Back Door Inside Handle.

(a) Pull out the lock pin with a wire or other means and take off the handle.

Installation

Reverse REMOVAL procedure.

* Install the back door inside handle with the slot in handle seat (shown by arrow) positioned upward.

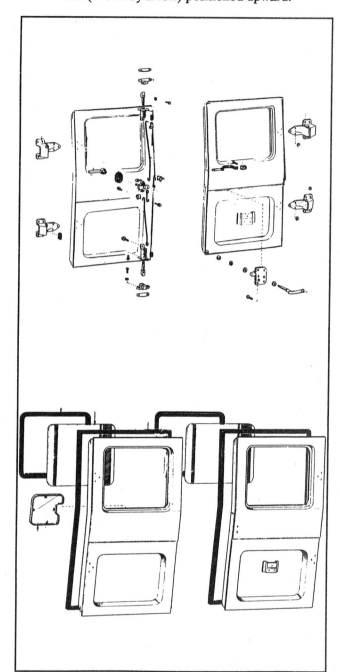

Adjustment

1.Adjust the door alignment by shifting the positions of the door hinges at the body.

2.Adjust the door closing action:

(a) Right side door.

(b) Left side door.

3.Adjust the inside handle play.

FJ 55 SERIES

HOOD

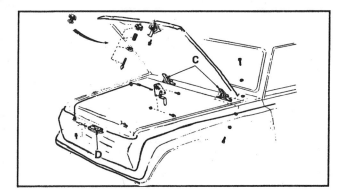

Adjustment

1.Hood.

(a) Adjust the hood in front-rear direction by loosening the bolts attaching the hood to the hood hinges.

(b) Adjust the hood in lateral direction by loosening the bolts attaching the hood hinges to the body.

2.Hood Lock.

(a) If the hood lock dowel and hood lock are out of alignment with each other, correct by loosening the mounting bolts.

(b) If the hood is loose in vertical direction, or the hood lock does not catch properly, correct by adjusting the hood lock hook.

3.Hood Auxiliary Catch Hook. If the catch hook does not latch on properly, correct by loosening the bolts.

FRONT DOOR

Removal

1.Door Window Glass and Regulator. Remove in the following order:

1)Inside Handle Bezel.

2)Arm Rest.

3)Regulator Handle.

4)Door Trim.

5)Service Hole Cover.

6)Window Glass.

(a) Remove the 2 bolts attaching the glass channel.

(b) Pull out the window glass (with the glass channel attached) toward the top.

7)Glass Weatherstrip.

8)Window Regulator.

(a) Remove the bolts attaching the window regulator.

(b) Take out the window regulator through the service hole.

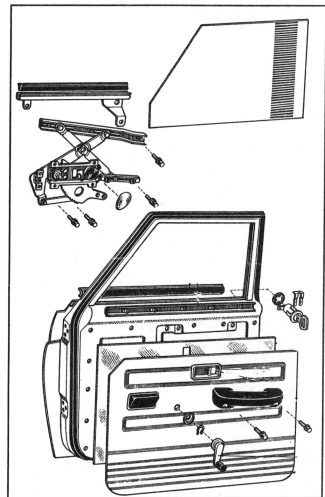

Inspection

1.Window Regulator. Check the regulator to see if properly lubricated, and apply grease if found insufficient.

2.Door Lock. Grease the frictional surfaces of the door lock.

Adjustment of Door

1. Adjust the door in front-rear direction by loosening the bolts attaching the door to the door hinges.

2.Correct surface difference with fender by loosening the bolts attaching the door hinges to the body.

3.If the door does not close properly, correct by adjusting the door lock striker.

4.Adjust the window glass tilt.

5.Adjust the outside door handle play.

6.Adjust the inside door handle play.

REAR DOOR

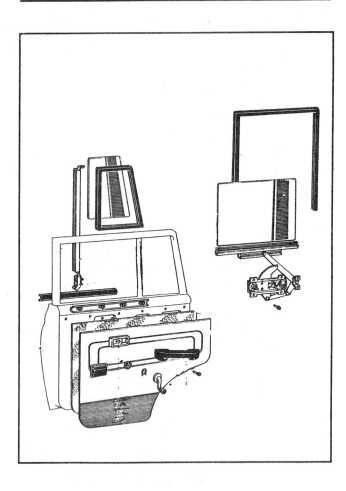

Removal of Window Glass & Quarter Window Glass.

Remove in the following order:

1.Arm Rest.

2.Regulator Handle.

3.Bezel.

4.Trim Board.

5.Service Hole Cover.

6.Division Bar Support. Remove the division bar support by loosening the 3 attaching bolts.

7.Window Regulator. Remove the 2 bolts attaching the window regulator and disconnect the roller from the glass channel.

8.Division Bar. Remove the division bar by loosening the 2 screws from upper part of door.

9.Window Glass. Remove the window glass.

10. Quarter Window Glass. Remove the quarter window glass after shifting it to the centre.

WINDSCREEN

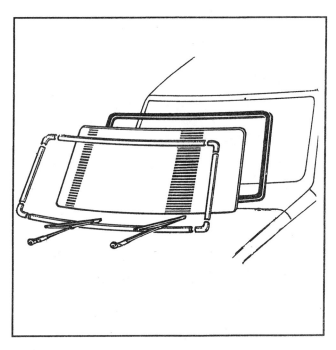

Removal of Glass

Remove in the following order:

1.Wiper Arm.

2.Windscreen Moulding. Remove the moulding with a screwdriver or similar tool.

3.Inner Rear View Mirror.

4.Windscreen Glass.

(a) Using a screwdriver, remove the adhesive attaching the weatherstrip to the body.

(b) From inside the car, push out the weatherstrip (upper side toward the outside) with a screwdriver.

(c) Push the glass surface near the upper side of the weatherstrip toward the outside and remove the glass with the weatherstrip attached.

* Apply force uniformly on the glass when pushing it out.

5.Windscreen Weatherstrip.

TAIL GATE

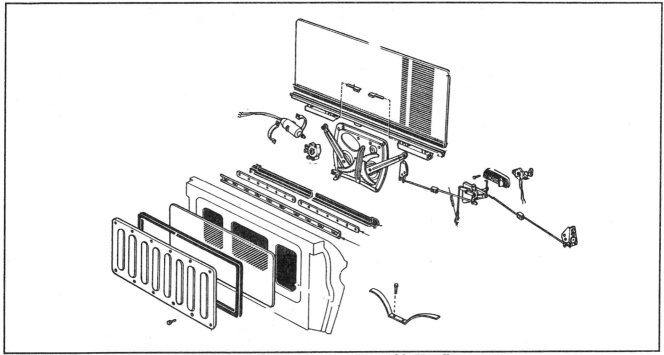

13.Outside Handle.

Removal of Tail Gate Glass, Regulator & Tail Gate Lock

Remove in the following order:

1.Back Door Trim Board.
2.Service Hole Cover.
3.Stopper Plate.
(a) Press the safety switch when taking out the glass.
(b) After lifting out the glass about half way, remove the stopper plate.
4.Roller Hinge. Remove the roller hinge from the glass holder.
5.Glass Damper. Remove the glass damper and have the glass all the way down.
6.Weatherstrip. Remove the inner and outer weatherstrips and take out the glass.
7.Tail Gate Glass.
8.Regulator Motor Wire harness. Disconnect the wire harness.
* Have the battery fusible link disconnected beforehand.
9.Lock Off Lever Connecting Rod. Disconnect the connecting rod and spring from the lock off lever.
10.Tail Gate Regulator.
(a) Remove the 4 bolts.
(b) Remove the regulator.
11.Tail Gate Lock.
12.Tail Gate Control Switch.

Adjustment

1.In case the parts pertaining to the tail gate lock had been removed, pull the tail gate handle and verify that the tail gate lock turns freely. If the tail gate lock does not turn freely, correct by adjusting the length of the connecting rod.
2.In case the parts pertaining to the regulator had been removed, verify the lock off lever operation.
(a) With the glass lowered all the way down, pulling the tail gate should allow the tail gate lock to turn freely.
(b) At conditions other than above, the tail gate handle should be such that it cannot be pulled.

Removal of Tail Gate Assembly, Hinge and Torsion Bar

1.Remove the tail gate glass.
2.Disconnect the battery fusible link, and disconnect the wire harness.
3.Remove in the following order:
1)Torsion Bar Adjust Bolt Cover.
2)Completely Loosen the Torsion Bar Adjust Bolt.
3)Tail Gate Hinge.
(a) Among the screws attaching the hinges to the tail gate, remove one screw (at lower side).

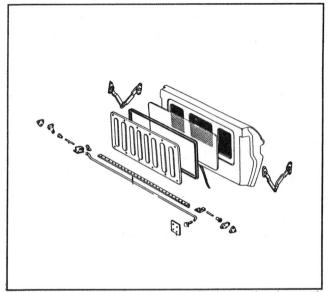

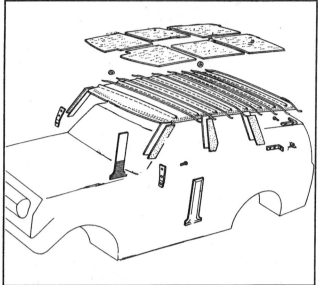

(b) Insert piece of wood between the torsion bar and body.

* Insert the piece of wood securely.

(c) While holding up the tail gate, remove the screws attaching the hinges to the body.

4)Remove the Tail Gate Support Stay from the tail gate and take off the tail gate.

5)Tail Gate Hinge. Remove the hinges from the body.

6)Torsion Bar Cover. Remove the torsion cover and pull out the torsion bar.

7)Torsion Bar.

Installation

Reverse the REMOVAL Procedure.

* When attaching the tail gate to the hinges, insert a piece of wood between the torsion bar and body.

Adjustment

1.Adjust the tail gate alignment and its closing action.
2.Adjust the tail gate support stay.
3.Adjust the torsion bar.

ROOF LINING

Removal

Remove in the following order:

1.Windscreen Glass.
2.Sun Visor.
3.Seat Belt Anchor.
4.Assist Grip.
5.Interior Light.
6.Door Opening Trim and Weatherstrip. Remove the door opening trim and weatherstrip at the parts attached to the roof lining.

(a) Remove the door opening.
(b) Remove the opening trim retainer.
7.Back Door Glass Weatherstrip.
8.Side Window Glass.
9.Centre Pillar Garnish Panel. Peel off the centre pillar garnish just enough to allow removing the headlining.
10.Headlining Front Side Garnish.
11.Headlining Rear Side Garnish.
12.Instrument Panel Outside Garnish.
13.Headlining.
(a) Peel off the adhered part of the headlining.
(b) Remove the headlining supports, starting from the front side.
14.Headlining Support.
15.Pillar Garnish Pad.
16.Roof Silencer Pad.

Installation

Reverse the REMOVAL Procedure.

* If there are any wrinkles after installing the headlining, heating about one-half to one minute with infra-red light or similar means will help remove the wrinkles.

FJ, BJ, HJ 6..ˢ SERIES

HOOD

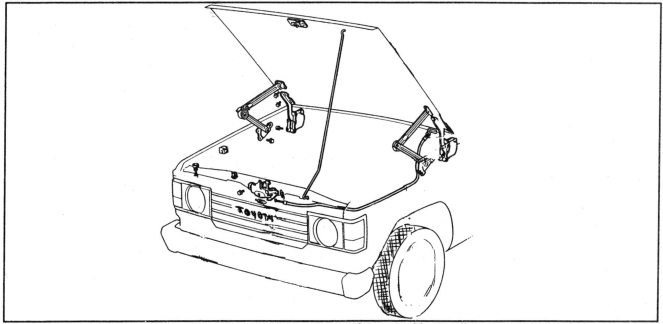

Adjustment

1.Loosen the 3 bolts and move the hood lock horizontally or vertically to adjust the hood.

2.Adjust so that the left and right clearances between the fender and hood are equal.

3.Adjust so that the heights of the fender and hood are equal.

FRONT DOOR

Door Trim and Service Hole Cover

Removal

1.Lower the door glass to full down position.
2.Remove the parts in the following order:
1)Window Regulator Handle.
2)Armrest or Pull Handle.
3)Door Inside Handle Bezel.
4)Door Trim Board.
5)Door Inside Handle.
6)Service Hole Cover.
7)Door.

3.Before removing the handle, pull off the snap ring with a piece of cloth and remove the window regulator handle.

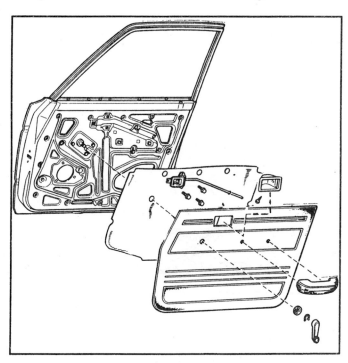

4.Insert a screwdriver between the door panel and retainers and pry out.

* Tape the screwdriver tip before use.

5.Disconnect the control link and remove the inside handle.

Installation

Install the parts in the following order:

1.Door.

2.Service Hole Cover.

(a) Seal the service hole cover with adhesive.

(b) Insert the lower edge of the service hole cover into the panel slit.

(c) Seal the service hole cover with cotton-covered tape.

* Do not block the trim board clip seating with the tape.

3.Door Inside Handle. Adjust the link play.

(a) Loosen the screws.

(b) Move the handle forward to the point where strong resistance is felt.

(c) Move handle back 0.5 - 1.0 mm (0.020 - 0.029 in) and tighten.

4.Door Trim Board.

5.Door Inside Handle Bezel.

6.Armrest or Pull Handle.

7.Window Regulator Handle.

(a) Raise the window to the fully closed position.

(b) Install the door inside handle as illustrated.

DOOR GLASS

Without Vent Window

With Vent Window.

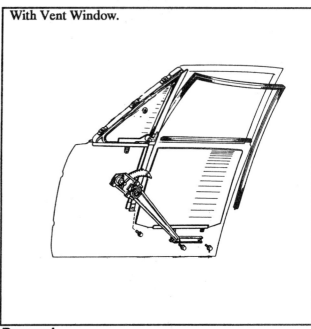

Removal

1.Remove the door trim and service hole cover as described in FRONT DOOR TRIM Section.

2.Remove the parts in the following order:

[without ventilator window]

1)Weatherstrip.

2)Channel Mounting Bolt.

3)Glass and Channel. Pull the glass upward to remove.

[with ventilator window]

1)Glass Run.

2)Division Bar.

3)Vent Window.

(a) Remove the bolt.

(b) Take out the ventilator window.

  (i) Pull up the ventilator window.

  (ii) Turn the ventilator window to the left.

4)Channel Mounting Bolt.

5)Glass and Channel. Pull the glass upward to remove.

Installation

1.Install the parts in the following order:

[without ventilator window]

1)Glass and Channel. With the door glass in position as illustrated, tighten the equaliser arm bracket.

2)Channel Mounting Bolt.

3)Weatherstrip.

[with ventilator window]

1)Glass and Channel. With the door glass in position as illustrated, tighten the equaliser arm bracket.

2)Channel Mounting Bolt.

3)Ventilator Window.

4)Division Bar.

5)Glass Run.

2.Install the service hole cover and door trim as described in FRONT DOOR TRIM Section.

WINDOW REGULATOR

Removal

1.Remove the door trim and service hole cover.
2.Remove the parts in the following order:
[without ventilator window]
1)Window Regulator Set Bolt.
2)Window Regulator. Remove the window regulator through the service hole.
[with ventilator window]
1)Window Regulator Set Bolt.
2)Window Regulator. Remove the window regulator through the service hole.

Inspection

Check the following:

1.Gears for wear or damage.
2.Spring for deterioration or breaks.
3.Lubrication of regulator sliding parts.

Installation

1.Install the parts in the following order:
[without ventilator window]
1)Window Regulator.
2)Window Regulator Set bolt.
[with ventilator window]
1)Window Regulator.
2)Window Regulator Set Bolt.
2.Install the service hole cover and door trim.

DOOR LOCK

Removal

1.Remove the door trim and service hole cover.
2.Remove the parts in the following order:
1)Door Inside Handle.
2)Door Glass Rail.

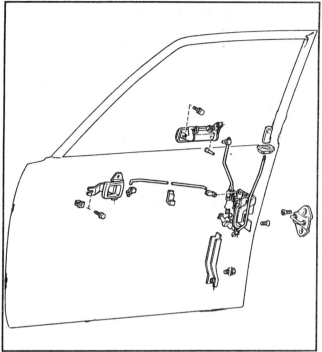

3)Door Lock through the Service Hole.
4)Door Inside Lock Button.
5)Door Outside Handle.
6)Door Lock Striker.

Inspection

1.Operation of moving parts.
2.Lubricate sliding parts of door lock with MP grease.

Installation

1.Install the parts in the following order:
1)Door Lock Striker.
2)Door Outside Handle.
3)Door Inside Lock Button.
4)Door Lock.
5)Door Glass Rail.
6)Door Inside Handle.
2.Install the service hole cover and door trim as described in FRONT DOOR TRIM Section.

Adjustment

1.Inside Handle.
 (a) Loosen the screws.
 (b) Move the handle forward to the point where strong resistance is felt.
 (c) Move handle back 0.5 - 1.0 mm (0.020 - 0.039 in) and tighten.

2.Outside Handle.

(a) Check the outside handle play.

Control link play: 0.5 - 1.0 mm (0.020 - 0.039 in)

(b) Adjust the control link play to within 0.5 - 1.0 mm (0.020 - 0.039 in).

3.Door Lock Striker. Open and close the door by the outside handle and adjust so that the door lock does not contact the striker.

DOOR HINGE

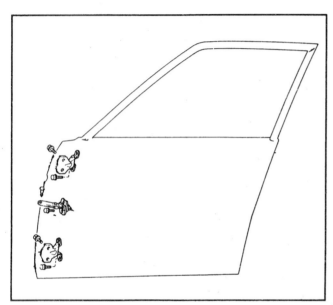

Removal

Remove the parts in the following order:

1)Door Check Pin. Push in the claw and pull up the pin.

* After removal, leave the claw raised.

2)Door Check.

3)Door Hinge.

4)Door Hinge Set Bolt.

5)Door Panel. Place a wooden block and cloth under the door panel and support it with a jack.

Installation

Install the parts in the following order:

1)Door Panel.

2)Door Panel Set Bolt.

3)Door Hinge.

4)Door Check.

5)Door Check Pin.

Adjustment

1.Loosen the body hinge bolts with special tool and adjust the door forward-backward and up-down positions.

2.Loosen the door hinge bolts and adjust the left-right and up-down positions of the door.

REAR DOOR

Door Trim

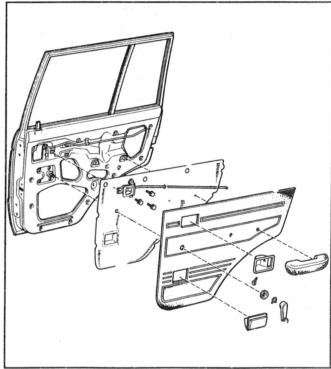

Removal

Remove the parts in the following order:

1.Window Regulator Handle. Before removing the handle, pull off the snap ring with a cloth and remove the window regulator needle.

2.Armrest or Pull Handle.

3.Door Inside Handle Bezel.

4.Door Trim Board. Insert a screwdriver between the panel and panel retainers and pry out.

5.Door Inside Handle.

(a) Disconnect the link.

(b) Remove the handle.

6.Service Hole Cover.

Installation

Install the parts in the following order:

1.Service Hole Cover.

(a) Seal the service hole cover with adhesive.

(b) Insert the lower edge of the service hole cover into the panel slit.

(c) Seal the service hole cover with cotton-covered tape.

* Do not block the trim board clip seating with the tape.

2.Door Inside Handle. Adjust the link play.

(a) Loosen the screws.

(b) Move the handle forward to the point where strong resistance is felt.

(c) Move handle back 0.5 - 1.0 mm (0.020 - 0.039 in) and tighten.

3.Door Trim Board.

4.Door Inside Handle Bezel.

5.Armrest or Pull Handle.

6.Window Regulator Handle.

(a) Raise the window to the fully closed position.

(b) Install the inside door handle on a 45° angle leaning forward.

DOOR GLASS

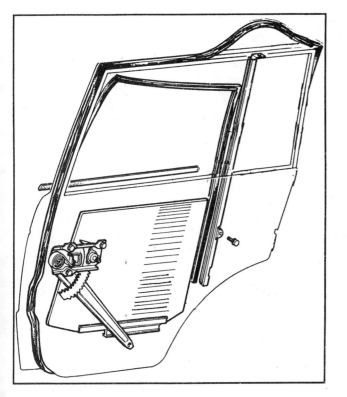

Removal

1.Remove the door trim and service hole cover.

2.Remove the parts in the following order:

1)Weatherstrip.

2)Division Bar and Set Screw. Remove the division bar and glass run.

3)Glass Run.

4)Door Glass.

(a) Remove the door glass from the regulator roller.

(b) Pull the glass upward to remove.

Replacement

1.Remove the glass channel from the glass with a screwdriver.

2.Apply soapy water to weatherstrip.

3.Install the new glass by tapping it with a plastic hammer.

Installation

Reverse REMOVAL procedure.

QUARTER WINDOW GLASS

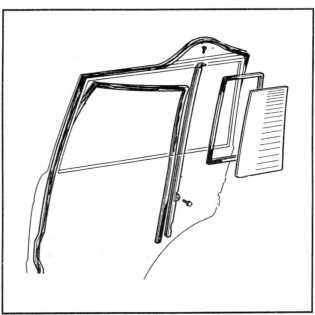

Removal

1.Remove the door trim, service hole cover and door glass.

2.Remove the parts in the following order:

1)Set Screw.
2)Set Bolt.
3)Division Bar. Remove the glass run and the division bar.
4)Quarter Glass Weatherstrip.
5)Quarter Glass.

Installation

Reverse REMOVAL Procedure.

* Apply soapy water to the weatherstrip.

WINDOW REGULATOR

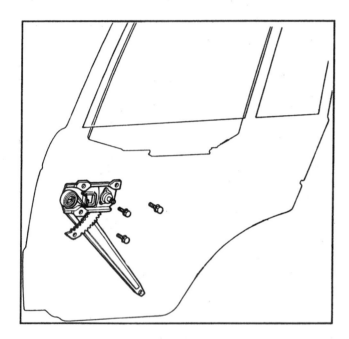

Removal

1.Remove the door trim and service hole cover.
2.Remove the parts in the following order:
1)Door Glass.
2)Set Bolt.
3)Window Regulator. After separating the glass from the regulator roller, raise the glass and remove the regulator from the service hole.

Inspection

Check the following:

1.Gears for wear or damage.

2.Spring for deterioration.
3.Other components for damage.
4.Lubrication of sliding parts.

Installation

1.Install the parts in the following order.
1)Regulator.
2)Set Bolt.
3)Door Glass.
(a) Raise the window to the fully closed position.
(b) Install the regulator handle in position as shown in the figure.
2.Install the service hole cover and door trim as described in INSTALLATION OF DOOR TRIM Section.

DOOR LOCK

Components

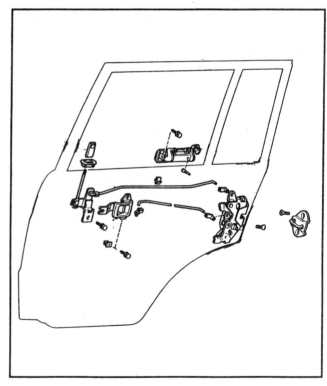

1.Door Inside Handle.
2.Door Lock.
3.Door Inside Lock Button.
4.Door Outside Handle.
5.Door Striker.

Inspection

1.Operation of moving parts.
2.Lubrication of lock sliding parts.

Adjustment

1.Inside Handle.
(a) Loosen the screws.
(b) Move the handle forward to the point where strong resistance is felt.
(c) Turn backward 0.5 - 1.0 mm (0.020 - 0.039 in) and tighten.
2.Outside Handle.
(a) Check the outside handle play.
Handle and lever gap: 0.5 - 1.0 mm (0.020 - 0.039 in)
(b) Set the outside handle and lever so that the gap between them is 0.5 - 1.0 mm (0.020 - 0.039 in).
3.Door Lock Striker. Open and close the door with the outside handle and ensure that the door lock does not contact the striker.

DOOR HINGE

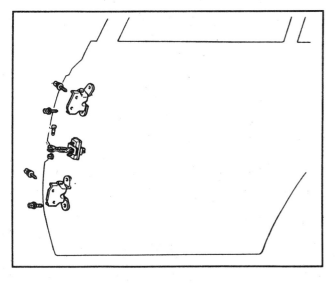

Removal

Remove parts in the following order:

1)Door Check Pin. Support door panel with jack wooden block.
2)Door Set Bolt.
3)Door Panel.
4)Hinge.

Installation

Reverse REMOVAL Procedure.

Adjustment

1.Adjust the door forward-backward and vertical directions by loosening the body side hinge bolts.
2.Adjust the door left-right and vertical directions by loosening the door side hinge bolts.

TAIL GATE [LIFT TYPE]

Components

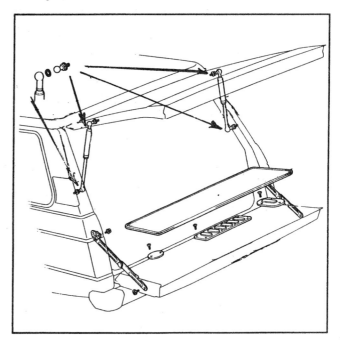

Damper Stay

Replacement

1.Remove the stud and stay together.
2.Remove the snap ring and separate the stud from the stay.
3.Install the stud.
* Apply MP grease to the stud.
4.First insert the snap ring and then tap with a plastic hammer.
5.If the damper is being replaced, drill a 2 - 3 mm (0.08 - 0.12 in) hole in the bottom of the removed damper cylinder to completely release the high pressure gas.

* The gas is colourless, odourless and not poisonous. However, when drilling, chips may fly out. Work carefully!

* Handling the back door damper:

- Do not dismantle the damper because the cylinder is filled with gas.

- When working, handle the damper carefully. Never score or scratch the exposed part of the piston rod and never allow paint or oil to adhere to it.

- Do not turn the piston rod and cylinder with the damper fully extended.

Tail Gate Stay

Check the following:
1. Spring for deterioration.
2. Other components for damage.
3. Lubrication of sliding parts.

Door Trim

Remove the clips by prying with a screwdriver.

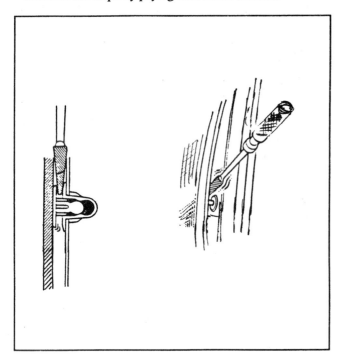

Components

1. Pull Handle.
2. Service Hole Cover.
3. Lock.
4. Lock Cylinder.
5. Protector or Pad.
6. Inside Handle.
7. Slide Block.
8. Striker.
9. Handle Lever.
10. Lock Knob.
11. Left Lock.
12. Right Lock.
13. Link Turn Block.
14. Striker.

Inspection

Lift Door Lock

1. Operation of moving parts.
2. Lubrication of lock sliding parts.

Gate Door Lock

1. Operation of moving parts.
2. Lubrication of lock sliding parts.
* Assemble the child protector lever in a free state.

Adjustment

Lower Gate Door Lock Striker

Open and close the door and adjust so that the door lock does not contact the striker.

Upper Lift Door Lock Striker

Open and close the door and adjust so that the door lock does not contact the striker.

DOOR PANEL AND HINGE

Removal

Remove the parts in the following order:
1. Lift Door Hinge.
2. Lift Door Panel.
3. License Light.
4. Inside Handle.
5. Gate Door Stay.
6. Gate Door Stay.

7.Gate Door Hinge.
8.Gate Door Panel.

Before removing the panel, disconnect the number plate light connector.

Installation

Reverse REMOVAL Procedure.

Adjustment

1.Check the door framework.
2.Loosen the body hinge bolts and adjust the back door left-right and u-down positions.
3.Loosen the door hinge bolts and adjust the left-right and forward-backward positions of the door.
4.Adjust the door lock striker.

SWING OUT BACK DOOR

Removal

Remove the parts in the following order:

1.Door Inside Handle Bezel.
2.Door Trim. Insert a screwdriver between the door panel and retainers and pry out.
* Tape the screwdriver before use.

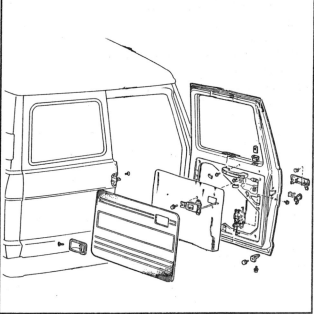

3.Door Inside Handle and Link.
4.Service Hole Cover.
5.Door Lock.
6.Door Inside Lock Lever.
7.Door Outside Handle.
8.Door Lock Cylinder.
9.Door Lock Striker.
10. Door Pull Handle.
11. Right Door.

Inspection

1.Operation of moving parts.
2.Lubrication of lock sliding parts.

Installation

Install the parts in the following order:

1.Right Door.
2.Door Pull Handle.
3.Door Lock Striker.
4.Door Lock Cylinder.
5.Door Outside Handle.
6.Door Inside Lock Lever.
7.Door Lock. Seal the service hole cover with adhesive.
8.Service Hole Cover.
9.Door Inside Handle and Link.
10. Door Trim.
11. Door Inside Handle Bezel.

Adjustment

1.Outside Handle.

(a) Check the outside handle play.

Control link play:

0.5 - 1.0 mm (0.020 - 0.039 in)

(b) Adjust the control link play.

2.Inside Handle.

(a) Loosen the screws.

(b) Move the handle forward to the point where strong resistance is felt.

(c) Turn backward 0.5 - 1.0 mm (0.020 - 0.039 in) and tighten.

3.Door Lock Striker. Open and close the door by the outside handle and adjust so that the door lock does not contact the striker.

LEFT BACK DOOR LOCK

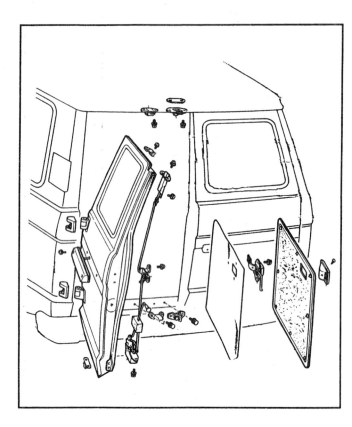

Removal

Remove the parts in the following parts:

1.Door Inside Handle Bezel.

2.Door Trim. Insert a screwdriver between the door panel and retainers and pry out.

* Tape the screwdriver tip before use.

3.Door Inside Handle and Link.

4.Service Hole Cover.

5.Lower Door Lock. Remove the link.

6.Upper Door Lock.

7.Slide Block.

8.Link Turn Block.

9.Slide Block.

10. Upper Lock Striker and Spacer.

11. Lower Lock Striker.

12. Slide Block.

13. License Light.

14. Left Door.

15. Slide block.

Installation

Reverse the REMOVAL procedure above.

Adjustment

1.Inside Handle.

(a) Loosen the screws.

(b) Move the handle forward to the point where strong resistance is felt.

(c) Turn backward 0.5 - 1.0 mm (0.020 - 0.039 in) and tighten.

2.Upper Door Lock Striker. Loosen set screws and adjust so that the door closes softly.

* When closing the door be careful of the door upper indentations.

* When opening the door be sure that there is no interference between the door check and upper lock. If there is interference adjust the up-down direction.

3.Lower Door Lock Striker. Loosen the set screws and adjust so the door closes softly.

* When closing the door be careful of the door indentations.

* If there is a door sag, adjust with the door hinge, not with the door lock striker.

4.Slide Block. Loosen the set screws and adjust so the door closes softly.

* When closing the door be careful of the door lower indentations.

* When opening the door be sure that there is no interference between the door check and upper lock. If there is interference, adjust the upper lock protrusion.

5.Upper Door Lock. Before installing, turn the door upper lock rod and adjust the lock protrusion.

Protrusion:

Limit 14.5 +/- 1.5 mm (0.571 +/- 0.059 in)

WINDSCREEN GLASS

Removal

Remove the parts in the following order:

1.Sun Visor and Holder.
2.Inside Rear View Mirror.
3.Wiper Arm.
4.Glass with Weatherstrip.
(a) Remove the glass by one of the following methods:
   (i) When reusing the weatherstrip. Working from the inside of the vehicle, push the weatherstrip lip with a screwdriver to the outside of the body flange.
   (ii) When no reusing the weatherstrip. From the out-side, cut off the weatherstrip lip with a knife.
(b) Push the glass surface near the upper side of the weatherstrip toward the outside and remove the glass.
* Use a uniform force when pushing out glass.

Installation

Install parts in the following order:

1.Glass with Weatherstrip.
(a) Wipe off any adhesive left on the body or glass with alcohol or white spirits (for windscreen glass only).
(b) Mount the weatherstrip on the glass, and fit the installation cord in the weatherstrip body groove.
(c) Apply soapy water to the weatherstrip and body contacting surfaces.
(d) Position the windscreen accurately on the body.

(e) Pull the cords from inside, and at the same time, tap the glass surface near the weatherstrip with the palm of the hand from the outside. Begin installation from the lower centre.
(f) After installing the glass, tap it from the outside with the palm of the hand until it is fully seated.
(g) Put adhesive between the weatherstrip and vehicle body and between weatherstrip and glass.
   (i) Before putting on adhesive, place masking tape on the glass and vehicle body to allow easy removal of excess adhesive that oozes out.
   (ii) Fill in the adhesive from the outside.
2.Wiper Arm.
3.Inside Rear View Mirror.
4.Sun Visor and Holder.

SIDE WINDOW

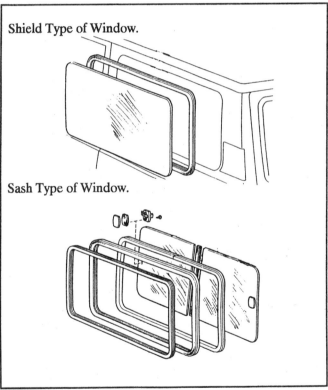

Shield Type of Window.

Sash Type of Window.

Removal

Remove the parts in the following order:

[Shield Type]
1.Remove the weatherstrip adhesive from the body with a scraper.

2.From the inside, push out the weatherstrip lip with a screwdriver.

[Sash Type]

1.Remove the window frame clips.

2.Remove the window frame by cutting the adhesive.

3.Spread the upper and lower portions of the centre frame and take out the glass.

* To prevent glass from dropping, support it with fingers.

Installation

Install the parts in the following order:

[Shield Type]

1.Weatherstrip.

2.Side Window.

(a) Apply adhesive to the body side.

(b) Attach string as illustrated.

* Apply adhesive to the weatherstrip inside.

(c) Install glass by pushing from the outside and pull the string from the inside.

(d) Tap the glass from the outside to work in the weatherstrip

3.Install the clips on the body and frame edge.

[Sash Type]

1.Glass Run.

2.Inner Sash. Pull apart the sash and install the inner sash.

3.Side Glass.

4.Outer Sash.

(a) Clean the body side.

(b) Apply adhesive tape around the body.

(c) Install the window frame.

5.Sash Clip. To compress the adhesive tap squeeze the frame and body edge portion together with a pair of pliers.

6.Install the clips on the body and frame edge.

BACK DOOR GLASS

Components

[Lift Gate Type]

1.Rear Wiper.

2.Rear Window Glass.

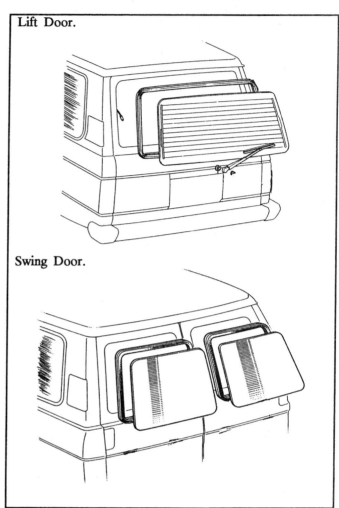

Lift Door.

Swing Door.

3.Rear Window Glass.

[Swing Out Door Type]

4.Left Door Glass.

5.Left Door Glass Weatherstrip.

6.Right Door Glass.

7.Right Door Glass Weatherstrip.

Removal

From inside, push out weatherstrip lip with screwdriver.

Installation

1.Apply adhesive to the body side.

2.Attach string as illustrated.

3.Install glass by pushing from the outside and pull the string from the inside.

4.Tap the glass from the outside to work in the weatherstrip.

SEAT

Front Seat.

Back Parallel Seat.

Rear seat.

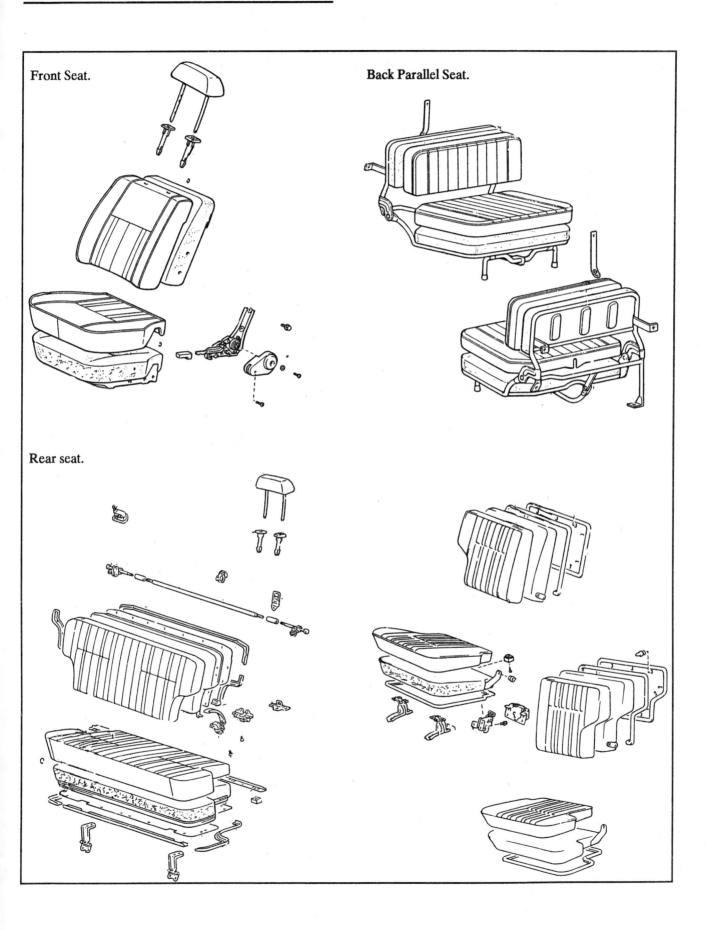

SEAT BELTS

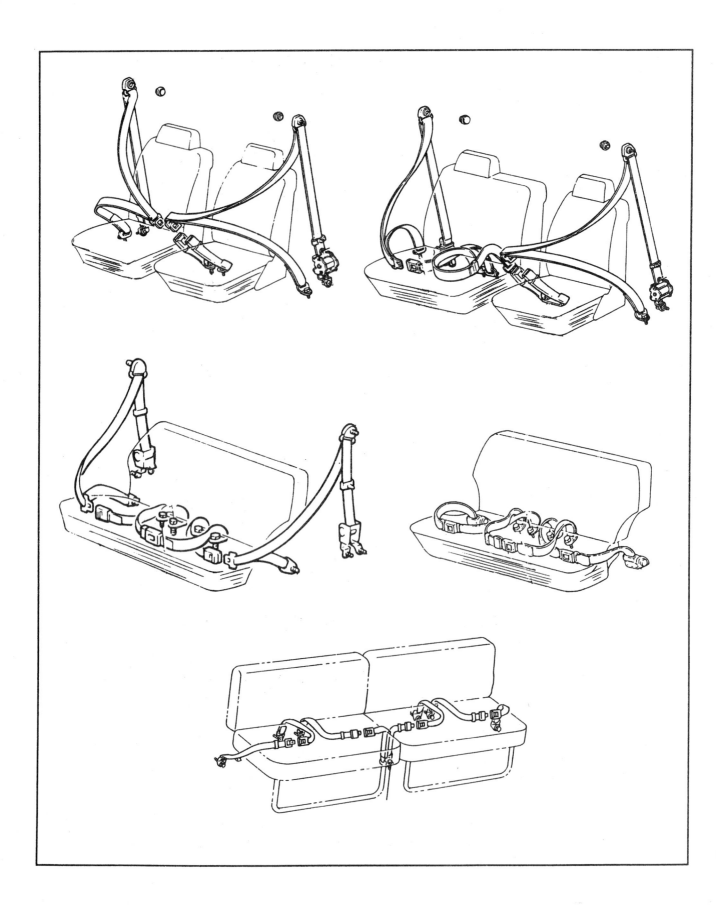

FJ, BJ, HJ, RJ, LJ 7..ˢ

HOOD

Adjust Hood. 6...'s.

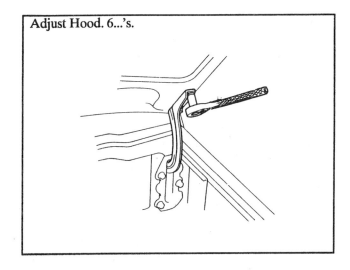

Adjust Hood 7...'s.

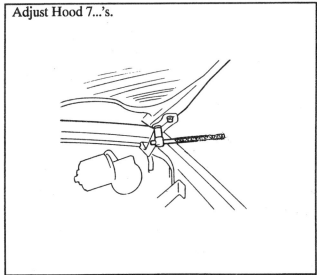

Adjustment

1.Adjust Hood in Forward/Backward and Left/Right Directions. Adjust the hood by loosening the hood side hinge bolts.

2.Adjust Front Edge of Hood in Vertical Direction. Adjust the hood by turning the hood cushions.

3.Adjust Rear Edge of Hood in Vertical Direction.

(a) Disconnect the washer hose and remove the 4 bolts and hood.

(b) Remove the 2 clips and 6 screws and cowl louvre.

(c) Adjust the hood by increasing or decreasing the number of shims.

(d) Install the cowl louvre with 2 clips and 6 screws.

(e) Install the hood with 4 bolts and connect the washer hose.

4.Adjust Hood Lock by Loosening the Mounting Bolts.

FRONT DOOR

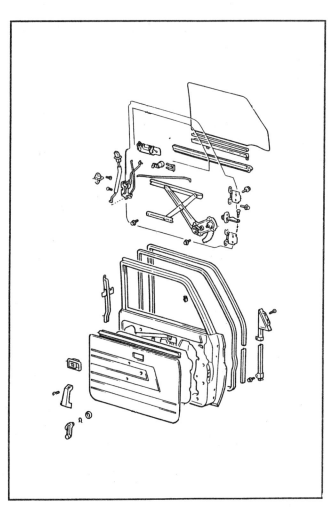

Dismantle

1.Remove Window Regulator Handle. Pull off the snap ring with a cloth and remove the regulator handle.

2.Remove Armrest or Pull Handle.

3.Remove Inside Handle.

(a) Remove the screw.

(b) Slide forward and pull off the inside handle.

(c) Disconnect the link from the inside handle.

4.Remove Door Trip.

[With Soft Top]

(a) Remove the screw and service cover.

(b) Insert a screwdriver between the trip retainers and door panel to pry it loose.

* Tape the screwdriver tip before use.

[With Power Window]

(a) Disconnect the connector from the switch.

5.Remove Rear View Mirror.

6.Remove Inner and Outer weatherstrip.

(a) Using a screwdriver, remove the inner weatherstrip.

(b) Pull off the outer weatherstrip.

7.Remove Service Hole Cover.

8.Disconnect Inside Opening Control Link from Door lock.

9.Remove Glass Run.

10.**[With Ventilator Window Type]** Remove Ventilator Window.

(a) Peel off the weatherstrip on the upper side of the ventilator window.

(b) Remove the 3 screws.

(c) Remove the division bar set bolt.

(d) Remove the ventilator window by pulling it up.

11.**[Without Ventilator Window Type]** Remove Clip.

12.Remove Door Glass.

(a) **[without ventilator window type]** Remove two glass channel mounting bolts.

(b) Incline the door glass and pull it up.

13.Remove Window Regulator.

(a) **[without ventilator window type]** Remove the 2 equaliser arm bracket mounting bolts.

(b) **[with power window]** Disconnect the connector from the motor and remove the 4 bolts.

[without power window] Remove the 3 bolts.

(c) Remove the regulator through the service hole.

14.**[Without Ventilator Window Type]** Remove Front Lower Frame.

[with soft top] Remove the 2 bolts and front lower frame.

[without soft top] Remove the 2 screws, 2 bolts and front lower frame.

15.Remove Rear Lower Frame.

[with soft top] Remove the 2 bolts and rear lower frame.

[without soft top] Remove the bolt and rear lower frame.

16.Disconnect Inside Locking Control Link From Door Lock.

17.Remove Door Lock Cylinder.

(a) Disconnect the link from the cylinder.

(b) Remove the retainer and cylinder.

18.Remove Outside Handle.

(a) Disconnect the link from the outside handle.

(b) Remove the 2 bolts and outside handle.

19.Remove Door Lock.

[with door lock solenoid] Remove the 3 screws, bolt and door lock, and disconnect the connector from the solenoid.

[without door lock solenoid] Remove the 3 screws and door lock.

Replacement of Glass

1.Prise out Glass Channel.

2.Apply Soapy Water to Inside of Weatherstrip.

3.Tap on Channel with Plastic Hammer.

Assembly

1.Apply MP Grease to Parts Before Installing.

(a) Apply MP grease to the sliding surface and gear of the window regulator.

(b) Apply MP grease to the sliding surface of the door lock.

2.Install Door Lock.

[with door lock solenoid] Connect the connector to the door lock solenoid and install the door lock with the 3 screws and bolt.

[without door lock solenoid] Install the door lock with the 3 screws.

3.Install Door Lock Cylinder. Install the door lock cylinder with the retainer and connect the control link to it.

4.Install Outside Handle. Install the outside handle with the 2 bolts and connect the control link to it.

4.Install Outside Handle. Install the outside handle with the 2 bolts and connect the control link to it.

5.Connect INside Locking Control Link to Door Lock.

6.Check Door Lock Operation.

7.Install Rear Lower Frame.

[with soft top] INstall the rear lower frame with 2 bolts.

[without soft top] Install the rear lower frame with bolt.

8.**[Without Ventilator Window Type]** Install Front Lower Frame.

[with soft top] Install the front lower frame with 2 bolts.

[without soft top] Install the front lower frame with 2 screws and 2 bolts.

9.Install Window Regulator.

(a) **[with power window]** Connect the connector to the motor and install the regulator with the 4 bolts.

[without power window] Install the regulator with the 3 bolts.

(b) **[without ventilator window type]** Install the 2 equaliser arm bracket mounting bolts.

10.Install Door Glass.

(a) Incline the door glass and install it to the window regulator.

(b) **[without ventilator window type]** Install the 2 glass channel mounting bolts.

11.**[With Ventilator Window Type]** Install Ventilator Window.

(a) Install the 3 screws.

(b) Install the division bar set bolt.

12.**[Without Ventilator Window Type]** Install Clip.

13.Install Glass Run.

14.connect Inside Opening Control Link to Door Lock.

15. Adjust Door Glass. Adjust the equaliser arm up or down and tighten it where the top of the door glass is horizontal when the door glass is approximately 2.5 cm from the top of the door.

16. Install Inner and Outer Weatherstrip.

17. Install Rear View Mirror.

18. Install Service Hole Cover.

(a) Seal the service hole cover with adhesive.

(b) Insert the lower edge of the service hole cover into the panel slit.

(c) Seal the panel slit with cotton tape.

* Do not block the trip clip seating with the tape.

19. Install Door Trip.

(a) **[with power window]** Connect the connector.

(b) Install the door trim with clips to the inside door panel by tapping.

(c) **[with soft top]** Install the service cover with screw.

20. Install Inside Handle.

(a) Connect the link to the inside handle.

(b) Push the inside handle in the door panel and slide it backward.

(c) Install the screw.

21. Install Armrest or Pull Handle.

22. Install Window Regulator Handle. With the door glass fully closed, install the window regulator handle with a snap ring as illustrated.

Adjustment

1.Adjust Door in Forward/Backward and Vertical Directions. Adjust the door by loosening the body side hinge bolts.

2.Adjust Door in Left/Right and vertical Directions. Adjust the door by loosening the door side hinge bolts.

3.Adjust Door Lock Striker.

(a) Check that the door fit and door lock linkages are adjusted correctly.

(b) Adjust the door lock striker by loosening the screws.

BACK DOOR [LIFT-UP TYPE]

Components

Dismantle (Upper Back Door)

1.Remove Pull Handle.

2.Remove Service Hole Cover.

3.Disconnect Inside Locking Control Link from Door Lock.

4.Remove Door Lock Cylinder.

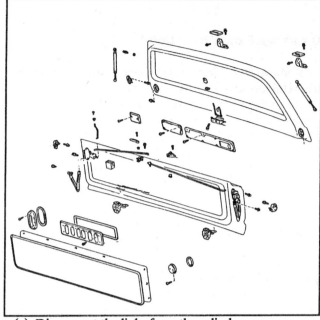

(a) Disconnect the links from the cylinder.

(b) Using a screwdriver, remove the E-clip and lever.

(c) Using snap ring pliers, remove the snap ring and control bracket.

(d) Remove the retainer and cylinder.

5.Remove Door Lock. Remove the 3 bolts and door lock.

Assembly (Upper Back Door)

1.Apply MP Grease to the Sliding Surface of Door Lock.

2.Install Door Lock with 3 Bolts.

3.Install Door Lock Cylinder.

(a) Install the cylinder with retainer.

(b) Install the control bracket.

(c) Using snap ring pliers, install snap ring.

(d) Install the lever and E-clip.

(e) Connect the links to the cylinder.

4.Connect Inside Locking Control Link to Door Lock.

5.Check Door Lock Operation.

6.Install Service Hole Cover and Pull Handle.

Adjustment (Upper Back Door)

1.Adjust Door in Forward/Backward and Left/Right Directions. Adjust the door by loosening the door side hinge bolts.

2.Adjust Door in Left/Right and Vertical Directions. Adjust the door by loosening the body side hinge bolts.

3.Adjust Door Lock Striker.

(a) Check that the door fit and door lock linkages are adjusted correctly.

(b) Adjust the door lock striker by loosening the screws.

RIGHT BACK DOOR

Dismantle (Lower Back Door)

1.Remove Door Trip. Insert a screwdriver between the trip retainers and door panel to pry it loose.
* Tape the screwdriver tip before use.
2.Remove Service Hole Cover.
3.Remove Door Lock Control.
(a) Disconnect the links from the door lock control.
(b) Remove the screw and inside handle.
(c) Remove the 2 bolts and door lock control.
4.Disconnect Inside Locking Control Link from Door Lock.
5.Remove 2 Bolts and Door Lock.

Adjustment (Lower Back Door)

1.Adjust Door in Forward/Backward and Left/Right Directions. Adjust the door by loosening the door side hinge bolts.
2.Adjust Door in Left/Right and Vertical Directions. Adjust the door by loosening the body side hinge bolts.
3.Adjust Door Lock Striker.
(a) Check that the door fit and door lock linkages are adjusted correctly.
(b) Adjust the door lock striker by loosening the screws.

BACK DOOR [SWING OUT TYPE]

Dismantle

1.Remove Spare Wheel and Carrier. Remove the 4 bolts and spare wheel carrier.
2.Remove Pull Handle.
3.Remove Door Trip. Insert a screwdriver between the trim retainers and door panel to pry it loose.
* Tape the screwdriver tip before use.
4.Remove Service Hole Cover, Door Stopper and Door Stopper Bracket.
5.Remove Lower Door Lock.
(a) Disconnect the link from the door lock control.
(b) Remove the 3 bolts and lower door lock.
6.[Without Soft Top] Remove Upper Door Lock.
(a) Remove the 6 screws and link cover.
(b) Disconnect the link from the door lock control.
(c) Remove the 2 bolts and upper door lock.
7.Remove Door Lock Control.
(a) Remove the screw and inside handle.
(b) Remove the 2 screws, bushing and door lock control.

Assembly

1.Apply MP Grease to Parts Before Installing.
(a) Apply MP grease to the sliding surface of the door lock.
(b) Apply MP grease to the sliding surface of the door lock control.
2.Install Door Lock Control.
(a) Install the bushing and door lock control with 2 screws.

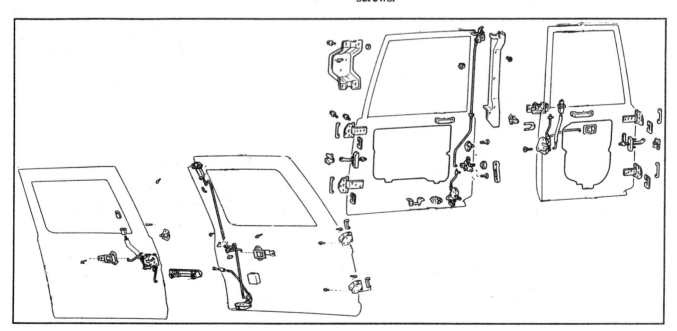

(b) install the inside handle with a screw.

3.[Without Soft Top] Install Upper Door Lock.

(a) Install the upper door lock with the 2 bolts.

(b) Connect the link to the door lock control.

(c) Install the link cover with the 6 screws.

4.Install Lower Door Lock.

(a) Install the lower door lock with the 3 bolts.

(b) Connect the link to the door lock control.

5.Check Door Lock Operation.

6.Install Door Stopper Bracket. Install the door stopper bracket with the 2 bolts.

7.Install Door Stopper. Install the door stopper with the 2 bolts.

8.Install Service Hole Cover.

(a) Seal the service hole cover with adhesive.

(b) Insert the lower edge of the service hole cover into the panel slit.

(c) Seal the panel slit with cotton tape.

* Do not block the trip clip seating with the tape.

9.Install Door Trim. Install the door trip with clips to the inside door panel by tapping.

10. Install Pull Handle.

11. Install Spare Wheel Carrier. Install the spare wheel carrier with 4 bolts.

Adjustment

1.Adjust Door in Forward/Backward and Vertical Directions. Adjust the door by loosening the body side hinge bolts.

2.Adjust Door in Left/Right and Vertical Directions.

(a) Remove the pull handle and door trim.

(b) Peel off the outer ridges of the service hole cover.

(c) Adjust the door by loosening the door side hinge bolts.

3.Adjust Door Lock Striker.

(a) Check that the door fit and door lock linkages are adjusted correctly.

(b) Adjust the door lock striker by loosening the bolts or screws.

LEFT BACK DOOR

Dismantle

1.Remove Inside Handle.

(a) Remove the screw.

(b) Slide and pull off the inside handle.

(c) Disconnect the link from the inside handle.

2.Remove Pull Handle.

3.Remove Door Trim. Insert a screwdriver between the trim retainers and door panel to pry it loose.

* Tape the screwdriver tip before use.

4.Remove Service Hole Cover.

5.Disconnect Inside Locking Control Link from Door Lock.

6.Remove Door Lock Cylinder.

(a) Disconnect the link from the door lock cylinder.

(b) Remove the retainer and cylinder.

7.Remove Outside Handle.

(a) Disconnect the link from the outside handle.

(b) Remove the 2 bolts and outside handle.

8.Remove Door Lock. Remove the 3 screws and door lock.

Assembly

1.Apply MP Grease to Door Lock. Apply MP grease to the sliding surface of the door lock.

2.Install the Door Lock with 3 Screws.

3.Install Outside Handle.

(a) Install the outside handle with the 2 bolts.

(b) Connect the link to the outside handle.

4.Install Door Lock Cylinder.

(a) Install the door lock cylinder with retainer.

(b) Connect the link to the cylinder.

5.Connect Inside Locking Control Link to Door Lock.

6.Install Service Hole Cover.

(a) Seal the service hole cover with adhesive.

(b) Insert the lower edge of the service hole cover into the panel slit.

(c) Seal the panel slit with cotton tape.

* Do not block the trim clip seating with the tape.

7.Install Door Trim with Clips to the Inside Door Panel by Tapping.

8.Install Pull Handle.

9.Install Inside Handle.

(a) Connect the link to the inside handle.

(b) Push the inside handle in the door panel and slide it.

(c) Install the screw.

10. Check Door Lock Operation.

Adjustment

1.Adjust Door in Forward/Backward and Vertical Directions. Adjust the door by loosening the body side hinge bolts.

2.Adjust Door in Left/Right and Vertical Directions.

(a) Remove the pull handle, inside handle and door trim.

(b) Peel off the outer ridges of the service hole cover.

(c) Adjust the door by loosening the door side hinge bolts.

3.Adjust Door Lock Striker.

(a) Check that the door fit and door lock linkage are adjusted correctly.

(b) Adjust the door lock striker by loosening the screws.

WINDSCREEN

Components

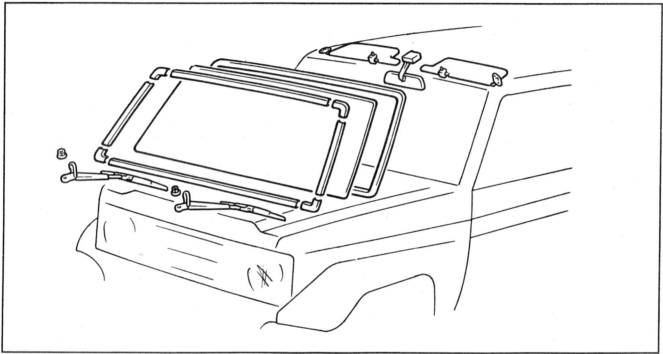

Removal

1.Remove Following parts:

1) wiper arms,

2) windscreen mouldings,

3) inner rear view mirror,

4) sun visors and holders.

2.Remove Windscreen.

(i) [if reusing weatherstrip]

(a) Working from the vehicle outside with a screwdriver, loosen the weatherstrip lip from the body.

(b) From inside of vehicle, stuff lip of weatherstrip under flange with screwdriver.

(c) To remove, push the glass out.

(ii) [if not reusing weatherstrip]

(a) From the outside, cut off the weatherstrip lip with a knife.

(b) From the vehicle interior, push the windscreen with an even force.

Installation

1. Clean Body and Glass. Using alcohol, wipe off any adhesive left on the body or glass.

2.Install Weatherstrip on Glass.

(a) Attach the weatherstrip to the glass.

* If the weatherstrip has hardened, it may develop water leaks. Use a new one if possible.

(b) Insert a cord into the groove of the weatherstrip all the way around and so the ends overlap.

3.Install Glass.

(a) Apply soapy water to the contact face of the weatherstrip lip and to the body flange.

* Begin installation in the middle of the lower part of the glass.

(b) Hold the glass in position on the body.

(c) From the inside, pull on one cord at an angle so it pulls the lip over the flange. From the outside, press the glass along the weatherstrip until the glass is installed.

4.Snug Down Glass. To snug down the glass, tap from the outside with your open hand.

5.Apply Adhesive.

(a) Pull masking tape around the weatherstrip to protect the paint and glass.

(b) Apply adhesive to the No. 1 weatherstrip lip and glass lip until it oozes out.

6.Clean Adhesive Surface.

(a) When adhesive is dry, remove the masking tape.

(b) Clean off the adhesive oozing out from the masking tape with a clean rag saturated in cleaning fluid.

WINDSCREEN (CANADA)

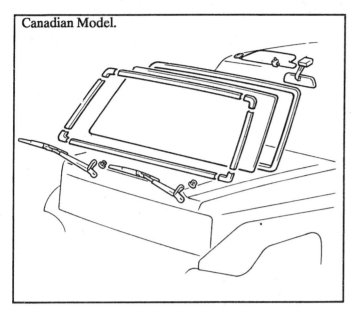

Canadian Model.

Preparation for Replacement

Prepare the following parts in advance:

Weatherstrip cleaner - cleaning fluid
Weatherstrip primer - AP131 (ADHESION PROMOTER UNION CARBIDE CORPORATION) or such
Primer dilution - toluene
Weatherstrip adhesive - 366ET (CEMEDINE), IMRON SEALANT (E1 DUPONT DE NEMOURS CO.) or such.

Removal

1.Remove Following Parts:
1) wiper arms,
2) windscreen mouldings (use screwdriver or similar instrument),
3) inner rear view mirror,
4) sun visors and holders.
2.Remove Windscreen Glass.
(a) From the exterior, cut off the weatherstrip lip.
(b) Push piano wire or strong nylon cord (or similar) through from the interior.
(c) Tie both wire ends to a wooden block or equivalent.
* When separating, take care not to damage the paint or interior and exterior ornaments.
* To prevent scratching the safety pad when removing the windscreen, place a plastic sheet between the piano wire and safety pad.

(d) Cut the adhesive by pulling the piano wire around it.
(e) Remove the glass.

Installation

1.Clean the Body and Glass. Using cleaning fluid, clean the weatherstrip contacting surface of the body and glass.
2.Clean Weatherstrip.
(a) Clean the weatherstrip surface with a piece of cloth saturated with cleaning fluid.
(b) Then, with another rag saturated in cleaning fluid, clean portions that will contain the glass and metal section of the body.
* Do not use cleaning fluid that appears dirty.
(c) Apply primer to the cleaned section of the rubber in (b) after the cleaning fluid has dried at least 3 minutes.
* Use AP131 grade primer or such. The primer is volatile and will form deposits under humid conditions. Therefore, always store primer in a cool, dry place away from direct sunlight. Use toluene to dilute the primer.
(d) Allow the primer to dry for at least 15 minutes.
* Be careful not to touch the sections of the weatherstrip after applying the primer, and attach the weatherstrip within 3 days.
3.Install Weatherstrip on Glass.
(a) Attach the weatherstrip to the glass.
(b) Apply a working cord along the weatherstrip groove as shown.
4.Install Glass.
(a) Clean the rest of the weatherstrip with cleaning fluid. Do not coat sections covered with primer.
* Do not sue soapy water.
* Begin installation in the middle of the lower part of the glass.
(b) Hold the glass in position on the body.
(c) From the inside, pull on one cord at an angle so it pulls the lip over the flange. From the outside, press the glass along the weatherstrip until the glass is installed.
5.Snug Down Glass. Tap from the outside with your open hand.
6.Apply Adhesive.
(a) Put masking tape around the weatherstrip to protect the paint and glass.
(b) Apply adhesive to the No. 1 weatherstrip lip and glass lip until it oozes out.
* Use a CEMEDINE 366ET, IMRON SEALANT or equivalent.
7.Clean the Adhesive Surface.
(a) When adhesive is dry, remove the masking tape.
* The adhesive will harden in about 15 hours.
(b) Clean off the adhesive oozing out from the masking tape with cleaning fluid.
8.Check For Water Leaks. If necessary, apply adhesive.

* Use a CEMEDINE 366ET, IMRON SEALANT or equivalent.

9.Install Following Parts:

1) sun visors and holders,

2) inner rear view mirror,

3) windscreen mouldings,

4) wiper arms.

SIDE WINDOW

Components

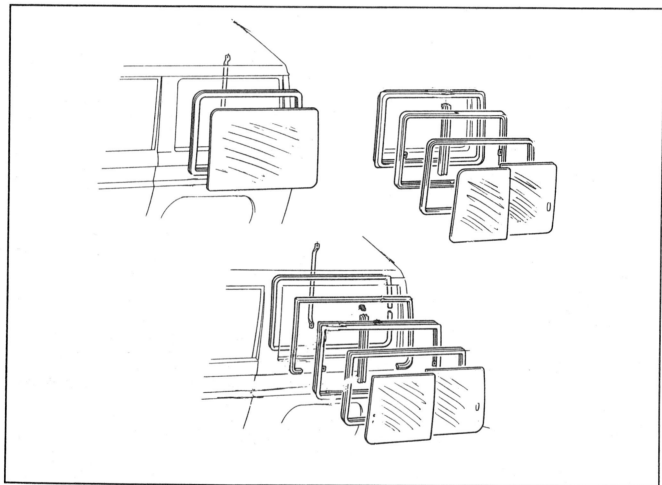

Installation

1.Install Side Window.

(a) Insert a cord into the groove of the weatherstrip all the way around with the ends overlapping.

(b) Apply soapy water to the contact surface of the weatherstrip lip and to the body flange.

* Begin installation in the middle of the lower part of the side window.

(c) Hold the window in position on the body.

(d) From the inside, pull on one cord at an angle so it pulls the lip over the flange. From the outside, press the glass along the weatherstrip until the window is installed.

(e) Tap on the outside of the glass until it is securely in place.

BACK DOOR GLASS

Installation

1.Install Weatherstrip on Glass.
(a) Attach the weatherstrip to the glass.
* If the weatherstrip has hardened, it may develop leaks. Use a new one if possible.

Components

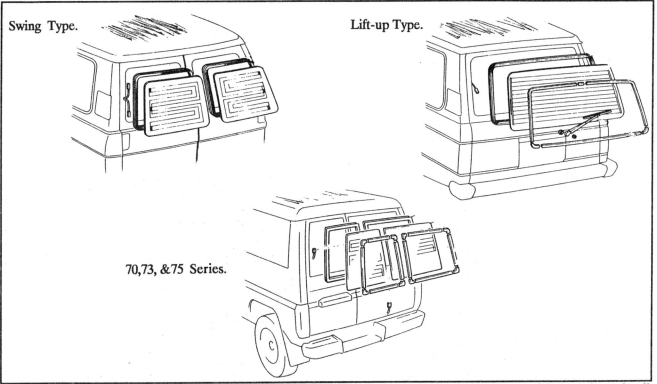

Swing Type.

Lift-up Type.

70,73, &75 Series.

(b) Insert a cord into the groove of the weatherstrip all the way around with the ends overlapping.

2.Install Back Door Glass.
(a) Apply soapy water to the contact surface of the weatherstrip lip and to the body flange.
* Begin installation in the middle of the lower part of the back door glass.
(b) Hold the glass in position on the body.
(c) From the inside, pull on one cord at an angle so it pulls the lip over the flange. From the outside, press the glass along the weatherstrip until the glass is installed.
(d) Tap on the outside of the glass until it is securely in place.

3.Check for Leaks. Pour water on glass and weatherstrip, check seal for leaks and apply sealant where necessary.

4.Install Back Door Control Link Cover with 6 Screws.
5.Install Following Parts:
1) defogger connector,
2) back door moulding,
3) rear wiper arm,
4) spare wheel.

Removal

1.Remove Following Parts:
1) spare wheel,
2) rear wiper arm,
3) back door moulding (use screwdriver or similar instrument),
4) defogger connector.

2.[Except Soft Top] Remove Door Control Link Cover. Remove the 6 screws and link cover.

3.Remove Back Door Glass.

[If reusing the weatherstrip]
(a) From inside of vehicle, stuff lip of weatherstrip under flange with screwdriver.
(b) Push the glass out to remove.

[If using a new weatherstrip]
(a) From outside of the vehicle, cut off the weatherstrip lip with a knife.
(b) Push the back door glass out and remove the back door glass.
(c) Remove the remaining weatherstrip.

BACK WINDOW

Components

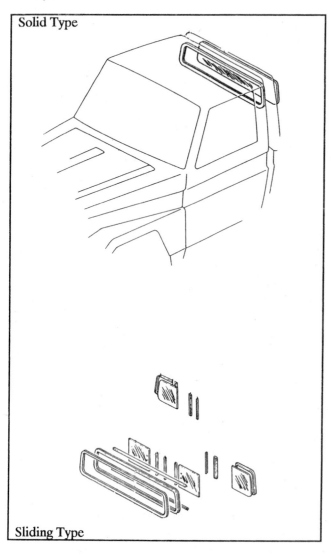

Solid Type

Sliding Type

Assembly

1.Install Weatherstrip. Align the grooves on the channel and weatherstrip and install.

2.Install Fixed Glass.

(a) Apply soapy water to the contact face of the weatherstrip and to the glass channel flange.

(b) Pull apart the channels and install the 2 fixed glass panes with the weatherstrip.

3.Install Fix Frames.

(a) Apply soapy water to the contact face of the weatherstrip and to the fix frames.

(b) Pull apart the channels and install the 2 fixed frames.

4.Install Slide Glass. Pull apart the channels and install the slide glass in the centre of the glass channel.

5.Install 4 Fix Frame Screws and 4 Packings.

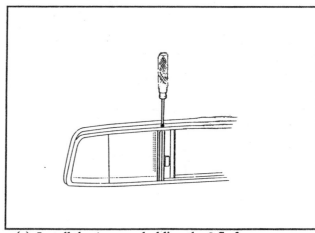

(a) Install the 4 screws holding the 2 fix frames.

(b) Install packing (4 pieces).

6.Install Sliding Glass Stopper. Install the sliding glass stopper with the screw.

Installation

1.Install Weatherstrip on Back Window.

(a) Attach the weatherstrip to the back window.

* If the weatherstrip has become hard, it may develop leaks. Use a new one if possible.

(b) Insert a cord into the groove of the weatherstrip all the way around with the ends overlapping.

2.Install Back Window.

(a) Apply soapy water to the contact surface of the weatherstrip lip and to the body flange.

* Begin installation in the middle of the lower part of the glass.

(b) Hold the back window in position on the body.

(c) From the inside, pull on one cord at an angle so it pulls the lip over the flange. From the outside, press the glass along the weatherstrip until the glass is installed.

(d) Tap on the outside of the glass until it is securely in place.

3.Check for Leaks. Pour water on glass and weatherstrip, check seal for leaks and apply sealant where necessary.

SUN ROOF

Components

1.Remove Sliding Roof Headlining. Before making adjustments, loosen the clips and slide the headlining to the

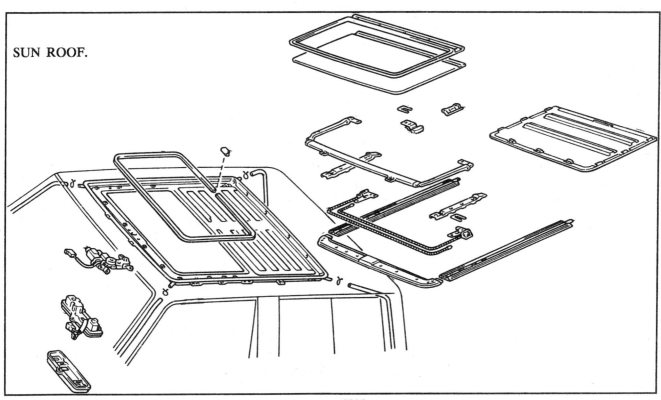

SUN ROOF.

rear.

* When checking adjustment, reattach the headlining before sliding the roof.

2.To Adjust Level Difference. Adjust by increasing or decreasing the number of shims.

* If the front end is high, even without a shoe shim, check to see if the front shoes are in contact with the stoppers.

3.To Adjust Forward or Backward. Adjust by moving the front shoe on both sides.

* When the sliding roof is fully closed, confirm that the front shoes are in contact with the stopper.

4.To Adjust Right or Left. Adjust by loosening the rear shoe nuts and move the sliding roof to the right and left.

5.To adjust Clearance. (Difference in left and right front clearance).

[If the difference is about 2 mm (0.08 in)]:

(a) Remove the drive motor and shift the cable one notch on the side with the larger clearance.

(b) Reinstall the motor.

[If the difference is about 1 mm (0.04 in)]: Loosen the rear shoe bolts and readjust the sliding roof to the proper position.

On-Vehicle Inspection

1.Start the Engine and Check the Operation of the Sun Roof.

Operation time: approx. 10 secs.

2.Check for Abnormal Noise or Binding During Operation.

3.With the Sun Roof Fully Closed, Check for Water Leakage.

4.Check for a Difference in Level Between the Sliding Panel and Roof Panel.

Front side:	0 (+ 1.0) mm [0 (+ 0.039) in]
	0 (- 2.0) mm [0 (- 0.079) in]
Rear side:	0 (+ 1.0) mm [0 (+ 0.039) in]
	0 (- 2.0) mm [0 (- 0.079) in]
Left & right side:	0 (+ 1.0) mm [0 (+ 0.039) in]
	0 (- 2.0) mm [0 (- 0.079) in]

If the sliding roof does not operate:

(a) Remove the grommet in front of the control switch.

(b) Remove the screw inside.

* Be careful not to lose the spring washer or washer.

(c) Manually operate the sun roof by inserting a screwdriver into the hole and turning the drive shaft.

FRP TOP

Components

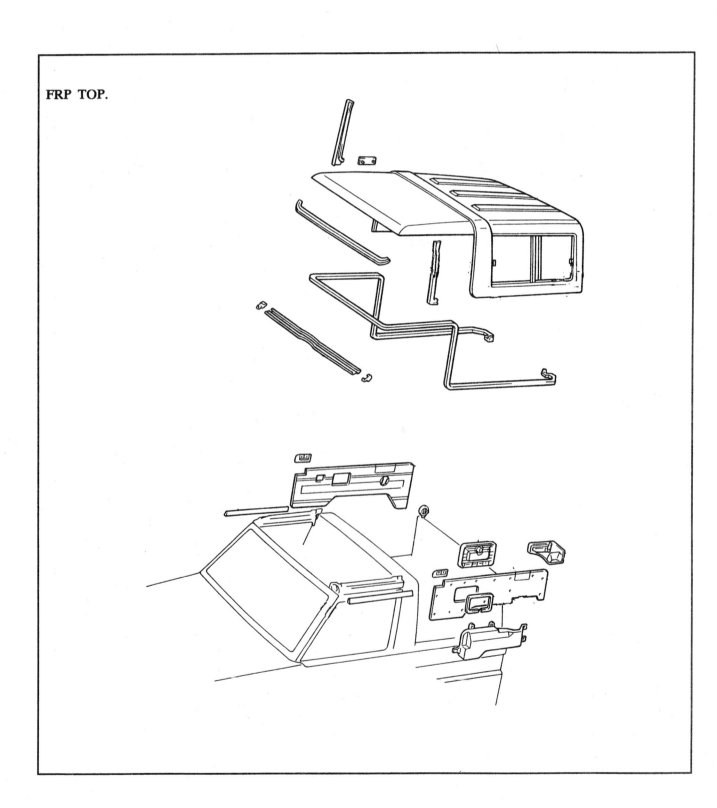

FRP TOP.

ROLL BAR

Components

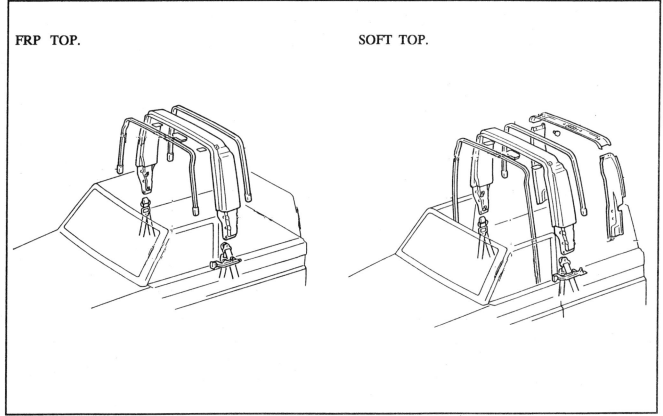

FRP TOP.   SOFT TOP.

SEAT BELTS.

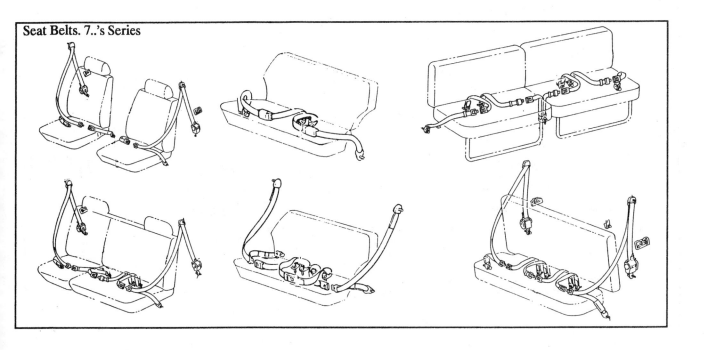

Seat Belts. 7..'s Series

SEATS

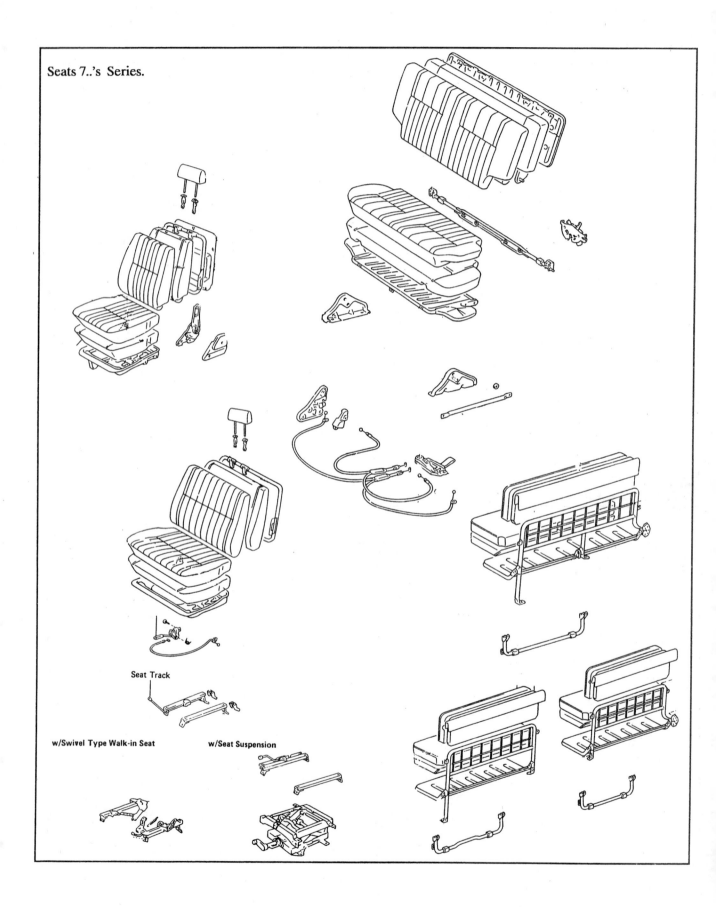

Seats 7..'s Series.

Seat Track

w/Swivel Type Walk-in Seat   w/Seat Suspension

WINCH

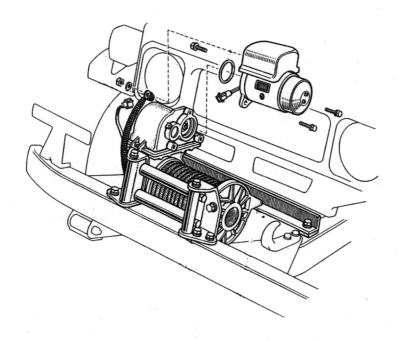

WINCH

WINCH [MECHANICAL]

Dismantle

Dismantle the parts in the following order:

1.Member and bracket. Remove the front and rear base members, and the roller bracket support.
2.End Bracket and Clutch Lever. Remove the winch end bracket assembly.

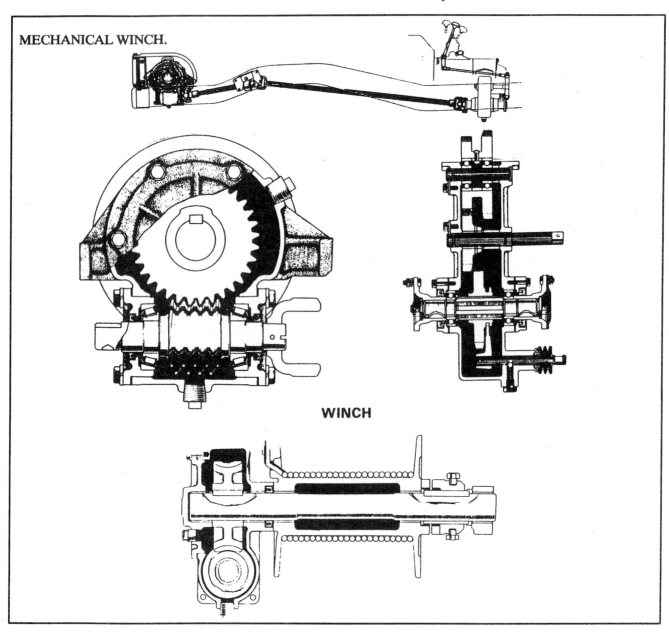

MECHANICAL WINCH.

WINCH

3.Spacer, Key and Clutch.
4.Winch Drum.
5.Case Cover.
6.Retainer and Shim.
7.Worm.
8.Worm Gear and Key.
9.Shaft.

Inspection

1.Worm and Bearing. Inspect for wear or damage.
2.Worm Gear and Shaft. Inspect for wear or damage.
3.Clutch and Spacer. Inspect for wear or damage.
4.Gear Case and Cover. Inspect for cracks or wear.

Assembly

Assemble the parts in the following order:

1.Shaft.
(a) Apply MP grease on all bushings, shaft and the clutch mechanism when assembling.
(b) Pack MP grease into the drum to about 3/4 of the drum volume.
2.Key and Worm Gear. Place the worm into the case with the straight pin hole towards the rear.
3.Worm.

(a) Install the worm bearing retainers with the adjusting shims and tighten the bearing retainer attaching bolts.
Tightening torque: 1.9 - 3.1 kg-m (14 - 22 ft-lb)
  * Apply liquid sealer onto the gasket surfaces to prevent oil leak.
(b) Rotate the worm and check the condition for looseness or tightness. Also rock the worm to and fro to check the worm end play. The worm end play should be zero and it should rotate smoothly.
Adjusting shim thickness:

Part No.	Thickness mm (in)
38123-60010	0.228 (0.0090)
38124-60010	0.5 (0.020)

4.Retainer and Shim.
5.Case Cover. Install the case cover with its filler hole positioned downward.
6.Winch Drum.
7.Spacer Key and Clutch.
8.End Bracket and Clutch Lever.
9.Member and Bracket.
10.Plug. Fill the gear case with gear oil.
Gear case oil capacity:
0.6 lts (0.6 US qts, 0.5 Imp.qts)
Type: SAE 90, API GL-4

POWER TAKE OFF

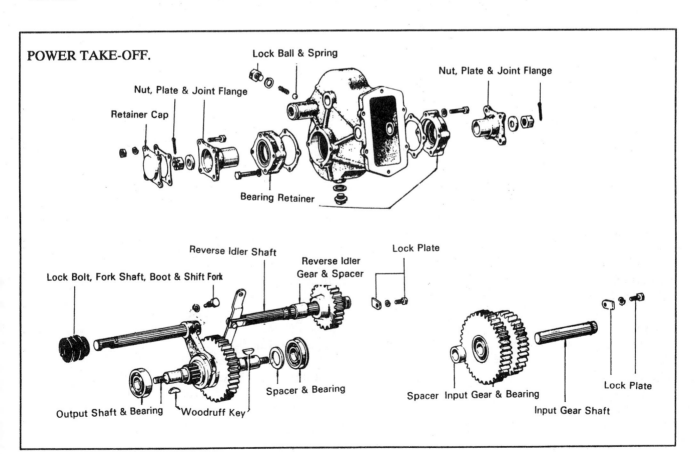

POWER TAKE-OFF.

Dismantle

Dismantle the parts in the following order:

1. Lock Plate
2. Input Gear Shaft.
   * If difficult to remove the shaft, first tap the shaft lightly towards the front, and remove the expansion plug.
3. Spacer, Input Gear and Bearing.
4. Lock Plate.
5. Reverse Idler Shaft.
6. Reverse Idler Gear and Spacer.
7. Lock Ball and Spring.
8. Lock Bolt, Fork Shaft, Boot and Shift Fork.
9. Retainer Cap.
10. Nut, Plate and Joint Flange. Remove the joint flange by lightly tapping its portion of woodruff key groove.
11. Bearing Retainer.
12. Woodruff Key.
13. Output Shaft and Bearing with a Press.
14. Spacer and Bearing.

Inspection

1. Input Gear and Bearing.
   (a) Inspect the gears for teeth wear or damage.
   (b) Inspect the bearings for wear or damage.
2. Replace the Input Gear Bearing.
   (a) Remove the bearings with a drift pin.
   (b) Install the bearings with socket wrench.
3. Reverse Idler Gear and Shaft. Inspect for wear or damage.
4. Output Gear, Shaft and Bearing. Inspect for wear or damage.
5. Replace the Output Gear Bearing.
   (a) Remove the bearing with a press.
   (b) Install the bearing with a press.

Assembly

Assemble the parts in the following order:
1. Output Shaft and bearing. Position the output gear into the case with the shift fork groove towards the rear.
2. Spacer and Bearing. Install the bearing with a press.
3. Woodruff Key.
4. Bearing Retainer.
5. Joint Flange.
6. Bearing Retainer.
7. Joint Flange. Tighten the nut.
   Tightening torque: 3.5 - 5.5 kg-m (26 - 39 ft-lb)
8. Retainer Cap.
9. Shift Fork, Shaft and Boot.
10. Lock Ball and Spring.
11. Reverse Idler Gear, Spacer and Shaft.

(a) Place the reverse idler gear and the idler gear spacer into the case with the gear hub to the rear side.
(b) The spacer should be installed between the gear hub and the case.
12. Input Gear and Shaft. Install the input gear with the larger gear towards the rear.
13. Lock Plate.

WINCH [ELECTRICAL]

Removal

Remove the parts in the following order:

1. Negative Battery Terminal.
2. Wiring Harness.
3. Connector.
4. Motor and O-Ring.
5. Winch with Rear Base Member.
6. Rear Base Member.

Dismantle

Dismantle the winch in the following order:

1. Housing Cover.
2. Cable.
3. Winch Set Plate.
4. Winch Housing.
5. Drum Spacer.
6. Case Cover.
   (a) Loosen each bolt a little at a time and in the following order:
   1) E-Clip and Spacer.
   2) Input Shaft.
   3) Slotted Spring Pin using a pin punch.
   4) No. 1 Counter Shaft. Tap the case cover with a plastic hammer and remove shaft.]
   * If No. 1 counter shaft is difficult to remove, lightly tap out the case cover with a plastic hammer while rotating the clutch subassembly by hand.
   5) Clutch.
   6) Clutch Outer Race.
   7) Thrust Bearing and Race.
   8) Snap Ring.
   9) One-way Clutch.
   10) No. 1 Counter Gear.
   11) Clutch Outer Disc, Inner Disc and Plate.
   (b) Dismantle the winch case in the following order:
   1) Winch Drum and Spacer. Before removing the winch drum, shift the lever to the lock position.

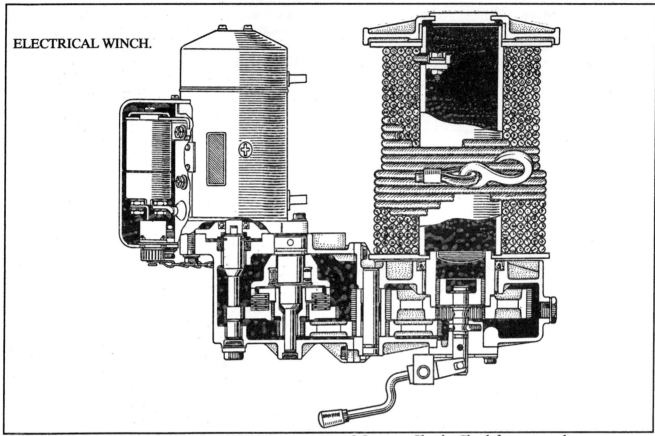

ELECTRICAL WINCH.

2) Shift Lever.

3) Tap out No. 2 Counter Shaft.

4) No. 3 and No. 4 Counter Gear.

5) Free Spool.

6) Output Gear.

Inspection and Repair

1. Case Cover.

(a) Check for damage.

(b) Check the slotted spring hole for bits of debris.

(c) Thoroughly remove all debris from the hole as it will cause damage to the O-ring.

2. Oil Seal.

(a) Check the lip for wear or damage.

(b) Replace the oil seal.

(i) Remove the oil seal.

(ii) Install the oil seal.

(c) Coat the lip with MP grease.

3. Bushing. Check for wear or damage. If found, replace the case cover.

4. Input Shaft. Check for wear or damage.

5. No. 1 Counter Shaft and Slotted Spring Pin. Check for wear or damage.

6. Outer Race and Bushing. Check for wear or damage.

7. Thrust Bearing and Race. Check for burning, wear or damage.

8. One-way Clutch. Check for wear or damage.

9. No. 1 Counter Gear. Check for wear or damage.

10. No. 2 Counter Gear.

(a) Check for wear or damage.

(b) Check the bushing for wear or damage.

11. Clutch Outer Disc. Check for burning, wear or damage.

12. Clutch Inner Disc and Plate. Check for burning, wear or damage.

13. Winch Drum. Check for damage.

14. Shift Lever.

(a) Check for damage.

(b) Check the bushing for wear or damage.

15. No. 2 Counter Shaft. Check for wear or damage.

16. No. 3 Counter Gear. Check for wear or damage.

17. No. 4 Counter Gear.

(a) Check for wear or damage.

(b) Check the bushing for wear or damage.

18. Output Gear. Check for wear or damage.

19. Shift Shaft Retainer, Spring and Ball. Check for wear or damage.

20. Sleeve Shift Shaft and Pin. Check for wear or damage.

21. Inner Hub. Check for wear or damage.

22. Winch Case.

(a) Check for wear or damage.

(b) Check the bushing for wear or damage.

(c) Check the oil seal for wear or damage.

23. Replace the Oil Seal.

(a) Remove the oil seal.

(b) Install a new oil seal.

(c) Coat the oil seal with MP grease.

Assembly

(b) Align the notch and tab and assemble the clutch disc to the counter gear.

(c) Hold the clutch disc and plate by hand and assemble the No. 1 and No. 2 counter gears as illustrated.

4. Clutch Outer Disc, Inner Disc and No. 1 Counter Gear.

5. Thrust Bearing and Race.

(a) Coat the thrust bearing and race with MP grease.

(b) Before assembling the outer race, align the disc

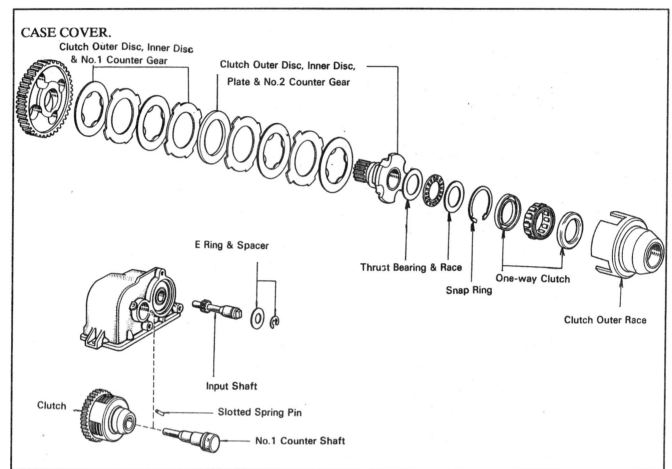

CASE COVER.

ASSEMBLE THE CASE COVER IN THE FOLLOW-ING ORDER:

1. One-way Clutch.

(a) Before assembling new inner discs, soak them in automatic transmission fluid for at least 30 minutes.

Fluid: ATF Type F.

(b) Coat the outer race bushing with MP grease.

(c) Coat the one-way clutch with MP grease.

2. Snap Ring.

(a) Assemble the one-way clutch as illustrated.

(b) Install the snap ring.

* Confirm that the snap ring is securely installed.

(c) Check the one-way clutch.

3. Clutch Outer Disc, Inner Disc, Plate and No. 2 Counter Gear.

(a) Coat the No. 2 counter gear with MP grease.

contours.

6. Clutch Outer Race. Turn the No. 2 counter gear clockwise and lock.

7. Clutch.

(a) Confirm that the thrust bearing and race are aligned in the centre.

(b) Coat the bearing parts of the case cover with MP grease.

8. No. 1 Counter Shaft.

(a) Install a new O-ring and coat with MP grease.

(b) Hold No. 1 counter gear by hand and push in No. 1 counter shaft.

* At this stage, align the case cover hole and counter shaft hole.

(c) After assembling No. 1 counter shaft, if the holes are not aligned, rotate the outer race counterclockwise and align the holes.

9. Tap in Slotted Spring Pin with Pin Punch.

10. Input Shaft.
11.E-Clip and Spacer.

ASSEMBLE THE WINCH CASE IN THE FOLLOW-
ING ORDER:

1.Winch Case. Coat the winch case bushing with MP
grease.
  2.Output Gear.
  3.Free Spool.
  (a) Coat the sleeve shift shaft and O-ring with MP
grease.
  (b) Install the shift shaft retainer and steel ball.
  (c) Make sure that the position of the shift shaft retainer
is as illustrated.
  4.No. 3 and No. 4 Counter Gear.
  5.No. 2 Counter Shaft.
  (a) Coat No. 2 counter shaft and a new O-ring with MP
grease.
  (b) Tap in the No. 2 counter shaft.
  6.Shift Lever.
  7.Winch Drum and Spacer. Coat spacer with MP
grease.

ASSEMBLE THE WINCH IN THE FOLLOWING ORDER:

1.Case Cover.
2.Drum Spacer.
3.Winch Housing.
4.Winch Set Plate.

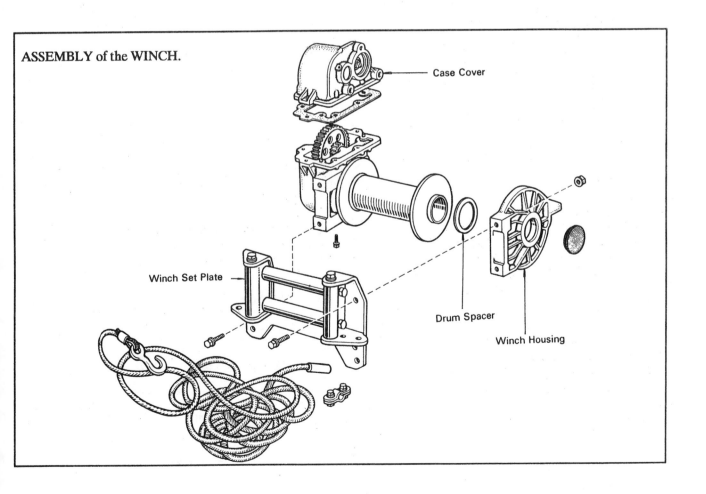

ASSEMBLY of the WINCH.

Case Cover

Winch Set Plate

Drum Spacer

Winch Housing

WINCH MOTOR

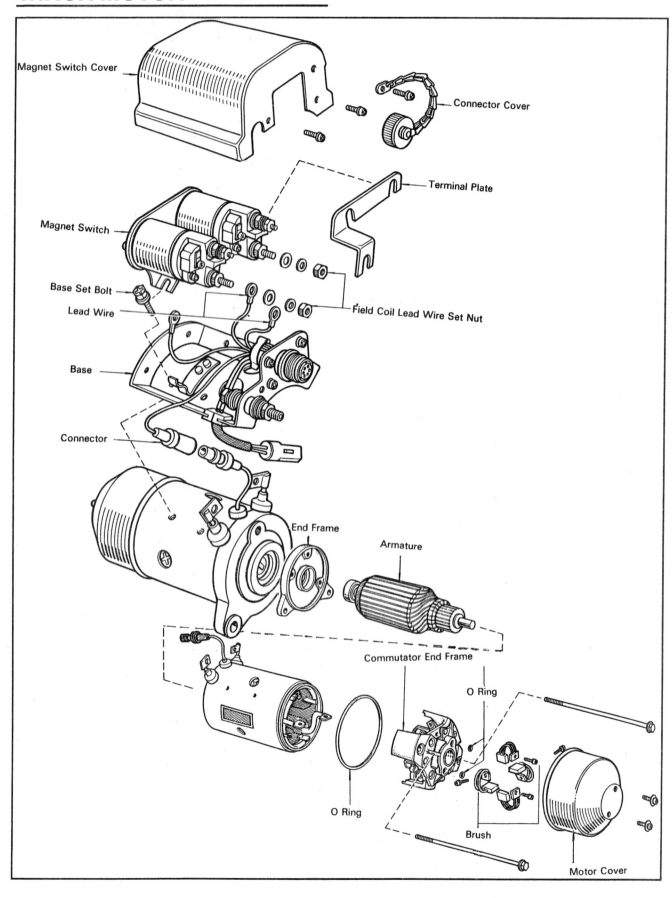

Magnet Switch Cover

Connector Cover

Terminal Plate

Magnet Switch

Base Set Bolt

Lead Wire

Field Coil Lead Wire Set Nut

Base

Connector

End Frame

Armature

Commutator End Frame

O Ring

O Ring

Brush

Motor Cover

AIR CONDITIONING SYSTEM

PRECAUTIONS

When handling refrigerant (R-12), the following precautions should be observed:

1.Always wear eye protection.
2.Keep the refrigerant container (service drum) below 40°C (104°F).
3.Do not handle refrigerant in an enclosed area or near an open flame.
4.Discharge refrigerant slowly when purging the system.
5.Be careful that liquid refrigerant does not get on your skin.

If liquid refrigerant gets in your eyes or on the skin:

1.Do not rub.
2.Wash the area with a lot of cool water.
3.Apply clean petroleum jelly to the skin.
4.Seek medical attention IMMEDIATELY.
5.Do not attempt to treat yourself.

When tubing:

1.Apply a few drops of refrigeration oil to the seats of the O-ring fittings.
2.Tighten the nut using 2 wrenches to avoid twisting the tube.
3.Tighten the O-ring fitting to the specified torque.
Torque specification for O-ring fittings:

Fitting size	Torque
0.31 in Tube	135 kg-cm (10 ft-lb, 13 N·m)
0.50 in Tube	225 kg-cm (16 ft-lb, 22 N·m)
0.62 in Tube	325 kg-cm (24 ft-lb, 32 N·m)

ON-VEHICLE INSPECTION

1.Check Condenser Fins for Blockage or Damage. If the fins are clogged, clean them with pressurised water.

* Be careful not to damage the fins.

2.Check Drive Belt Tension.

(a) [Except Canada]:

Drive belt tension at 10 kg (22 lb, 98 N):

Engine	New Belt	Used Belt
3F	12-15 (0.47-0.59)	15-21 (0.59-0.83)
3B, 13B-T	9-12 (0.35-0.47)	12-16 (0.47-0.63)
2H, 12H-T	14-19 (0.55-0.75)	19-25 (0.75-0.98)

" F " Type Engines.

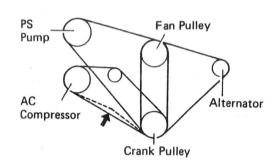

" B, 3B & 13 B-T " Type Engines.

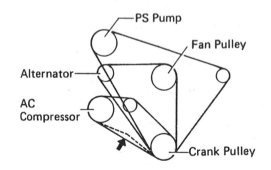

" H, 2H & 12 H-T " Type Engines.

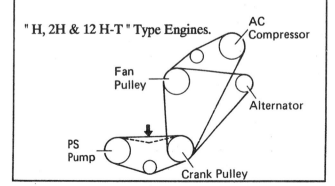

(b) [Canada]: Using a belt tension gauge, check the drive belt tension.

Belt tension gauge:

Nippondenso BTG-20 (95506-00020) or

Borroughs No. BT-33-73F

Drive belt tension:

New belt 125 +/- 25 lb

Used belt 80 +/- 20 lb

* "New belt" refers to a new belt which has never been used.

* "Used belt" refers to a belt which has been used on a running engine for 5 minutes or more.

3.Start Engine.

4.Position the Temperature Control Resistor on "MAX COOL" or Turn on A/C Switch. Check that the A/C operates at each position of the blower switch. If A/C does not operate, check A/C fuse.

5.Check Magnetic Clutch Operation.

6.Check That Idle Increases. When the magnetic clutch engages, engine revolution should increase.

Standard idle-up rpm:

3F, 3B & 13B-T 900 - 1,000 rpm

2H, 12H-T 800 - 900 rpm

7.Check Amount of Refrigerant. If you can see bubbles in the sight glass, additional refrigerant is needed.

8.If No (or Insufficient) Cooling, Inspect for Leakage. Using a gas leak tester, inspect each component of the refrigeration system.

REFRIGERATION SYSTEM CHECK

Checking Refrigerant Charge

1.Run Engine at Fast Idle.

2.Operate Air Conditioner at Maximum Cooling for a few Minutes.

3.Check Amount of Refrigerant. Observe the sight glass on the receiver.

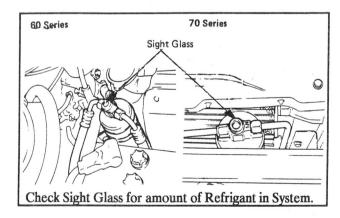

Check Sight Glass for amount of Refrigant in System.

Item 1:
Symptom: Bubbles present in sight glass.
Amount of refrigerant: Insufficient.

Item 2:
Symptom: No bubbles present in sight glass.
Amount of refrigerant: None, too much or sufficient.

Item 3:
Symptom: No temperature difference between compressor inlet and outlet.
Amount of refrigerant: Empty or nearly empty.

Item 4:
Symptom: Temperature between compressor inlet and outlet is noticeably different.
Amount of refrigerant: Proper or too much.

Item 5:
Symptom: Immediately after the air conditioner is turned off, refrigerant in slight glass stays clear.
Amount of refrigerant: Too much.

Item 6:
Symptom: When the air conditioner is turned off, refrigerant foams and then stays clear.
Amount of refrigerant: Proper.

WARNING: For service to Air Conditioning System please take your vehicle to an Air Conditioning Service Specialist. This is necessary because of Environmental and Laws associated to Environmental reasons.

PROBLEM DIAGNOSIS

Problem: No cooling or warm air!
Possible Causes:
* Magnetic clutch does not engage:
(a) A/C fuse blow.
(b) Magnetic clutch faulty.
(c) A/C switch faulty.
(d) Temperature control resistor faulty.
(e) Thermostat faulty.
(f) A/C amplifier faulty.
(g) Wiring or ground faulty.
(h) Refrigerant empty.
(i) Heater relay faulty.
(j) Circuit breaker faulty.
(k) Pressure switch faulty.
* Compressor does not rotate properly:

(a) Drive belt loose or broken.
(b) Compressor faulty.
* Expansion valve faulty.
* Leak in system.
* Fusible plug on receiver blown or clogged screen.
* Blower does not operate:
(a) Heater circuit breaker blown.
(b) A/C switch faulty.
(c) Temperature control resistor faulty.
(d) Heater relay faulty.
(e) Blower motor faulty.
(f) Wiring faulty.
(g) Magnetic valve faulty.

Problem: Cool air comes out intermitently!
Possible Causes:
* Magnetic clutch slipping.
* Expansion valve faulty.
* Wiring connection faulty.
* Excessive moisture in the system.

Problem: Limited amount of cool air at high speed!
Possible Causes:
* Thermostat faulty.
* A/C amplifier faulty.

Problem: Cool air comes out only at high speed!
Possible Causes:
* Condenser clogged.
* Drive belt slipping.
* Compressor faulty.
* Insufficient or too much refrigerant.
* Air in system.

Problem: Insufficient cooling!
Possible Causes:
* Condenser clogged.
* Drive belt slipping.
* Magnetic clutch faulty.
* Compressor faulty.
* Expansion valve faulty.
* Thermistor faulty.
* A/C amplifier faulty.
* Insufficient or too much refrigerant.
* Air or excessive compressor oil in system.
* Receiver clogged.
* Water valve set faulty.

Problem: Insufficient velocity of cool air!
Possible Causes:

* Evaporator clogged or frosted.
* Air leakage from cooling unit or air duct.
* Air inlet blocked.
* Blower motor faulty.

Air Conditioning Components for a Dual System 6..'s Series.

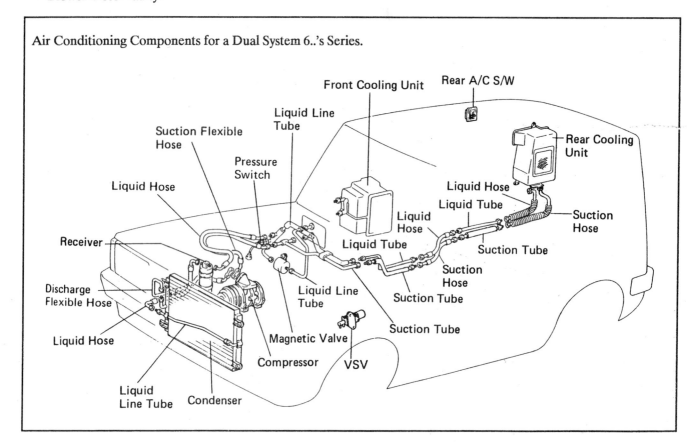

Air Conditioning System for a 7.'s Series.

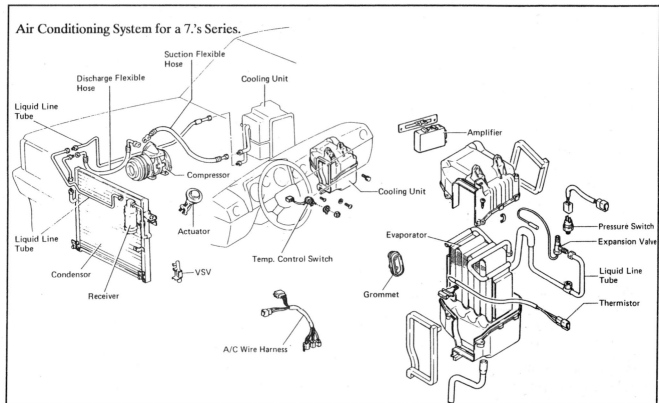

ELECTRICAL

Description **Page**

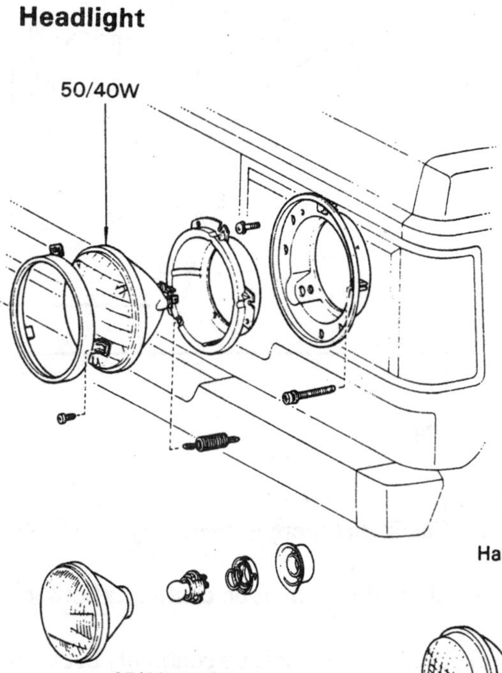

Headlight
50/40W
45/40W 12V
55/50W 24V

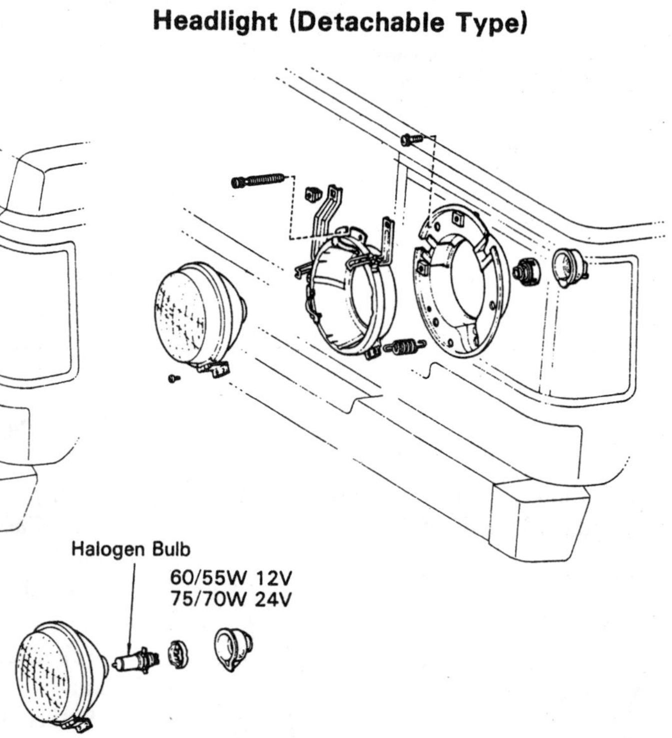

Headlight (Detachable Type)
Halogen Bulb
60/55W 12V
75/70W 24V

ELECTRICAL

LIGHTING.

LIGHT CONTROL SWITCH & HEADLIGHT DIMMER SWITCH

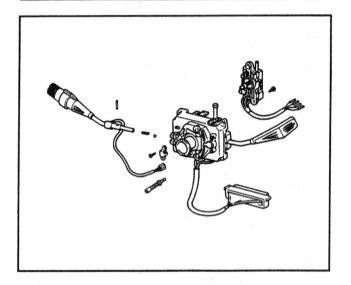

Replacement

1. Remove the Terminals From the Connector, the Light Control Switch and the Headlight Dimmer Switch.

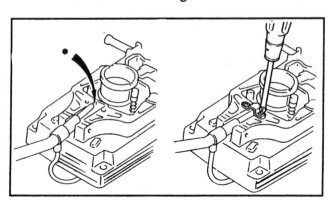

2. Install the Headlight Dimmer Switch.

3. Insert the Spring into the Lever and Install the Lever with the Pin.

4. Place the Ball on the Spring, Position the Lever at "HI" and Install the Plate.

5. Ensure that the Switch Operates Smoothly.

6. Install the Terminals to the Connector.

HEADLIGHT CONTROL RELAY

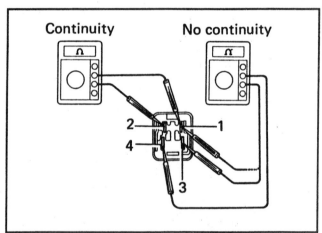

Inspection

1. Inspect Relay Continuity.

(a) Check that there is continuity between terminals 1 and 2.

(b) Check that there is no continuity between terminals 3 and 4.

(c) Check that there is no continuity between terminals 1 and 4.

* If continuity is not as specified, replace the relay.

2. Inspect Relay Operation.

(a) Apply battery voltage across terminals 1 and 2.

(b) Check that there is continuity between terminals 3 and 4.

(c) Check that there is no continuity between terminals 1 and 4.

* If operation is not as described, replace the relay.

TAILLIGHT CONTROL RELAY

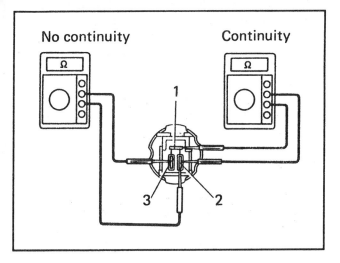

No continuity   Continuity

Inspection

1.Inspect Relay Continuity.

(a) Check that there is continuity between terminals 1 and 2.

(b) Check that there is no continuity between terminals 2 and 3.

* If continuity is not as specified, replace the relay.

2.Inspect Relay Operation.

(a) Apply battery voltage across terminals 1 and 2..

(b) Check that there is continuity between terminals 2 and 3.

* If operation is not as described, replace the relay.

DIMMER RELAY

Inspection

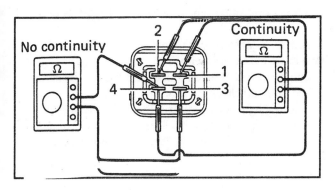

No continuity   Continuity

1.Inspect Relay Continuity.

(a) Check that there is continuity between terminals 1 and 4.

(b) Check that there is continuity between terminals 2 and 4.

(c) Check that there is no continuity between terminals 3 and 4.

* If continuity is not as specified, replace the relay.

2.Inspect Relay Operation.

(a) Apply battery voltage across terminals 2 and 4.

(b) Check that there is continuity between terminals 3 and 4.

(c) Check that there is no continuity between terminals 1 and 4.

* If operation is not as described, replace the relay.

TURN SIGNAL & HAZARD WARNING SWITCH

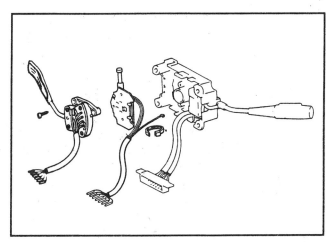

Inspection

Inspect the Switch Continuity Between Terminals:

Switch Position	Terminal
Turn Signal L	9 - 3 and 2 - 7
Turn Signal N	2 - 7
Turn Signal R	3 - 8 and 2 - 7
Hazard	9 - 3 and 3 - 8 and 7 - 1

* If continuity is not as specified, replace the switch.

Replacement

1.Remove the terminals from the connector.

2.Remove the 3 screws, and remove the wiper and washer switch.

3.Remove the turn signal and hazard switch.

4.Install the turn signal and hazard switch.

5.Install the wiper and washer switch.

6.Connect the terminals to the connector.

TURN SIGNAL FLASHER

Inspection

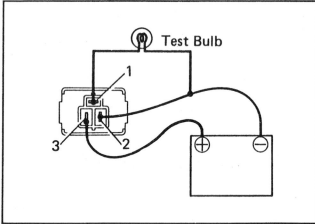

1.Connect the positive (+) lead from the battery to terminals 3. Connect the negative (-) lead to terminals 2.

2.Connect a test bulb between terminals 1 and 2 and check that the bulb goes on and off.

Test bulb: 12V system 55W

            24V system 50W

* The turn signal lights should flash 75 to 95 times/minute.

* If one of the front or rear turn signal lights has an open circuit, the number of flashes would be more than 120/minute.

* If operation is not as described, replace the flasher.

PROBLEM DIAGNOSIS

Problem: Only 1 light does not light (all exterior)!
Possible Causes and Remedies:

* Light bulb burned out. Remedy - replace bulb.

* Socket, wire or ground faulty. Remedy - repair as necessary.

Problem: No headlights light!
Possible Causes and Remedies:

* Fusible link blown. Remedy - replace fusible link.

* Headlight control relay faulty. Remedy - check relay.

* Light control switch faulty. Remedy - check switch.

* Wiring or ground faulty. Remedy - repair as necessary.

Problem: High beam headlights or headlight flashers do not operate!
Possible Causes and Remedies:

* Light control switch faulty. Remedy - check switch.

* Wiring faulty. Remedy - repair as necessary.

Problem: Tail, parking and license lights do not light!
Possible Causes and Remedies:

* TAIL fuse blown. Remedy - replace fuse and check for short.

* Fusible link blown. Remedy - replace fusible link.

* Taillight control relay faulty. Remedy - check relay.

* Light control switch faulty. Remedy - check switch.

* Wiring or ground faulty. Remedy - repair as necessary.

Problem: Stop lights do not light!
Possible Cause and Remedy:

* Stop light switch faulty. Remedy - adjust or replace switch.

Problem: Instrument lights do not light (taillights light)!
Possible Causes and Remedies:

* Light control rheostat faulty. Remedy - check rheostat.

* Wiring or ground faulty. Remedy - repair as necessary.

Problem: Turn signal does not flash on one side!
Possible Causes and Remedies:

* Turn signal switch faulty. Remedy - check switch.

* Wiring or ground faulty. Remedy - repair as necessary.

Problem: Turn signals do not operate!

* TURN fuse blown. Remedy - replace fuse and check for short.

* Turn signal flasher faulty. Remedy - check flasher.

* Turn signal/hazard switch faulty. Remedy - check switch.

* Turn signal relay faulty (24V, 60 Series). Remedy - check relay.

* Wiring or ground faulty. Remedy - repair as necessary.

Problem: Hazard red indicator light does not operate!

Possible Causes and Remedies:

* Hazard red indicator light relay faulty. Remedy - check relay.

* Wiring or ground faulty. Remedy - repair as necessary.

Problem: Rear fog lights do not light!

Possible Causes and Remedies:

* DOME or HEAD RH-LWR fuse blown. Remedy - replace fuse and check for short.

* Rear fog light switch faulty. Remedy - check switch.

* Rear fog light relay faulty. Remedy - check relay.

* Wiring or ground faulty. Remedy - repair as necessary.

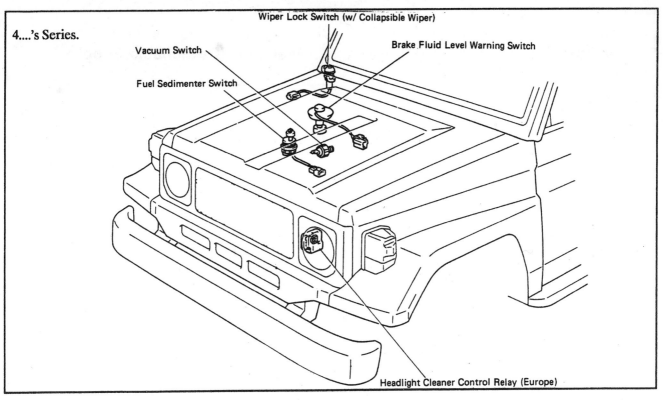

4....'s Series.

Wiper Lock Switch (w/ Collapsible Wiper)

Vacuum Switch

Brake Fluid Level Warning Switch

Fuel Sedimenter Switch

Headlight Cleaner Control Relay (Europe)

Turn Signal & Hazard Light

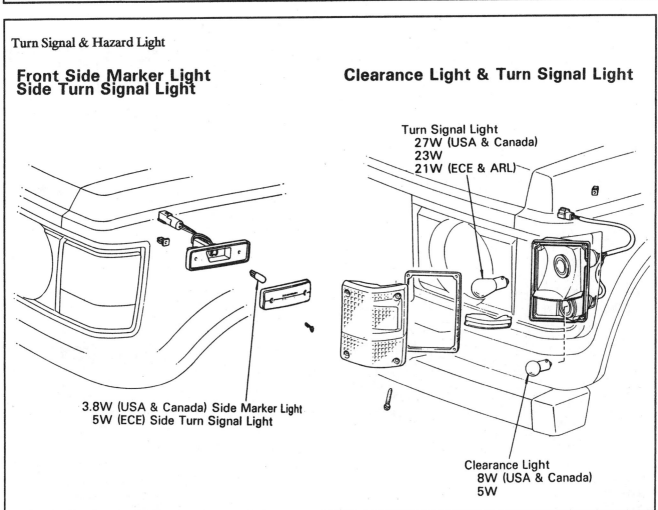

Front Side Marker Light
Side Turn Signal Light

Clearance Light & Turn Signal Light

Turn Signal Light
27W (USA & Canada)
23W
21W (ECE & ARL)

3.8W (USA & Canada) Side Marker Light
5W (ECE) Side Turn Signal Light

Clearance Light
8W (USA & Canada)
5W

6...'s Series.

Headlight

50/40W

Headlight (Detachable Type)

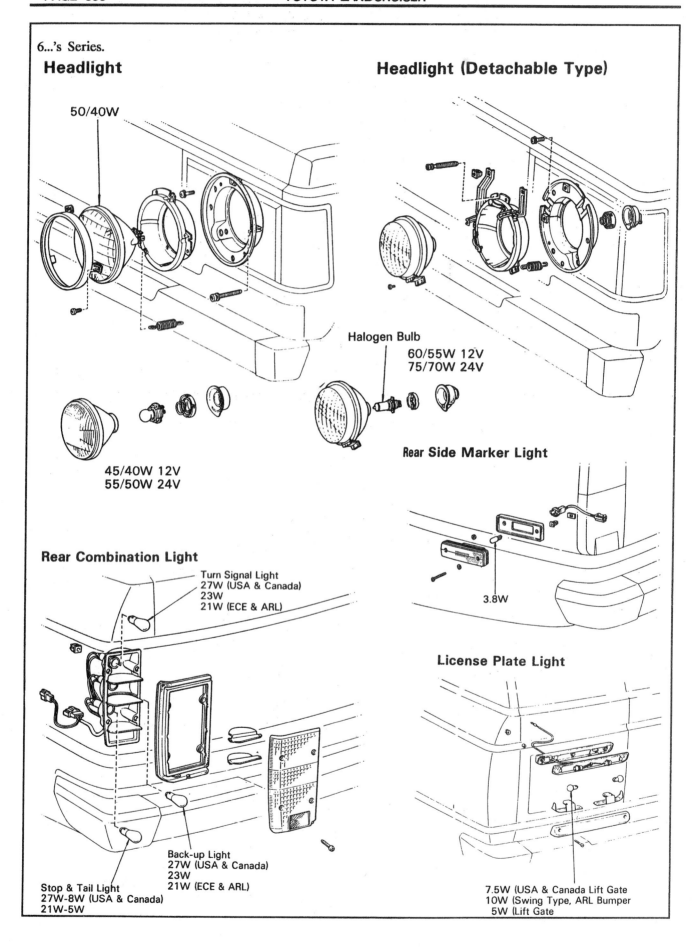

Halogen Bulb
60/55W 12V
75/70W 24V

45/40W 12V
55/50W 24V

Rear Side Marker Light

3.8W

Rear Combination Light

Turn Signal Light
27W (USA & Canada)
23W
21W (ECE & ARL)

Back-up Light
27W (USA & Canada)
23W
21W (ECE & ARL)

Stop & Tail Light
27W-8W (USA & Canada)
21W-5W

License Plate Light

7.5W (USA & Canada Lift Gate
10W (Swing Type, ARL Bumper
5W (Lift Gate

WIPERS AND WASHERS

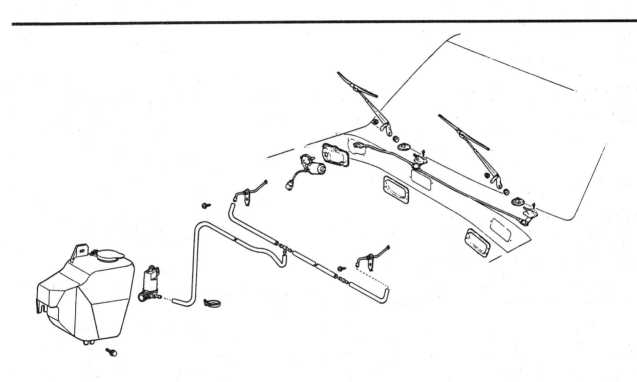

WIPERS AND WASHERS

Inspection of Switch

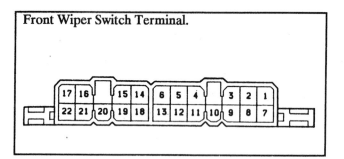

Front Wiper Switch Terminal.

Inspect Continuity between Terminals:
1) MIST   -   Terminal 21 - 17
2) OFF   -   "   20 - 21
3) INT   -   "   20 - 21
              &   "   19 - 14
4) LO   -   "   21 - 17
5) HI   -   "   17 - 22
6) Washer OFF -
   Washer ON -   "   14 - 15

Replacement

1. Remove the terminals from the connector.
2. Remove the wiper and washer switch.
3. Install the wiper and washer switch.
4. Connect the terminals to the connector.

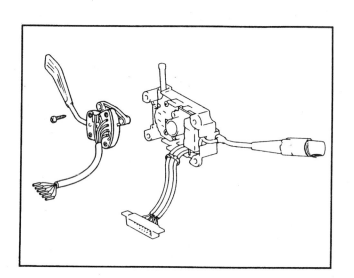

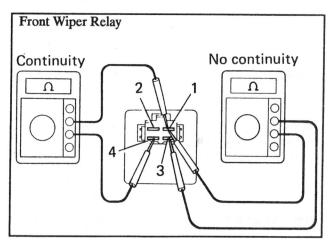

Front Wiper Relay

Continuity   No continuity

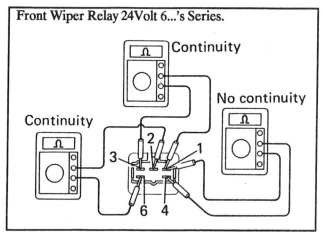

Front Wiper Relay 24Volt 6...'s Series.

Continuity

Continuity   No continuity

FRONT WIPER MOTOR

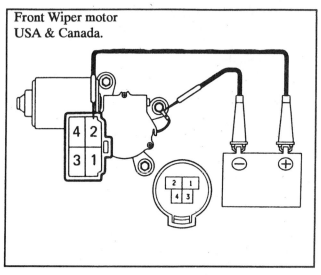

Front Wiper motor
USA & Canada.

Front Wiper Motor

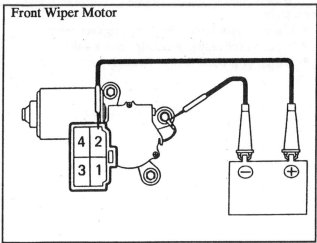

Inspection

1.Inspect that Motor Operates at Low Speed.

(a) Disconnect the connector from the wiper motor.

(b) Connect the positive (+) lead from the battery to terminal 2. Connect the negative (-) lead to the motor body.

(c) Check that the motor operates at low speed.

2.Inspect that Motor Operates at High Speed.

(a) Connect the positive (+) lead from the battery to terminals 1. Connect the negative (-) lead to the motor body.

(b) Check that the motor operates at high speed.

3.Inspect that Motor Operates, Stopping at Stop Position.

(a) Operate the motor at low speed.

(b) Stop the motor operation anywhere except the stop position by disconnecting the battery positive (+) terminal.

(c) Connect the positive (+) lead from the battery to terminal 4. Connect the negative (-) lead to the motor body. Connect terminals 2 and 3.

(d) Check that the motor stops running at the stopped position after the motor operates again.

* If operation is not as described, replace the motor.

REAR WIPER MOTOR

Inspection

1.Inspect that Motor Operates.

(a) Connect the positive (+) lead from the battery to terminal 3. Connect the negative (-) lead to the motor body.

(b) Check that the motor operates.

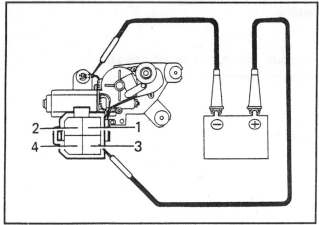

2.Inspect that Motor Operates, Stopping at Stop Position.

(a) Connect the positive (+) lead from the battery to terminal 3. Connect the negative (-) lead to the motor body. Operate the motor.

(b) Stop motor operation anywhere except stop position by disconnecting terminal 3.

(c) Connect terminals 3 and 4.

(d) Connect the positive (+) lead from the battery to terminal 1.

(e) Check that the motor stops running at stop position after the motor operates again.

* If operation is not as described, replace the motor.

PROBLEM DIAGNOSIS

Problem: Wipers do not operate or return to off position!

Possible Causes and Remedies:

* WIPER fuse blown. Remedy - replace fuse and check for short.

* Wiper motor faulty. Remedy - check motor.

* Wiper switch faulty. Remedy - check switch.

* Wiper relay faulty (24V, 60 series). Remedy - check relay.

* Wiper lock relay faulty. Remedy - check relay.

* Wiper lock switch faulty. Remedy - check switch.

* Wiring or ground faulty. Remedy - repair as necessary.

Problem: Wipers do not operate in INT position!

Possible Causes and Remedies:

* Wiper relay faulty (24V, 60 series) Remedy - check relay.

* Wiper control relay faulty. Remedy - check relay.

* Wiper motor faulty. Remedy - check motor.

* Wiring or ground faulty. Remedy - repair as necessary.

Problem: Washer does not operate!
  Possible Causes and Remedies:

* Washer hose or nozzle clogged. Remedy - repair as necessary.
  * Washer motor faulty. Remedy - replace motor.
  * Wiper switch faulty. Remedy - check switch.
  * Wiring or ground faulty. Remedy - repair as necessary.

Front Wipers.

Rear Wipers.

Front Windscreen Washer.

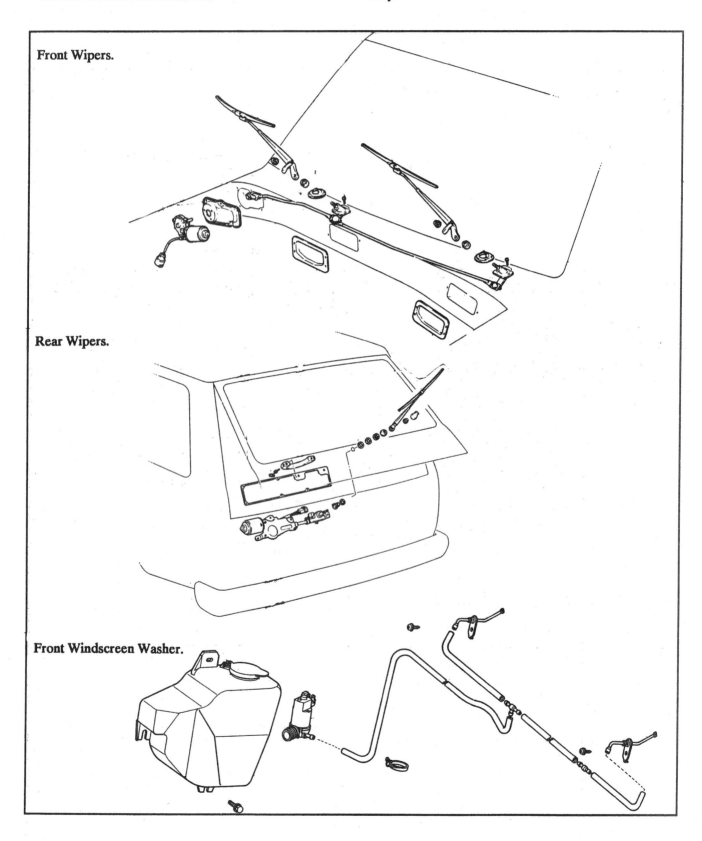

HEATER UNIT

HEATER UNIT.

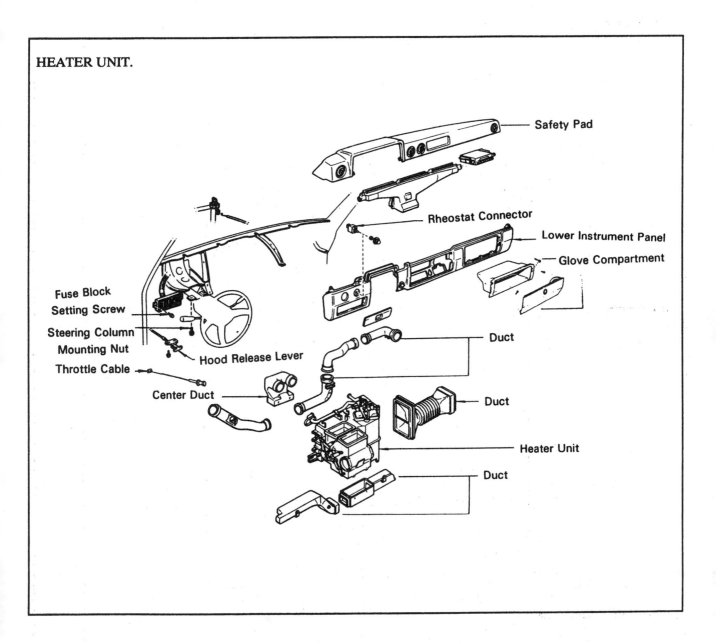

Safety Pad

Rheostat Connector

Lower Instrument Panel

Glove Compartment

Fuse Block

Setting Screw

Steering Column

Mounting Nut

Hood Release Lever

Throttle Cable

Center Duct

Duct

Duct

Heater Unit

Duct

PROBLEM DIAGNOSIS

Problem: Blower does not work when fan switch is on!

Possible Causes and Remedies:

* Heater circuit breaker OFF. Remedy - reset breaker and check for short.

* Heater relay faulty. Remedy - check relay.

* Heater blower switch faulty. Remedy - check switch.

* Heater blower resistor faulty. Remedy - check resistor.

* Heater blower motor faulty. Remedy - replace motor.

* Wiring or ground faulty. Remedy - repair as necessary.

Problem: Incorrect temperature output!

Possible Causes and Remedies:

* Control cables broken or binding. Remedy - check cables.

* Heater hoses leaking or clogged. Remedy - replace hose.

* Water valve faulty. Remedy - replace valve.

* Air dampers broken. Remedy - repair dampers.

* Air ducts clogged. Remedy - repair ducts.

* Heater radiator leaking or clogged. Remedy - repair radiator.

* Heater control unit faulty. Remedy - repair control unit.

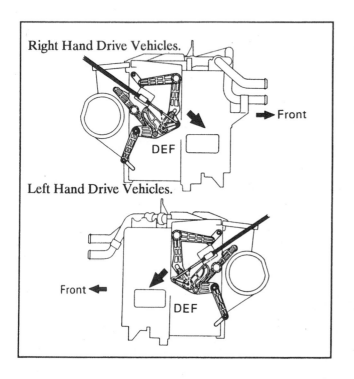

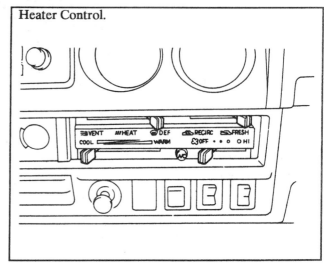

Heater Control.

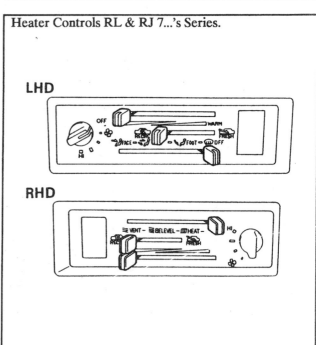

Heater Controls RL & RJ 7...'s Series.

LHD

RHD

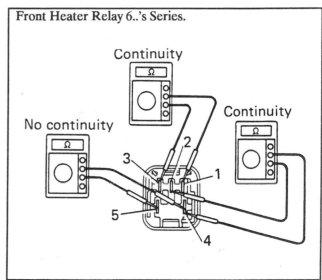

Front Heater Relay 6..'s Series.

RADIO AND STEREO TAPE PLAYER

RADIO and STERO TAPE PLAYER.

RADIO ANTENNA.

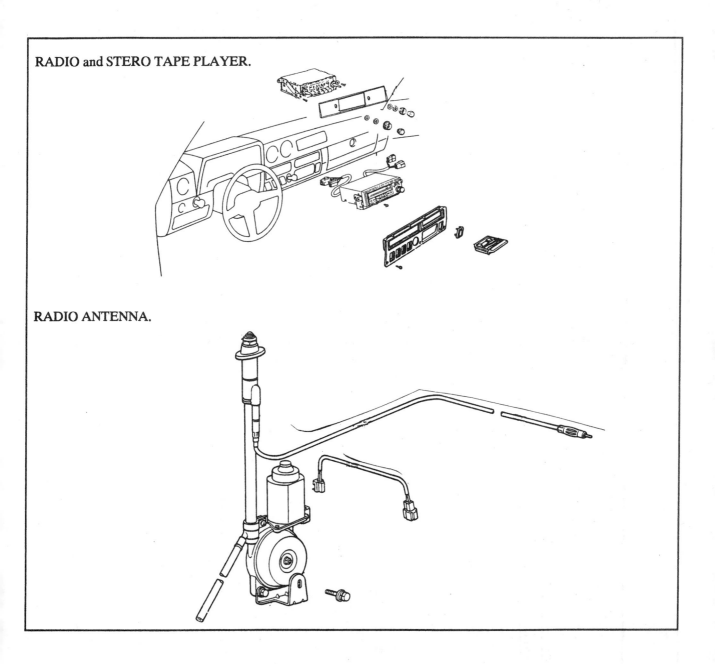

RADIO and STERO TAPE PLAYER CIRCUIT DIAGRAM.

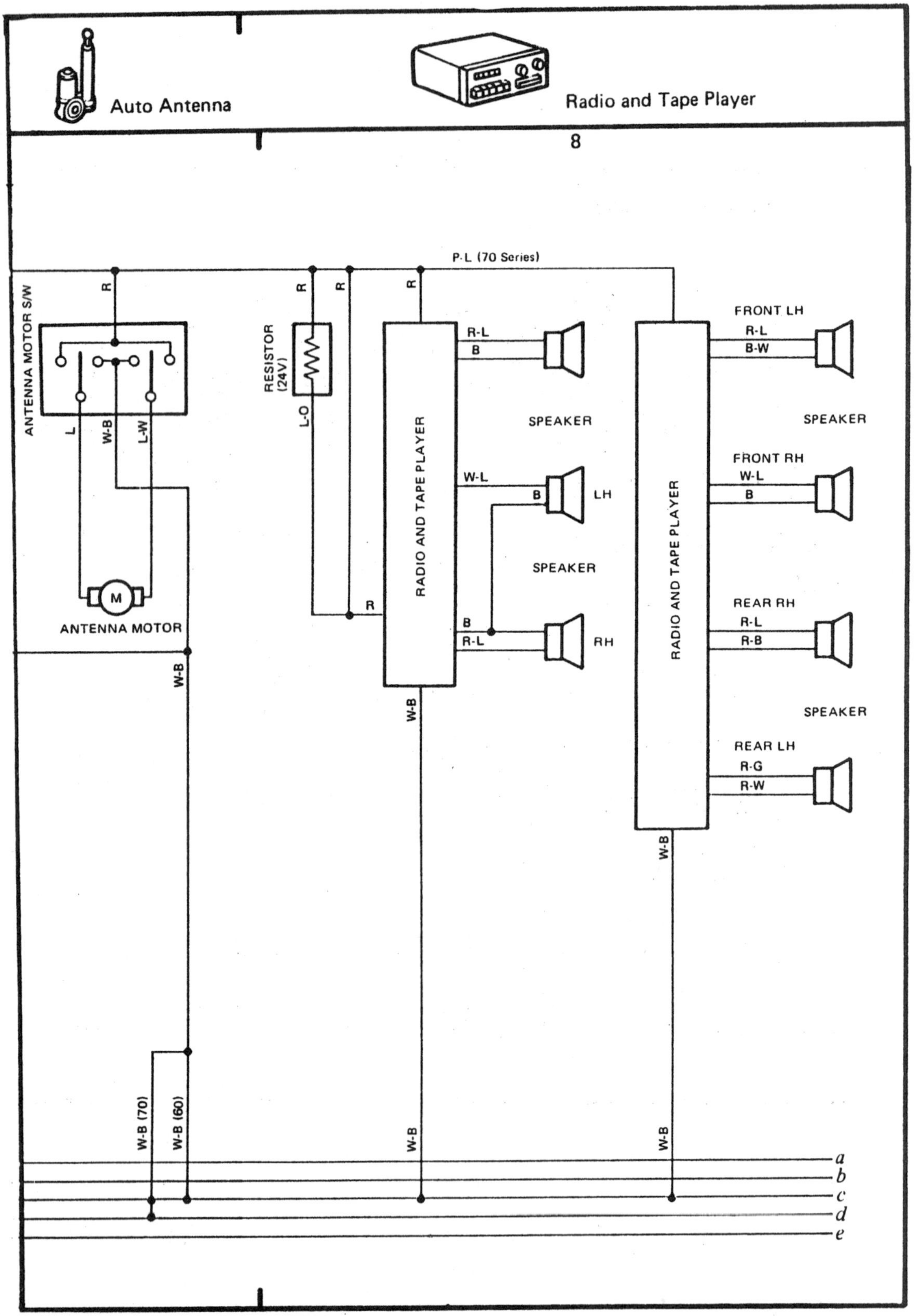

Auto Antenna

Radio and Tape Player

8

P·L (70 Series)

ANTENNA MOTOR S/W

ANTENNA MOTOR

RESISTOR (24V)

RADIO AND TAPE PLAYER

SPEAKER

LH

SPEAKER

RH

RADIO AND TAPE PLAYER

FRONT LH
R·L
B·W

SPEAKER

FRONT RH
W·L
B

SPEAKER

REAR RH
R·L
R·B

SPEAKER

REAR LH
R·G
R·W

W-B (70)
W-B (60)

a
b
c
d
e

INSTRUMENT CLUSTERS

INSTRUMENTATION 4..'s and 6..'s Series.

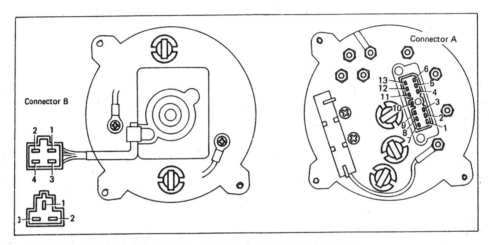

COMBINATION METER CIRCUIT

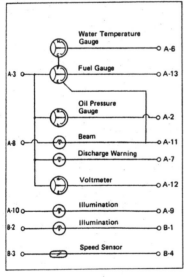

No.		Wiring Connector Sides
A	2	Oil Pressure Sender Gauge
	3	GAUGE Fuse
	6	Water Temperature Sender Gauge
	7	CHARGE Fuse
	8	Headlight Dimmer Switch Terminal
	9	Ground
	10	TAIL Fuse
	11	Ground
	12	Ground
	13	Fuel Sender Gauge
B	1	Ground
	2	TAIL Fuse
	3	Emission Computer
	4	Ground

INSTRUMENTATION 7...'s Series with Tachometer.

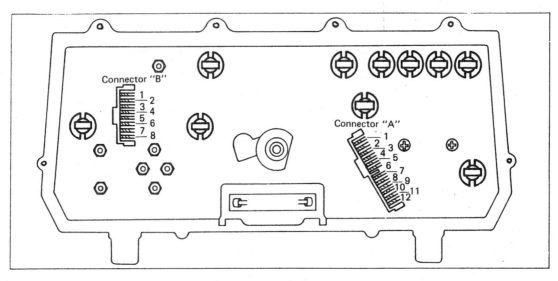

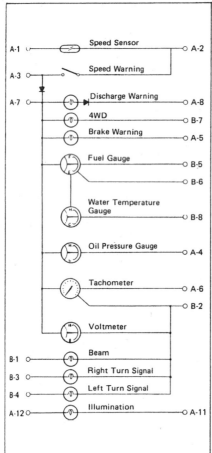

COMBINATION METER CIRCUIT

No.		Wiring Connector Sides
A	1	Emission Computer
	2	Ground
	3	Speed Warning Buzzer
	4	Oil Pressure Sender Gauge
	5	Vacuum Switch, Parking Brake Switch and Brake Fluid Level Warning Switch
	6	Ignition Coil or Tach. Sensor
	7	ENGINE Fuse
	8	CHARGE Fuse
	11	Light Control Rheostat Terminal or Ground
	12	TAIL Fuse
B	1	Headlight Dimmer Switch Terminal
	2	Ground
	3	Turn Signal Switch Terminal
	4	Turn Signal Switch Terminal
	5	Fuel Sender Gauge Terminal 1
	6	Ground
	7	4WD Indicator Switch
	8	Water Temperature Sender Gauge

INSTRUMENTATION 7...'s Series With out Tachometer.

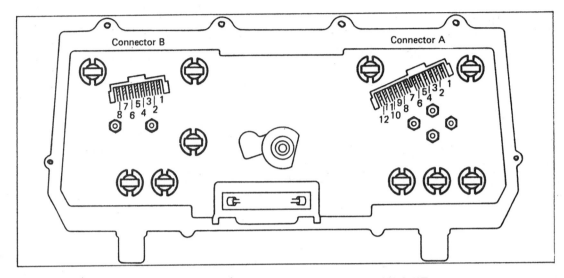

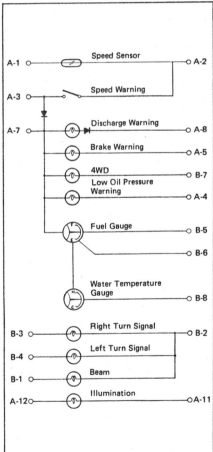

COMBINATION METER CIRCUIT

No.		Wiring Connector Sides
A	1	Emission Computer
	2	Ground
	3	Speed Warning Buzzer
	4	Oil Pressure Switch
	5	Vacuum Switch, Parking Brake Switch and Brake Fluid Level Warning Switch
	7	ENGINE Fuse
	8	CHARGE Fuse
	11	Ground
	12	TAIL Fuse
B	1	Headlight Dimmer Switch Terminal
	2	Ground
	3	Turn Signal Switch Terminal
	4	Turn Signal Switch Terminal
	5	Fuel Sender Gauge Terminal 1
	6	Ground
	7	4WD Indicator Switch
	8	Water Temperature Sender Gauge

PROBLEM DIAGNOSIS

Problem: Tachometer does not work!
  Possible Causes and Remedies:
  * Fuses blown. Remedy - replace in-line fuses and check for short.
  * Tachometer faulty. Remedy - check tachometer.
  * Wiring faulty. Remedy - repair as necessary.

Problem: Tachometer does not work!
  Possible Causes and Remedies:
  * "GAUGE" fuse blown. Remedy - replace fuse and check for short.
  * Tachometer faulty. Remedy - check tachometer.
  * Wiring faulty. Remedy - repair as necessary.

Problem: Fuel gauge does not work!
  Possible Causes and Remedies:
  * "GAUGE" fuse blown. Remedy - replace fuse and check for short.
  * Fuel gauge faulty. Remedy - check gauge.
  * Sender gauge faulty. Remedy - check sender gauge.
  * Wiring or ground faulty. Remedy - repair as necessary.

Problem: Water temperature gauge does not work!
  Possible Causes and Remedies:
  * "GAUGE" fuse blow. Remedy - replace fuse and check for short.
  * Water temperature gauge faulty. Remedy - check gauge.
  * Water temperature sender gauge faulty. Remedy - check sender gauge.
  * Wiring or ground faulty. Remedy - repair as necessary.

Problem: Low oil pressure warning light does not work!
  Possible Causes and Remedies:
  * "GAUGE" fuse blown. Remedy - replace fuse and check for short.
  * Bulb burned out. Remedy - replace bulb.
  * Oil pressure warning switch faulty. Remedy - check switch.
  * Wiring or ground faulty. Remedy - repair as necessary.

Problem: Brake warning light does not light!
  Possible Causes and Remedies:
  * "GAUGE" fuse blown. Remedy - replace fuse and check for short.
  * Bulb burned out. Remedy - replace bulb.
  * Brake fluid level warning switch faulty. Remedy - check switch.
  * Wiring or ground faulty. Remedy - repair as necessary.

Problem: Discharge warning light does not light!
  Possible Causes and Remedies:
  * "GAUGE" fuse blown. Remedy - replace fuse and check for short.
  * Bulb burned out. Remedy - replace bulb.
  * Wiring or ground faulty. Remedy - repair as necessary.

Problem: Parking brake indicator light does not light (Australia only)!
  Possible Causes and Remedies:
  * "GAUGE" fuse blown. Remedy - replace fuse and check for short.
  * Bulb burned out. Remedy - replace bulb.
  * Parking brake switch faulty. Remedy - check switch.
  * Wiring or ground faulty. Remedy - repair as necessary.

SPECIFICATIONS

3F ENGINE

ENGINE MECHANICAL

Specifications

Engine coolant capacity					
FJ70, 73, 75 series	w/o Heater		15.0 liters	15.9 US qts	13.2 Imp. qts
	w/ Front heater		17.0 liters	18.0 US qts	15.0 Imp. qts
	w/ Front and rear heaters		19.0 liters	20.1 US qts	16.7 Imp. qts
FJ62 series	w/o Heater		15.5 liters	16.4 US qts	13.6 Imp. qts
	w/ Front heater		17.5 liters	18.5 US qts	15.4 Imp. qts
	w/ Front and rear heaters		19.5 liters	20.6 US qts	17.2 Imp. qts
Engine oil capacity					
Drain and refill	w/o Oil filter change		7.0 liters	7.4 US qts	6.2 Imp. qts
	w/ Oil filter change		7.8 liters	8.2 US qts	6.9 Imp. qts
Dry fill			8.0 liters	8.5 US qts	7.0 Imp. qts
Battery gravity when fully charged at 20°C (68°F)			1.25 – 1.27		
High-tension cord	Resistance	Limit	25 kΩ per cord		
Spark plug					
Type		ND	W14EX-U		
		NGK	BP4EY		
Correct electrode gap			0.8 mm	0.031 in.	
Drive belt deflection with 10 kg (22.0 lb, 98N)					
Alternator – Water pump		New belt	7.0 – 9.0 mm	0.278 – 0.354 in.	
		Used belt	9.0 – 12.0 mm	0.354 – 0.472 in.	
PS pump – Crankshaft		New belt	7.0 – 9.5 mm	0.278 – 0.374 in.	
		Used belt	8.0 – 10.0 mm	0.315 – 0.393 in.	
A/C compressor – Crankshaft		New belt	12.0 – 15.0 mm	0.472 – 0.590 in.	
		Used belt	15.0 – 21.0 mm	0.590 – 0.827 in.	
Valve clearance	at hot	IN	0.20 mm	0.008 in.	
		EX	0.35 mm	0.014 in.	
Distributor	Dwell angle		41 ± 4°		
Ignition timing			7° BTDC @ Max. 900 rpm		
Idle speed		M/T	650 rpm		
		A/T	750 rpm		
Maximum speed (w/ Anti-over run)			4,600 ± 200 rpm		
Idle mixture speed		M/T	690 rpm		
		A/T	790 rpm		
Fast idle speed			1,800 rpm		
TP setting speed			1,000 rpm		
Idle CO concentration			1.5 ± 1.0%		
Intake manifold vacuum	at idle speed		420 mmHg (16.54 in.Hg, 56.0 kPa) or more		
Compression pressure	at 200 rpm	STD	10.5 kg/cm² (149 psi, 1,030 kPa) or more		
		Limit	8.0 kg/cm² (114 psi, 785 kPa)		
Pressure difference between each cylinder			1.0 kg/cm² (14 psi, 98 kPa) or less		

2F engine

ENGINE TUNE-UP

Drive belt tension (Genuine deflection)		
Deflection with 10 kg (22 lb) force		
Fan – Alternator	N.S.W & Victoria	13 – 16 mm / 0.51 – 0.59 in
	Other australian states ex Australia	7 – 10 mm / 0.28 – 0.39 in
Fan – Air Pump	New belt	7 – 9 mm / 0.28 – 0.35 in.
(USA & Canada)	Used belt	9 – 12 mm / 0.35 – 0.47 in
	N.S.W & Victoria	7 – 10 mm / 0.28 – 0.39 in
Burroughs belt tension gauge No. BT-33-73F		
	Air con. New belt	100 – 150 lbs
	Used belt	60 – 80 lbs
	Fan New belt	120 – 170 lbs
	Used belt	80 – 120 lbs
Battery electrolyte specific gravity		
When fully charged at 20°C (68°F)		1.25 – 1.27
Engine oil capacity	Dry fill	8.0 liters / 8.5 US qt / 7.0 Imp qt
	Drain & refill w/ Oil filter change	7.8 liters / 8.2 US qt / 6.9 Imp qt
	w/o Oil filter change	7.0 liters / 7.4 US qt / 6.2 Imp qt
Radiator cap valve opening pressure	STD	0.75 – 1.06 kg/cm² / 10.7 – 14.9 psi
	Limit	0.6 kg/cm² / 8.5 psi
Coolant capacity	w/ Heater or Air con.	
	FJ40, 43, 4b series	16.0 liters / 16.9 US qt / 14.1 Imp qt
	FJ60 series	16.5 liters / 17.4 US qt / 14.5 Imp qt
	FA series	25.0 liters / 26.4 US qt / 22.0 Imp qt
Spark plugs Type	FJ series ND	W14EXR-U (USA & ECE)
	NGK	BPR4EY (USA & ECE)
	ND	W14EX-U (Others)
	NGK	BP4EY (Others)
	FA series ND	W14EX-U
	NGK	BP4EY
Gap		0.8 mm / 0.031 in
High tension cord resistance		Less than 25 kΩ per cord
Distributor	Air gap (USA FJ series)	0.2 – 0.4 mm / 0.008 – 0.016 in
	Rubbing block gap (Others)	0.30 mm / 0.0118 in.
Dwell angle (except USA FJ series)		41°
Ignition timing		7° BTDC / Max 950 rpm
Firing order		1 – 5 – 3 – 6 – 2 – 4
Valve clearance Hot	Intake	0.20 mm / 0.008 in
	Exhaust	0.35 mm / 0.014 in
Idle speed		650 rpm
Idle mixture speed (except USA)		690 rpm
Fast idle speed	USA	1,800 rpm (w/ EGR & EVAP systems OFF and vacuum advancer OFF)
	N.S.W. & Victoria	1,800 rpm (w/ EGR & EVAP systems OFF)
	Others	1,800 rpm
Throttle positioner setting speed	N.S.W. & Victoria	1,200 rpm (w/ EGR & EVAP systems OFF)
	Others	1,000 rpm
Compression pressure at 250 rpm	STD	10.5 kg/cm² / 149 psi
	Limit	8.0 kg/cm² / 114 psi
Pressure difference between each cylinder		Less than 1.0 kg/cm² (14 psi)

Crankshaft and bearing

Thrust clearance	STD	0.015 – 0.204 mm	0.0006 – 0.0080 in.
	Limit	0.30 mm	0.0118 in.
Thrust washer thickness	STD	2.430 – 2.480 mm	0.0957 – 0.0976 in.
	O/S 0.125	2.493 – 2.543 mm	0.0981 – 0.1001 in.
	O/S 0.250	2.555 – 2.605 mm	0.1006 – 0.1026 in.
Main journal oil clearance	STD	0.016 – 0.056 mm	0.0006 – 0.0022 in.
	U/S 0.25 and 0.50	0.021 – 0.067 mm	0.0008 – 0.0026 in.
	Limit	0.10 mm	0.0039 in.
Main journal diameter	STD No. 1	66.972 – 66.996 mm	2.6367 – 2.6376 in.
	No. 2	68.472 – 68.496 mm	2.6957 – 2.6967 in.
	No. 3	69.972 – 69.996 mm	2.7548 – 2.7557 in.
	No. 4	71.472 – 71.496 mm	2.8139 – 2.8148 in.
	U/S 0.25 No. 1	66.745 – 66.755 mm	2.6278 – 2.6281 in.
	No. 2	68.245 – 68.255 mm	2.6868 – 2.6872 in.
	No. 3	69.745 – 69.755 mm	2.7459 – 2.7463 in.
	No. 4	71.245 – 71.255 mm	2.8049 – 2.8053 in.

Torque Specifications

Part Tightened	kg-cm	ft-lb	N·m
Cylinder head x Cylinder block	1,250	90	123
Valve rocker support x Cylinder head			
12 mm bolt head	240	17	24
14 mm bolt head and nut	340	25	33
Manifold x Cylinder head			
14 mm bolt head	510	37	50
17 mm bolt head	700	51	69
Nut	570	41	56
Water outlet housing x Cylinder head	250	18	25
Water outlet x Water outlet housing	185	13	18
Cylinder head cover x Cylinder head	90	78 in.-lb	8.8
Camshaft thrust washer x Cylinder block	120	9	12
Timing gear cover x Front end plate or cylinder block			
10 mm bolt head	50	43 in.-lb	4.9
14 mm bolt head	250	18	25
Crankshaft pulley x Crankshaft	3,500	253	343
PS pulley x Crankshaft pulley	185	13	18
Valve lifter cover x Cylinder block	40	35 in.-lb	3.9
Main bearing cap x Cylinder block			
19 mm bolt head	1,375	99	135
17 mm bolt head	1,175	85	115
Connecting rod cap x Connecting rod	600	43	59
Front end plate x Cylinder block			
Screw	250	18	25
Bolt	310	22	30
Flywheel x Crankshaft	890	64	87
Drive plate x Crankshaft	890	64	87
Fuel pipe x Carburetor	150	11	15

SERVICE SPECIFICATIONS 21R, 21R-C and 22R

ENGINE TUNE-UP

Drive belt deflection (General countries)

Deflection at 10 kg (22 lb) force

Fan – Alternator	New belt	5 – 7 mm	0.20 – 0.28 in
	Used belt	7 – 10 mm	0.28 – 0.39 in
Crank – Air pump	New belt	8 – 10 mm	0.31 – 0.39 in
	Used belt	10 – 14 mm	0.39 – 0.55 in
Tension with SST (Reference)	New belt	45 – 55 kg	99 – 121 lb
	Used belt	20 – 35 kg	44 – 77 lb

(USA & Canada)

Borroughs belt tension gauge No BT-33-73F

	New belt	100 – 150 lbs
	Used belt	60 – 100 lbs

Battery electrolyte specific gravity
When fully charged at 20°C (68°F)   1.25 – 1.27

Engine oil capacity

21R & 21R-C	Dry fill	4.8 liters	5.1 US qt	4.2 Imp qt
	Drain & refill	4.3 liters	4.5 US qt	3.8 Imp qt
	w/o Oil filter change	3.6 liters	3.8 US qt	3.2 Imp qt
22R	Dry fill	4.8 liters	5.1 US qt	4.2 Imp qt
	Drain & refill	4.6 liters	4.9 US qt	4.0 Imp qt
	w/o Oil filter change	3.8 liters	4.0 US qt	3.3 Imp qt

Radiator cap valve opening pressure

	STD	0.75 – 1.05 kg/cm²	10.7 – 14.9 psi
	Limit	0.6 kg/cm²	8.5 psi

Coolant capacity

w/ Heater	21R & 21R-C	8.0 liters	8.5 US qt	7.0 Imp qt
	22R RN, RU	12.0 liters	12.7 US qt	11.0 Imp qt
	RJ	8.4 liters	8.9 US qt	7.4 Imp qt
	RJ	10.3 liters	10.9 US qt	9.1 Imp qt
RJ (w/o Heater)		8.1 liters	8.6 US qt	7.1 Imp qt

Spark plugs

Type	21R/RA Before '84/8, RX60)ND	W20EXR-U
		RPR6FY
	22R RU, RB ND	W16EX-U
		RP5EY
	Others ND	W16EXR-U
	NGK	RPR5FY
Gap	0.8 mm	0.031 in
High tension cord resistance	Less than 25 kΩ per cord	

Distributor

Breaker points type	Rubbing block gap	0.45 mm	0.0177 in
	Damping spring gap	0.1 – 0.4 mm	0.004 – 0.016 in
	Dwell angle	52°	
Breaker points less type	Air gap	0.2 – 0.4 mm	0.008 – 0.016 in

Ignition timing

21R	RA (Since '83/8). RX70	5° BTDC/Max. 750 rpm	
	RA (Before '83/8). RX60 (Ex. South Africa)	8° BTDC/Max. 750 rpm	
	RX60 (South Africa)	12° BTDC/Max. 750 rpm	
21R-C	Australia A/T	˟5° BTDC/Max. 600 rpm	
	Switzerland, Sweden	˟5° BTDC/Max. 650 rpm	
22R	RB20 (Since '84/8. 85 RON version)	˟0° BTDC/Max. 750 rpm	
	RJ (Australia)	˟0° BTDC/Max. 860 rpm	
	RB20 (Since '84/8, 90 RON version). RN, RU.	˟0° BTDC/Max. 950 rpm	
	RJ (Ex Australia)	˟5° BTDC/Max. 850 rpm	
	RB20 (Before '84/8, 85 RON version)	5° BTDC/Max. 950 rpm	
	RB20 (Before '84/8, 90 RON version), RB13	8° BTDC/Max. 950 rpm	

Firing order   1 – 3 – 4 – 2

Valve clearance

	Hot	Intake	Exhaust
		0.20 mm	0.30 mm
		0.008 in	0.012 in

Idle speed
(Ex. Canada RN 4x4)

M/T		700 rpm
A/T	Fed. RN w/ 4-speed A/T	700 rpm
	Canada RA, RT-A/T	850 rpm
	Others A/T	750 rpm

Idle speed and idle mixture

RN (Canada 4x4). RJ (Australia)		700 rpm
HJ (Ex Australia). RN (South Arabia). RU, RB, RA60.		800 rpm
61. HX. RT133		750 rpm
Idle speed		
RN (Canada 4x4). RJ (Australia)		600 rpm (M/T), 650 rpm (A/T)
HJ (Ex Australia). RX		740 rpm
RA (Australia). RT133		800 rpm
Idle mixture speed	Canada RN 4x4	2,600 rpm
	RB	
	21R & 21R-C	2,600 rpm
	(RA (Since '84/8). RX70)	2,400 rpm
Fast idle speed	22R RN, RJ	
	Others	1,050 rpm
Throttle positioner setting speed		1,200 rpm
Calif. HN 4x4 and HN C&C		
RX ex ECE M/1, HA60 61. RT133, HN		1,400 rpm
& RJ		
RB		

Cylinder Block

Warpage	Limit	0.05 mm	0.0020 in
Cylinder bore	STD 21R & 21R-C	84.00 – 84.03 mm	3.3071 – 3.3083 in
	22R Before '84/R	91.938 – 91.968 mm	3.6196 – 3.6208 in
	Since '84/8	91.96 – 91.99 mm	3.6205 – 3.6216 in
	O/S 0.50 21R & 21R-C	84.46 – 84.49 mm	3.3254 – 3.3264 in
	22R Before '84/8	92.438 – 92.468 mm	3.6393 – 3.6405 in
	Since '84/8	92.46 – 92.49 mm	3.6402 – 3.6413 in
	O/S 1.00 21R & 21R-C	84.96 – 84.99 mm	3.3449 – 3.3461 in
	22R Before '84/8	92.938 – 92.968 mm	3.6590 – 3.6602 in
	Since '84/8	92.96 – 92.99 mm	3.6598 – 3.6610 in
Wear	Limit 21R & 21R-C	0.03 – 0.05 mm	0.0012 – 0.0020 in
	22R	0.2 mm	0.008 in
Taper and out of round	Limit 21R & 21R-C	0.01 mm	0.0004 in
Difference between each cylinder	22R	Less than 0.03 mm (0.0012 in)	

Piston & Piston Ring

Piston diameter	STD 21R & 21R-C	83.96 – 83.99 mm	3.3055 – 3.3067 in
	22R Before '84/R	91.938 – 91.968 mm	3.6196 – 3.6208 in
	Since '84/8	91.96 – 91.99 mm	3.6205 – 3.6216 in
	O/S 0.50 21R & 21R-C	84.46 – 84.49 mm	3.3254 – 3.3264 in
	22R Before '84/8	92.438 – 92.468 mm	3.6393 – 3.6405 in
	Since '84/8	92.46 – 92.49 mm	3.6402 – 3.6413 in
	O/S 1.00 21R & 21R-C	84.96 – 84.99 mm	3.3449 – 3.3461 in
	22R Before '84/8	92.938 – 92.968 mm	3.6590 – 3.6602 in
	Since '84/8	92.96 – 92.99 mm	3.6598 – 3.6610 in
Cylinder to piston clearance	21R & 21R-C	0.03 – 0.05 mm	0.0012 – 0.0020 in
Piston ring end	No 1 21R & 21R-C	0.0052 – 0.0072 mm	0.0020 – 0.0028 in
gap STD	22R Before '84/R	0.25 – 0.47 mm	0.0098 – 0.0185 in
	Since '84/8	0.24 – 0.39 mm	0.0094 – 0.0154 in
	No 2 21R & 21R-C	0.15 – 0.42 mm	0.0059 – 0.0165 in
	22R Before '84/R	0.18 – 0.42 mm	0.0071 – 0.0165 in
	Since '84/8. Ex Australia RJ	0.60 – 0.70 mm	0.0236 – 0.0276 in

Crankshaft

Circle runout	Limit	0.1 mm	0.004 in
Thrust clearance	STD	0.02 – 0.22 mm	0.0008 – 0.0087 in
	Limit	0.3 mm	0.012 in
Main journal			
diameter	STD	59.98 – 60.00 mm	2.3614 – 2.3622 in
	U/S 0.25	59.70 – 59.71 mm	2.3504 – 2.3508 in
Main journal oil clearance	Limit	0.01 mm	0.0010 in
Taper and out of round	Limit	0.08 mm	0.0031 in
Bearing type		STD. U/S (0.25)	
Crank pin journal			
diameter	STD	52.99 – 53.00 mm	2.0862 – 2.0866 in
	U/S 0.25	52.70 – 52.71 mm	2.0748 – 2.0752 in
Oil clearance	Limit	0.01 mm	0.0004 in
		0.022 – 0.055 mm	0.0010 – 0.0022 in
		0.08 mm	0.0031 in
Bearing type		STD. U/S (0.25)	

Piston & Piston Ring

Piston diameter	STD	93.96 – 94.01 mm	3.6992 – 3.7012 in
	O/S type 0.50	94.46 – 94.51 mm	3.7189 – 3.7209 in
	O/S type 1.00	94.96 – 95.01 mm	3.7386 – 3.7405 in
	O/S type 1.50	95.46 – 95.51 mm	3.7583 – 3.7602 in
Piston to cylinder clearance		0.03 – 0.05 mm	0.0012 – 0.0020 in
Piston ring end gap (compression)	No. 1	0.20 – 0.56 mm	0.0079 – 0.0220 in
	No. 2	0.20 – 0.58 mm	0.0079 – 0.0228 in
	Oil	0.20 – 0.88 mm	0.0079 – 0.0346 in
	Rham		0.0017 in
Ring to ring groove clearance	No. 1	0.03 – 0.07 mm	0.0012 – 0.0028 in
	No. 2	0.02 – 0.06 mm	0.0008 – 0.0024 in
	Oil	0.03 – 0.07 mm	0.0012 – 0.0028 in
Piston pin diameter	No. 1	0.04 – 0.19 mm	0.0016 – 0.0075 in
Piston pin to piston oil clearance		0.008 – 0.012 mm	0.0003 – 0.0005 in

Crankshaft

Thrust clearance	STD	0.06 – 0.16 mm	0.0024 – 0.0063 in
	Limit	0.3 mm	0.012 in
Main journal oil clearance	STD	0.020 – 0.044 mm	0.0008 – 0.0017 in
	Limit	0.10 mm	0.0039 in
Main journal diameter	STD No.1	69.972 – 66.996 mm	2.6367 – 2.6376 in
	No.2	68.472 – 68.496 mm	2.6367 – 2.6367 in
	No.3	69.972 – 69.996 mm	2.7548 – 2.7557 in
	No.4	71.472 – 71.496 mm	2.8139 – 2.8148 in
	Bearing U/S type	0.05, 0.25, 0.50	
Crank pin diameter	STD	53.98 – 54.00 mm	2.1252 – 2.1260 in
Circle runout	Limit	0.1 mm	0.004 in
Main journal taper and out of round	Limit	0.01 mm	0.0004 in
Crank pin journal taper and out-of-round	Limit	0.01 mm	0.0004 in

IGNITION SYSTEM

Distributor

Rubbing block gap (except USA)		0.30 mm	0.0118 in
Dwell angle (except USA)		41°	
Governor shaft thrust clearance (except USA)		0.05 – 0.50 mm	0.0059 – 0.0197 in
Air gap (USA)		0.2 – 0.4 mm	0.008 – 0.016 in

Distributor advance angle

		Governor		Vacuum		
(Part No.)	Dis rpm	Advance angle	Advance begins	in. Hg	mmHg	Advance begins
General FJ & FA series	450		Advance begins	3.94	100	Advance begins
(19100-61010)	900	9°	5°	7.87	200	5°
	1,600	15°	8.5°	11.81	300	8.5°
	3,000	14.6°				
	750		Advance begins	3.94	100	Advance begins
	1,600	12°	5°	7.87	200	5°
			8.5°	11.81	300	8.5°
ECE	600		Advance begins	3.94	100	Advance begins
(19100-61071)	900	5.0°	4.4°	7.49	190	4.4°
	1,322	6.9°	8.5°	11.81	300	8.5°
	1,900	10°				
	3,000	9.7°				

Distributor advance angle

		Governor			Vacuum		
(Part No.)	Dis rpm	Advance angle	Advance begins		in. Hg	mmHg	Retard angle
Australia	450		Advance begins	Main			Retard begins
(ex N.S.W. & Victoria)	900	9.0°	4.4°		3.15	80	−3°
(19100-61130)	1,600	13.0°	8.5°		5.35	136	
	3,000	14.6°			7.87	200	
	500		Advance begins	Sub			
	900	5.5°	5.8°		3.94	100	
USA	1,383	6.5°	10.0°		5.31	135	
(19100-61102)	2,000	8.5°					
	3,000	7.8°					

Distributor angle

		Governor			Vacuum		
(Part No.)	Dis rpm	Advance angle	Advance begins		mmHg	mmHg	Retard begins
Australia	600		Advance begins				Retard begins
(NSW & Victoria)	900	5°	6.9°		3.15	80	−3°
(19100-61023)	1,322	6.9°	10°		5.51	140	
	1,900	10°					
	3,000	9.7°					

"B, 3B & 13B-T" ENGINES

Engine tune-up	Engine coolant capacity (w/ Heater)			
	BJ60	13.3 liters	14.1 US qts	11.7 Imp qts
	BJ70, 71, 73, 74, 75			
	3B	13 8 liters	14 6 US qts	12 1 Imp qts
	13B-T M/T	14 2 liters	15 0 US qts	12 5 Imp qts
	13B-T A/T	13.6 liters	14 4 US qts	12 0 Imp qts
	Engine oil capacity			
	Drain and refill			
	w/o Oil filter change	5 8 liters	6.1 US qts	5.1 Imp. qts
	w/ Oil filter change	6.7 liters	7.1 US qts	5 9 Imp qts
	Dry fill	7 3 liters	7 7 US qts	6 4 Imp qts
	Battery specific gravity	1.25 – 1.27 when fully charged at 20°C (68°F)		
	Drive belt			
	Tension (Canada) New belt	145 ± 25 lb		
	Used belt	100 ± 20 lb		
	Deflection (Others)			
	Single belt New belt	8 – 12 mm		0.31 – 0 47 in.
	Used belt	11 – 16 mm		0 43 – 0 63 in
	Double belt New belt	12 – 15 mm		0.47 – 0 59 in.
	Used belt	14 – 20 mm		0 55 – 0 79 in.
	Tension (Reference)			
	Single belt New belt	55 – 65 kg		
	Used belt	30 – 45 kg		
	Double belt New belt	45 – 55 kg		
	Used belt	20 – 35 kg		
	Injection nozzle opening pressure			
	B and 3B New nozzle	115 – 125 kg/cm² (1,636 – 1,778 psi, 11,278 – 12,258 kPa)		
	Reused nozzle	105 – 125 kg/cm² (1,493 – 1,778 psi, 10,296 – 12,258 kPa)		
	13B-T New nozzle	200 – 210 kg/cm² (2,845 – 2,987 psi, 19,613 – 20,594 kPa)		
	Reused nozzle	180 – 210 kg/cm² (2,560 – 2,987 psi, 17,652 – 20,594 kPa)		
	Valve clearance (Hot) IN	0.20 mm		0 008 in.
	EX	0.36 mm		0.014 in.
	Injection timing			
	B and 3B	14° BTDC		
	13B-T	11° BTDC		
	Injection order	1–3–4–2		
	Idle speed			
	M/T	650 rpm		
	A/T (13B)	770 rpm		
	A/T (13B-T)	820 rpm		
	Maximum speed	4,100 rpm		
	A/C idle-up setting speed			
	BJ[illegible]	950 rpm		

Cylinder block and cylinder	Cylinder head surface warpage Limit	0.20 mm	0.0079 in.
	Cylinder bore diameter STD B,	95.00 – 95 03 mm	3.7402 – 3.7413 in.
	3B, 13B-T	102.00 – 102.03 mm	4 0157 – 4.0169 in.
	Limit B,	95 23 mm	3 7492 in.
	3B, 13B-T	102.23 mm	4 0248 in
	Cylinder liner ridge protrusion	0.01 – 0.10 mm	0.0004 – 0.0039 in.
Piston and piston ring	Piston diameter B	94 90 – 94 93 mm	3.7362 – 3.7374 in.
	3B	101 90 – 101.93 mm	4 0118 – 4 0130 in.
	13B-T	101.92 – 101.95 mm	4.0126 – 4.0138 in.
	Piston oil clearance STD B, 3B	0.09 – 0.11 mm	0.0035 – 0.0043 in
	13B-T	0.07 – 0.09 mm	0.0028 – 0.0035 in.
	Limit	0.15 mm	0.0059 in.
	Piston ring groove clearance		
	B, 3B,	0.04 – 0.08 mm	0.0016 – 0.0031 in.
	13B-T	0.06 – 0.10 mm	0.0024 – 0.0039 in.
	Oil	0.03 – 0.07 mm	0.0012 – 0.0028 in.
	Piston ring end gap		
	STD No. 1 B	0.35 – 0.64 mm	0.0138 – 0.0252 in.
	3B 13B-T	0.30 – 0.54 mm	0.0118 – 0.0213 in.
	No. 2 B,	0.35 – 0.64 mm	0.0138 – 0.0252 in.
	3B 13B-T	0 45 – 0.69 mm	0.0177 – 0.0272 in.
	Oil B,	0.35 – 0.64 mm	0.0138 – 0.0252 in.
	3B, 13B-T	0.40 – 0.69 mm	0.0157 – 0.0272 in.
	Limit No. 1 B	1.44 mm	0.0567 in.
	3B 13B-T	1.34 mm	0.0528 in.
	No. 2 B,	1.44 mm	0.0567 in.
	3B, 13B-T	1.49 mm	0.0587 in.
	Oil B,	1.44 mm	0.0567 in.
	3B, 13B-T	1.49 mm	0.0587 in.
Connecting rod	Thrust clearance STD	0.200 – 0.320 mm	0.0079 – 0.0126 in.
	Limit	0.40 mm	0.0157 in.
	Bushing inside diameter B	29.009 – 29 019 mm	1.1421 – 1.1425 in.
	3B	32 009 – 32.019 mm	1.2602 – 1.2606 in.
	13B-T	34 009 – 34.019 mm	1.3389 – 1.3393 in.
	Piston pin diameter B	29 000 – 29.010 mm	1.1417 – 1.1421 in.
	3B	32 000 – 32.010 mm	1.2598 – 1.2602 in.
	13B-T	34 000 – 34 010 mm	1.3386 – 1.3390 in.
	Piston pin oil clearance	0.004 – 0.014 mm	0.0002 – 0.0006 in.
		0 05 mm	0.0020 in.
	Bend Limit per 100 mm (3.94 in.)	0.05 mm	0 0020 in.
	Twist Limit per 100 mm (3 94 in.)	0.05 mm	0.0020 in.

Rocker arm and shaft	Rocker arm inside diameter	18 512 – 18 533 mm	0.7288 – 0.7296 in.
	Rocker shaft diameter	18.472 – 18 493 mm	0.7272 – 0.7281 in.
	Rocker arm to shaft oil clearance STD	0.019 – 0.061 mm	0 0007 – 0.0024 in.
	Limit	0.10 mm	0 0039 in.
Push rod	Circle runout	0.50 mm	0.0197 in.
Intake and exhaust manifold	Manifold surface warpage Limit	0.20 mm	0.0079 in.
Combustion chamber (B, 3B)	Protrusion	Minus 0.05 – Plus 0.05 mm	Minus 0 0020 – Plus 0 0020 in.
Camshaft	Circle runout Limit	0.06 mm	0.0024 in.
	Cam lobe height STD IN B, 3B	45 067 – 45 157 mm	1 7743 – 1 7748 in
	13B-T	44 909 – 44 999 mm	1.7681 – 1.7716 in
	EX B, 3B	45.065 – 45 155 mm	1.7742 – 1.7778 in
	~~11B, 13B~~, 13B-T	44.774 – 44 864 mm	1.7628 – 1.7663 in.
	Limit IN B, 3B	44.63 mm	1.7571 in.
	13B-T	44 47 mm	1.7508 in
	EX B, 3B	44 63 mm	1.7571 in.
	13B-T	44 34 mm	1 7457 in.
	Journal diameter No. 1	53.459 – 53 475 mm	2.1047 – 2.1053 in
	No. 2	53 209 – 53.225 mm	2.0948 – 2.0955 in
	No. 3	52.959 – 52.975 mm	2 0850 – 2 0856 in
	No. 4	52.709 – 52 725 mm	2.0752 – 2.0758 in
	No. 5	52.459 – 52 475 mm	2.0653 – 2.0659 in.
	Bearing inside diameter No. 1	53.495 – 53.568 mm	2.1061 – 2.1090 in
	No. 2	53 245 – 53.318 mm	2.0963 – 2.0991 in
	No. 3	52.995 – 53.068 mm	2.0864 – 2.0893 in
	No. 4	52 745 – 52.818 mm	2.0766 – 2.0794 in.
	No. 5	52.495 – 52.568 mm	2.0667 – 2.0696 in.
	Journal oil clearance STD	0.020 – 0.109 mm	0.0008 – 0.0043 in.
	Limit	0.15 mm	0.0059 in.
	Thrust clearance STD	0.06 – 0.13 mm	0.0024 – 0.0051 in.
	Limit	0.30 mm	0.0118 in.
Timing gear	Gear backlash (each gear) STD	0.058 – 0.162 mm	0.0023 – 0.064 in.
	Limit	0.30 mm	0.0118 in
	Idle gear thrust clearance STD	0.06 – 0.17 mm	0 0024 – 0.0067 in.
	Limit	0.30 mm	0.0118 in.
	Idle gear shaft diameter	44.935 – 44 955 mm	1.7691 – 1.7699 in.
	Idle gear inside diameter	44.969 – 44 995 mm	1.7704 – 1.7715 in.
	Idle gear oil clearance STD	0.014 – 0.060 mm	0.0006 – 0.0024 in.
	Limit	0.15 mm	0.0059 in.
Valve lifter	Valve lifter diameter	26 972 – 26.985 mm	1.0619 – 1 0624 in
	Valve lifter bore diameter	27 010 – 27 030 mm	1.0634 – 1 0642 in.
	Oil clearance STD	0.025 – 0.065 mm	0 0010 – 0.0026 in.
	Limit	0 10 mm	0.0039 in.

Compression pressure	Engine revolution at 250 rpm STD	30 0 kg/cm² (427 psi, 2,942 kPa) or more	
	Limit	20 0 kg/cm² 284 psi 1,961 kPa	
	Difference of pressure between each cylinder	2.0 kg/cm² (28 psi, 196 kPa) or less	
Turbocharger	Turbocharging pressure	0 42 – 0.56 kg/cm² (6 0 – 8.0 psi, 41 – 55 kPa)	
	Impeller wheel axial play	0.13 mm (0.0051 in.) or less	
Cylinder head	Cylinder block side warpage Limit	0.20 mm	0.0079 in.
	Manifold side warpage Limit	0.20 mm	0.0079 in.
	Valve seat		
	Refacing angle	30°, 45°, 60°	
	Contacting angle	45°	
	Contacting width	1.9 – 2.3 mm	0.075 – 0 091 in
Valve guide busing	Inner diameter	9.010 – 9.030 mm	0.3547 – 0.3555 in.
	Outer diameter	14 023 – 14.041 mm	0.5521 – 0.5528 in.
Valve	Valve overall length STD IN	127.95 mm	5.0374 in.
	EX B, 3B	127.75 mm	5.0295 in.
	13B-T	127.95 mm	5 0374 in.
	Limit IN	127.45 mm	5.0177 in.
	EX B, 3B	127.25 mm	5.0098 in.
	13B-T	127.45 mm	5.0177 in.
	Valve face angle	45.5°	
	Stem diameter IN	8.968 – 8.984 mm	0.3531 – 0.3537 in.
	EX B, 3B,	8.954 – 8.970 mm	0.3525 – 0.3531 in.
	13B-T	8.940 – 8.956 mm	0.3520 – 0.3526 in.
	Stem oil clearance STD IN	0.026 – 0.062 mm	0.0010 – 0.0024 in.
	EX B, 3B,	0.040 – 0.076 mm	0 0016 – 0.0030 in.
	13B-T	0.054 – 0.090 mm	0 0021 – 0.0035 in.
	Limit IN	0.10 mm	0.0039 in.
	EX B, 3B,	0.12 mm	0.0047 in
	13B-T	0 13 mm	0 0051 in.
	Margin thickness STD IN	1.4 mm	0.055 in.
	EX B, 3B	1.8 mm	[illegible] in.
	13B-T	1.7 mm	0.067 in.
	Limit IN	0.9 mm	0.035 in.
	EX B, 3B	1.3 mm	0.051 in.
	13-T	1.2 mm	0 047 in.
Valve spring	Free length STD Inner B, 3B	45 50 mm	1.7913 in.
	13B-T	54.84 mm	2.1591 in.
	Outer B, 3B	47.52 mm	1.8709 in.
	13B-T	58.30 mm	2.2953 in.
	Installed tension Inner B, 3B	5.95 kg (13.1 lb, 58 N) at 36.05 mm (1 4193 in.)	
	13B-T	14.2 kg (31.3 lb, 139 N) at 42.25 mm (1 6634 in.)	
	Outer B, 3B	25.53 kg (56 3 lb, 250 N) at 39.55 mm (1 5571 in.)	
	13B-T	27 8 kg (61.2 lb, 273 N) at 44 75 mm (1.7618 in.)	
	Squareness	2 0 mm	0 079 in.

Crankshaft	Thrust clearance STD	0 040 – 0.250 mm	0.0016 – 0.0098 in.
	Limit	0.40 mm	0 0157 in
	Thrust washer thickness STD size	2 430 – 2.480 mm	0 0957 – 0.0976 in
	O/S 0 125	2.493 – 2 543 mm	0 0981 – 0 1001 in
	O/S 0 250	2 555 – 2 605 mm	0 1006 – 0 1026 in
	Main journal diameter STD size	69 98 – 70.00 mm	2 7551 – 2 7559 in
	U/S 0.25	69 74 – 69 75 mm	2 7457 – 2 7461 in
	U/S 0.50	69 49 – 69 50 mm	2 7358 – 2 7362 in
	U/S 1.00	68 99 – 69 00 mm	2 7161 – 2 7165 in
	Main journal oil clearance STD	0.030 – 0.074 mm	0 0012 – 0 0029 in
	Limit	0.15 mm	0.0059 in.
	Main bearing thickness at center wall		
	STD size Yellow	2 480 – 2 485 mm	0 0976 – 0 0978 in.
	STD size Green	2 485 – 2.490 mm	0.0978 – 0 0980 in.
	Crank pin diameter B STD size	58.98 – 59 00 mm	2.3220 – 2.3228 in.
	U/S 0.25	58 74 – 58.75 mm	2.3126 – 2.3130 in
	U/S 0.50	58 49 – 58 50 mm	2.3028 – 2.3031 in.
	U/S 1 00	57.99 – 58.00 mm	2.2831 – 2 2835 in.
	13B-T STD size	60.98 – 61.00 mm	2 4008 – 2.4016 in
	U/S 0.25	60.74 – 60 75 mm	2 3913 – 2.3917 in.
	U/S 0 50	60 49 – 60.50 mm	2.3815 – 2.3819 in.
	U/S 1.00	59.99 – 60 00 mm	2.3618 – 2.3622 in
	Crank pin oil clearance STD	0.030 – 0.070 mm	0 0012 – 0.0028 in.
	Limit	0.10 mm	0.0039 in
	Crank pin (connecting rod) bearing thickness at center wall		
	STD size Brown or Yellow	1.480 – 1.485 mm	0.0583 – 0.0585 in.
	STD size Black or Green	1.485 – 1.490 mm	0.0585 – 0.0587 in.
	Circle runout Limit	0.08 mm	0.0031 in.
	Taper and out-of round		
	Main journal and crank pin Limit	0.02 mm	0.0008 in.

Torque Specifications

Part tightened		kg-cm	ft-lb	N·m
Turbine outlet elbow x Turbocharger (13B-T)		375	27	37
Turbocharger x Exhaust manifold (13B-T)		465	34	46
Water by-pass pipe x Turbocharger		75	65 in.-lb	7.1
Turbocharger oil pipe x Cylinder block	Unit bolt	130	9	13
	Bolt	185	13	18
Turbocharger oil pipe x Turbocharger		185	13	18
Cylinder head x Cylinder block		1,200	87	118
Valve rocker support x Cylinder head		185	13	18
Cylinder head cover x Cylinder head		125	9	12
Exhaust manifold x Cylinder head		475	34	47
Water outlet housing x Cylinder head		185	13	18
Intake manifold x Cylinder head		185	13	18
Glow plug x Cylinder head (B, 3B)		125	9	12
Camshaft timing gear x Camshaft		375	27	37
Camshaft thrust plate x Cylinder block		185	13	18
Idle gear x Cylinder block		475	34	47
Idle gear shaft union bolt		110	8	11
Timing gear cover x Cylinder block	12 mm bolt head	185	13	18
	14 mm bolt head	375	27	37
Crankshaft pulley x Crankshaft		2,450	177	240
Push rod cover x Cylinder block		185	13	18
Main bearing cap x Cylinder block		2,000	145	196
Connecting rod cap x Connecting rod	B	750	54	74
	3B, 13B-T	1,200	87	118
Rear oil seal retainer x Cylinder block		185	13	18
Flywheel x Crankshaft (M/T)		1,800	130	177
Drive plate x Crankshaft (A/T)		1,200	87	118

Torque Specifications

Part tightened		kg-cm	ft-lb	N·m
Nozzle holder retaining nut x Nozzle holder body	B, 3B	700	51	69
	11B, 13B, 13B-T	350	25	34
Injection nozzle x Cylinder head	B, 3B	700	51	69
	11B, 13B, 13B-T	185	13	18
Nozzle leakage pipe x Injection nozzle	B, 3B	450	33	44
	11B, 13B, 13B-T	250	18	25
Injection pipe x Injection nozzle		250	18	25
Chamber plug x Feed pump housing	19 mm bolt head	500	36	49
	32 mm bolt head	1,500	109	147
Priming pump x Feed pump housing		500	36	49
Feed pump x Injection pump		95	82 in.-lb	9.3
Fuel pipe x Feed pump		375	27	37
Delivery valve holder x Injection pump body		375	27	37
Spline shaft x Injection pump camshaft	B, 3B	650	47	64
	11B, 13B, 13B-T	925	69	91
Plate plug x Injection pump body		650	47	64
Steel ball guide x Injection pump camshaft (B, 3B)		550	40	54

Feed pump	Suction test		
	Suction pipe Inner diameter	8 mm	0.31 in.
	length	2 m	78 7 in
	Suction height	1 m	39 4 in.
	Priming pump at 60 stroke/ min.	Fuel must discharge within 25 strokes	
	Feed pump at 150 rpm	Fuel must discharge within 40 seconds	
	Discharge test		
	Pressure at 600 rpm	1 8 – 2 2 kg/cm² (26 – 31 psi, 177 – 216 kPa)	
	Discharge nozzle diameter	1 54 mm	0 0606 in.
	Volume at 1,000 rpm	900 cc/min (54 9 cu in./min) or more	

"H" ENGINES

Periodical Service

Battery	Electrolyte level		10 to 25 mm (0.4 to 1.0") (above plates)
	Specific gravity		1,260 (at 20°C)
	Capacity		70AH or 100AH
Coolant capacity	w/Heater HU	15.2 liters	16.1 US qt / 13.4 Imp. qt
	HU	14.9 liters	15.8 US qt / 13.1 Imp. qt
	for Europe	14.3 liters	15.1 US qt / 12.6 Imp. qt
Radiator cap valve opening pressure			0.9 kg/cm² (12.8 psi)
"V" belt deflection (Water pump X alternator)			11 to 14 mm (0.4 to 0.6") at 10 kg (22 lb) pressure
Injection timing (stationary)			12° BTDC
Idling speed			625 – 675 rpm
Maximum rpm	Maximum instantaneous rpm		3,950 rpm
	Maximum created rpm		3,900 rpm
Compression	Limit		20 kg/cm² (284 psi) at 320 rpm
	Standard		30 kg/cm² (427 psi) at 320 rpm
	Variation limit between cylinders		2.0 kg/cm² (28 psi)
Valve clearance (Hot)	Intake		0.20 mm (0.008")
	Exhaust		0.36 mm (0.014")
Engine oil capacity	Dry refill	9.8 liters	10.4 US qt / 8.6 Imp. qt
	Drain & refill w/Oil filter	9.1 liters	9.6 US qt / 8.0 Imp. qt
	w/o Oil filter	8.0 liters	8.5 US qt / 7.0 Imp. qt

Engine

Cylinder Head

Underside surface warpage limit		0.20 mm (0.008")
Manifold mounting surface warpage limit		0.20 mm (0.008")
Valve seat	Seating width	1.3 to 1.6 mm (0.051 to 0.063")
	Seating angle	45°
	Refacing angles	30° 60°

Valve Guide Bushing

Overall length	Intake	56 mm (2.21")
	Exhaust	60 mm (2.36")
Inner diameter		9.01 – 9.03 mm (0.355 – 0.356")
Protrusion above head upper surface (from valve spring contact surface)		16.2 to 16.8 mm (0.64 to 0.66")
Stem oil clearance	STD Intake	0.02 – 0.06 mm (0.0008 – 0.0024")
	STD Exhaust	0.04 – 0.08 mm (0.0016 – 0.0031")
	Limit Intake	0.10 mm (0.004")
	Limit Exhaust	0.12 mm (0.005")

Valve

Head outside diameter	Intake	40.3 to 40.7 mm (1.587 to 1.602")
	Exhaust	33.3 to 33.7 mm (1.311 to 1.327")
Overall length	Intake	120.6 mm (4.748")
	Exhaust	120.4 mm (4.740")
Stem outside diameter	Intake	8.97 to 8.99 mm (0.3531 to 0.3539")
	Exhaust	8.95 to 8.97 mm (0.3523 to 0.3531")
Valve seating angle		45.5°
Stem end refacing limit		0.5 mm (0.020")
Head thickness limit	Intake	0.9 mm (0.035")
	Exhaust	1.0 mm (0.039")

Compression Spring (Valve)

Free length	45.1 mm (1.776")
Installed length	40.0 mm (1.575")
Installed load limit	18.5 kg (40.8 lb)
Installed load	21.7 kg (47.8 lb)
Squareness limit	1.6 mm (0.063")

Valve Rocker Shaft and Arm

Shaft diameter limit		18.44 mm (0.7260")
Rocker arm bore limit		18.60 mm (0.7323")
Rocker arm bushing to shaft oil clearance	Limit	0.1 mm (0.004")
	Standard	0.01 to 0.05 mm (0.0004 to 0.0020")

Valve Lifter and Push Rod

Lifter diameter limit	STD	22.170 to 22.190 mm (0.87283 to 0.87362")
Lifter to block bore clearance	Limit	0.1 mm (0.004")
	Standard	0.010 to 0.061 mm (0.00039 to 0.00201")
Push rod bend limit		0.5 mm (0.020")

Manifold

Cylinder head mounting surface warpage limit	Intake	0.3 mm (0.012")
	Exhaust	0.5 mm (0.020")

Cylinder Block

Block upper surface warpage limit		0.15 mm (0.0059")
Valve lifter bore limit	STD	22.20 to 22.22 mm (0.8740 to 0.8748")
Cylinder bore	STD	88.00 to 88.03 mm (3.4646 to 3.4657")
Liner	Max. wear limit	0.3 mm (0.01")
	Protrusion	0.03 to 0.12 mm (0.0012 to 0.0047")

Crankshaft

Bend limit		0.04 mm (0.0016")
Thrust clearance	Limit	0.3 mm (0.012")
	Standard	0.04 to 0.24 mm (0.0016 to 0.0095")
Main Journal Diameter	STD	69.98 to 70.00 mm (2.7551 to 2.7559")
	U/S 0.06	69.89 to 69.90 mm (2.7516 to 2.7520")
	U/S 0.25	69.74 to 69.75 mm (2.7457 to 2.7461")
	U/S 0.50	69.49 to 69.50 mm (2.7358 to 2.7362")
	U/S 0.75	69.24 to 69.25 mm (2.7260 to 2.7264")
	U/S 1.00	68.99 to 69.00 mm (2.7161 to 2.7165")
Journal and Crankpin	Tapered limit	0.05 mm (0.0020")
	Out-of-round limit	0.02 mm (0.0008")
Crank pin Journal Diameter	STD	54.98 to 55.00 mm (2.1646 to 2.1654")
	U/S 0.06	54.94 to 54.95 mm (2.1630 to 2.1634")
	U/S 0.25	54.74 to 54.75 mm (2.1551 to 2.1555")
	U/S 0.50	54.49 to 54.50 mm (2.1453 to 2.1457")
	U/S 0.75	54.24 to 54.25 mm (2.1354 to 2.1358")
	U/S 1.00	53.99 to 54.00 mm (2.1256 to 2.1260")
Main Journal Oil clearance	Limit	0.1 mm (0.004")
	Standard	0.038 to 0.072 mm (0.0012 to 0.0028")

Flywheel

Run-out limit	0.2 mm (0.008")

Connecting Rod

Bend limit [per 100 mm (3.9")]		0.05 mm (0.0020")
Twist limit [per 100 mm (3.9")]		0.15 mm (0.0059")
Thrust clearance	Limit	0.3 mm (0.012")
	Standard	0.08 to 0.16 mm (0.0031 to 0.0063")
Solid bushing to pin clearance	Limit	0.05 mm (0.0020")
	Standard	0.004 to 0.012 mm (0.0002 to 0.0005")
Connecting rod bearing	Oil clearance limit	0.10 mm (0.0039")
	Oil clearance std.	0.030 to 0.070 mm (0.0012 to 0.0028")

Piston and Piston Ring

Piston	Diameter	STD	87.81 to 87.84 mm (3.4571 to 3.4583")
		O/S 1.00	88.81 to 88.84 mm (3.4964 to 3.4976")
	Piston to cylinder clearance		0.18 to 0.20 mm (0.0071 to 0.0079")
	Pin diameter		27.00 to 27.012 mm (1.0630 to 1.0635")
	Pin fitting temperature		60°C (140°F)
Piston ring	End gap	Compression ring No.1	0.25 to 0.45 mm (0.0098 to 0.0177")
		No.2	0.25 to 0.45 mm (0.0098 to 0.0177")
		Oil ring No.1	0.20 to 0.40 mm (0.0079 to 0.0157")
	Ring to groove clearance	Compression ring No.1	0.01 to 0.06 mm (0.0004 to 0.0024")
		No.2	0.05 to 0.09 mm (0.0020 to 0.0035")
		Oil ring No.1	0.03 to 0.07 mm (0.0012 to 0.0028")

Timing and Idle Gear

Gear backlash	Idler gear to timing drive gear — Limit	0.3 mm (0.012")
	Standard	0.1 mm (0.004")
	Crankshaft gear to idle gear & cam gear — Limit	0.3 mm (0.012")
	Standard	0.1 mm (0.004")
Idle gear thrust clearance	Limit	0.25 mm (0.01")
	Standard	0.08 to 0.18 mm (0.0032 to 0.0071")
Idle gear oil clearance	Limit	0.15 mm (0.0059")
	Standard	0.04 to 0.09 mm (0.0016 to 0.0035")
Idle gear bore		50.00 to 50.03 mm (1.9685 to 1.9697")
Idle gear shaft diameter	Limit	49.90 mm (1.9646")
	Standard	49.94 to 49.96 mm (1.9661 to 1.9669")

Camshaft and Bearing

Bend limit		0.03 mm (0.0012")
Thrust clearance	Limit	0.3 mm (0.012")
	Standard	0.06 to 0.13 mm (0.0024 to 0.0051")
Oil clearance	Limit	0.1 mm (0.004")
	Standard	0.025 to 0.066 mm (0.0010 to 0.0026")
Cam height limit	Intake	38.92 mm (1.5323")
	Exhaust	38.91 mm (1.5319")
Cam height standard	Intake	39.467 to 39.557 mm (1.5538 to 1.5574")
	Exhaust	39.465 to 39.555 mm (1.5537 to 1.5573")
Journal diameter (STD)	No.1	47.150 to 47.175 mm (1.8566 to 1.8573")
	No.2	46.959 to 46.975 mm (1.8488 to 1.8494")
	No.3	46.769 to 46.775 mm (1.8409 to 1.8415")
	No.4	46.559 to 46.575 mm (1.8330 to 1.8337")
Journal Bearing U/S		0.125, 0.50, 0.500

Fuel System

Fuel Pump (Part Number 22510-48010)

Fuel pump	Housing to piston clearance	0.009 to 0.013 mm (0.0004 to 0.005")
	Housing to push rod clearance	0.003 to 0.006 mm (0.0001 to 0.0002")
	Feed pump tappet stroke	8 mm (0.31") approx
	Priming pump stroke	25 mm (0.98") approx

Fuel Pump Performance Test (Part Number 22510-48010)

Test item	Conditions	Performance
Suction test	Suction pipe spec: Inside dia. 8 mm (0.31"), Length 2 m (78.7"), Height 1 m (39.4")	Fuel pump: Start discharge within 40 seconds at 150 rpm. Priming pump: Start discharge within 25 strokes when pumped at 60 stroke/min
Discharge test	600 rpm	Discharge pressure 1.8 to 2.2 kg/cm² (25.6 to 31.3 psi)
	1000 rpm	Discharge quantity More than 900 cc/min (54.9 cu in.) (Discharge nozzle diameter 1.54 mm (0.0006"))

Injection Pump (Part Number 22103-47042-HJ) (Part Number 22100-47032-HU)

Direction of rotation		Clockwise as seen from driven side
Cam lift		6 mm (0.24")
Pump element	Bore	7 mm (0.28")
	Shape	Lift hand load
Injection order		1-4-2-6-3-5
Control rack sliding resistance		Less than 150g (5.3 oz) / Less than 50g (1.8 oz)
Pin stroke		1.9 to 2.0 mm (0.075 to 0.079")
Injection interval angle		59.5 to 60.5 degrees
Tappet clearance		More than 0.2 mm (0.008")
Camshaft thrust clearance		0.03 to 0.05 mm (0.0012 to 0.0020")
Camshaft shim plate thickness		0.10, 0.12, 0.14, 0.16, 0.18, 0.50 mm (0.0039, 0.0047, 0.0055, 0.0063, 0.0071, 0.0197")
Plunger spring	Free length	49.4 mm (1.945")
	Installed length	44.0 mm (1.732")
	Installed load	15.1 kg (33.3 lb)
Delivery valve spring	Free length	37.0 mm (1.457")
	Installed length	25.9 mm (1.020")
	Installed load	4.42 kg (9.7 lb)
Model and Type		Model MN, vacuum type
Pneumatic governor (HJ)	Main spring: Free length	106.0 mm (4.134")
	Installed length	36.0 mm (1.417")
	Installed load	1.04 kg (2.3 lb)
	Idling spring: Free length	23.7 mm (0.933")
	Shim & washer thickness (for idling capsule)	0.1, 0.2, 0.5, 1.0 mm (0.004, 0.008, 0.020, 0.039")

Nozzle and Nozzle Holder (Part Number 23600-48011)

Nozzle holder model		
Nozzle	Type	KCA, Throttle
	Opening pressure: New nozzle	115 to 125 kg/cm² (1,633 to 1,775 psi)
	Reused nozzle	105 to 125 kg/cm² (1,491 to 1,775 psi)
	Injection angle	Approx. 4 degrees
Adjust washer thickness (for adjusting nozzle opening pressure)		1.00 ... 1.95 mm (0.0394 to 0.0768"); 20 sizes in 0.05 mm (0.0020") increments

Lubricating System

Oil Pump and Oil Cleaner

		Type	Gear pump
Discharge		Oil temperature	98 to 102°C (208 to 216°F)
		Discharge pressure	3 kg/cm² (42.7 psi)
		Discharge quantity	40 liters/min. (10.6 US or 8.8 Imp. gal.)
		Speed	1800 rpm
Oil clearance	Drive shaft		0.013 to 0.051 mm (0.0005 to 0.0020 mm)
	Driven shaft		0.014 to 0.042 mm (0.00055 to 0.0016A mm)
Tip clearance	Limit		0.025 to 0.105 mm (0.0010 to 0.0041")
	Standard		0.2 mm (0.008")
Side clearance	Limit		0.2 mm (0.008")
	Standard		0.03 to 0.09 mm (0.0012 to 0.0035")
Relief valve	Valve opening pressure		3.0 to 4.5 kg/cm² (42.7 to 64.0 psi)
Filter valve	Valve opening pressure		0.8 to 1.2 kg/cm² (11.4 to 17.1 psi)

Cooling System

Radiator

Coolant Capacity	w/Heater	15.2 liters (16.1 US qt, 13.4 Imp. qt)
	HU	14.9 liters (15.8 US qt, 13.1 Imp. qt)
	HJ for Europe	14.3 liters (15.1 US qt, 12.6 Imp. qt)
Valve opening pressure		0.9 kg/cm² (12.8 psi)

Water Pump

Discharge capacity (liter/min.)		220 liter (58 US gal. 48 Imp. gal.)
Pump speed		4300 rpm

Thermostat

	Type	Wax
Full open temperature		90°C (194°F)
Valve opening temperature		74.5 to 78.5°C (166 to 173°F)
Valve lift		10 mm Min. (0.39")

ENGINE MECHANICAL

Specifications

Engine tune-up	Engine coolant capacity (w/ Heater): HJ80, 61 series		15.4 liters / 16.3 US qts / 13.6 Imp qts
	HJ75 series		14.2 liters / 15.0 US qts / 12.5 Imp qts
	Engine oil capacity — Drain and refill w/o Oil filter change		8.1 liters / 8.6 US qts / 7.1 Imp qts
	w/ Oil filter change		9.7 liters / 10.3 US qts / 8.5 Imp qts
	Dry fill		10.3 liters / 10.9 US qts / 9.1 Imp qts
	Battery specific gravity — 12V type		1.25 - 1.27 when fully charged at 20°C (68°F)
	24V type		1.27 - 1.29 when fully charged at 20°C (68°F); 1.25 - 1.27 when fully charged at 20°C (68°F)
	Drive belt — Tension (Canada)	Used belt	115 ± 15 lb
		New belt	125 ± 25 lb
	Deflection (Others)	Used belt	10 - 13 mm (0.39 - 0.51 in)
		New belt	8 - 9 mm (0.31 - 0.35 in)
	Injection nozzle opening pressure — 2H	Reused nozzle	105 - 125 kg/cm² (1,493 - 1,778 psi, 10,296 - 12,258 kPa)
		New nozzle	115 - 125 kg/cm² (1,636 - 1,778 psi, 11,278 - 12,258 kPa)
	12H-T	Reused nozzle	180 - 210 kg/cm² (2,560 - 2,987 psi, 17,652 - 20,594 kPa)
		New nozzle	200 - 210 kg/cm² (2,845 - 2,987 psi, 19,613 - 20,594 kPa)
	Valve clearance (Hot)	IN	0.20 mm (0.008 in)
		EX	0.36 mm (0.014 in)
	Injection timing — 2H		18° BTDC
	12H-T		11° BTDC
	Injection order		1-4-2-6-3-5
	Idle speed — 2H	M/T	650 rpm
		A/T	750 rpm
	12H-T	M/T	650 rpm
		A/T	770 rpm
	Maximum speed — 2H	w/ Fluid coupling	4,170 rpm
		w/o Fluid coupling	4,100 rpm
	12H-T		4,170 rpm
	PS lift-up setting speed (12H-T A/T)		820 rpm
	A/C idle-up setting speed (12H-T A/T)		950 rpm (Transmission in neutral); 800 rpm (Transmission in D range)

Timing Gear

Gear backlash	Automatic timer drive gear	STD	0.050 - 0.111 mm (0.0019 - 0.0043 in)
		Limit	0.30 mm (0.0118 in)
	Camshaft timing gear	STD	0.050 - 0.113 mm (0.0019 - 0.0044 in)
		Limit	0.30 mm (0.0118 in)
	No. 1 idle gear	STD	0.050 - 0.116 mm (0.0019 - 0.0045 in)
		Limit	0.30 mm (0.0118 in)
	No. 2 idle gear	STD	0.050 - 0.113 mm (0.0019 - 0.0044 in)
		Limit	0.30 mm (0.0118 in)
Idle gear thrust clearance (No. 1 and No. 2)		STD	0.050 - 0.150 mm (0.0019 - 0.0059 in)
		Limit	0.30 mm (0.0118 in)
Idle gear inside diameter (No. 1 and No. 2)			45.000 - 45.025 mm (1.7717 - 1.7726 in)
Idle gear shaft diameter (No. 1 and No. 2)			44.950 - 44.975 mm (1.7697 - 1.7707 in)
Idle gear oil clearance (No. 1 and No. 2)		STD	0.025 - 0.075 mm (0.0010 - 0.0030 in)
		Limit	0.20 mm (0.0079 in)

Valve lifter

Item	STD/Limit/O/S	Value
Cylinder block lifter bore diameter		22.200 - 22.221 mm (0.8740 - 0.8748 in)
Lifter diameter	STD	22.17 - 22.19 mm (0.8728 - 0.8736 in)
	O/S 0.05	22.22 - 22.24 mm (0.8748 - 0.8756 in)

Cylinder block

Item	STD/Limit/O/S	Value
Warpage		0.20 mm (0.0079 in)
Cylinder bore diameter	STD	91.000 - 91.030 mm (3.7008 - 3.7020 in)
	Limit	91.23 mm (3.5886 in)
	O/S 0.50	91.73 mm (3.6045 in)

Piston and piston ring

Piston diameter	2H	STD	90.930 - 90.960 mm (3.5799 - 3.5811 in)
		O/S 0.50	91.430 - 91.460 mm (3.5996 - 3.6008 in)
	12H-T	STD	90.940 - 90.970 mm (3.5803 - 3.5815 in)
		O/S 0.50	91.440 - 91.470 mm (3.6000 - 3.6012 in)
Piston oil clearance	2H		0.060 - 0.080 mm (0.0024 - 0.0032 in)
	12H-T		0.050 - 0.070 mm (0.0020 - 0.0028 in)
Piston ring groove clearance	2H	No. 1	0.097 - 0.137 mm (0.0038 - 0.0054 in)
		No. 2	0.020 - 0.060 mm (0.0008 - 0.0024 in)
		Oil	0.139 - 0.204 mm (0.0055 - 0.0080 in)
	12H-T	No. 1	0.060 - 0.100 mm (0.0024 - 0.0039 in)
		No. 2	0.020 - 0.060 mm (0.0008 - 0.0024 in)
Piston ring end gap	2H	No. 1	0.200 - 0.440 mm (0.0079 - 0.0173 in)
		No. 2	0.200 - 0.440 mm (0.0079 - 0.0173 in)
		Oil	0.150 - 0.490 mm (0.0059 - 0.0193 in)
		Limit	1.24 mm (0.0488 in)
	12H-T	No. 1	0.200 - 0.470 mm (0.0079 - 0.0185 in)
		No. 2	0.200 - 0.440 mm (0.0079 - 0.0173 in)
		Oil	0.150 - 0.490 mm (0.0059 - 0.0193 in)
		Limit	1.29 mm (0.0508 in)

"2H & 12H-T" ENGINES

COOLING SYSTEM

Specifications

Engine coolant capacity			
Thermostat	Valve opening temperature — 82°C type		80 - 84°C (176 - 183°F)
	88°C type		86 - 90°C (187 - 194°F)
	Valve opening travel — 82°C type	at 95°C (203°F)	10 mm (0.39 in) or more
	88°C type	at 100°C (212°F)	10 mm (0.39 in) or more
Radiator	Relief valve opening pressure	STD	0.75 - 1.05 kg/cm² (10.7 - 14.9 psi, 74 - 103 kPa)
		Limit	0.6 kg/cm² (8.5 psi, 59 kPa)

Torque Specifications

Part tightened	kg-cm	ft-lb	N·m
Water pump cover x Water pump body	185	13	18
Water pump x Cylinder block	375	27	37
Water outlet x Water outlet housing	185	13	18

LUBRICATION SYSTEM

Specifications

		at idle	at 3,000 rpm
Oil pressure	STD	0.3 kg/cm² (4.3 psi, 29 kPa) or more	2.5 – 5.0 kg/cm² (36 – 85 psi, 245 – 589 kPa)
Frame oil capacity		See page A-2	
Oil Pump	Rotor body clearance	STD 0.144 – 0.219 mm (0.0057 – 0.0086 in)	
		Limit 0.40 mm (0.0157 in)	
	Rotor side clearance	STD -0.035 – 0.090 mm (-0.0014 – 0.0035 in)	
		Limit 0.15 mm (0.0059 in)	
	Rotor tip clearance	STD 0.110 – 0.240 mm (0.0043 – 0.0094 in)	
		Limit 0.30 mm (0.0118 in)	
	Drive spline to rotor backlash	STD 0.541 – 0.790 mm (0.0213 – 0.0311 in)	
		Limit 1.00 mm (0.0394 in)	

Torque Specifications

Part tightened	kg-cm	ft-lb	N·m
Engine chain plug	400	29	39
Plug of oil pump relief valve	500	36	49
Timing gear case x Cylinder block	250	18	25
Timing gear cover x Injection pump retainer	250	18	25
Oil strainer x Main bearing cap	185	13	18
Oil strainer x Timing gear case	185	13	18
Oil pipe x Cylinder block	450	33	44
Oil pipe x Timing gear case	185	13	18
Oil can x Cylinder block	130	9	13
Oil can x Timing gear case	130	9	13
Oil can x Rear oil seal retainer	130	9	13
Oil cooler x Oil cooler case	250	18	25
Oil cooler case x Cylinder block	185	13	18
Oil filter bracket x Oil cooler case	185	13	18
Plug of oil cooler relief valve	500	36	49
Oil nozzle x Cylinder block	275	20	27

Injection Pump Adjustment (Pump Body)

Preparations of pump tester	Test nozzle type	2H	DN 4 SD 24 A
		12H-T	DN 12 SD 12 A
	Test nozzle opening pressure	2H	115 – 125 kg/cm² (1,636 – 1,778 psi, 11,278 – 12,258 kPa)
		12H-T	170 – 180 kg/cm² (2,418 – 2,560 psi, 16,671 – 17,651 kPa)
	Injection pipe	Outer diameter	6.0 mm (0.236 in)
		Inner diameter	2.0 mm (0.079 in)
		Length	600 mm (23.6 in)
		Minimum bending radius	25 mm (0.98 in) or more
	Fuel temperature		40 – 45°C (104 – 113°F)
	Fuel feeding pressure	2H	0.5 kg/cm² (7.1 psi, 49 kPa)
		12H-T	2.0 kg/cm² (28.4 psi, 196 kPa)
Control Rack	Sliding resistance	Pump at 0 rpm	120 g (4.2 oz) or less
		Pump at 1,000 rpm	50 g (1.8 oz) or less
Injecting timing	Pre-stroke	2H	1.90 – 2.00 mm (0.0748 – 0.0787 in)
		12H-T	3.55 – 3.65 mm (0.1398 – 0.1437 in)
	Injection interval		59°30' – 60°30'
	Tappet clearance		0.2 mm (0.008 in) or less
	Adjusting shim thickness		0.10 mm (0.0039 in)
			0.15 mm (0.0059 in)
			0.20 mm (0.0079 in)
			0.30 mm (0.0118 in)
			0.40 mm (0.0157 in)
			0.50 mm (0.0197 in)
			0.60 mm (0.0236 in)
			0.70 mm (0.0276 in)
			0.80 mm (0.0315 in)
			0.90 mm (0.0354 in)
			1.00 mm (0.0394 in)

STARTING SYSTEM

Pre-heating system	Light lighting time	2H (Super glow type) / 12H-T	Approx. 2 seconds
		2H (Fixed delay type)	15 – 19.5 seconds
		12H-T w/ Water temp. sensor disconnected	12V type 20 seconds
			24V type 14 seconds
Starter	Rated voltage and output power		12V 2.5 kw / 24V 4.5 kw
	No-load characteristic	Ampere	12V 180 A or less at 11 V; 24V 90 A or less at 23 V
		rpm	3,500 rpm or more
	Brush length	STD	12V 20.5 mm (0.807 in); 24V 13.0 mm (0.512 in)
	Spring installed load	STD	3.2 – 4.0 kg (7.1 – 8.8 lb, 31 – 39 N)
	Commutator	Outer diameter STD	36 mm
		Limit	35 mm
		Undercut depth STD	0.7 mm
		Limit	0.2 mm
		Circle runout Limit	0.05 mm (0.0020 in)

CHARGING SYSTEM

Battery specific gravity			
Drive belt tension or deflection			
Alternator	Rated output		12V 40 A; 12V 55 A; 12V 80 A; 24V 25 A; 24V 30 A; 24V 40 A
	Rotor coil resistance	w/o IC regulator	12V type 3.9 – 4.1 Ω; 24V type 18.8 – 19.2 Ω
		w/ IC regulator	12V type 8.8 – 9.2 Ω
	Slip ring diameter	STD	32.3 – 32.5 mm (1.272 – 1.280 in)
		Limit	32.1 mm (1.264 in)
	Brush exposed length	STD	20.0 mm (0.787 in)
		Limit	5.5 mm (0.217 in)
Alternator regulator	Regulating voltage at 25°C (77°F)	w/o IC regulator	12V type 13.8 – 14.8 V; 24V type 27.0 – 29.0 V
		w/ IC regulator	12V type 13.8 – 14.4 V; 24V type 27.9 – 28.5 V

Torque Specifications

Part tightened	kg-cm	ft-lb	N·m
Turbine outlet elbow x Turbocharger (12H-T)	530	38	52
No.2 water by-pass pipe x Turbocharger (12H-T)	75	65 in-lb	7.1
Turbocharger x Exhaust manifold (12H-T)	530	38	52
Turbocharger x Cylinder head (12H-T)	185	13	18
Turbocharger oil pipe x Turbocharger (12H-T)	250	18	25
Turbocharger oil pipe x Cylinder block (12H-T)	75	65 in-lb	7.1
No.1 water by-pass pipe x Cylinder block (12H-T)	176	13	17
No.1 water by-pass pipe x Turbocharger (12H-T)	75	65 in-lb	7.1
Turbocharger stay x Turbocharger (12H-T)	700	51	69
Turbocharger stay x Cylinder block (12H-T)	700	51	69
PCV pipe x Intake air connector (12H-T)	185	13	18
Cylinder head x Cylinder block	1,150	83	113
Valve rocker support x Cylinder head	185	13	18
Cylinder head cover x Cylinder head	70	69 in-lb	6.9
Water outlet housing x Cylinder head	375	27	37
Exhaust manifold x Cylinder head	210	15	21
Intake manifold x Cylinder head	185	13	18
Fuel filter bracket x Cylinder head	375	27	37
Fuel pipe x Injection pump	280	20	28
Fuel hose x Injection pump (12H-T)	280	20	28
Glow plug x Cylinder head (2H)	125	9	12
Camshaft turning gear x Camshaft	450	33	44
Automatic timer drive gear x Automatic timer (12H-T)	230	17	23
No.1 idle gear x Cylinder block	475	34	47
No.2 idle gear x Cylinder block	475	34	47
Camshaft thrust plate x Cylinder block	375	27	37
Automatic timer x Injection pump	750	54	74
Timing gear cover x Timing gear case	250	18	25
Timing gear cover x Cylinder block	250	18	25
Injection pump retainer x Timing gear case	250	18	25
Oil pipe union bolt	185	13	18
Crankshaft pulley x Crankshaft	4,500	325	441
Push rod cover x Cylinder block	130	9	13
Connecting rod cap x Connecting rod	900	65	88
Main bearing cap x Cylinder block	1,300	100	136
Rear oil seal retainer x Cylinder block	185	13	18
Rear end plate x Cylinder block 12 mm head bolt	185	13	18
17 mm head bolt	650	47	64
Flywheel x Crankshaft (M-T)	1,200	87	118
Drive plate x Crankshaft (A-T)	1,000	72	98

Engine Mechanical Specifications

			STD	Limit
Compression pressure	Engine revolution at 250 rpm	2H	28.0 kg/cm² (398 psi, 2,746 kPa) or more	20.0 kg/cm² (284 psi, 1,961 kPa)
		12H-T	30.0 kg/cm² (427 psi, 2,942 kPa) or more	
	Difference of pressure between each cylinder		2.0 kg/cm² (28 psi, 196 kPa) or less	
Turbocharger	Turbocharging pressure		0.39 – 0.53 kg/cm² (5.6 – 7.5 psi, 38 – 52 kPa)	
	Impeller wheel axial play		0.13 mm (0.0051 in) or less	
Cylinder head	Cylinder block side warpage			0.20 mm (0.0079 in)
	Manifold side warpage			0.20 mm (0.0079 in)
	Valve seat Refacing angle	12H-T IN	30°, 45°, 60°	
		Others	30°, 45°, 75°	
	Contacting angle		45°	
	Contacting width		1.4 – 2.0 mm (0.055 – 0.079 in)	
Valve guide bushing	Inner diameter		9.010 – 9.030 mm (0.3547 – 0.3555 in)	
	Outer diameter		14.023 – 14.041 mm (0.5521 – 0.5528 in)	
Valve	Valve overall length	STD IN	120.7 mm (4.752 in)	120.2 mm (4.732 in)
		STD EX	120.6 mm (4.748 in)	120.1 mm (4.728 in)
	Valve face angle		44.5°	
	Stem diameter	STD IN	8.973 – 8.989 mm (0.3533 – 0.3539 in)	
		STD EX	8.964 – 8.970 mm (0.3529 – 0.3531 in)	
	Stem oil clearance	STD IN	0.021 – 0.057 mm (0.0008 – 0.0022 in)	0.10 mm (0.0039 in)
		STD EX	0.040 – 0.076 mm (0.0016 – 0.0030 in)	0.12 mm (0.0047 in)
	Margin thickness	STD IN	1.4 mm (0.055 in)	0.9 mm (0.035 in)
		STD EX	1.8 mm (0.071 in)	1.3 mm (0.051 in)
Valve spring	Free length	Inner	44.3 mm (1.744 in)	
		Outer	48.1 mm (1.894 in)	
	Installed tension	Inner at 35.0 mm (1.417 in)	7.6 kg (16.9 lb, 75 N)	
		Outer at 40.0 mm (1.575 in)	22.5 kg (49.6 lb, 221 N)	
	Squareness		2.0 mm (0.079 in)	
Rocker arm and shaft	Rocker arm inside diameter		18.500 – 18.521 mm (0.7283 – 0.7292 in)	
	Rocker shaft diameter		18.472 – 18.493 mm (0.7272 – 0.7281 in)	
	Rocker arm to shaft oil clearance	STD	0.007 – 0.049 mm (0.0003 – 0.0019 in)	0.10 mm (0.0039 in)
Push rod	Circle runout			0.50 mm (0.0197 in)
Connecting rod	Thrust clearance	STD	0.200 – 0.340 mm (0.0079 – 0.0134 in)	0.40 mm (0.0157 in)
	Bushing inside diameter	2H	29.008 – 29.020 mm (1.1420 – 1.1425 in)	
		12H-T	32.008 – 32.020 mm (1.2602 – 1.2606 in)	
	Piston pin diameter	2H	29.000 – 29.012 mm (1.1417 – 1.1422 in)	
		12H-T	32.000 – 32.012 mm (1.2598 – 1.2603 in)	
	Piston pin oil clearance		0.004 – 0.012 mm (0.0002 – 0.0005 in)	0.03 mm (0.0012 in)
	Connecting rod oil clearance	STD	0.030 – 0.070 mm (0.0012 – 0.0028 in)	0.10 mm (0.0039 in)
		U/S 0.25, 0.50, 0.75 and 1.00	0.030 – 0.072 mm (0.0012 – 0.0028 in)	
	Connecting rod bearing center wall thickness	STD Mark 1	1.490 – 1.495 mm (0.0583 – 0.0585 in)	
		STD Mark 2	1.485 – 1.490 mm (0.0585 – 0.0587 in)	
	Bend	Limit per 100 mm (3.94 in)		0.05 mm (0.0020 in)
	Twist	Limit per 100 mm (3.94 in)		0.05 mm (0.0020 in)
Crankshaft	Thrust clearance	STD	0.040 – 0.240 mm (0.0016 – 0.0094 in)	0.30 mm (0.0118 in)
	Thrust washer thickness	STD	2.930 – 2.980 mm (0.1154 – 0.1173 in)	
		O/S 0.125	2.993 – 3.043 mm (0.1178 – 0.1198 in)	
		O/S 0.250	3.055 – 3.105 mm (0.1203 – 0.1222 in)	
	Main journal diameter	STD	69.980 – 70.000 mm (2.7551 – 2.7559 in)	
		U/S 0.25	69.730 – 69.740 mm (2.7453 – 2.7457 in)	
		U/S 0.50	69.480 – 69.490 mm (2.7354 – 2.7358 in)	
		U/S 0.75	69.230 – 69.240 mm (2.7256 – 2.7260 in)	
		U/S 1.00	68.980 – 68.990 mm (2.7157 – 2.7161 in)	
	Main journal oil clearance	STD	0.032 – 0.068 mm (0.0013 – 0.0027 in)	0.10 mm (0.0039 in)
		U/S 0.25, 0.50, 0.75 and 1.00	0.030 – 0.074 mm (0.0012 – 0.0029 in)	
	Main bearing center wall thickness	STD Mark 1	1.981 – 1.985 mm (0.0780 – 0.0781 in)	
		STD Mark 2	1.985 – 1.989 mm (0.0781 – 0.0783 in)	
		STD Mark 3	1.989 – 1.993 mm (0.0783 – 0.0785 in)	
	Crank pin diameter	STD	54.980 – 55.000 mm (2.1646 – 2.1654 in)	
		U/S 0.25	54.730 – 54.740 mm (2.1547 – 2.1551 in)	
		U/S 0.50	54.480 – 54.490 mm (2.1449 – 2.1453 in)	
		U/S 0.75	54.230 – 54.240 mm (2.1350 – 2.1354 in)	
		U/S 1.00	53.980 – 53.990 mm (2.1252 – 2.1259 in)	
	Circle runout	Limit		0.06 mm (0.0024 in)
	Taper and out-of-round	Main journal and crank pin Limit		0.02 mm (0.0008 in)

L, 2L and 2L-T

ENGINE MECHANICAL

Specifications

Drive belt deflection with 10 kg or 22 lb				
Water pump - Alternator			7 – 10 mm	0.28 – 0.39 in.
Crankshaft - FE vane Pump	New belt	10 – 14 mm	0.39 – 0.55 in.
	Used belt	8 – 10 mm	0.31 – 0.39 in.
Crankshaft - A/C compressor	New belt	13 – 17 mm	0.55 – 0.65 in.
	Used belt	17 – 23 mm	0.67 – 0.91 in.
Engine oil capacity	Drain and refill	w/o Oil filter change	4.8 liters	5.1 US qt	4.2 Imp qt
		w/ Oil filter change	5.6 liters	5.9 US qt	4.9 Imp qt
	Dry fill		8.5 liters	8.9 US qt	7.5 Imp qt
Valve clearance	at hot	L	0.25 mm	0.0098 in.
		EX	0.36 mm	0.0142 in.
Injection timing		L	0.94 – 1.06 mm	0.0370 – 0.0417 in.
Plunger stroke	at 0°TDC	2L w/o ACSD	1.06 – 1.22 mm	0.0417 – 0.0480 in.
		2L w/ ACSD	0.82 – 0.98 mm	0.0323 – 0.0386 in.
		2L-T	0.76 – 0.87 mm	0.0299 – 0.0343 in.
Injection order			1 – 3 – 4 – 2	
Idle speed			700 rpm	
Maximum speed	M/T (ex. U/I)		4,800 rpm	
	L, 2L (ex. LY & UNSAE) A/T		4,600 rpm	
Compression pressure at 250 rpm	STD	L, 2L-T	30.0 kg/cm²	427 psi	2,942 kPa
		2L	32.0 kg/cm²	465 psi	3,138 kPa
	Limit		20.0 kg/cm²	284 psi	1,961 kPa
Pressure difference between each cylinder			Less than 5.0 kg/cm² (71 psi, 490 kPa)	

Torque Specifications

Part tightened		kg-cm	ft-lb	N·m
Nozzle holder retaining nut × Nozzle holder body	2H	700	51	69
	12H-T	350	25	34
Injection nozzle × Cylinder head	2H	700	51	69
	12H-T	185	13	18
Nozzle leakage pipe × Injection nozzle	2H	500	36	49
	12H-T	125	9	12
Injection pipe × injection nozzle		300	22	29
Chamber plug × feed pump head	19 mm bolt head	500	36	49
	32 mm bolt head	1,500	109	147
Priming pump × feed pump housing		500	36	49
Feed pump × injection pump		95	82 in.-lb	9.3
Fuel pump × injection pump		280	20	27
Automatic timer × injection pump		750	54	74
Steel ball grade × Camshaft (2H M/T)		550	40	54
Flyweight × Camshaft (2H A/T and 12H-T)		550	40	54
Injection pump retainer × injection pump		375	27	37
Injection pump × Timing gear case		250	18	25
Fuel pipe × injection pump (12H-T)		280	20	27
Fuel hose × injection pump (12H-T)		280	20	27
Oil pipe union bolt		185	13	18

WIRING DIAGRAMS

LAND CRUISER (BJ40, BJ43 & HJ47 Series) ELECTRICAL WIRING DIAGRAM – 1981 PRODUCTION VEHICLE

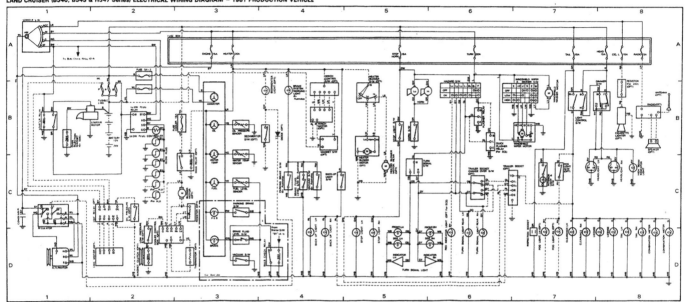

LAND CRUISER (BJ60 & HJ60 Series) ELECTRICAL WIRING DIAGRAM – 1981 PRODUCTION VEHICLE

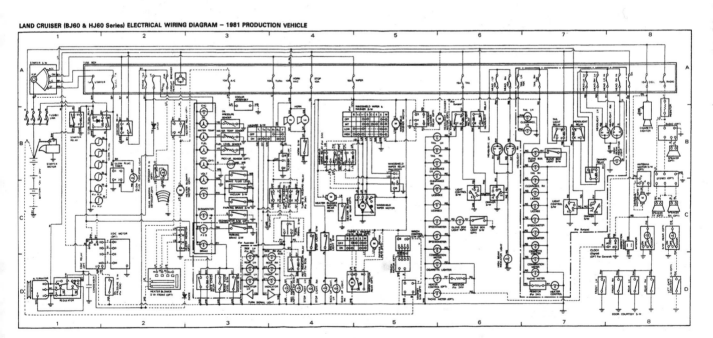

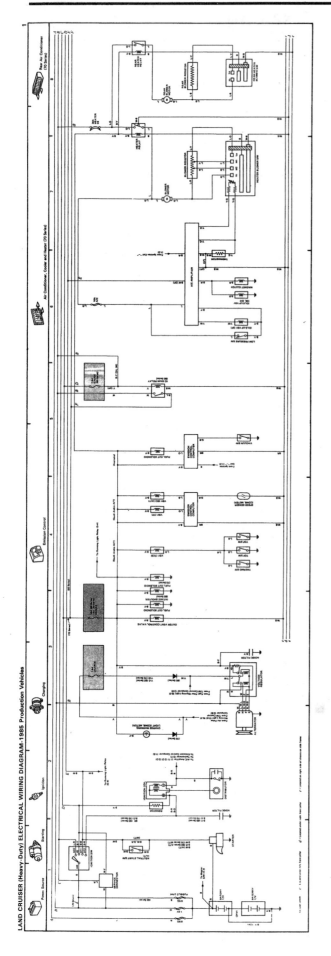

LAND CRUISER (Heavy-Duty) ELECTRICAL WIRING DIAGRAM-1985 Production Vehicles

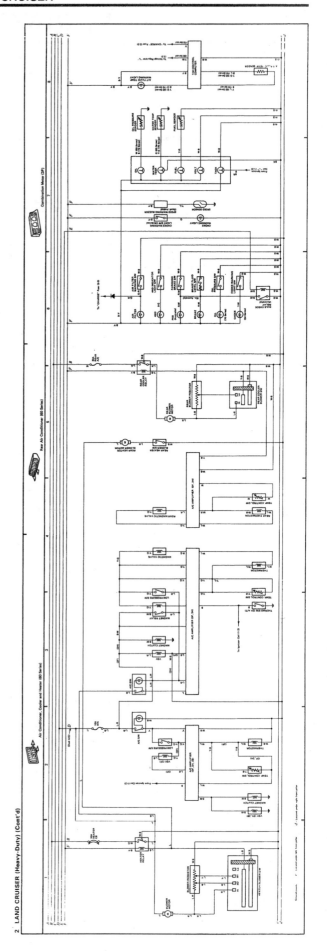

2   LAND CRUISER (Heavy-Duty) (Cont'd)

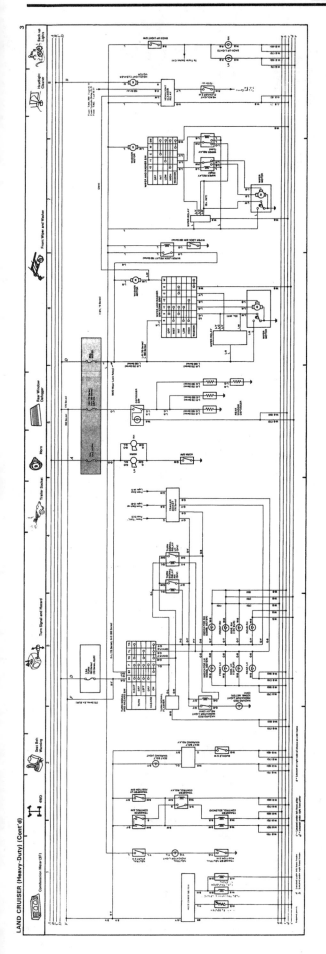

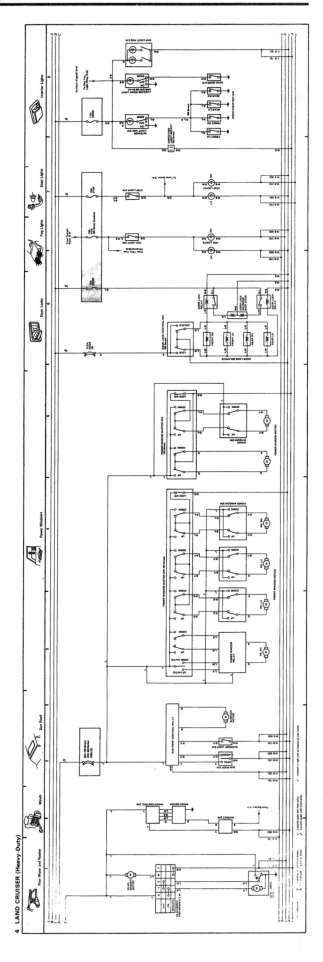

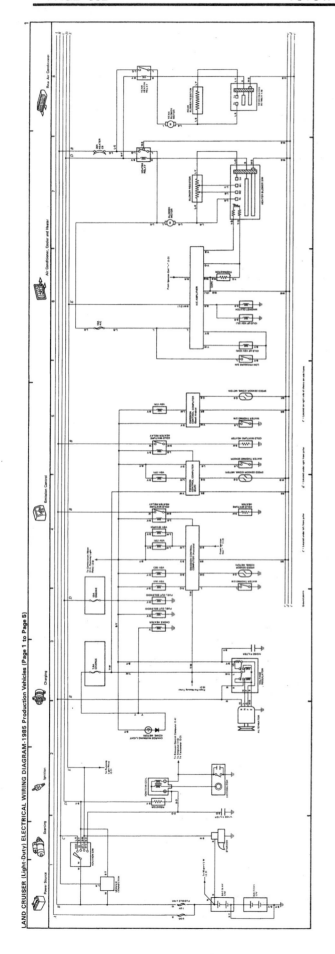

LAND CRUISER (Light-Duty) ELECTRICAL WIRING DIAGRAM—1985 Production Vehicles (Page 1 to Page 5)

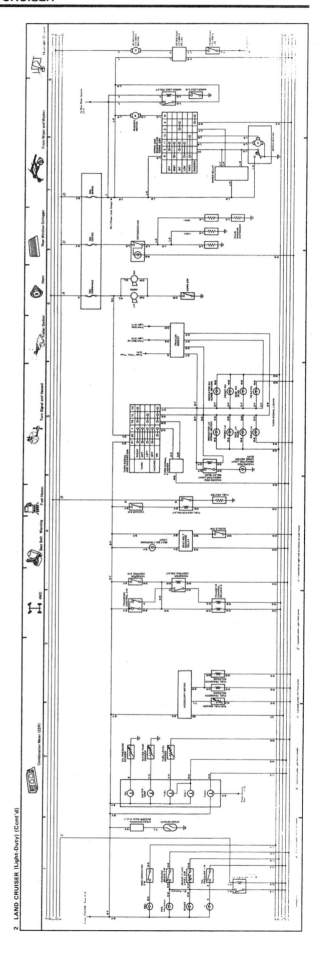

2 LAND CRUISER (Light-Duty) (Cont'd)

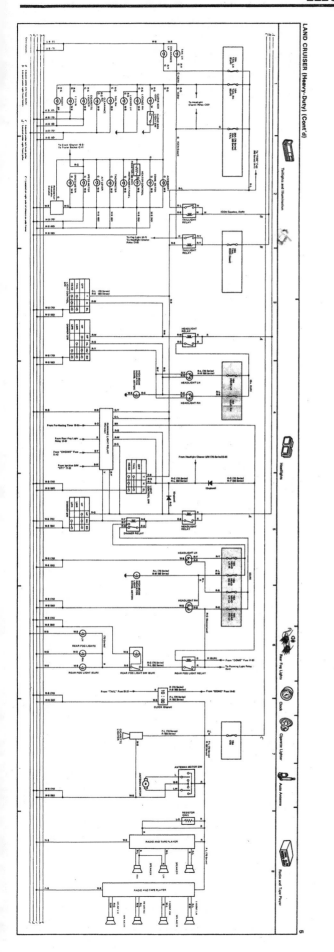

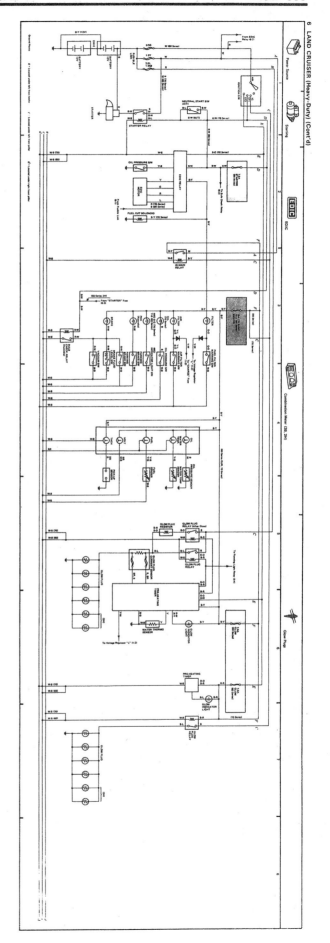

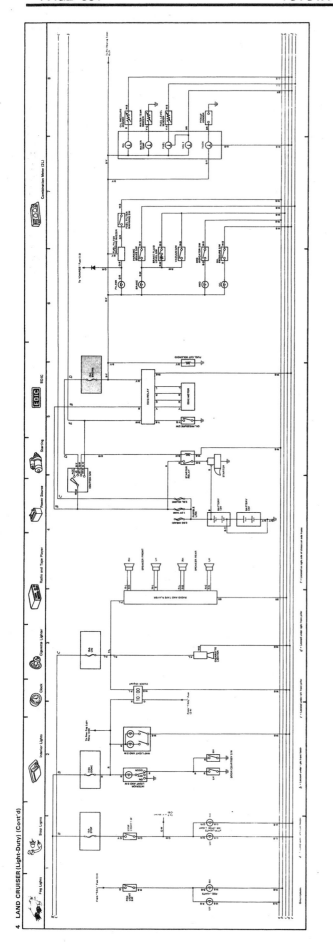

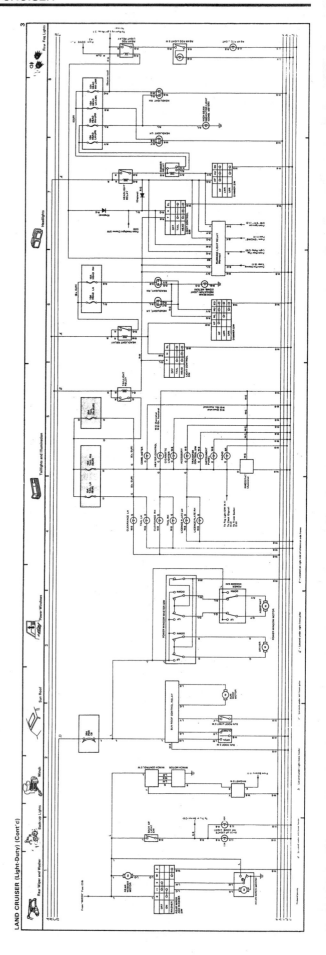

BRAKE SYSTEM

BRAKE SYSTEM

ADJUSTMENT AND CHECKING

Check and Adjust Brake Pedal

1.Check That Pedal Height is Correct.

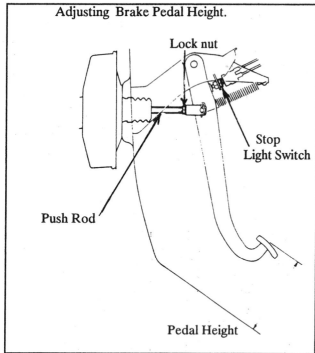

Adjusting Brake Pedal Height.

Lock nut

Stop Light Switch

Push Rod

Pedal Height

Pedal height from asphalt sheet:

Model	Distance mm (in)
HJ, FJ, BJ 4..^{s} 1962/71	190 (7.48)
FJ 55 68/71	170 (6.69)
HJ, FJ, BJ 4..^{s} 1972/74	245 (9.65)
FJ 55 72/74	170 (6.69)
HJ, FJ, BJ 4..^{s} 1975 on w/ Booster	215 (8.46)
HJ, FJ, BJ 4..^{s} 1975 on w/o Booster	198 (7.80)
FJ 55 1975 on w/ Booster	185 (7.28)
FJ 55 1975 on w/o booster	172 (6.77)
HJ, FJ, BJ 6..^{s} to 1984 light chassis	192 (7.55)
HJ, FJ, BJ 6..^{s} 1984 on. light chassis	180 (7.09)
HJ,FJ,BJ,RJ,LJ70's 84/90 light chas	169-179(6.65-7.05)

Heavy Chassis
FJ, BJ, HJ, 60 series

Front disc brakes	more than 90mm (3.54 in)
Front drum brakes	more than 103mm (4.06 in)

FJ, BJ, HJ, 70', series

Front disc brakes	more than 80mm (3.15 in)
Front drum brakes	
FJ,BJ,HJ 75 series	more than 90mm (3.54 in)
Except 75 series	more than 100mm (3.94 in)

If incorrect, adjust the pedal height.

2.If Necessary, Adjust Pedal Height.

(a) Disconnect the stop light switch connector and sufficiently loosen the switch.

(b) Adjust the pedal height by turning the pedal push rod.

(c) Return the stop light switch until its body lightly contacts the pedal stopper.

(d) After adjusting the pedal height, check and adjust the pedal freeplay.

3.Check Pedal Freeplay.

(a) Stop the engine and depress the brake pedal several times until there is no more vacuum left in the booster.

(b) Push in the pedal until the beginning of resistance is felt. Measure the distance, as shown.

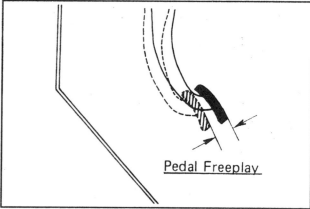

Pedal Freeplay

Pedal freeplay: 3 - 6 mm (0.12 - 0.24 in)

* The pedal freeplay is the amount of the stroke until the booster air valve is moved by the pedal push rod.

4.If Necessary, Adjust Pedal Freeplay.

(a) If incorrect, adjust the pedal freeplay by turning the pedal push rod.

(b) Start the engine and confirm that pedal freeplay exists.

(c) After adjusting the pedal freeplay, check the pedal height.

Test Brake Booster

* If there is leakage or lack of vacuum, repair before testing.

1.Operating Check.

(a) Depress the brake pedal several times with the engine off, and check that there is no change in the pedal reserve distance.

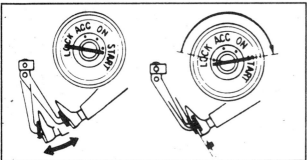

(b) Depress the brake pedal and start the engine. If the pedal goes down slightly, operation is normal.

2.Air Tightness.

(a) Start the engine and stop it after one or two minutes. Depress the brake pedal several times slowly. If the pedal goes down further the first time, but gradually rises after the second or third time, the booster is air tight.

(b) Depress the brake pedal while the engine is running and stop it with the pedal depressed. If there is no change in pedal reserve travel after holding the pedal for 30 seconds, the booster is air tight.

Bleeding Brake System

* If any work is done on the brake system or if air is suspected in the brake lines, bleed the system of air.

* Do not let brake fluid remain on a painted surface. Wash it off immediately.

1.Fill Brake Reservoir with Brake Fluid. Check the fluid level in the reservoir. If necessary, add brake fluid.

2.Bleed Master Cylinder.

* If the master cylinder was dismantled or if the reservoir becomes empty, bleed the air from the master cylinder.

(a) Disconnect the brake tubes from the master cylinder.

(b) Depress the brake pedal and hold it.

(c) Block off the outlet holes with your fingers and release the brake pedal.

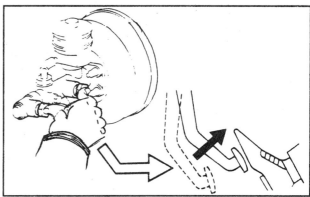

(d) Repeat (b) and (c) 3 or 4 times.

3.Begin Bleeding Air from Wheel Cylinder with Longest Hydraulic Line.

(a) Connect the vinyl tube to the brake cylinder bleeder plug, and insert the other end of the tube in a half-full container of brake fluid.

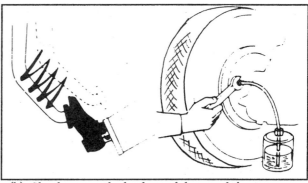

(b) Slowly pump the brake pedal several times.

(c) While having an assistant press on the pedal, loosen the bleeder plug until fluid starts to run out. Then close the bleeder plug.

(d) Repeat (b) and (c) until there are no more air bubbles in the fluid.

(e) Tighten the bleeder plug.

4.Repeat Procedure for Each Wheel.

Parking Brake Adjustment

1.Check that Parking Brake Lever Travel is Correct. Pull the parking brake lever all the way up, and count the number of clicks.

2.If Necessary, Adjust Parking Brake Lever Travel.

* Before adjusting the parking brake, make sure that the rear brake shoe clearance has been adjusted.

(a) Remove the console assembly and/or parking brake lever cover.

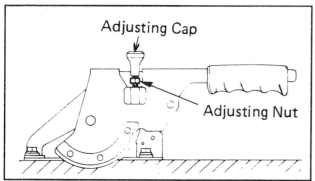

(b) Loosen the adjusting cap and turn the adjusting nut until the travel is correct.

(c) Tighten the adjusting cap.

(d) Install the console assembly and/or parking brake lever cover.

Drum Brake Adjustment

Adjust Brake Shoe Clearance:

(a) Jack up and support the vehicle.

(b) Remove the shoe adjusting hole plugs from the backing plate.

(c) Using a brake adjusting tool, turn the adjusting nut until the wheel locks.

(d) Using a brake adjusting tool, turn the adjusting nut until the wheel turns freely.

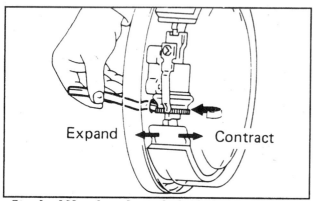

Standard No. of notches to be backed off: 5 notches.

(e) Repeat the steps (c) and (d) for other wheels.

(f) Install the shoe adjusting hole plugs.

(g) Check that the pedal reserve distance is correct.

MASTER CYLINDER

Removal

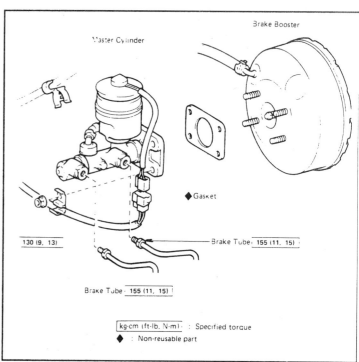

1.Disconnect Level Warning Switch Connector.

2.Drain out Brake: Do not allow fluid to remain on paint.

3.Disconnect 2 Brake Tubes.

4.Remove Master Cylinder.

(a) Remove the 4 nuts.

(b) Remove the master cylinder, clamp and gasket from the brake booster.

Dismantle

1.Remove Reservoir and Hose.

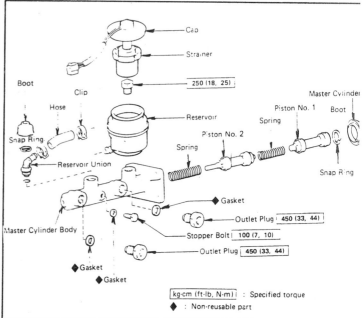

(a) Remove the set bolt from the reservoir.

(b) Remove the reservoir with the hose from the master cylinder.

2. Remove Boot.

3. Remove Reservoir Union.

(a) Using a snap ring pliers, remove the snap ring.

(b) Remove the reservoir union and O-ring.

4. Remove 2 Outlet Plugs.

5. Remove Piston Stopper Bolt. Using a screwdriver, push the pistons in all the way, and remove the piston stopper bolt and gasket.

6. Remove 2 Pistons and Springs.

(a) Push in the piston with a screwdriver and remove the snap ring with snap ring pliers.

(b) Remove the 2 pistons and springs from the master cylinder. If necessary, inject compressed air into the outlet hole to force out the piston.

Inspection

* Clean the dismantled parts.

1. Inspect Cylinder Bore for Rust and Scoring.

2. Inspect Cylinder for Wear or Damage. If necessary, clean or replace the cylinder.

Assembly

1. Apply Lithium Soap Base Glycol Grease (non-petroleum grease) to Rubber parts of Piston.

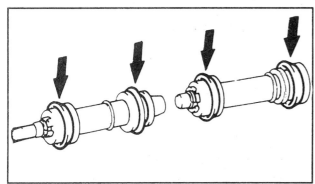

2. Install 2 Springs and Pistons.

* Be careful not to damage the rubber lips on the pistons.

(a) Insert 2 springs and pistons straight in, not at an angle.

(b) Using snap ring pliers, install the snap ring.

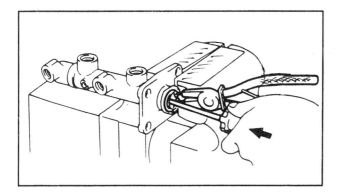

3. Install Piston Stopper Bolt and New Gasket. Using a screwdriver, push the pistons in all the way and install the piston stopper bolt through the new gasket. Torque the bolt.

Torque: 100 kg-cm (7 ft-lb, 10 N·m)

5. Install Reservoir Union.

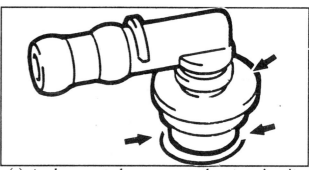

(a) Apply non-petroleum grease to the reservoir union.

(b) Pack the non-petroleum grease on the union.

(c) Install the union through the new O-ring.

(d) Using snap ring pliers, install the new snap ring.

(e) Install the boot.

Installation

1. Clean out Groove on Lower Installation Surface of Master Cylinder.

2. Confirm that "UP" Mark on Master Cylinder Boot is in Correct Position.

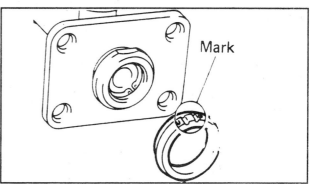

Mark

3. Adjust Length of Brake Booster Push Rod before Installing Master Cylinder. See INSTALLATION OF BRAKE BOOSTER Section.

4. Install Master Cylinder and clamp on the brake booster with 4 nuts through the new gasket.

Torque: 130 kg-cm (9 ft-lb, 13 N·m)

5. Connect 2 Brake Tubes.

6. Connect Level Warning Switch Connector.

BRAKE BOOSTER

Removal

1. Remove Master Cylinder.

2. Disconnect Vacuum Hose from Brake Booster.

3. Remove Clutch Booster.

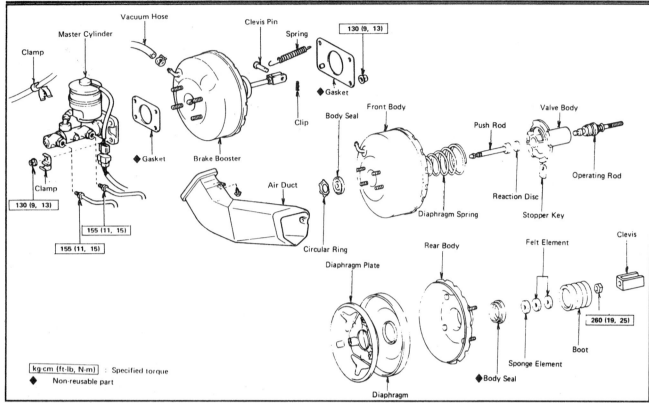

kg·cm (ft-lb, N·m) : Specified torque
◆ Non-reusable part

4. Remove the 2 Screws and Air Duct under Dash.

5. Remove Pedal Return Spring.

6. Remove Clip and Clevis Pin.

7. Remove Brake Booster. Remove the 4 nuts, and pull out the brake booster with gasket.

Dismantle

1. Remove Clevis and Lock Nut.

2. Separate Front and Rear Bodies.

(a) Place the matchmarks on the front and rear bodies.

(b) Set the booster in clamp.

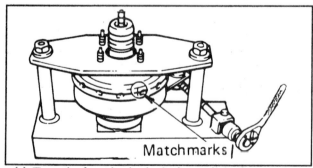

Matchmarks

(c) Turn the front body clockwise until the front and rear bodies separate.

(d) Evenly tighten the 4 booster mounting nuts to separate the front and rear bodies.

(e) Remove the diaphragm spring and push rod.

3. Remove Boot from Rear Body.

4. Remove Diaphragm Assembly from Rear Body.

5. Remove Body Seal from Rear Body.

6. Remove Valve Body and Diaphragm from Diaphragm Plate.

(a) Put the diaphragm assembly on special tool and turn it to separate the valve body and diaphragm plate.

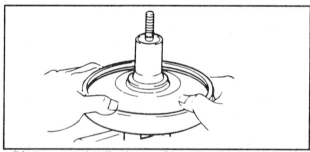

(b) Remove the diaphragm from the plate.

7. Remove Operating Rod from Valve Body.

(a) Push the operating rod in the valve body and remove the stopper key.

(b) Pull out the operating rod with the 3 elements.

8. Remove Reaction Disc from Valve Body.

9. Remove Body Seal from Front Body. Using a screwdriver, pry out the circular ring and remove the seal.

Inspection

Inspect Check Valve Operation.

(a) Check that air flows from the booster side to the hose side.

(b) Check that air does not flow from the hose side to the booster side.

Assembly

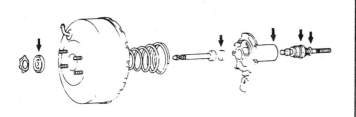

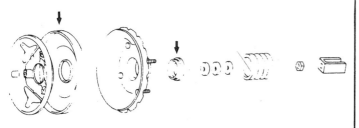

1.Apply Silicone Grease as Illustrated.

2.Install Body Seal to Front Body.

(a) Place the body seal in position.

(b) Secure the body seal with the circular ring.

3.Install Operating Rod to valve Body.

(a) Insert the operating rod in the valve body.

(b) Push the operating rod in the valve body and install the stopper key.

(c) Pull the operating rod and confirm that the stopper key is working.

4.Install Reaction Disc to valve Body.

5.Install Valve Body and Diaphragm to Diaphragm Plate.

(a) Install the diaphragm to the plate.

(b) Insert the valve body to the plate.

(c) Put the diaphragm assembly on, and turn it to install.

6.Install Body Seal to Rear Body.

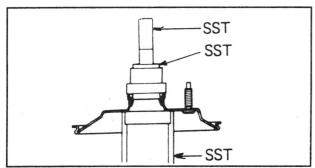

7.Install Diaphragm Assembly to Rear Body.

8.Install Following Parts to Rear Body: 1) felt elements, 2) sponge element, 3) boot.

9.Assemble Front and Rear Bodies.

(a) Place the spring and push rod in the front body.

(b) Using special tool, compress the spring between the front and rear bodies.

(c) Assemble the front and rear bodies by turning the front body counterclockwise until the alignment marks match.

* If the front body is too tight to be turned, apply more silicone grease on the diaphragm edge that contacts the front and rear bodies.

10.Install Clevis and Lock Nut.

Installation

1.Adjust Length of Booster Push Rod.

(a) Set special tool on the master cylinder with the gasket, and lower the pin until its top slightly touches the piston.

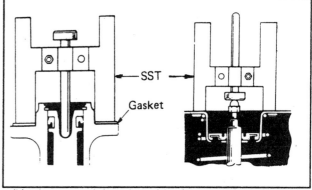

(b) Turn special tool upside down, and set it on the booster.

(c) There should be no clearance between the booster push rod and pin head (special tool).

(d) Adjust the booster push rod length until the push rod lightly touches the pin head.

2.Install Brake Booster. Install the brake booster and torque the 4 nuts.

Torque: 130 kg-cm (9 ft-lb, 13 N·m)

3.Connect Clevis to Brake Pedal. Insert the clevis pin into the clevis and brake pedal and install the clip to the clevis pin.

4.Install Pedal Return Spring.

5.Install Air Duct.

6.Install Clutch Booster.

7.Install Master Cylinder.

8.Connect Hose to Brake Booster.

9.Fill Brake Reservoir with Brake Fluid and Bleed Brake System.

10.Check for Leaks.

11.Check and Adjust Brake Pedal.

VACUUM PUMP

Components

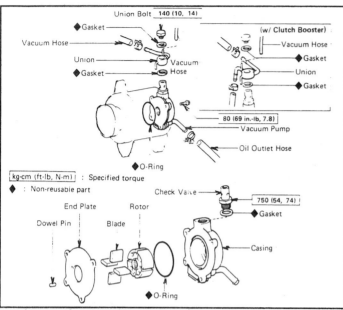

FRONT BRAKE (DRUM)

Components

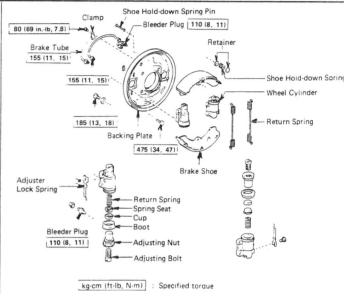

Inspection

1.Inspect Blade.

(a) Check for wear or damage.

(b) Using callipers, measure the height, width and length of the blade.

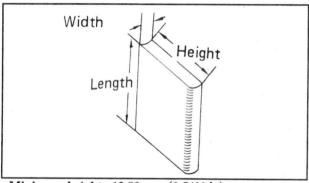

Minimum height: 13.80 mm (0.5433 in)
Minimum width: 5.95 mm (0.2343 in)
Minimum length: 39.98 mm (1.5740 in)

2.Inspect Rotor.

(a) Check for wear or damage.

(b) Assemble the rotor to the alternator and check the amount of play in the direction of rotor spline rotation.

Maximum play: 1.0 mm (0.039 in)

3.Inspect Check Valve Operation.

(a) Check that air flow from the union side to the pump side.

(b) Check that air does not flow from the pump side to the union side.

(c) If Necessary, replace the check valve.

Removal

1.Remove Drum. Remove the screw and then remove the drum.

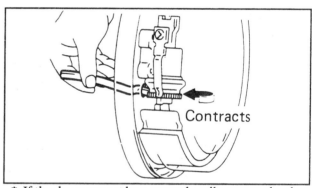

* If the drum cannot be removed easily, return the shoe adjuster until the wheel turns freely.

2.Remove Front Side Return Spring.

3.Remove Shoe Hold-Down Springs, Retainers and Pin.

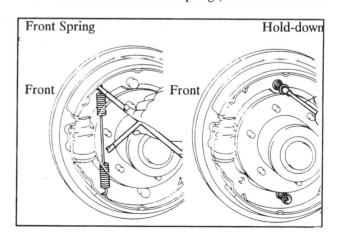

4.Remove Brake Shoes and Rear Side Return Spring. Slide the shoes and remove them together with the rear side return spring.

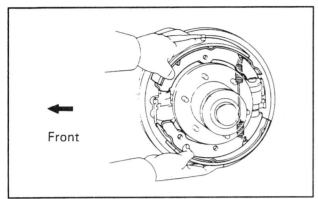

Front

5.If Necessary, Remove Wheel Cylinder.
6.If Necessary, Dismantle Wheel Cylinder.
(a) Remove the following parts from the wheel cylinder: 1) adjusting bolt and nut, 2) boot, 3) cup, 4) spring seat, 5) return spring.
(b) Remove the screw and adjuster lock spring.

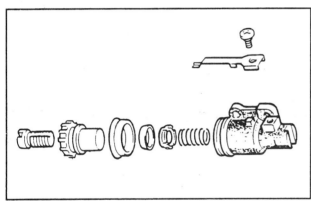

Inspection

1.Inspect Dismantled Parts for War, Rust or Damage.
2.Measure Brake Shoe Lining Thickness.

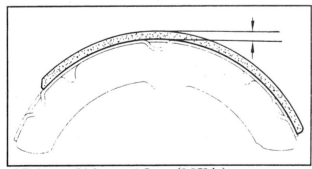

Minimum thickness: 1.5 mm (0.059 in)

If the shoe lining is less than minimum or shows signs of uneven wear, replace the brake shoe.

3.Inspect Brake Lining and drum for Proper Contact. If the contact between the brake lining and drum is improper, repair the lining with a brake shoe grinder, or replace the brake show assembly.

Assembly

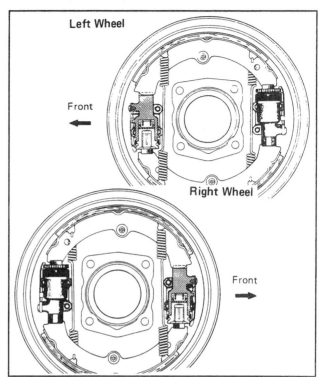

Left Wheel

Front

Right Wheel

Front

* Assemble the parts in the direction shown.
1.Assemble Wheel Cylinder.
(a) Apply non-petroleum grease to parts as shown.

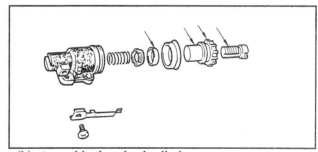

(b) Assemble the wheel cylinder.
* Fit in the following order: 1) return spring, 2) spring seat, 3) cup, 4) boot.
(c) Install the adjusting bolt and nut to the wheel cylinder. There are 2 kinds of adjusting nuts and bolts. Use each at the proper location.
  RH wheel cylinder - Right-hand threads
  (R mark on cylinder) (Yellow colour)
  LH wheel cylinder - Left-hand threads
  (L mark on cylinder) (White colour)

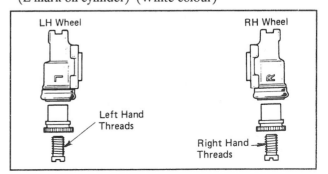

LH Wheel

RH Wheel

Left Hand Threads

Right Hand Threads

(d) Install the adjusting lock spring with the screw.

2. Install Bleeder Plug. Temporarily install the bleeder plug as shown.

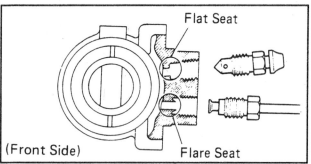

Flat Seat

(Front Side)   Flare Seat

3. Install Wheel Cylinder to Backing Plate.

(a) Install the front wheel cylinder with the adjuster facing downward.

(b) Install the rear wheel cylinder with the adjuster facing upward.

4. Install Brake Tube to Wheel Cylinder.

5. Install Brake Shoes and Return Springs.

(a) Apply high temperature grease to the brake shoe contact surfaces as shown.

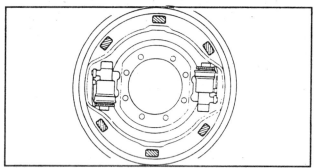

(b) Hook the return spring to the brake shoe rear inner side.

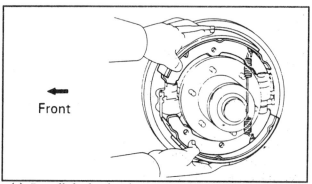

Front

(c) Install the brake shoes assembly.

(d) Install the shoe hold-down spring, 2 retainers and spring.

(e) Install the other side return spring.

6. Clean Lining and Inner Drum with "Wet & Dry" Sandpaper.

7. Install Drum. Install the drum with screw.

FRONT BRAKE (DISC)

Components

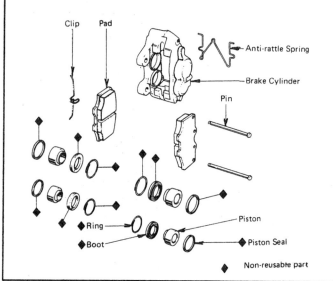

Clip   Pad   Anti-rattle Spring

Brake Cylinder

Pin

Piston

Ring

Boot   Piston Seal

Non-reusable part

Replacement of Disc Pads

1. Inspect Pad Lining Thickness. Check the pad thickness through the cylinder inspection hole and replace pads if not within specification.

Standard Thickness: 10.0mm (0.394 in)
Minimum Thickness: 1.0mm (0.039 in)

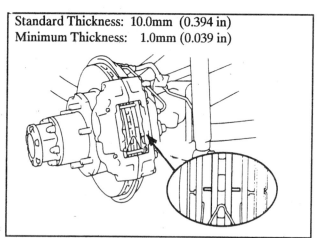

2. Remove Following Parts: 1) anti-rattle clip, 2) 2 anti-rattle pins, 3) anti-rattle spring, 4) 2 pads.

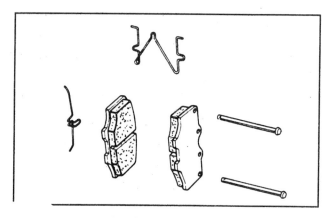

3.Check Rotor Disc. (later on this page)

4.Install New Pads.

(a) Draw out a small amount of brake fluid from the reservoir.

(b) Press in the piston with a hammer handle or such.

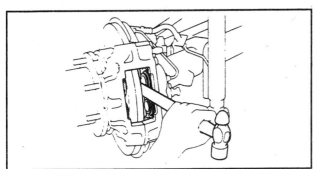

* Always change the pad on one wheel at a time as there is a possibility of the opposite piston flying out.

(c) Install the new pads into the cylinder.

* Do not allow oil or grease to get on the rubbing face.

5.Install Anti-Rattle Spring.

6.Install 2 Pins.

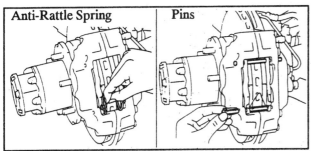

| Anti-Rattle Spring | Pins |

7.Install Anti-Rattle Clip.

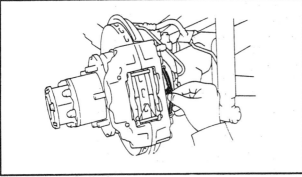

Removal of Cylinder

1.Disconnect Brake Line.

2.Remove Cylinder. Remove the 2 mounting bolts and cylinder.

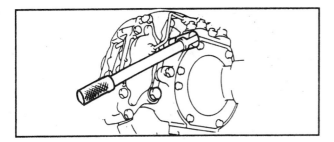

3.Remove following parts: 1) anti-rattle clip, 2) 2 anti-rattle pins, 3) anti-rattle spring, 4) 2 pads.

Dismantle of Cylinder

1.Using a Screwdriver, Remove Cylinder boot Set Ring and Boot.

2.Remove Piston From Cylinder.

(a) Place a wooden block between the pistons and insert a pad at one side.

(b) Use compressed air to remove the pistons alternately from the cylinder.

3.Remove Piston Seal.

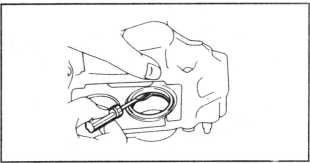

Inspection and Repair of Brake Components

1.Measure Pad Lining Thickness. Replace the pad if the thickness is less than the minimum (the 1.0 mm slit is no longer visible) or it if shows signs of uneven wear.

2.Measure Rotor Disc Thickness.

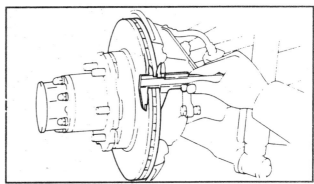

HJ, FJ & BJ:

Standard thickness: 20.0 mm (0.787 in)

Minimum thickness: 19.0 mm (0.748 in)

RJ & LJ:

Standard thickness: 12.5 mm (0.492 in)

Minimum thickness: 11.5 mm (0.453 in)

3.Measure Rotor Disc Runout at 10 mm (0.39 in) from the Outer Edge of the Rotor Disc.

Maximum disc runout: 0.15 mm (0.0059 in)

If the runout is greater than the maximum, replace the disc.

* Before measuring the runout, confirm that the front bearing play is within specification.

4.If Necessary, Replace Disc.

(a) Remove the axle hub (see FRONT AXLE Section).

(b) Using rod, press the hub bolts out of the axle hub.

(c) Remove the 2 bolts and separate the disc and hub.

(d) Install a new disc to the axle hub and tighten the 2 bolts.

Torque: 475 kg-cm (34 ft-lb, 47 N·m)

(e) Using a collar and rod, press the hub bolts into the hub.

(f) Install the axle hub and adjust the front bearing preload (see FRONT AXLE Section).

Assembly of Cylinder

1.Apply Non-petroleum grease to Parts.

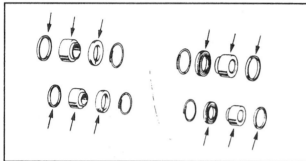

2.Install Piston Seal in Cylinder.
3.Install Piston in Cylinder.

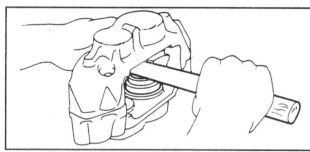

4.Install Cylinder boot and Set Ring in Cylinder.

Installation of Cylinder

1.Install Cylinder. Install and torque the mounting bolts.

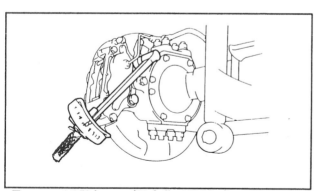

Torque: 1,250 kg-cm (90 ft-lb, 123 N·m)

2.Install following parts: 1) 2 pads, 2) anti-rattle spring, 3) 2 anti-rattle pins, 4) anti-rattle clip.

3.Connect Brake Line.

4.Fill Brake Reservoir with Brake Fluid and Bleed Brake System.

REAR BRAKE

Components

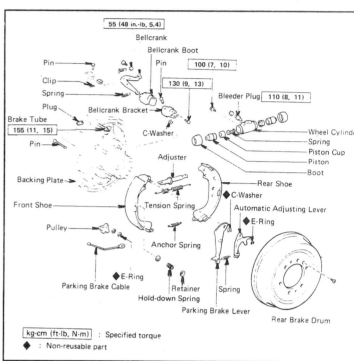

kg-cm (ft-lb, N·m) : Specified torque
◆ : Non-reusable part

Removal

1.Remove Rear Wheel and Brake Drum.

* If the brake drum cannot be removed easily, perform the following:

 (i) Insert a screwdriver through the hole in the backing plate, and hold the automatic adjusting lever away from the adjusting bolt.

 (ii) Using another screwdriver, reduce the brake shoe adjustment by turning the adjusting bolt clockwise.

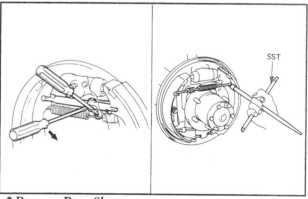

2.Remove Rear Shoe.

(a) Remove the tension spring.

(b) Remove the rear shoe hold-down spring and pin.

(c) Remove the rear brake shoe and anchor spring.

3.Remove Front Shoe.

(a) Remove the hold-down spring and pin.

(b) Disconnect the parking brake cable from the parking brake bellcrank.

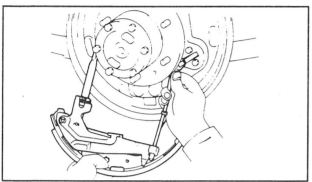

(c) Remove the front shoe with adjuster.

(d) Disconnect the parking brake cable from the front shoe.

4.Remove Adjuster from Front Shoe. Remove the adjusting lever spring and the adjuster.

5.If Necessary, Remove and Dismantle Wheel Cylinder.

6.Dismantle Wheel Cylinder. Remove the following parts from the wheel cylinder: 1) 2 boots, 2) 2 pistons, 3) 2 piston cups, 4) spring.

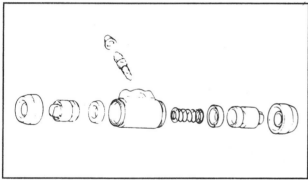

7.If Necessary, Remove and Dismantle Parking Brake Bellcrank Assembly.

(a) Remove the clip and disconnect the parking brake cable.

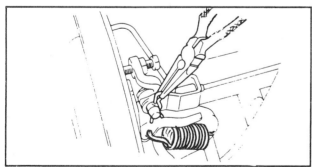

(b) Remove the 2 tension springs.

(c) Remove the parking brake bellcrank assembly with the 2 bolts.

(d) Remove the boot from the parking brake bellcrank assembly.

(e) Using a screwdriver, remove the C-washer and pin.

(f) Remove the parking brake bellcrank from the crank bracket.

Inspection

1.If the drum is scored or worn, the brake drum may be lathed to the maximum inside diameter.

Maximum inside diameter: 297.0 mm (11.693 in)

2.Measure Brake Shoe Lining Thickness. If the shoe lining is less than minimum or shows signs of uneven wear, replace the brake shoes.

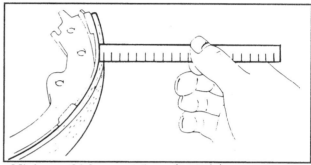

Minimum thickness: 1.5 mm (0.059 in)

* If any of the brake shoes have to be replaced, replace all of the brake shoes in order to maintain even braking.

3.Inspect Brake Lining and Drum for Even Contact. If the contact between the brake lining and drum is uneven, repair the lining with a brake shoe grinder, or replace the brake shoe assembly.

4.If Necessary, Replace Brake Shoes.

(a) Using a screwdriver, remove the automatic adjusting lever from the front shoe.

(b) Using a screwdriver, remove the parking brake lever from the front shoe.

(c) Using pliers, install the parking brake lever with a new C-washer.

(d) Install the automatic adjusting lever with a new E-clip.

5.Inspect Wheel Cylinder for Corrosion or Damage.

6.Inspect Backing Plate for Wear or Damage.

7.Inspect Bellcrank Parts for Bending, Wear or Damage.

Assembly

1.If Necessary, Assemble and Install Parking Brake Bellcrank Assembly.

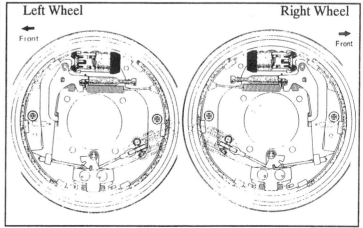

Left Wheel   Right Wheel
Front   Front

(a) Install the parking brake bellcrank to the crank bracket.

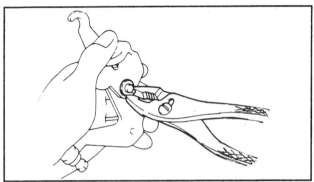

(b) Install the pin with the new C-washer.

(c) Apply non-petroleum grease to the boot.

(d) Install the parking brake bellcrank assembly on the backing plate with 2 bolts.

(e) Torque the bolts.

Torque: 130 kg-cm (9 ft-lb, 13 N·m)

2.If Necessary, Assemble and Install Wheel Cylinder.

(a) Apply non-petroleum grease to the piston cups and pistons.

(b) Install the spring and 2 piston cups in the wheel cylinder. Make sure flanges of the cups are pointed inward.

(c) Install the 2 pistons, boots and spring in the cylinder.

(d) Install the wheel cylinder on the backing plate with 2 bolts.

Torque: 100 kg-cm (7 ft-lb, 10 N·m)

(e) Connect the brake line.

Torque: 155 kg-cm (11 ft-lb, 15 N·m)

3.Apply High-Temperature Type Grease on Backing Plate as Shown.

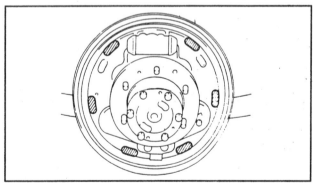

4.Apply High-Temperature Type Grease to Adjuster bolt Threads and End.

5.Install Adjuster to front Shoe.

(a) Install the adjuster to the adjust lever.

(b) Install the adjust lever spring.

6.Install Front Shoe.

(a) Install the parking brake cable to the parking brake shoe lever.

(b) Install the parking brake cable to the bellcrank as shown.

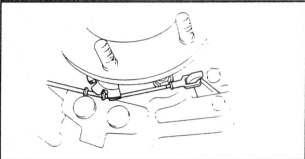

(c) Set the front shoe in place with the end of the shoe inserted in the piston.

(d) Install the shoe hold-down spring and pin.

7.Install Rear Shoe.

(a) Install the anchor spring to the front shoe and rear shoe.

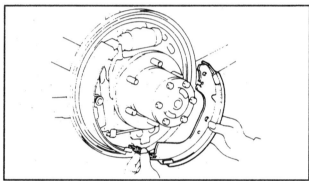

(b) Set the rear shoe in place with the end of the shoe inserted in the piston.

(c) Install the shoe hold-down spring and pin.

(d) Install the tension spring.

8.Check Operation of Automatic Adjuster Mechanism.

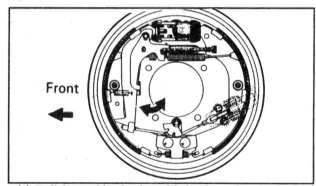

Front

(a) Pull the parking brake cable backward as shown, and release. Check that the adjusting bolt turns. If the bolt does not turn, check for incorrect installation of the rear brakes.

(b) Adjust the adjuster to the shortest possible length.

(c) Install the drum.

(d) Turn the brake drum in the reverse direction and depress the brake pedal. Repeat this procedure several times.

9.Check Clearance Between Brake Shoes and Drum.

(a) Remove the drum.

(b) Measure the brake drum inside diameter and diameter of the brake shoes. Check that the difference between the diameters is the correct shoe clearance.

Shoe clearance: 0.6 mm (0.024 in)

If incorrect, check the parking brake system.

10.If Necessary, Adjust Bellcrank.

(a) Lightly pull the bellcrank in the opposite direction to when the brakes are applied until there is no slack with the hand/park brake cable.

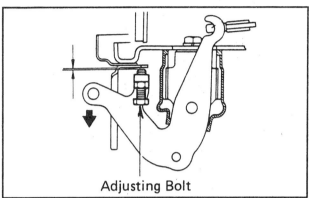

Adjusting Bolt

(b) Turn the adjusting bolt so that there is a clearance of between 0.4 and 0.8 mm (0.016 and 0.031 in). Then lock the adjusting bolt with the lock nut.

(c) Connect the parking brake cable No. 2 to th bellcrank.

(e) Install the tension spring.

11.Install Brake Drum and Rear Wheel.

BRAKE TUBES

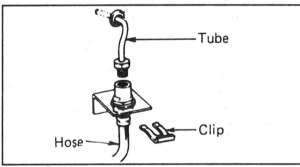

Inspection

1.Inspect Brake Hoses.

(a) Inspect the hose for damage, cracks or swelling.

(b) Inspect the threads for damage.

2.Inspect Brake Tubes.

(a) Inspect the tube for damage, cracks, dents or corrosion.

(b) Inspect the threads for damage.

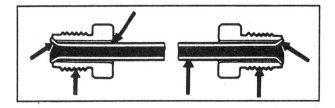

LOAD SENSING PROPORTIONING VALVE

Components

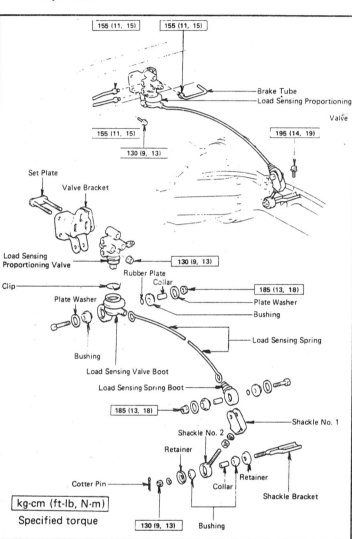

Adjustment of Fluid Pressure

1.Adjust the length of the No. 2 shackle.

Low pressure: lengthen A

High pressure: shorten A

Initial Set:	mm (in)
FJ40	90 (3.54)
FJ, BJ, HJ 4..[s] (except FJ40)	120 (4.72)
FJ, BJ, HJ 6..[s]	78 (3.07)
FJ, BJ, HJ 7..[s]	90 (3.54)
RJ & LJ 7..[s]	120 (4.72)

Adjusting Range:	
FJ40	84- 93 (3.31-3.66)
FJ, BJ, HJ 4..[s] (except FJ40)	114-126 (4.49-4.96)
FJ, BJ, HJ 6..[s]	72- 84 (2.83-3.31)
FJ, BJ, HJ 7..[s]	84- 93 (3.31-3.66)
RJ & LJ 7..[s]	114-126 (4.49-4.96)

* One turn of the No. 2 shackle changes the fluid pressure about 0.6 kg-cm^2 (8.5 psi,59 kPa).

2.In event pressure cannot be adjusted by the No. 2 shackle, raise or lower the valve body.

Low pressure: lower

High pressure: raise

3.Torque the nuts.

Torque: 130 kg-cm (9 ft-lb, 13 N·m)

4.Adjust the length of the No. 2 shackle again. If it cannot be adjusted, inspect the valve housing.

PROBLEM DIAGNOSIS

* Care must be taken to replace each part properly as it could affect the performance of the brake system and result in dangerous driving.

* It is very important to keep parts clean, otherwise brake system may not work properly.

Problem: Low or spongy pedal!
Possible Causes and Remedies:
* Linings worn. Remedy - replace brake shoes or pads.
* Leak in brake system. Remedy - repair leak.
* Master cylinder faulty. Remedy - repair or replace master cylinder.
* Air in brake system. Remedy - bleed brake system.
* Wheel cylinder faulty. Remedy - repair wheel cylinder.
* Piston seals worn or damaged. Remedy - repair brake callipers.
* Rear brake automatic adjuster faulty. Remedy - repair or replace adjuster.

Problem: Brakes drag!
Possible Causes and Remedies:
* Parking brake out of adjustment. Remedy - adjust parking brake.
* Parking brake wire binding. Remedy - repair as necessary.
* Booster push rod out of adjustment. Remedy - adjust push rod.
* Lining cracked or distorted. Remedy - replace brake shoes and pads.
* Wheel cylinder or calliper piston sticking. Remedy - repair as necessary.
* Automatic adjuster broken. Remedy - replace adjuster.

Problem: Brakes pull!
Possible Causes and Remedies:
* Tyres improperly inflated. Remedy - inflate tyres to proper pressure.

* Oil or grease on linings. Remedy - check for cause/replace shoes.
* Brake shoes distorted, linings worn or glazed. Remedy - replace brake shoes.
* Drum or disc out of round. Remedy - replace drum or disc.
* Return spring faulty. Remedy - replace spring.
* Wheel cylinder faulty. Remedy - repair wheel cylinder.
* Piston frozen in calliper. Remedy - repair calliper.
* Disc brake pad sticking. Remedy - replace pads.

Problem: Brakes grab/chatter!
Possible Causes and Remedies:
* Oil or grease on linings. Remedy - check for cause/replace shoes.
* Drum or disc scored or out of round. Remedy - replace drum or disc.
* Brake shoes distorted, linings worn or glazed. Remedy - replace brake shoes.
* Wheel cylinder faulty. Remedy - repair wheel cylinder.
* Disc brake pad sticking. Remedy - replace pads.

Problem: Hard pedal but brakes inefficient!
Possible Causes and Remedies:
* Oil or grease on linings. Remedy - check for cause/replace shoes.
* Brake shoes distorted, linings worn or glazed, drums worn. Remedy - replace as required.
* Disc brake pads worn. Remedy - replace pads.
* Piston frozen in calliper. Remedy - repair calliper.
* Brake booster faulty. Remedy - repair booster.
* Brake line restricted. Remedy - repair as necessary.
* Vacuum leaking. Remedy - repair as necessary.
* Vacuum pump faulty. Remedy - repair or replace vacuum pump.

Problem: Scraping or grinding noise when brakes are applied!
Possible Causes and Remedies:
* Worn brake linings. Remedy - replace, resurface drums or rotors if heavily scored.
* Calliper to wheel or rotor interference. Remedy - replace as required.
* Dust cover to rotor or drum interference. Remedy - correct or replace.
* Other brake system components - warped or bent brake backing plate - cracked drum or rotor. Remedy - inspect and service.
* Tyres rubbing against chassis and body. Remedy - inspect and service.